D1243093

SPARROWS
AND BUNTINGS

A GUIDE TO THE SPARROWS AND BUNTINGS
OF NORTH AMERICA
AND THE WORLD

SPARROWS
AND BUNTINGS

A GUIDE TO THE SPARROWS AND BUNTINGS
OF NORTH AMERICA
AND THE WORLD

CLIVE BYERS

JON CURSON

AND

URBAN OLSSON

Houghton Mifflin Company
Boston New York
1995

For information about this and other Houghton Mifflin
trade and reference books and multimedia products, visit
The Bookstore at Houghton Mifflin on the World Wide Web at
(http://www.hmco.com/trade/).

Library of Congress Cataloging-in-Publication data

Byers, Clive.
   Sparrows and buntings / Clive Byers, Jon Curson and Urban Olsson.
   344p. 24cm.
   Includes bibliographical references and index.
   ISBN 0-395-73873-3
   1. Sparrows — Identification. 2. Buntings (Birds) — Identification.
  I. Curson, Jon. II. Olsson, Urban. III. Title.
  QL696.P246B95   1995
  598.8'83 — dc20

                             95 - 4862
                             CIP

Printed in Great Britain
10 9 8 7 6 5 4 3 2 1

CONTENTS

To my parents,
Gustav and Inger-Maja

Urban Olsson

INTRODUCTION

Buntings and American sparrows, Emberizinae, are a great challenge to all birdwatchers interested in identification. Many of the long-distance migrants are notable wanderers, with a strong tendency to vagrancy, while others are rare and local. Some of the Asian buntings and tropical sparrows are still poorly known, and a few have not even had all their plumages described. Many fit the description of "little brown job" very well, but a closer look will reveal intricate and quite beautiful plumage detail. Most males of the buntings acquire a bright breeding plumage, which is usually easily identified, but in the American sparrows this is the exception rather than the rule. With some of the dull species and plumages, the features that will enable positive identification are to be found in minute feather detail, which requires highly specialised knowledge; the skulking habits of some of the species adds to the challenge.

This book is the first comprehensive guide to all the Old World buntings and the Nearctic sparrows and is designed to enable identification of each species, plus ageing, sexing and racial determination, wherever possible. Although the book is intended primarily as an identification guide, the habitat, habits and breeding biology, moult, status and movements of each species is outlined where known, and references are provided for those who wish to follow these topics up further. Several of the species are rare, local and little known. In several cases descriptions of plumage are based on very few individuals. Songs may have been described from a single recording or observation, or from a limited area in a wider range. For many species breeding biology and ecology are insufficiently known. We recognise these shortcomings and invite anyone who has additional information to contact us.

The scope of the book, as indicated in the subtitle, is the buntings and sparrows of the Holarctic region. All species which occur in the Holarctic are included. However, to avoid treating some species of a widespread genus and excluding others, a few tropical species are also described. Thus, for example, the African buntings are included, as they are all in the genus *Emberiza*. The extralimital Crested Bunting is also included for completeness. With the Nearctic members of the subfamily Emberizinae, the decision on the limits of treatment was a little more tricky. Three of the North American genera have representatives in South America, and these are all included. However, to include all the South American species would really be beyond the scope of the book and would create a very bulky guide. The problem was that there are several genera which are very closely related and whose taxonomic relations are not yet fully resolved, namely *Pipilo, Melozone, Arremon, Arremonops* and *Atlapetes*. All of these, except for *Pipilo,* have tropical as well as temperate species within them. The genus *Melozone* has three species which are restricted to Mexico and Central America, in montane and other temperate biomes, and therefore they are included. The genus *Arremonops* is quite a mixture: one species is restricted to South America, another occurs in Central and South America, and the other two occur in Mexico and Central America (with one of them, Olive Sparrow, occurring north to southern Texas). This genus is therefore also included in the book. The remaining two genera, *Arremon* and *Atlapetes,* are primarily tropical, with just one species of the former and a handful of the latter occurring north of South America. These two genera are therefore excluded.

ACKNOWLEDGEMENTS

The production of a book such as this relies on the help of many people, and the authors and artist gratefully acknowledge the support and assistance of the people listed below for helping to make this book far more complete and readable than it would otherwise have been.

Urban Olsson would first of all like to thank Per Alström. Much of the information about the buntings was gathered on field trips in Asia in his company. He also gave free access to his wealth of field notes and excellent sound recordings.

Special thanks are due to Yoshimitsu Shigeta and Kiyoaki Ozaki, at the Yamashina Institute for Ornithology, for freely sharing their great expertise of the eastern Palearctic species during and after Urban Olsson's stay at Japanese bird observatories. Yoshimitsu Shigeta also provided numerous photographs of previously undescribed juvenile plumages of Japanese buntings.

Urban Olsson would also like to thank Martin Reid, who not only helped in locating longspurs and read and improved the texts, but also served as a wind shield while Urban Olsson watched Smith's Longspur during an Oklahoma blizzard.

Jon Curson would like to thank Richard Knapton of Ontario, Canada, for reading and offering valuable comments on the North American sparrow texts, for providing him with several useful references, and for help and encouragement in many other ways.

Both authors and the artist would like to thank the staff at the Natural History Museum (BMNH), UK, particularly Robert Prys-Jones, Peter Colston and Michael Walters, for arranging access to the skin collection at the museum and for help in many other ways throughout the project. Effie Warr assisted in seeking out obscure references. Jon Fjeldså at the University Zoological Museum, Copenhagen, provided generous access to the collections at the museum. We also wish to thank Mary LeCroy at the American Museum of Natural History, New York; R. A. Paynter, Jr. at the Museum of Comparative Zoology, Cambridge, Mass.; Phil Angle at the Smithsonian Institution, Washington, DC; David Willard at the Field Museum of Natural History, Chicago; Mark Robbins at the Academy of Natural Sciences, Philadelphia.

Jon Curson and Urban Olsson sincerely thank Richard Ranft at the British Library of Wildlife Sounds (National Sound Archive), for arranging access to numerous recordings of American sparrows (including his own) and African buntings, and to the many people who have deposited copies of their private sound recordings at BLOWS over the years.

Unique photographs, useful to both authors and the artist, were provided by: Mark Beaman (winter plumage of Koslov's Bunting), Alan Greensmith (many of the Mexican endemic sparrows), Shawneen Finnegan (non-breeding Smith's Longspur and several American sparrows), and George Wallace (Zapata Sparrow).

In addition, several people helped in various ways. The texts and illustrations were greatly improved by those who commented on early drafts, or provided useful references and unpublished material, sound recordings or photographs. Others provided invaluable information about sites, or assisted in the field. We are grateful to them all for stimulating discussion and support throughout the project: Duncan Brooks, Clide Carter, Dave Curson, Jon Dunn, Shaween Finnegan, Ulf Hassel, Carl Haynie, Jim Hoffman, Hannu Jännes, Guy Kirwan, Mikal Käll, Greg Lasley, Paul Lehman, Lars-Göran Lindgren, Rod Martins, Bob Medland, Krister Mild, Joe Moreland, Paul Mosimann, Richard Mundy, Raimo Neergaard, Anders Paulsrud, Peter Post, Robert Prys-Jones, Carsten Rahbek, Nigel Redman, Craig Robson, Ken Seyffert, Alexandr Soldatov, Mats Strömberg, Tim Wacher, George Wallace, David Wege and Claudia Wilds.

Last, but definitely not least, Urban Olsson, Jon Curson and Clive Byers are indebted to their often neglected families, Eva, Joel and Emilia, Carole, and Audrey, for their support, tolerance and understanding.

EXPLANATION OF THE SPECIES ACCOUNTS

Species sequence

Each species has been given a reference number which serves as a useful label, both on the plates and in the text. This number is intended for use within the confines of this book only and has no taxonomic significance. The order of the species and their scientific names generally follow Sibley & Monroe (1990), with a few minor exceptions.

Vernacular name

Nomenclature is often a problem, with vernacular names differing between different regions and field guides. In this guide, the vernacular names follow Beaman (1994) for Palearctic species and Sibley & Monroe (1990) for American sparrows.

Nomenclature

The name under which the species was originally described, as well as author and year in which it was first described are given. The full reference for each species can be found in Paynter & Storer (1970). Other scientific names under which the species (or part of it) has been described are given as synonyms.

Identification

The species' average total length is given in centimetres (a range is given where the species is quite variable in size). This is intended to give a general idea of the size of the bird, rather than being an accurate mean average or range. The information given here is designed to facilitate identification to species level. The more important plumage variations and criteria for ageing and sexing are summarised here, as knowledge of these often aids identification, but these are all discussed more fully in subsequent sections. Similar species are discussed and cross-referenced.

Hybridisation

This section gives details of hybridisation between two species where relevant, including typical characters of individual hybrids.

Description

A detailed description of each species is given for each plumage, starting with adult male in breeding plumage and finishing with the juvenile. The description follows the same pattern throughout: first the head is described, followed by the upperparts, wings, tail and underparts. The bare parts are described last of all, under the first plumage to be described; if they differ in other plumages this is discussed where appropriate. Generally, the first described plumage is given a full, feather-by-feather description, and the differences from this plumage are described for the subsequent plumages. However, where subsequent plumages are very different from the first described (as is the case with many Eurasian buntings), these are described more fully where appropriate. It may seem slightly misleading to use the terms breeding and non-breeding plumage, as in most species they largely represent the same set of feathers in different stages of wear. However, for tropical species the terms summer or winter plumage would be highly inappropriate. A terminology suggested by Humphrey and Parkes (1959) addresses this problem. These alternative terms are given in parentheses in the 'Moult and Ageing' section on p.6 and in 'Plumage sequence' on p.12. Nevertheless, we have chosen to link the plumage terminology to the breeding cycle, as this is easy to relate to. The description section is intended to enable all the described plumages to be identified, where possible, and so all the main feather groups are included. Obscure feather tracts which are not normally visible on buntings, such as underwing-coverts, are not described unless they are of value for identifying, ageing or sexing the species. This section may at times seem to require a magnifying glass rather than field glasses, but it is also intended to be useful for identifying, sexing and ageing birds in the hand and museum skins.

Sexing

A summary of the most useful criteria for sexing is given where appropriate. Where the sexes are very similar, but may sometimes be identified, such as when a mated pair is seen together (as is the case with certain North American sparrows), these subtle differences are described here. Generally, among buntings and longspurs, the females are less brightly coloured than males. In breeding plumage, some females may show features reminiscent of the male's breeding plumage. Presumably this tendency becomes more pronounced with increasing age. Conversely first-summer males may be very similar to breeding females. Female traits in breeding males may indicate birds in first-, second- or perhaps even third-summer plumage, although very little is known about this in buntings. However, it has been demonstrated that Yellowhammer males become brighter with increasing age.

In the species covered by this book, males are on average larger than females. Very often the measurements overlap, but wing length in particular may help to determine the sex of an individual bird.

Moult and Ageing

The plumage of a bird is continuously worn and bleached and the feathers have to be renewed at regular intervals. Each species has its own moult strategy, with all the members of the species following the same pattern (sometimes with minor variations); most closely related species also follow a similar basic pattern. Occasionally there are differences between races. The flight feathers are renewed symmetrically on both wings, the moult generally starting with the shedding of the innermost primary on both. The primaries are then renewed outwards in sequence. When four to seven primaries have been renewed, or are still growing, the outermost secondary is shed, the moult of the secondaries then proceeding inwards. Accidentally lost feathers may be renewed at any time of the year, but are rarely replaced symmetrically.

In buntings and sparrows, the most common strategy is to renew all the feathers at the same time once a year. A moult in which all the feathers are replaced during the same period and the flight feathers are replaced symmetrically is called a *complete moult*. Since moult is very costly in terms of energy expenditure, it is best done at a time of year when the bird is subjected to a minimum of stress from other activities. In the northern hemisphere, this moult usually occurs after the bird has finished breeding and before it starts migrating. The moult which occurs after the breeding season is called the *post-breeding moult* (pre-basic of Humphrey and Parkes). The duration of this process is often a compromise between the need for flight, protection from heat-loss, etc., and the time available. In a species breeding in the far north, such as the Snow Bunting, the season is short and time is therefore very limited. In order to complete its moult before it is forced to move south, the flight feathers are shed so rapidly that the bird may become virtually flightless for a short period. Species breeding further south replace their flight feathers at a slower pace, so that only a few are growing at a particular time. An alternative strategy for northern breeders is for the moult to begin on the breeding grounds, then be suspended over migration and completed on the winter grounds. When this results in the presence of new, fully grown flight feathers during migration which show a contrast in colour compared to older, worn and bleached ones, it is referred to as *suspended moult*. Beware that accidentally lost feathers which have been replaced will also result in a contrast. However, except in exceptional cases, this contrast differs from suspended or normal moult by being asymmetrical and at odds with the normal moult sequence.

The first set of feathers of a young bird grow simultaneously, while it is still in the nest. These feathers differ from subsequent plumages not only in pattern but also in shape. The body feathers are very loose in structure and tail feathers are narrower and more pointed than in adults. Juvenile buntings and sparrows usually moult to first-winter plumage when they are between a few weeks and a few months old, before they leave the breeding grounds (in the case of migratory species). This is more often a *partial moult*, in which only the body feathers and some of the wing-coverts (usually at least the lesser and median coverts) are replaced. In a partial moult, none of the flight or tail feathers is replaced. Some species may have a moult which is intermediate between a partial and a complete moult; i. e. some flight feathers (usually the tertials) and/or some of the tail feathers are replaced. In this book, this is referred to as an *incomplete moult*. The first moult to occur after the bird fledges from the nest is called the *post-juvenile moult* (first pre-basic of Humphrey and Parkes). It usually occurs on the breeding grounds, but odd individuals migrate in juvenile plumage. The fact that the post-juvenile moult is often partial can be important in ageing a bird, at least in the hand, as the retained juvenile wing and tail feathers of first-year birds are noticeably more worn and faded than those of the adults. Tail feathers, primaries and secondaries are in many species not moulted for the first time until the bird is just over a year old. Details are mentioned in the species accounts, where appropriate.

After the annual complete moult, males of many buntings and all the longspurs attain a relatively dull non-breeding (winter) plumage. Often a difference between male and female which was obvious during the breeding season becomes less noticeable and in some species the sexes are then virtually identical. The reason for this is presumably the higher survival value in being less conspicuous. The bright breeding (summer) plumage which many male buntings acquire in the breeding season is used to attract a mate and defend a territory. In many species this plumage is acquired largely through wear. In fresh plumage the individual head and throat feathers are quite large, and only the broad, dull fringes are visible. In late winter, these wear off to reveal the more brightly coloured feather bases, thus producing the breeding attire. The speed of this transition indicates that mechanisms other than simple wear may be responsible for the rapid loss of the feather fringes in late winter/early spring. Most buntings also moult at least some of the head and throat feathers prior to breeding; in particular the short feathers of the forehead, lores and chin are almost always replaced, as they would otherwise wear into breeding plumage too quickly. This restricted *pre-breeding moult* (pre-alternate of Humphrey and Parkes), which involves only some or all of the head feathers and a few body feathers is referred to in this guide as a *limited moult*.

Each species' moulting strategy and timing, where known, is given under this heading. Ageing criteria that result from the moulting strategy are given here as well. Plumage-related ageing criteria may be summarised here, but are discussed more fully in the Description section. See also Plumage sequence on page 12.

The shape of tail feathers, colour of iris and skull ossification are usually useful for determining age. In all species the juvenile tail feathers are narrower and more pointed than in adults. With experience it is usually possible to see the differences, but note that in some species adults also have narrow and pointed tail feathers. The colour of the iris changes with age, usually from a dull to a clearer colour. In species with dark eyes, the change is usually from duller greyish-brown to clearer chestnut-brown. This difference is not always obvious and can only be discerned when the bird is held in the hand and in good light. In some cases the differences are extremely difficult to see, but with experience this character can be very useful, particularly since it is still valid in the spring. In some species it is still possible to recognise second-year birds in the autumn. Skull ossification is an excellent way of ageing birds during the months following the breeding season. Thorough presentations of ageing techniques are given in Svensson (1992) and Pyle *et al.* (1987).

Measurements

The measurements are a combination of our own measurements of live birds and museum specimens, and those compiled from the literature. As many of the measurements in the literature relate to the same specimens as the ones measured by us, it has not always been possible to give the number of specimens measured or the standard deviation. Where the number of specimens measured can be given it is abbreviated as, for example, (n47). Anyone working on morphometry is encouraged to contact the authors directly.

The four standard measurements of wing, tail, bill and tarsus are given here, in millimetres. Other measurements are given where they are useful for identification, ageing or sexing. There are standard ways of taking these measurements but, unfortunately, the standard European and American literature use different methods of measuring wing lengths; these are both briefly described below. The tail length is the total length of the tail, from the tip of the longest feather to the point of insertion of the central feathers into the body. The bill length is the chord of the culmen, from the tip to the feathering at the base, or to the skull. The tarsus length is the chord from the intertarsal joint to the distal end of the last undivided scale before the toes diverge. Methods for taking all these measurements are given in Svensson (1992) and Pyle *et al.* (1987).

For wing measurements, the European literature measures the maximum wing length, with the wing flattened and straightened against the ruler. The American literature measures the wing chord, with the wing lying in a natural position along the ruler and only touching it at the shoulder and the tip. Again, methods for taking both these measurements can be found in Svensson (1992) and Pyle *et al.* (1987). The wing chord may be up to 5% less than the maximum wing length. As a result of this discrepancy, the maximum wing length is given for the Old World buntings and the wing chord is given for the New World sparrows. However, for those Nearctic species which have occurred as vagrants to the Western Palearctic a range of maximum wing lengths is given at the end. European and Asian ringers fortunate enough to trap a North American sparrow, or indeed any American bird, are strongly advised to measure the wing chord as well as the maximum wing length.

Wing shapes and emarginations are given in abbreviated form. Thus 'P6-P8 emarginated' indicates that the sixth, seventh and eighth primaries are emarginated. 'P8=P5' indicates that the fifth and eighth primaries are equal in length, and 'P6=WP' indicates that the sixth primary is the wing point (i.e. the longest). Similarly, tail feathers (rectrices) are abbreviated as T1, T2 etc. (see page 11 for feather numbering).

Geographical Variation

Taxonomy and its sister science, systematics, seek to classify all living things. Traditionally, the classification has been based mainly on degree of similarity, and this is largely the foundation for bunting and sparrow taxonomy. However, most modern systematic studies concentrate instead on evolutionary history and common descent of species. Taxonomy is then based on monophyletic groups, i.e. groups of closely related species which include all the descendants from a single common ancestor. As past evolutionary events and the ancestors of modern species are largely unknown, similarities in morphology and genetic composition are used to evaluate relationship. New evidence sometimes results in rearrangements to the systematic order being proposed and these are sometimes quite radical: witness the recent rearrangement suggested by Sibley *et al.* (1988) as a result of extensive DNA-DNA hybridisation experiments. The classification of most of the species in this book has not been thoroughly revised recently and will probably see some change in the future.

All the normally recognised races are listed, along with a summary of their range and distinguishing characteristics. Although many races are identifiable in the field, it should be remembered that many are extremely similar and intergrade extensively where their ranges overlap. Such examples can often only be identified by comparison with a large series of museum skins and, even then, birds from an area of overlap between two similar races will often remain unidentifiable to race. A selection of the more striking races is illustrated in the plates. Race is synonymous with subspecies. The nominate race is the one first named, and its subspecific name is always the same as the specific, e.g. *Emberiza cia cia*.

Relationships

This section is used for some species to emphasise close relationships between species (e.g. as part of a monophyletic group or superspecies) or close relationships between genera, particularly for monotypic species.

Voice

The song and most commonly used contact and alarm calls are described here, along with a brief description of the bird's normal behaviour when singing (e.g. from an exposed perch, during a display flight, etc.). It is beyond the scope of this book to describe all possible vocalisations of a species, and it should be noted that most species have a wider vocal repertoire than is indicated here.

Transcribing bird songs and calls is notoriously difficult. The ones given are our interpretations, based in some cases on the published literature, and it is hoped that they will be sufficient to emphasise the general quality of the song and calls and, in particular, to point out the main differences between similar species.

Habits

In a work of this nature space does not allow a full discussion of the habits of each species. This section summarises the information available on breeding biology, feeding and flocking behaviour, and any other habits of specific interest. It is worth noting that, although this group are principally seed-eaters, most species also eat insects and other invertebrates, especially in the breeding season, and most species feed their young on insects. For those interested in pursuing these subjects further, the references at the end of each species account will indicate useful sources in the bibliography.

Status and Habitat

Each species' status is very briefly summarised, but details are given only when the bird is particularly rare or highly localised. The availability of preferred habitat often determines both the distribution and abundance of a species. The main habitats where the species can be expected in each season are summarised. It should be remembered that this section is only a guide to the favoured habitats, and many species will occasionally turn up in unlikely places, especially on migration.

Distribution and Movements

The distribution (breeding and non-breeding where different) is outlined here. It should be remembered that, within the distribution range given, the species will only occur in suitable habitat; therefore distribution should be used in conjunction with the information on habitat given in the previous section. For migrants, an indication of the route and the timing is given where known. Once again, it should be borne in mind that this is a summary of the main migration routes and timing, and individuals of a species may occur outside the routes or timing indicated. More sedentary species may also move locally at various times of year (for example, some montane species move to lower elevations after breeding) and these localised movements are also summarised where known.

Notes

This section is used, occasionally, to bring attention to relevant details of a particular species which do not readily fit into any of the above categories (e.g. taxonomic notes).

References

The most useful sources of information used in compiling the species accounts are given (author and year) at the end of each account. These refer mostly to specialised papers, monographs and other sources of specific information which will provide further information on the species concerned. All references are given in full in the bibliography.

The Maps

Each species has a distribution map, showing breeding and non-breeding ranges. For tropical species, the situation may be complex, and breeding is usually timed to coincide with wet or dry seasons, which often vary locally. Black dots indicate isolated or restricted breeding ranges. It can generally be taken that a particular species can be expected to occur on migration in unmarked areas between the breeding and non-breeding ranges. A cross on the map indicates a vagrant record (or a series of records). A question mark indicates uncertain occurrence during the breeding season. Note that the maps are only a guideline, and that within a given range a species may be sparsely distributed to abundant, depending on habitat availability and/or population density. More details are given under the Distribution and Movements heading for each species.

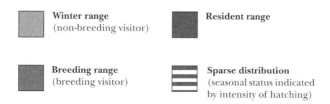

Winter range (non-breeding visitor)　　**Resident range**

Breeding range (breeding visitor)　　**Sparse distribution** (seasonal status indicated by intensity of hatching)

The Plates

Each species is illustrated, usually in a selection of plumage and racial variations. Important identification features are mentioned in a succinct text on the facing page. It is important to refer to the main text for a full treatment of identification criteria. Figures are to scale on each plate. The choice of plumages for the illustrations is designed to show representative individuals covering as many plumage and racial variations for each species as possible, subject to space constraints.

HOW TO IDENTIFY BUNTINGS AND NORTH AMERICAN SPARROWS

Bunting topography

In order to correctly describe the intricate differences that separate the often very similar plumages in buntings and sparrows, it is often necessary to go into great detail. Many terms are self-explanatory, whereas the use of others, e.g. back, moustache and lores differs from the use in some widely used field guides. We consistently use the terms shown in the figures below in the way demonstrated, and urge readers to familiarise themselves with the terminology.

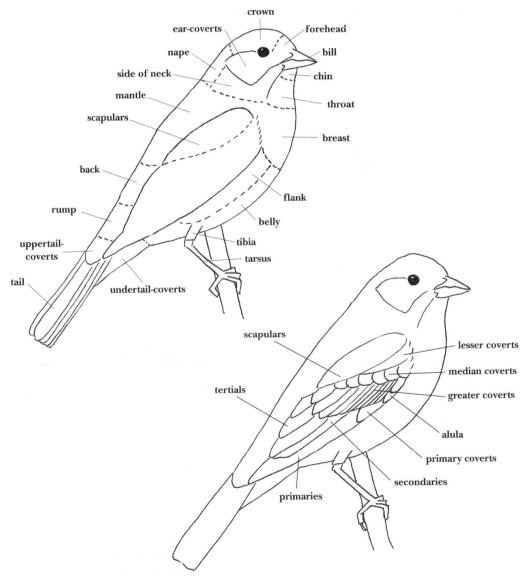

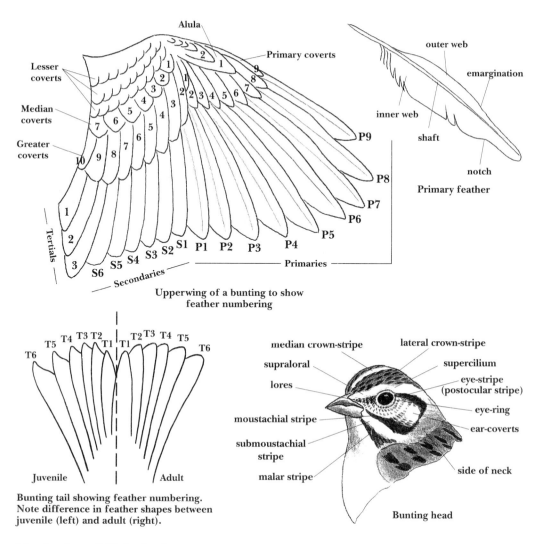

Upperwing of a bunting to show
feather numbering

Bunting tail showing feather numbering.
Note difference in feather shapes between
juvenile (left) and adult (right).

Bunting head

Numbering of flight feathers

There are two ways of numbering the primaries, descendently and ascendently. Both methods have their advantages and advocates. When numbered descendently, the primaries are numbered from the centre of the wing and outwards. When numbered ascendently, the outermost primary becomes number one.

In this work, the primaries are numbered descendently. The basis for this is the moult sequence; the first primary is shed first, and so on. As the outermost primary is vestigial, a descendent numbering will avoid mistakes and make comparison with ten-primaried passerines more straightforward. If numbered ascendently, the outermost visible primary is counted as number two, as the first one is not visible.

The six 'true' secondaries, however, are numbered ascendently. The innermost three secondaries differ in shape and pattern from the rest, and are commonly known as tertials. They are here numbered from the inside.

Emberiza pattern

Many members of the genus *Emberiza* (and two of the longspurs) show a unique pattern on the tertials. The pale edges on the outer webs are broad near the tip, and then abruptly become narrow. In some species the pale edges even appear to protrude like wedges into the dark centres. The bases of the dark centres may then be visible as isolated dark patches, suggesting a second row of tertials.

The common pattern for other passerines is that the pale edges are of even width, which may be diffusely or contrastingly set off. All the Eurasian members of the genus *Emberiza* show this '*Emberiza* pattern', with the exception of the Rock Bunting group, Red-headed and Black-headed Buntings, and all the African buntings. In White-capped Bunting the *Emberiza* pattern is so faint as to appear to be lacking in most individuals.

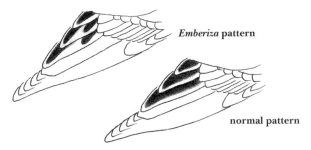

Tertial patterns showing well developed *Emberiza* pattern (left), compared to the pattern typical for many common passerines (right).

Plumage sequence

Most species follow the same basic pattern in plumage sequence, but some, e.g. Black-headed and Red-headed Buntings, deviate markedly.

As not all parts of the world experience winter, terms like first-winter plumage is not always appropriate. Alternative terminologies have addressed this problem. The terminology of Humphrey & Parkes (1959), which is widely used in North America, is given in brackets.

first-winter plumage (first basic plumage)   first-summer plumage (first alternate plumage)
non-breeding plumage (basic plumage)   breeding plumage (alternate plumage)

The first set of feathers acquired by a young bird is called the **juvenile plumage**. The feathers are grown simultaneously, and initially the wings and tail are shorter than in full-grown birds. At an early age, the gape is yellow. The juvenile plumage is normally noticeably different from subsequent plumages, usually duller and more inconspicuous. The body feathers are very loose in structure and the resistance to wear is poor. This causes colours to change rapidly, and fringes and feather edges often wear to whitish. The pattern is often scalloped or more diffusely streaked than in older birds. Juvenile birds frequently differ from birds in subsequent plumages by showing more prominent streaking on the breast. Typically, the dark centres of the median and greater coverts, and often also of the tertials, are of a different shape than in subsequent plumages. Often the dark centres are more well-defined and more pointed, and the edges and tips paler. The tip of the dark centres is often in the shape of a spike or a blunt 'tooth'. The shape of the feathers is also different from subsequent plumages, and in particular the tail feathers are narrower and more pointed than in adults. The shape and extent of white patterning on the outermost pairs may be slightly different from adults. In some species, where adults have all-dark tails, juveniles may show rusty edges or tips to the outermost pair. In most species, this plumage is only retained for a few weeks, or up to a few months, and is replaced (in the post-juvenile moult) by the first-winter plumage.

In **first-winter plumage** (first basic plumage), certain feathers may be retained from the juvenile plumage. In most species the primaries and flight feathers are not replaced. Frequently some or all of the tail feathers, tertials, greater coverts, primary coverts and alula are also retained. This varies both individually and between species. In most species, with the exception of some feathers of the head that may be renewed before the breeding season, all feathers are retained until after the following breeding season. In many cases, the bases of the feathers show coloration reminiscent of adult birds, causing the first-winter birds to become increasingly similar to adults as wear proceeds. This worn plumage is then termed **first-summer plumage** (first alternate plumage), even in cases where all the feathers are the same as in first-winter plumage. As some feathers, most notably tail and flight feathers, have then been worn for over a year, these may be extremely abraded.

At the end of the breeding season, adults and first-summer birds alike undertake a post-breeding moult into a **non-breeding plumage** (basic plumage). In most species, adults and one-year-old birds now become inseparable. This plumage is often very similar to first-winter plumage, and in many cases the only difference is absence of retained juvenile feathers. Apart from differences in shape or colour pattern, there is also a difference in amount of abrasion. Juvenile feathers are grown a couple of weeks before the non-breeding plumage, which as stated above is attained at the end of the breeding season, and throughout the year there is an average difference in wear.

The **breeding plumage** (alternate plumage) is normally attained by a combination of wear and moult. The extent of the moult differs between species, and females normally moult considerably less than males. The breeding attire develops as the fringes wear off and the concealed bases of the longer feathers of the head become visible. The short feathers of the forehead, lores, ear-coverts and chin usually do not show the colour of the breeding plumage, and are replaced before the breeding season. Thus, the breeding plumage is largely made up of the same feathers as the non-breeding plumage, only more abraded.

Other factors affecting colours and patterns

For a variety of reasons, individual birds may show a plumage that does not conform with what is typical of the species. One well-known factor influencing coloration is the inherited trait causing lack of pigmentation, albinism. Often only one or a few feathers are white, but rarely the whole bird may be white. Such individuals are rare in nature as they are easily detected by predators, and soon succumb. Individuals with scattered white feathers may show a similarity to species that normally show white patterns, but it is extremely rare that the white feathers are symmetrically distributed.

Other aberrations include melanism and leucism, producing very dark or washed-out pale brownish individuals, respectively.

Occasionally, individuals showing unnatural wear may be encountered. White portions of the plumage are less resistant to wear than dark ones, and pale fringes, edges and other white parts may be lost altogether. Other effects of unnatural or extremely heavy wear may be that (usually) dark bases of feathers become visible, causing the bird to appear darker than normal. Strong bleaching causes black feathers to turn brown, and pale colours to become whitish.

Birds in transition from non-breeding plumage to breeding plumage may show a wide range of unexpected features.

Size and shape

General impression and shape (jizz) of a species plays an important part in identification. However, it is in most cases very difficult to describe subtle differences in jizz in a way that an observer unfamiliar with a species will find useful. We have in this book largely omitted describing differences in jizz, not because they are unimportant, but because we believe that such knowledge is subjective and best acquired by each observer by direct experience in the field.

Some structural differences are less subjective, and we have described differences in primary projection, primary spacing, tail length and shape where appropriate. In all buntings, the tips of the primaries are not covered by the folded wing, which is the case in, for example, most larks. The distance from the tip of the tertials to the tip of the wing, when folded, is called the primary projection. The length of the visible part of the primaries and the length of the tertials can be compared relatively reliably, and the relative differences between species used as an aid in identification.

The relative length of the primaries and the number of emarginations influence the aerodynamic properties of a wing. For example, a long and narrow wing is best used for fast flight, whereas a short and broad wing decreases the speed and manoeuvring skills. Thus aspects such as distance of migration, flight action and feeding behaviour of a species are indicated by the shape of the wing. The taxonomic usefulness of the differences in wing shape is linked to a species' unique habits, even if these habits are not always known to ornithologists. In the species covered by this book, these differences are of much less use for identification than in, for example, Old World warblers, but in a few cases they are important. Differences in relative length of primaries lead to different spacing of the tips on the folded wing, which is sometimes useful in the identification process.

Behaviour

Differences in behaviour are often useful for identification, or at least as pointers. For a few species covered by this book we describe characteristic song flights. Whether the song is delivered during a song flight, from an exposed perch, or within the cover of vegetation may be useful indications for identifying certain species. Different tendencies to congregate in flocks may also aid identification.

Taxonomy and Relationships

In traditional taxonomy, buntings and sparrows form part of the subfamily Emberizinae, which is in turn part of the vast family Emberizidae - the nine-primaried passerines. Although morphologically similar to the 'true finches' and Old World sparrows they are not particularly closely related to them. The true finches belong to the family Fringillidae and the Old World sparrows to the family Passeridae. Both of these families evolved in the Old World (although several species, especially in the genera *Carduelis* and *Carpodacus*, now occur widely in the Americas and two Old World sparrows have been introduced there) whereas the Emberizidae family has its origins in the New World. The vast Emberizidae family consists of seven subfamilies (Parulinae, Thraupinae, Coerebinae, Catamblyrhynchinae, Icterinae, Cardinalinae and Emberizinae) and contains groups as diverse as the tiny parula warblers and the (relatively) huge oropendolas. These were formerly considered separate families and, as the amalgamated family is so huge, the seven subfamilies are generally still treated separately within it for practical purposes.

Sibley and Ahlquist (1990) have further revised the taxonomy of the nine-primaried passerines by merging Emberizidae and Fringillidae into one gigantic superfamily (called Fringillidae) with Emberizinae and Fringillinae (along with the monotypic subfamily Peucedraminae) as subfamilies within it. Following this arrangement, the emberizine sparrows, buntings and Neotropical emberizine finches become a tribe Emberizini within the Emberizinae subfamily. The other tribes within the Emberizinae subfamily are Parulini, Thraupini etc.

These two taxonomic arrangements are shown below, using Smith's Longspur *Calcarius pictus* as an example.

Traditional taxonomy

    Family Emberizidae

            Subfamily Emberizinae, (also Parulinae etc.)

                  Genus *Calcarius*

                        Species *pictus*

Sibley & Ahlquist DNA-based taxonomy

    Family Fringillidae

            Subfamily Emberizinae, (also Fringillinae and Peucedraminae)

                Tribe Emberizini, (also Parulini etc.)

                  Genus *Calcarius*

                      Species *pictus*

The subfamily Emberizinae (or tribe Emberizini) appears to have evolved in South America and this is where the greatest diversity of species occurs (see below). From there they spread north into Central and North America and then across into Eurasia, with relatively few species reaching western Europe and Africa.

The Emberizinae subfamily may be divided into three main groups: the Old World buntings of Eurasia and Africa, the North American (Nearctic) sparrows and the South American (Neotropical) emberizines (seedeaters, grassquits and emberizine finches). It must be stressed that this is a generalisation and not a cut and dry division. Central America (southeastern Mexico to Panama) is quite a melting pot of North American sparrows and South American emberizines: representatives of five North American genera are found in Central America as breeding species (with more occurring as winter visitors) and 11 genera of South American emberizines have representatives with ranges which extend north into Central America, with a few reaching northern Mexico (which is geographically part of the Nearctic region). In addition, three emberizine genera (*Acanthidops*, *Pezopetes* and *Pselliophorus*) are endemic to the Neotropical region of Central America, the genus *Melozone* contains two species endemic to Central America and one endemic to western Mexico, and the genus *Arremonops*, while ranging from southern Texas to northern South America, may have its origins in Central America. Three North American genera also have representatives in South America, with four of the six species involved being endemic to the continent. In contrast, there is far less overlap between the Old and New World regions; they share just two breeding species in two genera, both of which are circumpolar and breed in the arctic.

The Old World buntings comprise 43 species in just six genera. This lower number of genera compared to North American sparrows may seem to indicate a lower diversity. However, it should be remembered that taxonomic ranks such as genera and families are entirely human inventions, reflecting human opinion about grouping of species, rather than being a measurement of biodiversity. Such a comparison is better based on number of species.

It is generally believed that this group arrived in the east, across the Bering Strait from the Americas, and spread west across the region; thus it is not surprising that the greatest diversity occurs in eastern Asia. Of the two species which also breed in North America one (Lapland Longspur) belongs to a primarily North American genus (*Calcarius*), while the other (Snow Bunting) belongs to a truly Holarctic genus (*Plectrophenax*); the only other member of the genus, McKay's Bunting, is sometimes regarded as conspecific with Snow Bunting, and breeds only on islands in the Bering Strait. Of the four genera endemic to the Old World, three are monotypic with the other (*Emberiza*) containing all the other species.

The Pink-tailed Rosefinch *Urocynchramus pylzowi* is sometimes placed in the subfamily Emberizinae (e.g. Sibley & Monroe 1990). The authors state that the relationships are uncertain, based on Zusi (1978), and mention that B. King, P. Alström and U. Olsson are convinced it is related to rosefinches. The Pink-tailed Rosefinch is similar to other rosefinches in plumage, but differs in having a pink lower mandible and a long tail which is pink in the male. It is also similar in behaviour to rosefinches, occurring in scrubby vegetation at high altitude where it is relatively unobtrusive. The species displays a unique songflight, different from both rosefinches and buntings. The male rises to about five metres and glides down in a pipit-like manner, with the pink tail raised and slightly spread. We adhere to the opinion that a species should be classified according to relationship rather than differentiation, and as evidence for a closer relationship to buntings than to anything else seems to be wanting at present, we have chosen not to include Pink-tailed Rosefinch in this guide.

The North American sparrows contain 69 species in 20 genera (this includes the longspurs and the *Melozone* and *Arremonops* genera). As explained below, the differences between this group and the South American emberizines are not as clear cut as those with the Old World buntings. The genus *Melozone* appears to have evolved in Central America but it has clear affinities with certain South American genera (see below). *Pipilo* also appears to have affinities with this group, although it is obviously a North American genus, probably with its origins in the southern part of that area.

The third group, the South American emberizines, comprise approximately 150 species in 41 genera, occurring in South America and associated islands, southern Central America and the West Indies, with a few species reaching Mexico. Their relationship to the North American sparrows is not fully understood. In particular, the genera *Pipilo*, *Melozone*, *Arremon*, *Arremonops* and *Atlapetes* appear to be closely related within the subfamily, although it is possible that convergent evolution may be partly responsible for this. Of these *Pipilo* is clearly a North American genus with no species occurring south of the highlands of Mexico and Guatemala. *Melozone* consists of three species endemic to Mexico and Central America. *Arremon* is clearly a South American genus with only one of the five species reaching Central America (north to southeastern Mexico). *Arremonops* is quite a mixture; one species is restricted to northeastern South America, one occurs in South America and also in Central America north to Honduras, one is endemic to Central America (southeastern Mexico to Honduras) and the fourth occurs from Costa Rica north to northern Mexico and southern Texas. *Atlapetes* is principally a South American genus with only seven of the 27 species occurring in Central America (although it is noteworthy that four of these seven are endemic to Mexico). The reasons for including *Melozone* and *Arremonops* (as well as *Pipilo*) in this guide have already been given in the introduction.

There are five emberizine genera endemic to the West Indies. One of these, *Loxipasser*, is similar to the *Tiaris* grassquits, differing principally in its decidedly larger nest, though it is also slightly larger.

Melopyrrha, *Loxigilla* and *Melanospiza* recall the *Oryzoborus* seed-finches in plumage and bill shape. The fifth genus, *Torreornis*, resembles *Aimophila* in its morphology and *Zonotrichia* or *Pipilo* in its behaviour. Therefore, although the West Indies are not strictly part of the Holarctic region, *Torreornis* is included in this guide as it appears to have evolved from the North American group, whereas the other four genera seem to be derived from the South American group.

Dark-eyed Junco

White-capped Bunting

BREEDING BIOLOGY

The following brief notes refer mainly to the group as a whole. Each species' breeding biology, as far as it is known, is summarised in the Habits section of the species accounts.

In the Holarctic breeding species the breeding season is timed to coincide with the northern summer; this not only provides longer hours of daylight for rearing young, but also coincides with the maximum abundance of invertebrates on which they are fed. Most northerly breeding species are migratory; the birds arrive on the breeding grounds from early spring with the males arriving a few days before the females in order to set up breeding territories (males which already have a territory by the time the females arrive are more likely to attract a mate).

In the African buntings and Neotropical sparrows breeding is generally closely tied to the rainy season. Although there seems to be more variability in the timing of breeding (for example, in certain places Rufous-collared Sparrow may nest at any time of year), in areas with relatively heavy rainfall there is generally a peak of breeding activity at the end of the main rainy season, which often continues into the beginning of the dry season.

In areas with lighter, or more unpredictable rainfall, such as in southern USA and Mexico or in sub-Saharan Africa or other arid habitats in Africa or Asia, the breeding seasons are closely tied to seasonal rainfall, and are usually timed to coincide with the onset of the rains.

In tropical species, the breeding season is often protracted compared to temperate and arctic zone species. Furthermore, the clutch size is smaller (typically 2-4 for tropical species and 3-6 for temperate species), the growth rate of the young is slower and the perinatal mortality is higher. However, once fledged they are longer lived and suffer lower mortality rates than temperate zone species, which are, to a greater degree, subject to the dangers of migration and inclement weather.

Buntings and sparrows generally build an open cup nest which is usually well hidden on the ground or low in a bush or shrub. The nest is often built by the female alone and although she is generally responsible for incubating the eggs, the male often takes short turns, particularly towards the end of the incubation. In some cases the female also takes responsibility for feeding the young, with the male in turn providing her with food during this period, but generally both sexes help rear the young.

As is evident from the bill shape, seeds form a large (sometimes exclusive) part of the diet of buntings and sparrows. However, comparison of the digestive tracts to similar groups, such as finches, reveals that buntings and sparrows are more adapted to animal food than the former. Consequently, as far as is known, the young are almost exclusively fed on insects and other invertebrates and do not start taking seeds until after they fledge. At this time of year the seeds are unripe, and softer and more moist than at other times of year. In all buntings the adults switch to a largely insectivorous diet during the breeding season as well, and in some species invertebrates make up the largest part of their diet throughout the year.

ESCAPED CAGEBIRDS

Many emberizine species, especially buntings, are commonly kept as cagebirds. Such birds frequently escape and as they are often not ringed, nor particularly tame, it can be difficult to tell whether an unusual bunting or sparrow is an extralimital vagrant or an escape from captivity. The problem seems to be most serious in western Europe, due to the rampant cagebird trade. For some species the escape potential is considered so high by most rarities committees that records are automatically assumed to be at least possible escapes from captivity. One such example is the Red-headed Bunting, where wild origin of the many records is in question. For example, the British Birds Rarities Committee (BBRC) currently excludes the species from the main British list (category A). However, the species is strongly migratory and natural vagrancy to Britain and western Europe is a possibility. Some of the many records almost certainly refer to genuine vagrants, but the problem is deciding which.

The shadow of doubt will fall on most buntings from the eastern Palearctic turning up as vagrants in western Europe, as long as these species continue to be imported. Short-distance migrants like Meadow Bunting are thus unlikely ever to become accepted as genuine vagrants while Yellow-browed Buntings generally seem to be admitted to category A. Others, however, such as Black-faced and Chestnut Buntings, although far more common than Yellow-browed in their more or less overlapping ranges, seem to be more difficult to assess. Being commoner in their natural ranges also allows more of them to be caught and sent to Europe. Birds caught in China during the autumn migration may be shipped out via Hong Kong to, for example, Brussels or Madrid within a few weeks, and thus be potential escapes at just the time of year when genuine vagrants are to be expected. These birds are wild, and will have retained their migrational instinct. This may take them south for the winter, but the following spring survivors are likely to return to the north.

Monitoring of the cagebird trade as a whole and submitting records, even of obviously escaped birds, will provide us with useful information about what species are common in captivity, as well as giving us an idea of their behaviour and patterns of movements if they escape. Apart from the circumstances surrounding the individual records, these are the only methods currently available when assessing the likelihood of wild origin of a record.

Yellow-throated Bunting

HYBRIDS

Hybrids are rarely reported among buntings and sparrows, except among certain species-pairs, although bizarre combinations such as White-throated Sparrow x Dark-eyed Junco have occurred several times.

There are three species-pairs that are especially prone to hybridisation. Yellowhammers and Pine Buntings hybridise regularly where their ranges overlap in western Siberia. The hybrids are fertile and this has led to a well-established hybrid zone, with up to 15% of Pine Buntings showing signs of mixed ancestry in some areas of this zone. Black-headed and Red-headed Buntings also hybridise regularly south of the Caspian Sea where their ranges meet. On the other side of the Atlantic, Rufous-sided and Collared Towhees hybridise extensively in certain regions in the highlands of Mexico.

In the case of the towhees, hybrids are very variable but generally quite distinctive and identification is straightforward. As hybrids back-cross with one or other parent species, however, the intermediate characteristics of the hybrid will be diluted through the generations. Pine Bunting x Yellowhammer hybrids are generally fairly straightforward to identify, though again back-crossing complicates the issue. A Pine Bunting with yellow anywhere in its plumage (sometimes only on the underwing-coverts) can be assumed to have a hybrid origin. Male Black-headed x Red-headed Bunting hybrids are quite straightforward to identify but females (which can be extremely difficult to separate when pure) are generally impossible to identify, at least in the field and probably often in the hand too, and many such hybrids are presumably overlooked.

With all birds of hybrid origin it is worth remembering that a bird may appear phenotypically pure but may still be carrying hidden recessive genes from the other species; these hidden genes can sometimes show again in subsequent generations.

It may be tempting to regard the extent of hybridisation in these three species-pairs as evidence that they are conspecific; however, it is notable that, with the exception of Black-headed and Red-headed Buntings, the members of each pair co-exist in other areas of their range with no apparent hybridisation taking place. It is in this context also worth keeping in mind that the biological species concept, based on reproductive isolation, is not the only way of defining a species; indeed, the species concept itself is an invention by humans. The evolutionary process proceeds gradually, producing a broad spectrum of stages from local populations to universally undisputed species.

Olive-backed Towhee

PLATES
1-39

PLATE 1:   ASIAN BUNTINGS (1)

7   Koslov's Bunting *Emberiza koslowi*   **Text and map page 119**

Restricted range in E Tibet. Probably resident. Dwarf rhododendron and scrub at high altitude.

   7a   **Adult male breeding** Black crown and ear-coverts, and broad white supercilium. Peculiar dark chestnut lores and chin. Black breast-band separating white throat from grey belly. Mantle uniformly chestnut, contrasting with grey rump.

   7b   **Adult female breeding** Broad whitish supercilium and rather uniformly dark greyish ear-coverts distinctly set off from pale buffish throat, and indistinct malar stripe, create unique facial expression. Brownish-grey mantle often contrasts with chestnut scapulars, but may be quite prominently tinged chestnut. Rump greyish. Breast buffish, with some fine dark streaking, grading into pale greyish belly. Undertail-coverts pale cinnamon.

   7c   **First-winter male** Mantle prominently streaked buffish, recalling female. Pale fringes also obscure crown, ear-coverts and breast-band to some extent. Supercilium and throat streaked blackish.

---

11   Jankowski's Bunting *Emberiza jankowskii*   **Text and map page 128**

NE China, formerly extreme SE Russia and North Korea. Dispersive or short-distance migrant. Overgrown sand-dunes with stunted bushes, interspersed with grassy patches.

   11a   **Adult male breeding** Similar to Meadow Bunting (10), but grey ear-coverts, heavier streaking on mantle, whiter wing-bars, lack of breast band, and dark belly patch distinctive.

   11b   **Adult female breeding** Similar to breeding male, but duller, lores paler, and with belly patch reduced or lacking. Often shows some streaks or spots on the upper breast, and may be heavily marked. Differs from female Meadow Bunting by greyer ear-coverts, more prominent streaking on mantle, whiter wing-bars, and pale greyish central breast.

   11c   **Adult male non-breeding** Paler than breeding male, but shows same characters separating from Meadow Bunting. The patch on the belly may be largely obscured.

---

2   Slaty Bunting *Latoucheornis siemsseni*   **Text and map page 105**

C and SE China. Short-distance migrant. Secondary forest and scrubs.

   2a   **Adult male breeding** Junco-like uniformly dark blue plumage, but with white area on belly more restricted. Outer tail feathers white as in juncos. Bill usually blackish, but may be pale.

   2b   **Adult female** Unstreaked dull brown with head tinged rufous. Rump and belly greyer, grading to dirty whitish on central belly and undertail-coverts. Double rusty wing-bars.

   2c   **First-summer male** Similar to adult male, but traces of brown fringes may be present on head and body. The flight feathers and primary coverts are brown, and the greater coverts are tipped whitish.

---

1   Crested Bunting *Melophus lathami*   **Text and map page 103**

Himalayas east to SE China. Altitudinal and short-distance migrant. Dry rocky slopes and cultivation. In winter often in rice stubbles.

   1a   **Adult male breeding** (*subcristatus*; Kashmir to Burma) Prominent crest, and shining bluish-black plumage, with striking chestnut wings and tail distinctive.

   1b   **Adult female** (nominate; S China) Prominent crest. Breast and throat sullied sandy-grey, with brownish streaks. Tail usually with less rufous than in males.

   1c   **First-winter male** (nominate) Prominent crest. Similar to adult female, but darker, with underparts heavily blotched blackish. Glossy feathers often present on the crown.

   1d   **First-winter female** (nominate) Worn individual shown. Similar to adult female, but rufous edges on wings heavily abraded. Crest slightly shorter. Tail devoid of rufous colour.

PLATE 2: CORN BUNTING AND YELLOWHAMMER GROUP (1)

41 Corn Bunting *Miliaria calandra* — Text and map page 203

Distributed from Europe to W China. Sedentary in most of range, but migratory in north-east. Cereal crops, grassy areas and steppe.

41a **Adult male fresh** (nominate; most of Europe) Uniformly streaked dull brownish plumage, large head and large pale bill. No white in tail.

41b **Juvenile** (nominate) Mantle scalloped. Breast spotted rather than streaked. Dark border to ear-coverts more well-defined than in adults.

3 Yellowhammer *Emberiza citrinella* — Text and map page 107

N and C Europe, east to C Siberia. Introduced New Zealand. Dispersive or migratory. Occurs in a variety of scrubby habitats, intermixed with open areas.

3a **Adult male breeding** (nominate; Europe) Head yellow, with narrow lateral crown-stripes, eye-stripe and moustache dark. Crown lemon yellow. Rump rufous. Underparts yellow, with rusty-red mottling, often forming breast-band.

3b **Adult male breeding** (nominate) Extensively yellow individual. The amount of yellow in the plumage of an individual increases with age.

3c **Adult male non-breeding** (nominate) Blotchy crown pattern characteristic of males. Paler appearance than in breeding plumage.

3d **Adult female non-breeding** (nominate) Streaking on crown denser on forehead, forming dark brows, unlike Cirl Bunting (6). Very similar to some first-winter males, but face pattern on average more obscured. Usually lacks rufous and greyish breast-band; ill-defined if present. Streaking on breast and flanks on average more distinct than on males. Belly less bright yellow than on most males.

3e **First-winter female** (nominate) Dull individual. Reminiscent of Pine Bunting (4), but belly not silky white, and edges of primaries yellow.

3f **Juvenile** (nominate) Paler than adult, with blacker and more diffuse streaking. Dark centres to median coverts more pointed. Combination of nondescript head pattern, rufous rump and yellow tinge to underparts separate from juveniles of other species.

3g **Adult male breeding** (*erythrogenys*; Russia) Similar to nominate race, and not always separable. Typical characters are paler mantle, with slightly less prominent streaking, more extensively rufous sides of breast, and paler flanks.

3h **Adult female non-breeding** (*erythrogenys*) Similar to nominate, and most not separable in the field. Some may be identified by mantle being a trifle paler and rufous streaking on sides of breast on average more extensive. Belly and flanks may be whiter.

6 Cirl Bunting *Emberiza cirlus* — Text and map page 116

S Europe, NW Africa and NW Turkey. Introduced New Zealand. Largely sedentary. Lightly wooded country, like parkland, orchards and vineyards, usually close to cultivated land.

6a **Adult male breeding** (nominate; most of range) Striped black and yellow face, black throat, relatively dark crown and greyish olive-green band across breast characteristic.

6b **Adult female breeding** (nominate) Similar to female Yellowhammer (3), but rump grey and underparts paler yellow, with finer streaks. Crown more uniformly streaked, without darker forehead. Eye-stripe and moustache often in shape of parallel stripes, not appearing to encircle the ear-coverts.

6c **Adult male non-breeding** (nominate) Breeding attire obscured by pale fringes, but characteristic pattern of male still apparent. First-winter male very similar.

6d **First-winter female** (nominate) Very similar to adult female non-breeding, and not safely separated in the field. Differences from first-winter Yellowhammer same as those described for adult female.

6e **Juvenile** (nominate) Differs from first-winter birds primarily by pattern of median coverts. Very similar to juvenile Yellowhammer, but rump grey.

4 Pine Bunting *Emberiza leucocephalos*   **Text and map page 111**

Siberia, N Mongolia and NE Inner Mongolia, and mountains south to the E Tien Shan range. Also NE Qinghai to S Gansu. Winters in Afghanistan, Pakistan and NW India, and in N China. Forest edge and clearings. In winter in arable fields, waste ground and orchards.

4a   **Adult male breeding** (nominate; Siberia) Characteristic chestnut head pattern, with relatively narrow white stripe on ear-coverts and white crown.

4b   **Adult female breeding** (nominate) Individual showing rufous tinge to supercilium, submoustachial stripe and throat, and whitish central crown. The collar of distinct black spots across breast is characteristic of worn plumage.

4c   **Adult male non-breeding** (nominate) Rufous throat obscured by pale fringes, but still clearly visible.

4d   **First-winter female** (nominate) Individual showing normal amounts of rufous. Compared to Yellowhammer (3) underparts are silky white, entirely lacking yellow. Never shows yellow on edges of primaries, tail feathers or underwing-coverts.

4e   **First-winter female** (nominate) Dull individual.

4f   **Juvenile** (nominate) Similar to juvenile Yellowhammer, but lacks yellow in plumage. Breast buffish, contrasting with whitish belly and throat.

4g   **Adult male breeding** (*fronto*; Qinghai and Gansu, China) Lateral crown-stripes broader than nominate and forehead blacker. Chestnut colour on supercilium and throat darker.

3x4 Hybrid Pine Bunting x Yellowhammer

Hybrids occur regularly in parts of the zone of overlap in W Siberia, and may show a variety of intermediate characters.

3x4a   **Male hybrid breeding** (*leucocephalos* x *citrinella*) Presence of yellow colour on breast reveals hybrid origin.

3x4b   **Male hybrid breeding** (*leucocephalos* x *citrinella*) Base colour of head pale yellow; amount of rufous on head reduced compared to Pine Bunting.

3x4c   **Male hybrid breeding** (*leucocephalos* x *citrinella*) Besides distinctive face pattern very similar to male *E. c. erythrogenys*, but whiter on belly, with white outer edges to primaries.

3x4d   **Variant adult male** (Probably hybrid *leucocephalos* x *citrinella*) Males in plumage similar to this one are known primarily from the Altai Mountains.

5 White-capped Bunting *Emberiza stewarti*   **Text and map page 114**

Turkmenistan to S Kazakhstan and Kashmir. Winters mainly in NW India. Bare grassy and rocky slopes, sometimes with sparse bushes and trees, or in open pine or oak forest, usually between 1200 and 2500m. In winter in grassy scrub forest, dry hillsides with scattered bushes and waste ground.

5a   **Adult male breeding** Very pale head, with black eye-stripe and throat characteristic. Upperparts and sides of breast chestnut.

5b   **Adult female breeding** Plumage relatively nondescript, with more indistinct streaking on head than similar species. Rump rusty. Usually a chestnut patch on sides of breast.

5c   **Adult male non-breeding** Bright breeding plumage obscured by pale fringes, but head pattern still clearly visible. Mantle sandy-brown, streaked dark.

5d   **First-winter female** Most similar to female Pine Bunting (4). Differs by greyer plumage, less prominent streaking on crown and mantle, less prominent wing-bars, more white in tail, and lack of *Emberiza* pattern on tertials. Rufous rump less extensive than in Pine Bunting.

5e   **Juvenile** Head rather pale, with indistinct streaking. Bill grey. Mantle dull grey-brown, relatively finely streaked, in obvious contrast to rusty rump. Tertials lack *Emberiza* pattern. Breast rather uniformly and finely streaked.

PLATE 4: ROCK BUNTING GROUP

10 Meadow Bunting *Emberiza cioides* **Text and map page 126**

S Siberia, Mongolia, N and E China to Japan. Resident or short-distance wanderer. Open scrubby habitats or forest edge, usually in hilly or montane country, descending to plains in winter.

10a   **Adult male breeding** (nominate; Altai to Transbaikalia and Mongolia) Chestnut crown and ear-coverts, and prominent breast-band. Streaked mantle separates from *castaneiceps*.

10b   **Juvenile** (nominate) Dark centres of median coverts pointed. Very similar to juvenile of both Godlewski's (9) and Rock Bunting (8). Central pair of tail feathers almost entirely rufous, with only a narrow area along the shaft dark. Rump on average less prominently streaked than eastern races of Rock Bunting.

10c   **Adult male breeding** (*castaneiceps*; E China, Korea) Mantle almost uniformly chestnut. Breast-band broader than nominate.

10d   **Adult male breeding** (*ciopsis*; Japan) Ear-coverts black. Often blackish blotches on breast. Bill longer and more slender than other races.

10e   **Adult male non-breeding** (*ciopsis*) Lores black. Ear-coverts blackish, with white and brown intermixed. Dark pattern of breast concealed.

10f   **Adult female non-breeding** (*ciopsis*) Ear-coverts may appear blackish, but the lores are never as black as in males.

10g   **First-winter female** (*ciopsis*) At least some individuals display this nondescript plumage, lacking dark submoustachial stripe. Underparts may be almost unstreaked.

10h   **Adult female breeding** (*weigoldi*; SE Siberia, NE China) Extreme end of variation. Most females are more male-like. See also Jankowski's Bunting (11).

---

9 Godlewski's Bunting *Emberiza godlewskii* **Text and map page 124**

The Altai Mountains, Transbaikalia, Mongolia, N and C China, south to Yunnan. Resident or dispersive. Bushy and rocky slopes, often near forest. In winter often also in farm fields.

9a   **Adult male breeding** (nominate; S Siberia, Mongolia, N China) Lateral crown-stripes chestnut. Lores and moustachial stripe black; eye-stripe and rear border to ear-coverts chestnut. Base colour of head and breast grey. Scapulars chestnut. Wing-bars white.

9b   **Adult female non-breeding** (nominate) Very similar to male, but on average shows broader dark centres on scapulars. Pale fringes obscure breeding plumage.

9c   **Adult male breeding** (*yunnanensis*; N Yunnan, SE Tibet east to C Sichuan, China) The darkest and most saturated race.

9d   **Juvenile** (*yunnanensis*) Similar to juveniles of other races, but deeper rufous.

9e   **First-winter female** (*decolorata;* Tien Shan Mts, China) Plumage similar to nominate race, but pale and washed out. Rear border to ear-coverts may be pale.

---

8 Rock Bunting *Emberiza cia* **Text and map page 121**

NW Africa and S Europe to Central Asia and the Himalayas. Resident or partly migratory. Dry, sparsely vegetated rocky hillsides, slopes and ravines. Sometimes vineyards and cultivations. In the east often in forests. In winter in open habitats, with hedges and bushes.

8a   **Adult male breeding** (nominate) Distinct narrow blackish border surrounding pale grey ear-coverts, black lores, and black lateral crown-stripes characteristic. Rump rufous. Lacks *Emberiza* pattern on tertials. Underparts rather uniformly rufous.

8b   **Adult female breeding** (nominate) Distinctive narrow dark border around the ear-coverts. Bill grey. Similar to male, but contrast between head and underparts less prominent. Supercilium not as white and lores browner.

8c   **Juvenile** (nominate) Rufous tinge on rump and belly, in combination with narrow dark border to ear-coverts, distinguish from most other juvenile buntings except Godlewski's (9) and Meadow (10). Central tail feathers mostly dark, with only a narrow pale edge.

8d   **Adult male breeding** (*stracheyi*; W Himalayas) Wing-bars buff, base colour of head paler and belly darker and more uniformly rusty-brown than nominate race.

8e   **Adult male breeding** (*par*; Crimea and Caucasus to Iran and C Asia) Wing-bars buff and belly paler than nominate race.

PLATE 5: ORTOLAN GROUP (1)

12   Grey-necked Bunting *Emberiza buchanani*   **Text and map page 130**

E Turkey to W Mongolia. Winters in NW India. Barren arid foothills and mountains. In winter in dry stony semi-desert and cultivated areas.

12a   Adult male breeding (*cerruti*; Turkey, Iran) Uniformly grey head, with whitish eye-ring, and yellowish submoustachial stripe and throat. Bill pinkish-orange. Differs from Ortolan (14) and Cretzschmar's (15) in that there is no clear division between belly and breast. The mantle is sandy-brown, indistinctly streaked dark brown, showing a prominent contrast with the rufous scapulars. Rump sandy-greyish.

12b   Adult female breeding (*cerruti*) Usually duller than males, but some virtually indistinguishable. Head and nape buffier, showing little contrast with the mantle. Crown and nape often show some streaking. Scapulars less bright than in males. Breast slightly paler.

12c   First-winter female (*cerruti*) Crown and nape pale greyish-brown, streaked dark. Rufous mottling on underparts restricted. Breast intermixed with small dark spots. Retained juvenile greater coverts, if present, show narrower and whiter lower wing-bar.

12d   Juvenile (*cerruti*) Crown sandy-grey with diffuse streaking. Nape almost unstreaked, slightly paler than mantle and crown. Breast buffy with some rufous and dark spots intermixed. The dark centres of the median coverts are more pointed than in adult, with a broader tooth.

13   Cinereous Bunting *Emberiza cineracea*   **Text and map page 132**

W Turkey to W Iran. Dry rocky slopes, with shrubby vegetation. In winter in dry open country, often in coastal areas.

13a   Adult male breeding (nominate; W Turkey; Lesbos) Greyish, with yellowish grey-green head. There is a prominent yellowish eye-ring and a short yellowish supercilium in front of the eye. Throat yellow, lacking prominent malar stripe.

13b   Adult female breeding (nominate) Uniform grey-brown appearance, with prominent eye-ring, buffish-yellow throat and only faint malar stripe separates from other bunting species. Differs from male in being duller and browner, often faintly streaked on the crown.

13c   First-winter (nominate) Duller than adults, with streaked breast, and more diffuse streaking on the mantle. Throat pale buff, not yellow.

13d   Adult male breeding (*semenowi*; SE Turkey; Zagros Mts, Iran) Head and underparts largely yellowish. Upperparts similar to nominate race, but tinged brownish or greenish. The scapulars are often dull rufous-brown.

13e   Adult female breeding (*semenowi*) Face and underparts tinged dull yellowish.

13f   First-winter (*semenowi*) Duller than adults, with streaked breast and more diffuse streaking on the mantle. Throat and underparts washed dingy yellow. Wings like adult, but edges buffy and narrower and more distinct. Differs from Black-headed (33) and Red-headed (34) by showing white in the tail. The undertail-coverts are never brighter yellow than the belly, and the rump is concolorous with the mantle, never yellow. The tertials show broad and diffuse pale edges.

15   Cretzschmar's Bunting *Emberiza caesia*   **Text and map page 138**

S Balkans to Israel and Jordan. Winters primarily in Sudan and in Eritrea. Dry stony slopes, wadis and hillsides, with sparse vegetation. In winter in dry open areas.

> **15a**   **Adult male breeding** Head uniformly bluish-grey with rusty submoustachial stripe and throat. Lores rufous-cinnamon. Prominent eye-ring whitish or pale buff. Mantle slightly ruddier than in Ortolan Bunting (14), and belly deeper rufous-brown. Rump unstreaked rufous-brown.
>
> **15b**   **Adult female breeding** Crown tinged brown, finely streaked dark, the demarcation between nape and mantle less prominent than in male. Breast with buffish intermixed, streaked dark on the lower throat. Submoustachial stripe and throat paler and less contrasting than in males. From female Ortolan by blue-grey tinge on head, and rusty submoustachial stripe and throat.
>
> **15c**   **First-summer** Very similar to adult female, and not always possible to distinguish on plumage.
>
> **15d**   **First-winter** This plumage is only worn until about December, when first-summer plumage is acquired. Very similar to Ortolan, but wing-bars indistinct. However, retained outer juvenile greater coverts may form narrow whitish lower wing-bar. Supercilium broad in front of the eye, almost meeting above the bill. Throat and submoustachial stripe similar in colour to breast and belly, but slightly paler. The malar stripe is marginally paler than in Ortolan, making the pattern of the throat slightly less contrasting. Streaking on breast tends to be less black in Cretzschmar's, but marginally more extensive, and often in the shape of streaks, rather than spots as in Ortolan. The belly is slightly deeper cinnamon-buff than in Ortolan. Plumage rather warm brown.

14   Ortolan Bunting *Emberiza hortulana*   **Text and map page 135**

W Europe, through Central Asia, to the Altai Mts. Winters locally in West Africa and in E Sudan and Ethiopia. Open areas with scrub and sparse trees. In winter in dry open country.

> **14a**   **Adult male breeding** Head uniformly greenish-grey, slightly paler on lores, with prominent yellowish-white eye-ring, pinkish bill, and yellow submoustachial stripe and throat. Grey breast sharply set off from rufous-buff belly and flanks.
>
> **14b**   **Adult male breeding** Individual with greyer head and paler yellow throat.
>
> **14c**   **Adult female breeding** Uniform head pattern, lack of supercilium, but with prominent submoustachial stripe characteristic. Similar to adult male, but head more olive with distinct streaking on crown, malar stripe blackish, and breast tinged buffish, grading into belly, with a varying amount of dark streaking. Flanks unstreaked. Contrast between nape and mantle not very prominent compared to male.
>
> **14d**   **First-summer female** Differs from adult female in more prominent streaking on crown, duller underparts, and narrow dark streaking on flanks. Very similar to Cretzschmar's Bunting (15), but usually shows traces of greenish on crown and nape.
>
> **14e**   **First-winter** This plumage is only worn until about December-March, when first-summer plumage is acquired. Very similar to Cretzschmar's, but throat usually whitish or pale yellow, showing some contrast with the pale rufous-buff belly. The malar stripe is more prominent and the breast is spotted blackish. The supercilium is usually narrow in front of the eye and the forehead darker than in Cretzschmar's. Wing-bars often, but not always, whiter.

15a

14a

14b

15b

14c

15c

14d

15d

14e

PLATE 7:   HOUSE BUNTING GROUP

18   Cinnamon-breasted Bunting *Emberiza tahapisi*　　　Text and map page 145

Africa south of the Sahara and the SW Arabian peninsula, avoiding the equatorial forest, the highest mountains and deserts. Migratory or dispersive in many regions, but resident in others. Bushy or lightly wooded rocky ridges, escarpments, quarries and eroded mountainsides.

18a　**Adult male** (nominate; E and S Africa) Head prominently striped black and white, throat black.

18b　**Adult female** (nominate) Rather nondescript cinnamon-brown appearance, but striped crown and face and dark throat characteristic.

18c　**Juvenile** (nominate) Similar to adult female, but pattern of head duller and less contrasting. Throat paler with some dark streaking. Dark centres of median coverts with blunt 'tooth'.

18d　**Adult male** (*goslingi*; Gambia to Sudan) Relatively pale grey throat and more extensively rufous wings render males of this sub-Saharan race very different from nominate males.

18e　**Adult female** (*goslingi*) Similar to female of nominate race, but throat pale and wings more extensively rufous.

18f　**First-winter female** (*insularis*; Socotra) Extreme end of variation. Crown and face pattern typical of species, but throat pale. Wing-coverts lack rufous. No white in tail.

16   House Bunting *Emberiza striolata*　　　Text and map page 141

Occurs from Morocco and Mauretania in the west, and N Kenya in the south, to NW India, but absent from large areas of unsuitable habitat. Mostly resident, with some local wandering to lower elevations in winter. Arid rocky slopes and stony hillsides with sparse scrub, usually within reach of water. In NW Africa, largely adapted to human settlements.

16a　**Adult male** (*sahari*; NW Africa) Uniform in appearance, with upperparts almost unstreaked, wings almost uniformly rufous, and underparts similar to mantle in colour. The head pattern is more uniform than in the nominate, with eye-stripe, moustachial stripe, and streaking on throat and breast paler grey, and the bill is longer.

16b　**Adult female** (*sahari*) Rather nondescript rufous-brown plumage, with head slightly more grey-brown. Wings uniformly rufous.

16c　**Juvenile** (*sahari*) Very pale and nondescript, with rufous wings. Generally browner than subsequent plumages. Bill duller than in adult female.

16d　**Adult male** (nominate; Sinai to India) Mantle and rump sand-coloured, streaked dark. Underparts relatively pale greyish-brown, tinged rufous. Crown uniformly streaked blackish, sometimes more densely on the sides. Face striped black and white, the stripes more parallel than in most other buntings. Wings less uniform than in *sahari*.

16e　**Adult male** (nominate) Pale individual representative of eastern populations.

16f　**Adult female** (nominate) Differs from male in that the crown is pale sandy-brown streaked dark brown, instead of white distinctly streaked black. Supercilium and submoustachial stripe pale sandy-brown rather than white.

16g　**Adult female** (nominate) Pale individual representative of eastern populations. Differs from male in that the crown is pale sandy-brown, streaked dark brown, instead of white, distinctly streaked black. Supercilium and submoustachial stripe pale sandy-brown.

16h　**Adult male** (*jebelmarrae*, W Sudan) Similar to nominate race, but considerably darker rufous-brown, with bolder streaking on crown, breast, mantle and scapulars. The underparts are even darker than Cinnamon-breasted Bunting.

16i　**Adult female** (*jebelmarrae*) Similar to nominate female, but darker and more prominently streaked. Differs from nominate Cinnamon-breasted Bunting (18) by more uniformly streaked crown, less prominent face pattern, and more extensively rufous wings. From Cinnamon-breasted Bunting of the race *goslingi* by dark throat.

16j　**Juvenile** (*jebelmarrae*) Similar to nominate juvenile, but darker and more heavily streaked on crown, breast, mantle and flanks. Face pattern less distinct than subsequent plumages, with streaking on crown, breast and upperparts paler and more diffuse. Dark shaft streak on median coverts with blunt end. Tail feathers show diffuse rufous-brown tip of outermost pair.

PLATE 8:   AFRICAN BUNTINGS

19   Socotra Bunting *Emberiza socotrana*   **Text and map page 148**

Endemic to Socotra Island in the Indian Ocean. Breeds in rugged terrain with steep cliffs and boulders at relatively high altitudes, probably descending to lower altitude after the breeding season.

> **19a**   **Adult male** Resembles Cape Bunting (20), but crown with prominent white median crown-stripe, bill yellow, underparts white with russet-brown breast-band, and a pale band across the back.
>
> **19b**   **Adult female** Less saturated colours than male, with less contrasting head pattern.

17   Lark-like Bunting *Emberiza impetuani*   **Text and map page 143**

SW Angola, Namibia, S Botswana, S Zimbabwe and W South Africa. Irruptive and nomadic. Hard stony eroded ground and open hillsides, with sparse growth of stunted scrub, grass and weeds.

> **17a**   **Adult** Sand-coloured and featureless. Wing-coverts, tertials and secondaries relatively dark with narrow and contrasting rufous edges, forming a wing panel on the folded secondaries. No white in the tail. Breast unstreaked.
>
> **17b**   **Juvenile** Very similar to adult, but slightly browner, with streaking on upperparts more diffuse, breast faintly streaked or spotted and wing more uniform.

20   Cape Bunting *Emberiza capensis*   **Text and map page 150**

Southern Africa. Mainly sedentary. Rocky, boulder-strewn hills and dry stony ground with sparse short grass and scattered scrub.

> **20a**   **Adult male** (*smithersii*; Chimanimani Mts, E Zimbabwe) A rather dark race, with upperparts olive-grey heavily, streaked blackish. Underparts, including the throat, olive-greyish. The median coverts show dark shaft streaks. Similar to *basutoensis*, but slightly darker below.
>
> **20b**   **Adult male** (*reidi*; E South Africa) Rich cinnamon-brown plumage. The races *media* and *limpopoensis* from neighbouring areas are generally similar. The race *basutoensis*, occurring at higher altitude in the Drakensberg mountains, is more olive-grey, and shows dark shaft streaks on the median coverts.
>
> **20c**   **Adult male** (*nebularum*; SW Angola) The palest race. The buffish mantle shows less streaking than any other race, with only fine blackish shaft streaks. Underparts very pale grey. The bill is proportionately longer. Wings contrastingly rufous.
>
> **20d**   **Adult male** (nominate; W South Africa, S Namibia) Distinct black border to ear-coverts, uniformly streaked crown, unmarked throat, uniform underparts and rufous wings contrasting with greyish plumage (except *reidi*-group) diagnostic for species. Nominate race rather grey in appearance, with diffuse streaking on mantle. Underparts vinaceous-grey.
>
> **20e**   **Juvenile** (nominate) Paler than adult, showing streaking on breast and flanks; the breast lacks greyish cast. Base colour of mantle paler and greyer than adult, but streaking heavier. Tips of primary coverts paler than in adult. Tips of outer tail feathers rusty-brown.
>
> **20f**   **Adult male** (*vincenti*; S Malawi, and adjacent Tanzania, Zambia and Mozambique) Very dark plumage, only diffusely streaked above, with slaty-black underparts, contrasting with white throat. Amount of chestnut in the wings less extensive than other races, creating chestnut wing-bars instead of a panel.

PLATE 9: ASIAN BUNTINGS (2)

21 Chestnut-eared Bunting *Emberiza fucata* Text and map page 152

W Himalayas, China, SE Siberia, Mongolia and Japan. Winters in southern parts of range, north to Korea and S Japan, and south to N Indochina. Scrubby hillsides, open marshland, meadows and riverside thickets. In winter often in bushes and grasses adjoining fields and marshes.

21a   **Adult male breeding** (nominate; NE China, Japan) Unmistakable. Unique breast pattern. Chestnut ear-coverts contrast with grey crown and sides of neck.

21b   **Adult male non-breeding** (nominate) Similar to adult male breeding, but crown tinged olive-brown, and breast-bands less well developed. The contrast between breast and belly is more prominent than in female, and the ear-coverts tend to show more black.

21c   **Adult female breeding** (nominate) Duller than male. Crown tinged olive. Supercilium whiter. Ear-coverts paler. Throat and upper breast show less contrast with belly. Breast-bands less prominent.

21d   **First-winter female** (nominate) Crown pale olive-brown, always lacking dark lateral crown-stripes. Ear-coverts brown. Eye-ring well-marked. Little contrast between breast and belly. Traces of the lower breast-band sometimes visible.

21e   **First-winter female** (nominate) Dull individual resembling Ortolan (14). Differs by heavier streaking on mantle, ear-coverts usually noticeably browner than crown, more prominent supercilium, blacker and more well-defined malar stripe, darker bill and rufous lesser coverts.

21f   **Juvenile** (nominate) Dark lateral crown-stripes, prominent whitish supercilium, and whitish centre to ear-coverts. Breast sparsely streaked, flanks often tinged rufous.

21g   **Adult male breeding** (*arcuata*; N India, SW China) Darker and more richly coloured than nominate. Black streaking on mantle on average narrower. Throat whiter, the black gorget broader. Lower breast-band more extensive.

21h   **First-winter female** (*arcuata*) Colours more saturated compared to nominate, with streaking on breast heavier, orange on flanks more extensive, and wing-bars less prominent, pale rufous.

23 Tristram's Bunting *Emberiza tristrami* Text and map page 157

NE China and adjacent Russia. Winters in S China, and rarely to N South-East Asia. Forest with dense underbrush, usually on hillsides. In winter on the forest floor in wooded hills.

23a   **Adult male breeding** Unmistakable. Striking head pattern and black throat. Rump unstreaked reddish-brown. Centre of ear-coverts black or dark brown.

23b   **Adult female breeding** Similar to male, but throat buffish-white, and lores and ear-coverts browner. Black malar stripe contrasts with rufous pattern on the breast, unlike in Yellow-browed.

23c   **Adult male non-breeding** Lateral crown-stripes, lores and ear-coverts slightly obscured by pale fringes. Throat dark.

23d   **First-winter female** Pale parts of head tinged buffish. Lateral crown-stripes fringed brownish. Breast rufous-brown, indistinctly streaked.

23e   **Juvenile** Very similar to 24e, but rump rufous.

24 Yellow-browed Bunting *Emberiza chrysophrys* Text and map page 159

C Siberia. Winters in C and SE China. Taiga, and edges of clearings. In winter in scrubby and weedy areas, often near edges of forest.

24a   **Adult male breeding** Striking head pattern. Anterior supercilium yellow.

24b   **Adult female breeding** Similar to male, but lores and ear-coverts browner.

24c   **Adult male non-breeding** Contrasting head pattern indicates male, but most autumn birds not safely sexed or aged in the field. Yellow supercilium usually obvious. Mantle shows brown central stripe characteristic of this species and Tristram's Bunting.

24d   **First-winter female** Most birds in fresh plumage cannot be sexed or aged in the field. Lateral crown-stripes on average browner, due to broader fringes.

24e   **Juvenile** Very similar to 23e, but rump similar to mantle. Supercilium may be yellow.

22 Little Bunting *Emberiza pusilla*   Text and map page 154

N Scandinavia to NE Siberia. Winters from Nepal to S China. Open taiga with undergrowth of dwarf birch and willows, and bushy tundra. In winter found in a variety of open habitats.

22a **Adult breeding** Well-defined lateral crown-stripes, chestnut ear-coverts and pale eye-ring distinctive. Moustache never dark. Sexes indistinguishable except in breeding pairs.

22b **Adult breeding** Commonly seen plumage with extensively chestnut face.

22c **First-winter** Virtually identical to adult non-breeding, but head pattern on average duller.

22d **Juvenile** Similar to adult non-breeding, but crown-stripes more streaked, dark centres to median coverts pointed, and streaking on breast and mantle less neat.

25 Rustic Bunting *Emberiza rustica*   Text and map page 161

N Scandinavia to Kamchatka. Winters in Japan, Korea and China. Damp forest and scrub bordering fens, river banks or bogs. In winter in woods, cultivated land and open areas.

25a **Adult male breeding** (nominate; N Scandinavia to C Siberia) Striking head pattern, and reddish nape, breast-band and streaking on flanks and rump. Crown feathers often slightly raised. Underparts white.

25b **Adult male non-breeding** (nominate) Generally similar to breeding female. Ageing and sexing of autumn birds in the field not recommended.

25c **Adult female breeding** (nominate) Prominent whitish spot on rear corner of ear-coverts, rufous nape, prominent white wing-bars, reddish-brown rump and white breast and flanks, with reddish streaking distinctive. Similar to breeding male, but head pattern less striking and reddish-brown colours paler and more orange-brown.

25d **Adult female breeding** (nominate) Somewhat like male, but median crown-stripe reaches bill, and ear-coverts and lores paler. Shallow V-shape of breast-band typical.

25e **First-winter female** (nominate) Similar to 25c but duller. Cf. Yellow-throated Bunting (26). Lesser coverts reddish-brown.

25f **Juvenile** (nominate) Face pattern similar to adult female, but duller. Usually some reddish visible on neck or nape. Dark centres of median coverts pointed. Breast prominently streaked dark brown. Rump and streaking on flanks reddish-brown.

26 Yellow-throated Bunting *Emberiza elegans*   Text and map page 164

Two disjunct populations. NE China, Korea, and adjacent Russia; and C China. Winters from Korea and W Japan, to SE China and Taiwan. Partly resident, with some southward dispersal, in C China. Dry deciduous forest in hills. Winters in woods and scrubby areas.

26a **Adult male breeding** (nominate; NE China, SE Siberia) Erect black crest, black mask and breast patch. Supercilium, throat and hindcrown yellow.

26b **Adult female breeding** (nominate) Breast smudged rufous-buff, with indistinct rufous-brown streaking. Chin never black.

26c **Adult female breeding** (nominate) Individual resembling male, but crown and ear-coverts brown. Supercilium and throat yellowish-buff. Dark spots on breast, ghosting pattern of male.

26d **Adult male non-breeding** (nominate) Crown, ear-coverts and breast patch obscured by pale fringes. Yellow colours paler, mantle and rump browner.

26e **First-winter female** (nominate) Similar to 25e, but ear-coverts uniformly dark brown and pale spot much reduced. No dark malar stripe. Crest more prominent. Throat pale buffish. Central breast poorly marked. Lesser coverts and rump grey.

26f **Juvenile** (nominate) Short crest. Dark centres of median coverts pointed. Breast finely streaked dark.

26g **Adult male breeding** (*elegantula*; C China) Dark, with blackish streaking on the mantle. Nape dark grey, with more blackish intermixed on rear crown. Black patch on breast more extensive. Streaking on sides of breast and flanks blacker and more extensive.

26h **Adult female breeding** (*elegantula*) Darker than nominate, with blacker streaking on the mantle. Dark patch on breast more extensive.

27 Yellow-breasted Bunting *Emberiza aureola* **Text and map page 166**

Finland to Japan, south to Hebei, China. Win ters from Nepal to S China, south to S Thailand. Meadows with tall herbage and scattered shrubs, riverside thickets, and areas with secondary scrub. Ricefields, reedbeds, grasslands and scrubby arable land in winter.

27a **Adult male breeding** (nominate; N Scandinavia to Kamchatka) Upperparts rather uniformly dark chestnut. Face and throat jet black. Underparts bright yellow with narrow chestnut breast-band. Prominent white patch on the wing.

27b **Adult female breeding** (nominate) Distinguished by distinct narrow dark border to ear-coverts, prominent supercilium and virtually no malar stripe, in combination with prominently streaked mantle, and whitish-yellow underparts. The streaking on the underparts is most prominent on flanks, and usually faint or absent on the breast. Wing-bars fairly obvious.

27c **Adult male non-breeding** (nominate) Although partly obscured by pale fringes, traces of breeding plumage usually apparent, and white lesser and median coverts still obvious.

27d **Adult female non-breeding** (nominate) Similar to 27b, but brighter yellow, unstreaked below. Very similar to first-winter birds of both sexes, and single birds are not safely aged or sexed in the field.

27e **First-winter male** (nominate) Similar to non-breeding female, and most cannot be told apart. Plumage may be more contrasting, and concealed chestnut on upperparts may show through. Safely told from females only if upper wing-bar obviously broader.

27f **Juvenile** (nominate) Similar to 27d, but breast streaked, and a dark malar stripe sometimes present. Dark centres of the median coverts more pointed. Migrates in juvenile plumage.

27g **Adult male breeding** (*ornata*; Japan, Sakhalin, Manchuria and S Russian Far East) More black on forehead. Darker above. Sides of breast blackish. Underparts on average brighter yellow.

27h **Adult female non-breeding** (*ornata*) Brighter than nominate with streaking on sides of breast.

28 Chestnut Bunting *Emberiza rutila* **Text and map page 169**

S Siberia and Dauria. Winters in N South-East Asia and S China. Forest with shrubby ground cover, often on ridges, hillocks or mountain slopes. In winter usually in open woodland, clearings or cultivated land with cover nearby.

28a **Adult male breeding** Head and upperparts uniformly chestnut, belly yellow.

28b **Adult female breeding** Greyish-buff and rather featureless head and mantle contrasts with yellow underparts (including undertail-coverts) and rufous rump. Wing-bars indistinct. The throat is buffish and never yellow. Malar stripe relatively prominent.

28c **Adult male non-breeding** Very similar to breeding plumage, but narrow fringes obscure chestnut parts to some extent.

28d **Immature male spring/summer** Ageing of immature males is not fully understood. Streaked mantle, white throat and dark-centred median and greater coverts are all characters of immaturity.

28e **First-winter male** Very similar to first-winter female, but concealed chestnut often shows through on crown, ear-coverts and/or breast.

28f **First-winter female** Very similar to adult female non-breeding. Never shows rufous on crown, mantle, scapulars and lesser coverts, but most cannot be aged in the field.

28g **Juvenile** Mantle and breast more heavily streaked than adults, rump less bright and head pattern more striking. Rufous rump and yellowish undertail-coverts separate it from Yellow-breasted Bunting (27).

PLATE 12: AFRICAN YELLOW-BREASTED BUNTINGS

31 Brown-rumped Bunting *Emberiza affinis*　　　　**Text and map page 176**

Gambia to Ethiopia and Uganda. Short-distance migrant. Open woodlands and forest.

31a　**Adult male breeding** (nominate; S Sudan, N Uganda and adjacent Zaïre) Lack of significant wing-bars, brown rump and very white face distinctive of species.

31b　**Adult female breeding** (nominate) Similar to adult male, but head pattern slightly duller.

31c　**Juvenile** (nominate) Lateral crown-stripes sandy chestnut. Slightly paler tips to median and greater coverts may form inconspicuous wing-bars.

31d　**Adult male breeding** (*nigeriae*, Gambia to E Nigeria and N Cameroon) From nominate by paler appearance, evidence of wing-bars and streaked mantle.

31e　**Adult male non-breeding** (*nigeriae*) Mantle very pale. Inconspicuous wing-bars, all yellow underparts and brown rump distinctive.

29 Golden-breasted Bunting *Emberiza flaviventris*　　　**Text and map page 172**

Most of Africa south of Sahara except the equatorial forest region. Dry open woodland habitats, wooded acacia steppe and dry savanna.

29a　**Adult male** (nominate; S Sudan to South Africa) Bold black and white head pattern, orange-yellow breast, chestnut mantle, grey rump, and prominent white wing-bars. Lores dark just in front of the eye. Orange-yellow breast clearly set off from yellow throat.

29b　**Adult female** (nominate) Similar to male, but dark pattern of head browner, and whitish parts buffier. Mantle usually with narrow dark shaft streaks. Yellow underparts less bright, the difference between throat and breast less obvious.

29c　**Juvenile** (nominate) Duller than adult; head pattern brown and pale buff, underparts paler. Narrower wing-bars, median coverts with pointed dark centres.

29d　**Adult male** (*flavigaster*, S edge of Sahara) Mantle paler, more rufous. Rump paler grey, tinged sandy. Yellow underparts paler, and flanks whiter. Very little black on lores.

30 Somali Golden-breasted Bunting *Emberiza poliopleura*　**Text and map page 174**

E Ethiopia, Somalia and Kenya, except central highlands. Arid tropical subdesert steppe, edges of wooded steppe, and coastal savanna.

30a　**Adult male** Mantle streaked whitish. Scapulars dark. Back spotted blackish. Flanks pale grey. Face whiter than Golden-breasted (29): supercilia nearly meet on forehead, lores white, and eye-ring white above eye. Short primary projection.

30b　**Adult female** Lateral crown-stripes and border around the ear-coverts browner than male.

30c　**Juvenile** Resembles 29c, but mantle more contrastingly striped, underparts whiter, with breast streaked dark. Head browner and duller than adults. Median coverts dark-centred.

32 Cabanis's Bunting *Emberiza cabanisi*　　　　**Text and map page 177**

Discontinuous distribution from Sierra Leone to Uganda, south to Cameroon; Gabon; Angola to Tanzania and Zimbabwe. Savanna and miombo woodlands with little or no undergrowth.

32a　**Adult male** (nominate; Sierra Leone to Cameroon) Crown, mantle and rump dark grey, mantle diffusely streaked dark. Ear-coverts uniformly blackish. Throat white. Underparts yellow faintly tinged greenish, with no difference in colour between breast and belly.

32b　**Adult female** (nominate) Similar to male, but crown, lores and ear-coverts paler brown and supercilium and throat tinged buffish. The central breast is washed orange-brown.

32c　**Juvenile** (nominate) Ear-coverts dark, upperparts virtually unstreaked, wing-bars inconspicuous, and underparts unstreaked.

32d　**Adult male** (*orientalis*, Zambia to Tanzania and Zimbabwe) Differs from nominate by prominent whitish median crown-stripe, and paler buffy-grey mantle, with distinct blackish streaking. Throat yellow, with only chin white.

32e　**Adult female** (*orientalis*) Similar to male, but head pattern duller.

32f　**Juvenile** (*orientalis*) Browner than adult, with pale rufous supercilium and dark-centred median coverts. From nominate by streaking on mantle and breast. Wing-bars paler.

PLATE 13: RED-HEADED AND BLACK-HEADED BUNTINGS

34 Red-headed Bunting *Emberiza bruniceps*   **Text and map page 182**

C Asia. Winters in India. Scrubby areas in open country, cultivated and steppe areas.

34a **Adult male breeding** Head and breast chestnut, underparts and rump yellow. Mantle yellowish-green, streaked blackish.

34b **Adult male breeding** Individual with limited amount of chestnut, showing yellow crown.

34c **Adult male non-breeding** After partial post-breeding moult during summer, bright colours often obscured to some extent, but still visible enough for a safe identification.

34d **Adult female breeding** (spring-early summer) Extremely similar to Black-headed (33), and most cannot be safely identified. Subtle differences include slightly browner ear-coverts, contrasting less with the throat; on average less streaking on forehead and crown, often virtually unstreaked; no significant colour difference between crown and mantle; back never rufous, and rump usually brighter yellow. The throat tends to be paler yellow or buffier compared to the breast, which often shows a rusty wash. The wing-bars tend to be buffier.

34e **Adult female breeding** (summer-autumn) Rufous tinge on the forehead, yellow tinge on the crown and mantle, greyish back, and yellow rump typical. Usually no difference in colour between crown and mantle, although nape paler. In birds with a yellow belly, the throat is usually noticeably buffier.

34f **Probable first-summer female** (spring-early summer) Plumage attained on wintering grounds. Similar to 34d, but yellow on underparts restricted to undertail-coverts. Extremely similar to Black-headed; wing-bars virtually identical in this plumage.

34g **First-winter** Extremely similar to Black-headed Bunting in corresponding plumage. Plate shows heavily patterned individual, so far not confirmed for Black-headed.

33x34 Hybrid Black-headed x Red-headed Bunting

In a limited area south-east of the Caspian Sea, the two species are sympatric and hybridisation is relatively frequent.

33x34a **Hybrid** (*melanocephala* x *bruniceps*) Most similar to Red-headed Bunting, but ear-coverts speckled black, and throat yellow. Some rufous visible on the otherwise mainly greenish mantle.

33x34b **Hybrid** (*melanocephala* x *bruniceps*) Plumage intermediate. Mantle predominantly rufous, but head extensively yellow, and breast with some chestnut.

33x34c **Hybrid** (*melanocephala* x *bruniceps*) Similar to Black-headed Bunting, but yellow intermixed in otherwise black crown reveal hybrid origin.

33 Black-headed Bunting *Emberiza melanocephala*   **Text and map page 179**

The E Mediterranean to Iran. Winters in India. Maquis, thickets and cultivated areas.

33a **Adult male breeding** Black cap, chestnut upperparts and bright yellow underparts.

33b **Adult male non-breeding** Plumage acquired during summer after breeding season. Similar to breeding plumage, but bright colours obscured by pale fringes.

33c **Adult female breeding** (spring-early summer) Extremely similar to Red-headed (34), and most cannot be safely identified. Subtle differences include slight colour difference between crown and mantle, more uniformly coloured underparts, darker ear-coverts, and whiter wing-bars.

33d **Adult female breeding** (summer-autumn) Some, but not all, females show plumage reminiscent of washed-out male when worn.

33e **First-winter** Extremely similar to first-winter Red-headed Bunting, and not safely separable on plumage. Differs from subsequent plumages by streaked breast, whiter and more well-defined fringes on tertials and wing-coverts, and little or no yellow on rump.

33f **Juvenile** This golden-buff nestling plumage is moulted soon after leaving the nest.

36 Black-faced Bunting *Emberiza spodocephala*   Text and map page 187

Siberia, C China and Japan. Winters from the E Himalayas to S China. Favours moist shrubby undergrowth; in Japan also in broadleaf mountain forest. In winter in hedges and shrubs near water, clearings or other open habitats.

36a **Adult male breeding** (nominate; Siberia) Base colour of head grey. Underparts pale yellow or almost whitish. Lores and chin blackish; bill pale. Upperparts brown, streaked blackish, slightly greyer and unstreaked on the rump.

36b **Adult female breeding** (nominate) Nondescript; crown and ear-coverts rather uniform. Supercilium less prominent than submoustachial stripe. Pattern of crown and ear-coverts often similar to 36g. Male-like individuals never show black lores or chin, and breast never prominently set off from belly.

36c **First-winter male** (nominate) Crown feathers and sides of neck usually greyer than female. The streaking on the breast is less prominent than in females.

36d **First-winter female** (nominate) Rather featureless, lacking obvious distinguishing characters. Lower mandible pale; culmen dark and straight. Supercilium duller and less prominent than submoustachial stripe. Malar stripe not very prominent. Lesser coverts grey-brown. Wing-bars pale. Streaking on breast fainter than on flanks.

36e **Adult male breeding** (*sordida*; C China) Similar to nominate, but base colour of head greenish, and underparts often more yellow.

36f **Adult male breeding** (*personata*; Japan) Throat and breast yellow like belly. Streaks on flanks blacker. Underparts yellow, brighter than other races.

36g **Adult female breeding** (*personata*) Often similar to nominate, apart from yellow colour, and heavier streaking. Individual shown approaches male in appearance, but lacks black lores and chin.

36h **First-winter female** (*personata*) Similar to nominate, but plumage yellow, and streaking on breast blacker.

35 Japanese Yellow Bunting *Emberiza sulphurata*   Text and map page 185

Japan. Winters in Taiwan, S China and the Philippines. Second growth and forest edge in deciduous and mixed forest in foothills.

35a **Adult male breeding** Brighter green than female, with lores and chin blackish.

35b **Adult female non-breeding** Rather uniformly yellowish-green, with mantle streaked dark, and white double wing-bars. Head uniformly plain greenish with a prominent white eye-ring. Bill relatively uniformly blue-grey. Streaking on underparts largely restricted to flanks.

35c **First-winter female** Similar to 35b, but plumage tinged rufescent. Malar stripe short and indistinct.

37 Grey Bunting *Emberiza variabilis*   Text and map page 190

S Kamchatka to Japan; winters mainly in Japan. Bamboo and undergrowth in temperate mountain forests.

37a **Adult male breeding** Dark slaty-blue, mantle streaked dark. Lacks white in tail.

37b **Adult female non-breeding** Face rather dull, reminiscent of 36d. Crown rather dark, with pale median crown-stripe. Rump unstreaked rufescent brown. Underparts whitish with olive-brown wash, and relatively indistinct dark streaking. Undertail-coverts dark-centred. Lacks white in tail.

37c **First-winter male** Head pattern slightly duller than female. Rump a mixture of blue-grey and rufous-brown. Breast, flanks and belly blue-grey, uniform or slightly mottled, lacking dark streaking.

39   Common Reed Bunting *Emberiza schoeniclus*   Text and map page 196

Breeds over large parts of Europe and Asia, north of Tibet and E China. Southern populations sedentary or dispersive, others migrating mainly to southern parts of range. Marshy areas with shrubs or reeds or with tall herbage. Outside breeding season along lake shores or in fields and weedy areas.

39a   **Adult male breeding** (nominate; N and W Europe) Head, including throat, black, except for a prominent white submoustachial stripe, and bordered behind by a conspicuous white nape. Mantle grey-brown and rufous, streaked blackish. Rump greyish. The wings are extensively rufous, with rather inconspicuous wing-bars. Underparts whitish, with some dark streaking on the flanks. The outermost pair of tail feathers is extensively white.

39b   **Adult female breeding** (nominate) Head pattern typical of the genus. Crown brown, with a pale median crown-stripe, unless too worn. Supercilium, sides of neck, submoustachial stripe and throat pale buffish. Ear-coverts and lores relatively pale brownish, with eye-stripe, moustachial stripe and rear edge of ear-coverts darker brown. Malar stripe prominent, dark brown. Lesser coverts rufous. Wing-bars relatively inconspicuous. The streaking on the flanks relatively prominent. Bill blue-grey, the culmen slightly convex.

39c   **Male in transitional plumage** (nominate) In spring, when part of the breeding plumage is attained by moult, and part by wear, unexpected patterns may occur. In this individual, moult proceeds faster than wear. Confusion with species with dark ear-coverts and white supercilium, like Rustic Bunting (25), conceivable. See also Pallas's Reed Bunting.

39d   **Adult female non-breeding** (nominate) Similar to 39b, but plumage paler, the under parts buffier, the dark streaking less well-defined. Crown paler, particularly the centre.

39e   **Juvenile** (nominate) Similar to adult female, but streaking broader and more diffuse. Dark centres of median coverts more pointed.

39f   **Adult male breeding** (*lusitanica*; Portugal) The darkest race. Bill average size.

39g   **Adult female breeding** (*lusitanica*) Darker than nominate, in worn plumage often with almost blackish crown and indistinct supercilium.

39h   **Adult male breeding** (*reiseri*; Albania, Greece) Large, with heavy bill. One of the darkest races. Most similar to *witherbyi*, *intermedia* and *caspia*.

39i   **Adult female breeding** (*reiseri*) Darker than nominate, in worn plumage often with almost blackish crown and indistinct supercilium.

39j   **Adult male breeding** (*pyrrhuloides*; Kazakhstan and neighbouring areas) Large, with heavy bill. Very pale plumage, with whitish rump. In coloration most similar to *korejewi*, *incognita*, *pallidior*, *harterti* and *centralasiae*.

39k   **Adult male non-breeding** (*zaidamensis*; Zaidam depression, China) Large, with heavy bill. Buffier, less grey, than *pyrrhuloides*.

39l   **Adult female non-breeding** (*pyrrhulina*; Kamchatka, E Siberia, NE China) Very pale, with pale unstreaked rump and no or inconspicuous streaking on breast and belly. Confusion with non-breeding Pallas's Reed Bunting (38) conceivable, but the bill is larger, with convex culmen, the lesser coverts are rufous, and there is a clear difference between the pale median crown-stripe and darker rufous lateral crown-stripes.

39f

39g

39k

39e

39a

39b

39d

39j

39h

39i

39l

39c

38 Pallas's Reed Bunting *Emberiza pallasi*   **Text and map page 192**

N Siberia, mountain and plains in S Siberia, Mongolia and N China. Tundra and steppe. In winter in reedbeds and shrubs, ricefields and arable land. The geographical variation is not fully understood, and the races *pallasi*, *polaris* and *montana* are not differentiated here.

> **38a** **Adult male breeding** Very worn individual. Similar to Common Reed Bunting (39), differing by combination of darker mantle and paler rump. The lesser coverts are blue-grey and the wing-bars whiter.
>
> **38b** **Adult male breeding** Individual in less worn plumage than 38a. The pale stripes on the mantle are more prominent, and the lesser coverts are paler.
>
> **38c** **Adult female breeding** Individual in moderately worn and relatively dull plumage. Uniformly streaked crown, grey-brown lesser coverts and prominent wing-bars separate from female Common Reed Bunting.
>
> **38d** **Adult female breeding** Individual in typical worn plumage. Differs from female Common Reed Bunting by same characters as 38c.
>
> **38e** **Male in transitional plumage** In spring, when part of the breeding plumage is attained by moult and part by wear, unexpected patterns may occur. In this individual, wear has preceded moult. See also Common Reed Bunting.
>
> **38f** **Adult male non-breeding** Similar to non-breeding female, but the concealed black bib often shows through. The crown and ear-coverts may also show more black than females, particularly when plumage becomes worn in late winter. The lesser coverts are blue-grey.
>
> **38g** **Adult female non-breeding** Pale, with pale rump and very sparse streaking on the underparts, prominent pale double wing-bars, two-toned bill, with dark upper and pinkish lower mandible, and greyish-brown or blue-grey colour of lesser coverts. Crown rather uniformly sandy-brown, with some faint streaking. Supercilium indistinct. Ear-coverts rather uniform in colour and relatively pale, with a dark spot at the lower rear corner and narrow dark moustachial stripe creating a distinct dark lower border. Bill pointed with more or less straight culmen.
>
> **38h** **Juvenile** Streaked on the underparts. Crown rather uniformly dark without pale median crown-stripe. No dark eye-stripe behind eye.
>
> **38i** **Adult male breeding** (*lydiae*, Mongolia) Paler and buffier than other races, with less contrast between rump and mantle.
>
> **38j** **Juvenile** (*lydiae*) Paler than other races, with breast sparsely spotted.

40 Japanese Reed Bunting *Emberiza yessoensis*   **Text and map page 200**

Japan, NE China and extreme SE Siberia. Winters in coastal areas of Japan, Korea and E China. Reedbeds, marshes and wet meadows. Winters in coastal marshes.

> **40a** **Adult male breeding** (nominate; Japan) Head all black, lacking whitish submoustachial stripe. Nape brown. Mantle heavily streaked, but underparts unstreaked.
>
> **40b** **Adult female breeding** (nominate) Crown and ear-coverts uniformly blackish. Mantle heavily streaked. Malar stripes prominent, but streaking on breast inconspicuous.
>
> **40c** **Adult male non-breeding** (nominate) Dark bases to throat feathers usually show through, and both crown and ear-coverts usually show more black than in younger males.
>
> **40d** **First-winter male** (nominate) Shows more black on ear-coverts than female in corresponding plumage, and often a less neat crown pattern.
>
> **40e** **First-winter female** (nominate) Lack of dark pattern on throat separates from males. Ear-coverts are on average paler than in males, and the pale median crown-stripe is usually more well-defined. Compared to similar species, the mantle is more heavily streaked, but the underparts are paler, often with no or only faint streaking. The rump is pale, pinkish grey-brown. The wing is uniform in colour, with inconspicuous wing-bars.
>
> **40f** **First-winter female** (nominate) Individual with streaked breast, showing extreme end of variation.

PLATE 17: LAPLAND LONGSPUR AND LARK BUNTING

43   Lapland Longspur *Calcarius lapponicus*   Text and map page 209

Distributed throughout the Arctic region, breeding on tundra. Winters on steppes, prairie and sea coasts further south.

43a   **Adult male breeding** (nominate; N Norway to E Siberia) The breeding male is unmistakable, showing characteristic black face and breast, corn yellow bill, rufous nape and whitish zigzag pattern on the side of the head. The upperparts are relatively dark, blackish narrowly streaked pale buff.

43b   **Adult female breeding** (nominate) Rather nondescript, but shows rufous nape and greater coverts. The head is very pale, with blackish lateral crown-stripes and prominent blackish border to ear-coverts. Pale lores, whitish supercilium and pale centres to ear-coverts create open-faced expression. Upperparts like adult male, underparts whitish, with blackish streaking on breast and flanks.

43c   **Adult male non-breeding** (nominate) Not separable from first-winter male, except in the hand. In non-breeding males, concealed black breast pattern often visible, causing breast to appear erratically spotted or even barred, rather than streaked.

43d   **Adult female non-breeding** (nominate) Very similar to first-winter female. May show more rufous on nape, and breast usually lacks streaking.

43e   **First-winter female** (nominate) Similar to 43b, but browner and paler on crown and mantle, and buffier on breast. Differs from buntings by combination of bulky appearance, yellowish bill, open-faced expression, chestnut greater coverts, and white wing-bars. The eye-stripe (behind the eye) and moustachial stripe, bordering the ear-coverts, are inconspicuous in front and broad, almost triangular at rear, bordered behind by whitish sides of the neck. The sides of the crown are dark, and the pale median crown-stripe conspicuous. The nape is pale rufous-buff, almost unstreaked (in males often with concealed rufous colour showing through), and contrasts with darker crown and heavily streaked mantle. The underparts are noticeably whitish, the breast washed buffish, with dark streaking.

43f   **Juvenile** (nominate) Juveniles are duller and darker than adults. The mantle and crown are heavily streaked yellowish-brown and blackish, the nape similar in colour with no trace of chestnut. The breast is darker yellowish-olive and more prominently streaked than adults, clearly demarcated from the pale buffish belly.

48   Lark Bunting *Calamospiza melanocorys*   Text and map page 225

Breeds in prairies of N America; winters in Mexico.

48a   **Adult male breeding** Unmistakable; black with prominent white wing patch.

48b   **Adult female** Crown and upperparts brown, streaked darker; ear-coverts dark brown with pale surrounds; buffy wing patch; underparts whitish with dark brown streaks. Like male, has a fairly large bill.

48c   **Male moulting from first-winter to first-summer** Moulting males in spring look patchy; first-years can be told from adults by the contrast between fresh and worn wing feathers (as in first-winter).

48d   **Adult male non-breeding** More similar to adult female but has blackish wings, mostly blackish throat, heavier black streaking on underparts and larger (buffy) wing patch.

48e   **First-winter male** Resembles adult female but underparts are more heavily streaked (with blackish), there is often some blackish mottling in the throat, and the fresh black outer primaries contrast with worn brownish primary coverts and remainder of remiges.

48f   **Juvenile** Resembles female but is buffier; upperparts appear scaled rather than streaked, due to obvious whitish fringes to the feathers.

42   **McCown's Longspur** *Calcarius mccownii*   **Text and map page 206**

The northern Great Plains in United States and S Canada. Short-grass prairie. Main wintering area centred around W Oklahoma, and adjacent areas of surrounding states.

     42a   **Adult male breeding** Plumage mainly grey, except black crown, breast-patch and moustache, and chestnut median coverts.

     42b   **Adult female breeding** Pale plumage, unstreaked below, with nondescript face pattern and large pinkish bill characteristic. The median coverts and scapulars are often tinged rusty. The breast may show a trace of a dark patch. Note characteristic tail pattern of species, and relatively long primary projections.

     42c   **Adult male non-breeding** Very similar to adult female breeding, but concealed black patch on breast often shows through. The crown often appears spotted rather than streaked. Median coverts and scapulars extensively chestnut.

     42d   **First-winter female** Underparts unstreaked, breast slightly darker than belly. Bill large and pinkish. Cf. first-winter Chestnut-collared Longspur (45f).

     42e   **Juvenile** Uniform sandy appearance, lacking whitish 'braces' on mantle. Base colour of breast contrasts with whiter belly.

---

45   **Chestnut-collared Longspur** *Calcarius ornatus*   **Text and map page 215**

The Great Plains in United States and S Canada. Prairie and grasslands. Winters in SW United States and N Mexico.

     45a   **Adult male breeding** Upperparts virtually identical to Lapland Longspur (43), but throat yellow, and breast and belly black.

     45b   **Adult male breeding** Some individuals show chestnut instead of whitish fringes to feathers of breast.

     45c   **Adult female breeding** Reminiscent of washed-out male. Underparts densely covered with dark 'arrow-heads'. Note characteristic tail pattern and short primary projection.

     45d   **Adult female breeding** Individual with much chestnut on nape and extensively black breast and belly, ghosting pattern of male.

     45e   **Adult male non-breeding** Concealed black pattern on breast usually shows through.

     45f   **First-winter female** Underparts diffusely streaked, base colour of breast and belly similar. Bill average-sized and not strikingly pale. Cf. first-winter McCown's Longspur (42d).

     45g   **Juvenile** Uniform greyish appearance, often with whitish 'braces' on mantle. Base colour of breast and belly similar.

---

44   **Smith's Longspur** *Calcarius pictus*   **Text and map page 212**

Alaska to the Hudson Bay in Canada. Meadows and grassy areas with scattered conifers and scrubs along the edge of the tundra. Winters from Missouri and Kansas south to Texas.

     44a   **Adult male breeding** Characteristic head pattern and golden-buff underparts unmistakable.

     44b   **Adult female breeding** Distinct dark border to ear-coverts. Underparts golden-buff. Very little white on lesser coverts. Note relatively long primary projection and spacing of primaries, typical of species. Cf. Lapland Longspur (43).

     44c   **Adult male non-breeding** White patch on lesser coverts. Nape golden-buff. Streaking on upperparts blacker and bolder than female. Band of streaks across breast narrower.

     44d   **First-winter female** Very similar to adult female breeding. Some individuals may appear similar to Lapland Longspur, but are buffier below, show less prominent chestnut on greater coverts, and different primary spacing.

     44e   **Juvenile** Prominent supercilium and ear-covert pattern reminiscent of adult. Upperparts a mixture of white, buff, chestnut and black. Belly buffish.

PLATE 19: SNOW BUNTING GROUP

46 Snow Bunting *Plectrophenax nivalis*　　　　　Text and map page 217

Distributed throughout the Arctic region. Barren tundra, rocky terrain, scree and sea cliffs. In winter in steppes, prairie and along sea coasts further south.

46a　**Adult male breeding** (nominate; N Scandinavia) Unique black and white plumage. White primary coverts and greater coverts characteristic of adult male.

46b　**Adult female breeding** (nominate) Mantle browner and less uniform than male, and crown and ear-coverts faintly streaked dark. Primary coverts mostly dark and greater coverts show dark bases.

46c　**First-winter male** (nominate) Generally whiter than female. Primary coverts white with blackish tips. Greater coverts white. Scapulars with blunt black centres.

46d　**First-winter female** (nominate) Duller and greyer than male. Primary coverts dark and greater coverts show dark base. Dark centres of scapulars pointed.

46e　**Juvenile female** (nominate) Rather uniformly greyish head and breast, and prominent eye-ring slightly reminiscent of Ortolan, but belly white. This individual shows darkest wings possible for the species, with only narrow white wing-bars and panel on secondaries (a pattern also possible for first-winter female).

46f　**Adult male breeding** (*insulae*, Iceland) Often shows dark patch on hindcrown or nape and rusty tinge on ear-coverts.

47 McKay's Bunting *Plectrophenax hyperboreus*　　　　　Text and map page 222

Hall and St. Matthew's Islands in the Bering Strait. Migrates to coasts of Alaska. Sea coasts and tundra.

47a　**Adult male breeding** Very white individual shown. In most, there is some black in the central tail feathers, and both primaries and tertials may be more extensively black. In all plumages, the alula and primary coverts are all white.

47b　**Adult female breeding** White head and extensively white wings more similar to male than female of Snow Bunting, but mantle streaked black and white. Female Snow rarely shows as large a white rump patch or broad white streaking on mantle, but some adult female Snow Buntings of Aleutian race may be confusingly similar.

47c　**First-winter male** Much paler than female McKay's, or any plumage of Snow Bunting. No black on mantle. Compare variation in pattern of alula and primary coverts to juvenile male, which shows a wing pattern which is also possible for first-winter male.

47d　**First-winter female** Much paler than Snow Bunting, particularly on mantle. Wings, tail and rump more extensively white. Compared to first-winter male Snow Bunting, often more white on base of primaries, but on average blacker on greater coverts and primary coverts.

47e　**Juvenile male** Very similar to juvenile Snow Bunting, but generally paler (except compared to Aleutian race of Snow). White in wings more extensive. All-white primary coverts of juvenile male distinguishes from all plumages of Snow Bunting except adult male.

50   Song Sparrow *Melospiza melodia*   **Text and map page 229**

Widespread in North America; also occurs on Mexican Central Plateau. Most northern birds are migratory, wintering in S USA. Very variable; a selection of races is shown to illustrate the range of size and plumage variation.

50a   Adult (nominate; breeds NE North America) Longish rounded tail; warm brown crown with narrow grey median stripe; prominent grey supercilium and broad whitish submoustachial stripe, bordered below by broad blackish malar; dark brown streaking on breast and flanks often forms a noticeable spot in centre of breast.

50b   Juvenile (nominate) Buffier than adult; face pattern less distinct and median crown-stripe virtually absent. Can be very similar to juvenile Swamp Sparrow (52); juvenile Song usually has less rufous in wings and tail, less heavily streaked crown and a larger, less slender bill.

50c   Adult (*morphna*; coastal W Canada) The darkest race; upperparts very dark grey, with indistinct blackish streaking; underparts white, heavily streaked blackish.

50d   Adult (*rivularis*; Baja California) A very pale race; upperparts pale greyish-brown, indistinctly streaked dark; underparts white, sparsely streaked.

50e   Adult (*saltonis*; interior SW US) A pale, rufous race; upperparts pale grey, streaked rufous, wings and tail mostly rufous; underparts lightly streaked with rufous.

50f   Adult (*mexicana*; C Mexico) Wings distinctly dark rufous, underparts heavily streaked with blackish.

50g   Adult (*samuelis*; coastal C California) Rather similar to *mexicana* in plumage but noticeably smaller and with a smaller, slenderer bill.

50h   Adult (*maxima*; Aleutian Islands, Alaska) Very large and large-billed; appears greyer than other races shown, with dull rufous streaks above and below.

---

51   Lincoln's Sparrow *Melospiza lincolnii*   **Text and map page 233**

Breeds in N and W North America; winters in S USA and N Central America. Races very similar.

51a   Adult (nominate; range of species except Pacific coast and Rockies) Prominent grey supercilium and broad buffy submoustachial stripe, bordered below by narrow dark malar; underparts whitish with buffy breast and fine black streaks on throat, breast and flanks.

51b   Juvenile (nominate) Buffier overall than adult, particularly on head. Throat is streaked, unlike juvenile Song and Swamp Sparrows.

---

52   Swamp Sparrow *Melospiza georgiana*   **Text and map page 234**

Breeds in N and E North America; winters in S and E USA and N Mexico. Races very similar.

52a   Adult breeding (nominate; SE part of range) Grey face with rufous crown; wings distinctly rufous; underparts pale grey with whitish throat and belly.

52b   Adult non-breeding (nominate) Similar to breeding but duller; crown less rufous, with black streaking and a greyish median stripe.

52c   First-winter (nominate) Duller than non-breeding adult and distinctly buffier on the head; crown generally has little or no rufous.

52d   Juvenile (nominate) Noticeably buffy overall and with prominent dark streaks on breast and flanks. Can be very similar to juvenile Song; juvenile Swamp generally has more rufous in wings and tail, more blackish streaking in the crown and a slenderer bill, but identification of lone juveniles can be extremely difficult. See text for further details.

56   White-throated Sparrow *Zonotrichia albicollis*   Text and map page 242

Breeds in N North America; winters mainly in S and E North America.

56a   Adult white-striped Head striped black and white, with noticeable yellow supraloral; white throat usually clearly demarcated from pale greyish underparts.

56b   Adult tan-striped Head striped blackish-brown and grey-buff, supraloral usually dull buffy-yellow; some (probably females) may have indistinct dark mottling/streaking on breast and flanks.

56c   First-winter (dull individual) First-years resemble tan-striped adults in non-breeding (first-winter) plumage but have greyish (not dark reddish) eyes. First-winter birds are quite dull on the head and have relatively extensive mottling/streaking on under parts, but there is considerable overlap with adult tan-striped birds; eye colour is the best ageing character through first-winter but it can be difficult to see in the field.

56d   Juvenile Resembles first-year but head pattern is duller, buffy-yellow supraloral is absent and underparts have distinct dark streaks on breast and flanks.

55   White-crowned Sparrow *Zonotrichia leucophrys*   Text and map page 239

Breeds in N and W North America; winters mainly in the S USA and N Mexico.

55a   Adult (nominate; breeds in NE Canada) Bill pinkish; head striped black and white with the black stripes meeting on black supraloral; sides of head and underparts pale grey, throat slightly paler but not contrastingly white.

55b   First-winter (nominate) Head pattern as adult but stripes are dark brown and grey-buff; upperparts noticeably buffer than adult's.

55c   Juvenile (nominate) Greyer and streakier than first-year with less distinct head pattern; conspicuous dark streaks on underparts.

55d   Adult (*gambelii*; breeds in NW North America) Black stripes on head separated by white supraloral; eye-stripe narrower than in nominate; bill slightly paler and more orange-pink. First-year has similar head pattern but colours are as first-year nominate.

55e   Adult (*nuttalli*; resident in coastal California) Similar to *gambelii* but underparts have a distinct brownish wash on the breast and the upperparts are also slightly browner. Bill is also duller and more yellowish.

57   Golden-crowned Sparrow *Zonotrichia atricapilla*   Text and map page 243

Breeds in NW North America; winters mainly in coastal W USA.

57a   Adult breeding Black crown with bright yellow patch in centre; sides of head grey, underparts grey-brown with whiter belly.

57b   Adult non-breeding Variable but always duller on head than in breeding, often considerably so (dullest birds overlap with bright first-winters and are not distinguishable from them).

57c   First-winter (dull individual) Crown dark brown, streaked darker, crown patch yellowish-brown, quite indistinct and often also streaked darker. Brighter birds overlap with non-breeding (winter) adults.

57d   Juvenile Distinct dark streaks on underparts; head pattern very indistinct and crown with fine dark streaks throughout.

54 Harris's Sparrow *Zonotrichia querula*   Text and map page 238

Breeds in NC Canada; winters in C USA.

54a   **Adult breeding** Black crown and throat contrast with pink bill, sides of head grey with black mark on ear-coverts.

54b   **Adult non-breeding** (bright individual) Pattern similar to breeding but sides of head buffier, rear-crown with pale feather edges.

54c   **Adult non-breeding** (dull individual) Entire crown has pale feather edges, giving a scaled appearance; throat with large white patch; lores blackish.

54d   **First-winter** Crown mostly grey-buff with black scalloping; lores brownish; throat white, bordered on sides by black malar and below by blotchy black breast-band.

53 Rufous-collared Sparrow *Zonotrichia capensis*   Text and map page 236

Resident in Central and South America. Quite variable over its large range; a selection of races is shown.

53a   **Adult** (*costaricensis*; S Central America and N South America, east to NW Venezuela and south to Ecuador) Striking head pattern, rufous collar, black patches on breast-sides usually extending across breast as narrow band.

53b   **Juvenile** (*costaricensis*) Streaked underparts; duller than adult with indistinct head pattern.

53c   **Adult** (*peruviensis*; W Peru) Underparts paler than *costaricensis*; black on breast restricted to patch on sides.

53d   **Adult** (*insularis*; Curaçao and Aruba in the Netherlands Antilles) Paler overall than *costaricensis* with head pattern less distinct; black on breast restricted to small patch on sides.

53e   **Adult** (*australis*; S Chile and Argentina) Head mostly grey with black stripes more or less lacking.

54a

54b

54c

54d

53a

53c

53e

53b

53d

59 Dark-eyed Junco *Junco hyemalis*   Text and map page 246

North America; breeds mainly in the north and west, wintering birds reaching the SE and N Mexico. Highly variable; races representing the five main groups are shown.

Slate-coloured Junco (E North America)

59a **Adult male** (nominate; most of range) Mostly slate-grey with white outer tail feathers and belly, pink bill.

59b **Adult female** (nominate) Duller than male with a brown wash, especially on mantle.

59c **First-winter female** (nominate) Typically duller than adult female, often mostly brownish although brighter individuals ovelap with adult female. First-winters of both sexes have grey (not dark reddish) eyes and brown tertial edges, which often contrast with the grey edges of the freshly moulted inner greater coverts.

59d **Juvenile** (nominate) Brownish overall and heavily streaked.

White-winged Junco (Black Hills area, S Dakota and adjacent states)

59e **Adult male** (*aikeni*; S Dakota and adjacent states) Bluish-grey on hood and upperparts; usually has two white wing-bars.

59f **Adult female** (*aikeni*) Similar to male but slightly duller and browner.

Oregon Junco (W North America)

59g **Adult male** (*oreganus*; Pacific coast) Blackish hood, rufous mantle and flanks, grey rump, white belly.

59h **Adult female** (*oreganus*) Similar to male in pattern but paler on hood and duller on mantle and flanks.

59i **Adult male** (*mearnsi*; SE Alberta and SW Saskatchewan south to E Idaho and NW Wyoming) Paler than *oreganus*, especially on head, with more pinkish sides; dark lores contrast with paler grey head.

Grey-headed Junco (S Rockies)

59j **Adult male** (*caniceps*; S Idaho and Wyoming south to N New Mexico) Mostly fairly pale grey with sharply defined chestnut-brown mantle and pale bill. Pattern recalls Yellow-eyed Junco (60) but eye is dark.

59k **Adult male** (*dorsalis*; New Mexico and Arizona) Resembles *caniceps* but bill is larger and dark with a yellowish-flesh lower mandible.

59X Guadalupe Junco *Junco (hyemalis) insularis*   Text and map page 249

59x **Adult male** Head dark grey with black lores; mantle dull olive-brown, rump grey; flanks pinkish-buff. Female very similar. Only junco on Guadalupe island.

PLATE 24: SOUTHERN JUNCOS AND BLACK-CHINNED SPARROW

60   Yellow-eyed Junco *Junco phaeonotus*   **Text and map page 250**

Resident in Mexico, Guatemala and extreme SW USA.

60a   Adult male (nominate; SC Mexico) Eye yellow, bill bicoloured; head and rump grey with contrasting rufous mantle. Similar to Grey-headed form of Dark-eyed Junco (59) but note eye colour and rufous (not grey) edges to tertials and inner greater coverts. Female very similar but slightly duller.

60b   Juvenile (nominate) Duller than adult and streaked overall; eye brown or greyish. Very similar to juvenile of Grey-headed form of Dark-eyed Junco but the greater covert and tertial edges are bright rufous (pale buff in juvenile Grey-headed).

60c   Adult male (*bairdi*; S Baja California) Paler than nominate with buffy rump and pinkish-brown flanks.

60d   Adult male (*alticola*; SE Chiapas and W Guatemala) Noticeably duller and darker than northern races, also larger and larger-billed.

58   Volcano Junco *Junco vulcani*   **Text and map page 245**

Resident in Costa Rica and W Panama.

58a   Adult Lacks the white outer tail feathers of other juncos and generally duller, upperparts streaked darker; bill pink, iris yellow.

58b   Juvenile Iris dark, underparts with dark streaking; crown and upperparts brighter brown than in adult and more heavily streaked.

76   Black-chinned Sparrow *Spizella atrogularis*   **Text and map page 276**

SW USA and W Mexico; north-western populations are migratory. Races very similar.

76a   Adult male breeding (nominate; C Mexico) Mostly grey with dark-streaked brown mantle, black lores and throat; pink bill. Lores and throat slightly greyer in non-breeding plumage.

76b   Adult female (nominate) Slightly duller than male with less contrasting, blackish-grey lores and throat. Lores and throat greyer in non-breeding plumage.

76c   Juvenile (nominate) Similar to non-breeding female but underparts have faint dark streaks, head and rump are faintly mottled brownish and wing-bars are broader and buffier.

60a

60b

60c

60d

58a

58b

76a

76b

76c

62   Seaside Sparrow *Ammodramus maritimus*   **Text and map page 254**

Atlantic and Gulf coasts of USA; extreme northern populations are migratory. Quite variable; a
selection of races is shown.

   62a   **Adult** (nominate; N Atlantic coast) Mostly greyish with contrasting yellow
              supraloral and rufous patch in wing; white throat and submoustachial separated by dark
              malar stripe; obscure darker streaking above and below; note also long, pointed bill,
              typical of all races.

   62b   **Juvenile** (nominate) Buffier than adult with pale buff supraloral; fine, sharply
              defined streaks on underparts.

   62c   **Adult** (*macgillivrai*; S Atlantic coast) Brighter than nominate with buffier breast,
              browner mantle and distinct brown lateral crown-stripe; supraloral extends behind eye
              as greenish-yellow supercilium.

   62d   **Adult** (*fisheri*; Gulf coast from Alabama east to E Texas) Similar to *macgillivrai* but
              brighter.

   62e   **Adult** (*mirabilis*; S Everglades) Olive above, heavily streaked dark brown below.

   62f   **Adult** (*peninsulae*, NW Florida) Darker and sootier above than nominate and with more
              distinct sooty streaking.

   62g   **Adult** (*nigrescens*; extinct; formerly occurred on Merritt Island, Florida) Blackish
              above, whitish below with heavy black streaking.

63   Sharp-tailed Sparrow *Ammodramus caudacutus*   **Text and map page 256**

Breeds in NC North America, wintering on the Gulf coast; also resident populations on the
northern Atlantic coast. Quite variable; a selection of races is shown.

   63a   **Adult** (nominate; Atlantic coast of New England) Grey ear-coverts broadly
              surrounded by orange-buff; neck-sides and median crown-stripe dark grey, lateral
              crown brownish; pale buff lines on mantle sides; narrow dark streaks on breast and
              flanks.

   63b   **Juvenile** (nominate) Duller and buffier than adult, especially on head; pale lines
              on mantle lacking; streaking on underparts browner and more diffuse.

   63c   **Adult** (*nelsoni*; breeds NC North America, winters coastal SE USA) Brighter than
              nominate with orange-buff extending to breast and flanks (which are less heavily
              streaked), buffier and less contrasting ear-coverts and whiter, more contrasting, lines
              on mantle.

   63d   **Adult** (*subvirgatus*; N Atlantic coast from Nova Scotia south to Maine) Duller and
              greyer than other races, with greyish-buff surrounds to ear-coverts, streaking on
              underparts and whitish lines on mantle very indistinct.

62a

62g

62b

62d

62e

62c

62f

63c

63a

63b

63d

66 Baird's Sparrow *Ammodramus bairdii*   Text and map page 260

Breeds in NC North America, winters mainly in N Mexico.

  66a Adult Dark moustachial and malar stripes separated by broad pale submoustachial; head bright buff with blackish lateral crown-stripes, ear-coverts framed darker; breast and flanks streaked blackish; upperparts grey-buff, streaked with blackish and some chestnut.

  66b Juvenile Resembles adult but feathers of upperparts are broadly fringed pale buff, giving a scaly rather than streaked appearance.

65 Henslow's Sparrow *Ammodramus henslowii*   Text and map page 259

E North America; breeds in NE USA and SE Canada, wintering in Gulf lowlands. Races very similar.

  65a Adult (nominate; western part of range) Shares dark moustachial and malar stripes with Baird's Sparrow (66); top of head and nape olive with blackish lateral crown-stripes; submoustachial stripe buff; wings and upperparts largely rufous, feathers of upperparts with black streaks and narrow whitish fringes; underparts have dark streaks on breast and flanks and buffy wash to breast.

  65b Juvenile (nominate) Duller than adult, especially on upperparts; streaking on under parts very indistinct or lacking; dark malar stripe lacking.

64 Le Conte's Sparrow *Ammodramus leconteii*   Text and map page 258

Breeds in N North America, winters in SE USA.

  64a Adult (bright individual) Less chunky than Baird's (66) or Henslow's (65); broad buff supercilium, blackish lateral crown-stripes, whitish median crown-stripe and grey ear-coverts give a distinctive head pattern; rufous streaks on nape also distinctive; submoustachial and breast bright buff, blackish streaks on flanks.

  64b Adult (dull individual) Some birds are relatively dull, apparently due to individual variation rather than age or sex differences.

  64c Juvenile Duller and less intricately marked than adult; nape streaks dark brown; breast as well as flanks with dark streaks.

69   **Yellow-browed Sparrow** *Ammodramus aurifrons*   **Text and map page 264**

Resident in South America. Races quite similar; two shown to illustrate extent of variation.

69a   **Adult** (nominate; lowlands east of Andes from SE Colombia south to Bolivia and in the Amazon Basin) Very similar to Grassland Sparrow (68) but typically yellow on face is quite extensive (including eye-ring), streaks on upperparts are browner and lack chestnut edging, and tertials and inner secondaries have warm brown edges.

69b   **Juvenile** (nominate) Buffier overall than adult with fine dark streaks on breast and flanks; lacks yellow on face.

69c   **Adult** (*apurensis*; NE Colombia and S Venezuela) Less yellow on face than *aurifrons* and heavier and blacker streaking on upperparts; some can be very difficult to separate from Grassland (which occurs within the range of this race).

68   **Grassland Sparrow** *Ammodramus humeralis*   **Text and map page 263**

Resident in South America. Races quite similar; two shown to illustrate extent of variation.

68a   **Adult** (nominate; N South America) Very similar to Yellow-browed Sparrow (69) but typically yellow is restricted to supraloral, eye-ring is whitish, streaks on upperparts are blackish with chestnut edging, and tertials and inner secondaries have rufous edges. Some can be very difficult to separate by plumage, however.

68b   **Juvenile** (nominate) Buffier overall than adult with dark streaks on breast and flanks; lacks yellow supraloral.

68c   **Adult** (*xanthornus*; C and S South America) Streaking on upperparts heavier than in nominate; yellow supraloral extends back slightly behind eye.

67   **Grasshopper Sparrow** *Ammodramus savannarum*   **Text and map page 261**

North and Central America and West Indies, also very locally in N South America; North American races are migratory except in extreme south. The many races are all fairly similar; a selection is shown.

67a   **Adult** (*pratensis*; breeds E North America) Chunky and large-billed; orange-buff supraloral, buffy median crown-stripe, dark lateral crown-stripes; nape streaked with rufous; buffy breast and flanks.

67b   **Juvenile** (*pratensis*) Duller than adult with dark streaks on breast and flanks; lacks buffy-orange supraloral spot.

67c   **Adult** (*perpallidus*; breeds W North America) Smaller-billed and duller than *pratensis*, especially on head and underparts.

67d   **Adult** (*cracens*; N Guatemala to NE Nicaragua) Darker than *perpallidus* and buffier on underparts; resembles *pratensis* but is darker above, with less rufous.

67e   **Adult** (nominate; Jamaica) Resembles *perpallidus* but is slightly duller above with blackish streaks on nape and relatively dull brown streaks on upperparts.

PLATE 28: *SPIZELLA* SPARROWS (1)

75   Field Sparrow *Spizella pusilla*   **Text and map page 273**

SE North America, north to Great Lakes; northern populations are migratory.

75a   **Adult** (nominate; breeds E North America west to Mississippi) Pink bill, white eye-ring, flesh legs; crown mostly rufous with a narrow grey median stripe; ear-coverts narrowly framed with rufous-brown.

75b   **Juvenile** (nominate) Buffier overall with pale brown crown; crown and breast with indistinct dark streaks.

75c   **Adult** (*arenacea*; breeds NC USA south to N Texas) Paler and greyer than nominate, especially on the head, with very little rufous-brown outlining the ear-coverts and a broader grey median crown-stripe.

75X Worthen's Sparrow *Spizella (pusilla) wortheni*   **Text and map page 275**

Resident in NE Mexico; local.

75x   **Adult** (nominate; most of range) Quite similar to *arenacea* race of Field Sparrow (75) but sides of head are entirely grey, lacking rufous edges to ear-coverts, crown is rufous, lacking a grey median stripe, the white eye-ring appears more prominent and the nape is grey, forming a noticeable collar which separates the crown from the upperparts.

71   American Tree Sparrow *Spizella arborea*   **Text and map page 267**

Breeds across N North America, winters across C North America.

71a   **Adult breeding** (nominate; breeds from C North-west Territories east) Bicoloured bill; grey head with rufous crown (stripe on centre of forehead usually grey); rufous patches on breast-sides and black spot in centre of breast; black legs.

71b   **Adult non-breeding** (nominate) Slightly duller overall; rufous crown has pale grey feather fringes and a grey median stripe.

71c   **Juvenile** (nominate) Duller overall with dark streaks on head and underparts; lacks rufous crown.

71d   **Adult breeding** (*ochracea*; breeds from W North-west Territories west) Slightly larger and paler than nominate with a richer buff wash to the flanks.

75a

75b

75c

75x

71b

71d

71c

71a

72   Chipping Sparrow *Spizella passerina*   **Text and map page 268**

North America and N Central America; North American populations are migratory except in the
south. Races similar; two shown to illustrate extent of variation.

72a   **Adult breeding** (nominate; E North America) Rufous crown with long white
supercilium and black eye-stripe, black bill, pale grey face and nape.

72b   **Adult non-breeding** (nominate) Crown duller rufous or tawny-brown and streaked
black; supercilium and ear-coverts pale grey-buff; bill more flesh-coloured.

72c   **First-winter** (nominate) Resembles non-breeding (winter) adult but has a duller
crown, lacking any rufous tones, an all-flesh bill and a brownish wash to the
underparts. Some retain juvenile streaking through the autumn. Can be similar to
winter Clay-coloured (73) but the head pattern is much less striking, and the lores are
dark.

72d   **Juvenile** (nominate) Distinct dark streaking on breast and flanks; otherwise similar
to first-winter.

72e   **Adult breeding** (*pinetorum*; Guatemala to NE Nicaragua) Brighter and 'cleaner-
looking' than nominate with a darker rufous crown.

73   Clay-coloured Sparrow *Spizella pallida*   **Text and map page 270**

Breeds in NC North America, winters mainly in Mexico.

73a   **Adult breeding** Lateral crown brown, streaked black, with pale median crown-stripe;
broad whitish supercilium; buff-brown ear-coverts, narrowly framed with dark
brown; dark malar stripe conspicuous, separated by whitish submoustachial stripe and
throat; grey neck-sides, narrowly streaked darker.

73b   **Adult non-breeding** Slightly buffer overall, especially on supercilium, breast and
flanks; grey neck-sides unstreaked and more contrasting; median crown-stripe may be
slightly less conspicuous (but still obvious).

73c   **First-winter** Similar to non-breeding (winter) adult but generally has buffer breast
and flanks (forming a clear contrast with white throat and belly); some are more similar
to adults and may not always be distinguishable. Some may retain juvenile streaking
on flanks well into the autumn. Head pattern much stronger and more contrasting
than on Chipping Sparrow (72) (with pale lores) and never shows contrasting grey
rump.

73d   **Juvenile** Buffer than adult, with only a trace of the adult head pattern, and dark
streaking on breast and flanks; distinctly buffer than juvenile Chipping.

74   Brewer's Sparrow *Spizella breweri*   **Text and map page 272**

Breeds in interior W North America, winters in Mexico and extreme SW USA.

74a   **Adult** Duller and greyer overall than Clay-coloured (73); crown grey-brown, finely
streaked with black throughout, no median crown-stripe; pale eye-ring more
prominent than on Clay-coloured; no grey patch on neck-sides.

74b   **Juvenile** Buffier than adult with dusky streaks on breast and flanks.

74X Timberline Sparrow *Spizella (breweri) taverneri*   **Text and map page 273**

74x   **Adult** Very similar to Brewer's and possibly not reliably separated in the field, but is
slightly darker and greyer above, with heavier streaking.

PLATE 30: LARK AND FOX SPARROWS

78 Lark Sparrow *Chondestes grammacus*　　　　　　**Text and map page 279**

North America and Mexico; northern populations are migratory.

78a　**Adult** (nominate; E North America) Chestnut, black and white pattern on head is distinctive, as is long, white-cornered tail; note also black spot on breast.

78b　**Juvenile** (nominate) Streaked on underparts and adult head pattern only vaguely indicated, but tail pattern remains distinctive.

78c　**Adult** (*strigiceps*; W North America and N Mexico) Very similar to nominate but upperparts are slighty paler and less heavily streaked, and head has slightly less black.

---

49 Fox Sparrow *Passerella iliaca*　　　　　　　　**Text and map page 227**

Breeds in N and W North America, winters in S North America and on the west coast. Very variable; a selection of races from the three main groups is shown.

Northern and eastern group

49a　**Adult** (nominate; breeds in NE North America) Bicoloured bill; crown, nape and mantle grey with 'untidy' rufous streaks, rump and tail rufous; underparts with 'blotchy' rufous streaks which generally merge into a spot on centre of breast.

49b　**Adult** (*altivagans*; eastern slope of the Rockies in Canada) Duller and more uniform above than nominate, with less noticeable streaking.

Northern Pacific coast group

49c　**Adult** (*unalaschcensis*; breeds on Alaska Peninsula and the Aleutians) Pacific north-western birds are sooty above and have sooty streaks on underparts, but the bill pattern is similar to eastern birds; *unalaschcensis* is the palest and largest-billed of this group.

49d　**Adult** (*fuliginosa*; breeds from SE Alaska south to NW Washington) Darkest of this group, uniform dark sooty-brown above.

Southern Rocky Mountain and Sierra group

49e　**Adult** (*schistacea*; breeds in the C Rockies) Head and mantle unstreaked grey, contrasting with rufous rump and tail; the smallest-billed of the south-western group.

49f　**Adult** (*stephensi*; breeds in the Sierra Nevada in S California) Similar to *schistacea* in plumage but much larger-billed; the largest-billed of the south-western group.

PLATE 31: NORTH AMERICAN AND MEXICAN SPARROWS

77   Vesper Sparrow *Pooecetes gramineus*   Text and map page 277

Breeds widely across North America, winters in the S USA and Mexico. Races very similar.

> **77a   Adult worn** (nominate; E North America) Rather stocky and short-tailed; white outer tail feathers distinctive; note also conspicuous white eye-ring, chestnut lesser coverts (sometimes difficult to see), and dark ear-coverts with paler centre.
>
> **77b   Adult fresh** (nominate) Paler, with narrower streaking than in worn plumage.

---

61   Savannah Sparrow *Passerculus sandwichensis*   Text and map page 251

Widespread in North America and Mexico; North American races (except on the Pacific coast) are migratory, wintering in southern USA, Central America and West Indies.

> **61a   Adult** (*savanna*; breeds from Nova Scotia south to New England) Fairly short, notched tail; supercilium yellow on supraloral, becoming whitish behind eye; narrow dark malar stripe; obscure pale median crown-stripe.
>
> **61b   Juvenile** (*savanna*) Slightly buffier than adult with wider wing-bars.
>
> **61c   Adult** (*wetmorei*; S Guatemala) Darker and browner above than N American races; supercilium extensively yellow.
>
> **61d   Adult** (*princeps* Ipswich Sparrow; breeds on Sable Island) Larger and paler than mainland races with paler brown streaking on underparts.
>
> **61e   Adult** (*beldingi* Belding's Sparrow; coastal California) Small, dark and heavily streaked with blackish.
>
> **61f   Adult** (*rostratus* Large-billed Sparrow; extreme coastal NW Mexico) Large bill; paler than most other forms with indistinct streaking; lacks obvious yellow supraloral.

---

70   Sierra Madre Sparrow *Xenospiza baileyi*   Text and map page 265

Resident in C Mexico; very local.

> **70a   Adult male worn** Very short wings with extensive rufous; rufous-brown crown and upperparts, heavily streaked with black; pale supercilium contrasts with dark ear-coverts; white underparts with heavy black streaking.
>
> **70b   Adult female fresh** Females are less heavily streaked below than males; on all birds the crown, ear-coverts and upperparts appear paler and more rufous (less blackish) in fresh plumage.

77a

77b

61f

61c

61e

61a

61d

61b

70b

70a

PLATE 32: WESTERN AND MEXICAN SPARROWS

81   **Five-striped Sparrow** *Amphispiza quinquestriata*   **Text and map page 283**

NW Mexico and extreme S Arizona; extreme northern populations are migratory. Races similar.

     81a   **Adult** (*septentrionalis*; NW Mexico except N Jalisco, and extreme S Arizona) Dark and dull with distinctive head pattern; note also black spot in centre of breast and barred undertail-coverts.

     81b   **Juvenile** (*septentrionalis*) Belly pale yellow, lacks broad black malar stripe.

---

82   **Bridled Sparrow** *Aimophila mystacalis*   **Text and map page 285**

Resident in C Mexico.

     82   **Adult** Distinctive head pattern; scapulars and rump rufous; crown and upperparts streaked blackish; flanks and undertail-coverts cinnamon-buff; bold white wing-bars.

---

79   **Black-throated Sparrow** *Amphispiza bilineata*   **Text and map page 280**

SW US and N Mexico; northern populations are migratory. Races similar; two examples shown.

     79a   **Adult** (nominate; most of Texas and NE Mexico) Black throat and breast, and blackish ear-coverts contrast with broad white submoustachial stripe; prominent white supercilium; crown and upperparts brownish-grey; white outer web of outer tail feather and spots at tip of outer two feathers.

     79b   **Juvenile** (nominate) Lacks black throat but breast and flanks have fine brown streaks, head grey-brown with prominent supercilium, upperparts buff-brown; rather similar to juvenile Sage (80) but supercilium long, broad and continuous, crown lacks darker streaks and tail with white outer edges.

     79c   **Adult** (*deserticola*; W USA south to NW Mexico) Slightly paler and browner above than nominate.

---

80   **Sage Sparrow** *Amphispiza belli*   **Text and map page 282**

W US and NW Mexico; northern interior populations are migratory. Coastal and interior groups quite different; one example of each shown.

     80a   **Adult** (nominate; coastal California and NW Baja, and mountains of W California) Head dark grey with white supraloral; prominent white submoustachial stripe, bordered below by distinct black malar stripe; black spot in centre of breast.

     80b   **Adult** (*nevadensis*; breeds in the Great Basin) Head and upperparts paler than nominate with fine darker streaking; malar stripe is narrow and greyer.

     80c   **Juvenile** (*nevadensis*) Crown and upperparts buffier than adult with more prominent darker streaking; lacks black breast spot but breast and flanks have brown streaks; similar to Black-throated Sparrow (79) but supercilium short and indistinct, crown and upperparts with darker streaks, tail lacks distinct white edges.

PLATE 33: *AIMOPHILA* SPARROWS (1)

88 Bachman's Sparrow *Aimophila aestivalis* Text and map page 290

SE USA; northern populations are migratory. Two races shown; a third is very similar to *bachmani*.

88a **Adult** (nominate; Atlantic coastal plain) Crown dark rufous, streaked blackish, and with obscure grey median crown-stripe; grey upperparts with dark brown and chestnut streaking; grey-buff breast contrasts with whitish belly; narrow but conspicuous dark malar stripe.

88b **First-winter** (nominate) First-winters of all races have a variable number of rounded streaks on the breast.

88c **Juvenile** (nominate) Buffier overall than adult with little chestnut and blackish streaking; breast and flanks have distinct rounded streaks.

88d **Adult** (*bachmani*; central part of range) Paler and more rufous than nominate, with rufous streaking on upperparts; crown rufous with obscure grey median stripe and lacking black streaking; buffy breast contrasts with paler throat and belly.

89 Botteri's Sparrow *Aimophila botterii* Text and map page 291

Mexico to Costa Rica, also extreme S USA; northern populations are migratory. Races quite similar; a selection is shown.

89a **Adult** (nominate; highlands of E and SE Mexico) Crown greyish with fine blackish streaks throughout, lacks dark malar stripe; upperparts also greyish with blackish streaks (narrowly edged with rufous); underparts pale grey-buff, throat and belly paler but not greatly contrasting.

89b **Juvenile** (nominate) Buffier overall than adult, dark streaks on underparts.

89c **Adult** (*arizonae*, SE Arizona and NW Mexico) Paler than nominate with rufous streaks on crown and upperparts.

89d **Adult** (*petenica*; lowlands of SE Mexico, N Guatemala and Belize) Smaller and darker than nominate with broader black streaks on upperparts; underparts are also whiter.

89e **Adult** (*vulcanica*; highlands of Nicaragua and Costa Rica) Larger, darker and duller than other races, with duskier underparts.

90 Cassin's Sparrow *Aimophila cassinii* Text and map page 293

S USA and N Mexico; northern populations are migratory.

90a **Adult fresh** Very similar to *texana* race of Botteri's Sparrow (89) but tail has noticeable white tips to the feathers, stronger cross-barring on the tail, faint but distinct streaking on rear flanks and more variegated (less neatly streaked) upperparts.

90b **Adult worn** Adults become very worn in late summer and most of the features listed above are lost; Botteri's Sparrow never becomes as worn as this.

90c **Juvenile** Buffier than adult; upperparts have less variegated pattern and underparts have indistinct darker streaking on breast and flanks.

88a

88d

88b

88c

89c

89d

89a

89e

90a

89b

90b

90c

91   Rufous-winged Sparrow *Aimophila carpalis*   Text and map page 295

Resident in NW Mexico and extreme S Arizona. Races very similar.

91a   **Adult** (nominate; S Arizona and N Mexico) Blackish moustachial and malar stripes are prominent in greyish face, crown rufous, streaked grey; indistinct pale wing-bars; lesser coverts chestnut.

91b   **Juvenile** (nominate) Buffier than adult with dark streaks on breast and flanks; crown lacks rufous and is streaked with dark brown.

92   Rufous-crowned Sparrow *Aimophila ruficeps*   Text and map page 296

S USA and Mexico; extreme north-eastern populations are migratory. Races quite similar; one example each from coastal and interior groups shown.

92a   **Adult** (nominate; WC California) Rufous crown, sometimes with vague, narrow greyish median stripe at front; prominent black malar stripe; greyish supercilium becomes whitish on supraloral; broad dark rufous streaks on upperparts; bill dark grey with greyish-flesh lower mandible.

92b   **Juvenile** (nominate) Buffier than adult with dark streaks on breast and flanks; crown buff-brown with darker streaking.

92c   **Adult** (*eremoeca*; north-east of range, south to NE Mexico) Larger and paler than nominate with paler and less distinct rufous streaking on upperparts.

93   Oaxaca Sparrow *Aimophila notostricta*   Text and map page 297

Resident in S Mexico, where only known from Oaxaca.

93a   **Adult** Crown rufous with grey median stripe; bill and lores blackish, emphasising white supraloral and broken eye-ring; black malar stripe; upperparts streaked with blackish; tertial edges rufous; sides washed with cinnamon-buff.

93b   **Juvenile** Similar to Rufous-crowned Sparrow (92) but has warmer brown upperparts, brighter rufous tertial edges and a noticeably stronger buff wash to underparts.

94   Rusty Sparrow *Aimophila rufescens*   Text and map page 298

Resident from Mexico to Costa Rica. Races quite different; a selection is shown.

94a   **Adult** (nominate; S and SW Mexico) Large *Aimophila*; rufous crown with grey median stripe; black malar stripe; bicoloured bill; wings extensively rufous; upperparts streaked rufous and grey.

94b   **Juvenile** (nominate) Duller than adult with indistinct head pattern; underparts washed pale yellow with dark streaks on breast and flanks.

94c   **Adult** (*discolor*; S Belize to NE Nicaragua) Smaller than nominate, greyer on head, brighter and darker rufous on upperparts with darker streaking, and richer buff on flanks.

94d   **Adult** (*pyrgitoides*; E Mexico to El Salvador) Buffier above and below than nominate with darker streaks on upperparts; larger than *discolor* and buffier above.

83   Black-chested Sparrow *Aimophila humeralis*   Text and map page 286

Resident in WC Mexico.

83a   **Adult fresh** Broad black breast-band separates white throat and belly; dark grey head with narrow rufous feather edges; white submoustachial and black malar stripes; mantle and scapulars rufous.

83b   **Adult worn** In worn plumage, rufous feather edges on head are largely lost and head appears darker.

95   Zapata Sparrow *Torreornis inexpectata*   Text and map page 300

Resident on Cuba. Races differ slightly; two examples shown.

95a   **Adult** (nominate; Zapata Swamp) Grey head with dull rufous crown; black malar separating white submoustachial stripe and throat; lower underparts pale yellowish.

95b   **Adult** (*sigmani*; SE Cuba) Duller than nominate; crown with little rufous, and upperparts greyer and unstreaked.

84   Stripe-headed Sparrow *Aimophila ruficauda*   Text and map page 286

Resident from Mexico to Costa Rica. Races differ slightly; two examples shown to illustrate extent of variation.

84a   **Adult** (nominate; Guatemala to Costa Rica) Boldly black and white striped head; bicoloured bill; rump and tail rufous-brown, mantle and scapulars with dark streaks.

84b   **Juvenile** (nominate) Duller than adult, especially on head, with dark streaks on breast.

84c   **Adult** (*acuminata*; W Mexico) Smaller than nominate with blacker head stripes and ear-coverts; body duller, with browner upperparts and tail, and paler underparts with less cinnamon-buff wash on flanks.

85   Cinnamon-tailed Sparrow *Aimophila sumichrasti*   Text and map page 287

Resident in S Mexico; very local.

85   **Adult** Rufous tail; black moustachial and malar stripes; rufous-brown crown, streaked blackish, with grey median stripe; cinnamon-rufous wash on flanks.

96   Striped Sparrow *Oriturus superciliosus*   Text and map page 301

Resident in Mexico. Races very similar.

96a   **Adult** (nominate; NW Mexico) Duller than Stripe-headed Sparrow (84); rufous-brown crown lacks obvious white median stripe, bill all dark, upperparts more variegated, rump and tail lack rufous.

96b   **Juvenile** (nominate) Buffier overall than adult and crown duller brown; supercilium and throat washed yellowish-buff; dark streaks on breast and flanks.

PLATE 36: RUFOUS-SIDED/COLLARED TOWHEE COMPLEX

98 Collared Towhee *Pipilo ocai* Text and map page 303

Resident in C Mexico. Very variable due to geographical variation and hybridisation with Rufous-sided Towhee (99).

98a **Adult** (*alticola*; W Jalisco and NE Colima) Variable through hybridisation with Rufous-sided Towhee and pure birds may no longer occur; typically has narrow and indistinct supercilium, and lacks white stripe on forehead.

98b **Adult** (nominate; E Puebla and WC Veracruz) Rufous crown and black ear-coverts separated by white supercilium, black forehead has white stripe through centre; white throat, bordered below by broad black breast-band; upperparts olive-green.

98c **Adult** (*nigrescens*; Michoacán) Very variable through hybridisation with Rufous-sided and pure birds may no longer occur; extensive black on head.

98d **Juvenile** (*guerrerensis*; Guerrero) Juveniles of all races have duller crowns than adults with dark streaking, brownish or rufous-brown upperparts, cinnamon wing-bars and blackish streaks on breast in place of breast-band.

98x **Chestnut-capped Brush-Finch** (*Atlapetes brunneinucha*; S Mexico) Similar to Collared Towhee but slightly smaller, duller olive above, white on head restricted to small supraloral spot, and undertail-coverts olive.

98x99 Hybrid Collared x Rufous-sided Towhee

Hybridisation occurs extensively where the ranges of the two species overlap. Hybrids are very variable; two examples are shown.

98x99a Collared x Rufous-sided hybrid.
98x99b Collared x Rufous-sided hybrid.

99 Rufous-sided Towhee *Pipilo erythrophthalmus* Text and map page 305

North America and Mexico; most northern populations are migratory. Quite variable; a selection from the four main groups is shown.

Rufous-sided Towhee (north-east of range)

99a **Adult male** (nominate; range of group except SE USA) Black hood and upperparts; white-cornered tail; rufous sides; white in wings; red eye.

99b **Adult female** (nominate) Pattern as male but black replaced with rufous-brown.

99c **Juvenile** (nominate) Head and upperparts brown, streaked darker; underparts pale buff, streaked darker on breast and flanks.

99d **Adult** (*alleni*; C and S Florida) Similar to nominate but eye white.

Spotted Towhee (coastal north-west of range)

99e **Adult male** (*oreganus*; Pacific coast) White wing-bars and spots on scapulars and sides of mantle.

99f **Adult female** (*oreganus*) Pattern as male but black replaced by dark grey-brown.

Olive-backed Towhee (C Mexico)

99g **Adult** (*macronyx*; C Mexico) Upperparts olive-green with yellowish wing-bars and spots on mantle and scapulars; sexes similar.

Socorro Towhee (Socorro Island)

99h **Adult** (*socorroensis*; Socorro Island) Much smaller than other races; hood and upperparts olive-grey, small spots on upperparts; sexes similar.

97 Green-tailed Towhee *Pipilo chlorurus*   Text and map page 302

Breeds in W USA, winters in S USA and Mexico.

97a Adult male breeding Grey head with contrasting rufous rear-crown and nape, and white supraloral; white throat contrasts with pale grey breast; upperparts grey, tinged olive, tail dark olive. Female similar but averages slightly duller.

97b First-winter female Non-breeding (winter birds) are duller, especially on the head; first-winter females average dullest, with relatively dull rufous cap, but there is considerable overlap.

97c Juvenile Lacks adult head pattern; head and upperparts grey-brown with darker streaks on crown, nape and mantle; underparts with dark streaks on breast and flanks; buffy wing-bars.

100 California Towhee *Pipilo crissalis*   Text and map page 308

Resident in S Oregon, California and Baja California. Races quite similar; two examples shown to illustrate extent of variation.

100a Adult (nominate; coastal C California) Throat buffy with narrow gorget of dark streaks on lower border; head and upperparts brown; cinnamon-rufous undertail-coverts.

100b Adult (*albigula*; S Baja California) Paler than northern races with distinct pale rufous crown; upperparts greyer, underparts whiter; throat bicoloured with white lower part.

101 Canyon Towhee *Pipilo fuscus*   Text and map page 310

Resident in interior S USA and Mexico. Races similar, varying mainly in strength of rufous on crown.

101a Adult (nominate; WC Mexico) Upperparts grey-brown with faint rufous crown; under parts similar to California Towhee (100) but throat paler buff and black spot in centre of breast, below gorget of streaks.

101b Juvenile (nominate) Slightly paler and buffier than adult with buffy wing-bars; under parts are streaked dark brown and lack the gorget and breast spot.

103 White-throated Towhee *Pipilo albicollis*   Text and map page 312

Resident in SC Mexico. Races very similar.

103 Adult (nominate; range of species except Mt. Zempoaltepec, Oaxaca) White throat with narrow gorget of dark streaks below; black and rufous patches on sides of neck, rufous sometimes extending across throat.

102 Abert's Towhee *Pipilo aberti*   Text and map page 311

Resident in SW USA and adjacent NW Mexico. Races very similar.

102 Adult (nominate; range of species except SE Arizona and SW New Mexico) Black front of face contrasts with grey-brown upperparts and cinnamon-buff underparts; undertail-coverts rich cinnamon-rufous.

97a

97b

97c

100a

100b

101b

101a

103

102

PLATE 38: GROUND-SPARROWS

104 Rusty-crowned Ground-Sparrow *Melozone kieneri*   **Text and map page 313**

Resident in W and C Mexico. Races similar; two examples shown.

104a **Adult** (nominate; Sinaloa south to Colima) Rufous rear-crown, nape and neck-sides, white supraloral and eye-ring; whitish underparts with black spot in centre of breast.

104b **Adult** (*rubricatum*; SC Mexico) Similar to nominate but smaller and smaller-billed, rufous on head paler and brighter.

104c **Juvenile** (*rubricatum*) Lacks adult head pattern and buffier overall; faint dark streaks on throat and breast.

105 Prevost's Ground-Sparrow *Melozone biarcuatum*   **Text and map page 314**

Resident from S Mexico to Costa Rica. Northern and southern races differ, as shown.

105a **Adult** (nominate; Chiapas, Guatemala, El Salvador and Honduras) White face with blackish spot on rear of ear-coverts, rufous rear-crown and nape.

105b **Juvenile** (nominate) Lacks adult head pattern and buffier overall, with dark streaks on breast.

105c **Adult** (*cabanisi*; Costa Rica) White on face restricted to large eye-ring and supraloral; rufous on head paler and extending to cover most of ear-coverts; black malar stripe; large black spot in centre of breast.

106 White-eared Ground-Sparrow *Melozone leucotis*   **Text and map page 315**

Resident from S Mexico to Costa Rica. Northern and southern races differ, as shown.

106a **Adult** (nominate; Costa Rica) Blackish head with large white spots on supraloral and ear-coverts, and white eye-ring; yellow patch on neck-sides; throat and breast black, separated by narrow rufous and white bands.

106b **Juvenile** (nominate) Duller and buffier than adult with cinnamon wing-bars; lower breast and flanks streaked with dark brown.

106c **Adult** (*occipitalis*; SE Chiapas, Guatemala and El Salvador) Yellow supercilium from behind eye to nape; throat black, breast white with large black spot in centre.

PLATE 39: *ARREMONOPS* AND S AMERICAN *AIMOPHILA* SPARROWS

107 Olive Sparrow *Arremonops rufivirgatus*   Text and map page 316

Resident from S Texas to Costa Rica. Races differ slightly; examples from the two groups shown.

Caribbean group (Olive Sparrow)

107a **Adult** (nominate; S Texas and NE Mexico) Greyish-olive above, pale grey-buff below; greyish head with relatively indistinct rufous lateral crown- and eye-stripes.

107b **Adult** (*verticalis*; Yucatan Peninsula) Brighter than *rufivirgatus* with darker and more sharply defined rufous head stripes, which are narrowly streaked with black.

Pacific group (Pacific Sparrow)

107c **Adult** (*superciliosus*; Pacific coast of N Costa Rica) Brighter than *verticalis* and noticeably buffier on face and underparts; head stripes darker rufous and more sharply defined.

108 Tocuyo Sparrow *Arremonops tocuyensis*   Text and map page 317

Resident in NE Colombia and NW Venezuela.

108 **Adult** Similar to Olive Sparrow but lateral crown- and eye-stripes are darker (blackish), and median crown- and eye-stripes are paler (buffy-white).

109 Green-backed Sparrow *Arremonops chloronotus*   Text and map page 318

Resident in N Central America. Races very similar.

109 **Adult** (nominate; range of species except NC Honduras) Upperparts olive-green, underparts whitish with greyer breast; head grey with black lateral crown- and eye-stripes. Very similar to some races of Black-striped Sparrow (110) but pale area on lower mandible is less sharply defined and head stripes may be less pure black.

110 Black-striped Sparrow *Arremonops conirostris*   Text and map page 319

Resident in Central America and N South America. Races differ slightly; a selection is shown.

110a **Adult** (nominate; N South America except Pacific slope, upper Magdalena Valley and Maracaibo Basin area) Black stripes on grey head; relatively dull, greyish-olive upperparts; pale grey breast separates white throat and belly.

110b **Adult** (*inexpectatus*; upper Magdalena Valley, Colombia) Duller than nominate with brownish-olive upperparts.

110c **Adult** (*richmondi*; Honduras to W Panama) Brighter than nominate with bright olive-green upperparts and purer grey head.

110d **Adult** (*striaticeps*; E Panama, and W Colombia and Ecuador) Similar to *richmondi* but underparts whiter, lacking greyish breast-band.

110e **Juvenile** (*striaticeps*) Head dull olive with indistinct dusky head stripes; upperparts brownish-olive with faint dusky streaks; underparts pale yellowish with dusky streaks.

87 Tumbes Sparrow *Aimophila stolzmanni*   Text and map page 289

Resident in SW Ecuador and NW Peru.

87 **Adult** Large-headed and large-billed; rufous lateral crown- and broad grey median crown-stripe, both faintly streaked with black; whitish supercilium and dark eye-stripe; narrow dark malar stripe; rufous lesser coverts; bend of wing pale yellow.

86 Stripe-capped Sparrow *Aimophila strigiceps*   Text and map page 288

Resident in S South America. Races differ slightly; both are shown.

86a **Adult** (nominate; SC Paraguay and NE Argentina) Similar to Tumbes Sparrow (87) but smaller-billed, slimmer-looking and slightly longer-tailed; bend of wing white.

86b **Adult** (*dabbenei*; NW Argentina) Larger than nominate with blackish lores, warmer brown upperparts and rufous edges to coverts and tertials.

SYSTEMATIC
SECTION

MELOPHUS

One species, which is characterised by a prominent crest, rufous wings and tail, and otherwise dark plumage. It is restricted to foothills in southern Asia, from Pakistan to China.

1 CRESTED BUNTING
Melophus lathami   Plate 1

Described as *Emberiza lathami* Gray 1831.
Synonyms: *Fringilla melanictera, Melophus melanicterus, Emberiza subcristata, Emberiza erythroptera.*

The Crested Bunting is widespread but local in open habitats in Himalayan and south Chinese hill country.

IDENTIFICATION 17cm. The unmistakable adult male is black with chestnut wings and tail and a long erect crest. Immature males are variable, some resembling adult male, but duller, streaked on the upperparts, and heavily blotched below, with wings and tail browner, less deep chestnut. Others are paler both above and below, and may be very similar to females in general coloration, but show less streaking on the breast than female.

The female is paler and browner than male, with shorter crest and less chestnut in wings and tail. The upperparts are olive-brown, diffusely streaked dark, and the underparts paler olive-brown, diffusely streaked dark on the breast. The chestnut edges of the wing-coverts and flight feathers are variable in width, depending on age and stage of wear. In fresh plumage the chestnut colours of the wing are prominent, making identification straightforward. In very worn plumage, the edges may become narrow and quite inconspicuous, but the chestnut colours are still visible, particularly on the edges of the secondaries and tips of greater coverts. However, the inner webs of the remiges are still extensively chestnut and in flight the wings flash chestnut, even in the otherwise dullest bird. The tail is browner with considerably less chestnut in females than in males of the same age. There is never any white in the tail.

Differs from most *Emberiza* buntings by lacking white in the tail. Unmistakable in fresh plumage, but uniform plumage of heavily worn female probably makes confusion with rosefinch conceivable. However, the crest, finer bill, chestnut wing panel and outer tail feathers in combination with bunting-like jizz make confusion with finches unlikely. Dull females may also be confused with female House Bunting, particularly in flight, when both species show similar extensively chestnut wings. Given reasonable views, confusion should not arise.

DESCRIPTION
Adult male breeding Entire head, mantle, back, rump, breast and flanks brownish-black with a blue gloss. Some narrow brown fringes, which are most obvious on the mantle. The central crown feathers elongated, held upright like a crest. Uppertail-coverts chestnut, blackish towards tip. Entire wing chestnut, except dark tips to primaries, secondaries and tertials. Occasionally the secondaries may be almost uniformly chestnut, lacking dark tip. In the tertials a large part of the inner web is dark. Some of the primary coverts may show a tiny dark spot at the tip. A varying number of lesser coverts along the leading edge of the wing are dark. The tail feathers are chestnut, all but the outer ones with some dark at the tip. The belly is tinged brown and lacks the bluish gloss. Thighs chestnut. Vent and undertail-coverts mottled chestnut and black. Upper mandible and tip of lower dark grey-brown, remainder of lower mandible flesh-coloured, or entire bill blackish. Tarsus fleshy brown to purplish-brown. Iris dark brown.

Adult male non-breeding Like breeding plumage, but plumage fresh and black feathers edged with buffish-grey.
Second-winter male Very similar to adult male, but apparently with dark tips on alula and primary coverts.
First-winter male Crown blackish-brown, with some faint olive-brown streaking. Crest shorter than in adult male. Supercilium concolorous with crown. Ear-coverts dark brown, palest at the rear, lores slightly paler. Submoustachial stripe rather ill-defined. Malar stripe blackish-brown. Throat heavily streaked blackish-brown. Mantle usually rather dark, broadly streaked blackish-brown. Back and rump like mantle but less heavily streaked. Uppertail-coverts similar, but with a faint rufous tinge. Lesser coverts olive-brown with a faint rufous tinge and dark centres. Median coverts chestnut, with dark base extending like a thin streak along the shaft. Greater coverts dark brown with broad rufous outer webs and tips. Tertials dark brown with broad rufous outer webs. Alula mainly brownish. Primary coverts brown, with pale rufous edges and some chestnut along the shafts. Primaries and secondaries chestnut, with brown tips and outer webs, paler rufous along the edge. The 2-4 outer pairs of tail feathers are largely chestnut, remainder brown. Breast and belly olive-grey, boldly blotched blackish-brown. In some individuals, the breast is more uniform in colour, similar to female, but with very little streaking. Flanks and lower belly with a faint rufous tinge and less contrastingly streaked. Undertail-coverts pale rufous-brown with dark centres.

Adult female breeding Crown brown, with some faint paler streaking. Crest much shorter than in breeding male. Supercilium concolorous with crown and ear-coverts, the latter with some fine whitish streaking. Lores slightly paler. Submoustachial stripe pale sandy-brown. Malar stripe very faint. Throat pale sandy-brown. Mantle sandy-brown, streaked brown. Back, rump and uppertail-coverts similar in colour, but more or less unstreaked. Lesser coverts olive-brown with dark pointed centres, sometimes with an element of chestnut. Median coverts brown with chestnut edges, pale rufous-sandy at the tips. Greater coverts dark brown with narrow sandy edges and rufous tips. Tertials brown. Primary coverts brown, with pale edges and chestnut inner webs. Primaries and secondaries chestnut, with broad brown tips and outer webs, paler along the edge. The 1-3 outer pairs of tail feathers are largely chestnut, remainder brown. Breast and belly sullied sandy-grey, with brownish streaks across the breast. Rear flanks and lower belly pale cinnamon and less contrastingly streaked. Undertail-coverts pale cinnamon.

Adult female non-breeding Similar to breeding female, but plumage fresh. General colour darker and more saturated. Malar stripe very faint. Throat pale sandy-brown. Mantle sandy-brown, streaked brown, streaking more diffuse than breeding female. Back, rump and uppertail-coverts similar, more or less unstreaked. Lesser coverts rufous olive-brown with dark centres, usually without chestnut tinge. Median coverts with dark base extending like a thin streak along the shaft and chestnut tips. Greater coverts dark brown with broad rufous outer webs and tips. Tertials dark brown with olive-rufous outer webs. Primary coverts brown, with pale rufous edges and some chestnut along the shafts. Breast and flanks olive-brown, with brownish streaks across the breast, most well-defined in the centre. Central belly tinged yellow. Undertail-coverts cinnamon-rufous.

First-winter female Very similar to adult female. No reliable differences found, but usually on average more coarsely streaked on the underparts, and with less rufous in wings and tail.

Juvenile Very similar to female in fresh plumage, but slightly darker, and with very short crest. The underparts are buffier, and the streaking on the breast tends to be more extensive and more diffuse. The dark centre of the median coverts ends in a blunt tooth.

SEXING Adult males are black on most of body. Immature males are heavily blotched blackish or similar to adult females. Those similar to females are best separated by little or no streaking on breast and throat and slightly darker upperparts. The border between rufous inner webs and brown tip of primaries is more well-defined in males, particularly on the outermost primary. A few blue-black feathers may be present on the crown. Males show on average more chestnut in the tail. In adult males all the tail feathers are largely chestnut. In first-winter males two to four outer pairs of tail feathers are chestnut. In some winter females, possibly first-winter birds, only the outermost pair shows any significant amount of chestnut. In others up to three outer pairs are largely chestnut.

MOULT AND AGEING The extent of the moult from juvenile to first-winter plumage is incompletely known. It is probably partial, not involving alula, primary coverts, flight feathers and tail. Adults apparently moult completely between September and November.

First-winter males can be told from adults by the blotched underparts and dark-centred wing-coverts. Males showing wings like adult, but with dark tip to alula and primary coverts, are presumably second year birds. First-winter females are very similar to adult females. They usually show on average less rufous in wings and tail and on average more coarsely streaked underparts, but single individuals can not usually be safely aged on plumage. The tail feathers of first-winter birds are narrower and slightly more pointed than adults. Skull ossification and iris colour not studied, but probably useful.

MEASUREMENTS Wing: (max) male 79.0-89.0mm; female 76.0-88.0mm. Tail: male 64.5-73.0mm, female 62.5-71.0mm. Bill: (to skull) male 14.3-16.6mm; female 13.0-15.7mm. Tarsus: male 18.9-21.1mm; female 18.7-20.0mm. P5-P8 emarginated.

GEOGRAPHICAL VARIATION Two subspecies have been described, but are not recognised by all authors. There is an extensive zone from Assam to Guangdong, where many birds show intermediate characters.

    M. l. lathami (S China) Not quite as shining blue-black as *subcristatus*, with a stronger element of brown. Shorter crest. Broader pale fringes in winter. The most typical birds are found to the east of Hong Kong.

    M. l. subcristatus (Kashmir to Burma) Shining blue-black plumage. Wings and tail deeper chestnut. More extensively blackish in upper- and undertail-coverts.

VOICE The song is given from a conspicuous perch, such as a telephone wire, the top of a pine tree or the top of a boulder. It is a brief, monotonously repeated strophe, falling in pitch, always starting with one or two hesitant, slightly grating notes, followed by a couple of clearer ones at a lower pitch, ending with a more variable note, e.g. *tzit dzit dzit see-see-suee* or *tzit dzit tzit-tzitswe-e-ee-tiyuh*.

The call is a soft, somewhat squeaky, repeated *tip* or *tup*, which is more emphatic in flight.

HABITS Breeding takes place some time between April and August, coinciding with local wet season. In southeastern China, usually in April-June. In Pakistan and Uttar Pradesh mainly July and August. The nest is placed on the ground, under a rock or bush or in crevices or under roots on steep banks, walls or precipitous slopes. In southeastern China, often nests in tea fields. The nest is a neat cup of woven grass, moss, fibrous plant stems and thin rootlets, lined with fine grass and animal hair. Eggs: 3-5, dull white, tinged pale greenish or greyish yellow, blotched and speckled with red, purple and brown, especially at the large end. Incubation apparently by female alone. Feeds mainly on small grass seeds, but also seeds from weeds and cereal. Has been observed flycatching flying ants or flies. Monogamous, but gregarious outside breeding season, when often found in small loose flocks, occasionally congregating in large flocks. Forages on the ground in fields, along roadsides, etc.

STATUS AND HABITAT Rather local and unpredictable in occurrence, but generally fairly common where present. Breeds on open hillsides, dry rocky slopes and open cultivation, with grass and sparse scrubs, sometimes with scattered trees. In winter also found in rice stubbles and open stony scrub country in dry-deciduous jungle, particularly areas of charred grass.

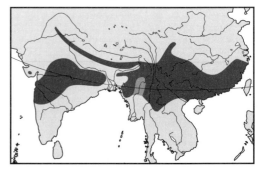

DISTRIBUTION AND MOVEMENTS Mainly resident in foothills up to 2400m. In Pakistan found mainly along the Kashmir border in the north-east. In India from eastern Rajasthan and Gir Forest, south-western Maharashtra, northern Andhra Pradesh, eastern Madhya Pradesh and southern Bihar, through Meghalaya, Cachar and Manipur, south to the Chittagong region. Hills of Nepal, Sikkim, Bangladesh, Bhutan, northern and eastern Burma. In South-East Asia, only found in northernmost regions, north-western Thailand, northern Laos and northern Vietnam. In China from south-eastern Tibet, where perhaps only recorded from areas claimed by India; south-western Sichuan, to southern edge of Red Basin, but also recorded in the north, close to Shaanxi border. Found through-out southern China, from most of Yunnan, through Guizhou, Hunan, and Jiangxi, to Anhui and Zhejiang. Subject to local altitudinal movements, withdrawing from higher elevations to foothills and plains in October, returning in April.

NOTE The name *Fringilla melanictera* Gmelin 1788 has been attributed to this species. However, this description is based on a painting depicting a bird which is not a Crested Bunting. Nevertheless the name *melanictera* has been widely used for this species in the literature.

REFERENCES Ali & Ripley (1974), Baker (1926), Bates & Lowther (1952), Latouche (1925-30), Roberts (1992), Smythies (1986), Ticehurst (1932).

LATOUCHEORNIS

One little-known species, endemic to China, superficially similar to the 'Slate-coloured' form of Dark-eyed Junco in plumage. Males are mainly dark blue and females brown.

2   SLATY BUNTING
Latoucheornis siemsseni   Plate 1

Described as *Junco siemsseni* Martens 1906. Monotypic. Synonym: *Emberiza siemsseni*.

A rare and local species, from central and south-eastern China, where it occurs in second growth and degraded forest in valleys and in low and mid-altitudes in mountains.

IDENTIFICATION 13cm. The adult male is uniformly dark slaty-blue, with white centre of belly and white outer tail feathers. The female is rather uniformly dull brown with head tinged rufous, and faint rusty double wing-bars. The centre of the belly and the undertail-coverts are whitish. A narrow white wing-bar, formed by white bases to the secondaries and inner primaries, is sometimes visible in flight in both sexes. Confusion of females with females of Gold-naped Finch *Pyrrhoplectes epauletta*, Crimson Rosefinch *Carpodacus rubescens* and Dark-breasted Rosefinch *C. nipalensis* conceivable as all are rather uniform brown, with unstreaked breast. Female Gold-naped Finch shows a reverse contrast in colour, compared to female Slaty Bunting. The belly and mantle are rufous-brown, but the crown is contrastingly grey-green, and the nape greyish. The primary coverts and flight feathers are black, in obvious contrast with mantle, greater coverts and belly. The bill is heavier and more finch-like. The Crimson Rosefinch is rather uniformly brown, with some rufescent on the upperparts, especially on the rump, but does not show the rufescent head of Slaty Bunting. The Dark-breasted Rosefinch differs by being heavily streaked dark on the mantle. Both these Rosefinches differ by having heavier bills and lacking white bellies and white outer tail feathers.

The North American "Slate-coloured" form of Dark-eyed Junco is superficially similar to male Slaty Bunting and has a similar call, but the general coloration is not as bluish, more dark grey, and the bill is always pale pinkish. Slaty Bunting shows only a rather narrow wedge of white from the undertail-coverts towards the breast, while in Dark-eyed Junco the dark colour is restricted to the flanks with most of the belly whitish, squarely set off against the dark breast.

DESCRIPTION
Limited seasonal variation. Sexes clearly different.
Adult male Head dark slaty-blue, except area between eye and bill, which is blackish. Entire upperparts dark slaty-blue. Lesser coverts dark slaty-blue. Median and greater coverts blackish with dark slaty blue edges and tips, forming blue, not very prominent wing-bars. Tertials blackish with dark slaty-blue outer web and tip of inner. Alula, primary coverts and flight feathers blackish with dark slaty-blue edges. Base of inner web of secondaries white. Tail feathers dark slaty-blue, outermost pair (T6) with much of inner web white. Underparts dark slaty-blue, except white central belly and undertail-coverts. Bill black. Birds in male plumage, of unknown age, have been observed in winter showing very pale cutting edge and lower mandible. Tarsus pale flesh-coloured. Iris dark brown.

Outermost tail feather (T6). Note unusual shape, with very narrow base.

First-winter male Very similar to adult male, but differs by showing narrow olive-brown fringes to body feathers when fresh. The tips of the greater coverts are white, forming a narrow wing-bar. The primary coverts are brownish, with very narrow pale edges, contrasting with the blue edges of the median and greater coverts. Flight and tail feathers are comparatively more worn and browner than in adult. The tail feathers are slightly more pointed, but note that adults also have rather pointed tail feathers.
Adult female Most of head rufescent brown, slightly paler on throat. Mantle olive-brown, tinged rufescent, with very narrow, not very prominent shaft streaks. Back and uppertail-coverts olive-brown, rump somewhat greyer. Lesser coverts olive-brown. Median and greater coverts dark brown, with rufescent brown tips, forming two wing-bars. Tertials blackish with olive-brown outer web. Alula and primary coverts dark brown with narrow olive-brown edges. Flight feathers dark brown with rufescent brown edges. Base of inner web of secondaries white. Tail feathers olive-brown, outer pair with much of inner web white. Upper breast rufescent brown. Sides of breast and flanks olive-brown. Central belly and undertail-coverts whitish.
First-winter female Very similar to adult female. Lores and

ear-coverts slightly browner. Mantle and scapulars with more obvious streaking. Back and rump paler than in adult, contrasting with darker uppertail-coverts. Tips on median and greater coverts paler rufous than in adult forming narrower but more distinct wing-bars. Primary coverts brownish, more uniform than adult. Flight and tail feathers are comparatively more worn and browner. Tail feathers slightly more pointed.

Juvenile Crown, throat and nape rufescent brown, duller than first-winter female and faintly streaked dark. Ear-coverts greyer brown. Mantle medium brown, with some dark streaking. Back, rump and uppertail-coverts undescribed. Lesser coverts undescribed. Median and greater coverts dark brown, with buffy tips, forming narrow double wing-bars, rather inconspicuous on the median coverts. Tertials dark brown with relatively broad buffish outer web. Rest of wings and tail similar to first-winter female. Breast and upper flanks rufescent buff, duller than crown and nape. Sides of breast olive-brown. Belly mottled greyish-white.

SEXING No differences in juvenile plumage known. After post-juvenile moult, males are predominantly blue and females brown.

MOULT AND AGEING Juveniles undergo a partial post-juvenile moult, involving head, body, lesser, median and greater coverts, but not alula, primary coverts, tertials, flight feathers and tail feathers. In adults there is probably a complete moult between July and September. There is no evidence of a partial pre-breeding moult in spring.

Juvenile similar to first-winter female, but streaked dark on crown and breast. First-winter males have narrow rufescent brown fringes to body feathers when fresh. They also show whitish tips on the greater coverts forming narrow wing-bars. Adult males have the entire outer web blue. The primary coverts are blackish with blue edges on the outer web in adult males. In first-winter males they are brownish, with very narrow paler edges, contrasting with the blue edges of the median and greater coverts. First-winter females are somewhat duller than adults, with more prominent streaking on the mantle, paler rumps and more prominent wing-bars. Flight feathers and tail feathers are relatively more worn and browner in first-winter birds. The tail feathers are slightly more pointed in first-year birds, but note that adults also have rather pointed tail feathers.

MEASUREMENTS Wing: (max) male 67.5-72.5mm; female 64.0-66.5mm. Tail: male 50.0-58.0mm, female 50.5-54.5mm. Bill: (to skull) male 11.6-12.3mm, female 12.5-12.8mm. Tarsus: (sexes not separated) 17-19mm. P5-P8 emarginated. The wing is strongly rounded: P9=P5/4, P8=P5, P7=P6=WP.

GEOGRAPHICAL VARIATION None.

RELATIONSHIPS A peculiar species without obvious close affinities. Plumage most similar to the American juncos, with which the species was originally considered congeneric. As the shape of the bill is more similar to the *Emberiza* buntings, some researchers have suggested placing it in that genus. The strongly rounded wing, the short tail, with feathers broad near the tip and narrow at the base, the central ones not differing from the others in shape, the strongly curved hind claws and the slender bill are the main reasons for the species being retained in its own genus, *Latoucheornis*.

VOICE The song is high-pitched and metallic, quite variable and often with a *Parus*-like quality and melody. Some song variants perhaps also slightly reminiscent of Tree Pipit *Anthus trivialis*. A common motif starts with drawn-out, high-pitched initial notes, followed by a twitter, and ends with a whistled note of quite different quality *ziiii ziiiu tz-itzitzitzi hee*. A more monotonous variant could be described *siii tsiu zhiu zhiu zhiu zhiu*, others begin with a fast trill *ze-ze-ze-ze swee twiitwit*, or *tze-tze-tze teeez teeez teeez*. Examples of *Parus*-like strophes are *siii-suu siii-suu zezezezet*, and *sui-tiu wui-tiu wui-tiu weee*.

The call note is a sharp *zick*, often repeated with about a second's interval, sometimes doubled.

HABITS Nothing is known about the breeding habits, except that territory-defending males have been observed in June. Diet in summer largely insects, like beetles, small cicadas, ants, larvae and insect eggs, but also small seeds. In winter often in loose flocks, feeding on ground. Often attracted to heaps of kitchen refuse.

STATUS AND HABITAT Perhaps not rare, but presumed breeding area rarely visited. Listed as near-threatened by BirdLife International. Most often found in bamboo, secondary growth and semi-open degraded habitats. Breeds in valleys 1500-2100m above sea level. In winter usually lower down, 500-1700m, often in forest, sometimes near human habitation or in city parks.

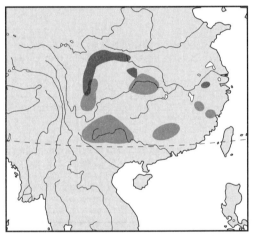

DISTRIBUTION AND MOVEMENTS Endemic to China. Described from a bird collected in April 1905 at Kuatun, Fujian province. This and further observations from the same place between December and April are all from the non-breeding season. Also observed on Huang Shan, Anhui province, in October. One bird collected on Huang Shan in June indicates that these birds may originate from isolated south-eastern breeding population. Main population probably in Sichuan province, from Nanchuan in the south in valleys on the edge of the Tibetan plateau, to the southern parts of adjacent Gansu province and Taibai Shan in southern Shaanxi province, where also recorded during breeding season in the extreme south-eastern parts. Probably also occurs in mountains of north-eastern Sichuan. In winter recorded from the provinces of Sichuan, Yunnan, Guizhou, western Hubei, northern Guangdong, Fujian and Anhui. Apparently a short- or medium-distance migrant.

REFERENCES Cheng & Stresemann (1961), Collar *et al.* (1994), Latouche (1925-30), Martens (1906).

EMBERIZA

A large and rather heterogeneous group with 38 species, distributed throughout Europe, Asia and Africa. Most of the species show strong sexual dimorphism in plumage in the breeding season. The genus is held together mainly by the characteristic bill shape. The upper mandible is curved inwards, and there is a sharp angle on the upper mandible just below the nostrils, less obvious on the broader lower mandible, and most species have a hump in the roof of the mouth for crushing seeds. Many species show a characteristic tertial pattern, unique to this genus and the two northern members of the genus *Calcarius*. Several well-defined subgroups can be recognised, some of them perhaps better treated as separate genera. The members of the following groups are probably closely related, and share combinations of several characteristic features that make the groups unique: the Yellowhammer group (Yellowhammer, Pine, Cirl and White-capped Buntings), the Rock Bunting group (Rock, Godlewski's, Meadow and Jankowski's Buntings), the Ortolan Bunting group (Ortolan, Grey-necked, Cinereous and Cretzschmar's Buntings), the House Bunting group (House, Lark-like and Cinnamon-breasted Buntings), the Golden-breasted Bunting group (Golden-breasted, Somali Golden-breasted, Brown-rumped and Cabanis's Buntings), and the species-pair Black-headed and Red-headed Buntings. Among the remaining species, some well-defined species-pairs can be identified (Tristram's and Yellow-browed; Rustic and Yellow-throated; Pallas's Reed and Common Reed), but the relationships between these and the rest of the members of the genus are less clear.

3 YELLOWHAMMER
Emberiza citrinella   Plate 2

Described as *Emberiza citrinella* Linnaeus 1758.
Synonyms: *Emberiza septentrionalis*, *Emberiza erythrogenys*, *Emberiza major*.

The Yellowhammer is one of the most well-known buntings in the Western Palearctic, occurring in a variety of open habitats over most of Europe, except in the vicinity of the Mediterranean, extending far eastwards into Siberia.

IDENTIFICATION 16.5cm. The Yellowhammer is characterised by a combination of relatively nondescript face pattern, yellow coloration on head and underparts, rufous rump and white in the outer tail feathers. In males in worn plumage, the head is extensively yellow, with dark pattern sometimes restricted to narrow blackish streak above supercilium and narrow border around ear-coverts. In exceptional cases, the head may become almost uniformly yellow. The breast is rufous, most prominently on the sides.

In fresh plumage, when males and females are similar, the head pattern is rather dull, but a more or less obvious yellow cast is normally apparent, particularly on central crown, supercilium and throat. The dark border encircling the ear-coverts is rather diffuse, grading into the paler centre, and often appears broken at the upper rear corner. Both mantle and underparts are streaked dark. The streaking on breast and flanks is blackish, most prominent on the rear flanks, with a strong element of rufous, particularly on the sides of the breast and upper flanks. The base colour of the mantle is a mixture of rufous and olive-brown, streaked blackish-brown, the lower scapulars mainly rufous on the outer web.

The most similar species is Pine Bunting, from the east Palearctic, which entirely lacks yellow in plumage. In Yellowhammer, there is usually a prominent yellow cast to the plumage, but in the palest birds this may be difficult to determine. The central belly, the edge of the base of the outer tail feathers, the edge of the outer primaries

and, above all, the underwing-coverts should show traces of yellow. However, the latter are not easily scrutinised in the field. In the theoretical case of a Yellowhammer completely lacking yellow tones in the plumage, the separation from Pine Bunting becomes extremely difficult. However, it remains to be proven that such individuals really exist. Apart from the yellow tones in the plumage, there are several details that differ on average between the two species (see Pine Bunting), but no single diagnostic character where there is no overlap.

Female and immature Cirl Buntings (which see for further differences) may appear very similar to Yellowhammer, but rump is grey-brown, instead of rufous.

Female Yellow-breasted Bunting shows yellow underparts and some rufous on the rump, but displays much bolder streaking on the mantle and only sparse and fine streaks on the underparts; in autumn, adult females in fresh plumage are unstreaked below, and juveniles show fine, distinct streaking which is much sparser than in Yellowhammer. In Yellow-breasted Bunting the border around the ear-coverts is narrow and distinct, which is not normally the case in Yellowhammer, and the supercilium prominent. However, male Yellowhammers in worn plumage may show a similar ear-covert pattern, but are easily separated by lack of broad lateral crown-stripes and less prominent supercilium.

The juvenile is much duller than adults, more evenly streaked, and with yellow colour less evident. The base colour of the underparts is usually paler whitish-yellow than in adults. The rump may be less rufous than in adults. Confusion is possible with juveniles of Pine and Cirl Bunting, which see. Juvenile Rock Bunting is similar in general pattern, but is much more buffish, particularly on the underparts.

DESCRIPTION
Adult male breeding Centre of crown lemon yellow, usually with traces of narrow blackish streaks or spots. Blackish lateral crown-stripe often very faint above eye, sometimes restricted to small dark area at base of bill and at the rear. Supercilium lemon yellow behind eye. In front of eye slightly more greenish-yellow like lores. Eye-stripe dark

greenish-grey, curving down around rear ear-coverts to lower rear corner. Ear-coverts yellow, moustache usually concolorous, but sometimes slightly darker. Submoustachial stripe and throat lemon yellow. Malar stripe usually absent, but may be rufous and quite prominent. Sides of neck greenish-grey, yellow just behind ear-coverts. Nape a mixture of yellow and greenish-grey. Mantle and scapulars a mixture of rufous and olive-brown, streaked blackish-brown, the lower scapulars mainly rufous on the outer web. Back olive-brown, tinged rufous, with narrower dark streaks than the mantle. Rump and uppertail-coverts rufous, the latter sometimes with narrow shaft streaks. Lesser coverts olive-green. Median coverts blackish-brown tipped rufous, pale sandy at the edge. Edges of greater coverts more olive-tinged. Tertials of similar colour as median coverts, showing *Emberiza* pattern. Alula dark brown. Primary coverts dark brown with greenish-grey edges. Primaries dark brown with very narrow greenish-grey edges, the outer one with whitish edge. Secondaries dark brown with greenish-brown edges, sometimes with a rufous cast. Tail feathers dark brown with greenish-grey edges, the two outermost pairs with white wedge on inner web. Underwing-coverts lemon yellow. Breast yellow with a varying amount of rusty-red mottling, particularly on the sides, forming breast-band in many individuals. There is usually some olive-grey in the centre and bordering the throat, continuous with the sides of the neck. Flanks yellow with diffuse rusty and distinct narrow blackish streaking. Belly unstreaked, lemon yellow. Undertail-coverts lemon yellow with greyish-brown or rufous centres and narrow dark shaft streaks, the longest ones often with extensive greyish-brown centres and prominent dark shaft streaks. Bill blue-grey, paler on cutting edge, slightly darker on culmen and gonys. Tarsus flesh-brown. Iris dark brown.

Juvenile   Adult

Median coverts of juvenile (left) and adult (right). Dark centre more pointed in juvenile.

Adult male non-breeding Similar to adult male breeding, but crown pattern obscured by olive-brown tips. Some yellow often shows through, at least on the central crown. Yellow ear-coverts and sides of neck also partially obscured by greenish-grey fringes. Malar stripes may be present and there are often dark spots on the throat. The mantle is more uniformly olive-rufous, streaked blackish. Rump and uppertail-coverts have pale yellowish edges, usually distinctly set off. The fringes on wing-coverts and tertials are broader than in breeding plumage, and the underparts are more diffusely streaked. On the upper breast, bordering the throat, there are often diffuse greenish-grey blotches and spots that will wear off later. Dark streaks on flanks are to some extent obscured.

First-winter male Similar to adult male non-breeding, but yellow base of crown feathers more efficiently obscured by olive-brown fringes and streaks. In some individuals the crown is greenish-grey, uniformly streaked dark, but usually some yellow shows through on the central crown. Some individuals are very similar to adults, but others show more obscured face pattern, with browner ear-coverts and sides of neck and less bright yellow base colour. In these

birds the malar stripe is more prominent and there are often more dark spots on the throat. The breast is often similar to adult, but some individuals show quite prominent streaking, with rufous and greenish-grey breast-band almost lacking. The tail feathers are pointed and more worn than in adults.

Adult female breeding Similar to adult male breeding, but less bright. The crown is distinctly streaked, particularly at the rear. The lateral crown-stripes are more prominent. The ear-coverts have broader and more diffuse borders and are usually browner. The sides of neck are greenish-grey, showing less yellow. The streaking on the breast and anterior flanks is on average more prominent. The uppertail-coverts on average have broader shaft streaks.

Adult female non-breeding Similar to adult male non-breeding, but the crown is yellowish-brown and the mantle slighlty less olive-tinged, uniformly streaked dark, very similar to some first-winter males. The face pattern is duller than adult male, quite similar to first-winter male, with browner ear-coverts and sides of neck and less bright yellow base colour. The malar stripe is well developed and there are dark spots on the throat. The breast is quite prominently streaked, the streaks often narrow and well-defined. The rufous and greenish-grey breast-band present in most males is usually ill-defined or lacking. The yellow colour of the belly is less bright than most males.

First-winter female Most individuals are virtually identical to adult female non-breeding. Best told from adult female by pointed and more worn tail feathers, and from first-winter males by less yellow on base of crown feathers.

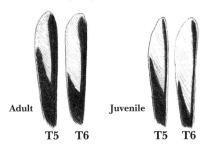

Adult   Juvenile

T5   T6   T5   T6

Outermost and second outermost tail feathers (T6 and T5) of adult and juvenile. Tips of adult feathers rounded; more pointed in juvenile. Dark pattern of outer web extends onto inner web near tip of feather in adult. Difference in amount of white between adult and juvenile indicates general variation within the species and is not age-related.

Juvenile Crown pale sandy-brown, often tinged yellow, boldly streaked blackish. The centre of the crown is slightly less heavily streaked, showing only a hint of a pale median crown-stripe. Supercilium pale sandy-brown, faintly streaked blackish. Lores pale yellowish-brown. Ear-coverts pale sandy-brown with dark borders. Submoustachial stripe and throat pale sandy-brown with a yellow tinge. Throat covered with small dark spots. Malar stripe usually ill-defined. Sides of neck pale sandy-brown. Nape sandy- or olive-brown, diffusely streaked. Mantle and scapulars uniformly olive-brown, streaked blackish-brown, the lower scapulars slightly rufescent. Back greyish-brown, tinged rufous, with narrower dark streaks. Rump and uppertail-coverts rufous-brown, with narrow dark shaft streaks. Lesser coverts olive-green. Median coverts tipped and edged rufous-sandy, with dark brown centres showing characteristic rounded tooth. Edges of greater coverts nar-

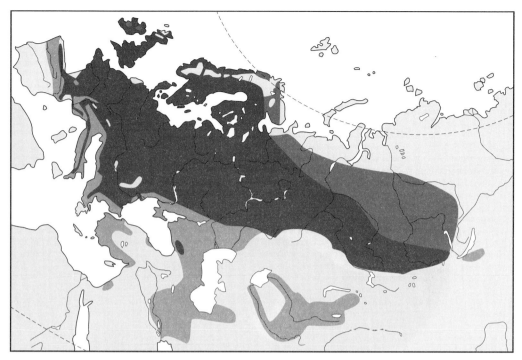

rower and more well-defined than in adults, more olive-tinged. Tertials similar to adults, as is rest of wing. Tail like adult, but feathers pointed. Two outermost pairs with white wedge on inner web, dark pattern of outer web extending onto inner web near tip of outermost pair. Underwing-coverts lemon yellow. Breast pale sandy-brown with a yellow tinge, prominently streaked dark brown. Flanks similar, but streaking more diffuse. The streaks become very narrow towards the belly, which is unstreaked pale sandy-brown with a yellow tinge. Undertail-coverts pale sandy-brown tinged yellow, with greyish-brown or rufous centres and narrow dark shaft streaks. Some feathers of belly or breast are often moulted quite early, resulting in more or less irregular yellow spots on the underparts.

Crown feathers of male (left) and female (right). Dark tip well-defined and square in male; less well-defined, with dark shaft streak in female.

SEXING The pattern of the crown feathers is the best difference between the sexes, but can usually only be determined in the hand. In males, most of the crown feather is yellow (turning to white towards the base of the feather), with a relatively well-defined border between yellow base and greyish-green or greyish-brown tip. There is a tiny dark spot or narrow dark shaft streak. In first-year males, the greyish-brown tip is more extensive and the amount of yellow is reduced, so pattern may be identical to that of adult female. In this case, correct ageing is necessary for determining the sex. Females always have more

extensive greyish-brown tip, with longer and more prominent dark shaft streak, and reduced amount of yellow. The border between the grey-brown tip and the yellow base is usually more diffuse, compared to males of similar age. In first-year females, there is often very little or no yellowish tinge at the base of the crown feathers, and much of the feather is brownish, to the tip, with a long dark shaft streak. Males have a tendency to have an unstreaked greenish breast-band, while females are usually streaked, with breast-band less pure green. Males are on average larger (wing: male 80-97, female 77-91).

MOULT AND AGEING Juveniles undergo a partial post-juvenile moult that starts not long after fledging. It involves head, body, lesser, median and usually all greater coverts and tertials, often also central pair of tail feathers (rarely a few more tail feathers are moulted), and is completed between August and October. Adults moult completely between July and October. Total duration has been estimated to c. 54 and 80 days in different studies. A limited pre-breeding moult may occur in some individuals.

In males, the amount of yellow in the plumage increases with age, but this is of limited value for ageing. As first-year birds usually moult all wing-coverts, ageing is best done according to relative amount of wear of primaries and tail feathers. Adults have these feathers relatively less worn than first-year birds until the next complete moult, but difference become more and more difficult to interprete with time. The shape of the tail feathers is also useful. The tips of the tail feathers are rounded in adults, while in first-year birds they are more pointed. Skull ossification is useful up to stage C, as a few adults may show incompletely ossified skull. Iris colour useful.

MEASUREMENTS Wing: (max) male 80-97, female 77-91. Tail: male 62-79, female 60-76. Bill: (to skull) male 10.7-13.9, female 10.3-13.4. Tarsus: male 17.0-21.3, female 17.4-21.8. P6-P8 emarginated.

GEOGRAPHICAL VARIATION The variation is largely clinal and rather slight. Single individuals usually difficult to diagnose, as individual variation almost as great as geographical variation.

E. c. citrinella (Scandinavia, and W and C Europe, intergrading with *erythrogenys* eastwards from a broad zone starting in W Russia, the Baltic states, Belarus, Ukraine, Romania, E Hungary and Serbia) Includes *nebulosa* and *sylvestris*. Described above.

E. c. caliginosa (Ireland, Scotland, Wales, and N and W England) Slightly smaller than nominate. Darker and more heavily streaked, with greenish tinge to yellow of head and underparts. The olive breast-band is reduced compared to nominate, but the chestnut pattern on flanks is more extensive.

E. c erythrogenys (Russia, east to Siberia) Yellow colour on crown and throat often brighter. Mantle paler than nominate, more sandy or pinkish-brown and less greenish-olive, and slightly less heavily streaked. Nape and scapulars somewhat greyer. Wing-bars usually somewhat whiter. Pale edges to feathers of rump whiter. Flanks and undertail-coverts often whiter, with rufous streaking on average more extensive.

VOICE The song is normally given from tree or bush. It is a series of usually 5-7 similar notes, usually ending in a drawn out note of a different pitch, *ze-ze-ze-ze-ze-ze ziiiii* or *chi-chi-chi-chi-chi-chi ziii-hüüü*.

The call notes are as characteristic as they are difficult to transcribe. Common call notes are single *ztif*, or *trp*, or more complex *perett* or similar variations. The alarm call is a thin *dzee*.

HABITS Breeding normally begins in early May, but sometimes earlier; in southern populations regularly in early April. Often 2-3 broods; late broods sometimes started as late as September. The nest is placed on or near the ground, hidden among grass or herbage, against a bank or tree, or relatively low in a bush. It is built by the female alone, of dry grass, plant stems, straw, leaves and moss, lined with rootlets and fine grass, sometimes hair. Eggs 3-5, variable in colour, from glossy purplish-white to pale bluish, greyish- or pinkish-buff, occasionally unmarked, but usually with a few small spots and an intricate network of irregularly spaced dark lines. Underlying smears sometimes cause marbled appearance. Incubation 12-14 days, usually by female alone. Young fledge after 11-13 days. Brooding by female, but male assists in bringing food, which is made up of invertebrates, such as moths, caterpillars, beetles, grasshoppers and flies. During the breeding season adults feed mainly on a wide range of invertebrates, particularly beetles, caterpillars and grasshoppers. During remainder of year grass and cereal seeds dominate diet, although a few birds may specialise in animal prey. Gregarious outside breeding season, sometimes in flocks of several hundreds. Not shy, but flocks wary.

STATUS AND HABITAT Common in a variety of open woodland, scrub, heathland and cultivation and similar habitats, favouring areas with a mosaic of open habitats and patches of forest or shrubs. Open ground for foraging, low woody vegetation and tall song-posts seem to be common denominators. Changing land use and farming practices affect population densities locally. Has declined in Ireland, Belgium, Netherlands, Germany, Austria, Italy and Latvia. Occurs in woodland edge, with no marked preference for coniferous or deciduous forest, even occu-

pying the margin between forest tundra and true tundra. Prefers traditional agricultural landscapes, like farmland with hedges, to modern monocultures. Avoids dense forest, wetlands and towns. In winter, often in stubble fields and other agricultural land.

DISTRIBUTION AND MOVEMENTS Widespread in Europe, breeding throughout Scandinavia, except above tree-limit and in arctic zone; most of Great Britain, except parts of Scotland; most of continental Europe, except most of western Netherlands, parts of southern France, the highest altitudes in the Alps and the Carpathian Mountains, and immediate vicinity of Mediterranean, including the Mediterranean islands. Absent from most of Iberian peninsula, but breeds in Pyrenees and Cantabrian Mountains, in northern Spain, and locally in northern Portugal. In Italy, breeds at mid-altitudes in the Alps, in the Appenine range, and locally in the upper Po Valley. Breeds in most of the Balkans, except along Adriatic Sea; absent from most of Greece, but breeds in Macedonia and in the Pindu Mountains; breeds locally in north-western Turkey, and probably also along the Black Sea in the north-east, and in the western and central Taurus Mountains. Most of Ukraine, except south. Breeds in much of Russia, north of Volgograd, with isolated population in western Caucasus. Southern limit of range roughly follows Kazakhstan border to the Altai Mountains and to Irkutsk in Siberia. Recorded in Kentei in Mongolia. Occurs locally in extreme northern Kazakhstan, e.g. in the Petropavlovsk and Semipalatinsk areas. In the north, range extends roughly to northern limit of taiga, but occurs locally in the tundra. In the east known to occur at the Nizhnyaya Tunguska River, and as far north-east as the Vilyuy River.

Successfully introduced in New Zealand between 1862 and 1871. It is now widespread throughout the country, except in the high mountains.

Sedentary or partial migrant in Europe. Only northernmost part of range is vacated in winter, otherwise winters mainly within breeding range. Winter visitor to northern Spain; much of Italy; the Balkans, except southernmost Greece; western Turkey; and northern Israel. In cold winters regularly found further south, reaching Morocco, Algeria, Tunisia, Sicily, Malta, Cyprus and Jordan in very low numbers. In eastern part of range most of population vacates breeding range, but winters locally, even in Siberia. Southward migration begins in September, and continues until late autumn. Main wintering range in east in Transcaucasia, north-eastern Iraq, and northern and western Iran. Also winters, mainly along Amu-Darya and Syr-Darya Rivers, but probably also elsewhere in Turkmenistan, Uzbekistan and southern Kazakhstan, but extent not well known. Some winter in Transbaikal area. Migration largely influenced by weather conditions, so timetable different between different years. Usually arrives in winter range in October or November, and present until February or March, when northward migration begins at first signs of spring. Returns to breeding grounds late March-April. Accidental Svalbard, Iceland, United Arab Emirates, Egypt and Ladakh. Vagrant or rare regular winter visitor to Nepal.

REFERENCES Bezzel (1993), Cramp & Perrins (1994), Dementiev & Gladkov (1966), Glaubrecht (1989 & 1991), Harrison (1954), Horváth & Keve (1956), Madge (1979), Sundberg & Larsson (1994), Svensson (1992), Tucker & Heath (1994), Vaurie (1956).

4   PINE BUNTING
Emberiza leucocephalos   Plate 3

Described as *Emberiza leucocephalos* Gmelin 1771.
Synonym: *Emberiza leucocephala*.

The Pine Bunting is a bird of clearings and forest edge in the southern parts of the Siberian taiga. It is closely related to Yellowhammer, hybridising regularly in certain areas.

IDENTIFICATION 17cm. Males are unmistakable and always characterised by their distinctive head pattern. The female is very similar to female Yellowhammer, but lacks all traces of yellow in the plumage. In particular, the edges of the outer tail feathers, the edge of the outer primaries and, above all, the underwing-coverts, which are white in Pine Bunting, never showing traces of yellow, which is always the case in Yellowhammer. Compared with normal Yellowhammers, female Pine Buntings are paler on the mantle with an almost pinkish tinge. The underparts are silky whitish. Most female Pine Buntings are readily identified, but matters are complicated by the frequent occurrence of hybrids in certain areas and the suspicion that there may be Yellowhammers lacking yellow pigmentation. It is not clear how a true Yellowhammer without a trace of yellow in the plumage could be safely identified, if such birds exists. There are several details that differ on average between the two species, but apart from presence or absence of yellow colour in plumage no single diagnostic character exists.

The lower mandible is paler and greyer than the upper mandible in Pine Bunting. In Yellowhammer there is little or no contrast. The streaks on the crown are slightly more distinct in Pine Bunting, but there is a great deal of overlap. The lateral crown-stripes are usually longer in Pine, continuing onto the nape, enhancing the nape spot, which is whiter than in Yellowhammer. The submoustachial stripe is usually whiter and more distinct in Pine, in combination with, on average, a broader and blacker malar stripe. The streaking on the upper breast, bordering the throat, is often more distinct and more in the shape of spots in Pine Bunting, particularly in worn plumage. Yellowhammer may show the same feature, but normally the pattern is more diffuse and paler. The rump is usually a deeper rufous-brown with whiter and more well-defined pale fringes in Pine, more orange-rufous with less prominent pale fringes in Yellowhammer. However, the Siberian race *erythrogenys* of Yellowhammer is very similar to Pine in this respect. The colour of the median covert wing-bars in Pine is buffish, wearing to white. In western Yellowhammers the median covert wing-bars are yellowish-rufous, wearing to pale yellow, but in the race *erythrogenys* the wing-bars are as in Pine. The marginal coverts and underwing-coverts are white in Pine, yellow in Yellowhammer. Pine Bunting shows on average more white in the tail, and always shows more rufous on the sides of the breast. In birds with the least amount of rufous, the streaking appears more contrasting in Pine, as it is set against white background. The undertail-coverts are whiter in Pine, with less dark on the centres. Quite often, they appear uniformly white, or with just a narrow blackish shaft streak. In Yellowhammer, the undertail-coverts are usually noticeably streaked dark.

The juvenile is similar to juvenile Yellowhammer, but lacks yellow colour in plumage, rendering it slightly more contrasting brown and white. In particular the median

crown-stripe often appears whitish. The breast is washed brownish, streaked dark, contrasting with whiter belly and throat. In Yellowhammer, the underparts appear more uniform, with little difference in base colour between breast and belly, and with more extensive dark streaking.

Confusion with Rustic Bunting is concievable, as both species show rufous rump, and white underparts are streaked rufous. Normally, the face and throat pattern of Rustic is more contrasting, with more prominent supercilium and submoustachial stripe, but worn adult female Pine may approach appearance of Rustic. However, blackish border to ear-coverts always more prominent in Rustic, and at least some traces of rufous nape apparent. The breast-band is usually narrower and more distinct in Rustic. Rustic is also a clearly smaller bird, with shorter tail.

HYBRIDISATION Closely related to Yellowhammer as shown by extensive local hybridisation in western Siberia, and sometimes considered conspecific. However, also occurs side by side over large areas in Siberia without hybridisation. The offspring of mixed pairs, which are fully fertile, or following generations, can show a variety of intermediate characters, and about 15% of the Pine Buntings do so in some areas of overlap. Some are complete intermediates, while others closely resemble one of the parental species. Second, third, fourth, etc., generation offspring of hybrids will presumably look increasingly like one of the ancestors as the genes of one species become diluted. Any type of intermediate plumage can be expected, up to the stage where the plumage only shows the characters of one of the ancestral species, but where the individual still carry genes from the other species. It is, in fact, possible that some of the traits of the race *erythrogenys* of Yellowhammer are a result of genetic overflow from Pine Bunting.

Most hybrids are easily diagnosed as they show obvious intermediate characters. Others are more similar to one of the parent species. Yellowhammers with Pine Bunting genes show paler mantle and flanks and increased amount of rufous on the underparts. Males tend to show blacker foreheads, lateral crown-stripes and a blacker and more prominent border to the ear-coverts. Pine Buntings with Yellowhammer genes show a yellowish tinge to pale parts of plumage. The question of hybrid origin arises every time a vagrant Pine Bunting is observed west of its normal range. Any bird with a yellow tinge anywhere in the plumage is a hybrid, if not a pure Yellowhammer. Yellowhammers always show yellow on the belly, the edge of the outer primaries, the edges of the base of the tail feathers or the underwing-coverts. Birds with all these areas whitish or at least without yellow, showing no other signs of hybrid origin, can for all practical purposes be identified as Pine Buntings. Beware that there are hybrids lacking yellow tinge on belly, edge of outer primaries and edges of tail feathers, looking exactly like Pine Buntings, but with yellow underwing-coverts, revealing their hybrid origin.

A male morph, probably of hybrid origin, shows a much paler face than normal males and seems to be most frequent in the Altai Mountains. The base colour of the head is usually pure white but may be pale yellow. These birds differ from normal males by a prominent white supercilium and more extensive white on the ear-coverts. The lores are rufous or white. The submoustachial area is rufous to a varying degree and the throat is white or rufous. Individuals lacking rufous throat may show a superficial similarity to Rock Bunting.

DESCRIPTION

Adult male breeding Central crown white. Rather narrow black lateral crown-stripes. Lores, broad supercilium, sides of neck and throat chestnut-brown. Ear-coverts white, with rather narrow dark border at the rear. Mantle rufous-brown, prominently streaked blackish. Scapulars slightly more prominently rufous-brown, streaked dark. Back, rump and uppertail-coverts almost uniformly rufous-brown, of same colour as sides of breast. Lesser coverts grey-brown. Median coverts blackish-brown with pale buffish, almost whitish tips. Greater coverts and tertials blackish, with pale rufous-brown outer webs, paler at the edges. Primaries and primary coverts dark brown with narrow off-white edges. Underwing-coverts white. Edges of outer webs of central tail feathers rufous-brown. Tail feathers dark brown with buffish-grey edges, the two outermost pairs with white wedge on inner web. Breast extensively mottled rufous, in odd individuals with a greyish upper edge, separated from chestnut-brown throat by white crescent. Flanks prominently streaked rufous, with some dark streaks especially at the rear. Belly whitish. Undertail-coverts white with inconspicuous narrow dark shaft streaks. Upper mandible dark brown, cutting edge and lower mandible blue-grey. Tarsus flesh-brown. Iris dark brown.

Adult male non-breeding Similar to adult male breeding, but head pattern somewhat obscured. Central crown white, the feathers tipped greyish-buff, creating blotchy appearance. Lateral crown-stripes with grey-brown fringes. Throat chestnut-brown, to some extent obscured by whitish tips. A few dark spots on breast, rufous colour much obscured. Back, rump and uppertail-coverts with prominent whitish fringes.

First-winter male Similar to adult male non-breeding, but pale fringes of head pattern broader. Central crown white, the feathers tipped brownish-grey with blackish shaft streaks. Rufous-brown pattern of head clearly visible, but more obscured than in adult male. Back almost like mantle, feathers with rufous centres, streaked dark. Rump and uppertail-coverts slightly duller, streaked. Shaft streak of uppertail-coverts narrower than in Yellowhammer. Breast-band blotchy, with some brownish admixed. Very diffuse streaking. Iris dark grey-brown.

Adult female breeding Central crown grey-brown, often quite pale, even whitish, streaked dark brown. Lateral crown-stripes appear more streaked than in males, but still relatively prominent dark brown. Supercilium, submoustachial stripe and throat whitish, often with a varying amount of pale rufous admixed. Especially when worn, resemblance to male may increase, as crown becomes whiter and supercilium and throat become more rufous. Ear-coverts whitish. Malar stripe variable, often prominent. Mantle like male, but slightly paler. Scapulars rufous-brown, streaked dark. Back, rump and uppertail-coverts paler than in adult male, rather uniformly rufous-brown, the uppertail-coverts with dark shaft streaks. Lesser coverts grey-brown. Median coverts blackish-brown with pale tips. Greater coverts and tertials blackish, with pale rufous-brown outer webs, paler at the edges. Primaries and primary coverts dark brown with narrow off-white edges. Edges of outer webs of central tail feathers pale rufous-brown, fading to white. Sides of breast blotched rufous, extending towards flanks and central breast. Upper breast with prominent spotting, especially near centre.

Lower breast and sides of breast more diffusely streaked. Belly whitish. Undertail-coverts white with very narrow shaft streaks.

Adult female non-breeding Very similar to adult female breeding, but broader fringes make plumage duller. Central crown brownish-grey streaked dark brown, usually with white at the base, and very faint darker lateral stripes. Ear-coverts pale brownish-grey, bordered behind by brownish eye-stripe and moustachial stripe. Throat off-white, sometimes with some pale rufous on the bases of the feathers. Mantle slightly paler than in summer. Back, rump and uppertail-coverts with distinct pale fringes. Edges of upperwing-coverts broader. Varying amount of rufous on breast, largely concealed by pale fringes. Dark streaking is more diffuse.

First-winter female Very similar to adult female non-breeding, but plumage even duller, although there is a great deal of overlap. Crown with on average less white at the base of the feathers than in adult female. Supercilium off-white, with some faint streaking. Ear-coverts slightly darker. Submoustachial stripe and throat buffier than adult female, with more small blackish spots on throat. Scapulars browner, with more distinct central streak. Back and rump similar to first-winter male but paler. Less rufous on breast than adult female, with more extensive streaking.

Juvenile Crown pale sandy-brown, boldly streaked blackish-brown. Central crown-stripe whitish. Supercilium whitish or pale sandy-brown, faintly streaked blackish. Lores pale whitish to buffy-brown. Ear-coverts pale sandy-brown with dark borders. Submoustachial stripe and throat whitish. Throat sparsely spotted. Malar stripe blackish-brown. Sides of neck pale sandy-brown. Nape sandy-brown, streaked dark. Mantle and scapulars sandy-brown tinged rufescent, streaked blackish-brown, the lower scapulars slightly more rufescent. Back sandy-brown, tinged rufous, indistinctly streaked. Rump and uppertail-coverts rufous-brown, with narrow dark shaft streaks. Lesser coverts grey-brown. Median coverts with dark brown centres, showing characteristic rounded tooth, tipped rufous-sandy. Edges of greater coverts narrower and more well-defined than in adults. Tertials similar to adults, as is rest of wing. Tail like adult, but feathers pointed. Underwing-coverts white. Breast pale fulvescent brown, prominently streaked dark brown. Flanks similar, but the streaking more diffuse. Belly whitish, almost unstreaked. Undertail-coverts whitish with narrow dark shaft streaks. Some feathers of the underparts may be moulted quite early, resulting in chestnut spots on the sides of breast or flanks.

T5   T6

Outermost and second outermost tail feathers (T6 and T5) of nominate race. White pattern on average more extensive than in Yellowhammer.

SEXING Except in juvenile plumage, males differ from females by having chestnut-brown throat and most of cen-

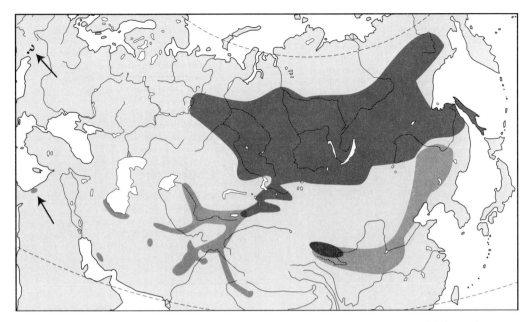

tral crown feathers white. In fresh plumage the crown feathers have greyish-buff tips, and the throat feathers have pale fringes, extent depending age, but these wear off during spring. In females there is usually very little white at the base of the central crown feathers, and little or no rufous on the throat. Some, presumably adult, females may show quite extensive white bases of the crown feathers and rufous on the throat, particularly in worn plumage, thus ghosting male plumage. The rufous on the throat is limited to rufous spots on the throat feathers, not extending to the base of the feather, and never the whole feather as in males.

MOULT AND AGEING Juveniles undergo a partial post-juvenile moult, which is completed before onset of autumn migration. It normally involves head, body, lesser, median and greater coverts, and tertials. Primaries, secondaries and primary coverts are not moulted. Adults moult completely July to September.

As first-year birds usually moult all wing-coverts, ageing best done according to relative amount of wear of primary coverts, primaries and tail feathers. Adults have these feathers relatively less worn than first-year birds until the next complete moult, but difference become more and more difficult to interpret with time. The shape of the tail feathers is also useful. The tip of the tail feathers in adults is rounded, while in first-year birds they are more pointed. In males, the tips of the crown feathers are a purer greyish-buff, while in first-year males they are browner grey, with dark shaft streaks. The pale tips of throat feathers are broader in first-year males, more effectively obscuring the rufous pattern. Skull ossification probably useful, but no detailed study. Iris colour useful.

MEASUREMENTS Wing: (max) male 88-100, female 83-95. Tail: male 68-83, female 64-75. Bill: (to skull) male 10.2-12.9, female 10.8-13.0. Tarsus: male 17.6-20.8, female 18.8-19.8. P6-P8 emarginated.

GEOGRAPHICAL VARIATION Normally only one sub-species recognised beside nominate race. A few races have been described from Siberia and western China, but are generally considered synonymous with the nominate race.

E. l. leucocephalos (Siberia) Includes *stachanovi* and *karpovi*. Described above. Width of black band across forehead 2-6mm.

E. l. fronto (NE Qinghai and adjacent Gansu, China) More extensively black on forehead (7-9mm) and lateral crown-stripes. Chestnut markings more saturated. Wing on average longer than nominate race, male 94.5-100.5mm (mean c. 97), female 88-94mm (mean c. 91), compared to approximate mean of nominate: male 94 and female 89.

VOICE The song is delivered from a tree or a bush, and is very similar to song of Yellowhammer, *ze-ze-ze-ze-ze-ze ziiiii*. Certain identification is usually not possible. Sonagrams reveal that the *ze* elements consist of two parts in both species, one higher and one lower in pitch. The lower part is consistently more drawn out in Pine Bunting, which may cause the elements to sound less discrete, and the whole song softer.

The call notes are very similar to those of Yellowhammer, which see, and no useful differences have been detected.

HABITS Breeding takes place from late April or early May to July. The nest, which is tightly woven of grass, rootlets and stalks and lined with soft grass and hair, is placed in a depression on ground, usually sheltered by grass, bush or fallen branch. It is built by the female alone. Two broods are regularly raised. Eggs 4-5 pale whitish-blue or -green to pinkish-cream, moderately glossy, marked with small dark dots, specks, streaks and a few fine lines, with small, faint underlying lilac-grey smears. Incubation 13 days by female alone. The young usually leave nest 9 days after hatching, and fledge 1-3 days later. There is often a second brood. Both sexes care for young, which are fed grasshoppers and other insects like bugs, flies, beetles and caterpillars, and some seeds. Diet of adult during breeding season dominated by a variety of invertebrates, like grasshoppers, bugs, beetles, caterpillars, flies, spiders and snails. Outside breeding season the diet consists mainly of grains of wheat, oats, barley, rye and rice, and to a lesser degree seeds from a variety of wild grasses and herbs. Gregarious outside breeding season, sometimes in flocks of hundreds, freely associating with other buntings and finches.

STATUS AND HABITAT Common in most of range. Occurs in southern part of Siberian taiga, where it prefers forest edge and clearings, or burnt or logged areas in more continuous pine or mixed forest. Sometimes also in clumps of trees on steppe. In winter usually found in arable fields, waste ground, orchards and similar open areas.

DISTRIBUTION AND MOVEMENTS Breeds from the the Perm area west of the Ural Mountains, east through Siberia to the mountains north of the Sea of Okhotsk in the north and on Sakhalin in the south. Northern limit of distribution generally south of the Arctic Circle, but on the Yenisey River and at Verkhoyansk extends somewhat further north. In the south, limit of range roughly along 50°N, including northern Mongolia and north-eastern Inner Mongolia. Range extends further south in Central Asia, where found in the Altai, Tarbagatay, Dzhungarian Ala Tau and the eastern Tien Shan ranges. An isolated population, the race *fronto*, inhabits north-eastern Qinghai, from the eastern edge of the Zaidam depression, eastwards to southern Gansu. This race appears to be non-migratory.

Autumn migration begins in August or September, earlier than Yellowhammer in areas of sympatry. Peak passage across the Tien Shan Mountains late September and October. Regular in low numbers on passage on Hegura-jima in Japan in October. Usually arrives on wintering grounds in Afghanistan and north-west India in November. Bulk of population winters in Afghanistan, Pakistan and north-western India, and in northern China, where found from eastern Qinghai through southern Gansu to southern Shaanxi and Henan, and from southern Hebei to Heilongjiang in the north-east. Locally fairly common in Nepal. Occurs regularly in smaller numbers over a large area, with some birds wintering as far north as the Lake Baikal area during mild winters. Regularly winters in southern Sakhalin, northern Honshu and Hokkaido in Japan, Mongolia, southern Turkmenistan, south-eastern Uzbekistan, Tajikistan, southern and south-eastern Kazakhstan, the Kashi region, China, and northern and south-western Iran. Probably winters regularly further west, as the species is annual in small numbers in well-watched Israel. There are also more than 100 records from north-eastern Italy, where winter trapping rampant.

Spring migration starts fairly early, with first birds normally leaving wintering grounds around mid March. Northward migration rapid during late March and first half of April, and birds are present in Yakutia from second half of April, by which time wintering grounds are deserted.

There is a sprinkling of records from all over Europe, with more than ten records from the British Isles, France, Belgium, the Netherlands, Italy and Yugoslavia. Rarer in Norway, Sweden, Finland and Germany and only encountered once or twice in Iceland, Denmark, Ireland, Spain, Gibraltar, Switzerland, Austria, Poland, Czech Republic, Hungary, Greece, Bulgaria and Malta. Outside Europe, vagrant to Morocco, Turkey, Cyprus, Iraq, UAE, Saudi Arabia, Korea and Alaska.

REFERENCES Ali & Ripley (1974), Alström *et al.* (1992), Anon. (1993), Bezzel (1993), Bradshaw (1990), Bradshaw & Gray (1993), Cramp & Perrins (1994), Dementiev & Gladkov (1966), Dorzhiev & Jumov (1991), Holloway (1990), Johansen (1944), Lewington (1990), Mauersberger (1971), Roberts (1992), Svensson (1992), Wallschläger (1983), Vaurie (1956).

5 WHITE-CAPPED BUNTING
Emberiza stewarti   Plate 3

Described as *Euspiza stewarti* Blyth 1854. Monotypic. Synonyms: *Emberiza caniceps*.

The White-capped Bunting inhabits dry mountains of Central Asia.

IDENTIFICATION 15cm. Adult male shows characteristic whitish or pale grey head and breast, with black throat and a black supercilium. The upperparts and sides of the breast are rufous. Only buntings with somewhat similar head pattern are Pine Bunting and extralimital Cirl Bunting. In Pine Bunting the throat is chestnut, but even if distance or light conditions make colours impossible to see, the more extensive whitish areas on crown and ear-coverts of White-capped Bunting should be evident. Also, in White-capped Bunting the ear-coverts are not bordered by a dark area at the rear as in Pine Bunting. In fresh plumage male White-capped has a head pattern somewhat similar to male Cirl Bunting, but the striped crown, yellow supercilium and yellow ear-coverts of latter make confusion unlikely. Also, the rump is never rufous in Cirl.

Females differ from most other buntings by their nondescript streaked plumage and combination of rufous rump and white in the tail. In worn plumage, there is usually a chestnut patch on the side of the breast. In winter most similar to female Pine Bunting. Best identified by combination of greyer plumage, less prominent streaking on crown and mantle, less prominent wing-bars, more white in tail, and inconspicuous *Emberiza* pattern on tertials. The underparts are pale buffy, with more extensive and blacker streaking on breast and flanks. Any rufous present should be confined to patch on sides of breast. In fresh plumage the rufous rump is less extensive in White-capped than in Pine.

The juvenile is dull grey-brown and rather uniformly and finely streaked, both above and below. The combination of uniformly rusty rump and white outer tail feathers distinguishes it from accentors, pipits, etc. Told from juvenile Rock Bunting by much less prominent streaking on crown, breast and upperparts, and more pronounced contrast between rump and mantle. From juvenile Grey-necked Bunting by dark bill, rufous rump, and heavier and more diffuse streaking on the upperparts. The breast of juvenile Grey-necked is buffish with relatively few rufous and dark spots intermixed, pale sandy-buff and streaked dark in White-capped. From juvenile Pine Bunting by greyer plumage, much less prominent streaking on crown, mantle and breast, more white in tail and lack of *Emberiza* pattern on tertials.

DESCRIPTION
Adult male breeding Crown grey, sometimes almost white. Supercilium black. Ear-coverts whitish. Throat black. Nape brownish-olive, sometimes plain grey. Mantle, back, rump and uppertail-coverts rufous-brown. The mantle some-

times show traces of dark streaking, especially in early summer. The scapulars are rufous-brown, usually unstreaked. Lesser coverts rufous-brown with narrow pale edges, slightly paler and greyer than the mantle. Median coverts rufous-brown with grey-brown base to the inner web and sandy-brown edge on the outer web, forming wing-bar unless too worn. Greater coverts with dark centres and sandy-brown or sandy-rufous edge on the outer web, broader at tip. Tertials with even, fairly narrow pale edges, showing no or very faint *Emberiza* pattern. Tail feathers blackish-brown, except central pair, which are brown, with pale edges. Outermost pair largely white, outer web brown towards the tip. Most of inner web of second outermost pair white, outer web brown. Breast pale creamy-white, whiter towards the throat. Chestnut breast-band broad on the sides, narrow, sometimes broken, in the centre. Flanks sometimes with rufous streaks or blotches. Belly creamy-white. Undertail-coverts whitish with chestnut centres. Bill dark horn, rather thin. Tarsus rather pale straw-coloured. Iris dark brown.

Outermost and second outermost tail feathers (T6 and T5) of adult. White pattern more extensive than in Pine Bunting.

Adult male non-breeding Similar to adult male breeding, but pattern much obscured. Crown diffusely blotched olive grey-brown, underlying grey usually showing through. Supercilium black in front of eye, narrowly fringed whitish behind eye. Ear-coverts sullied pale sandy-brown. Throat black, fringed pale sandy-brown. Nape brownish-olive. Mantle and scapulars heavily fringed sandy-brown, streaked dark. Back, rump and uppertail-coverts rufous-brown, with neat narrow fringes. Wing as in adult male breeding, but fringes broader. Chestnut breast-band partly obscured. Some diffuse rufous streaking on the flanks.

Median coverts of juvenile (left) and adult (right). Dark centre in first-winter male more extensive than in adult male and edges show less rufous-brown. In adult male, visible part of feather rufous-brown on outer web with less well-defined sandy-brown edge.

First-winter male Very similar to adult male non-breeding, but pattern even more obscured. Flight feathers, tertials and tail comparatively more worn. Tail feathers less rounded. The crown is more uniformly grey-brown, sometimes faintly streaked. Supercilium less black in front of eye. Ear-coverts darker. Fringes of throat broader. Lesser coverts grey-brown. Median coverts with pointed dark brown centres and sandy-brown edge, forming slightly

more prominent wing-bar. Edges of greater coverts paler and tips broader. Tertials with narrower pale edges.
Adult female breeding Crown sandy-grey, evenly streaked dark. Supercilium pale grey. Ear-coverts olive-brown, slightly paler in the middle, and often with a pale patch at the rear. Submoustachial stripe and throat sandy-white. Fairly prominent dark malar stripe. Some females show a head pattern reminiscent of male, with darker supercilium and throat. Mantle greyish-brown, streaked darker grey-brown. Scapulars chestnut with a dark shaft stripe. Back rusty, rump and uppertail-coverts darker rusty-red, the longest tail covert almost chestnut, with dark shaft streaks. Lesser coverts greyish-brown. Median coverts darker grey-brown, with pale sandy-brown tips. Greater coverts dark grey-brown with greyish sandy-brown edges and paler sandy-brown tips. Alula and primary coverts brown with narrow buffy edge. Primaries brown with narrow pale edges. Secondaries similar, but with a rufous tinge to the edges. Tertials dark grey-brown with even dull rufous-brown edges, which may become very worn, showing no or very faint *Emberiza* pattern. Tail similar to that of adult male. The underparts are sandy-white, with fine streaking on the breast and flanks. The central breast is streaked or spotted. A varying amount of chestnut on the sides of the breast, like a wedge towards the centre of the breast. Some females may be similar to males in this respect. Flanks show some streaking. Belly almost without streaking. Undertail-coverts with dark shaft streaks.

Adult female non-breeding Similar to adult female breeding, but upperparts browner and more heavily streaked, particularly on crown, which is concolorous with mantle. Streaking on breast rather prominent, in some almost pipit-like. Little or no chestnut visible on the sides of the breast.

First-winter female Very similar to adult female non-breeding, but flight feathers, tertials and tail comparatively more worn. Tail feathers more pointed.

Juvenile Crown greyish sandy-brown, indistinctly streaked darker grey-brown. Supercilium pale buffy, with grey-brown streaks. Ear-coverts almost uniformly olive sandy-brown. Submoustachial stripe and throat pale sandy-buff with streaks and spots. Malar stripe ill-defined. Mantle and scapulars greyish sandy-brown, diffusely streaked darker grey-brown, darker than crown. Back tinged rufous. Rump and uppertail-coverts darker rusty-red, the longest tail covert almost chestnut, sometimes with dark shaft streaks. Lesser coverts greyish-brown, edged pale. Median coverts darker grey-brown, showing characteristic rounded tooth, tipped pale sandy-brown. Greater coverts dark grey-brown with greyish sandy-brown edges and pale sandy-brown tips. Alula dark grey-brown with rather sharply set-off pale buffy edge, becoming paler and very narrow at the tip. Primary coverts dark grey-brown with narrow grey-brown edges. Primaries dark grey-brown with narrow pale sandy-brown edges. Secondaries dark grey-brown with dull olive rufous-brown edges. Tertials dark grey-brown with dull rufous-brown edges. Central tail feathers blackish-brown, with rather narrow paler edges. Most of two outer pairs white, except for some dark on outer webs and base of inner. Breast and flanks pale sandy-buff rather uniformly streaked. Some chestnut may be concealed on the sides of the breast. Belly paler, faintly streaked. Undertail-coverts pale buff, with narrow dark streaks.

SEXING Generally, sexing is straightforward, with males showing black throat and prominent chestnut patches on

115

sides of breast. Females normally lack dark on the throat, and show only limited amounts of chestnut on the sides of the breast. However, some females ghost male plumage and look like dull males. The supercilium and throat may be quite dark, but the base of the feathers are only diffusely dark, not distinctly blackish. Occasionally the breast-band may be almost complete in females.

MOULT AND AGEING Partial moult of juveniles August to September does not involve primaries, secondaries, tertials and tail feathers. Adults moult completely after the breeding season, July to early October. Some birds in late summer show arrested moult, with outer primaries worn and inner ones fresh.

First-year males can be told from adults by dark centred median coverts and comparatively more worn tertials, primaries and tail feathers. Females more difficult, but most first-year birds can be told from adults by the comparatively more worn tertials, primaries and tail feathers. Iris colour probably helpful.

MEASUREMENTS Wing: (max) male 74.5-88.5, female 71-79.5, tail: male 65.5-82.5, female 59.5-77.5, bill: (to skull) male 12.0-12.9, female 12.2-12.6, tarsus: male 15.8-17.6, female 16.0-17.2. P5-P8 emarginated.

GEOGRAPHICAL VARIATION None.

VOICE Sings from an exposed perch, such as a boulder, rock or top of a bush. The song is often reminiscent of Yellowhammer, but usually slower, consisting of 10-12 similar units, lacking the last drawn-out note *chew-chew-chew-chew-chew-chew-chew-chew-chew-chew* or *tzree-tzree-tzree-tzree-tzree-tzree- tzree-tzree-tzree-tzree*. Other variants may recall song of Ortolan, *tree tree tree tree tree tri tri*. A different type of song, faster and higher in pitch, has been described as a rapid short-noted twitter, *tih-tih-tih-tih-tih*.

The flight call is a twitter, *turrit*, or *tjuriritt*, recalling Linnet *Carduelis cannabina* or Serin *Serinus serinus*. A sharp *tit* and a variety of similar short calls may be heard from perched birds.

HABITS Breeds April-July. Usually 2 broods. The nest is placed on the ground, concealed by small bush, tuft of grass or overhanging rock, or in a crevice. The nesting hollow is lined with thin blades of dry grass and plant stems, lined with hair or wool. Building and incubation probably by female alone. Eggs 3-5, dull white, tinged blue or grey, with evenly spread thick purplish-grey mottling and deep reddish-brown spots and blotches, without any tendency of concentration at large end. Incubation 11-14 days. Young leave nest after 8-9 days, but cannot fly until about 14 days old. They are fed insects and arthropods, mainly by the female. Diet of adults includes grass seeds, in summer also insects and berries. Feeds on the ground. Gregarious in winter, sometimes with other buntings. Hops. Fairly tame.

STATUS AND HABITAT Common on relatively bare grassy and rocky slopes, with or without sparse bushes and trees, sometimes orchards, juniper scrub or open pine or oak forest. In places breeds as high as 3600m, but elevations between 1200 and 2500m more normal. In areas where Rock Bunting present, usually occurs at lower altitudes on more open arid ground. In winter in grassy scrub forest, dry hillsides with scattered bushes and waste ground.

DISTRIBUTION AND MOVEMENTS Breeds in a restricted area in central Asian mountains, from south-eastern

corner of Turkmenistan, northern Afghanistan, western and northernmost Pakistan and Kashmir, through southern Uzbekistan and Tajikistan, to southern and western Kyrgyzstan and the Kara Tau range in southern Kazakhstan. Occurs in the south to north-western Himachal Pradesh, and possibly further south-east along the Himalayan foothills. Migration patterns incompletely known. Southward migration apparently begins in August in the north, with main migration September. Further south, where migration partly altitudinal, birds may remain on the breeding grounds until late October. Winters in India in Haryana, western Uttar Pradesh, Rajasthan, Madhya Pradesh, north-eastern Maharashtra and Gujarat. Also winters locally in southern Afghanistan, and in northern Punjab in Pakistan. Return migration March to mid April, arriving on the breeding grounds in north-eastern Afghanistan in mid April. Vagrant to south-eastern Iran and to western and central Nepal.

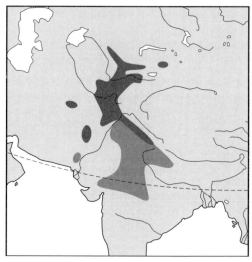

REFERENCES Ali & Ripley (1974), Baker (1926), Bates & Lowther (1952), Dementiev & Gladkov (1966), Mauersberger & Portenko (1971), Paludan (1959), Roberts (1992), Wallschläger (1983).

6   CIRL BUNTING
Emberiza cirlus   Plate 2

Described as *Emberiza cirlus* Linnaeus 1766.

The Cirl Bunting is a relatively unobtrusive inhabitant of lightly forested areas and other semi-open habitats primarily in southern Europe.

IDENTIFICATION 16.5cm. The male is distinctive and should not be confused with other buntings due to the unmistakable black and yellow head pattern which is still apparent in winter.

Female resembles female Yellowhammer but displays several distinctive plumage features, in particular an olive-grey or grey-brown rump quite different in colour from that of Yellowhammer. Usually a pale buff or yellowish-buff below, not clear pale yellow. The streaking on breast and flanks is narrower, more distinct and pencil-like. Cirl

Bunting is duller and browner above in general, but does show some chestnut on the scapulars and on the wing that contrasts with greyer mantle and sides of breast. The pattern on the ear-coverts, with prominent eye-stripe and well-marked moustachial stripe bordering paler grey ear-coverts above and below, broken at the rear, creates impression of two parallel stripes. The crown is more uniformly streaked than Yellowhammer, the difference most clearly seen on the forehead, when viewed from the front. Yellowhammer usually shows denser streaking on the forehead, and a paler centre on the crown, creating "brows", a feature usually lacking in Cirl.

Female in first-winter plumage resembles adult female but is duller and less distinctly marked. May seem slightly smaller, slimmer or more compact than Yellowhammer. Cirl Bunting calls are a particularly useful aid to identification, being soft and quiet unlike that of Yellowhammer.

Juvenile similar to juvenile Yellowhammer, but rump not more rufous than mantle. Streaking on belly usually finer and breast often with brownish wash.

DESCRIPTION

Adult male breeding Crown, nape, sides of neck and band across breast greyish olive-green, lightly streaked with black on crown and nape. Supercilium, centre of ear-coverts, upper breast, centre of lower breast and belly yellow. Throat, lower and hind edge of ear-coverts, eye-stripe and lores black. Mantle chestnut with blackish centres and paler olive edges. Scapulars chestnut fringed with paler olive. Rump greyish-olive or pale greyish-brown very lightly streaked darker. Lesser coverts olive-grey. Median coverts dark grey with whitish edges. Greater coverts and tertials reddish-brown with brownish-black centres, the *Emberiza* pattern being more ill-defined than Yellowhammer. Primary coverts blackish, edged olive-grey. Primaries blackish edged pale yellow. Secondaries blackish edged with pale greenish-yellow. Underwing-coverts greenish-yellow. Tail feathers brownish-black with paler edges, the outermost two pairs with white wedge on inner web, similar to Yellowhammer. Sides of breast chestnut with pale feather fringes, darker brownish streaking down flanks. Undertail-coverts pale yellow to whitish, usually with dark shaft streaks. Upper mandible dark horn, lower mandible pale blue-grey. Tarsus brownish-flesh. Iris dark brown.

T6   T5

Outermost and second outermost tail feathers (T6 and T5) of adult.

Adult male non-breeding Similar to adult male breeding, but plumage somewhat obscured by pale tips of the new feathers, particularly on the head and throat where the black feathers are tipped with buffish-white.

First-winter male Very similar to adult male non-breeding, but tail feathers slightly less rounded. Flight feathers and primary coverts comparatively more worn.

Adult female breeding Crown greyish, distinctly streaked dark. No apparent lateral crown-stripes. Supercilium pale yellowish. Eye-stripe and moustaschial stripe grey-brown, bordering paler yellowish ear-coverts above and below, but not at the rear. Submoustachial stripe and throat pale, tinged yellowish-buff, becoming yellower towards the breast. In some individuals the throat can be tinged rufous-brown. Dark malar stripe prominent, but may be lacking, especially in individuals ghosting male plumage. Mantle rufous-brown, with an element of olive-grey, streaked brownish-black. Scapulars chestnut with relatively broad dark shaft streaks. Back, rump and uppertail-coverts greenish-grey, with diffuse streaking on the back and distinct shaft streaks on the uppertail-coverts. The rump is often almost without streaking. Wing like adult male, but greater coverts slightly paler. Breast and flanks greenish-grey, often distinctly streaked. Sides of breast tinged rufous. Belly pale yellowish, unstreaked. Undertail-coverts pale yellowish with distinct dark shaft streaks.

Adult female non-breeding Very similar to adult female breeding. The face pattern is slightly obscured, with less contrast between supercilium and central ear-coverts, and eye-stripe and moustachial stripe. Crown, mantle and rump more prominently streaked. Less contrast between crown and mantle. The breast is more uniform, with less contrast between upper greenish-grey breast-band and lower rufous sides of breast.

First-winter female Very similar to adult female non-breeding, but tail feathers slightly less rounded. Flight feathers and primary coverts comparatively more worn, but differences slight.

Juvenile Crown pale sandy-brown, boldly streaked blackish, except pale central crown-stripe. Supercilium pale buff, whiter than adult female, faintly streaked blackish. Lores pale buff. Ear-coverts pale buff with dark borders, pattern recalling adult female. Submoustachial stripe and throat pale sandy-brown, often with a yellow tinge. Throat covered with small dark spots. Malar stripe usually ill-defined. Sides of neck pale sandy-brown. Nape olive- or greyish-brown, diffusely streaked. Mantle and scapulars pale rufous-buff, streaked blackish-brown, the lower scapulars slightly rufescent. Back, rump and uppertail-coverts similar to mantle, but slightly less prominently streaked. Lesser coverts dark brown with pale sandy-brown fringes. Median coverts with dark brown centres, showing characteristic rounded tooth, tipped rufous-sandy. Edges of greater coverts narrower and more well-defined than in adults. Tertials similar to adults, as is rest of wing. Tail like adult, but feathers pointed. Two outermost pairs with white wedge on inner web. Underwing-coverts white with a yellow tinge. Breast pale sandy-brown, often with an olive or rufescent tinge, prominently streaked dark brown. Flanks similar, but the streaking more diffuse. The streaks become very narrow and ill-defined on the belly, which is often tinged yellow. Undertail-coverts pale sandy-brown with a yellow tinge and prominent dark shaft streaks. Bill like adult, but paler and with yellowish cutting edge and pinkish tinge to base. Tarsus paler, pinkish-flesh. Iris duller brown.

SEXING Generally, sexing is straightforward, with males showing black throat and greyish olive-green band across breast. In fresh plumage, the dark pattern is obscured by pale fringes, but usually still apparent. Males show less streaking on crown and more chestnut on mantle. In females the crown is heavily streaked dark, and there is little chestnut on the mantle. Some females ghost male plumage to some extent, exceptionally being very similar. The throat may be quite dark, but the bases of the feathers are only diffusely dark, not distinctly blackish. The greyish-green breast-band may resemble that of male, but is usually streaked, showing at least dark spots along the upper edge. In males the breast-band is unmarked. The flanks are also more prominently streaked than in males. Males are on average larger (wing: male 75-86, female 71-82).

MOULT AND AGEING Juveniles undergo a partial moult, starting when c. 30 days old, June to October, including head, body, lesser, median and greater coverts and some tertials, sometimes also the central tail feathers, but not primary coverts. Adults moult completely July to October.

First-year birds told from adults by comparatively more worn primary coverts, tertials, primaries and tail feathers. Sometimes moult central tail feathers, making these contrast with older and more worn outer ones. Iris colour probably helpful.

MEASUREMENTS Wing: (max) male 75-86, female 71-82. Tail: male 60-81, female 60-73. Bill: (to skull) male 10.0-14.8, female 10.9-15.0. Tarsus: male 17.2-19.7, female 17.6-19.5. P5-P8 emarginated, sometimes also P4.

GEOGRAPHICAL VARIATION Three races have been suggested. The differences are slight, comprising coloration and amount of streaking.

E. c. cirlus (Most of range). Described above.

E. c. nigrostriata (Corsica and Sardinia) Slightly darker and on average more heavily streaked on crown and mantle than nominate. The streaking on the sides of the breast and flanks is more extensive in males.

E. c. portucaliae (Portugal) Slightly smaller and darker than nominate. Crown greener with slightly more prominent streaking.

VOICE In the north of its range the male sings persistently from early spring throughout the summer, although nesting rarely takes place before late May. The song may also be heard intermittently throughout the winter on fine days. The song is composed of a series of very short, clear, metallic notes rapidly repeated to form a rattle or trill *zr-r-r-r-r-r-r-r-r*. The pitch and speed of delivery are variable but it is usually quite similar to the song of Arctic Warbler *Phylloscopus borealis*. The slowest variants may bear a resemblance to Yellowhammer, at least in tone. The song may also be percieved as slightly reminiscent of the song of Lesser Whitethroat *Sylvia curruca*.

Call usually a quiet, soft, and high-pitched *tsi* or a slightly longer *tsiip*, sometimes repeated rapidly, *tsitsi tsitsi tsi*, particularly when alarmed. Also a rapid clicking and a thin *siu*, reminiscent of Reed Bunting. Begging call of young *dsidsidsidsi...*, louder than other buntings, audible up to c. 70m away.

HABITS The breeding season is protracted, and two, occasionally three, broods are raised in a season. The first nests are normally started between mid April and mid May, and the last ones may be started in late August, resulting in young fledging in mid September. The well-concealed nest is probably built by female alone, and placed low in dense shrub, conifer, creeper, or similar; usually below 2m, but only rarely on the ground. It is a bulky cup of stalks, grass, roots and moss, lined with finer grass and hair. Eggs 2-5, pale blue, green or pinkish, finely speckled brown, with sparse bold blackish scrawls and dots. Incubation (by

female alone) 12-14 days. Young fledge after 11-13 days, and become independent after 8-16 days. Young are fed by both sexes on invertebrates such as butterflies and caterpillars, craneflies, crickets, beetles, flies, spiders, and earthworms, but also seeds. Dominating food items change over the season, with more caterpillars and larvae brought to early nests, moths and crickets becoming common later on. When grain ripens, this is preferred to invertebrates. Adult takes invertebrates during the breeding season, but during most of year diet made up of seeds of herbs and grasses, preferably couch-grass, rye-grass, meadow-grass, and soft cereal grain. A rather unobtrusive bird. Where it occurs in the same areas as Yellowhammer it tends to be less often seen, being shyer and generally less conspicuous. In winter it forms flocks, and wanders in search of food. In some regions rarely mixes with other species, but in many parts often in flocks with Yellowhammers and finches.

STATUS AND HABITAT Usually a common bird in suitable habitats except in the northern and north-westernmost parts of its range, where it has suffered a serious decline in the last 30 to 40 years. This is probably due to a combination of climatic and environmental factors such as have affected the Corn Bunting. Added to this, the Cirl Bunting's plight in these areas has undoubtedly been compounded by competition with the ubiquitous and adaptable Yellowhammer. Population in southern Europe stable or increasing, with some northward spread in the east. In the northern parts of its range it prefers more sheltered areas with more tree cover than Yellowhammer, often on warmer south-facing slopes. In general it is a bird of parkland and lightly wooded country usually close to cultivated land. Orchards, vineyards and large gardens are all typical habitats. Further south it inhabits a wider variety of habitats up to an altitude of about 1500m.

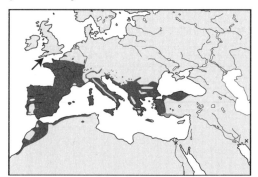

DISTRIBUTION AND MOVEMENTS Occurs in the western temperate and warm temperate areas of Europe and North Africa. The northern limit of the range roughly corresponds to a line drawn from northern France to the northernmost point of Turkey on the southern shore of the Black Sea. The species therefore has a decidedly southern and western range in Europe, from the extreme south of England, where it is now very rare, south through France and the Iberian peninsula to Morocco, coastal Algeria and extreme north-western Tunisia. Found in most of Italy, but absent from higher altitudes, and also from most of the Po Valley. Scattered localities in south-western Germany; Switzerland; Austria, where only a handful of pairs; Hungary; southern Carpathian foothills in Romania; mainly coastal Slovenia and Croatia; most of the Balkans; northern and north-western Turkey. Breeds on most of the large Mediterranean islands except Cyprus. Sight records from Georgia and old reports of breeding near Kiev in Ukraine need verification.

Successfully introduced in New Zealand, where seven birds were released in 1871 and four in 1880. From these few birds, and possibly other unrecorded liberations, the species established itself mainly in the South Island, where it occurs in the coastal plains along the east coast, from Cape Farewell in the north to Damaru in the south. Also in inland valleys, south to Lake Wakatipu. In the North Island it occurs in the south and in a few scattered localities along the coast north to East Cape.

Largely sedentary, winter wanderings tending to be rather local, and to some extent altitudinal, but there is a general southerly movement according to climatic conditions.

Vagrant to the Netherlands, Denmark, Poland, Czech Republic, Crimea, Russia and Egypt.

REFERENCES Bezzel (1993), Cramp & Perrins (1994), Harris *et al.* (1989), Kreutzer & Güttinger (1991), Pinter (1991), Svensson (1992), Tucker & Heath (1994).

7   KOSLOV'S BUNTING
Emberiza koslowi   Plate 1

Described as *Emberiza koslowi* Bianchi 1904. Monotypic.

Koslov's Bunting breeds in scrub in alpine areas in a restricted area along the upper Mekong and Yangtze Rivers. It is little known and apparently uncommon.

IDENTIFICATION 16cm. A rather large, long-tailed bunting. Breeding male unmistakable. Blackish crown and ear-coverts in combination with very broad white supercilium and white throat, somewhat reminiscent of Rustic Bunting, but similarity ends there. Uniformly chestnut mantle and prominent black pectoral band makes appearance quite different. Peculiar dark chestnut lores and chin look dark at a distance and are not always conspicuous. Most of the upperparts are unstreaked reddish-chestnut, except for narrow grey nuchal band and paler grey rump. The belly is bluish-grey below the blackish breast-band. Vent and undertail-coverts cinnamon. In fresh plumage pale fringes partly obscure crown and breast pattern, and males become more similar to females. Both supercilium and submoustachial stripe are narrowly streaked blackish. The mantle is striped chestnut and buffish. First-year males have narrower black collar than adults and whitish instead of greyish median covert wing-bar.

In females, the facial expression is somewhat different from other buntings. The supercilium is rather broad and prominent, pale buff with some thin streaking. The ear-coverts are relatively uniformly dark grey-brown, sharply set off from the pale yellowish-buff throat, and the malar stripe is inconspicuous, enhancing the contrast between throat and ear-coverts. As in the male, the pale throat contrasts with greyer breast and belly, although the difference is less pronounced. There is a narrow collar of dark spots and streaks across the upper breast. The undertail-coverts are chestnut. The crown and mantle are streaked dark, contrasting with unstreaked olive-grey rump and chestnut scapulars and greater coverts. There is a often, but not always, a prominent chestnut cast on the mantle.

Yellow-throated Buntings of both sexes have more or less uniformly dark ear-coverts and the male has a black breast patch, but crest and prominently streaked mantle of male make confusion highly unlikely. The greater coverts are extensively chestnut-brown in Koslov's, blackish with narrow edges tinged rufous and tips pale buffish in Yellow-throated. Females may also be perceived as similar, but Koslov's Bunting lacks crest, and shows an obvious contrast between the pale throat and the greyer belly. The mantle of Koslov's is uniformly streaked, lacking the contrasting brown stripe along the centre. The scapulars are obviously rufous, usually in marked contrast to mantle, wings and underparts. The sides of breast and flanks are virtually unstreaked.

DESCRIPTION The individual variation is not well known, as much of the information is gathered from a very small sample.

Adult male breeding Crown and upper nape black, a small white spot at the rear crown, dusky brownish-grey band across lower nape. Supercilium broad and white, extending to above bill. Chin and lores dark reddish-brown. Ear-coverts black. Mantle and scapulars chestnut-brown. Back, rump and uppertail-coverts steel-grey, tinged olive. Lesser coverts grey. Median coverts dark grey with grey tips. Greater coverts, except outer one which is grey, same colour as mantle or slightly paler, with whitish tips to the outer ones. Tertials blackish-brown with chestnut-brown outer edge, widest on the shortest tertial, where the entire outer web is chestnut-brown. Primary coverts dark brownish-grey, edged pale grey. Primaries and secondaries brownish-black, with outer edges pale buff. Edges of inner secondaries somewhat browner. The tail feathers are dark brown, median pair paler with whitish edges and the two outermost pairs largely white, all the others without white. Lower throat and upper breast white, bordered below by blackish feathers, forming a band across lower breast. The colours of the underparts become lighter towards the rear, the dusky bluish-grey of the chest becomes grey on the belly and whitish-grey around the crissum. The undertail-coverts are washed brownish-red, becoming darker towards the tip. Bill bluish-black. Tarsus light orange-yellow, feet darker. Iris brown.

T6   T5

Outermost and second outermost tail feathers (T6 and T5) of adult.

Adult male non-breeding Similar to adult breeding, but more streaked. Crown feathers have narrow grey fringes, making the crown appear greyer. The supercilium is prominently streaked blackish, particularly at the rear. The reddish-brown chin and lores appear dirtier than in breeding plumage. The ear-coverts are blackish intermixed with grey. The throat is white with relatively thick blackish streaking on the sides. The median coverts are blackish, with whitish tips and outer web, and greyish inner web. The mantle is reddish-chestnut, prominently streaked buffish. The scapulars may show broad blackish shaft streaks. The grey rump and uppertail-coverts are sometimes streaked dark. The outer web of the central pair of tail feathers is edged pale rufous. The breast-band is obscured by grey fringes, its prominence varying between different individuals. The sides of the breast and the flanks are brownish-grey, showing some faint streaking, most prominent on the rear flanks. Lower mandible pale yellowish-grey with dark tip.

First-winter male Fresh plumage undescribed. In spring, when plumage becomes worn, similar to adult, but differs in a number of details. The throat is sometimes washed pale buff. The nape is more olive-tinged. The mantle is paler, retaining traces of pale fringes longer than adult. Back and rump grey with a stronger olive wash. Uppertail-coverts with dark centres, fading to chestnut and with narrow olive-buff fringes. Median coverts with whitish tips forming obvious wing-bar. Juvenile outer greater covert (blackish-brown, tipped pale rusty) sometimes retained. Tail feathers pointed, with little or no white in outer ones. Dark collar across breast browner and narrower. Breast and flanks more prominently washed olive. Belly paler. Undertail-coverts pale lemon yellow.

Adult female breeding Crown olive-grey, streaked dark brown with some chestnut. Supercilium pale buff with some faint streaks, bordered above by narrow black stripe. Lores, to below eye, tinged yellowish-brown. Ear-coverts greyish-brown with some faint pale streaks. Submoustachial stripe pale buff, with some thin streaking. Throat whitish-buff. Malar stripe broken and rather inconspicuous, dark grey-brown. Sides of neck grey. Upper breast washed yellowish with narrow collar of dark spots and streaks. A faint brownish patch on the side of the breast, like a trace of the male collar. Nape brownish-grey, paler than crown and mantle, slightly striped dull chestnut. Mantle brownish-grey, streaked black and chestnut. The amount of chestnut is rather variable. Scapulars chestnut with dark shaft streaks. Back, rump and uppertail-coverts grey with an olive wash. Lesser coverts grey, washed olive. Median coverts dark grey with broad white tips. Greater coverts dark grey, with broad rufous edges on the outer veins and whitish tips. Tertials blackish, with thin pale rusty edge on the inner vein and broader on the outer one. Primary coverts dark brownish-grey, narrowly edged pale grey. Primaries and secondaries brownish-black, with outer edges pale buff. Edges of inner secondaries somewhat browner. Tail similar to male. Lower breast and belly ash grey. Undertail-coverts a lighter cinnamon colour than in the male. Upper mandible grey, lower pale.

Adult female non-breeding Undescribed.

First-winter female Undescribed.

Juvenile Undescribed.

SEXING From the limited material available, first-year males appear to be similar to adults. Thus males from first spring onwards can be recognised by mostly black crown feathers, extensively chestnut mantle and blackish breast-band. In fresh plumage these patterns may be obscured to some extent by pale fringes. Sexing in first-winter plumage not studied, but birds conforming with description above are males. Females in breeding plumage differ from males in that the crown is olive-grey, streaked dark, and the mantle is brownish-grey, streaked black and chestnut.

There is no black breast-band. Instead the upper breast is washed yellowish with narrow collar of dark spots and streaks.

GEOGRAPHICAL VARIATION None.

MOULT AND AGEING The handful of available specimens, all from April and May, are in worn plumage, as well as birds seen in late June. This suggests that there is probably a complete post-breeding moult from August to September or October. Birds in fresh plumage have been observed in late autumn. Presumably a partial post-juvenile moult takes place at roughly the same time or slightly later. The extent is not known, but apparently some juvenile greater coverts may be retained. There may be a pre-breeding moult, but again extent is unknown. Birds in fresh plumage showing dark-centred scapulars have been observed, a feature not noted in available first-summer birds. The character may be age-related, but it is also possible that the scapulars are moulted in a pre-breeding moult.

First-summer males are less bright than adults. The breast-band is also appreciably narrower. Most can probably be told by white-tipped median coverts. Brownish and chestnut uppertail-coverts with pale fringes, as opposed to dark grey in adults males, may also be a useful character. Ageing of females is unknown. Skull ossification, iris colour, shape of rectrices, retained juvenile feathers and wear should provide clues.

MEASUREMENTS Wing: male 93-95mm, female 91mm. Tail: male 82-95mm, female 80mm. Bill: (to skull) male 9mm, female 9mm. Tarsus: male 21-22, female 23mm.

VOICE The song is a short twittering phrase, very similar to that of sympatric Godlewski's Bunting, *cheep chüüp tererep cheechüü*, or *tsip tsi tsi chiriree teetew*, or starting with a slightly lower-pitched *chip* note and ending with a quiet jumble: *chep chip-chip chiriree chip-chee-(chü-ee tsi)*.

What seems to be a contact or possibly alarm call, given from the ground, is a thin drawn out *seee*. The flight call is a *tsip tsip*.

HABITS A pair collected in mid April had enlarged gonads. Apparently start breeding late June or July, as birds are paired in last third of June, and have been observed gathering nest material. No other signs of nesting observed. Nothing is known about breeding habits or food choice. Small flocks are formed outside the breeding season.

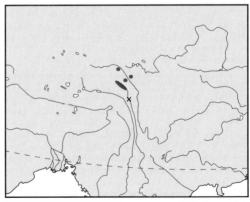

STATUS AND HABITAT Not common within its restricted range, but very little information available. Listed as near-threatened by BirdLife International. Found at high altitudes in areas of *Cotoneaster* and other low bushes interspersed with grassy patches on rocky slopes and ridges. Prefers higher elevations than geographically sympatric Godlewski's Bunting.

DISTRIBUTION AND MOVEMENTS Restricted to the high mountain ridges between the dry tributary valleys of the upper Mekong and Yangtse Rivers in north-eastern Tibet at an altitude of 3800-4300m. Recorded roughly from the area between Qumarleb, Zhadoi, Yushu and Chamdo. As far as known sedentary or only slightly dispersive.

REFERENCES Collar *et al.* (1994), Olsson (1995), Robson (1986), Schäfer (1938).

---

8   ROCK BUNTING
Emberiza cia   Plate 4

Described as *Emberiza cia* Linnaeus 1766.
Synonyms: *Emberiza stracheyi, Emberiza hordei, Emberiza giglioli.* There is some confusion surrounding the name *Emberiza giglioli* which has also been attributed to Meadow Bunting.

Fairly common in dry rocky terrain, from Europe to Central Asia and the Himalayas.

IDENTIFICATION 16cm. Adult males are distinguished by grey head, with characteristic distinct narrow blackish border surrounding pale grey ear-coverts, black lores, and black lateral crown-stripes. The underparts are rather uniformly rufous, in marked contrast with the pale grey breast. The rump is unstreaked rufous, darker than the underparts. Females are usually duller, with less prominent contrast between head and underparts, but the border around the ear-coverts is still narrow and distinct and the lores are dark. In both sexes, the bill is rather dark grey. Both Yellow-breasted Bunting and Lapland Bunting may show similar dark border to the ear-coverts, but have pale lores and bills and are very different in other respects. The combination of unstreaked deep rufous rump and contrast between grey throat and rufous breast and belly will prevent confusion with most species. Dull individuals of Yellowhammer show similarly coloured rump and white outer tail feathers, but lack the rufous tone to the belly. Ortolan and Cretzschmar's Bunting have a more or less rufous tone on the underparts, but lack rufous on the rump and have pinkish instead of grey bill. In all plumages, the tertial pattern is a further difference from most other similar buntings, except the African buntings and the Meadow Bunting group (*cia, cioides, godlewskii, jankowskii*). The pale edge on the outer web of the tertials is of even width, without the characteristic *Emberiza* pattern. Godlewski's Bunting, which see for differences, is similar in many respects. Meadow Bunting and Jankowski's Bunting do not show the narrow dark border around the ear-coverts. Juveniles and some first-winter birds may be very similar to Meadow Bunting in respective plumage and some juveniles are next to identical. See Meadow Bunting.
  The rufous rump and contrasting head pattern may make confusion with females of extralimital Tristram's Bunting conceivable, particularly if viewed from behind.

However, the head-pattern and underparts are significantly different. The centre of the ear-coverts in Tristram's are usually much darker, and even in the palest individuals the centre of the ear-coverts are in marked contrast with the pale supercilium and submoustachial stripe. In Rock, there is no great difference in colour between the centre of the ear-coverts and the supercilium and submoustachial stripe. The belly in Tristram's is whitish, contrasting with the buffy-brown breast-band. In Rock, the underparts are almost uniformly rufous, creating a totally different impression. Pine Bunting and White-capped Bunting both show rufous rump, but pattern of head and underparts is very different. House Bunting, Cinnamon-breasted Bunting, Socotra Bunting and Cape Bunting show some degree of similarity and occurs in similar habitat, although only House occur within the range of Rock Bunting. These four species also lack *Emberiza* pattern on the tertials, and at least Socotra and Cape show similar pattern on the ear-coverts. However, all lack any significant amounts of white in the tail, and all show more prominent rufous edges to secondaries and wing-coverts.

| Rock | Godlewski's | Meadow |

Classic pattern of central pairs of tail feathers (T1), but note that Godlewski's may overlap extensively with both Rock and Meadow Buntings.

DESCRIPTION
Adult male breeding Crown grey, narrowly streaked black, with prominent black lateral stripes. Supercilium very pale grey, often appearing whitish. Lores, eye-stripe, moustachial stripe and rear border of ear-coverts black. Ear-coverts pale grey, almost whitish below eye and in upper rear corner. No malar stripe. Throat pale grey. Sides of neck grey, whiter just behind ear-coverts. Nape brown, with some dark streaking. Mantle sandy-brown, tinged rufescent, with blackish streaks. Scapulars with amount of rufous varying from almost nothing to quite prominent. Back similar to mantle, but more rufous. Rump deep rufous. Uppertail-coverts rufous-brown, with darker centres. Lesser coverts grey, faintly tinged brownish. Median coverts blackish with white tips, less on the inner web. Greater coverts blackish with rather broad pale rufous edge on the outer web, becoming white at the tip. Tertials blackish with pale rufous edge on the outer web, slightly narrower on the inner web. No *Emberiza* pattern. On the shortest tertial more than half of the outer web is usually pale. Primaries and secondaries blackish-brown, with narrow pale margin on the outer web. The tail feathers are blackish, except the central pair which are dark brown, with narrow rufous edges. The outermost pair (T6) are white on the outer half of the inner web, and most of the outer web. The second outermost pair (T5) are white on the outer third of the inner web. The third outermost pair (T4) frequently show

a small white tip, but are more often blackish. Breast grey, slightly darker than throat. Sides of breast and flanks rufous, paler than the rump. Central belly paler, rusty-pink. Undertail-coverts rusty-pink, with narrow dark shaft streaks. Bill dark grey with blackish tip, lower mandible paler bluish-grey, with some yellowish or pinkish at the base. Tarsus orange-brown. Iris dark rufous-brown.

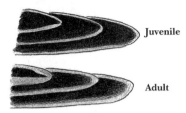

Juvenile

Adult

Tertials of juvenile and adult. This species lacks typical *Emberiza* pattern. Note difference between adult and juvenile in pattern of dark centre of shortest feather, and more well-defined pale fringes in juvenile.

Adult male non-breeding Similar to adult male breeding, but especially head pattern slightly obscured by buffy fringes. The crown is buffy, narrowly streaked blackish. The grey bases of the feathers are well-defined. The lateral crown-stripes are browner and less uniform. Both supercilium, ear-coverts, throat and breast are tinged brownish. The dark border around the ear-coverts, including the lores, is browner. The streaking on the upper parts is slightly less contrasting. The wing-bars are tinged buffish.

First-winter male Very similar to adult male non-breeding. Some birds can be distinguished by retained juvenile tertials, showing neat narrow pale margins of similar width on both inner and outer web, or browner uppertail-coverts. The difference from adults is best seen on the shortest tertial, where the width of the pale edge is usually less than half the width of the outer web. Lacks white tip on the fourth tail feather. At corresponding time of year, shows more abrasion and browner alula, primary coverts, flight and tail feathers. Bill, tarsus and iris similar to juvenile.

Adult female breeding Similar to adult male breeding, except that pattern of head and breast is often duller. The crown is buffy-grey, narrowly streaked dark brown. The lateral crown-stripes are often narrower, and not as black. Supercilium and chin are tinged pale sandy-brown. The ear-coverts have a similar tinge and are also often browner than in males. The grey breast is often sullied brownish and the demarcation from the rusty belly is less well marked than in males. The sides of breast and flanks often show some sparse streaking.

Adult female non-breeding Similar to adult female breeding, but head pattern even more obscured by buffy fringes.

First-winter female Similar to adult female non-breeding. Bill, tarsus and iris similar to juvenile. Head pattern may be further obscured. Age differences as described under first-winter male.

Juvenile Crown buffy, or rufous-buff, streaked dark brown. Supercilium, submoustachial stripe and throat pale buffy, finely streaked or spotted. Ear-coverts brown, paler in the centre. Malar stripe ill-defined, grading into streaking on breast. Nape, mantle and scapulars buffy, or rufous-buff, prominently streaked dark brown. Rump and uppertail-coverts tinged rufous, streaked dark. Lesser coverts dirty brown with buffish fringes (but are moulted at a very ear-

ly stage). Median coverts blackish-brown with buffish tips, dark centre with a blunt tooth. Greater coverts with pointed blackish centre and pale rufous tip. Tertials blackish with almost even pale rufous edge on the outer web, narrower on the inner web. Primaries and secondaries like first-winter birds, but fresh. Breast and flanks buffy, the former prominently, the latter finely streaked dark. Belly and undertail-coverts unstreaked pale buff. Bill bluish-grey, the upper mandible soon becoming darker. Tarsus pale flesh-brown. Iris dull brown.

SEXING The differences are relatively slight, and sexing of single individuals is occasionally difficult. However, in breeding pairs differences are usually apparent.

Adult males are characterised by jet black lores and lateral crown-stripes. The breast is grey, in clear contrast with the rufous flanks. Some first-year males are duller, with browner lores and lateral crown-stripes, and may be difficult to tell from females.

Females usually appear somewhat duller than males, but some adult females approach males in appearance. The supercilium is washed pale brownish, and the lores and lateral crown-stripes are dark brown, paler than in males and never jet black. The breast tends to be less pure grey, and the breast and flanks are sometimes diffusely streaked.

In ambiguous cases, ageing will separate most adult females from immature males. A very male-like individual, which is a first-year bird, is never a female. Conversely, a male-like adult bird not showing jet black lores and lateral crown-stripes is a female. Males are on average larger (wing: male 74-87, female 71-83).

MOULT AND AGEING Juveniles undergo a partial moult August to October, involving at least head, body, lesser and median coverts. First-winter birds often retain juvenile greater coverts and tertials, the latter having narrow pale edges that are of equal width on both inner and outer webs. The moult starts earlier in eastern populations, often in July. Adults moult completely, late July to September, before leaving breeding grounds.

Retained juvenile greater coverts differ in pattern from adults in that the edge is uniformly buffish, and the tip of the dark centre is blunt. The edges of the greater coverts are uniformly buffish, and the tip of the dark centre is blunt. The edges of the retained tertials are narrower and of more even width. Primaries and tail feathers are relatively more worn in first-year birds, the latter being more pointed than in adults. In adults, the tip of the third outermost tail feather is white, while in first-year birds the white tip is lacking. In spring, presence of white tip means that the bird is adult. If it is lacking, the character is useless, as the reason may be either because the bird is immature or because the tip has worn off. Skull ossification is useful up to about December, but should only be relied upon to stage C (Svensson 1992), as a few adults may show incompletely ossified skull. Iris colour useful.

MEASUREMENTS Wing: (max) male 74-87, female 71-83. Tail: male 65-75, female 62-77. Bill: (to skull) male 10.4-13.9, female 9.4-13.8. Tarsus: male 16.8-21.1, female 17.7-21.3. P5-P8 emarginated.

GEOGRAPHICAL VARIATION The variation is mainly clinal, with races grading into each other. The clines go from dark to pale, as well as from smaller to larger size. Generally the clines seem to go from drier (paler birds) to slightly more humid habitats (darker birds). Paler pop-

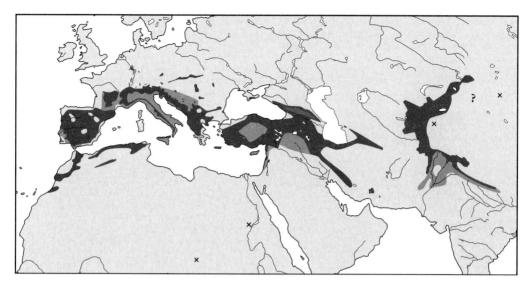

ulations are in many cases larger than dark ones. Birds
from northern Europe are somewhat darker than birds
from southern Europe or Central Asia. At the eastern limits
of distribution, however, birds from the north-east are
paler than those from the western Himalayas. Several different subspecies described, but differences are in many
cases slight.

E. c. cia (Europe, N Africa and W Turkey, including
barbata from S Europe, the Balkans and Turkey, *hordei*
from SE Europe, *meridionalis* from Sinai, *callensis* from
Portugal, *africana* from Morocco, Algeria, Tunisia and
S Spain, *mokrzechyi* from extreme W Caucasus) Described above. There are subtle differences in colour
and size from place to place. Differs from all following races by having white wing-bars, especially
noticeable on the median coverts.

E. c. par (Crimea and Caucasus to Iran and C Asia,
including *prageri* from Crimea and Caucasus, *sere-
browskii* from Altai and Tarbagatay and *lasdini* from
northern Pakistan) Slightly larger than nominate.
Paler, particularly on mantle. Wing-bars buffy and less
prominent. Juveniles are relatively pale. Particularly
the rump is sandy-buff without rufous tinge, more
prominently streaked than other races.

E. c. stracheyi (W Himalayas) Underparts darker and
more uniformly rusty-brown, more clearly demarcated from grey breast, which is paler than nominate.
The head pattern is very contrasting, as grey areas
replaced by whitish. Wing-bars, especially on median
coverts, buffy or greyish instead of white. In juveniles,
the streaking on the breast extends further down onto
the belly, and the base colour is warmer brown. The
rump is rufous, streaked dark.

E. c. flemingorum (W Nepal) Smaller and paler than
stracheyi. Wing-bars buffish.

RELATIONSHIPS Closely related to *E. godlewskii* and often considered conspecific. Together with *E. cioides* and
E. jankowskii, these four species form a group with similar
general plumage pattern, differing from many other *Emberizas* species in that they lack the typical *Emberiza* tertial
pattern.

VOICE The song is relatively long for a bunting, often

more prolonged in the beginning of the breeding season, becoming more stereotyped later. It is relatively
high-pitched, beginning somewhat hesitantly, accelerating into a clear twittering phrase, e.g. *tsiritt churr chu-chut
chirrirri tsirr chu-tsirririritt*. It is quite variable regionally,
and may be reminiscent of Dunnock *Prunella modularis*,
Rufous-breasted Accentor *P. strophiata*, Treecreeper *Certhia
familiaris*, Redstart *Phoenicurus phoenicurus*, Wren *Troglodytes
troglodytes* or Common Reed Bunting.

The call is a high-pitched, sharp *tsii*, slightly drawn out,
sometimes rapidly repeated in alarm. A high-pitched
drawn out *tseeeee*, slightly falling in pitch, may be an alarm
call. A short *tüp*, often given in flight, when various twitterings may also be heard. A rolling *trrr* may be given by
disturbed birds.

HABITS Nesting begins approximately first half of May
in Europe and in May-June in Afghanistan, but in some
areas sometimes as early as late March, if climatic conditions allow. Often two broods, the second one started about
one week after fledging of first one. The nest is placed on
the ground, in crevices, under a rock or a bush, or in
clumps of grass, occasionally low in bushes. It is built by
female of grass leaves, plant stems, moss, etc., lined with
thin grass stems and hair. Eggs 3-5, varying from greyish-
white to light plumbeous grey, with hairlines and squiggles
often forming a tangled belt around thick end, and a few
underlying grey or lilac-grey smears and veins. Incubation
by female 13-14 days. Young are fed insects, particularly
caterpillars, and fledge after 10-13 days. Main diet of adults
seeds, mainly of grasses, in summer also a variety of invertebrates, such as beetles, ants, snails, spiders, etc. Usually
stays on ground, where normal gait is a hop. Often in small
flocks outside breeding season, exceptionally as large as
100 or more.

STATUS AND HABITAT The Rock Bunting is a common
inhabitant of dry rocky hillsides, slopes and ravines, with
sparse vegetation. Sometimes in vineyards and cultivations
on poorer soil. Usually avoids forest, but in Afghanistan
common both in scrubby glades in coniferous forest, and
in scrub in valley bottoms and above the tree limit. Altitude varies with distribution, from sea level to 4000m, but
the species is more common in the mid-range. In Europe

123

usually below 1500m. In the eastern parts of the range often in more forested situations and also higher, including the alpine zone. In winter in open weedy and grassy habitats, with hedges and bushes.

DISTRIBUTION AND MOVEMENTS Widely distributed from north-western Africa through southern Europe to Central Asia and the Himalayas. In northern Africa, in the Atlas mountains from southern Morocco to northern Tunisia. In southern Europe, the Iberian peninsula, except along eastern coast; Massif Central and eastern France, north almost to Cologne along the Rhine valley in Germany; Switzerland, except north; western Italy; eastern Austria; southern Slovakia; central and northern Hungary; Slovenia; western Croatia; western Bosnia; central and southern Serbia; western and northern Greece; Bulgaria; Turkey, but absent from Thrace and much of western and central areas; Lebanon south to Mt. Hermon; Crimea; Caucasus; northern Iran through the Elburz Mountains east to the Kopet Dag range, and in the Zagros Mountains, perhaps as far east as the Jebal Barez area; northern Afghanistan; southern Tajikistan; Kyrgyzstan; eastern Kazakhstan, through the Tarbagatay Mountains, north to the southern foothills of the Altai Mountains. In the Tien Shan Mountains, occurs on the northern slope, east to Hami. From northern Pakistan and south-westernmost Tibet through the western Himalayas east to central Nepal. Northern populations partly migratory, in the south generally resident, but may descend to lower altitudes in winter or wander short distances. Winter visitor to Cyprus and Iraq.

Vagrant to Britain, Sweden, Poland, Canary Islands, Malta, Libya, Kuwait, Chad, Wadi Halfa in northern Sudan.

REFERENCES Ali & Ripley (1974), Baker (1926), Bezzel (1993), Cramp & Perrins (1994), Dementiev & Gladkov (1966), Reichenow (1911), Roberts (1992), Svensson (1992), Vaurie (1956).

9 GODLEWSKI'S BUNTING
Emberiza godlewskii   Plate 4

Described as *Emberiza godlewskii* Taczanowski 1874.
Synonym: *Emberiza yunnanensis*.

Often considered conspecific with Rock Bunting, which it replaces in eastern Asia, from about the Altai Mountains eastwards. Fairly common in treeless hill country.

IDENTIFICATION 17cm. A rather large bunting, superficially similar to Rock Bunting, but the grey colour of the head is darker, and the lateral crown-stripes are chestnut instead of black. The lores and moustachial stripe are black as in Rock, but the eye-stripe and rear border to ear-coverts are chestnut, unlike Rock Bunting, and often ill-defined. In combination with the darker base colour, this makes the head pattern far less striking than in Rock Bunting. The underparts are rufous, with a clear-cut border between the belly and the grey breast. The upper wing-bar is white, which is a further difference from the eastern races of Rock Bunting, which have buffish and less prominent wing-bars. The scapulars are chestnut, usually in obvious contrast with the grey-brown mantle. In Rock Bunting, this difference in colour between scapulars and mantle is present, but is not very striking.

Furthermore, Godlewski's Bunting differs from Rock Bunting in that the difference between the sexes is very slight.

The juvenile is virtually identical to juveniles of both Rock Bunting and Meadow Bunting, and safe identification may not always be possible. The pattern of the central tail feathers is intermediate between Rock and Meadow. Compared to juveniles of the eastern races of Rock Bunting, most juvenile Godlewski's show broader rufous edges to central tail feathers. Normally more than half of the inner web of the central pair of tail feathers is rufous, making confusion with juvenile Meadow more likely. In Rock, normally about a third or less of the outer web is rufous. The scapulars of juvenile Godlewski's usually show a stronger chestnut tinge than the mantle. In juvenile Rock, this is not always the case. In the race *stracheyi*, of Rock, which occurs close to the range of Godlewski's, the mantle is slightly richer in colour, lessening the contrast with the scapulars. The belly is also more richly coloured than in Godlewski's, showing a stronger contrast with the throat and breast. Juvenile Rock, of the race *par*, is very pale in base colour, with belly only slightly buffier than the throat, and often quite prominent rufous scapulars. The rump is more prominently streaked dark than in Godlewski's.

DESCRIPTION Very slight sexual or age-related differences in plumage.

Adult male breeding Crown grey, narrowly streaked black, with prominent chestnut lateral stripes. Supercilium, ear-coverts and throat grey. Lores and moustachial stripe blackish. Eye-stripe chestnut. Rear border of ear-coverts a greyish-chestnut, often ill-defined. Nape grey, with some dark streaking. Mantle sandy-brown, tinged rufescent, with blackish streaks. Scapulars chestnut, usually with dark shaft streak. Rump rufous. Uppertail-coverts rufous-brown, with darker centres. Lesser coverts grey. Median coverts blackish with whitish tips, narrower on the inner web. Greater coverts blackish with pale rufous edge on the outer web, becoming whitish at the tip. Tertials blackish with even pale rufous edge on the outer web, slightly narrower on the inner web, lacking *Emberiza* pattern. On the two shortest tertials much of the outer web is pale rufous. When plumage very worn, tertials become almost uniformly brown. Primaries and secondaries blackish-brown, with narrow pale margin on the outer web. The inner tail feathers are blackish, except the central pair which are dark brown, with rufous edges. The second outermost pair are white on the outer third of the inner web. The outermost pair are white on the outer half of the inner web, and most of the outer web. Breast grey like throat. Sides of neck grey. Sides of breast, flanks and belly rufous, slightly paler on the central belly. Undertail-coverts rusty-pink, sometimes with narrow dark shaft streaks or dark centres. Upper mandible blackish, lower bluish-grey with blackish tip. Tarsus pinkish-brown. Iris dark hazel brown.

Adult male non-breeding Similar to adult male breeding, but generally paler. The lateral crown-stripes are slightly less uniform. Grey parts of head slightly paler. The upperparts are noticeably paler and the streaking narrower. The wing-bars are tinged buffish.

First-winter male Very similar to adult male non-breeding. No age differences in plumage are known. Iris dark grey-brown.

Adult female breeding Almost identical to adult male breeding. The streaking on the central crown is darker and more prominent. The scapulars are not as prominently rufous, due to broader dark centres. The underparts may be slightly paler and there are frequently a few distinct dark streaks on the flanks.

Adult female non-breeding Like adult male non-breeding, except for slightly less prominent rufous scapulars.

First-winter female Like adult female non-breeding. No age differences in plumage are known. Iris dark grey-brown.

Juvenile Crown buffish, only slightly paler in the centre, prominently streaked dark brown. Supercilium, submoustachial stripe and throat buffy, finely streaked or spotted. Ear-coverts brown, paler in the centre. Malar stripe ill-defined, grading into streaking on breast. Nape and mantle buffish, prominently streaked dark brown. Scapulars tinged rufous. Back pale rusty-buff, streaked dark. Rump and uppertail-coverts rufous, streaked dark. Lesser coverts grey. Median coverts blackish-brown with buffish tips, dark centre with a blunt tooth. Greater coverts with pointed blackish centre and pale rufous tip. Tertials blackish with almost even pale rufous edge on the outer web, narrower on the inner web. Primaries and secondaries like fist-winter birds, but fresh. Breast buffish, prominently streaked. Flanks buffish, less prominently streaked than the breast. Belly and undertail-coverts unstreaked pale rusty-buff. Bill bluish-grey. Tarsus pale flesh-brown. Iris dull brown.

SEXING The sexes are very similar, and certain identification is not always possible on present knowledge. In both sexes, the scapulars show rufous, but the dark centres are on average less extensive in males, and in some individuals particularly the upper anterior ones are almost uniformly rufous. More often the dark centre is in the shape of a blackish shaft streak. The sides of breast and flanks are marginally darker in males, and usually lack dark streaking. However, some males show chestnut streaking on the rear flanks. The bases of the crown feathers are a cleaner grey, and the dark shaft streaks on the median crown-stripe are narrower in males.

In females the dark centres of the scapulars are usually prominent, sometimes broader than the rufous edge, but many are similar to males. In worn plumage, there is usually some sparse, fine, blackish streaking on the flanks. The dark streaking on the median crown-stripe is broader and more in the shape of arrow-heads in females, but the difference from males is slight. The tips of the crown feathers are tinged olive in both sexes, but the demarcation between the tip and the grey base is more diffuse in females. Females are on average smaller than males, but the available material is not sufficiently large to establish the range of overlap.

MOULT AND AGEING Juveniles have a partial post-juvenile moult, involving at least body, median and greater coverts. Some also moult the tertials. Flight and tail feathers are not moulted. Adults undergo a complete moult after the breeding season, July to mid September.

Ageing is very difficult, and most birds can probably not be safely aged on plumage. The difference in degree of wear is often difficult to judge, but tail feathers and primaries are on average more worn in first-year birds. Skull ossification and iris colour probably useful.

MEASUREMENTS Wing: (max) male 83.0-89.5, female 79.5-83.0. Tail: male 77.5-91.0, female 76.5-81.5. Bill: (to skull) male 12.2-14.9, female 12.3-14.3. Tarsus: male 16.6-

19.5, female 17.3-19.3. P5-P8 emarginated.

GEOGRAPHICAL VARIATION Clinal variation, mainly in saturation of colours, apparently to some extent influenced by humidity of habitat.

E. g. godlewskii (Russian Altai to Lake Baikal, Mongolia, Gansu and Qinghai provinces, China) Described above. The races *nanshanica* and *gobica* are included here but, as rather pale forms, they may deserve subspecific status.

E. g. decolorata (Foothills of the Tien Shan range on western rim of the Tarim basin, from the Urŭmqi area and Yining, south to Pishan) The palest race. Both mantle, edges of greater coverts and belly paler sandy-rufous. Females may be very pale and nondescript, showing ill-defined eye-stripe and moustachial stripe and hardly any dark rear border on the ear-coverts.

E. g. khamensis (From S Qinghai province and W Sichuan province, to the Lhasa region, grading into *yunnanensis* in the south-east) Somewhat darker than nominate race and more heavily streaked on the mantle.

E. g. yunnanensis (Northern half of Yunnan province, southern parts of SE Tibet, eastward to C Sichuan; to NE Burma in winter) The darkest and most saturated race.

E. g. omissa (From N and E Sichuan to S Heilongjiang province) Includes *styani* and *bangsi*. More richly coloured than *khamensis*, but paler and less reddish than *yunnanensis*.

RELATIONSHIPS This species is often treated as conspecific with *E. cia*. Godlewski's Bunting and Rock Bunting occur very close to each other, but are, as far as known, not actually sympatric anywhere. However, the situation in the eastern Tien Shan Mountains is complicated and merits further investigation. In winter the species penetrate each other's range, and occur side by side in the area around the Tien Shan Mountains. In spite of the proximity of the ranges, which in some places is no more than 60 km, there are no signs of significant hybridisation.

Morphological distinctness, absence of interbreeding, and separation between the two lineages for a substantial period, as indicated by the developement of independent clinal variation within each species, make treatment as full species reasonable.

VOICE The song is usually delivered from the top of a rock. The song is quite variable, and differences from Rock Bunting not well understood. Apparently the song usually begins with much more high-pitched *tsitt* notes than does song of Rock Bunting.

The call is very similar to Rock Bunting, a thin, drawn-out *tzii*. Also a hard *pett pett*.

HABITS In the north, most birds begin nesting around mid May, but some as late as the end of June. The nest is usually placed on the ground, under overhanging rocks, or under stones. It is a cup-shaped, fairly loose structure of withered grass and plant stems, lined with fine rootlets and hair. Eggs usually 3-5, very similar to those of Rock Bunting, white with characteristic purple-black or dark reddish-brown hairlines and squiggles forming a tangled belt around thick end, and a few underlying light grey, light green or light umber-yellow smears. Incubation probably 13-14 days. Young are fed invertebrates and fledge after 10-14 days. Diet of adults principally seeds, mainly of grasses, but in summer also a variety of invertebrates.

125

Usually found on ground, but often perches in trees. Normal gait a hop. Often congregates in small flocks outside the breeding season.

STATUS AND HABITAT Not uncommon on bushy and rocky mountainsides, often near forest. Avoids higher altitudes. Often visits farm fields, particularly outside the breeding season.

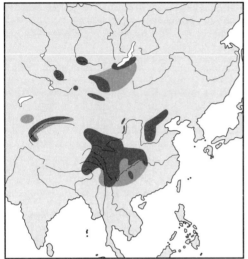

DISTRIBUTION AND MOVEMENTS From the Zmeinogorsk area on the northern slope of the western Russian Altai Mountains, eastwards to southern Lake Baikal; much of Mongolia, except south-east. In China, in foothills of the Tien Shan range on western rim of the Tarim basin, from the Urümqi and Yining areas, south to Pishan; Gansu and Qinghai provinces; northern and western Sichuan; eastern Tibet, west to the Everest region and Lhasa, mainly on the north side of the Himalayan range, but occurs locally in Arunachal Pradesh in north-eastern India; northern and western Yunnan, south to the Kunming area; mountains north of Beijing, south to the Qingling range. Resident or dispersive. Altitudinal movements apparent in many areas. In winter to northern Burma.

REFERENCES Dementiev & Gladkov (1966), Dorzhiev & Jumov (1991), Johansen(1944), Mauersberger (1971), Suschkin (1925), Vaurie (1956).

---

10   MEADOW BUNTING
Emberiza cioides   Plate 4

Described as *Emberiza cioides* Brandt 1843.
Synonyms: *Emberiza castaneiceps*, *Emberiza gigliolii*, *Emberiza ciopsis*. There is some confusion surrounding the name *Emberiza gigliolii* which has also been used for Rock Bunting.

The Meadow Bunting is fairly common on scrubby hillsides and semi-open habitats in eastern Asia.

IDENTIFICATION 16cm. The male is very characteristic. The face pattern differs from other species in that there is a short broad white moustachial stripe, enclosed between

dark ear-coverts and submoustachial stripe. The ear-coverts are uniformly chestnut or black, depending on race. The only other species with a similar face pattern is the rare Jankowski's Bunting, which see for differences. Apart from differences in face pattern, both Godlewski's Bunting and Rock Bunting are quite similar to Meadow Bunting. All lack *Emberiza* pattern on the tertials, and have rufous rump plus grey or whitish base colour on the face and throat, which contrasts with rufous underparts. A breeding male Meadow Bunting is readily distinguished by its dark breast, which contrasts strongly with both belly and throat. In Japanese birds of the race *ciopsis* the breast is paler, often with some black blotching. In both Godlewski's Bunting and Rock Bunting the breast shows contrast only with the throat, while flanks and belly are of more or less the same colour as the breast. In fresh winter plumage the dark breast patch of Meadow is partly obscured and may occasionally be difficult to discern.

Females are often similar to males, but always duller, appearing more washed out. Particularly the lores, ear-coverts and dark submoustachial stripe tend to be less prominent, this last feature virtually lacking in some individuals. The streaking on the crown and flanks is usually more prominent than in males, while the chestnut colour of the scapulars is less prominent. Also, the breast is usually rather uniform and the underparts generally paler. In fresh non-breeding plumage, pale fringes make the whole plumage appear paler. The upperparts are less rufous, with more well-defined streaking on the mantle. The breast patch is largely obscured, and reduced to some chestnut spots on the centre of the breast. First-winter birds are very similar to adults.

Juveniles are in many ways similar to adult females, but the face pattern is markedly different. The ear-coverts are brown, paler in the upper rear corner, bordered above and behind by blackish stripe. The dark submoustachial stripe is often more well-defined than in adults, and the underparts are paler, with some streaking on the breast and flanks.

Juvenile is very similar to juveniles of Godlewski's Bunting and Rock Bunting. The centre of the ear-coverts is often darker than the supercilium and pale moustachial stripe, whereas in juvenile Rock there is little difference in colour. The width of the rufous edge of the central tail feathers seems to be the most reliable difference from Rock Bunting. In Meadow Bunting most of the feather is rufous, with only a narrow area along the shaft being dark. In Rock Bunting most of the web is dark, with only a narrow pale edge. The pattern of the central tail feathers in Godlewski's Bunting varies between these two extremes, depending on race, and safe separation from juvenile Meadow is not always possible. The rump is on average less prominently streaked in Godlewski's than in Meadow. In juveniles of the races of Rock Bunting occurring closest to the range of Meadow, *par* and *stracheyi*, the rump is more prominently streaked than in either Godlewski's or Meadow.

DESCRIPTION

Adult male breeding Crown chestnut. Supercilium white. Lores black. Ear-coverts chestnut. The face pattern is peculiar, and part of it is difficult to compare with other buntings. Area from below lores to below centre of ear-coverts white. This feather tract most closely corresponds to the moustachial area in other species. The feather tract most closely corresponding to the submoustachial stripe

is black, often connecting with ear-coverts at rear. Throat whitish. Nape sandy-pink, mottled chestnut. Mantle and scapulars rufous-brown, with blackish streaks. Rump and uppertail-coverts rufous-brown, unstreaked. Lesser coverts sandy-grey. Median coverts blackish with chestnut or rufous outer web and narrow pale pinkish tips. Greater coverts blackish with rufous edge on the outer web, becoming paler at the tip. Tertials blackish with even, usually narrow, pale rufous edge on the outer web. On the inner web the edges are narrower, distinctly so on the middle tertial. On the two shortest tertials much of the outer web is pale. When plumage very worn, tertials become almost uniformly brown. Primaries and secondaries blackish-brown, with narrow pale margin on the outer web. The central tail feathers are rufous, with a narrow dark centre, often only a dark shaft streak. The breast is chestnut like crown. Sides of neck grey. Sides of lower breast and flanks rufous, central belly pale pinkish-buff. Undertail-coverts off-white. Upper mandible blackish, lower bluish-grey with blackish tip. Tarsus pinkish-brown. Iris dark hazel brown.

Outermost and second outermost tail feathers (T6 and T5) of adult. Note white outer web.

Adult male non-breeding Similar to adult male breeding, but with the breast patch obscured. There is a greyish-buff central crown-stripe. The streaking on the upperparts is less well-defined.

First-winter male Very similar to adult male non-breeding. Dark centres of median coverts more extensive than in adult, with a tiny tooth at the tip. Iris dark grey-brown.

Adult female breeding Some are almost identical to adult male breeding, but central crown is narrowly streaked dark, the supercilium is more buffish, the ear-coverts more brick-coloured, the submoustachial stripe is browner, the breast is paler without the dark patch shown by males, and the belly is buffier, less pinkish. Other individuals show a considerably more nondescript face pattern. In the least male-like individuals the lores are pale, the ear-coverts paler and the dark submoustachial stripe indistinct or lacking. The streaking on the central crown is more prominent than in males. The scapulars are not as prominently rufous, due to broader dark centres. There are frequently a few distinct dark streaks on the flanks.

Adult female non-breeding Like adult male non-breeding, except for slightly less prominent head pattern. White patterns are replaced by greyish or buffy-white. The crown is greyish-buff, finely streaked dark brown, with some chestnut admixed. The lateral crown-stripes are ill-defined, especially at the rear. The upperparts are less rufous and paler and the streaking of the mantle is more well-defined. The breast is paler than in male, with some chestnut spots on the centre of the breast.

First-winter female Like adult female non-breeding. Age

differences as described under first-winter male.

Juvenile Crown buffy, streaked dark brown. Supercilium, lores, moustachial stripe and throat pale buffy, finely streaked or spotted. Ear-coverts brown, paler in the centre, bordered above and behind by blackish stripe. Dark submoustachial/malar stripe ill-defined, grading into streaking on breast. Nape, mantle and scapulars buffy, prominently streaked dark brown. Rump and uppertail-coverts rufous, streaked dark. Lesser coverts grey, with dark centres. Median coverts dark grey with buffish tips, dark centre with a blunt tooth. Greater coverts blackish with pale rufous edge on the outer web, becoming whitish at the tip. Tertials blackish with almost even pale rufous edge on the outer web, narrower on the inner web. Primaries and secondaries like first-winter birds. Breast and flanks buffy, prominently streaked. Belly unstreaked pale rusty-buff. Undertail-coverts like first-winter, but shaft streaks short and well-defined.

SEXING Males are brighter than females. The lores and submoustachial stripes are blacker, and the supercilium whitish. Both the upperparts and ear-coverts are darker and more uniform than in females. The chestnut patch on the breast is prominent, and the belly is tinged pinkish. Females may be similar to males, but are greyer on the upperparts, with narrow dark streaking on the crown. The supercilium is buffier. The ear-coverts are paler, more orange. The submoustachial stripe is browner. The breast is pale rusty, normally lacking the chestnut breast patch. The belly is buffier. In the least male-like individuals the lores are pale, the ear-coverts are paler and the dark submoustachial stripe indistinct or lacking. The streaking on the central crown is more prominent than in males. The scapulars are not as prominently rufous, due to broader dark centres. There are frequently a few distinct dark streaks on the flanks.

MOULT AND AGEING Juveniles undergo a partial moult involving head, body, lesser and median coverts, July to August, usually completed before September, but late broods finish later. Japanese birds of the race *ciopsis* moult more extensively, including greater coverts, tertials, and tail feathers, possibly also flight feathers. Some even undergo a complete post juvenile moult. Adult moult complete July to September. Some individuals may have a limited moult in spring, restricted to lores, ear-coverts and chin.

First-winter birds are very similar to adults. The dark centres of the median coverts are more extensive than in adults, with a tiny tooth at the tip. Iris dark hazel brown in adults, dark grey-brown in first-year birds.

adult   first-winter

Median coverts of adult and first-winter. Dark centres of first-winter more extensive. In adult visible part of feather uniformly chestnut or rufous on outer web with narrow pale pinkish tip. Inner web with clear-cut dark base.

MEASUREMENTS Wing: (max) male 78-89, female 72-82. Tail: male 69-82, female 70-75. Bill: (to skull) male

10.1-13.5, female 11.2-13.6. Tarsus: male 18.0-20.8, female 18.2-20.0. P5-P8 emarginated.

GEOGRAPHICAL VARIATION Variation clinal, going from pale populations with more prominently streaked mantle to saturated ones with almost unstreaked mantle, with isolated Japanese race differing in many details.

E. c. tarbagataica (E Tien Shan, Bogda Shan and the Tarbagatay Mountains to SW Altai) Palest race. Upperparts sandy-brown, streaked dark. Less rufous on rump. Breast-band narrower.

E. c. cioides (Altai to Transbaikalia and Mongolia (including *tangutorum* from NE Qinghai province) Described above.

E. c. weigoldi (E Transbaikalia to N Korea and Hebei province, China) Brighter and more extensively chestnut than nominate race. Slightly smaller.

E. c. castaneiceps (From S Korea and S Hebei province, to S China) Smallest and darkest race. Upperparts with distinctly less streaking than nominate, sometimes almost uniform. Belly of both adults and juveniles warmer brown than in nominate race.

E. c. ciopsis (S Sakhalin and Japan) The most distinctive subspecies. Differs from all others by having nearly uniformly black ear-coverts. There is less difference in colour between breast and flanks than in other races. The breast varies from being almost concolorous with the flanks, to showing a deeper rusty breast-band with irregular blackish blotches. The bill is longer and more slender than in other races.

VOICE The song is given from an elevated position, most often the top of a bush. It is a rather short, hurried phrase quite similar to Godlewski's Bunting, which is often found in the same habitat. An apparently consistent difference is to be found in the initial note, a stressed *tit, ziu* or *chi-hu*, on a lower pitch than the high-pitched inital *tsitt*-note of Godlewski's Bunting. The geographical variation is not fully understood, but an example of a typical song phrase from continental Asia could be transcribed *chi-hu chee tsw-ee-tsweetuee*. The song of the Japanese race appears to be more twittering, *ziu chuhu tsitsirri tsetziiz*.

The call is a characteristic, sharp *zit-zit-zit*, not unlike Godlewski's Bunting, but almost always given in rapid series of three or four.

HABITS Nesting usually begins in May, but in some areas as early as April. Often two broods, sometimes even three, with last ones leaving nest in late August. The nest is placed on the ground, in depressions, under a bush or in clumps of grass, regularly in bushes just above the ground. It is built, probably by female alone, of grass leaves and fine twigs, lined with hair, often from horse, and thin grass rootlets. Eggs 3-6, usually pale greyish, with lines, patches and curls, usually forming characteristic tangled belt of hairlines around thick end. Incubation and fledging period insufficiently studied, probably not very different from Rock Bunting. Diet in summer mainly insects, such as locusts, larval Coleoptera and caterpillars, but also seeds, primarily of grasses. In winter grass seeds dominate. Often in flocks of 30-40 in midwinter, particularly in colder areas, but in autumn and spring usually only in small flocks.

STATUS AND HABITAT Fairly common in most parts of range and often locally common. Densities of 80 birds/km² have been recorded. Inhabits a wide range of dry open grassy, scrubby, lightly wooded habitats, or forest edge,

usually in hilly or montane country. At least in the north, often found on south-facing slopes. Descends to plains in winter.

DISTRIBUTION AND MOVEMENTS From the Tien Shan Mountains in the south-west and the Altai Mountains in the north-west through Mongolia and the Transbaikal area to Ussuriland, southern Sakhalin Island and Japan. In China in the Tien Shan Mountains and the southern Altai Mountains in the west, and in much of the area east of 100°E, south roughly to southern Sichuan, Guizhou, Hunan, Jiangxi and Fujian provinces. Resident in many parts of the range. In the north and in areas with severe winters, wanders to more favourable areas. Vast majority winter within breeding range of species. The presence of resident birds obscures movements but increase in numbers noted in winter in many areas, and movements apparent in March and April. Very rarely recorded away from breeding range. Vagrant to Taiwan in winter. Records from Europe now considered either escapes or insufficiently documented.

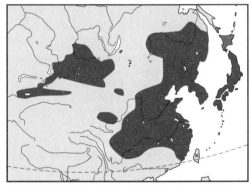

REFERENCES Alström *et al.* (1992), Anon. (1993), Austin & Kuroda (1953), Dementiev & Gladkov (1966), Dorzhiev & Jumov (1991), Jahn (1942), Johansen (1944), Komeda (1987), Latouche (1925-30), Vaurie (1956).

11   JANKOWSKI'S BUNTING
Emberiza jankowskii   Plate 1

Described as *Emberiza jankowskii* Taczanowski 1888. Monotypic.

Jankowski's Bunting has a relict distribution in north-eastern China and adjacent countries. It is rare and appears to have disappeared from large parts of its former range.

IDENTIFICATION 16cm. Adult male superficially similar to Meadow Bunting, but has grey ear-coverts, is paler above with more boldly streaked mantle, whiter and more prominent wing-bars in fresh plumage, pale underparts lacking contrast between throat and breast and a diagnostic dark patch on the central belly. In fresh plumage the belly patch may be partially obscured, but whitish breast differs from Meadow Bunting.

The female is very similar to Meadow Bunting and often lacks the dark patch on the belly or shows only a trace. Always differ from Meadow by showing whiter and more contrasting wing-bars, particularly on the median covert bar, and broader and bolder streaking on the mantle. The face pattern is usually more contrasting, with darker submoustachial stripe and ear-coverts. In Jankowski's Bunting the ear-coverts are a cold, rather dark, grey-brown, instead of a warm rufous-brown as in Meadow Bunting. Female Jankowski's Bunting shows no contrast between throat, breast and belly in worn plumage and has rufous colour on underparts restricted to sides of breast and flanks. In Meadow Bunting the rufous breast and belly are rather clearly set off from the whitish throat. Note that this difference may not be useful in fresh plumage, when the belly appears to be tinged rufous, contrasting with a paler throat also in female Jankowski's Bunting. Many female Jankowski's Buntings show a narrow gorget of blackish streaks or spots across the upper breast. In some individuals it may be very prominent, with rather large spots merging to form a band.

DESCRIPTION

Adult male breeding Crown rufous. Supercilium white. Lores black. Area below eye white. Ear-coverts grey with a brownish tinge. Submoustachial stripe blackish-chestnut. Throat whitish. Nape pale rufous. Mantle pale rufous with darker rufous intermixed, broadly streaked blackish. Scapulars rufous. Back, rump and uppertail-coverts orange-pink. Lesser coverts grey. Median coverts blackish with chestnut or rufous outer webs and white tips. Greater coverts blackish with brown outer edges and white tips. Central tail feathers dark brown with paler edges. Two outermost pairs with white outer web and extensive white on inner webs. Central breast very pale grey. Sides of breast rufous. Flanks pale rufous. Belly white with an oval blackish-chestnut patch. Bill two-toned, with dark upper and bluish-grey lower mandible with a distinctive dark tip. Tarsus pinkish-orange. Iris dark brown.
Adult male non-breeding Similar to adult male breeding, but slightly paler. Crown perhaps sometimes with some streaking. Ear-coverts browner. Dark streaks of mantle narrower. Median and greater coverts with broader white tips. Breast and belly tinged pale rufous-brown, the central patch paler and smaller. Tail feathers rounded.
First-winter male Similar to adult male breeding. Differences insufficiently known. Median coverts including outer web blackish, with tiny tooth and white tips. Probably more streaked on crown, higher tendency to have spots on breast. Belly patch often obscured. Tail feathers tapered.
Adult female breeding Crown rufous, paler than male and with narrow dark streaking. Supercilium white. Lores brownish-grey. Area below eye white. Ear-coverts brownish-grey, darker than male. Submoustachial stripe blackish-chestnut. In some individuals there is a trace of a malar stripe and a collar of streaks or spots, varying from virtually nothing to a complete blackish gorget. Throat whitish. Nape greyer than male. Mantle like male but colder in tone and more contrasting. Scapulars rufous with blackish streaks. Back, rump and uppertail-coverts like male. Wings and tail like adult male. Underparts like male, but less clean. Sides of breast tinged rufous, not as contrasting and clear-cut as male. Belly white with only traces of the central patch.
Adult female non-breeding Plumage insufficiently known. Breast probably tinged rufous, showing some contrast with the throat.
First-winter female Plumage insufficiently known. Median coverts probably like first-winter male, i. e. blackish with tiny tooth and white tips.
Juvenile Not seen. Described as blackish grey-brown on

crown. Supercilium and lores pale sandy-brown. Ear-coverts grey-brown. Throat sandy-whitish. Malar stripe sometimes quite prominent. Mantle pale sandy-brown, streaked blackish. Back, rump and uppertail-coverts sandy-rufous. Underparts sandy-whitish, faintly streaked on the sides of the breast.

SEXING Adult males have a prominent blackish patch in the centre of the belly and are brighter above, with little or no streaking on crown. The contrast between grey ear-coverts and black lores and submoustachial stripe is obvious in adult males. The scapulars are usually uniformly rufous.

In females the patch on the belly is smaller and paler, often almost lacking. The difference in colour between ear-coverts, lores and submoustachial stripe is not very prominent. There is a dark centre or shaft streak on the scapulars.

Sexing of first-year birds in fresh plumage is insufficiently studied, but the same differences as between adults are probably valid, although somewhat obscured.

MOULT AND AGEING Moult not studied in detail, but probably similar to Meadow Bunting. Post-juvenile moult not known, probably partial in late summer. Adults undergo complete moult July to September.

Shape of tail feathers useful for ageing, rounded in adults and tapered in first-year birds. Shaft of outermost tail feather is white in adults and brown in first-year birds, in the available specimens. However, the available material is very small and the range of variation has not been possible to determine.

MEASUREMENTS Wing: (max) male 74.0-80.0, female 70.5-76.0. Tail: male 73.5-78.0, female 71.5-74.0. Bill: (to skull) male 8.6-10.3, female 8.6-10.0. Tarsus: male 18.4-20.2, female 18.5-19.5. P5-P8 emarginated.

GEOGRAPHICAL VARIATION None.

VOICE The song is usually delivered from the top of a small bush. It is often a simple *chu-chu cha-cha cheee* or *hsuii dzja dzja dzjeee*, but more complicated songs have been recorded. Some strophes end in a note somewhat similar to the ultimate note in the song of Yellowhammer, but the beginning of the song has been likened to that of Rock Bunting or Dunnock *Prunella modularis*. The simple song has been recorded both in Jilin and in the Posyet Bay area, but the more elaborate song is only known from Jilin, and may represent a regional dialect.

A variety of calls have been recorded. Single or doubled *tsitt* notes are often heard, and may be contact calls. The alarm call is an explosive *sstlitt*, with an almost whip-like quality. At a distance it bears some resemblance to the flight call of Meadow Pipit *Anthus pratensis*. A thin *hsiu*, recalling Common Reed Bunting or Penduline Tit *Remiz pendulinus*, probably also serves as an alarm call.

HABITS The breeding biology is poorly known. There is conflicting evidence as to when breeding begins. Most probably begins during second half of May. Some apparently begin quite late, some time around mid June, but this may refer to second broods. The nest is built of grass, sometimes lined with horse hair, and placed on the ground in between sparse grass. Eggs 4-5, greyish-white, with faint purplish- or pale brown marks, evenly marked with rather sparse dark brown spots and short lines. The diet is little known, but young have been observed being brought grasshoppers, caterpillars, and spiders and their cocoons.

129

Forages on ground.

STATUS AND HABITAT Fairly common in restricted range in extreme southern Ussuriland early this century. Has declined steadily since and now reported to have disappeared from this region altogether. Traditional autumn or early spring burning of grass in the breeding habitat, to produce better grazing, may have been one of the main causes for the disappearance of the species in this region. In the Kaitong area and west of Changchun, currently the only known sites, the species is locally reasonably common in areas of favoured habitat. The total known breeding population has been estimated to between 330 and 430 pairs. Listed as vulnerable by BirdLife International.

Prefers dry overgrown sand-dunes with relatively scant ground cover and low bushes, particularly stunted dune elm *Ulmus macrocarpa* ssp. *mongolica*, *U. pumila*, and *Prunus sibirica*. In some areas also adapted to poplar and pine plantations. Absent from areas where bushes and young trees are higher than 2 to 3m. Historically reported from sandy areas with sparse oak and birch forests, interspersed with grassy patches. In the Kaitong area occasionally found in open grassy areas, interspersed with open patches of vegetationless soil, seasonally flooded during other times of the year.

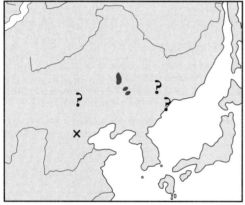

DISTRIBUTION AND MOVEMENTS The only known breeding populations at present are found in the western parts of Jilin province, China, where reported from Tong Yu, Li Shu, and Chang Ling counties. Previously reported from a locality in eastern Inner Mongolia, but no recent information available. In the past, the species occurred south of Lake Khanka, eastern Russia, particularly in the Posyet Bay area, but also on the Chinese side of the border. There have apparently been no records for the last 10-15 years in this area, but the core area of the distribution is within the politically sensitive and inaccessible border areas of China, Russia and North Korea. A record near Harbin, Heilongjiang province, China in late April may have been a local breeder, but there are no further records from this area during breeding season. Reported to be resident in some areas, but usually short-distance migrant. Most birds have left breeding areas before mid September. At least part of the Ussuriland population used to winter in North Korea, but there are no recent records. There are also scattered autumn and winter records from the Harbin, Jingpo Lake and Mudanjiang areas, Heilongjiang province, China. Recorded in the Beijing area

in early spring 1941. Return migration begins late March to early April. Arrives on the breeding grounds in late April or early May.

REFERENCES Collar *et al.* (1994), Dementiev & Gladkov (1966), Litwinenko & Schibajew (1966), Musilek (1928), Panov (1973), Yamashina (1957), Zhao *et al.* (1994).

12   GREY-NECKED BUNTING
Emberiza buchanani   Plate 5

Described as *Emberiza buchanani* Blyth 1844.
Synonyms: *Emberiza huttoni*, *Emberiza cerruti*.

The Grey-necked Bunting inhabits mid-altitudes in mountains in Central Asia. It favours barren ground, but avoids the driest areas.

IDENTIFICATION 15cm. Adults differ from most other species, except Cretzschmar's and Ortolan Buntings, by the plain greyish head and prominent eye-ring. The main difference from Cretzschmar's and Ortolan is that there is no clear division between belly and breast. In Cretzschmar's the underparts are more heavily mottled rufous, most intensely on the breast, and extend, to a varying degree, uninterrupted onto the throat. In Cretzschmar's and Ortolan Buntings the breast is uniformly grey or greenish, separating the pale throat from the rufous belly. The mantle is also paler in Grey-necked and considerably less heavily streaked, showing a prominent contrast with the rufous scapulars. Although the scapulars are more rufous than the mantle in Cretzschmar's and Ortolan, the difference is inconspicuous. Unlike in Cretzschmar's, the rump is sandy-greyish instead of bright rufous-brown. Differs structurally from Cretzschmar's and Ortolan Buntings in that both the bill and the tail are slightly longer.

Birds in immature plumages are reminiscent of Cretzschmar's and Ortolan Buntings in corresponding plumage. However, the malar stripe is more ill-defined, the streaking on the upperparts and breast is narrower and considerably less prominent, particularly on the breast where there is often very little streaking. In effect, Grey-necked is considerably plainer in appearance. Young Ortolan Buntings are more prominently streaked on the breast and usually show a contrast between the yellowish throat and rufous-buff belly. In Grey-necked Bunting the throat is usually tinged pinkish-rufous. Cretzschmar's differs from Grey-necked by being more heavily streaked on the upperparts and breast, and having rump and vent more prominently rufous.

DESCRIPTION
Adult male breeding Crown bluish-grey with no or only faint shaft streaking. Superciliary area virtually concolorous with crown. Eye-ring whitish. Lores and ear-coverts like crown. Submoustachial stripe and throat whitish or buffish, mottled rufous. Malar stripe usually ill-defined, pale grey, or slightly darker brown. Nape and sides of neck paler than crown, tinged sandy-brown, gradually blending into the mantle. Mantle sandy-brown, rather indistinctly streaked dark brown. Scapulars contrastingly rufous-brown, streaked dark. Back and rump unstreaked sandy-greyish. Uppertail-coverts slightly browner with indistinct shaft streaks. Lesser coverts sandy-brown. Median and greater coverts blackish-brown with buffy tips, often

with an element of rufous, forming double wing-bars. Alula blackish-brown. Primary coverts paler brown. Tertials dark brown, showing *Emberiza* pattern, with broad buffy-brown outer edge only on outer half of outer web. Edge on the inner web rather narrow. Primaries and secondaries dark brown, with narrow pale edge on the outer web. The central tail feathers are brown, with very narrow rufous-buff edges, remainder blackish-brown except two outermost pairs. On the outermost pair (T6), the distal two-thirds are white on both webs, except for brown smudge near tip of outer web. There is usually very little brown along the shaft on the inner web. The outer web is more extensively white than in Ortolan and ends more abruptly at the base. On the second outermost pair (T5), approximately the outer half is white on the inner web. The demarcation between the white tip and the dark base of the inner web of the two outer pairs of tail feathers is usually oblique. The tail feathers are usually rounded. Central breast vinous-rufous, with whitish fringes, becoming more mottled peripherally. Belly and flanks pinkish-buff, slightly mottled on the belly. Undertail-coverts pale yellowish-buff. Bill and tarsus pinkish-orange, the latter slightly browner. The iris is dark brown.

T6   T5

Outermost and second outermost tail feathers (T6 and T5) of adult. Note border between black and white pattern on inner web tapered.

Adult male non-breeding Very similar to adult male summer. There may be some faint streaking on crown and nape and the whole upperparts are slightly sandier. The rufous breast is obscured by pale fringes. The wing-bars are broader and more diffuse.

First-winter male Very similar to adult male winter. Differs mainly in having rufous mottling on underparts largely restricted to breast, and intermixed with small dark spots. Many retain juvenile greater coverts. These have narrower, paler and more distinct edges, forming a narrower and whiter lower wing-bar. The tail feathers are usually more pointed than in adults.

Adult female breeding Very similar to adult male summer, and some are indistinguishable. Many have distinct streaking on crown and nape, which are also sandier in base colour. The mantle is similar in colour, but perhaps more indistinctly streaked, and the demarcation from the nape almost non-existent. The amount of rufous on the breast is often less than in male and it is also usually paler and more broken up by pale fringes.

Adult female non-breeding More or less identical to first-winter male, but is more prominently streaked on crown and mantle and has fresh greater coverts. The scapulars are usually browner and less conspicuous.

First-winter female Virtually identical to first-winter males,

but usually slightly browner on crown and nape.

Juvenile Crown sandy-grey with diffuse streaking. Supercilium faint or lacking. Ear-coverts rather uniform sandy-brown. Submoustaschial stripe and throat pale buffy. Malar stripe ill-defined. Breast buffy, streaked brown, with some rufous and dark spots intermixed. Nape almost unstreaked, slightly paler than mantle and crown. Mantle sandy-brown with diffuse, not very prominent streaking. Scapulars browner. Back and rump unstreaked sandy-grey. Uppertail-coverts slightly browner, with dark shaft streaks. Lesser coverts sandy-grey. Median and greater coverts blackish-brown with buffy edges. The dark centres of the median coverts are more pointed than in adult, with a broader tooth. Alula has rather broad pale edge on the outer web. Tertials dark brown, edged pink-buff, bleaching to almost whitish. Rest of wing similar to adult. Outer tail feathers initially with white tips, which usually wear off rather soon. Belly and flanks mottled pinkish-buff. Undertail-coverts pale yellowish-buff, sometimes with narrow dark shaft streak.

SEXING The difference between the sexes is very slight, and many individuals are difficult to identify. Males are usually brighter, with purer grey head, showing a greater contrast with the mantle than in females, and with very faint streaking only in fresh plumage. The scapulars are brighter rufous-brown, and the colour of the breast deeper vinous-rufous and more extensive, but beware of age differences. Many females have distinct streaking on crown and nape, which are buffier in base colour. The mantle is perhaps more indistinctly streaked than in males, and there is virtually no contrast in colour between mantle and nape. The rufous colour on the breast is usually paler and more broken up by pale fringes and often less extensive than in males. First-winter birds are very difficult to sex on plumage alone. Males are on average larger.

MOULT AND AGEING Juveniles moult partially soon after leaving the nest, and usually while still near the breeding area, normally July to August. Post-juvenile moult includes head, body, lesser, median and a variable number of greater coverts and tertials, and usually the central pair of tail feathers. Greater coverts, tertials, and central pair of tail feathers, if unmoulted before migration, sometimes replaced after arrival on wintering grounds, but birds with these feathers still juvenile occur in late spring. Adults undergo a complete moult early June to late September. The majority moult July to August. There is probably no pre-breeding moult. If it exists it is very limited, perhaps involving cheek and central pair of tail feathers.

After the post-juvenile moult, first-winter birds may be recognised by being more worn than adults on the flight feathers and tail, and in many cases by showing retained juvenile greater coverts, tertials, and central pair of tail feathers. Juvenile greater coverts differ from those of adults in having paler buffy edges, as opposed to pale rufous-brown, and are comparatively more worn. The tip of the dark centre is more well-defined, and comes to a rounded tooth at the tip. If only some are moulted, the moult contrast is obvious. Juvenile tertials are mostly dark, edged pink-buff, bleaching to almost whitish. In adults, the tertials have broader buffy-brown edges, covering most of the outer web. First-winter birds with freshly moulted central pair of tail feathers can be recognised by different pattern of growth bars between fresh and older feathers. Iris colour and skull ossification probably useful, but not studied.

MEASUREMENTS Wing: (max) male 82.5-89.0, female 79.5-84.0. Tail: male 69.5-79.0, female 67.5-75.5. Bill: (to skull) male 13.4-14.5, female 13.3-14.6. Tarsus: male 17.9-20.1, female 18.6-19.6. P7-P8 emarginated, often faintly also on P6.

GEOGRAPHICAL VARIATION The variation is rather slight, and single individuals are often not possible to assign to race. Regarded as monotypic by many authors. The following races have been suggested.
   E. b. buchanani (N Afghanistan and W Pakistan) Including *huttoni*. Described above.
   E. b. cerrutii (E Turkey, Iran) On average darker rufous on the breast and browner on the mantle, with rufous on the scapulars more extensive. The rufous of the breast is more extensive, contrasting less with the belly. There seem to be significant plumage differences between Turkish and S Iranian populations, calling for further investigations.
   E. b. neobscura (Uzbekistan, S Kazakhstan, SW Siberia, W Mongolia and W China) Differs marginally from the nominate race in that the crown is greyer and the mantle more olive. Overall impression slightly darker above than *buchanani* and markedly so compared to Iranian birds. This race was originally described as *obscura*, but renamed as this name has also been applied to the race of Corn Bunting occurring on Corsica.

VOICE The song may be delivered from the ground, a slightly elevated point, like a stone or, less often, a low bush, or more prominent perch, like the top of a rock or outcrop. The song resembles that of both Ortolan and Cretzschmar's, but is typically divided into two similar parts, separated by an almost non-existent pause, with the last part usually shorter. Both parts have a rising inflection, with the penultimate note highest, falling markedly in pitch on the last note, *dzeee-zeee-zeeeo zee-zee-deo*. The song in Mongolia is said to differ from western populations, *ti-ti-ti tiu-tiu-tiuu u*, with the second strophe at a lower pitch.
   The flight call is a soft *tsip*. A *tcheup* or *chep* may be given both in flight and from the ground.

HABITS Breeding usually starts during first half of May, but in some places apparently later. The nest is probably built by the female alone, and is a fragile construction of stems and stalks, neatly lined with fine grass, wool and hair. It is placed in a sheltered spot on ground, concealed by vegetation or rocks. The 4-5 eggs are glossy and vary between bluish, greyish or pinkish, sparsely spotted, streaked and blotched with purplish- or chocolate brown, with a concentration towards the broad end. Incubation by female alone, but duration of incubation and length of fledging period not known. Young become independent about a week after they leave the nest. Young are raised on insects, by both parents. During the breeding season, diet of adults consists largely of invertebrates, like grasshoppers, cicada nymphs, beetles, bugs, ants and snails. After the breeding season switches to diet of seeds, buds and shoots of various plants, such as grasses, bistort, buckthorn and spurge. Gregarious during autumn migration and in winter, when flocks of up to 20 are formed. Often associates with other buntings. During spring migration apparently usually singly or in pairs.

STATUS AND HABITAT Fairly common in most of range, and in places common. Inhabits barren and arid slopes in rocky areas in foothills and mountains. Occurs both on open rocky ground, usually with grassy patches, and in ravines and screes. In winter in dry stony semi-desert and cultivated areas.

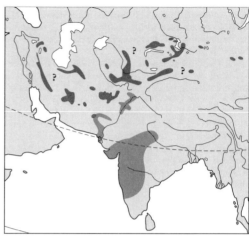

DISTRIBUTION AND MOVEMENTS Occurs from southeastern and eastern Anatolia in eastern Turkey, Azerbaijan and Armenia, the Elburz and Zagros Mountains, and mountains in the south-east of Iran; and southern Turkmenistan, through the Central Asian mountain ranges to western Altai and the Gobian Altai in south-western Mongolia approximately to 102°E, south to central Afghanistan and the Quetta area in north-western Pakistan. Leaves northern parts of range in first half of August. By mid September, most have left breeding grounds, and passage through southern Pakistan and north-western India is at its peak. Winters in India, from Gujarat, central Uttar Pradesh, eastern Maharashtra, northern Andhra Pradesh and central Karnataka. Northward migration begins in March, and by the end of April most birds have left wintering grounds. Normally arrives on breeding grounds during second half of April or early May.

REFERENCES Ali & Ripley (1974), Cramp & Perrins (1994), Dementiev & Gladkov (1966), Haffer (1989), Johansen (1944), Kozlova (1933), Paludan (1959), Roberts (1992), Svensson (1992), Wallschläger (1983).

13 CINEREOUS BUNTING
Emberiza cineracea   Plate 5

Described as *Emberiza cineracea* Brehm 1855.
Synonyms: *Emberiza (Hypocentor) semenowi*.

An uncommon inhabitant of barren mountains of relatively low altitude in Asia Minor, and perhaps the least known of the Western Palearctic buntings.

IDENTIFICATION 16cm. Shares many basic plumage features with the other members of the Ortolan group, but is considerably paler and more featureless. The head of adult male is yellowish grey-green, with a prominent yellowish eye-ring and a short yellowish supercilium in front of the eye. The throat is yellow, but there is no prominent malar stripe as in Ortolan. The breast is greyish-brown, grading into creamy-white belly. The overall impression is of a greyish bird with a yellowish cast on the head. The eastern race *semenowi* is dusky greenish instead of greyish on breast and flanks, and yellowish on the central belly.

The female is similar to the male, but duller and particularly the crown and ear-coverts are browner. The uniform appearance, with prominent eye-ring, buffish-yellow throat and only faint malar stripe separates it from other bunting species.

First-winter birds are similar to first-winter Ortolan and Cretzschmar's, but are paler and more featureless, with bill pale horn-grey instead of pinkish or flesh-coloured. The upperparts are greyer, with more diffuse streaking, the rump being almost unstreaked. The underparts lack all rufous colour. In Ortolan and Cretzschmar's, the upperparts are rather distinctly and uniformly streaked, and there is normally at least some rufous visible on the underparts. The streaking on the breast is more diffuse than in Ortolan and Cretzschmar's, and the breast is slightly darker than the belly, instead of slightly paler, as in the latter two species.

First-winter birds and females of Black-headed and Red-headed Bunting may appear similar, particularly compared to the race *semenowi* of Cinereous. Unlike Cinereous, which shows prominent white corners of the tail, neither Black-headed nor Red-headed shows any pure white in the tail. Instead the outer pair of tail feathers are usually pale brown, only slightly paler than the rest of the tail. In Cinereous, of the race *semenowi*, the undertail-coverts are usually yellowish or buffish-white, similar in colour to, or paler than, the belly, not bright yellow as in Black-headed and Red-headed. In the latter two species, the yellow undertail-coverts are in marked contrast with the pale buffish belly. In Black-headed or Red-headed with yellow bellies, the undertail-coverts are never less bright yellow than the belly. In Cinereous, the edges of the tertials are rather diffusely paler than the centres, and show *Emberiza* pattern. In Black-headed and Red-headed the edges are sharply set off, showing no trace of *Emberiza* pattern. Black-headed and Red-headed often shows a yellowish rump, unlike Cinereous, in which the rump is concolorous with the mantle.

DESCRIPTION

Adult male breeding Crown yellowish-green, with a grey cast and no or only faint shaft streaking. Supercilium yellowish in front of the eye, very indistinct behind. Ear-coverts like crown or slightly more olive-tinged. Eye-ring yellowish. Lores yellowish-white. Malar stripe virtually non-existent. Throat yellowish. Nape and sides of neck grey with a greenish cast, without streaking, blending into mantle. Breast pale grey-brown, sometimes with a greenish tinge. Mantle and scapulars grey-brown, with a faint rufous tinge, narrowly streaked dark brown. Back and rump unstreaked grey, with a brownish tinge. Uppertail-coverts slightly browner. Lesser coverts greyish. Median and greater coverts blackish-brown with pale buffy tips, forming double wing-bars. Alula blackish-brown. Primary coverts dark brown. Tertials dark brown, showing *Emberiza* pattern, with broad buffy-brown outer edge only on outer half of outer web. Inner web mainly dark brown, except at tip. Primaries and secondaries blackish-brown, with very narrow pale edge on the outer web. The central tail feathers are dark brown, with only narrow buff edges. The other ones are blackish-brown, with white outer third on second outermost pair and white outer half on outer pair. Belly, flanks and undertail-coverts creamy-white. Bill

pale horn-grey. Tarsus pale brown. Iris brown.

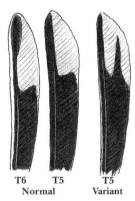

T6   T5   T5
Normal   Variant

Outermost and second outermost tail feathers (T6 and T5) of adult. Note square shape of white pattern on inner web.

Adult male non-breeding Very similar to adult male summer, but plumage fresh and colours of edges of tertials and wing feathers pale cinnamon.

First-winter male Crown relatively pale grey-brown, usually finely streaked, but sometimes more prominently. Supercilium ill-defined. Ear-coverts like crown, but lack streaking. Eye-ring whitish or pale buff. Lores buffy-white. Throat pale buff. Malar stripe rather broken up, spots scattered over lower throat. Sides of neck grey-brown, without streaking. Nape browner, faintly streaked. Breast buffish-brown, sometimes with a greyish tinge, streaked dark brown. Mantle and scapulars browner than adult male summer, the streaking more diffuse. Back and rump brown, faintly streaked. Uppertail-coverts slightly browner. Wings like adult, but edges buffy and narrower and more distinct. Tail like adult, but tail feathers usually more pointed and demarcation between black and white less square. Belly, flanks and undertail-coverts pale buff.

Adult female breeding Similar to adult male summer, but head duller and browner. Crown greyer, with faint streaking. Supercilium buff in front of the eye, concolorous with crown behind. Ear-coverts browner than crown. Eye-ring pale yellowish-buff. Lores yellowish-white. Malar stripe faint, but more prominent than in males. Throat buffish-yellow, duller than male. Nape and sides of neck tinged browner. Breast tinged browner, often with faint streaking. Mantle and scapulars similar to male, but back and rump browner. Wing and tail like male. Belly, flanks and undertail-coverts creamy-white, slightly duskier than male.

Adult female non-breeding More or less identical to adult female breeding, except plumage fresh.

First-winter female Virtually identical to first-winter males, and no differences known for certain.

Juvenile Crown yellowish-grey, streaked dark, forehead mottled darker. Lores yellowish-brown. Eye-ring relatively narrow, pale buff. Ear-coverts rather uniform brown grey. Whole head rather indistinctly patterned. Submoustachial stripe and throat pale buff. Mantle and scapulars streaked dark brown. Back, rump and uppertail-coverts uniformly brownish-grey. Wing similar to adult, but edges more distinct and buffier. White of outer tail feathers with less square base than in adult. Breast buffy-brown, heavily streaked. Belly and flanks pale buffy-brown distinctly streaked. Undertail-coverts pale buff, with dark shaft streaks.

SEXING Adult males are purer yellow and grey than females. The crown is unstreaked yellowish-green or yellowish-grey. The throat is bright yellow and lacks streaking. Adult female is rather similar to male, but the plumage is duller and browner. The crown is yellowish-brown or grey-brown, showing faint streaking. The throat is buffish-yellow or buffish-white, often finely streaked. First-winter birds are difficult to sex on plumage. Males are on average larger (wing: male 83-96, female 82-91), but only largest males can be recognised by size.

MOULT AND AGEING Incompletely known. Juveniles undergo a partial moult, involving head, body, lesser and median coverts, and tertials, and probably also greater coverts, prior to southward migration. Alula and sometimes a few median coverts are retained. Adults moult completely, probably during July and August, as moult is completed in migrating birds.

After the post juvenile moult, the tail feathers of first-year birds are more worn and slightly narrower than in adults. First-summer birds may show moult contrast between inner unmoulted primaries and fresh outer, retained median or greater coverts, and retained central tail feathers. Iris colour and skull ossification probably useful, but not studied.

MEASUREMENTS Wing: (max) male 83-96, female 82-91. Tail: male 63-73, female 64-72. Bill: (to skull) male 11.4-14.6, female 11.0-13.2. Tarsus: male 18.0-20.4, female 18.6-20.2. P7-P8 emarginated, sometimes also P6.

GEOGRAPHICAL VARIATION Two well-defined races recognised, differing mainly in colour of underparts. The ranges are disjunct, but some intergradation seems to occur.

E. c. cineracea (W Turkey) Described above.

E. c. semenowi (SE Turkey and SW Iran) Upperparts similar to nominate race when worn, but with a brownish or greenish tinge when fresh. Breast and flanks dusky greenish instead of greyish, and belly yellowish. Scapulars dull rufous-brown in some males. Marginally larger than nominate. Approximate average wing length male 93.5 and female 87.5 compared to male 89.5 and female 85.0 in nominate, but overlap extensive: male 85-98, female 84-95, compared to male 83-96, female 82-91 in nominate.

VOICE The song is delivered from an inconspicuous perch in a bush or a tree. It resembles the songs of both Ortolan, Cretzschmar's and Grey-necked Bunting, but is more ringing in quality, and the final unit is different *dzüu züü-züü-züü zee-üü*.

Call a soft metallic *tsik*, resembling one of the calls of Ortolan. Other calls are a *dju* and a short harsh *tshri*, resembling one of the calls of Yellowhammer.

HABITS Breeding usually begins second half of April. The nest is placed on the ground, concealed by rock or vegetation. It is built of stalks, stems and leaves, and lined with rootlets and hair, probably by female alone. Eggs 4-6, similar to Ortolan, but bluer and with smaller streaks and spots. Information about incubation, fledging and rearing of young is lacking. During the breeding season, diet seems to consist of invertebrates such as beetles, spiders, caterpillars, flies, pupae and snails. Remainder of year diet probably largely seeds, but has been seen to take invertebrates during migration. Usually singly or in small groups, but often associates with flocks of Ortolan and Cretzschmar's Bunting. Rather wary on breeding grounds, but migrants sometimes tame.

STATUS AND HABITAT Generally rare and local. The total world population appears to be stable at present and has been estimated at 550-5100 pairs. Listed as near-threatened by BirdLife International. Breeds on dry rocky slopes and uplands, with shrubby vegetation, sometimes as high as in the conifer region. On passage in lowland deserts and agricultural land. In winter in dry open country with short grass, semi-desert, low rocky hills, bare cultivated land, or in dry scrubby areas, often in dry coastal areas.

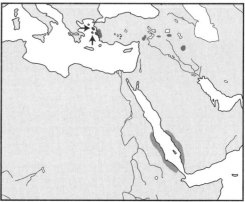

DISTRIBUTION AND MOVEMENTS Breeds in western Turkey along Aegean coast, approximately from Bergama south to Söke. Normally found within 70 km of coast. Range extends into Greece on Lesbos and Chios. In southeastern Turkey the race *semenowi* is found from the Gaziantep area in the west, eastwards towards Iran, where it occurs in an apparently isolated population in the Zagros Mountains in the south-west. Possibly also breeds in northern Syria and northern Iraq.

Southward migration commences in July, when birds start leaving breeding grounds. Rarely recorded on autumn migration. Apparently main passage through Middle East during late August and September, but recorded into November. The nominate race and small numbers of *semenowi* skirt the eastern Mediterranean (not passing through Cyprus) and migrate mainly through Lebanon, Israel, Jordan and Egypt southwards along the western coast of the Red Sea to the wintering grounds in coastal north-eastern Sudan and Eritrea. Eastern populations follow a more easterly route, around the Persian Gulf, to south-western Saudi Arabia and Yemen.

Leaves wintering grounds in February and March, to follow same route back. More often recorded on passage in spring, but still rare, except in Israel, where main passage late March to early April, but recorded as late as May. Rare on Cyprus in spring. Normally returns to breeding grounds in early April. Vagrant to Tunisia, Oman and Turkmenistan.

REFERENCES Collar *et al.* (1994), Cramp & Perrins (1994), de Knijff (1991), Svensson (1992), Tucker & Heath (1994), Wallschläger (1983).

14 ORTOLAN BUNTING
Emberiza hortulana   Plate 6

Described as *Emberiza hortulana* Linnaeus 1758.

The Ortolan Bunting is a relatively scarce inhabitant of open habitats, common only in certain areas. It is more insectivorous than most buntings, often foraging in trees, and even catching insects in flight.

IDENTIFICATION 16cm. Males are easily told from all other buntings, except perhaps Cretzschmar's. The head is uniformly greenish-grey down to the breast, with very characteristic pattern of yellow submoustachial stripe and throat. A prominent yellowish-white eye-ring and pinkish bill add to the characteristic facial expression. The grey breast is sharply set off from the rufous-buff belly and flanks.

Females are similar to adult male breeding in general appearance, but the head is more olive in base colour, and the breast is paler, with a varying amount of dark streaking. The lack of pale supercilium but presence of very prominent submoustachial stripe separate it from other species except members of ortolan group.

In juveniles the base colour of the upperparts is uniformly warm brown, streaked dark or almost scalloped, particularly on the mantle and rump. The submoustachial stripe and throat are buffish-white, noticeably paler compared to more buffish-brown breast and belly. The throat is spotted and the breast heavily streaked dark, often extending onto the flanks. Juvenile Cretzschmar's, which see for discussion, is very similar.

While most other buntings moult into a first-winter plumage similar to adult non-breeding, Ortolan acquires a first-winter plumage that is readily distinguished from subsequent plumages. The first-winter plumage roughly resembles juvenile plumage, but the streaking on the upperparts is less bold, particularly on the crown. First-winter birds are very similar to non-breeding females, but are duller and usually show streaking on the flanks and more prominent streaking on crown. Retained juvenile median or greater coverts, or tertials, differ from pattern of adult's, but beware that adult may show a moult contrast due to suspended moult. In an extensive partial moult on the wintering grounds, sometimes starting immediately upon arrival, the first-winter plumage is lost and a first-summer plumage, more similar to adult, is acquired.

Some plumages of Black-faced Bunting, notably males in fresh plumage and adult females in worn breeding plumage, may show some similarity in head pattern, as the submoustachial stripe and throat may then be pale on an otherwise grey head. However, they always lack the prominent eye-ring, usually have blackish lores (males), and are whitish or pale yellow instead of rufous-buff on the underparts.

Some first-winter Chestnut-eared Buntings show a rather plain head and a prominent eye-ring, and some may appear similar to first-winter Ortolans. However, in Chestnut-eared the ear-coverts are always browner than the surrounding areas, and the supercilium is paler. The malar stripe is blacker and more well-defined, the throat lacks significant streaking, the streaking on the breast is blacker and more prominent, and the belly paler. In Ortolan, the streaking on the breast extends onto the throat. The streaking on the mantle is considerably heavier in Chestnut-eared, showing marked contrast with the nape. In

Ortolan, the contrast is less pronounced. The rump is usually noticeably rufous in Chestnut-eared, concolorous with the mantle in Ortolan. The tail pattern differs in that the outermost pair of tail feathers show more white than in Ortolan, and the second outermost pair of tail feathers show less. The white pattern is also more in the shape of a wedge in Chestnut-eared. The resulting impression is that Ortolan shows white corners and Chestnut-eared white sides to the tail.

DESCRIPTION

Adult male breeding Crown greenish-grey with no or only faint shaft streaking. Superciliary area virtually concolorous with crown. Ear-coverts like crown or slightly more olive-tinged, often with slightly more pronounced streaking. Eye-ring yellowish-white. Lores and malar stripe darker, dusky green. Throat and submoustachial stripe pale yellow, wearing to whitish. Nape and sides of neck paler than crown and a trifle more greenish-grey, without streaking, clearly set off from mantle. Breast similar to crown, but paler still, less greenish, often with faint mottling. Mantle brown, streaked dark brown. Scapulars rufous-brown, streaked dark. Back and rump of similar colour to mantle, but with only faint streaking. Uppertail-coverts slightly darker brown with dark shaft streaks. Lesser coverts dark brown, with greenish-grey edges. Median and greater coverts blackish-brown with buffy tips, forming double wing-bars. Alula blackish-brown. Primary coverts dark brown. Tertials blackish-brown, showing *Emberiza* pattern, with broad buffy-brown outer edge only on outer half of outer web. Edge on the inner web very narrow. Primaries and secondaries blackish-brown, with very narrow pale edge on the outer web. The central tail feathers are dark brown, with only narrow rufous-buff edges. The other ones are blackish-brown, with white outer third on second outermost pair and white outer half on outermost pair. Both outermost pairs are tipped whitish on outer web. Belly and flanks rufous-buff, slightly mottled on the lower breast. Undertail-coverts slightly paler, with narrow dark shaft streaks. Bill and tarsus pinkish-flesh. Iris dark brown.

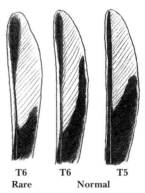

T6   T6   T5
Rare   Normal

Outermost and second outermost tail feathers (T6 and T5) of adult. Note border between black and white pattern on inner web tapered. Exceptionally, the pattern on outermost tail feather may resemble Cretzschmar's Bunting.

Adult male non-breeding Similar to adult male summer, but with more or less distinct streaking on crown and nape. The moustachial stripe is blacker. The breast is a mixture of greyish and yellowish, with some dark spots. The demarcation between the nape and the mantle is obscured.

First-winter male Crown, nape, mantle, scapulars, back, rump and uppertail-coverts greyish brown, prominently streaked blackish brown. Supercilium faint. Ear-coverts rather uniform warm brown, with a darker lower border. Submoustachial stripe and throat pale buffish-white, often with some yellow intermixed. Malar stripe dark brown. Breast pale buffish-brown, heavily streaked. Lesser coverts grey-brown, with blackish centres. Median and greater coverts, unless retained juvenile, blackish-brown, the edges buffish except at tip, where whitish. The dark centres of the median coverts are more pointed than in adult, with a broader 'tooth'. Tertials may be retained juvenile or similar to adult's. Rest of wing similar to adult. Outer tail feathers initially with white tips, which usually wear off rather soon. Brown and buffish parts bleach quickly to paler colours. Belly, flanks and undertail-coverts pale ochraceous-brown, distinctly streaked dark on flanks; the streaking clearly narrower than on the breast. The undertail-coverts often show narrow blackish shaft streaks.

Juvenile

Adult

Tertials of juvenile and adult. Note more extensively pale fringes on inner webs of juvenile.

Adult female breeding Similar to adult male summer, but with distinct streaking on crown, nape and breast. Base colour of crown marginally darker and greener. The malar stripe is blackish. The breast is more buffish than greyish and the underparts are ususally paler than in male, with some faint streaking on the flanks. The demarcation between the nape and mantle is not very prominent. The back, rump and uppertail-coverts are more distinctly streaked.

Adult female non-breeding More or less identical to adult female summer, except plumage fresh and crown tinged yellowish-buff. Most are indistinguishable from adult male winter, but crown tends to be yellower or browner, and there is no greyish breast-band.

First-winter female Virtually identical to first-winter males. Some may be on average more prominently streaked on the underparts, except the central belly. The streaking is most prominent on the breast, and there is little contrast between the base colour of the breast and belly. However, the individual variation and overlap, compared to first-year male, is great, and single individuals are usually impossible to separate on plumage.

Juvenile Crown, nape, mantle, scapulars, back, rump and uppertail-coverts uniformly warm brown, prominently streaked, or to some extent scalloped, blackish-brown. Supercilium faint. Ear-coverts rather uniform warm brown, with a darker lower border. Submoustachial stripe and throat buffish-white, the latter with numerous small dark spots. Malar stripe dark brown, often, but not always, prominent. Lesser coverts brown, with blackish centres. Median and greater coverts blackish-brown with buffish edges. The dark centres of the median coverts are more pointed than in adult, with a broader 'tooth'. Tertials similar to adult, but dark centres more bluntly pointed and more well-de-

fined. The pale edges are broader on the inner web than in adults, extending further towards the base. Rest of wing similar to adult. Outer tail feathers initially with white tips, which usually wear off rather soon. Brown and buffish parts bleach quickly to paler colours. Breast buffish-brown, heavily streaked. Belly and flanks pale ochraceous-brown, distinctly streaked dark on flanks, the streaking usually narrower than on the breast.

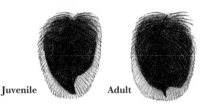

Juvenile   Adult

Median coverts of juvenile and adult. Tip of dark centre blunter in juvenile.

SEXING Adults in spring and summer are usually straightforward, but a few are ambiguous and should not be sexed on plumage. In adult males crown, malar stripe and breast are similar in colour, greenish-grey. The nape is clearly set off from the mantle.

Adult females differ by showing distinct streaking on crown (which tends to be browner), nape and breast, the latter being more buffish than greyish. The malar stripe is blackish. The demarcation between the nape and the mantle is not very prominent. The back, rump and uppertail-coverts are more obviously streaked in females.

Sexing in autumn is difficult, when most males are inseparable from females. Only birds identifiable by same criteria as in spring should be sexed. First-winter birds are equally difficult to sex, and should be left unsexed. Some females tend to be more prominently streaked on the underparts than males, and show little contrast between the base colour of the breast and belly. Males are on average larger (wing: male 83-96, female 77-92).

MOULT AND AGEING Juveniles moult partially into a first-winter plumage, starting at the age of 20 to 30 days, involving head, body, lesser and median coverts, and sometimes tertials and inner greater coverts. In the extensive pre-breeding moult, some time between early November and mid April, again moults head and body, but also a variable number of greater coverts and tail feathers, and acquires a first-summer plumage. Adults moult almost completely before leaving breeding areas, July to early September. A varying number of secondaries, and lesser, median and greater coverts are regularly left unmoulted. Duration of moult 4-6 weeks. Pre-breeding moult December-March extensive, involving both head and body.

First-year birds show relatively more wear and often a moult contrast between unmoulted outer greater coverts, with whitish edges, and fresh inner greater coverts, with pale rufous edges. The tail feathers are pointed, and outer is no or very little white on the outer webs of the outermost pairs of tail feathers (T5-T6). After complete moult, adults have fresh primaries, but may show an obvious moult contrast between these and unmoulted secondaries. Tertials and tail feathers, the latter with rounded tips, are normally fresh in adults. In adults, the two outermost pairs of tail feathers have white tips which extend onto the outer webs. Skull ossification useful.

MEASUREMENTS Wing: (max) male 83-96, female 77-

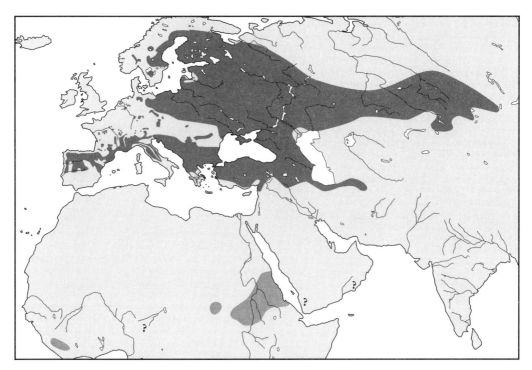

92. Tail: male 56-71, female 57-69. Bill: (to skull) male 10.1-13.8, female 11.0-13.9. Tarsus: male 17.0-20.3, female 16.8-19.7. P7-P8 emarginated, sometimes also P6.

GEOGRAPHICAL VARIATION Rather slight. Three races (*antiquorum* from southern Europe, *elisabethae* from Mongolia and *shah* from Iran) have been suggested, but are here considered insufficiently distinct to recognise.

VOICE Sings from posts on trees, wires, rocks and other elevated places, or in flight. The song usually begins with three or four similar units of a ringing quality that increase slightly in pitch, and ends with one to three, usually two, clear units at a lower pitch: *dzii dzii dzii dzii hüü hüü*. It varies to some extent, both individually and between geographical regions. Other variants could be transcribed *witt witt witt witt hüü hüü* and *zreee zreee zreee züü*. The latter variant is similar to some songs of Cretzschmar's, which see.

A common contact call is a dry *plet*. A characteristic call, often heard both during day and from nocturnal migrants is a clear metallic *ziie*. This call is often followed by a short *tew*, which may also be given separately.

HABITS The nest is usually placed on the ground in a rather deep depression, often in fields of cereals or other crops such as potatoes; also in forest clearings, heather or vineyards, etc. It is a cup of roots, blades of cereals, stems, stalks and leaves, lined with fine grasses, rootlets and hair. The eggs are laid from mid April in the south and second half of May in the north until late June or July. Clutch usually 4-5. The eggs are glossy and vary between bluish, greyish or pinkish, sparsely marked with dark dots, speckles and scrawls, sometimes forming a ring at broad end. Incubation by female alone, 11-12 days. Fledging period 12-13 days. Both parents attend young, which are principally fed caterpillars (often taken in oaks), grasshoppers, beetles and a variety of invertebrates. Adults feed on invertebrates, such as ants, beetles, caterpillars and grasshoppers, and cereal grain, grass seeds, pine seeds and seeds from a variety of herbs. Often forages in canopy of trees and also catches flying insects. Usually hops. Gregarious, even to some extent during breeding period, when birds may be seen feeding together in small flocks.

STATUS AND HABITAT Has suffered marked decline in western and central Europe. Destruction of trees lining country roads and small fields, often in combination with reduction in crop diversity, is major factor behind decline in most parts of European range. In northern Europe most common in southern Finland and northern Sweden along the Gulf of Bothnia. Also fairly common in southern France, Spain, Poland and Bulgaria. Rather scarce elsewhere. Numbers further east less well known, but said to be common in southern part of distribution in former USSR and in Turkey. Pairs often congregate during breeding period, being absent from many seemingly suitable areas. Average densities not very high, but local densities up to 180 pairs per km^2 have been recorded. Prefers open, relatively dry and sunny areas with shrubs and sparse trees, but is often found in tree plantations, or in more open habitats, like ravines or large forest clearings.

In winter in dry open country with short grass, semi-desert, low rocky hills, bare cultivated land, or in dry scrubby areas.

DISTRIBUTION AND MOVEMENTS Distribution fragmented, with only scattered occurrence in western and central Europe. Generally absent from coastal areas, except around the Baltic. In Norway, scattered localities in south-east. In Sweden, most common along Gulf of Bothnia, more local further south. Occurs in most of Finland, south of approximately 67°N. Formerly locally in eastern Netherlands and north-eastern Belgium, but now apparently extinct. In western and central Europe, in Germany,

137

between Lüneburger Heide and Dutch border in north-west, along the Main River, and in the Berlin region; in Switzerland, in scattered localities in south; in Austria, remnant population in west, south and around Vienna. In southern Europe, occurs in southern half of France, where more common in south-east; northern Spain; north-eastern Portugal; in Italy, in foothills of the Alps, and in Appenines south to about Naples, and locally further south; widely in former Yugoslavia, except in north-east; much of Greece, but more widespread in north; Crete. In eastern Europe, found in much of Poland; in Czech Republic, mainly in north and east; in Slovakia, at least around Bratislava; Matra Hills in Hungary; in Romania found in Carpathian foothills and in Dobrogea; Bulgaria, except central and south-eastern mountains. Distribution in former Soviet Union insufficiently known, but probably scarce in most of Estonia, Latvia and European Russia north of Moscow. More widespread in Lithuania, Belarus, Ukraine, southern European Russia, and Transcaucasia. In Asiatic part of Russia, found south of approximately 56°N, east to the Altai Mountains. In Kazakhstan, occurs roughly north of 50°N. Range reaches Altai and Khangai in north-western Mongolia. Range in south-western Asia includes Elburz Mountains, east to Kopet Dag in northern Iran, northernmost Iraq, and possibly north-western Syria. Widespread in Turkey, except south-eastern and inner Anatolia. On African continent only known as a breeder from northern Algeria, where rare.

Long-distance migrant. In most of range leaves breeding grounds mid-August to mid-September, but in some areas as early as mid-July. Western populations appear to migrate south on Atlantic side of the Sahara. Southward migration through Morocco, Mauretania, Senegal and Mali late September to November. Rare in Tunisia. Eastern populations migrate in south-westerly direction, passing north-western Iran and the Middle East mainly in September, to arrive on the wintering grounds in early October.

Winter range incompletely known, but appears to be entirely south of the Sahara. In the west, known to winter in mountains of Sierra Leone and on Mt. Nimba, Guinea. Rare in Nigeria. Only rarely and irregularly recorded between this area and other known wintering grounds in eastern Sudan, and western and northern Ethiopia, where common. May winter in small numbers in Yemen and Oman.

Leaves winter quarters during March. Main northward migration through the Middle East mid-March to April and through southern Europe second half of April, arriving around mid May in the northernmost breeding areas.

Vagrant Iceland, Faroes, Canary Islands, Kenya, Seychelles, Irkutsk, northern Pakistan, and India.

REFERENCES Åström & Stolt (1993), Bezzel (1993), Conrads (1976), Conrads & Conrads (1971), Cramp & Perrins (1994), Dement- iev & Gladkov (1966), Haffer (1989), Johansen(1944), Small (1992), Stresemann & Stresemann (1969), Stolt (1977 & 1993), Tucker & Heath (1994), Svensson (1992), Vaurie (1956).

15   CRETZSCHMAR'S BUNTING
Emberiza caesia   Plate 6

Described as *Emberiza caesia* Cretzschmar 1828. Monotypic.

Quite common on rocky slopes in restricted range in the east Mediterranean region.

IDENTIFICATION 16cm. Adults of both sexes share characteristic head pattern with male Ortolan, but are blue-grey instead of greenish-grey on head, with rusty instead of yellow submoustachial stripe and throat. The lores are rufous-cinnamon, contrasting with the surrounding blue-grey areas. In male Ortolan the lores are dusky green, often concolorous with rest of head, but sometimes show slight contrast. The belly is deeper rufous-brown than in Ortolan. The adult female is similar to the male, but duller, and shows less contrast between the nape and mantle. The lower throat usually shows some dark sreaking, and the breast band is less well-defined, with buffish intermixed. There is less contrast between the nape and mantle, the lower throat usually shows some dark streaking, and the breast-band is less well-defined, with buffish intermixed. The malar stripe is darker.

First-winter birds are very similar to first-winter Ortolan Bunting, and many are not safely identified as both species are quite variable. The colour of the underwing-coverts and axillaries is helpful in the hand (whiter in Cretzschmar's; usually with some pale yellow present in Ortolan). Typical individuals differ in a number of subtle ways, but the most reliable differences are the colour of the throat and wing-bars. The throat and submoustachial stripe of Cretzschmar's are tinged pale rufous or cinnamon (slightly richer than in Ortolan) and do not contrast very much with the only slightly darker breast and belly. Compared to Ortolan, both the streaking on the breast and the malar stripe are browner and less prominent. This results in the underparts appearing less contrasting in Cretzschmar's. In Ortolan the blackish malar stripe is often quite prominent, and there is usually a noticeable contrast in colour between the whitish or pale yellow throat, and the pale rufous-buff belly. The streaking on the breast is blackish, more restricted, and often in the shape of spots in Ortolan. The colour of the wing-bars varies a great deal, particularly in Ortolan, and careful examination of wear is necessary before using this character. In juvenile plumage, the wing-bars are similar in colour in both species, buffish bleaching to whitish. After moult, the tips of the fresh median coverts of Cretzschmar's are on average darker and buffier than Ortolan, in which they may be almost whitish. Freshly moulted Cretzschmar's thus show very indistinct wing-bars, whereas in Ortolan they are often, but not always, quite prominent whitish. However, beware of Cretzschmar's with retained juvenile coverts or with worn and bleached plumage. The upperparts are very similar between the two species, but first-winter males sometimes show traces of blue-grey on crown and nape in Cretzschmar's, greenish in Ortolan. The streaking on the crown is on average less prominent in Cretzschmar's. The supercilium of Cretzschmar's is broader in front of the eye, almost meeting above the bill. In Ortolan the supercilium is usually narrower in front of the eye and the forehead darker. The rump is somewhat warmer brown in Cretzschmar's.

The tail pattern differs between most Cretzschmar's and Ortolan Buntings. When viewed from below, the square border between the dark bases of the tail feathers and the white tips in Cretzschmar's causes more black to be visible at the base of the tail than in Ortolan.

Structural differences that may be useful with experience include shorter and more conical bill, proportionately longer tail and shorter primary projection in Cretzschmar's.

DESCRIPTION

Adult male breeding Whole head (crown, nape, sides of neck, ear-coverts and upper breast), including supercilium and malar stripe bluish-grey. Throat, lores and submoustachial stripe rufous-cinnamon. Eye-ring whitish or pale buff. Mantle brown, streaked blackish, slightly ruddier than in Ortolan Bunting. Scapulars rufous-brown, streaked dark. Back and rump unstreaked rufous-brown, brightest on rump. Uppertail-coverts slightly darker brown with dark shaft streaks. Lesser coverts dark brown, with greyish edges. Median and greater coverts blackish-brown with buffy tips, forming double wing-bars. Alula blackish-brown with pale edge. Primary coverts dark brown. Tertials blackish-brown, with broad buffy-brown outer edge only on outer two-thirds of outer web, showing *Emberiza* pattern. Edge on the inner web narrower, but not as narrow as in Ortolan Bunting. Primaries and secondaries blackish-brown, with very narrow pale edge on the outer web. The central tail feathers are dark brown, with fairly narrow rufous-buff edges. The others are blackish-brown, with white outer third on second outermost pair and white outer half on outermost pair. The division between dark and white is often more square than in Ortolan Bunting. Belly, flanks and undertail-coverts rufous-chestnut, the latter lacking dark shaft streaks. Bill and tarsus pinkish-flesh. Iris dark brown.

Outermost and second outermost tail feathers (T6 and T5) of adult. Note difference in angle of border between black and white pattern on inner web compared to Ortolan.

Adult male non-breeding Very similar to adult male breeding, but slightly duller and often with more or less distinct streaking on crown and nape. The rump and belly are often slightly paler and more tawny.

First-winter male Similar to adult female non-breeding, but flanks and belly often with rufous-cinnamon mottling and dark streaking. Some juvenile greater coverts are often retained, usually the outer ones. These have narrower, paler and more distinct edges, forming a narrower and whiter lower wing-bar. The tail feathers are usually more pointed than in adults.

Adult female breeding Similar to adult male breeding, but colours less clean. The crown and nape are tinged brown, with narrow streaking, and the demarcation between the nape and mantle is not very prominent. The colour of the submoustachial stripe and throat is paler and less contrasting, and the malar stripe is darker, often blackish near the bill. Upperparts slightly paler, tinged olive. The scapulars are browner, with broader dark centres. The breast is a mixture of buffish and greyish, with some dark streaking on the lower throat. The belly, flanks and undertail-coverts are usually slightly paler, appearing indistinctly mottled.

Adult female non-breeding Very similar to adult female breeding, but duller. The crown and sides of head are pale brownish, faintly streaked, with very little grey colour visible. The streaking on the breast is stronger and more extensive, and the underparts are paler still.

First-winter female Very similar to first-winter males, but streaking on head and across breast more prominent. Lacks grey colour on crown. Often more prominently streaked on the underparts, except the central belly, lacking rufous-cinnamon colour.

Juvenile Crown, nape, mantle, scapulars, back, rump and uppertail-coverts buff, prominently streaked, or to some extent scalloped, dark brown. Pale colours of plumage bleach quickly. Supercilium faint. Ear-coverts rather uniform grey-brown, with a darker lower border. Submoustachial stripe and throat buffy-white, spotted blackish. Malar stripe dark brown. Lesser coverts brown, with blackish centres. Median and greater coverts blackish-brown with buffy edges. The dark centres of particularly the median coverts are more pointed than in adult, with a broader tooth. Tertials with pale rufous edges. Rest of wing similar to adult. Tail similar to adult, but tips of feathers more pointed, less truncate. Breast, belly and flanks buffy-white, narrowly streaked dusky.

T4 Normal   T4 Variant

Third outermost tail feathers (T4) of adult. Normally shows little white on tip, but occasionally the tip is quite conspicuously white.

SEXING Adults are straightforward. In males crown, malar stripe and breast are similar in colour, bluish-grey, almost unstreaked, and the submoustachial stripe and throat are rufous-cinnamon. In females the crown is tinged brown and always shows streaking, the breast is a mixture of buffish and greyish, with some dark streaking on the lower throat, and the submoustachial stripe and throat are buffish, paler and less contrasting than in males. In first-winter birds, males show deeper rufous-cinnamon mottling on flanks and belly than females. There is also some grey on crown and breast, very little of which is visible in females; if present, it is restricted. Males may show some streaking on throat and breast, but females are always more prominently streaked on head, across breast and on flanks. Many young males are actually very similar to adult males in non-breeding plumage. Males are on average larger (wing: male 78.5-88.0, female 77-83).

MOULT AND AGEING Juveniles undergo a partial moult July to September, involving head, body, lesser and median coverts, usually all greater coverts, usually all tertials and usually also the central pair of tail feathers, in males often all tail feathers. In males, a comparatively extensive first pre-breeding moult in the wintering grounds usually involves head, neck, most of underparts, outer scapulars, scattered feathers of rump, median coverts, usually inner greater coverts, tertials, often also the central pair of tail feathers. In females, the first pre-breeding moult is less extensive than in males, involving the same feather tracts, but leaving a varying amount of feathers unmoulted. Adults moult completely July to August. Also in adults there is a comparatively extensive pre-breeding moult of head, neck, chin, breast, median coverts, inner greater coverts, tertials and a variable amount of scapulars, rump and underparts, often also the central pair of tail feathers.

After complete moult, adults have fresh primaries, greater coverts, tertials and tail feathers, the latter with rounded tips. First-year birds show relatively more wear and sometimes a moult contrast between unmoulted outer greater coverts, showing whitish edges, and fresh inner ones, showing pale rufous edges. The juvenile flight feathers, primary coverts and at least outer tail feathers of first-year birds are retained during the first year, except in some males. The tail feathers are pointed in first-year birds, truncate in adults. Skull ossification useful. Iris colour not studied, but probably useful.

MEASUREMENTS Wing: (max) male 78.5-88.0, female 77-83. Tail: male 55-70, female 56-62. Bill: (to skull) male 11.2-14.4, female 10.3-13.1. Tarsus: male 16.9-19.1, female 16.8-19.8. P7-P8 emarginated, usually faintly also on P6.

GEOGRAPHICAL VARIATION None.

VOICE Song, which can be heard between March and June, is delivered from a rock, bush or tree, sometimes also from ground or low perch. It is to some extent variable, and may be thin and weak or lower-pitched, and clear or buzzy, but usually consists of two or three initial units followed by a longer final one, *dzree-dzree-dzreee* or *ziii-ziii-ziii-ziiiii*. The song differs from Ortolan in that the final units are often similar to the initial ones, only more drawn-out. However, song types with a final unit on a different pitch occur, *zwiie-zwiie-zwiie ziüüü*, and these may be very similar to Middle East Ortolans which often have only one final unit. The song is generally harsher, lacking the ringing quality of Ortolan.

The call is a *tchipp*, harder and sharper than Ortolan, but less metallic. Other calls, like a harder *tchu*, and a *plet*, similar to Ortolan, are sometimes heard.

HABITS Breeding takes place from March to July. Regularly two broods. The nest is a cup of stalks, roots and grass, lined with rootlets and hair, in a depression on the ground, often sheltered by rocks or shrubs. Eggs 4-5 greyish-white, sometimes tinged yellow, blue, pink or pinkish-brown, marked all over with dark spots, lines and small chocolate brown blotches and faint grey underlying smears. Incubation 12-14 days, normally by female alone. Young fledge after 12-13 days and are fed by both parents. The food consists of seeds and small invertebrates, but information insufficient. Tame. The most terrestrial of the buntings in the region and normally stays on ground

except when singing, but may perch in bushes when alarmed. On migration in small flocks, sometimes associating with Ortolan.

STATUS AND HABITAT Fairly common on dry stony slopes and hillsides, usually below 1300m, with relatively sparse vegetation, more common nearer to the sea. Also found in other relatively barren areas like rocky wadis, but also near gardens and cultivation. On migration often in stubble fields and other cultivated fields. In winter mainly found in dry open areas, such as bare semi-desert, cultivated fields, grassy plains, steppe and savanna.

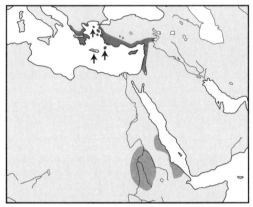

DISTRIBUTION AND MOVEMENTS Possibly breeds in south-western Albania. Breeds in southern Greece along western coast, on Peloponnisos, north to southern Thessalia, also on the Khalkidhiki peninsula and most islands in Aegean Sea. Locally on southern Crete. Western and southern Turkey, Cyprus, western Syria, Lebanon, Israel and Jordan, usually within 100km of the Mediterranean coast. Leaves breeding grounds gradually July to August. Main passage through Egypt and Israel from mid August to mid October. Arrives on the wintering grounds in Sudan in September. Bulk of population winters in Sudan, particularly along the Nile and in coastal areas, and in Eritrea, but also recorded in south-west Saudi Arabia in winter, although status there not well known. A few may winter regularly further north, in Egypt and north-western Saudi Arabia. Northward migration begins in February, with main passage across eastern Mediterranean in March and April.

Vagrant to Britain, Sweden, Poland, Austria, Georgia, Crimea, Malta, Algeria, Libya, Iran, Kuwait and Oman. Recorded from a number of European countries, but pattern obscured by likelihood of captive origin. Vagrant possibly also to Kenya.

REFERENCES Cramp & Perrins (1994), Haffer (1989), Tucker & Heath (1994), Small (1992).

16   HOUSE BUNTING
Emberiza striolata   Plate 7

Described as *Fringilla striolata* Lichtenstein 1823.
Synonyms: *Fringillaria saturiator, Fringillaria striolata, Emberiza sahari.*

In most of range a bird of desolate dry rocky hills, but in North-West Africa adapted to human habitation, and often common in villages and towns.

IDENTIFICATION 13-14cm. A small, rather nondescript species, lacking white in the tail. There are two distinct race groups. Males from eastern populations are sand-coloured with extensively rufous wings, and streaked or flecked throat and breast. The base colour of the head is whitish, with crown narrowly streaked blackish and face more prominently striped black and white.The dark streaking on the crown is usually rather uniform, but sometimes denser on the sides. The supercilium and submoustachial stripe, and sometimes the ear-coverts, are white. The ear-coverts and throat are pale greyish with blackish or dark grey streaking. The blackish eye-stripe and moustachial stripe are straighter than in most other *Emberiza* buntings, and do not encircle the ear-coverts at the rear, creating a slightly different facial expression. The upperparts are sandy-brown, narrowly streaked dark brown. The edges of the wing-coverts and flight feathers are rufous. Dark centres on the alula and on the median and greater coverts, particularly on the inner ones, are often visible on the folded wing. Slightly paler tips to median and greater coverts form relatively inconspicuous wing-bars. North African birds are much more uniform in appearance, rufous-brown with greyish head. The streaking on crown and breast is much reduced compared to eastern populations, and the upperparts are virtually unstreaked. The lesser, median and greater coverts, as well as the outer web of the secondaries, are uniformly rufous-brown, rendering the wing very uniform in colour, without any hint of paler wing-bars. The upperparts and wings are similar in colour, making the birds appear very uniformly rufous-brown. The colour of the belly varies from pale greyish-brown, to cinnamon-brown depending on race.

The Rock Bunting is superficially similar to eastern populations of House Bunting, but is larger, with greyish bill, and shows dark lateral crown-stripes and a prominent pale median crown-stripe, greyish lesser coverts, rufous rump and white outer tail feathers. The face pattern differs from House in that the dark border around the ear-coverts is narrower, and more well-defined, particularly at the rear. In House Bunting, the eye-stripe and moustachial stripe are broader and appear more as straight lines which not as clearly enclose the ear-coverts at the rear. Adult Rock Buntings show no or only very little streaking on the breast, and if streaking is present, it is always more prominent on the breast than on the throat. In House Bunting in most plumages the throat and breast are more uniformly streaked, and there is never a gorget.

The Cinnamon-breasted Bunting, which see for further differences, has bolder head pattern, with dark lateral crown-stripes and a pale median crown-stripe, and less rufous in the wings.

The Lark-like Bunting is nondescript, and similar to House Bunting in colour. However, the face pattern is very faint, the throat is paler, and the breast unstreaked rufous-brown, not greyish. Females and juveniles of North African populations are as plain-faced as Lark-like, but may be distinguished by their uniformly rufous wings, and darker belly.

Female Crested Bunting, which see, may resemble female House, particularly in flight, when wings appear extensively rufous in both species.

DESCRIPTION
Adult male breeding Crown white, distinctly streaked black, sometimes rather uniformly, but often more densely on the sides, forming darker lateral crown-stripes. Supercilium and submoustachial stripe white. The colour of the ear-coverts varies from white to grey. Eye-stripe and moustachial stripe black. Throat and upper breast greyish, heavily mottled or streaked blackish. Mantle, scapulars, back, rump and uppertail-coverts sandy-brown, finely streaked dark brown. Lesser coverts almost uniformly rufous. Median and greater coverts rufous with narrow dark brown centres, the medians often uniformly rufous. Primary coverts rufous with dark tips. Alula brownish. Tertials dark brown with narrow rufous-sandy edges, not showing typical *Emberiza* pattern. Primaries and secondaries dark brown, with rufous outer webs except at the tip. Overall effect is of a rather uniformly rufous wing. Tail feathers uniformly dark brown, except outer web of the outermost pair which is pale rufous-brown. Breast, flanks and belly rather pale sandy-brown, faintly tinged rufous or vinaceous. Undertail-coverts tinged cinnamon. Upper mandible blackish-brown, lower yellowish. Tarsus pale brown. Iris brown or orange-brown.
Adult male non-breeding Like adult male breeding, but fringes broader, especially noticeable on the tertials. Crown and breast somewhat paler due to broader pale fringes. Streaking on mantle slightly broader.
First-winter male Like adult male non-breeding. Retained juvenile tail feathers, if present, slightly more tapering than in adult, sometimes with diffuse rusty tip to outermost pair. Juvenile alula and primary-coverts retained, being relatively more worn than greater coverts.
Adult female breeding Crown pale sandy-brown, streaked dark brown. Rest of head pattern like male, but dark areas greyer or browner. Supercilium, ear-coverts and submoustachial stripe pale sandy-brown. Eye-stripe and moustachial stripe brown. Throat and upper breast pale greyish-brown, streaked brown. Upperparts, wings and tail as in male. Breast, flanks, belly and undertail-coverts slightly darker than in male.
Adult female non-breeding Like adult female breeding, but fringes broader, especially noticeable on median and greater coverts, and tertials.
First-winter female Like fresh adult female. Age differences as described under first-winter male.
Juvenile Similar to first-winter female, but generally browner, with less distinct face pattern. Streaking on crown, breast and upperparts paler and more diffuse. Dark shaft streak on median coverts with blunt end. Alula with slightly broader rusty edges. Tail feathers dark brown with distinct rufous-brown edges and diffuse rufous-brown tip of outermost pair. Underparts darker than subsequent plumages, more yellowish cinnamon. Bill dusky horn.

SEXING Males are characterised by whitish or purer grey base colour of head, depending on race, and black streaking on crown, eye-stripe, moustachial stripe and streaking on breast. Female differs from male in that the head pattern is duller. The crown is pale sandy-brown, streaked dark brown. Other dark areas of head and throat are also

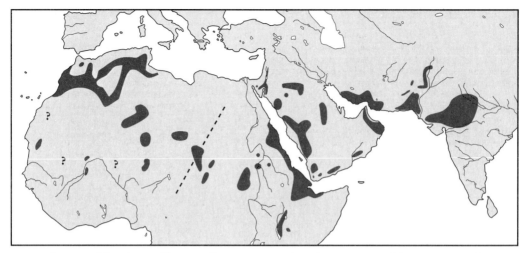

greyer or browner, while pale areas like supercilium, ear-coverts and submoustachial stripe are pale sandy-brown rather than white.

MOULT AND AGEING Juveniles undergo a partial moult April-August, involving head, body, lesser, median and greater coverts, usually some tertials, and often all tail. The alula, primary coverts and flight feathers are retained. Some (perhaps one-year-old) birds moult a varying number of flight feathers, showing a contrast between new and old feathers. Adults moult completely after the breeding season, April to October. Apparently no pre-breeding moult.

After the post-juvenile and post-breeding moults respectively, first-winter birds and adults are very similar. First-winter birds retain alula, primary coverts and flight feathers, which show a greater degree of abrasion, both compared to surrounding feathers and to corresponding feathers of adult. Some juvenile tail feathers are sometimes retained. They are slightly more tapering than in adult, sometimes with diffuse rusty tip to outermost pair, and show a greater degree of abrasion. The bill is duller in young birds, dusky horn, compared to relatively dark brown upper, and flesh-coloured or yellow lower mandible in adults. Skull ossification and iris colour probably useful, but not studied.

MEASUREMENTS Wing: (max) male 75.0-82.0, female 70.5-79.0. Tail: male 54.5-64.5, female 47.0-62.0. Bill: (to skull) male 10.8-11.9, female 10.9-12.3. Tarsus: male 14.6-15.4, female 14.5-16.2. P6-P8 emarginated, sometimes also P5.

GEOGRAPHICAL VARIATION Two distinct race groups, ecologically different, and both with clinal variation mainly in saturation of colours. The races from south-eastern and eastern Sahara and Asia are characterised primarily by dark streaking on the mantle and less rufous in the wings. Races from remainder of North African range are almost unstreaked above, with extensively rufous wings, and less prominent head pattern. There is no contact between the populations in eastern Sahara, but intergradation appears to be extensive in south-eastern Sahara.

NE African and Asian group.

   E. s. striolata (Coastal Sudan, Eritrea and N Somalia, W Saudi Arabia, north to Israel and east to NW India. Including *dankali* and *tescicola*) Described above. Birds from the eastern part of the range seem to be on average paler, but pale individuals occur in the west, and darker ones in the east.

   E. s. jebelmarrae (Typical birds only occur on Jebel Marra in W Sudan) Birds inhabiting Ennedi in eastern Chad, and lowlands of north-eastern Darfur are intergrades with *sahari*. Head pattern similar to nominate race, but dark streaking bolder. Rest of plumage darker rufous-brown. Streaking on mantle and scapulars bolder. Underparts darker, more brownish, darker even than in Cinnamon-breasted Bunting.

   E. s. saturiator (Kordofan, E Sudan, SW Ethiopia, NW Kenya) Similar to *striolata* but larger and darker.

NW African group.

   E. s. sahari (Morocco, Algeria, Tunisia, NW Libya) Birds from Hoggar, Tibesti, Aïr and Zinder are darker, but still almost unstreaked on the mantle. Vagrant to north-western Egypt. Slightly larger than nominate, with longer bill. Crown more uniformly streaked, eye-stripe, moustachial stripe, throat, and breast paler grey, making head pattern more uniform and less striking than in nominate race. The mantle, scapulars and rump are rufous-brown, with very ill-defined streaking confined to mantle. The underparts are darker and more uniform than in nominate race, rather distinctly set off from grey breast. The whole wing is very uniform in colour, more extensively rufous than *striolata*, showing no trace of wing-bars. Wing: male 73-87, female 72-78. Tail: male 59-64, female 55-60. Bill: male 12.1-13.1, female 12.0-13.0. Tarsus: male 16.4-19.2, female 16-1-19.8. P6-P8 emarginated, sometimes also P5.

   E. s. theresae (SW Morocco) Very similar to *sahari*, but darker and more saturated in colour. Contrast between breast and belly more well-defined. The underparts are a trifle darker even than *jebelmarrae*, but the streaking on the head is greyer and less prominent, and the mantle is almost unstreaked.

   E. s. sanghae (S Mali) Similar to *theresae* but slightly darker. The base colour of the crown and breast is darker grey than other races, and consequently the dark streaking is less apparent. Differs from *jebelmarrae* by almost unstreaked mantle, and from populations from Chad, Niger and southern Algeria in being darker.

VOICE The song may be given from a conspicuous perch, like a roof or rock, or from the ground on a rocky slope, and at least in the east sometimes also from the top of a bush. It is a simple repetitive phrase, e.g. *chippy chiwy chiwy chewy*. The song of the race *sahari* is similar, perhaps slightly more elaborate and less repetitive, *chippy cherr-pitchy cherr-pitchy*, or *chiwy cherr-chwii wi-cherr chwiiwy*, often resembling the end part of the song of Chaffinch *Fringilla coelebs*.

Common calls include a nasal *dschu*, perhaps resembling a very short version of call of Brambling *Fringilla montifringilla*, and a somewhat sparrow-like *tchiele* in flight. The call of the race *sahari* is a slightly higher-pitched *dzwee*.

HABITS The breeding season is drawn out, usually between February and August, but eggs recorded almost all months of the year from different regions. The nest is placed in crevices or on ground, in North-West Africa often in houses. It is built by female, possibly with the assistance of male, and is small and cup-shaped, constructed with dry grass, roots, twigs, etc., lined with hair, wool, plant down, and similar man-made materials. Eggs 2-4 greyish-white or pale bluish-white, densely speckled and mottled with reddish-brown, sometimes forming a ring at the larger end, with faint underlying blotches and smears of purplish-grey. Incubation 12-14 days by female alone. Young fed by both parents. Fledging period somewhere between 12 and 19 days. See Cinnamon-breasted Bunting for general comments on clutch size, growth rate, perinatal mortality, and length of nesting period in tropical compared to temperate and arctic zone species. The diet of adult is dominated by seeds of grasses, which the bird may reach by jumping up to pull down the stem. It then holds it down with one foot, while it extracts the seeds from the grasshead. The diet also includes various other seeds and berries. During the breeding season also invertebrates like ants and spiders. Outside breeding season gathers in small parties, sometimes associating with Rock Bunting or Cinnamon-breasted Bunting, and in western Sahara also with Desert Lark *Ammomanes deserti* and Trumpeter Finch *Bucanetes githagineus*. Sometimes follows sheep. Normal gait a hop.

STATUS AND HABITAT The eastern races shun human settlements and are found on arid rocky slopes and stony hillsides with sparse scrub, usually within reach of water. Rather capricious in occurrence, usually uncommon, but locally common or even abundant. Outside the breeding season sometimes wanders to plains and arable land. The north-west African race *sahari*, on the contrary, differs from other races in that it has largely adapted to human settlements. It is common in towns and villages, where it sings from roofs and ledges, and feeds in yards, streets and even inside houses, but may also occur in uninhabited places. It has continuously extended its range northwards for at least a century, and is now present in most large cities of Morocco.

DISTRIBUTION AND MOVEMENTS Distribution not known in detail due to desolate habitat. In Sahara, probably present in many suitable areas, but records mainly from the larger mountain massifs and along roads. Mostly resident, with some post-breeding wandering. From Morocco, where found in most of country, north to Rabat area and Fes, and still spreading north; eastwards through Algeria, where known distribution restricted to southern slope of Atlas mountains and Plateau de Tademait, and Hoggar in

extreme south; central Tunisia; to north-west Libya. Also locally in Ghat area in south-western Libya. Situation in Mauretania insufficiently known, but occurs in Adrar in west; northern Senegal; Mopti and Timbuktu in southern Mali; Aïr Massif and Zinder in Niger; Tibesti in northern Chad and Ennedi in eastern Chad; and Jebel Marra in western Sudan. Also along Red Sea coast, from south-eastern Egypt; coastal Sudan; Eritrea; north coast of Somalia; the Rift Valley of Ethiopia; south to the area east of Lake Turkana in northern Kenya. In Asia, breeds in central and southern Sinai in Egypt; the Judean Desert and Negev highlands in Israel; locally in western Jordan; in Saudi Arabia, mainly in mountains along Red Sea, but found inland to Riyadh; northern Yemen; scattered localities in Oman, mainly in north and south-east; northern United Arab Emirates; in Iran, south-eastern Zagros and Baluchistan; in Pakistan primarily in the Makran, Kirthar, and Sulaiman ranges, but present in scattered localities, from Quetta in the west, perhaps to as far north as Jhelum, and to Thatta in the south-east; in north-western India, from Pakistan border, locally south to the Vindhya and Ajanta ranges. Resident in many areas, but may wander locally in winter, when birds move to lower elevations and to plains. Vagrant Canary Islands, Cyprus, Kuwait, and perhaps Spain.

REFERENCES Archer & Godman (1961), Bannerman (1948 & 1953), Cramp & Perrins (19940, Etchécopar & Hüe (1967), Roberts (1992), Traylor (1960a), Vaurie (1956).

17   LARK-LIKE BUNTING
Emberiza impetuani   Plate 8

Described as *Emberiza impetuani* Smith 1836.
Synonyms: *Fringilla impetuani, Fringillaria impetuani, Fringillaria impetuana.*

The Lark-like Bunting inhabits arid stony terrain in southern Africa. It is nomadic and erratic, and may breed in large numbers after local rainfall.

IDENTIFICATION 14cm. The Lark-like Bunting is sand-coloured and featureless. Resembles House Bunting and Cinnamon-breasted Bunting in showing rusty edges to inner webs of flight feathers and a rufous panel on the folded wing. As in Cinnamon-breasted and House Bunting, there is no white in the tail. The general pattern resembles a very washed-out extralimital female House Bunting, but the nondescript face pattern makes confusion with this or any other African bunting highly unlikely. Even juveniles of Cinnamon-breasted and House Bunting, which are duller than adults, show more prominent face pattern than Lark-like, with the exception of north-west African races of House, which apart from being highly unlikely to cause confusion on geographical grounds, also differ in much more extensively rufous wings.

Although Lark-like Bunting may appear similar to a lark in coloration, there are actually no larks in the region that are more than superficially similar. The head is small, the bill shorter and more conical and the tail long compared to most larks. Lark-like Bunting lacks streaking on the breast, except in juvenile plumage, whereas most of the larks are streaked on the breast, or show some other dark pattern on the underparts. The wing-coverts, tertials and secondaries are relatively dark with narrow and contrasting edges, forming a wing panel on the folded secondaries. Some *Mirafra* larks show a similar rufous panel on the secondaries, but in most larks the edges of the wing-coverts and tertails are more diffuse, creating a less contrasting and more uniformly coloured wing pattern. Most larks have a relatively long or heavy bill, which in many species is pinkish or yellowish. The bill of Lark-like Bunting is relatively short and conical, blue-grey or dusky-flesh. Most larks have a short tail, where the part of the tail that is visible beyond the tip of the tertials is considerably shorter than the length of the tertials. Beware that a short-tailed juvenile Lark-like Bunting could perhaps be taken for a lark, as both shape and flight actions are different from that of adults. As juveniles also show some streaks or spots on the breast, birds in this plumage are the most likely candidates for confusion with larks. In many larks the tertials cover the wings completely, so that the primaries do not project beyond the tip of the tertials. In Lark-like Bunting, the outer pair of tail feathers are dark brown, with narrow pale brick-coloured edge on the outer web. Many larks have white outer pair of tail feathers, a character which, if seen, will rule out Lark-like Bunting.

Mirafra bush-larks differ by having longer bill, streaked breast or white in the tail, and there are no species that are particularly similar to Lark-like Bunting, with the exception of Fawn-coloured Lark *M. africanoides*, particularly the pale races in northern Namibia, in which the colour of the upperparts is similar, including a rusty wing panel. However, the underparts are pure white, showing a more obvious difference in colour between upperparts and underparts than in Lark-like Bunting, and the breast shows distinct, but restricted, dark streaking or spots. The bill is longer and the tail shorter. The pale edge of the tertials is broad and diffuse, not narrow and well-defined as in Lark-like. The face pattern differs from Lark-like in that the ear-coverts are more uniformly rufous, with a whitish crescent below the eye.

The Red-capped Lark *Calandrella brachydactyla* is unstreaked on the centre of the breast, but shows more prominent streaking on the sides of the breast, whiter belly, reddish cap and sides of breast, more prominent supercilium, and white in the tail. Lesser Short-toed Lark *C. rufescens*, Sclater's Lark *C. sclateri*, Stark's Lark *C. starki* and Pink-billed Lark *C. conirostris* (particularly of the race *damarensis*) are all short-tailed, with longer bills and a prominent breast pattern. All show a face pattern different from that of buntings, with a dark vertical stripe merging with a dark crescent below the eye. Stark's is also more prominently streaked on the upperparts, particularly on crown, and much whiter below. Pink-billed Larks of the pale race *damarensis* are very similar to Lark-like Bunting on the upperparts, and the breast-band is narrower and less prominent than in other races. The bill is also relatively similar to Lark-like. However, the wings are similar to the mantle, without rufous panel, the tertials cover the primaries, and the face pattern is contrasting and lark-like, with whiter and more prominent supercilium, white crescent below eye, and a short dark malar stripe.

Dune Lark *Certhilauda erythrochlamys* has unstreaked upperparts, with mantle and wings almost uniform in colour. The pale edges to the wing-coverts and tertials are more diffuse and less contrasting than in Lark-like Bunting. The breast is streaked dark, and the bill is longer.

Some female finch-larks are similar, but none should

be difficult to rule out on close inspection. The extralimital Black-crowned Finch-lark *Eremopterix nigriceps* is paler, with a more reddish sandy colour on the almost unstreaked upperparts. The wings are similar to the mantle, without the rufous panel of Lark-like Bunting. The bill is paler and the tail is shorter. Grey-backed Finch-lark *E. verticalis* has a larger, paler and more convex bill. The upperparts are paler, with less streaking on mantle than on crown. The wings are similar to the mantle, and lack rufous panel. The breast is spotted, there is a dark patch on belly and the outer pair of tail feathers are white. Chestnut-headed Finch-lark *E. signata* shows a strong contrast between the mantle, which resembles that of Lark-like Bunting, and much whiter underparts. The wings are similar to the upperparts, without rufous panel. The bill is yellowish and more convex. The outer pair of tail feathers are white.

DESCRIPTION
The differences both between the sexes and between different age groups are very slight.

Adult male breeding Crown sandy-brown, finely streaked dark brown. The supercilium is not very prominent, tinged rusty. Ear-coverts brown with a paler centre, encircled by creamy submoustachial stripe. The malar stripe is diffuse and ill-defined. Throat creamy-white. Mantle like crown. Back and rump sandy-brown, indistinctly streaked. Upper-tail-coverts browner, with some streaking. Lesser and median coverts with sandy edges, tinged rusty, and dark centres, well-defined and triangular in the median coverts. Greater coverts with well-defined pointed dark centres and pale rusty edges. Tertials rather narrowly edged rusty, showing no *Emberiza* pattern. Primaries dark brown with narrow sandy edges. Secondaries dark brown with rusty edges. Inner web of inner primaries and of all secondaries with rather broad rusty edge. Tail feathers uniformly dark chocolate brown, with narrow pale brick-coloured edges on the outer web of the outermost pair. Breast unstreaked pinkish-buff, faintly tinged vinaceous. Flanks buffish, very diffusely mottled. Belly yellowish-cream. Undertail-coverts pale pinkish-cream. Bill bluish-grey to dusky-flesh. Tarsus pinkish-orange to dusky-flesh. Iris dark hazel.

Adult male non-breeding Virtually identical to adult male breeding, but pale edges broader, most notably on greater coverts, tertials and central tail feathers. Base colour tinged browner, less grey, streaking on upperparts slightly broader.

First-winter male Like adult male non-breeding, but may have retained juvenile alula, primary coverts, primaries and tertials.

Adult female breeding Virtually identical to breeding adult male. The breast is often comparatively paler, contrasting slightly less with the belly, and there is often some faint streaking on the sides of the breast.

Adult female non-breeding Like adult female breeding. Differences as between adult males in breeding and non-breeding plumage.

First-winter female Like adult female breeding, but may have retained juvenile alula, primary coverts, primaries and tertials.

Juvenile Very similar to adults. Streaking on upperparts more diffuse. Lesser coverts almost uniformly rufous. Median coverts pale rufous, sometimes almost uniformly rufous. If centres are dark, they are less well-defined than in adults. Greater and primary coverts with less well-defined dark centres than in adults. Overall effect is much more uniform wing than adults. Alula with pale edge on inner web almost as broad as on outer web. Tertials with narrower edges than in adults. Primaries and secondaries like adult in non-breeding plumage. Tail feathers uniformly dark chocolate brown, central pair with well-defined pale rufous edge and almost all of outer web of the outermost pair pale brick-coloured. Breast slightly browner than adults, faintly streaked or spotted.

SEXING Sexing of single birds is not recommended. In pairs, males show darker, more vinaceous breast, and females duller breast and belly, with some diffuse streaking on the sides of the breast. The undertail-coverts of males are usually fairly uniform, whereas females usually show a dark shaft streak.

MOULT AND AGEING Juveniles undergo partial post-juvenile moult, involving body, lesser, median and greater coverts, tertials and some inner primaries. The outer primaries, primary coverts, alula and some tail feathers are usually left unmoulted. Adults moult completely, presumably after the breeding season, which is different in different regions. Moulting birds have been recorded March, May, June, August, October, November, December and January.

First-year birds can be told by moult contrast in the wing, between worn outer and fresh inner primaries, and un-moulted primary coverts, alula and usually some tail feathers. Adults show no moult contrast, and all feathers are in a similar stage of wear.

MEASUREMENTS Wing: (max) males 73.0-75.0, females 70.0-75.0. Tail: males 57.5-64.5, females 51.5-62.5. Bill: (to skull) males 12.3-12.7, females 11.7-13.0. Tarsus: males 16.4-17.9, females 15.6-16.8. P5-P8 emarginated.

GEOGRAPHICAL VARIATION Three races have been described. Differences are slight, and single birds cannot always be assigned a subspecific name.

    E. i. impetuani (N Cape province, adjacent Namibia, W Transvaal, W, S and E Botswana, and S Zimbabwe)
    E. i. eremica (SW Angola, Namibia, south to NW Cape province) Larger than nominate race (wing: males 75.0-80.0, females 72.0-78.0). Mantle more vinaceous or redder, with broader streaking than other two races.
    E. i. sloggeti (Cape province, south of Orange River, Griqualand West, and Orange Free State) Larger than nominate race (wing: males 76.0-81.5, females 74.0-77.5). Paler and greyer above than nominate race. Paler on breast and belly than other two races.

VOICE The song is rather monotonous and usually begins in a very quick tempo, followed by a more staccato part, often ending in a high-pitched, almost Corn Bunting-like jumble, *charra-dee-ur warrarett rett derwirr (zirrlirrlirr).*

The flight call is a single *chut* or a nasal *tweea*, higher in pitch, and more upwardly inflected than Cinnamon-breasted Bunting.

HABITS The time of breeding in relation to the rains seems complicated and may be opportunistic in areas with little rainfall. In the western Cape Province and southern Karoo breeding has been recorded at the outset of the dry season, September-December. In Namibia, northern Karoo and southern Zimbabwe, breeding has been recorded associated with rains March-May. In some of the Karoo localities, with two annual periods of rain, there are breeding records both from September-October and March-May. The nest is placed in depression on the ground among stunted scrub or weedy plants, against plant or tuft of grass, usually quite visible. It is a neat cup of fine grass and sometimes fine rootlets, surrounded by a loose structure of twigs and woody plant stems, built by the female. Eggs 3-4, white, finely spotted with brown and violet-grey. The diet consists of small seeds and insects taken on the ground. In the rainy season also green grass shoots and sprouting seeds. Runs and crouches on the ground in a lark-like fashion. Usually in small parties of about half a dozen birds, often mixing with other buntings or Black-headed Canaries *Serinus alario.* Often restless and wild.

STATUS AND HABITAT Local and perhaps nomadic in occurrence, but often common where found. Favours hard stony and much eroded ground and open hillsides, with sparse growth of stunted scrub, grass and weeds. May occur in grassveld, acacia scrub and even open grassy mopane woodland during non-breeding season dispersion.

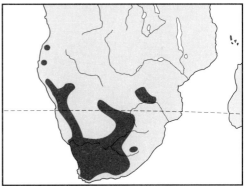

DISTRIBUTION AND MOVEMENTS Widespread in Namibia, but apparently absent from the north-east and the Caprivi Strip. Occurs in southern Botswana, but exact distribution insufficiently known. In South Africa throughout the Cape Province, except coastal areas, east to the western parts of the Orange Free State and western Transvaal. In Angola, the range extends north to Benguela along the arid coastal plain. In southern Zimbabwe occurs in the Limpopo River drainage, east to the lower Bubye River. May undertake nomadic wanderings to the north during dry periods in normal range. During irruptions recorded in Botswana and Zimbabwe north of normal range. Accidental north to Zambia, eastern Angola, and to the Kasai district (Kananga) in southern Zaïre.

REFERENCES Clancey (1989), Ginn *et al.* (1989), Maclean (1985), Priest (1936), Skead (1960), Vincent (1949).

---

18   CINNAMON-BREASTED BUNTING
Emberiza tahapisi   Plate 7

Described as *Emberiza tahapisi* Smith 1836.
Synonyms: *Fringillaria goslingi, Fringillaria arabica, Fringillaria insularis, Fringillaria tahapisi, Fringilloides tahapisi, Emberiza septemstriata.*

One of the most common and widespread of the African buntings, occurring on bushy or lightly wooded rocky or eroded hillsides, usually in dry country.

IDENTIFICATION 14cm. The male is strikingly striped black and white on the head, with uniformly black throat and upper breast. The upperparts are brown with dark streaking, and the underparts uniformly cinnamon-brown. The wing-coverts are dark brown with buffy edges. The tail is blackish-brown, completely lacking any white. The female is similar to the male, only slightly paler, differing mainly in head pattern, which is less contrasting, with stripes dark brown and pale buff instead of black and white. The throat and upper breast are paler than in males, dark grey-brown, with blackish mottling.

House Bunting may appear similar in some plumages, as the pattern on the ear-coverts may be very similar to Cinnamon-breasted, differing from other *Emberizas* in that the eye-stripe and moustachial stripe are broader and more parallel, and do not encircle the ear-coverts. The pattern on the crown is perhaps the best difference, with a prominent pale median crown-stripe and obvious dark lateral crown-stripes in Cinnamon-breasted. In House Bunting the dark streaking is more uniform, with no, or inconspicuous, pale median crown-stripe. In female Cinnamon-breasted the base colour of the throat and breast is greyish, and the dark pattern appears uniform or mottled. In House, the base colour of the throat and breast is paler and the dark pattern streaked or spotted. The streaking on the upperparts of Cinnamon-breasted is more prominent than in House, but some populations of the latter may be very similar to Cinnamon-breasted in this respect. The greater and median coverts are dark with only rufous edges in Cinnamon-breasted, rather uniformly rufous in House. The extralimital nominate race of House Bunting further differs by showing considerably paler underparts.

The race *goslingi*, of Cinnamon-breasted, differs from other races in that the throat is pale, uniformly grey in adult males, grey-brown in female and young, contrasting with the cinnamon breast. The rufous edges to flight feathers and wing-coverts are broader and more prominent than in the nominate race. In this respect *goslingi* is more similar to House Bunting, but general impression is that the wings appear darker, when folded, with rufous colour confined to a panel on the secondaries. In House, the whole wing appears more or less uniformly rufous. House Bunting occurs with two very different populations near the range of *goslingi*. The western ones, *sahari* and *sanghae*, differ from *goslingi* in being almost unstreaked on the upperparts, except on the crown, which is faintly and uniformly streaked. Females and juveniles of *goslingi* are always obviously streaked on mantle and rump, and show dark lateral crown-stripes and a contrastingly pale median crown-stripe. The supercilium is well-defined. House Bunting of the race *jebelmarrae*, in western Sudan, is quite different from the race *sahari*. It is as dark on the underparts as Cinnamon-breasted, sometimes even darker, and is similar in colour and amount of streaking on the upperparts. Main differences from *goslingi* are that the crown is more or less uniformly streaked, lacking obvious pale median and uniform lateral crown-stripes, and that the throat and breast are prominently streaked. In female *goslingi* there is a clear contrast between grey-brown throat and cinnamon breast. The greater and median coverts are rather uniformly rufous in *jebelmarrae*, dark with buffy edges in female *goslingi*.

The Cape Bunting shows a somewhat similar head pat-

tern, but most races of Cape are either paler on the underparts, or more olive-greyish or slaty-black than Cinnamon-breasted. However, the races in north-eastern South Africa are buffy or cinnamon on the underparts, and may be peceived as similar. In Cape, the throat is never darker than the breast, ruling out virtually all plumages of Cinnamon-breasted occurring in southern Africa. Any Cinnamon-breasted showing vaguely similar throat pattern would show very inconspicuous face pattern compared to Cape Bunting. The face pattern of Cape is always different, with blackish border surrounding ear-coverts and more uniform crown, instead of striped appearance of Cinnamon-breasted. In Cinnamon-breasted Bunting the wing-coverts are dark brown with buffy edges. The median and greater coverts of Cape appear more uniformly rufous on the folded wing.

DESCRIPTION There is very little seasonal variation. Adults vary mainly in stage of wear, particularly noticeable on fringes of median and greater coverts, and tertials. **Adult male** Central crown-stripe white, narrowly streaked black, lateral crown-stripes almost solid black anteriorly, becoming more broken up and streaked towards the rear. Broad eye-stripe, moustachial stripe, throat and central breast black. Supercilium, stripe on ear-coverts and submoustachial stripe white. Mantle, scapulars, back and uppertail-coverts brown, streaked blackish. Lesser, median and greater coverts blackish with buffy edges. Tertials blackish with rather narrow, well-defined rusty-buff edges, not showing *Emberiza* pattern. Alula blackish-brown with narrow whitish-buff edge on outer web. Primary coverts blackish-brown, narrowly edged pale buff. Underwing-coverts cinnamon. Primaries blackish-brown with narrow whitish edges, the inner ones with rather broad rusty inner web. Secondaries blackish-brown with narrow buffish edges to the outer web and, except for the tip, almost entirely rusty inner web. Tail blackish-brown. Sides of breast, flanks, belly and undertail-coverts cinnamon, the area bordering the black bib slightly tinged dusky. Upper mandible dark, lower yellowish, with blackish tip. Tarsus straw-coloured. Iris dark chestnut.

First-winter male Very similar to adult male. Tail feathers slightly more tapering than in adult, usually with narrow rusty tip to outermost pair. Moult contrast between darker fresh inner primaries and primary coverts, and browner worn outer ones. From females by blacker and whiter head pattern. Lower mandible flesh-coloured. Tarsus brownish-pink, slightly darker than in adult. Iris dark grey-brown.

Adult female Similar to adult male. Crown streaked blackish and greyish-buff. Rest of head pattern like male, but dark areas greyer or browner. Dark area on throat and breast less extensive and well-defined than in male and much greyer, with blackish blotching. Median crown-stripe, supercilium, stripe on ear-coverts and submoustachial stripe tinged buffish. Streaking on mantle, scapulars, back and uppertail-coverts paler than in male, dark brown rather than blackish. Wings like male, but inner primaries lacking or with only narrow rusty edges on the inner webs. Inner web of secondaries with less broad rusty edges than in male. Sides of breast, flanks, belly and undertail-coverts cinnamon, the area bordering the black bib slightly tinged dusky. Upper mandible dark, lower tends to be yellowish, rather than pinkish, as in males.

First-winter female Like fresh adult female, but head pattern on average paler and browner. Median crown-stripe, supercilium, stripe on ear-coverts and submoustachial stripe with stronger buffy tinge than adult female. Throat on average more uniform grey. Differences in shape and colour of tips of tail feathers, and moult contrast in wing, as in first-winter male.

Juvenile Similar to first-winter female, but median crown-stripe, supercilium, stripe on ear-coverts and submoustachial stripe obviously buffier. Throat paler, more brown than grey. Streaking on mantle, scapulars, back and uppertail-coverts brown, more indistinct. Dark centres of median coverts more pointed than in first-winter birds. Edges of tertials of more even width than in subsequent plumages. Alula blackish-brown with broader rusty edges, extending onto inner web, where often as broad as on outer web. Difference from adult most noticeable on middle alula feather. Primary coverts blackish-brown, narrowly edged rusty-brown. Small rusty wedge on tip of outermost pair of tail feathers. Breast often with faint streaks or spots. Bill grey. Iris dark grey-brown.

SEXING Males are characterised by black and white pattern of head, with rather uniformly black throat.

In females, the dark stripes on the head are browner than in males, and the median crown-stripe, supercilium, stripe on ear-coverts and submoustachial stripe are tinged whitish-buff. The throat patch is greyish, densely blotched black, and less extensive and less well-defined. The mantle, scapulars, back and uppertail-coverts are streaked dark brown in both sexes, but the streaking is not quite as dark in females as it is in males.

MOULT AND AGEING Juveniles moult partially after the breeding season. The extent of the moult is somewhat variable, but involves body feathers, lesser coverts, usually all median and greater coverts, although some medians may be retained, most tertials, inner primary coverts, inner primaries, outer secondaries and often a varying number of tail feathers. Adults undergo a complete moult after the breeding season. There is no evidence of a limited pre-breeding moult.

After the post-juvenile moult, first-year birds can be told in the hand from adults by the quite obvious moult contrast between both inner and outer primaries and inner and outer primary coverts. In adults all primaries and secondaries are of the same age, and there is no contrast. The lower mandible of adults is yellowish. In first-year birds it is flesh-coloured. Newly fledged individuals show greyish lower mandible. Skull ossification not studied, but first-year birds should be possible to identify at least in the first three or four months. Iris colour useful with caution and experience, being chestnut in adults, dark grey-brown in first-year birds.

MEASUREMENTS Wing: (max) males 77.0-84.5, females 72.5-79.0. Tail: males 61.0-68.0, females 58.5-64.5. Bill: (to skull) males 11.7-12.5, females 11.5-12.1. Tarsus: males 16.6-17.5, females 15.6-16.8. P5-P8 emarginated, sometimes faintly on P4.

GEOGRAPHICAL VARIATION There are two main groups of races. The West African race *goslingi*, and the *tahapisi* group in the rest of the range of the species.

E. t. tahapisi (Much of Africa, from S Ethiopia southwards) Described above.

E. t. arabica (S Arabian peninsula) Very similar to *tahapisi* but underparts slightly paler.

E. t. insularis (Socotra Island) Very similar to *tahapisi* but lateral crown-stripes blacker and dark bib more

restricted. Inner webs of flight feathers devoid of rufous. First-winter birds, particularly females, may be very pale on the underparts.

E. t. septemstriata (Sudan east of the Nile, Ethiopia, north of Addis Ababa) This race is quite variable, particularly regarding the amount of rufous in the wings, and seems to be a hybrid population between *goslingi* and *tahapisi*.

E. t. goslingi (Gambia to Sudan west of the Nile. Recorded in extreme NW Zaïre) The males have pale grey throats in strong contrast with the black stripes on the ear-coverts and crown, whereas males of the *tahapisi* group all have black throats. The lesser, median and greater coverts have darker centres than in the nominate race, but the primaries and secondaries are almost entirely rufous with only tips and outer webs of four outermost primaries brown.

VOICE The song is a short, fast, accelerating trill that ends with some twittering notes, rising in pitch. It is delivered from an elevated perch on a rock, bush or wire. Some song types start with a longer trill, *zrrrrrrrrr-zewiliwi* while others are shorter, *zrr-ze-ze-zewiliwi*, where the first part is shorter and more staccato. The initial part of the latter song resembles a short, very fast Yellowhammer.

The contact call is a nasal *per-wee-e*, in flight often just a subdued *dwee*. The alarm call is a very thin *tsiii-i*.

HABITS The breeding season is usually protracted, the dates varying between different regions, depending on the timing of the local rainy season. In regions with light rainfall, and in arid areas, the breeding season is usually throughout the rainy season. In areas with heavier rainfall, breeding begins at the end of the rains, or early in the dry season. In areas with two-season rainfall, breeding is normally during and just after the long rains.

In Arabia probably breeds throughout most of the year except summer, with eggs being recorded in January, February, May and October. The race *goslingi* breeds between September and March in West Africa. In Somalia in June. In East Africa breeding records are between January and July, with peak numbers between April and June. Breeding reported in south-west Tanzania between January and March, but in Malawi and Zambia breeding normally takes place May to July. Breeds April to June in northern Namibia. In Zimbabwe, there are two seasons, November to May and July to August, with peak numbers in the rains between January and March. In South Africa most breeding records are between October and May, with a peak around January-February in most areas. In Angola, probably breeds at end of rains, April-July.

The nest is built by female of twigs and grass, lined with fine grass and rootlets. In the race *goslingi*, the nest bottom has been observed to be impregnated with mud. It is placed on the ground in various situations, usually in a shady place, like the base of a rocky slope, a ledge in an earth bank, a crevice in a rock face, a shallow depression on the ground, or the base of a tuft of grass, stone or clod. Eggs 2-4, greenish-white or pale bluish-white, densely speckled or blotched and mottled with dark brown or reddish-brown. Incubation 12-14 days by both sexes, mostly female. Young are fed by both parents. They reach 90% of adult weight after about 12 days, and fledge after 14-16 days. The diet of adults, and presumably also juveniles, consists mainly of grass seeds and insects like small beetles. Usually seen singly, in pairs or in small parties, but sometimes in larger flocks outside the breeding season.

Feeds on the ground, hopping with rapid shuffling action. Unobtrusive.

STATUS AND HABITAT Generally fairly common, and numerous when habitat favourable, on relatively open rocky ridges, escarpments, quarries and mountainsides, with scattered trees and bushes, where often found in places with sparse grass and bare soil, such as eroded patches or roads. In some areas also occurs in open woodlands, like *Brachystegia* or pine forest. May enter towns.

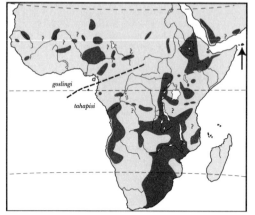

DISTRIBUTION AND MOVEMENTS Occurs in large parts of Africa south of the Sahara, but avoids the equatorial forest region, the highest altitudes in mountains, and deserts. Migratory or dispersive in many regions, but resident in others, and the exact breeding range is incompletely known, as records in many regions may refer to post-breeding wanderers. The nature of its movements is complicated and not fully understood. It is possible that the same birds may breed in different regions during the course of a year, but this remains to be proven.

Breeds in the Gambia and Senegal; south-western Mali; Burkina Faso; northern Ghana; Niger, north to northern Aïr; northern Nigeria, north of the great rivers; northern Cameroon; northernmost Central African Republic; the uplands of Ethiopia and Eritrea; Mt. Wagar in north-western Somalia. Distribution in Chad insufficiently known. In Sudan, an isolated population in Darfur and then from the Jeibal an Nubah eastwards to Ethiopia, also in extreme south. In the western parts of this region primarily a wet-season breeding visitor to the arid Sahel region, with a southward dispersion during the dry season.

On the Arabian peninsula, found in mountains along the Red Sea from the Mecca area southwards to north Yemen, and in south-western Oman. Breeding in south Yemen is likely, but needs clarification. Mainly resident, but some seasonal movement. Breeds on Socotra Island.

In eastern Africa, mainly found in the south-western and southern parts of Kenya, but locally to Marsabit and Lake Turkana basin; central and northern Tanzania; and along the western Rift, from extreme north-eastern Zaïre, and western Uganda, where also found in mountains along Kenya border, north to Kidepo Valley; southwards through Rwanda and Burundi; to southern Zaïre; northern and eastern Zambia; Malawi; central and north-western Mozambique, and along South African border; Zimbabwe; eastern Botswana; South Africa; where found in most of Transvaal, eastern Orange Free State, Lesotho, and Na-

tal, but absent from the coast. Also occurs from Cabinda and the lower Congo River, through Angola, to northern Namibia.

In the south-eastern parts of Kenya, most records are from December to February. In Zambia and Malawi a dry-season breeding migrant, most birds disappearing around October, at the end of the dry season. Returns to the southern parts of Zambia, where rainfall lowest, in February-March, and to northern Zambia and to Malawi in April. In Zimbabwe, eastern Botswana and South Africa absent from many parts in the dry season, April to November, but resident in others. May arrive in certain areas in Zimbabwe in large numbers in December.

Vagrant reported from Sinai, 19 and 20 April 1984, but this record was erroneous.

REFERENCES Archer & Godman (1961), Bannerman (1948 & 1953), Benson (1982), Brown & Britton (1980), Chapin (1954), Cumming & Steyn (1966), Curry-Lindahl (1981), Gartshore (1975), Ginn *et al.* (1989), Haydock (1949), Jennings (1995), Maclean (1985), Priest (1936), Skead (1960), Vincent (1949).

19 SOCOTRA BUNTING
Emberiza socotrana   Plate 8

Described as *Fringillaria socotrana* Ogilvie-Grant and Forbes 1899. Monotypic.

A little-known species, endemic to Socotra Island. It has only been observed on a few occasions, and virtually nothing is known about its life history.

IDENTIFICATION 13cm. A rather small bunting, with distinctive black and white head pattern similar to that of Cape Bunting and some of the African yellow-bellied buntings. It differs from the latter by lacking yellow on the underparts. The mantle is buffish-brown with dark streaking, separated from unstreaked grey-brown rump by unique pale cream band across back. The wing-coverts are chestnut with no or only very narrow pale tips, resembling Cape Bunting, but very different from the yellow-bellied buntings. The underparts are almost white except for russet-brown breast. White in the tail restricted to tiny spot on tip on the outer tail feather or lacking altogether. Most similar to extralimital Cape Bunting, from which it is readily told by the distinctive crown pattern, with blackish lateral and white median crown-stripe, yellow not slaty-grey bill, a pale band across the back and the contrast between the russet-brown breast and the whitish belly. Cinnamon-breasted Bunting, which occurs on Socotra, has dark or dark-streaked throat in most plumages, shows obvious wing-bars and a uniformly cinnamon breast and belly. Some first-year birds are very pale on the underparts, including more or less unstreaked throat. These birds are uniformly pale cinnamon in base colour, with no difference in colour between breast and belly, and lack any significant amounts of rufous in wings. House Bunting, occurring on the adjacent mainland, shows a superficially similar head pattern, but the eye-stripe and moustachial stripe form two parallel stripes rather than a distinct dark border surrounding the ear-coverts, as in Socotra, and the throat and breast are greyish with dark spots and streaks. Rock Bunting shows similar head pattern, but belly and rump are some shade of rufous and the outer tail feathers are white.

DESCRIPTION

Although the species is insufficiently studied, available data indicate that there is little seasonal variation. The sexes are very similar, as are adults and first-year birds.

Adult male breeding Lateral crown-stripes black, central crown-stripe white. Supercilium and ear-coverts white. Moustachial stripe and eye-stripe black, encircling ear-coverts. Loral stripe black, not reaching the bill. Submoustachial stripe white, throat pale grey. Very narrow dark malar stripe. Sides of neck greyish. Mantle buffy-brown with a greyish cast, streaked dark brown. Scapulars chestnut, streaked dark. Feathers of back with dark centres sharply set off from pale cream fringes, forming pale area. Rump grey-brown, unstreaked. Uppertail-coverts similar to rump, but with dark diffuse streaks. Lesser and median coverts chestnut, sometimes with thin shaft streaks on the latter. Greater coverts dark brown, with broad chestnut fringes. Alula dark brown. Primary coverts dark brown with paler vinaceous-chestnut outer fringes. Primaries and secondaries dark brown with pale chestnut outer fringes. Tertials uniformly dark brown. Breast rufous-brown with a pinkish cast. Flanks pale pinkish-cream with rufous blotching. Belly, vent and undertail-coverts pale pinkish-cream. Tail feathers blackish-brown. Upper mandible dark brown with a paler cutting edge. Lower mandible orange-yellow with a small dark tip. Tarsus yellowish-flesh. Iris dark brown.

Adult male non-breeding Undescribed, but probably very similar to adult male breeding.

First-winter male Similar to adult male breeding, but tail feathers narrower and slightly less blunt at the tip, the outermost pair tipped pale rufous. Shaft streak of median coverts broader and more diffuse than in adults, reaching the tip of the feather.

Adult female breeding Like adult male but less saturated colours. Supercilium and ear-coverts white. Moustachial stripe, encircling ear-coverts, eye-stripe and loral stripe blackish-brown, the latter not reaching the bill. Submoustachial stripe white, throat pale grey. Very narrow dark malar stripe. Lateral crown-stripes blackish-brown, central crown-stripe white. Sides of neck greyish. Mantle buffy-brown with a greyish cast, slightly more heavily streaked than in male. Scapulars chestnut, with broader dark streaking than in male. Feathers of back with dark centres diffusely set off from pale cream fringes, which are palest at the tip. Rump grey-brown, unstreaked. Uppertail-coverts similar but with dark diffuse streaks. Lesser and median coverts chestnut, the latter sometimes with dark shaft streaks, which may be more prominent than in males. Rest of wing much like male. Breast russet-brown, blotchier and showing less contrast with throat than in male. Flanks with russet blotching, less prominent than in the male. Belly, vent and undertail-coverts darker pinkish-cream than male. Tail feathers dark brown with a small whitish tip on the outer tail feather.

Adult female non-breeding Undescribed.

First-winter female Similar to adult female breeding, but tail feathers narrower and slightly less blunt at the tip, the outermost pair tipped pale rufous.

Juvenile Undescribed.

SEXING

Sexes very similar, but colours of males are more saturated. In males, the head pattern is more contrasting, with dark parts blacker and pale parts whiter. The contrast between the pale throat and the rufous-brown breast is slightly more obvious. Feathers of back (not to be confused with the mantle) show a more contrasting pattern.

MOULT AND AGEING Moult not sufficiently studied. Adults as well as juveniles appear to moult completely after the breeding season. Several specimens collected in May and June are in active moult of wing and tail. Some possibly show signs of arrested moult. These may be first-year birds.

The alula, which is retained after post-juvenile moult, is pointed in juveniles, more rounded in adults. The dark shaft streak in median coverts reaches tip of feather in juveniles and possibly first-winter birds. Juveniles and first-winter birds have pale rufous tips to the outer pair of tail feathers. In adults, the tips are white or concolorous with the rest of the feather.

MEASUREMENTS Wing: (max) male 68-73.5, female 63.5-69. Tail: male 55.5-60.5, female 50-58.5. Bill: (to skull) male 10.3-12.4, female 11.1-11.7. Tarsus: sexes combined 16.4-17.2. P5-P8 emarginated.

GEOGRAPHICAL VARIATION None.

VOICE The song is a ringing and somewhat metallic *huĕ-heee hu-hey*, given from a perch on a cliff or a tree. It is described as similar to the song of Golden-winged Grosbeak.

HABITS Judging from timing of moult, breeding probably takes place some time during the period December-April, but birds with slightly enlarged ovaries have been recorded in early June. Possibly lays two clutches, as a female collected on 15 February showed a well developed brood patch, and the ovaries indicated that breeding might take place after a further three weeks. The nest remains undescribed, and no data on breeding biology available. Feeds on grass seeds.

STATUS AND HABITAT Apparently uncommon. Listed as vulnerable by BirdLife International. Seems to be most common on the high plateau, in vicinity of the high granite peaks, and in rugged terrain with steep cliffs and boulders, where it often forages on ledges of steep precipices. The vegetation at Adho Dimellus is comparatively luxuriant, with shrubbery of *Hypericum* and thickets of *Cocculus*, interspersed by meadows of succulent herbage. Other records are from dry rocky hillsides at lower altitude, with short scrub and a few scattered small trees.

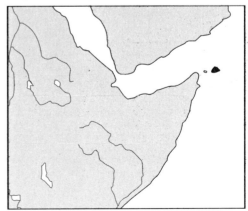

DISTRIBUTION Endemic to Socotra Island in the Indian Ocean, where singing birds have been recorded in the

Hagghier and Maggheer mountains above approximately 1000 m. Patterns of dispersion during the non-breeding season are not known. Some of the few records are from low altitudes, namely the pass south of Rookib and Qaysula near Kallansiya, suggesting that the birds descend to the lowlands after the breeding season.

REFERENCES Collar *et al.* (1994), Forbes & Ogilvie-Grant (1903), Ogilvie-Grant & Forbes (1899).

---

20   CAPE BUNTING
Emberiza capensis   Plate 8

Described as *Emberiza capensis* Linnaeus 1766.
Synonyms: *Fringillaria capensis, Fringillaria reidi, Fringillaria media, Fringillaria cinnamomea*.

The Cape Bunting is a fairly common breeder in rocky and grassy areas in the southern part of Africa. The species shows marked geographical variation.

IDENTIFICATION 16cm. A medium-sized, slender-built bunting. Despite marked geographical variation, all races are characterised by the combination of distinct narrow border around ear-coverts, pale throat, extensive chestnut in the wings, lack of yellow colours on the underparts, little contrast between breast and belly, and no white in tail. The pattern of the ear-coverts is similar to that of Golden-breasted Bunting, but the dark border around the ear-coverts is narrower and the lores are dark. The crown pattern is less prominent than other species with similar head pattern. Colour and streaking on the crown varies depending on subspecies, but there are no distinct lateral crown-stripes. The folded wing is extensively russet-brown. The underparts vary from almost white or different shades of buff to dark slaty-grey, but are never yellow. Except for narrow white edges on the outer web of the outermost pair of tail feathers, the outer tail feathers are all dark in adults. In juveniles, the tips of the outermost pair are paler brown.

The Cinnamon-breasted Bunting, which see, may appear superficially similar to some races. The extralimital and very localised Socotra Bunting, which see for differences, shows a similar face pattern. The chestnut lesser and median coverts separate this bird from all canaries, siskins and whydahs. Some female and non-breeding male widowfinches show reddish lesser coverts, but all these have a nondescript face pattern.

DESCRIPTION
Male and female are difficult to separate on plumage. The seasonal variation is very slight and after post-juvenile moult no plumage differences are known between adults and first-year birds. Juvenile slightly different from subsequent plumages.
Male Crown greyish-brown, streaked dark, with relatively narrow dark lateral crown-stripes. Supercilium whitish. Eye-stripe and fairly broad moustachial stripe blackish, forming blackish border that encircles the whitish ear-coverts. Some individuals show a very short malar stripe at the base of the bill. Throat whitish. Mantle and scapulars slightly browner than crown, with broad dark streaks. Back, rump and uppertail-coverts unstreaked greyish-brown. Lesser and median coverts uniformly russet-brown. Tip and outer web of greater coverts broadly edged russet-brown. Outer web of primary coverts, primaries and

secondaries russet-brown. Tertials dark, with even russet-brown edges. Underparts fairly uniform vinaceous-buff, slightly greyer on the breast and palest on the belly. Centres of undertail-coverts greyish-brown, tips pale. Tail dark sepia, except the outermost pair, which may show a very thin whitish edge on the outer web. Upper mandible slate-black, lower slaty-bluish, slightly paler at the base. Legs and feet dark horn. Iris dark brown.
Female Like male, except supercilium, ear-coverts and throat slightly more buffish. Eye-stripe and moustachial stripe dark brown to blackish. The demarcation between the pale throat and darker breast is less well-marked than in male.
Juvenile Mantle paler and greyer, more heavily streaked than adult. Tips of primary coverts paler than in adult. Breast and flanks streaked. Breast without greyish cast. Tip of outermost pair of tail feathers rusty-brown.

SEXING The difference between the sexes is slight, and some are difficult to sex. The dark patterns on the face are blacker in males, browner in females, who also show less contrast between throat and breast. Males are on average larger.

MOULT AND AGEING Timing of moult depends on local climate seasonality, and apparently occurs after the breeding season, which tend to be rather drawn-out. Adults and apparently also juveniles undergo a complete post-breeding moult, usually December-March, but some as late as May. Exceptions are *plowesi* and *vincenti* which undergo a complete post-breeding moult June-July.

Juveniles are streaked on the breast and flanks and paler than adults, but at least in the race *smithersii* adult females can also be streaked on the breast. The tips of the outermost pair of tail feathers are rusty-brown in juveniles, not concolorous with the rest of the feather, as in adults. No plumage characters for ageing after the post-breeding moult discovered. Skull ossification not studied, but first-year birds should be possible to identify at least in the first three or four months. Iris colour should be useful, with caution and experience.

MEASUREMENTS Wing: male 75-88mm, female 71-82mm; Tail: male 64-72mm, female 58-67mm; Bill: (to skull) (sexes combined) 10.5-12mm; Tarsus: 19-20mm. P5-P8 emarginated.

GEOGRAPHICAL VARIATION This is a very variable species, with recognisable forms on virtually every mountain massif. The pale forms in the west, and the cinnamon-coloured forms in eastern South Africa may represent the extremes of a cline. There is a clinal variation in colour from Angola and western Zimbabwe southwards to the Cape, going from pale to darker, although the differences between these races are slight. The races occurring in eastern South Africa vary in saturation of cinnamon colour, both above and below. The birds found at high altitude in the Drakensberg Mountains appear to represent a break in continuity of the colour cline. It is possible that they are more closely related to the isolated race in the Chimanimani Mountains in eastern Zimbabwe. The very distinct race in E Zambia and Malawi differs from all other races in several respects and again represents a break in continuity of the colour cline.

E. c. nebularum (Restricted range in SW Angola, in vicinity of Mossamedes) The palest race. The buffish mantle shows less streaking than any other race, with only fine blackish shaft streaks. The underparts are very pale grey. The bill is proportionately long (14.5-15.0mm). Greater coverts rufous on outer web. Shows a rufous panel on the secondaries.

E. c. bradfieldi (Eronga Mountains and Waterberg, N Namibia) Includes *cloosi* from Brandberg, N Namibia. Similar to the previous race, but colours more saturated. Shows a rufous panel on the secondaries.

E. c. plowesi (Zimbabwe, NE Botswana) Similar to *nebularum*, but the mantle is buffish, showing distinct streaking, and the bill is shorter. The underparts are very pale grey. Greater coverts with more extensive dark centres than *nebularum*, from which it also differs by lacking rufous panel on secondaries.

E. c. capensis (Namibia, south of Windhoek and the western parts of the Cape Province) Includes *klaverensis* and *ausensis*. Similar to previous races, but mantle greyer, with more diffuse streaking. Underparts vinaceous-grey.

E. c. vinacea (N Cape Province, to the east of *capensis*) Upperparts similar to *capensis*, but underparts, including throat, vinaceous-buff, intermediate in colour between *capensis* and *media*.

E. c. cinnamomea (W Cape Province) Similar to *vinacea*, but underparts buffier, less vinaceous.

E. c. media (Karoo and eastern districts of the Cape Province to the Orange Free State, Griqualand West and S Botswana) Underparts including throat buffish. Upperparts buffier than *capensis*, similar to *plowesi*. Streaking more distinct than *capensis*, but not as black as in *plowesi*.

E. c. reidi (E Orange Free State, N Lesotho, N Natal, and S and SE Transvaal) Rufous-brown above. The underparts, including throat, are pale olive-cinnamon, darker than any of the previous races, but not very different from *media*. The rufous colour of the wings is darker than previous races.

E. c. limpopoensis (C and SW Transvaal) Similar to *reidi*, but still richer brown above.

E. c. basutoensis (S Drakensberg area in E Lesotho and W Natal, occurring at higher altitudes than *reidi*) Underparts almost as dark as *reidi*, but greyish instead of olive-cinnamon. Much darker and more olive above than *reidi*, and more prominently streaked than any of the previous races. Streaking almost as heavy as *smithersii*, but mantle darker and browner. Differs from all previous races by median coverts showing a dark shaft streak.

E. c. smithersii (Chimanimani Mountains in E Zimbabwe and adjacent Mozambique) Mantle olive-grey, heavily streaked blackish. Underparts, including the throat, olive-greyish, slightly darker than *basutoensis*. The median coverts show a dark shaft streak.

E. c. vincenti (Easternmost Zambia, SW Tanzania, S and C Malawi, and adjacent Mozambique) A very distinctive race. Differs from all other races by its slaty-black underparts, contrasting with the white throat. Dark, almost unstreaked upperparts. Less extensive chestnut in the wings. Several inner median coverts are dark grey and the primary coverts are brownish-grey on the outer web. The outer webs, but not the tips, of several inner greater coverts are grey, unlike all other subspecies, which create chestnut wing-bars instead of a panel.

VOICE The song is delivered from the top of a rock or low bush, the male sometimes opening and closing the wings during the song. Regional variation is incompletely known, but may be extensive. The song of the nominate race is a series of chirping, sparrow-like notes, starting with a repetition of the same note, turning into a more varied section *chup chup chup chup chup cheep chu chichu chichu*, or *chip-chup chup-chup-chup chip-chup*, loudest in the middle. The song of the race *vincenti* is a simple *tre-re-ret tre-re-ret*.

The call is a nasal *wip dee-wee-wee-wip*.

HABITS Breeds some time between July and April in most of range, mainly September-October, timing dependent on local climate, usually during or just after the rains. South-western populations usually breed in the first half of the period, eastern and northern populations normally later. In Malawi, breeds April-June after the end of the wet season. The nest is a raggedly built cup of twigs and dry grass, lined with hair, very fine grass and rootlets. It is placed low in bushes or at the base of a grass tuft among rocks, often in a sheltered hollow on a hillside. Eggs 2-4, cream or pale bluish-white, heavily speckled and blotched with pale reddish-brown and a few pale lilac or grey undermarkings sometimes forming a ring at the larger end. Food consists of seeds, insects and spiders. Usually solitary, in pairs or small family groups. Does not flock. Forages on ground. Walks or hops. Flight low and somewhat jerky, not sustained.

STATUS AND HABITAT Common to fairly common in rocky, boulder-strewn hills, often in areas of xerophytic vegatation, from high mountains to the coast, where it also occurs in sandy areas with low scattered weedy scrub. Often near water. Originally generally distributed also in arid scrubby areas and dry stony ground with sparse short grass and scattered scrubs, but has disappeared from many places because of extensive ploughing. In the north-east, confined to rocky inselbergs.

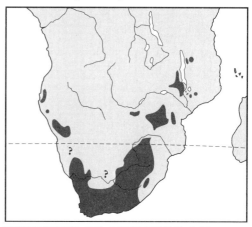

DISTRIBUTION AND MOVEMENTS Probably occurs from vicinity of Mossamedes in south-western Angola, southwards through mountain areas in western Namibia, to South Africa, but apparently thinly distributed in some areas. In South Africa distributed over much of the country, extending north to south-eastern Botswana, but absent from most of the Kalahari basin and the coastal lowlands in the east. In Zimbabwe primarily in mountains between Bulawayo and Harare, extending westwards into eastern Botswana, with an isolated occurrence in the Chimanimani Mountains. Further north, found to the north of the lower Zambezi River, in easternmost Zambia, extreme south-western Tanzania, southern and central Malawi, and adjacent Mozambique. Mainly sedentary, but apparently some seasonal movements in Botswana and Malawi.

REFERENCES Benson (1941), Ginn *et al.* (1989), Maclean (1985), Rudebeck (1958), Skead (1960), Vincent (1936, 1949 & 1950).

---

21   CHESTNUT-EARED BUNTING
Emberiza fucata   Plate 9

Described as *Emberiza fucata* Pallas 1776.
Synonym: *Spina fucata.*

The Chestnut-eared Bunting inhabits open shrubby marshland and meadows from Kashmir to Japan. It is generally not rare, but does not usually occur in high numbers anywhere.

IDENTIFICATION 16cm. The breeding male is unmistakable. The chestnut ear-coverts contrast prominently with the grey crown and sides of neck, and the eye-ring is well-marked. The breast pattern is unique. The throat and upper breast are white, with a gorget of dense blackish spots across the breast, separated from rufous band across lower breast by an unmarked whitish area. The flanks and belly are buffier than the throat, enhancing the breast pattern. Females show the same characters, but are duller and more washed out. The rufous breast-band is paler and reduced, and may be almost entirely lacking. The chestnut colour of the ear-coverts may be quite pale, but still contrasts rather obviously with the olive-grey crown and sides of neck.

In fresh plumage, much of the characteristic pattern is obscured, and first-year females in particular may become relatively nondescript. The ear-coverts are still noticeably darker rufous-brown than surrounding areas, but the crown is a pale olive-brown instead of grey. The throat and upper breast are buffy, and do not show the same contrast with the belly as in breeding plumage. In some individuals there is no contrast at all. The dark breast-band is less solidly black, but is relatively narrow, compared to other species, and consists of streaks and spots. The rufous lower breast-band is much obscured, and often lacking, although there is usually a faint rufous tinge at the sides of the breast.

Juveniles show prominent whitish supercilium and differ from other species by characteristic broad dark borders around almost whitish central ear-coverts. The breast is sparsely streaked dark, and there is sometimes a hint of the rufous lower breast-band.

Some first-winter Chestnut-eared Buntings show a rather plain head and a prominent eye-ring, inviting confusion with first-winter Ortolans. However, in Chestnut-eared the ear-coverts are always browner than the surrounding areas, and the supercilium is paler. The malar stripe is blacker and more well-defined, the throat lacks significant streaking, the streaking on the breast is blacker and more prominent, and the belly paler. In Ortolan, the streaking on the breast extends onto the throat. The streaking on the mantle is considerably more prominent in Chestnut-eared, showing marked contrast with the nape. In Ortolan, the contrast is less pronounced. The rump is usually noticeably rufous in Chestnut-eared, concolorous with the mantle in Ortolan. The tail pattern

differs in that the outermost pair of tail feathers show more white than in Ortolan, and the second outermost pair show less. The white pattern is also more in the shape of a wedge in Chestnut-eared. The resulting impression is that Ortolan shows white corners and Chestnut-eared white sides to the tail.

Confusion with other species is not very likely. Little Bunting also shows chestnut ear-coverts, but always differs in its dark lateral crown-stripes. Meadow Bunting may show combination of rufous rump and chestnut ear-coverts, but breast is more or less unstreaked, and the supercilium is more prominent. Eastern Common Reed Buntings, particularly the race *pyrrhulina*, may appear superficially similar in general coloration, and both species have rufous lesser coverts. However, most Eastern Reed Buntings are readily distinguishable by darker lateral crown-stripes, more prominent supercilium, shorter and stubbier bill, almost unstreaked underparts, and paler rump, lacking rufous tinge.

DESCRIPTION
Adult male breeding Crown grey, streaked black. Supercilium unstreaked, not very prominent, grey like crown or with some white intermixed. Lores relatively pale. Eye-ring whitish, most prominent below eye. Ear-coverts bright rufous-chestnut, greyish below and behind the eye, with some black below the lores. Submoustachial stripe and throat white or tinged pale buff. Malar stripe blackish and prominent. Sides of neck grey, whiter just behind ear-coverts. Nape grey with an olive tinge and some dark streaking. Mantle rufescent sandy-brown, with heavy blackish streaking. Scapulars rusty-brown, with prominent dark shaft streak. Rump rusty-brown, with a few scattered dark streaks. Uppertail-coverts grey-brown tinged ochre, with dark shaft streaks. Lesser coverts rusty-brown. Median coverts blackish with buffy tips, divided by a narrow zone of rusty-brown. Greater coverts blackish with rather broad pale sandy-rufous edge on the outer web and tip. Tertials with blackish centres and pale buffy edge on the outer web, separated by a narrow zone of rusty-brown, narrow pale edge on the inner web, showing the characteristic *Emberiza* pattern on the two outer tertials. Primaries and secondaries brown, with narrow pale margin on the outer web. The central tail feathers are dark brown, with sandy-brown edges. Remainder of tail dark brown, the outermost two pairs (T5-T6) with relatively narrow whitish wedge on inner web, sometimes lacking on second outermost pair (T5). Upper breast whitish, with dense collar of blackish spots, separated from rufous band across lower breast by whitish unmarked area. The rufous band becomes narrow and appears broken in the centre. Flanks buffish, tinged rufous, streaked dark. Central belly paler, sometimes almost whitish. Undertail-coverts like belly. Upper mandible blackish, with greyish or pinkish cutting edge. Lower mandible bluish-grey, with pinkish base. Tarsus pinkish-brown. Iris dark chestnut-brown.
Adult male non-breeding Similar to adult male breeding, but pattern much obscured. Grey colour of crown obscured by pale olive-brown fringes, streaked blackish. The pure grey bases of the feathers are well-defined, but usually only visible in the hand. Both supercilium, throat and breast are tinged buff, but the lores are greyish-white. The lower breast-band may be completely obscured. The pale streaking on the upperparts is slightly more prominent.
First-winter male Very similar to adult male non-breeding. At corresponding time of year, shows more abrasion

and browner alula, primary coverts, flight and tail feathers. Lower mandible on average more extensively pinkish than in adult. Iris dark grey-brown.

Adult female breeding Similar to adult male breeding, but base colour of head olive-grey. The supercilium is whiter and more prominent than in male. The throat and upper breast is not as white as in males and shows less contrast with the belly. The collar of blackish-brown spots is less well developed, as is the rufous band across the lower breast. The rump frequently shows more dark markings than in males.

Adult female non-breeding Very similar to adult female breeding, but head pattern even more obscured by buffy fringes. The lores are usually more buffish than in males. Shows on average less black than males on ear-coverts below eye. The underparts are buffier than in worn plumage.

First-winter female Similar to adult female non-breeding. Head pattern may be further obscured. Age differences as described under first-winter male. Lower mandible on average more extensively pinkish than in adult. Iris dark grey-brown.

Juvenile Lateral crown-stripes rather dark, particularly in front. Pale central crown-stripe narrow, pale grey or sandy. Supercilium prominent, whitish. Ear-coverts dark greyish-brown, with whitish centre, usually tinged buff. Submoustachial stripe and throat white or tinged pale buff. Malar stripe narrow. Nape buffy-grey with some dark streaking. Mantle rufescent sandy-brown or grey-brown, with heavy blackish streaking. Scapulars similar to mantle. Back, rump and uppertail-coverts ochre brown, plain or with a few indistinct streaks. Lesser coverts rusty or ochre brown. Median and greater coverts show bluntly pointed drawn-out tooth on blackish centres, and buffy tips. Tertials with blackish centres and relatively narrow pale buffy or rufous edge. Primaries, secondaries and tail similar to first-winter birds. Breast pale buff, sparsely spotted. Flanks buffy-white, almost unstreaked. Central belly almost white. Undertail-coverts buffy-white. Lower mandible on average more extensively pinkish than in adult. Iris dark grey-brown.

T6   T5   T4

Three outermost tail feathers (T6-T4) of adult. Note extremely pointed shape of adult feather, deceptively similar to typical shape of juvenile in other buntings.

SEXING In breeding plumage, males are brighter than females. The crown is grey; the ear-coverts uniformly chestnut; the throat, upper breast and submoustachial stripe are whitish; the upper breast-band blackish and relatively broad, and the lower breast-band darker and broader than in females. In fresh plumage, the differences are largely obscured. The bases of the crown feathers are grey, squarely and prominently set off from olive-grey tips. This can

usually only be determined in the hand, but is sometimes possible to see in the field. Similarly, the bases of the feathers of the throat are whiter in males, and there is a larger amount of concealed rufous on the sides of the breast, reflecting the breeding plumage. The lores usually appear whiter than the anterior supercilium.

In females, the crown is olive-grey; the ear-coverts paler chestnut with whitish intermixed, particularly at the upper rear corner; the throat, upper breast and submoustachial stripe are tinged pale buffish; the upper breast-band is blackish-brown rather than black, narrower and more broken up; and the lower breast-band is paler and may be reduced to a smudge on the side of the breast. In fresh plumage, females are more nondescript than males, with traces of breeding plumage less apparent. The lores are usually similar in colour to the anterior supercilium. In the hand, the bases of the crown feathers are more similar to the tips in colour, and the demarcation is diffuse. The bases of feathers of the throat are buffier than in males, and the concealed rufous feathers on the sides of the breast are paler and more diffusely rufous, with less well-defined pale fringes.

MOULT AND AGEING Juveniles undergo partial post-juvenile moult that starts relatively soon after fledging. It involves head, body, lesser, median and usually all greater coverts and tertials, often also central pair of tail feathers and some outer primaries, and is completed between August and September. Adults moult completely August-September.

In this species adults have unusually pointed tail feathers, which could easily be interpreted as juvenile feathers. With practice, the shape of the tail feathers is still useful for ageing, as first-year birds have still more pointed tail feathers. First-year birds retain alula, primary coverts, flight feathers and tail feathers, and these are relatively more worn than in adults. In first-year birds, the primary coverts usually show a more prominent colour difference compared to the edges of the flight feathers, and the edges of the alula are paler. In adults there is no obvious colour difference between the primary coverts and the edges of the flight feathers. Adults have chestnut iris and first-winter birds have dark grey-brown iris.

MEASUREMENTS Wing: (max) males 70.5-79.0, females 67.0-74.0. Tail: males 59.0-67.5, females 52.5-61.5. Bill: (to skull) males 14.0-15.7, females 13.8-15.3. Tarsus: males 18.7-19.8, females 19.2-20.4. P6-P8 emarginated.

GEOGRAPHICAL VARIATION Two rather distinct main groups, from China and India, respectively, differing mainly in saturation of colours and amount of chestnut on breast.

    E. f. fucata (NE China and Japan). Described above.
    E. f. kuatunensis (SE China) Includes *fluviatilis*. Smaller (wing: male 69.5-71.5, female 68-71), darker and redder on the upperparts. The breast band is similar to the nominate race, or narrower.
    E. f. arcuata (India, Yunnan) Darker and more richly coloured compared to the nominate race. The throat is whiter, and the black gorget broader. The black streaking on the mantle is on average narrower. The flanks and lower breast-band, which is markedly broader than in the nominate race, are warm chestnut-red. In females the breast-band is more well marked than in the nominate race. The median coverts are almost uniformly rusty-brown in males, and

in females with pale rufous rather than whitish tips, rendering the wing-bars less prominent.

VOICE The song, which is delivered from the top of a scrub or weed, is twittering and more rapid than most other buntings in the range. It usually starts with a few staccato *zwee* or *zip* notes, accelerating into a variable twitter, often ending with a very characteristic double *trüp-trüp* or *chürüpp*, lower in pitch than the rest of the song and not always audible at a distance. Typical song types may be transcribed *zwee zwizwezwizizi trüp-trüp* or *zip zizewüziwiziriri chüpee chürüpp*. The song may also be given in a slower tempo, with the different units more clearly audible, e.g. *zip chup chup cheechewee (tziri)*.

The call is an explosive typical bunting-like *pzick*, similar to Rustic Bunting. Alarmed birds may give a series of calls, with the *pzick*-call alternating with a higher-pitched *zii* or *zii-zii* and a lower-pitched *chutt*.

HABITS Breeding usually begins in May or early June, but late broods may be started as late as August. The nest is built of dry grass blades, weed stems, rootlets and twigs, lined with animal hair, fine roots and grass, and usually placed in a depression in the ground on dry patch of soil in marsh, well concealed by vegetation. Eggs 3-5 (rather rounded in subspecies *fucata*), glossy white to yellowish-white or pale greenish-grey, speckled and mottled brown, with underlying grey, sometimes with darker spots and fine lines. Breeding biology insufficiently known. The diet consists of grass seeds and some insects. Gregarious in winter, but never in large flocks.

STATUS AND HABITAT Uncommon in most of range, but locally fairly common. Found on scrubby hillsides, in open expanses of marshland and meadows with herbaceous and shrubby vegetation, and riverside thickets.

In the winter found in scrubby grassy areas, cultivated areas and rice stubble. Often in low bushes and high grasses adjoining fields and marshes.

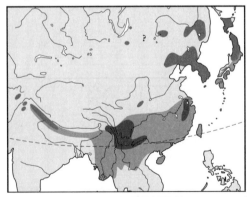

DISTRIBUTION AND MOVEMENTS Uncommon and local in the western Himalayas from Chitral, in northern Pakistan, and Kashmir, east to north-western Nepal. Recorded in northern Afghanistan, but probably only a vagrant. Appears to be absent from the eastern Himalayas, but reappears in south-eastern Tibet, and is widely distributed in southern and western Yunnan, western Guizhou, Sichuan and southern Shaanxi, in China, and possibly breeds in north-eastern Burma. An isolated population is found in the lower Yangtze River region and Fujian. Further north-east in China, found in south-eastern Jilin, Liaoning, adjacent Inner Mongolia, eastern

Heilongjiang and most of Korea. In Russia, occurs along upper and middle Amur River at least to Khabarovsk in the north-east. Eastern limit of range along Ussuri River, east at least to the western slope of the Sikhote Alin. Uncommon in scattered localities from Kentei in north-eastern Mongolia and eastern Transbaikalia to adjacent Hulun Buir region in northern Inner Mongolia. Breeds in the southern Kuril Islands, north to Kunashir, and in Japan from Hokkaido south to central Honshu.

Himalayan populations winter in foothills and adjacent plains, and may be replenished to some extent by birds from China, particularly in the east. Populations from south-eastern China winter in southern parts of range, and from Bangladesh and north-eastern India, Burma except Tenasserim, northernmost Thailand, to northern Indochina. North-eastern populations winter from southern Korea, southern Japan (but rare in the Nansei Shoto), Taiwan and throughout southern China, south of the Yangtze River, including Hainan, from November to April. Northward migration begins in April, with passage through north-east China in April and May. The first birds arrive on the breeding grounds in Korea and Japan in mid or late April. Accidental in Afghanistan and Uzbekistan.

REFERENCES Ali & Ripley (1974), Anon. (1993), Bezzel (1993), Baker (1926), Bates & Lowther (1952), Dementiev & Gladkov (1966), Dorzhiev & Jumov (1991), Jahn (1942), Latouche (1925-1930), Roberts (1992), Satou (1985), Vaurie (1956).

22   LITTLE BUNTING
Emberiza pusilla   Plate 10

Described as *Emberiza pusilla* Pallas 1776. Monotypic.

The Little Bunting is one of the most common birds in the northern parts of the Siberian taiga, extending its range into scrubby tundra. It is also one of the most common buntings in a variety of open habitats on the wintering grounds in southern Asia.

IDENTIFICATION 12-14cm. The Little Bunting is best recognised by its small size, chestnut ear-coverts and pale eye-ring. In breeding plumage, the lateral crown-stripes are very dark, and the prominent median crown-stripe, supercilium, ear-coverts, and chin often deep chestnut. The upperparts are greyish-buff, heavily streaked dark brown, the rump somewhat greyer with more diffuse streaking. The underparts are whitish-buff, prominently streaked blackish on breast and flanks. The sexes are very similar, and the seasonal plumage variation is limited, mainly restricted to the brightness of the head pattern. In fresh plumage the lateral crown-stripes are largely obscured, rusty-buff with some diffuse dark streaking, but still evident. The chestnut colour of median crown-stripe, supercilium and chin is often largely obscured and may be replaced by white. The ear-coverts are chestnut in all plumages, but may be quite pale in fresh plumage.

Common Reed Buntings in female and non-breeding plumage are similar to Little in many respects, but never show contrasting chestnut ear-coverts and the pale eye-ring is less prominent. The crown pattern is usually more contrasting in Little, with darker and more well-defined lateral crown-stripes and a usually narrower and more well-defined median crown-stripe. In Common Reed, the dark border around the relatively uniformly brown ear-coverts encircles the entire ear-coverts, including a dark moustachial stripe which reaches the bill. In Little, the moustache is chestnut like the ear-coverts, and there is usually a more distinct pale spot on the rear of the ear-coverts. In Little, the lesser coverts are greyish-brown, never rufous-brown as in Common Reed. The wing-bars are more prominent in Little, particularly on the median coverts, which are white in Little, pale rufous in Common Reed. The bill is proportionally slightly larger and more pointed in Little, with straight culmen. In Common Reed, the culmen is normally slightly convex, but may occasionally be almost straight. However, even then the bill does not appear as pointed as in Little. The tarsus is reddish-brown in Little, never as dark as is often the case in Common Reed. The clicking call of Little is completely different from the *seeoo* or *brzee* calls of Common Reed.

The Chestnut-eared Bunting, which see, shows prominent chestnut ear-coverts like Little, but lacks dark lateral crown-stripes and is more yellowish in fresh plumage. Juvenile Little Bunting is very similar to juvenile Pallas's Reed Bunting, which see for differences. Juvenile Dunnock *Prunella modularis* shows diffusely streaked breast, and may show chestnut ear-coverts and an eye-ring, and may thus appear similar to Little Bunting. Differs from Little by longer and more pointed bill, with pinkish base, darker moustachial area and indistinct median crown-stripe. The streaking on the underparts is more indistinct on the breast but broader and more prominent on the rear flanks.

DESCRIPTION
Small differences between sexes and ages with many intermediates occurring between extremes described below. Slight seasonal variation.

Adult male breeding Central crown-stripe, ear-coverts, lores, and supercilium in front of eye reddish-brown, the latter paler and more brownish behind eye, becoming almost white at the rear. Prominent pale eye-ring. Lateral crown-stripes jet black. Eye-stripe black, angling down along rear of ear-coverts. Moustache concolorous with ear-coverts. Submoustachial stripe and throat whitish, sometimes reddish-brown in front. Malar stripe blackish. Nape brownish-grey, streaked dark. Mantle greyish-buff, with an element of chestnut, heavily streaked dark brown. Scapulars similar, but more chestnut. Back and rump buffish-grey, diffusely streaked dark brown. Uppertail-coverts tinged chestnut-brown. Lesser coverts greyish-brown. Median coverts dark brown with whitish tips. Greater coverts dark brown with brown edges, slightly paler at the tips. Tertials similar in colour to greater coverts, showing *Emberiza* pattern. Alula, primary coverts, primaries and secondaries dark brown with narrow pale edges. Tail brown, outermost pair (T6) with long white wedge on inner web, outer web white except at tip. Second outermost pair (T5) variable; usually shows narrow white wedge on inner web, but occasionally all dark. Underparts whitish-buff, prominently streaked on breast and flanks. Bill dark grey, cutting edge and base of lower mandible paler pinkish-grey. Tarsus reddish-brown. Iris dark red-brown.

Adult male non-breeding Very similar to adult male breeding, but head pattern obscured by pale fringes. The lateral crown-stripes are rusty-buff, with some diffuse blackish streaking. The mantle is paler, due to broader pale fringes. Fringes of coverts and tertials are broader, contributing to more prominent wing-bars and overall paler appearance. Underparts buffier, with whitish belly, and slightly

more diffuse dark streaking.

First-winter male Virtually identical to adult male non-breeding, but head pattern often on average duller with less rusty colour and more streaking. Flight feathers and tail feathers slightly more worn. Tips of tail feathers more pointed.

Adult female breeding Very similar to adult male breeding, and many cannot be safely sexed on plumage, unless in breeding pair with male. In typical individuals the rusty colour of head is paler, with some dark streaking on central crown-stripe. The lateral crown-stripes are browner.

Adult female non-breeding
Virtually identical to both adult and first-winter male. Differences same as in summer, but head pattern obscured by pale fringes.

First-winter female Virtually identical to adult female non-breeding, but flight feathers and tail feathers slightly more worn. Tips of tail feathers more pointed.

Juvenile Central crown-stripe buff. Lateral crown-stripes rufous-brown with dark brown streaks. Supercilium sandy-buff, wearing to whitish. Ear-coverts rufescent brown, bordered above by a dark eye-stripe, encircling the upper rear corner. As in adults, the dark border along the lower margin of the ear-coverts does not reach the bill. Submoustachial stripe pale sandy-buff. Malar stripe prominent, blackish-brown. Throat pale sandy-buff. Nape olive-brown, similar to crown, but less prominently streaked. Mantle sandy-brown with some rufous-brown intermixed, heavily streaked blackish. Scapulars blackish with pale sandy-buff edges. Rump sandy-brown, often quite prominently streaked dark brown. Uppertail-coverts olive-brown with dark brown streaks. Lesser coverts grey-brown. Median coverts blackish-brown with whitish or buffish tips. The shape of the black centres is more pointed than in adults and there is a characteristic rounded tooth. Greater coverts blackish-brown with similar pale buffish tips, together with median coverts forming narrow double wing-bars. Alula dark brown. Primary coverts dark brown, with pale rufous-brown edges. Tertials similar to adult female non-breeding, as are the primaries and secondaries. The tail feathers are similar to first-winter male. Breast yellowish-buff, rather heavily streaked dark. Belly and undertail-coverts pale sandy-buff. Iris dark grey-brown.

Outermost (T6) and two examples of second outermost tail feathers (T5) of adult.

SEXING Many single individuals can not be reliably sexed, as differences are slight. The most typical males show jet black lateral crown-stripes and deep rufous median crown-stripe and ear-coverts. In breeding pairs, males are almost invariably brighter than females, and the dullest males seem to pair up with the dullest females.

In females, the lateral crown-stripes are browner, and

the rufous colour on the head is paler. The median crown-stripe is streaked. In autumn, when the plumage is fresh, the head pattern is obscured by pale fringes, and sexing is not recommended.

MOULT AND AGEING Juveniles undergo a partial post-juvenile moult, starting at the age of 17-23 days; duration 40-45 days. It normally involves head, body, lesser and median coverts, sometimes inner greater coverts and tertials. Adults moult completely July to September. There is a limited pre-breeding moult on the wintering grounds, February-April, involving side of head and throat.

First-winter birds are virtually identical to adults in non-breeding plumage, but on average less rufous on head. Retained juvenile greater coverts, primary coverts, flight feathers and tail feathers are slightly more worn. Tips of tail feathers more pointed. In the hand, iris colour useful, dark red-brown in adults, dark grey-brown in first-year birds.

MEASUREMENTS Wing: (max) male 69-78, female 64-75. Tail: male 51-58, female 46-55. Bill: (to skull) male 11.6-13.4, female 11.2-12.6. Tarsus: male 16.5-18.2, female 17.0-18.4. P6-P8 emarginated, sometimes also slightly P5.

GEOGRAPHICAL VARIATION None.

VOICE The song is delivered from an exposed perch in a tree top. A singing individual often repeats sequences, consisting of a handful of different song-types given in a certain order. The song is rather variable, and often somewhat metallic in timbre. Each song type usually consists of two or three parts, each of which consists of a number of similar units. The last part is sometimes more variable. Examples of common variants, beginning with repeated single units, followed by a more rapid part and ending with a higher-pitched, somewhat quavering unit, may be transcribed *zree zree zree tsütsütsütsü tzriitu* or *tzrü tzrü tzrü zee-zee-zee-zee zriiiiiru*. Other variants begin with a rapid trill, followed by single units, repeated at a slower pace *tser-ererere chu-chu-chu-chu* or *tserererere tswee-tswee chu-teee*. Some parts of the song may recall song of Common Reed Bunting. The way the units are repeated may also recall Ortolan Bunting.

The usual call is a hard *pwick* or *tzik*, recalling call of Hawfinch *Coccothraustes coccothraustes*, but weaker.

HABITS Breeding begins between early June and July. The nest is usually placed on the ground, often on grass tussock, but occasionally on tree stump or low in tree. It is built by female alone, of grass, twigs, stalks, moss and horsetail, and lined with fine grass, lichen and sometimes hair. There is usually only one brood per year. Eggs 4-6, sometimes similar to Common Reed Bunting, varying in base colour, from pale lavender-grey, pale ashy-blue, pale green to pale pinkish-buff, pale chestnut or dark brown, with faint blotches of lilac-grey and marked with sparse dark reddish-brown spots, streaks and twisted lines, blurred at the edges. Both sexes incubate, 11-12 days. Young leave nest already at age of 6-8 days, when unable to fly, but often fully fledged 3-5 days later. Both parents care for young, which are mainly fed craneflies, midges and defoliating caterpillars, plus a variety of other invertebrates like spiders and beetles. Diet of adults during breeding season largely invertebrates, mainly caterpillars, flies, craneflies, midges, beetles and spiders. During remainder of year, seeds of sedges, grasses and cereal dominate, but invertebrates still make up significant proportion of food intake. Gregarious outside breeding season, and mixes with a variety of species that utilise same habitat.

STATUS AND HABITAT Common in moist open taiga with undergrowth of dwarf birch and willows, and in more open tundra habitat, ranging from bushy tundra to areas with only low, sparse shrubs, with concentrations in river valleys. In favoured areas local densities of more than 100 pairs per km² are possible.

In winter found in a variety of open habitats, such as fringes of forest, shrubbery on hillsides, crops, stubble and paddyfields, roads and paths, river banks and marshes.

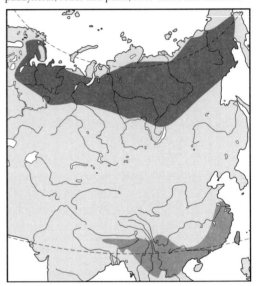

DISTRIBUTION AND MOVEMENTS Breeds from northern Scandinavia, eastwards through northern Russia and Siberia. In Norway mainly found along the Alta and Tana Rivers, and in the Pasvik Valley. In Finland main distribution is in eastern Lapland. Rare breeder in northern Sweden. In Russia and Siberia, mainly north of 60°N, but extends further south in mountains north of Lake Baikal. Northern limit of range roughly follows edge of taiga, but usually found in tundra some distance further north. In the east reaches the pacific coast in the Anadyr area. Southward migration starts August, and most birds have left the breeding grounds by mid September. Western populations migrate directly eastwards at first, and turn south-easterly when they reach western Siberia. Passage through Mongolia and Manchuria in September and early October and through north-eastern China about a month later, end of September to early November. During autumn migration regular in small numbers to north-western Europe, Israel and Japan. Arrives on the wintering grounds in October. Winters in eastern Nepal and north-eastern India, northern and central Burma, northern Thailand, northern Laos, northern Vietnam and China, generally south of the Yangtze River, but locally further north. Spring migration begins in March. Last birds leave the southern parts of the winter range in early May. Main passage through north-eastern China between last third of April and first half of May. Reaches breeding grounds between last third of May and early June.

Vagrant to most European countries, including Iceland, and to the Canary Islands, Morocco, Algeria, Turkey, Lebanon, Jordan, Egypt, Iran, Kuwait, Oman, the United Arab Emirates, Afghanistan, Pakistan, Borneo, the Philippines, Alaska and California.

REFERENCES Alström *et al.* (1991), Anon. (1993), Bezzel (1993), Bradshaw (1991), Cramp & Perrins (1994), Dementiev & Gladkov (1966), Harris *et al.* (1989), Johansen(1944), Kretchmar (1993), Svensson (1975 & 1992).

---

23   TRISTRAM'S BUNTING
Emberiza tristrami   Plate 9

Described as *Emberiza tristrami* Swinhoe 1870. Monotypic. Synonym: *Emberiza quinquelineata*.

Tristram's Bunting has a limited breeding range in the temperate zone of far eastern Asia, and is confined to forests throughout the year.

IDENTIFICATION 15cm. Male in breeding plumage is unmistakable. The striking head pattern and black throat, in combination with unstreaked reddish-brown rump and tail, separates it from other buntings within normal range. Most of the head is black, except for prominent white median crown-stripe, supercilium and submoustachial stripe. The centre of the ear-coverts are often brownish, and there is a small white spot in the upper rear corner. Females in breeding plumage are very similar to males, but throat is buffish-white instead of black and the lores and ear-coverts are noticeably browner. In fresh non-breeding plumage in autumn, buffish fringes make white parts buffier and black parts browner. The dark throat of males is obscured by pale fringes, but the black colour usually shows through.

The Yellow-browed Bunting is the most similar species in all plumages, except breeding male, but differs by having bright yellow anterior supercilium, prominently streaked breast and flanks, browner, less reddish, rump and always pale throat. The lateral crown-stripes are blacker in Tristram's. The yellow colour in the supercilium of Yellow-browed is usually obvious, but may occasionally be surprisingly difficult to discern in the field. The white supercilium of Tristram's is often buffish in front of the eye, and may occasionally appear very similar to Yellow-browed in the field. In worn plumage, in spring and summer, the streaking on the sides of the breast and flanks in Tristram's becomes darker, and the most prominently streaked individuals of Tristram's may resemble the most faintly streaked Yellow-browed in this respect. However, in Tristram's there is usually an obvious difference in colour between the blackish malar stripe and the rufous pattern on the breast. In Yellow-browed, the blackish malar stripe breaks up into blackish streaking on the breast, with no difference in colour between the malar stripe and the streaking on the sides of the breast. The breast and flanks are still washed buffish-brown in Tristram's and the streaking is not as distinct and blackish as in Yellow-browed, which also shows paler base colour to the breast and flanks.

In autumn, when the plumage is fresh, the breast and flanks are relatively uniformly buffish-brown in Tristram's, with only some indistinct mottling or brownish streaking. Particularly males may appear very uniform, and show very little mottling. Yellow-browed shows prominent dark streaking at this time of year. In both species the centre of

the belly is unstreaked whitish. Tristram's also shows a brighter and more uniformly rufous rump and the closed tail appears cinnamon-brown. In Yellow-browed, the rump is more mottled, less rufous, the uppertail-coverts tend to be browner and the tail is darker.

The juvenile is very similar to juvenile Yellow-browed, and best told by rufous- not ochraceous brown, rump. Extralimital Cinnamon-breasted Bunting is superficially similar, but has uniformly cinnamon underparts.

DESCRIPTION
Adult male breeding Crown black, with white median crown-stripe. Supercilium white. Lores and ear-coverts black, a small white spot in the upper rear corner. There is sometimes a faint brownish tinge to the centre of the ear-coverts. Submoustachial stripe white. Throat black. Sides of neck and nape grey-brown. Mantle grey-brown, streaked blackish, reddish-brown along the central mantle and on the scapulars. Back, rump and uppertail-coverts uniformly reddish-brown. Lesser coverts grey-brown. Median coverts blackish-brown tipped buffy. Edges of greater coverts pale grey-brown, tips pale buff. Tertials dark brown with rufous-brown edges, showing *Emberiza* pattern. Alula and primary coverts brown. Primaries dark brown with narrow pale edges. Secondaries dark brown with rufescent brown edges. Underwing-coverts whitish. Central tail feathers rufescent cinnamon-brown, the others brown. Two outermost pairs with white wedge on inner web, narrow and sometimes almost absent on second outermost pair. Breast rufous-buff, darker on the sides, mottled rufous. Flanks rufous-buff indistinctly streaked. Belly and undertail-coverts unstreaked, whitish. Upper mandible blue-grey, lower pinkish-flesh. Tarsus pale brown. Iris dark chestnut-brown.

T6   T5

Outermost and second outermost tail feathers (T6 and T5) of adult. White pattern on T5 sometimes almost absent.

Adult male non-breeding Very similar to adult male breeding, but lateral crown-stripes, lores and ear-coverts blackish-brown and the throat slightly obscured by pale fringes.
First-winter male Similar to adult male non-breeding, but lores and ear-coverts noticeably browner, contrasting with dark border. The dark pattern on the throat is apparent, but much obscured by pale fringes. Iris dark grey-brown.
Adult female breeding Very similar to adult male breeding, but lores and ear-coverts paler brown surrounded by blackish-brown moustache and eye-stripe like first-winter male. The crown is sometimes brownish, but may be very similar in colour to adult male. The throat is buffy-white with a few dark spots and the malar stripe well marked.
Adult female non-breeding Very similar to adult female breeding, but median crown-stripe, supercilium, submoustachial stripe and throat tinged buffish. Breast rufous-

brown, mottled rather than streaked.

First-winter female Very similar to adult female non-breeding, but median crown-stripe, supercilium and submoustachial stripe on average more buffish. The lateral crown-stripes are sometimes more broadly fringed brown. There may be some fine streaking on the breast.
Juvenile The head pattern is similar to that of adult female, with white median crown-stripe and blackish lateral crown-stripes. Supercilium white. Lores and ear-coverts dark, with white intermixed at the rear. Submoustachial stripe white. Throat white. Sides of neck and nape pale grey-brown. Mantle and scapulars grey-brown, streaked blackish, less rufous than adults. Back, rump and upper-tail-coverts rufous-brown, less bright than adults. Median coverts blackish-brown tipped whitish. Edges of greater coverts pale grey-brown, tips pale buff, broader and more prominently set off than in adults, creating more prominent wing-bars. Breast grey-brown, streaked dark. Flanks whitish streaked dark. Belly and undertail-coverts un-streaked, whitish.

SEXING In males in all plumages the base on the feathers of the throat are black. In fresh plumage, the dark bases may be almost completely obscured, particularly in first-year males, but are always evident in the hand.

In females, the base of the feathers of the throat are never black. The lores and ear-coverts are on average browner in females than in males in comparable plumage and age.

MOULT AND AGEING Juveniles undergo a partial post-juvenile moult, July-September. The extent is not clear, but involves at least head, body, lesser and median coverts, and usually innermost greater coverts, possibly also outer greater coverts and tertials. The primaries, secondaries, primary coverts and tail feathers are not moulted. Adults moult completely July - September. There is a limited pre-breeding moult in the winter quarters, involving at least parts of the head.

Adult males show black throat throughout the year. In fresh plumage, narrow pale fringes obscure the black colour slightly. In first-winter males, there is considerably less black visible on the throat in fresh plumage, and the lores and ear-coverts are browner. Ageing of females is more difficult, as characters overlap. The tail feathers of first-winter birds are more pointed than in adults. Tail and wings relatively more worn in first-winter birds. Adults show chestnut iris, first-winter birds dark grey-brown iris. Skull ossification is helpful during autumn.

MEASUREMENTS Wing: (max) males 70.0-78.5, females 67.0-72.5. Tail: males 53.5-61.5, females 52.0-60.0. Bill: (to skull) males 13.2-14.1, females 12.5-13.9. Tarsus: males 17.4-18.9, females 17.0-18.6. P5-P8 emarginated.

GEOGRAPHICAL VARIATION None.

VOICE The song is delivered from an inconspicuous perch in a tree. It always begins with a clear high-pitched unit, usually followed by another drawn-out unit, which may be higher or lower in pitch. The last part is quite variable, although fairly simple. One or two units are given one to four times each in rapid succession, often with a short *chit*, or similar, added at the end. Some examples of common variants are *hsiee swee-swee swee-tsirririri*, or *hsiee swee swiririchew*, or *hsiee swee tzrii-tzrii (chit)*, or *hsiee swiii chew-chew-chew*. The song is very similar to that of Yellow-browed Bunting, but is slightly faster, often more twittering, and

lacks the thrush-like quality. The initial unit is higher-pitched and weaker in Tristram's, slightly deflected in pitch, but flute-like and rich in Yellow-browed, clearly inflected in pitch.

The call is an explosive *tzick*, usually irregularly repeated.

HABITS Breeding begins in June. The nest is usually placed low in a bush. It is built of dry grass blades, often lined with horse hair. Eggs 4-5, pale pinkish with greenish tinge, marked with sparse blackish patches and lines. Breeding biology insufficiently known. During migration, beetles, flies, and other insects, as well as seeds have been observed to be included in diet. Outside breeding season often in small flocks.

STATUS AND HABITAT Fairly common in forest with dense underbrush, usually on hillsides. Often found in mixed forest, but occurs in understorey both in tall pine forest and spruce taiga. In winter on the forest floor in wooded hills.

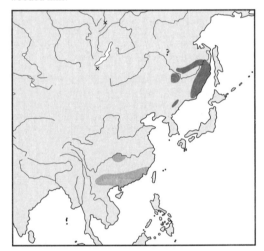

DISTRIBUTION AND MOVEMENTS Known from a relatively limited area in northern China and adjacent Russia. Breeds in the Lesser Khingan Mountains in Manchuria; from the Zeja river along the Amur river, north to the Gorin and Khungari rivers in Russia, and in the lower reaches of the Ussuri River and in the Sikhote Alin Mountains. Autumn migration begins in September, and majority of birds have evacuated breeding areas by October, with stragglers remaining into December.

Main passage in Korea during September, and at Beidaihe, in north-eastern China, during October. Vagrant to main islands of Japan, but annual both in spring and autumn on islands in Sea of Japan and Korea Strait. Winters in southern China from south-eastern Yunnan, where rare, to Fujian, and in Hunan and eastern Sichuan. Recorded on Emei Shan west of the Red Basin in Sichuan. Very rare winter visitor in northern Thailand and northern Laos, probably also Tonkin. Normally present in the winter quarters between November and March. Main spring passage in north-eastern China and Korea between the end of April and the beginning of June. First birds arrive on the breeding grounds at the end of April, occasionally earlier.

Vagrant to Burma. The species has also been reported from near Ulan-Ude, with a flock of 120 birds in spring

1974, and a flock of 7 birds in the same area the following year. The same source also reports a record from the upper Nizhnaja Tunguska.

REFERENCES Anon. (1993), Dementiev & Gladkov (1966).

24 YELLOW-BROWED BUNTING
Emberiza chrysophrys   Plate 9

Described as *Emberiza chrysophrys* Pallas 1776. Monotypic.

The Yellow-browed Bunting is a rather uncommon bird of the southern taiga in central Siberia, where it occurs in rather closed forest and at the edges of clearings.

IDENTIFICATION 15cm. The adult male is characterised by its striking head pattern. The most distinctive feature is the prominent supercilium, which is yellow in front of the eye, white at the rear. The crown is blackish with a prominent white median crown-stripe. Lores and ear-coverts are blackish. The underparts, including submoustachial stripe and throat, are white, with prominent blackish malar stripe and distinct blackish streaking on breast and flanks, the latter with a pale rufous-brown wash. The mantle is grey-brown, streaked blackish, with a broad chestnut stripe along the centre. The rump is rufous-brown, indistinctly streaked. In fresh plumage in autumn, the blackish parts of the head pattern become partly obscured by brownish fringes and the white parts become tinged buffish.

Females in breeding plumage are very similar to males, but dark parts of head are somewhat browner. Particularly the lores are paler and browner in females. The ear-coverts are often medium brown, with blackish border.

In fresh plumage in autumn the sexes are very similar. The head is still more boldly patterned than most similar species. The yellow colour in the supercilium is usually obvious, but may occasionally be surprisingly difficult to discern in the field. The lores and ear-coverts are relatively dark brown and the malar stripe dark brown and quite prominent. Tristram's Bunting, which see for discussion, is very similar in some plumages.

In winter, the Black-faced Bunting is similar in general appearance, and regularly occurs in mixed flocks together with Yellow-browed. Most obvious difference is more prominent supercilium of Yellow-browed. The lateral crown-stripes are darker, and the median crown-stripe is obvious. The dark borders to the ear-coverts are usually more prominent. The upperparts are duller in Black-faced, with rump grey-brown, not rufous-brown.

Rustic Bunting shows a degree of similarity, but nape, rump, and streaking on underparts rufous. The lateral crown-stripes and lores are usually paler, creating a different facial expression, with less distinct supercilium.

North American Savanna Sparrow shows yellow supercilium, and confusion could thus possibly arise. It is a smaller bird, with shorter tail, differing in lacking both white in the outer tail feathers and *Emberiza*-pattern on the tertials. It is also more uniformly greyish in general appearance, with much less prominent lateral crown-stripes, always lacking blackish ear-coverts. The breast is whiter and there is no chestnut stripe along the centre of the mantle.

DESCRIPTION
Adult male breeding Crown black, with white median crown-stripe. Supercilium yellow, white at the rear. Lores and ear-coverts blackish, a small white spot in the upper rear corner. There is sometimes a faint brownish tinge to the ear-coverts. Submoustachial stripe and throat white. Malar stripe rather prominent, blackish. Sides of neck and nape grey-brown. Mantle rather pale sandy-grey-brown, streaked blackish, scapulars and central mantle tinged chestnut. Back, rump and uppertail-coverts uniformly rufous-brown, indistinctly streaked. Lesser coverts greyish-brown. Median coverts blackish-brown tipped buffish-white. Edges of greater coverts pale sandy-brown, tips pale buff. Tertials dark brown with rufous-brown edges, showing *Emberiza* pattern. Alula and primary coverts brown. Primaries dark brown with narrow pale edges. Secondaries dark brown with slightly rufescent brown edges. Central tail feathers rufescent brown, the others dark brown. Two, sometimes three, outermost pairs with white wedge on inner web. Underwing-coverts whitish. Breast and flanks washed brownish, distinctly streaked blackish. Belly whitish. Undertail-coverts whitish with dark shaft streaks. Bill flesh-pink, with dark grey on culmen and tip of lower mandible. Tarsus pinkish-flesh. Iris dark chestnut-brown.

Outermost and second outermost tail feathers (T6 and T5) of adult.

Adult male non-breeding Crown blackish, obscured by brown fringes, with sandy-brown median crown-stripe. Supercilium yellowish, particularly above the eye. Lores brown, paler than ear-coverts. Ear-coverts brown, surrounded by narrow blackish border, with a buffy spot in the upper rear corner. Submoustachial stripe and throat buffish-white. Malar stripe dark brown, not always conspicuous. Sides of neck and nape brown. Mantle grey-brown, streaked blackish, scapulars and central mantle tinged chestnut. Back, rump and uppertail-coverts rufous-brown, indistinctly streaked. Lesser coverts greyish-brown. Median coverts blackish-brown tipped buffy. Edges of greater coverts pale rufous-brown, tips slightly paler. Tertials and rest of wing similar to adult male breeding, but slightly more rufous. Tail like adult male breeding. Breast and flanks pale rufous-brown, distinctly streaked blackish. Belly whitish.

First-winter male Like adult male non-breeding on plumage, but tail feathers more pointed. Tail and wings relatively more worn. Some may show streaked rump and uppertail-coverts. Iris dark greyish-brown.

Adult female breeding Very similar to adult male breeding, but lores and ear-coverts paler brown. The feathers of the lateral crown-stripes are fringed brownish, but may wear to become as blackish as adult male. The median

159

crown-stripe is tinged buffish. The dark eye-stripe angles down around the rear ear covert, but the moustachial stripe is lacking or ill-defined. The malar stripe is not as black as in males. The chestnut stripe on the centre of the mantle is slightly paler.

Adult female non-breeding Very similar to adult male non-breeding, and most cannot be sexed on plumage. The feathers of the lateral crown-stripes have on average slightly smaller dark centres and thus broader fringes. However, the differences are very slight.

First-winter female Very similar to adult female non-breeding, but tail feathers more pointed. Tail and wings relatively more worn. Some may show streaked rump and uppertail coverts.

Juvenile Similar to adult female breeding. The lateral crown-stripes are dark brown with sandy-brown fringes, but may appear blackish. Median crown-stripe and supercilium whitish, the latter without yellow. Lores pale brown. Ear-coverts brownish. Submoustachial stripe and throat buffish-white. Malar stripe dark brown. Sides of neck and nape whitish with dark spots. Mantle similar to adult female breeding, but streaking more distinct. Back, rump and uppertail-coverts ochraceous brown, streaked dark brown. Lesser coverts greyish-brown. Median and greater coverts with pointed dark brown centres, showing characteristic rounded tooth, tipped whitish. Tail like first-winter birds. The streaking on the breast is narrow and more distinct than in adults.

SEXING The sexes are very similar. In breeding plumage, males are brighter, with blackish lores and lateral crown-stripes, and white median crown-stripe. The ear-coverts are on average darker than in female. The chestnut stripe on the centre of the mantle is slightly darker and the belly tends to be whiter.

The lores and ear-coverts of female are paler brown and the feathers of the lateral crown-stripes are fringed brownish, but may wear to become as blackish as adult male. The median crown-stripe is tinged buffish. The malar stripe is not as black in females as in males and the chestnut stripe on the centre of the mantle is slightly paler.

In non-breeding plumage, the sexes are even more similar, and most cannot be identified on plumage. The feathers of the lateral crown-stripes have on average slightly smaller dark centres and thus broader fringes in females. However, the differences are very slight.

MOULT AND AGEING Juveniles undergo a partial post-juvenile moult, July-September, involving head, body, lesser and median coverts, and usually innermost greater coverts. Outer greater coverts, primaries, secondaries, tertials and primary coverts are not moulted. Adults moult completely July to September. There is a limited pre-breeding moult in the winter quarters, involving at least parts of the head.

After the post-juvenile moult is completed, ageing is difficult, as characters overlap. As in other species, tail feathers of first-winter birds are more pointed than in adults, but the difference is slight and not always useful. Tail and wings relatively more worn, but this, too, may be difficult to discern. Iris colour is dark greyish-brown in first-year birds, and dark chestnut-brown in adults, but experience or direct comparison is needed to determine the difference. Skull ossification is helpful during autumn. Note that birds with skull ossification almost completed cannot be aged based on this criterion, as some adults

apparently do not become fully pneumatised.

MEASUREMENTS Wing: (max) males 77.5-84.0, females 71.5-78. Tail: males 58.0-66.0, females 55.0-63.5. Bill: (to skull) males 13.4-14.8, females 13.4-15.0. Tarsus: males 19.2-21.5, females 19.2-20.8. P5-P8 emarginated.

GEOGRAPHICAL VARIATION None.

VOICE The song is delivered from a perch in a tree in dense forest. It begins with a characteristic clear drawn-out, almost thrush-like unit, usually followed by two high-pitched notes, ending with a more variable section, e.g. *chueee swii-swii chew-chew-chew*, or *chueee tzrrii tzrrii wee-wee-wee (tzitzi)-tueei*. The song of Tristram's Bunting, which see, is very similar.

The contact call is a short *ziit*, similar to Black-faced Bunting.

HABITS The breeding period is relatively drawn out. It usually begins in mid June, but clutches may be started between early June and mid July. It is not clear whether two broods may be raised. The nest is usually placed 1-2 metres high, rarely near the ground or up to 44 metres, close to the main trunk of a tree or bush, often a low pine or sprue. It is a loose, rather messy, construction, built of dry straw up to 60cm long that often sticks out of the sides. The inner parts are made of finer straw, lined with thin straw and animal hair, often from Elk *Alces alces* or horse, sometimes also moss. Eggs 3-5, lustreless greyish-white or cream-grey, clouded with lilac-grey, with irregular brown lines, dark streaks, or curls. Both sexes incubate 11-12 days. The diet of the young consists mainly of a variety of flying insects and spiders. Presumably the diet of adults is similar during the breeding season, with grasses and herbs dominating the remainder of year. Rather secretive. Often found in mixed flocks with other buntings during migration and in the winter.

STATUS AND HABITAT Uncommon in most of range. Usually found in mixed forests with a good proportion of relatively low conifers along the major rivers and their tributaries. Favoured habitats are along margins of regenerating clearings, but may occur well inside forest. In winter in scrubby and weedy areas, often near edges of forest.

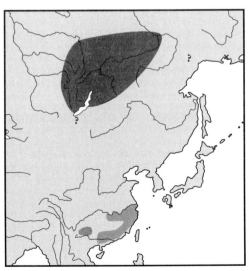

DISTRIBUTION AND MOVEMENTS Exact boundaries of breeding range imperfectly known. Central Siberia, from the upper Nizhnyaya Tunguska River, Bratsk and Irkutsk, in the west, east at least to the Vilyuy River and Yakutsk. Occurrence in Magadan in June may represent vagrant or extreme limit of range. South-eastern limit of range even less well known, but recorded in the Chamar Daban range, south of lake Baikal, and on the Vitim River in the Stanovoy Mountains, east of Lake Baikal.

Southward migration begins August or September, with main passage through north-eastern Mongolia, north-eastern China and Korea from September to November. Annual in small numbers to islands off western Japan.

Winters in central and south-eastern China, from Jiangsu, south to Guangdong, west along the Yangtze to eastern Sichuan. Accidental south to Hong Kong. Main spring passage through north-eastern China during April and May, arriving on breeding grounds late May and June. Vagrant to Britain, the Netherlands and Ukraine.

REFERENCES Alström *et al.* (1991), Cramp & Perrins (1994), Dementiev & Gladkov (1966), Dorzhiev & Jumov (1991), Svensson (1992).

---

25 RUSTIC BUNTING
Emberiza rustica   Plate 10

Described as *Emberiza rustica* Pallas 1776.

A bird of the northern Eurasian taiga, where it breeds fairly commonly in marshy areas, such as willow thickets along fens in damp spruce forest, or along margins of peat bogs. Migrates south-east to wintering grounds in China.

IDENTIFICATION 14-15cm. The adult male in breeding plumage shows a striking black and white head pattern, white underparts, and reddish nape, breast-band, and streaking on flanks and rump. The malar stripe is usually ill-defined and may be lacking altogether. Female is similar to male, but duller, with paler lateral crown-stripes and brown ear-coverts. The reddish colours of nape, rump and breast are marginally paler. Both sexes often raise feathers of crown slightly, particularly when alarmed.

Birds in fresh plumage, particularly first-winter female, are very similar to first-winter Yellow-throated, which see for differences. Confusion may possibly arise between Rustic in fresh plumage and small- or medium-billed western races of Common Reed Bunting, but less contrasting plumage of Common Reed will prevent misidentification in most cases. In Rustic, the supercilium is whiter and more contrasting, and the lateral crown-stripes and rear border to ear-coverts are blacker. A whitish spot on the upper rear corner of the ear-coverts is prominent in Rustic, usually not evident in Common Reed. The malar stripe is obvious in Common Reed, almost always less prominent in Rustic. Even though the rufous colour on the nape of Rustic may be largely concealed in fresh plumage, it often shows through to some extent, particularly as a narrow band between the hindcrown and the upper nape. Common Reed shows no rufous on nape. The tips of the median coverts are pure white in Rustic, forming a prominent wing-bar. In Common Reed, the median covert wing-bar is pale rufous and inconspicuous. The rump is reddish-brown, fringed pale sandy-brown. In western races of Common Reed, the rump is greyish-brown, usually streaked dark; eastern races are very pale on the rump. In Rustic, the underparts are whiter than in Common Reed, with more contrasting streaking, which is often more blotchy and less extensive on the breast, forming breast-band roughly shaped like a shallow V. The streaking both on the breast and flanks is reddish, not dark brown or blackish as in Common Reed.

Little Bunting, which occurs in similar habitats, never shows dark a moustachial stripe that reaches the bill. The supercilium is not as white behind the eye as in Rustic, and shows less contrast with the ear-coverts. In Little, the lores are not darker than the supercilium, unlike in Rustic, which shows obviously darker lores. The rump is greyish in Little, never rufous as in Rustic.

Females of Tristram's differ most notably by showing more prominent lateral crown-stripes, and usually more well-defined dark border to ear-coverts. The nape is never rufous. The flanks and breast are washed rufous-buff, with some indistinct dark streaking. In fresh plumage, the lateral crown-stripes of Tristram's are often less prominent, but in this plumage the breast is even more uniformly rufous-buff.

Male Yellow-browed Bunting shows similar head pattern to male Rustic, but the supercilium is bright yellow, instead of white, the nape is grey-brown, not rufous, and the streaking on the underparts is blackish, not rufous. Females of Yellow-browed show more distinct and longer lateral crown-stripes, usually more well-defined dark border to ear-coverts, more distinct malar stripe and blackish streaking on breast. The flanks are more prominently streaked, and the sides of the breast are washed brownish, not rufous.

Pine Bunting shows some similarities, like rufous rump, white belly and rufous streaking on sides of breast and flanks, but face pattern is indistinct, with less prominent supercilium, and usually very different. The median covert wing-bar is not as prominent as in Rustic, and the nape never shows any rufous.

The juvenile Rustic is very similar to juvenile Common Reed, but face pattern resembles adult female in respective species. In Rustic, the median crown-stripe, supercilium and dark border around ear-coverts are more prominent than in Common Reed, and there is usually some reddish visible on the sides of neck or on the nape. The median covert wing-bar is whiter in Rustic, and the rump and streaking on the flanks are reddish-brown.

DESCRIPTION

Adult male breeding Crown black, with white spot at the rear centre and trace of white median crown-stripe. Supercilium broad and white behind eye, ill-defined in front. Lores and ear-coverts black, a small white spot in the upper rear corner. Throat white, malar stripe ill-defined, not reaching bill. Many have some blackish feathers on the chin, just at the base of the lower mandible. Sides of neck and nape reddish-brown. Mantle and scapulars a mixture of reddish-brown and pale sandy-brown, streaked blackish. Back, rump and uppertail-coverts reddish-brown, fringed pale sandy-brown. Lesser coverts reddish-brown. Median coverts blackish-brown tipped white. Edges of greater coverts pale grey-brown, tips whitish. Tertials blackish-brown, with edges two-coloured, reddish-brown between dark centre and pale edge, forming *Emberiza* pattern. Alula and primary coverts brown. Primaries dark brown with very narrow pale edges. Secondaries dark brown with rufescent brown edges. Tail feathers dark brown with sandy-brown edges. Two outermost pairs with white wedge on inner web. Underwing-coverts whitish. Breast white with a reddish-brown breast-band. Flanks white with prominent reddish-brown streaking. Belly and undertail-coverts unstreaked, white. Bill dark grey, with pinkish-grey base. Tarsus pinkish-flesh. Iris dark chestnut-brown.

♂   ♀

Crown feathers of male and female. Note well-defined tip of male, and diffuse border between dark centre and pale edge of female.

Adult male non-breeding Similar to adult male breeding, but crown obscured by brown fringes. Supercilium, sub-moustachial stripe and throat buffy. Lores and ear-coverts buffy-brown, the latter with dark border, particularly at the rear. Malar stripe dark brown.
First-winter male Virtually identical to adult male non-breeding. Iris duller. Tail feathers more pointed.
Adult female breeding Similar to adult male breeding. Reddish-brown colour generally marginally paler. The median crown-stripe is sandy-brown, narrowly streaked dark brown, lateral crown-stripes dark brown. The supercilium is not as white as in male, but is more prominent in front of the eye. The ear-coverts are brown, paler in the centre. The malar stripe is usually better developed than in males. Uppertail-coverts browner.
Adult female non-breeding Very similar to adult male non-breeding, but crown sandy-brown, streaked dark, without any underlying black pattern showing through. The ear-coverts are browner. The malar stripe is on average more prominent than in males. There is usually less reddish-brown visible on the nape. The breast-band is less solid, often broken into reddish-brown streaking.
First-winter female Virtually identical to adult female non-breeding. Iris duller. Tail feathers more pointed.
Juvenile Resembles first-winter female. Crown more uniformly dark. Supercilium whitish. Median and greater coverts with pointed dark centres. Breast prominently streaked dark brown. Sides of breast streaked reddish-brown. Iris dark grey-brown.

Adult   Juvenile

Median coverts of adult and juvenile. Note dark centre more pointed in juvenile.

SEXING The sexes are very similar, and sexing in the field is not recommended except in breeding plumage, when males are characterised by black lateral crown-stripes, lores and much of ear-coverts, and bright reddish-brown nape, rump and streaking on underparts.
In females the face pattern is less striking. The lateral crown-stripes are not uniformly black, and the ear-coverts are brown, paler in the centre. The malar stripe is usually better developed than in males. The reddish-brown col-

our of the plumage is generally marginally paler, more orange-brown.
In fresh plumage, pale fringes obscure underlying pattern and sexes can only safely be separated in the hand. The most useful difference is the pattern of the crown feathers. Males have blacker and more well-defined dark centres, whereas in females the dark centres are less black, narrower and more diffuse. The reddish-brown bases of feathers of nape and rump differ in the same way as described for breeding plumage.

MOULT AND AGEING Juveniles undergo a partial post-juvenile moult, June-September, duration 50-60 days. It normally involves head, body, lesser, median and greater coverts, and tertials. Primaries, secondaries, primary coverts and tail feathers are not moulted, except sometimes a few median tail feathers. Adults moult completely June to September, duration 50-70 days. There is a limited pre-breeding moult of forehead, crown, ear-coverts and upper throat, March-May.
Ageing in autumn is difficult on plumage. In first-year birds, primaries are slightly more worn than in adults. There may also be a difference between fresh and older, unmoulted, feathers of the tail. The shape of the tail feathers differs between adults and first-year birds in the same way as in most buntings, in that the tips are more pointed in first-year birds. The colour of the iris is useful with experience. In adults, the iris is a clear dark chestnut-brown, whereas in first-year birds it is a duller greyer dark brown. Skull ossification useful in autumn.

MEASUREMENTS Wing: (max) male 74-85, female 70-81. Tail: male 48-59, female 49-57. Bill: (to skull) male 11.6-14.9, female 12.0-15.0. Tarsus: male 18.3-20.3, female 18.4-19.7. P6-P8 emarginated, sometimes faintly on P5.

GEOGRAPHICAL VARIATION Two races are sometimes recognised, although differences slight and boundary between them unclear.
E. r. rustica (N Scandinavia to C Siberia). Described above.
E. r. latifascia (Siberia, roughly part of range east of Lake Baikal) Crown blacker than nominate. Band across breast and streaks on flanks broader and deeper red. Juveniles darker.

VOICE The song is delivered from an elevated perch, usually the canopy of a tree, and is a rather hurried, melodious and mellow warble, *dudeleu-dewee-deweea-weeu*, reminiscent of Garden Warbler *Sylvia borin*, but less harsh.
The common call, given both as a contact call and in alarm, is a sharp *tzik*, very similar to call of Song Thrush *Turdus philomelos*, but often repeated at irregular intervals, especially when disturbed. A high-pitched *tsiee* is sometimes given in alarm.

HABITS Breeding usually begins in May or early June. The nest is built in a sheltered place on ground, e.g. in grass tussock, among thick roots, beside tree or in a hollow tree or a bush. It is a cup of grass, moss, horsetail stems, lichens, leaves, etc., lined with fine plant material, hair and sometimes feathers. There is normally no second brood. Eggs 4-6, moderately glossy greyish-green, greenish-blue to pale blue, finely spotted and blotched with a relatively pale lavender-grey and greenish-brown, sometimes with hairline streaks. Incubation by both sexes 11-13 days. Young fledge after 7-10 days and are cared for by both parents. They are fed invertebrates, such as cater-

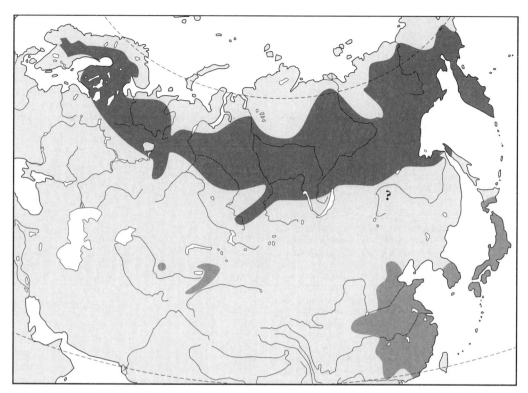

pillars, craneflies and sawflies. Diet of adult mainly invertebrates during breeding season, often those associated with water, e.g. damselflies, dragonflies, stoneflies, caddisflies, but also a variety of others like beetles, caterpillars, craneflies and mosquitoes, spiders, aphids and grasshoppers. After the breeding season, diet changes to seeds, mainly grasses, cereal and sedges, but also seeds and berries from a wide range of herbs, including seeds of conifers. Gregarious outside breeding season. Family parties form small nomadic flocks before onset of migration. During migration and early winter usually in small flocks, but later may form flocks of several hundreds.

STATUS AND HABITAT Common in northern taiga, where it prefers margins between damp spruce, pine or birch forest; also willow scrub along fens or river banks, and sphagnum and cloudberry bogs. In winter and on migration found in a variety of habitats, including woods, cultivated land and other open areas.

DISTRIBUTION AND MOVEMENTS Taiga from northern Scandinavia to Kamchatka. Breeds in south-eastern Norway. In northern Sweden, except in mountain region, locally south to 60°N. Common in Finland south of approximately 68°N, except in south-west. Common in Russia north of approximately 60°N, reaching further south in central Siberia, where range includes the Altai and Sayan Mountains, and comes close to Lake Baikal. Further east, occurs from the Stanovoy Range to the Sea of Okhotsk, on northern Sakhalin and on Kamchatka. Possibly breeds in northern Greater Khingan Mountains in north-eastern China. Northern limit of range not well known, but generally follows extension of taiga.

Southward migration begins in late July or August, with last birds having left breeding area by mid September in many northern areas, lingering through October further south. Migration route from western part of range follows forest regions eastwards, skirting steppes and deserts, bulk of population turning to southward direction only when in eastern Siberia, passing east of Mongolia. Small proportion migrate in south-westerly direction, with annual occurrence in Britain and several records from other north-west European countries.

Winters mainly in Japan, Korea and China. In Japan most common in northern and central Honshu, but regular from southern Hokkaido to Kyushu, rare further south. In China, from Hebei and Shandong in the north, south to Fujian and west along the Yangtze valley to eastern Sichuan and southern Shaanxi. Small numbers winter around the Tien Shan Mountains in southern Kazakhstan and western Xinjiang in China. Leave wintering grounds in China from February and migrate through northern China mainly in March, with few birds left in April. Japanese birds leave during April. Arrival on breeding grounds mainly in May.

Vagrant to Svalbard and Iceland, and several central and southern European countries, including Belgium, Switzerland, Austria, Poland, Czech Republic, Spain, Portugal, Italy, Malta, Yugoslavia, Greece and Bulgaria. Also recorded in Turkey, Egypt, Israel (annual), Syria, Iraq, Kuwait, Iran (rare migrant), Saudi Arabia, United Arab Emirates, Oman, Afghanistan, north-west India, Nepal, and Hong Kong. Rare in Alaska (mostly mid May to mid June), and vagrant to Washington, Oregon, California and Canada (British Columbia), mainly in late autumn or winter.

REFERENCES Anon. (1993), Bezzel (1993), Bradshaw (1991), Cramp & Perrins (1994), Dementiev & Gladkov

163

(1966), Portenko (1930), Shigeta & Mano (1982), Svensson (1992), Vaurie (1956).

26 YELLOW-THROATED BUNTING
Emberiza elegans   Plate 10

Described as *Emberiza elegans* Temminck 1835.
Synonym: *Emberiza elegantula*.

The Yellow-throated Bunting has a disjunct distribution, with a limited range in north-eastern China and adjacent Russia and Korea. Another race inhabits central China. It inhabits dry deciduous and mixed forest, and is fairly common.

IDENTIFICATION 15cm. Erect crest and black mask make the adult male unmistakable. The crest is black and the hindcrown yellow. The striking face-mask is formed by black lores and ear-coverts. The throat is bright yellow, and the remainder of the underparts mainly white, with a striking black crescent on the breast.

Breeding female resembles male, but the crown and ear-coverts are brown. The bright yellow colour of the supercilium and hindcrown of males is replaced by less extensive yellowish-buff. There is usually a pattern of blackish-brown spots on the breast, more or less evidently ghosting crescent of male.

Females and first-winter birds in fresh plumage in autumn display several similarities to Rustic Bunting in similar plumage, but the ear-coverts of Yellow-throated are almost uniformly dark brown, without the obvious dark borders of Rustic. The pale spot in the upper rear corner, characteristic of Rustic, is much reduced. Unlike in Rustic, there is no dark malar stripe in Yellow-throated. The crest of Yellow-throated is usually more prominent, revealing a yellowish-buff hindcrown. In Rustic, the crest is not very prominent, and there is no yellowish tinge on the hindcrown. The nape usually shows some rufous, particularly near the ear-coverts. In Yellow-throated, the nape is greyish-brown, and the lateral crown-stripes are less well-defined at the rear. The throat and breast are pale buffish in Yellow-throated, whitish in Rustic. In Yellow-throated, the central breast is very poorly marked in fresh autumn plumage. The sides of the breast and flanks show relatively narrow, brownish streaking. In Rustic, there is an obvious blotchy breast-band, and the streaking on the sides of the breast and flanks is broader and more prominent. The mantle appears paler in Yellow-throated than in Rustic, with a rufous-brown stripe along the centre of the mantle, and the dark streaking is browner. In Rustic, the mantle appears more uniformly striped. The lesser coverts of Yellow-throated are grey, reddish-brown in Rustic. The wing-bars are buffer and slightly less prominent in Yellow-throated than in Rustic. In Yellow-throated, the rump is grey, much paler than the mantle, while Rustic shows a reddish-brown rump.

DESCRIPTION
Adult male breeding Crown black. Rear crown yellow, occasionally concealed by elongated black crown feathers, but usually conspicuous as latter are almost always held erect. Supercilium whitish in front of eye, yellow behind. Lores and ear-coverts black. Narrow area on chin blackish. Upper throat and submoustachial area yellow. No malar stripe. Sides of neck and nape grey. Mantle a mix-ture of pale sandy-brown and rufous-brown, streaked blackish. There is a rufous-brown stripe along the centre of the mantle. Scapulars rufous-brown streaked blackish. Back, rump and uppertail-coverts pale grey-brown, unstreaked, at the most with some rufous streaking on the back. Lesser coverts slaty-grey. Median coverts blackish with whitish tips. Greater coverts blackish with edges tinged rufous and tips pale buffish, together with median coverts forming double wing-bars. Alula and primary coverts brown. Tertials blackish-brown, showing prominent *Emberiza* pattern, with rather pale buff outer edge. Concealed base of inner web whitish. Primaries and secondaries brown, with narrow pale edge on the outer web. Central tail feathers brown. Remaining ones are blackish-brown, with large white wedge on second outermost pair, outer pair extensively white. Underparts pale buffish-white, except sides of breast which are often smudged grey or buff, and a black crescent-shaped patch on the breast. There is some not very prominent streaking on the sides of breast and rear flanks. Undertail-coverts whitish. Bill blackish. Tarsus relatively pale grey-brown. Iris dark chestnut-brown.
Adult male non-breeding Crown and ear-coverts to some extent obscured by brown fringes. Nape brown instead of grey. Mantle and rump browner, with streaking on mantle less distinct than in breeding plumage. The breast patch is partly obscured by pale fringes.
First-winter male Similar to adult male non-breeding, but dark pattern of head and breast less well developed and more obscured. Throat buffier. Iris dark grey-brown.
Adult female breeding Similar to adult male non-breeding, but crown and ear-coverts browner, never black. The supercilium is buffish, grading into yellowish rear of crest. The throat shows some yellow, but is noticeably buffer than male. The chin is never black. The breast is smudged rufous-buff, with some indistinct rufous-brown streaking. There are often only a few dark spots on the breast, but frequently there is a pattern ghosting male breast patch. The amount of dark streaking on the mantle is reduced compared to adult male.
Adult female non-breeding Similar to adult male non-breeding, but crown and ear-coverts browner. The breast is buffish-brown with some indistinct rufous-brown streaking, showing only some dark spots instead of the breast patch. The throat shows some yellow, but is noticeably buffer than in male. The amount of black streaking on the mantle is reduced compared to adult male.
First-winter female Very similar to adult female non-breeding. The throat is buffish instead of yellowish and the breast is buffish-brown with some indistinct rufous-brown streaking, usually with no concealed dark bases to the feathers, consequently showing no traces of a breast patch. Tail feathers pointed and more worn.
Juvenile Crown, ear-coverts and lores more or less uniform brown. Rear crown paler, sandy-brown. Supercilium rather broad, pale buff. Upper throat and submoustachial stripe buffish-white. Malar stripe dark brown, sometimes ill-defined. Sides of neck and nape grey-brown. Mantle and scapulars a mixture of pale sandy-brown and rufous-brown, streaked blackish. Back, rump and uppertail-coverts pale buffish-brown, unstreaked. Lesser coverts brownish-grey. Median coverts blackish with blunt tooth and pale tips. Greater coverts with blackish pointed centres and pale edges. Rest of wing and tail similar to first-winter birds. The breast is buffish-brown finely streaked dark. Rest of underparts pale buffish-white, with some streaking on the rear flanks. Undertail-coverts buffish-white.

SEXING Males are characterised by blackish ear-coverts, blackish crown, a black crescent on the breast, and yellow throat. A small area on the chin, at the base of the bill, is black. In fresh plumage particularly the breast patch and the yellow throat are partly concealed, but examination in the hand will reveal blackish and yellow feather bases, respectively. The feathers on the crown have prominent blackish centres. Males show more white in the tail than females.

In females, the dark centres on the crown feathers are not as distinct and broad as in males, often just a dark streak. Both crown and ear-coverts are browner. The throat is buffish or yellowish-buff, never pure yellow, and the chin is never black. Sometimes show trace of malar stripe. The breast patch, if present, may be dark brown, but never black, and is also less clear-cut than in male.

MOULT AND AGEING Juveniles undergo a partial post-juvenile moult, June-September. It normally involves head, body, lesser, median and greater coverts, and tertials. Primaries, secondaries, primary coverts and tail are not moulted. Adults moult completely June to September. There may be a limited pre-breeding moult of forehead, crown, ear-coverts and upper throat, March-May.

Ageing in autumn is difficult on plumage. In first-year birds, primaries are slightly more worn than in adults. The tips of the primary coverts are round, and without buffish edges in adults, pointed and with buffish edges in first-winter birds. There may also be a difference between fresh and older, unmoulted, feathers of the tail, but note that the normal colour of the central tail feathers is a quite pale brown. The shape of the tail feathers differs between adults and first-year birds in the same way as in most buntings, in that the tips are more pointed in first-year birds, but the difference is not always obvious. In first-year males, the buffish tips to the black feathers on the crown, ear-coverts and breast are broader and more prominent than in adults. First-winter females are generally darker than adults, and particularly the wing-bars are whiter and more conspicuous in adults. The colour of the iris is useful with experience. In adults, the iris is a clear dark chestnut-brown, whereas in first-year birds it is a duller greyer dark brown. Skull ossification useful in autumn.

MEASUREMENTS Wing: (max) male 71.0-80.5, female 70.0-74.0. Tail: male 63.0-74.0, female 62.0-68.0. Bill: (to skull) male 12.1-13.2, female 12.0-13.5. Tarsus: male 18.3-19.8, female 18.5-19.4. P5-P8 emarginated.

GEOGRAPHICAL VARIATION Three races have been described, varying mainly in coloration. Two are based on birds taken on migration, presumed to breed in the Amur-Ussuri area. The validity of these forms may be questioned. Further studies on the breeding grounds, confirming the existence of two geographically separated races, and clarifying their breeding ranges, are called for.

E. e. elegans (E Siberia, Manchuria). Described above.

E. e. ticehursti (Range not known, alleged to be N Korea and adjacent China) Upperparts paler than nominate, with narrower streaks on the mantle.

E. e. elegantula (C China) Darker than nominate, with blacker streaking on the mantle. Nape dark grey, with more blackish intermixed on rear crown. Black patch on breast more extensive. Streaking on sides of breast and flanks blacker and more extensive.

VOICE The song is a rather monotonous twitter, *tswit-tsu-ri-tu tswee witt tsuri weee-dee tswit-tsuri-tu*, often given with close intervals, sometimes appearing almost continuous. It is given from a perch in a tree or bush, and is quite similar to the song of Rustic Bunting.

The call is an often repeated sharp *tzik*, similar to call of Rustic Bunting, but with a liquid quality to it.

HABITS Breeding begins in May. There are regularly two broods. The nest is placed in a hollow on the ground, under shrubs or bushes. It is a simple structure of loosely packed moss, plant stems, sedge and decayed leaves, sometimes animal hair. Eggs 4-6, glossy whitish, faintly washed lilac-grey, sparingly marked with small dark spots and a few irregular lines. The food during the breeding season consists mainly of insects, but some seeds are also taken. Often seen in small flocks on migration and in winter.

STATUS AND HABITAT Fairly common in relatively open dry deciduous forest. Usually found in hills and on the sides of ridges.

Winters in mixed woodland, shady conifer forest, and along forest edge, in orchards, and in rough vegetation along river banks.

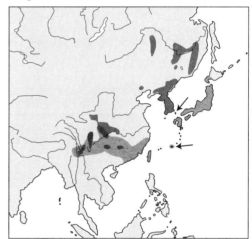

DISTRIBUTION AND MOVEMENTS Breeds in two disjunct populations. In the north-east, breeds in extreme eastern Russia, in the Amur River area, west at least to the Bureya River, and in Ussuriland; and in the Greater and Lesser Khingan Mountains, Heilongjiang, eastern Jilin and eastern Liaoning, China; to Korea. Also on Tsushima Island, Japan. May breed in eastern Hebei. Another race breeds in central China, from southern Gansu and southern Shaanxi, south to Yunnan, Guizhou, and Hunan. The northern population winters from Korea and western Japan, where present from November to early April, south to Guangdong and Fujian, and on Taiwan. The race in central China is partly resident, but most probably winter at low altitudes, and in southern part of range. Winter range includes mountains of north-east Burma, near Yunnan border.

There are at least six records from the western Palearctic – Finland, Denmark, the Netherlands, France (twice) and Germany – but these are not likely to refer to genuine vagrants.

REFERENCES Anon. (1993), Dementiev & Gladkov (1966), Mauersberger & Portenko (1971), Suschkin (1925), Vaurie (1956).

27 YELLOW-BREASTED BUNTING
Emberiza aureola   Plate 11

Described as *Emberiza aureola* Pallas 1773.
Synonyms: *Emberiza sibirica, Euspiza aureola, Hypocentor aureola*.

The Yellow-breasted Bunting is one of the most common buntings in wet meadows south of the taiga. Its pleasant song is one of the most characteristic sounds of Siberia.

IDENTIFICATION 15cm. Adult male in breeding plumage unmistakable. The upperparts, including rump and crown, are rather uniformly dark chestnut, and the face and throat are jet black. A yellow half-collar on the upper breast is separated from the yellow belly by a narrow chestnut breast-band. Unlike other buntings, pure white lesser and median coverts form a prominent patch on the wing, quite similar to the pattern of Chaffinch *Fringilla coelebs*. Golden-breasted Bunting of tropical Africa shows similar wing pattern, but head pattern differs significantly. After post-breeding moult in early autumn, pale fringes obscure breeding plumage and appearance becomes more similar to female, but traces of breeding plumage usually apparent, and white lesser and median coverts still obvious.

Young males apparently do not attain full adult plumage until their second summer. In first and second winter, the plumage is intermediate between adult male and female. Chestnut colour of upperparts is often visible, particularly on crown and rump. In second winter, the white tips on the median coverts are broader than in first-year males and females of all ages. Males frequently show more streaking on the breast than females, and in the second-year plumage there is often a collar of spots on the breast.

The female is characterised by distinct head pattern, distinctly streaked mantle, relatively plain yellow underparts, with streaking restricted to flanks, and comparatively little white in the outermost tail feathers. There is a well-defined pale sandy-grey median crown-stripe, bordered by dark lateral crown-stripes. The whitish supercilium is prominent and rather long, and enhanced by the lateral crown-stripes and narrow dark eye-stripe. The ear-coverts are pale and surrounded by a narrow, distinct dark border which reaches the base of the bill. Unlike most other similar species there is virtually no malar stripe. The nape is relatively pale and contrasts with the dark lateral crown-stripes and darker streaking on the mantle. The rump may be tinged chestnut, but rarely enough to be evident in the field except on close inspection. The tips of the median coverts are white, and normally broader and more prominent than the pale rufous-buff tips on the greater coverts. The colour of underparts vary from whitish-yellow in worn plumage to yellowish with a strong buffish tinge in fresh plumage, particularly prominent on breast and flanks. The streaking is normally restricted to the flanks, while the breast is usually unmarked. In some individuals there may be some fine streaking, and in worn plumage even a trace of a breast-band reminiscent of that of adult male.

Juveniles differ from other species by the same characters as adult and first-year females, but the breast is prominently but finely streaked, unlike adult female. A dark malar stripe may be present in the most well-marked individuals. The dark centres of the median coverts are

more pointed than in subsequent plumages or show a long prominent tooth. In most species, juvenile plumage is only seen on the breeding grounds, but in the nominate race of Yellow-breasted Bunting it is the norm that juvenile birds migrate before the post-juvenile moult. Consequently, most vagrant birds seen in western Europe are in juvenile plumage.

Females and juveniles share general appearance and yellow underparts with Chestnut Bunting, which see for differences. Female and non-breeding male of larger Bobolink *Dolichonyx oryzivorus* are surprisingly similar to female Yellow-breasted Bunting, but lack dark surround to ear-coverts. The tail feathers of Bobolink are sharply pointed and lack white in the outermost pairs. The colour of the underparts in Bobolink is buffish rather than yellow, making them more similar in general coloration to juvenile Yellow-breasted than to adult. However, juvenile Yellow-breasted is streaked on the breast, unlike Bobolink.

Female Rock Bunting shows a similar narrow dark border to the ear-coverts as female Yellow-breasted, but is pale rufous on the underparts and has blue-grey bill. The mantle is less boldly streaked and the rump is more prominently rufous than in female Yellow-breasted Bunting.

DESCRIPTION
Adult male breeding Forehead black. Crown, nape, mantle, back, rump and uppertail-coverts deep rufous-brown. Traces of pale fringes are often present on nape, mantle and rump. Some individuals show some dark streaking on the mantle. These individuals also tend to show more pale fringes, particularly on the mantle, worn brown uppertail-coverts, and on average less white in the second outermost pair of tail feathers. Some also show female-like greater coverts. It is likely that these features are age-related. Lores, ear-coverts and upper throat black. Lower throat bright yellow. Upper rows of lesser coverts dark grey, lower white. Median coverts white. Greater coverts dark brown, with deep rufous-brown outer web, squarely set off from white tip. Tertials with deep rufous-brown outer web, showing *Emberiza* pattern. Alula dark brown, edged pale. Primary coverts brown. Primaries and secondaries dark brown, narrowly edged pale. Tail feathers dark brown, outermost pair with subterminal white wedge, second outermost pair with narrow subterminal white wedge. Sides of breast and narrow band across breast deep rufous-brown. Breast, belly and flanks bright yellow, with blackish streaking on flanks. Undertail-coverts whitish. Upper mandible dark grey, cutting edge and lower mandible pinkish-brown. Tarsus pale brown. Iris dark chestnut-brown.

Crown feathers of female and male. Note well-defined pale tip and chestnut centre of male, and diffuse border between dark centre and pale edge and dark shaft streak of female.

Adult male non-breeding Very similar to breeding male, but with broad pale fringes on upperparts and yellow throat. Lores, supercilium and ear-coverts buffish, the latter surrounded by narrow dark rufous-brown border. Submoustachial area and throat yellowish, without concealed dark bases, malar stripe lacking.

Second winter male Birds intermediate between adult and first-winter male are presumably second-winter males. The head and breast patterns are mostly like adult, but the crown is more obscured than adult; greyish-brown with darker lateral crown-stripess that are dark brown at the front and deep rufous-brown at the rear. The concealed deep rufous bases to the crown feathers often show through. Nape greyish-brown, often with the concealed deep rufous bases showing through. Mantle greyish-brown, the feathers with rufous-brown centres, relatively weakly streaked dark. Back and rump like adult male breeding, broadly fringed greyish-brown, but uppertail-coverts browner. Wing as in adult male breeding, but outer web of greater coverts pale rufous-buff, and the white tips not squarely set off. Underparts like adult male breeding but with a buffish tinge, strongest on the breast, and sides of breast, breast-band and streaking on flanks to some extent obscured by pale fringes, but still clearly visible.

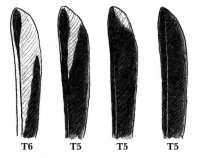

T6   T5   T5   T5

Outermost (T6) and three examples of second outermost tail feathers (T5) of adult indicating range of variation.

Second-summer male Birds tentatively of this age are superficially similar to adult male breeding, but are more prominently streaked black on the mantle. The greater coverts are not as prominently rufous-brown, and the white tip on the outer web is not squarely set off.

First-winter male Resembles adult male non-breeding, but shows very little concealed rufous-brown, except small amounts that may be visible on the rear crown or nape. The lateral crown-stripes are blacker and more prominent. The border around the ear-coverts is blacker. The nape is rufescent greyish-brown, faintly streaked. The mantle is brown, streaked blackish, the feathers lacking rufous-brown centres. Back, rump and uppertail-coverts greyish-brown, faintly streaked dark, tinged deep rufous. Lesser coverts grey. Median coverts blackish with buffish-white tips. Greater coverts dark brown, with pale greyish-brown edges, broader and paler at the tip, forming wing-bar less prominent than that on median coverts. Rest of wing and tail like adult male, but amount of white on second outermost tail feather often reduced. Underparts not as bright yellow. Breast-band narrow and less well-defined, or inconspicuous, largely replaced by some diffuse streaking. Undertail-coverts white or buffish. Iris dark grey-brown.

First-summer male Many are similar to adult male breeding, but several characters more reminiscent of female. Some individuals are actually confusingly similar to adult

females, differing primarily by considerably more heavily worn tertials, primaries and primary coverts. In individuals similar to adult male, the head pattern differs by black area on throat being less extensive. Both the throat and crown are usually to some extent obscured by pale fringes, and a pale supercilium is often present. The mantle is brown, streaked blackish. Back and rump more rufous-brown, fringed greyish-brown. Uppertail-coverts brown. Wing like first-winter male, but edges narrower and bleached. Tail like first-winter male. Underparts like adult male breeding, but less bright yellow, breast-band narrow, lacking or replaced by spots or streaks.

Adult female breeding Similar to first-winter male, but worn and bleached. The well-defined median crown-stripe is pale sandy-grey, lateral crown-stripes brown, streaked blackish. Supercilium, lores and ear-coverts are whitish or tinged buffish, the latter with distinct narrow dark border. Throat buffish-white. The malar stripe is usually faint, and may be lacking. Nape and mantle similar to first-winter male, but base colour paler. Rump and back duller, less rufous. Wings similar to first-winter male, but median covert wing-bar narrower and greater covert wing-bar whiter. Underparts whitish-yellow. Breast-band usually absent, but breast sometimes finely streaked. It is possible that some adult females become similar to first-summer males, making sexing difficult. Iris dark chestnut-brown.

Adult female non-breeding Upperparts similar to first-winter male, but slightly warmer brown. Face and underparts tinged buffish, quite prominently on breast and flanks. Only faint trace of breast-band if any. Undertail-coverts white or buffish.

First-winter female Very similar to adult female non-breeding, but paler below, with some fine streaking. Iris dark grey-brown.

Juvenile Similar to adult female breeding, but plumage fresh. Median coverts with more pointed dark centres or long prominent tooth. Colour of underparts varies from pale yellowish-buff to yellowish with a strong buffish tinge. The breast is prominently but finely streaked, unlike adult female breeding. Malar stripe is usually lacking or is very ill-defined, but may be present in the most well-marked individuals. Iris dark grey-brown.

Adult female   Juvenile

Median coverts of adult female and juvenile. In juveniles the tip of the dark centre is more pointed and elongated, and the pale tips are buffier than in adult females.

SEXING Adult males are easily sexed throughout the year as they show white lower row of lesser and all median coverts. Immature males showing mostly white median coverts and white in the lower lesser coverts can also be reliably sexed. In males in first-summer plumage the head and breast pattern is similar to adult male plumage, with the mantle similar to female. The median coverts are usually more extensively white than in females. Beware that some males in first-summer plumage are so similar to adult females on plumage that they can only be told by their more heavily worn tertials, primaries and primary coverts.

Breeding females lack black face, are streaked on the

upperparts and lack significant amounts of rufous-brown on crown and rump. Up to the completion of the post-breeding moult they can be told from first-year birds by their more worn plumage. However, some individuals showing only a few dark feathers on the throat in summer and a trace of a breast-band are intermediate between first-summer male and adult female. It is not clear whether these are males or females, and if no other evidence supports a verdict they are best left unsexed. Average differences in plumage between first-winter males, first-winter females and adult non-breeding females described above are not recommended for sexing of single birds. Wing length may indicate sex for some of these.

MOULT AND AGEING The timing of the moult differs between the two races. The eastern race *ornata* follows the same moult pattern as most other buntings in that both adults and juveniles moult on the breeding grounds, before migration. The western race *aureola* does not moult until in migration stop-over sites in China. Consequently, unlike all other Palearctic buntings, first-year birds normally migrate in juvenile plumage. Juveniles undergo a partial moult July to mid September (*ornata*) or late August to October (*aureola*), involving at least head, body, lesser, median and greater coverts and tertials. Adults moult completely, July to mid September (*ornata*) or late August to October (*aureola*). Males undergo a limited pre-breeding moult of the head in March-April.

In the western Palearctic, adults retain the breeding plumage throughout the summer and autumn, and are thus easily told from juveniles. Ageing of males is not sufficiently understood. Several different plumage types occur. Typical adult males can be recognised throughout the year by their white median and lesser coverts. They also show more or less uniformly rufous-brown feathers on the mantle, with narrow buffish edges in winter, and no or only narrow black streaking. Those showing dark streaking often also show other features not quite in accordance with typical adult plumage, and may be younger adults. What appear to be second-winter males show a crown pattern mostly like adult male, but mantle like female. Wing like first-winter male, except that the median coverts and lower row of lesser are mostly white. The underparts are slightly paler than adult, but the breast-band is similar to adult. When worn, apparent second-summer males become very similar to adult male breeding plumage, but dark streaking on the mantle relatively extensive and dark bases to the median and lower row of lesser coverts make white patch on wing less uniform. First-winter male resembles adult female non-breeding, and differs from older males by grey lesser coverts, blackish median coverts with narrow buffish-white tips, often reduced amount of white on second outermost tail feather, and breast-band usually inconspicuous, largely replaced by some diffuse streaking. In first-summer plumage male differs from adult and second-summer male by narrow median covert wing-bar and no white in lesser coverts. The mantle is brown with rather broad dark streaking. The underparts are like adult male breeding, but less bright yellow, and the breast-band is narrow, lacking or replaced by spots or streaks. The head pattern is often obscured by pale fringes, and there is usually a pale supercilium.

Juveniles are relatively similar to adult females, but plumage considerably fresher, apart from a number of differences in plumage details. The breast is prominently but finely streaked. In adult females there may be some limited streaking on the breast, but then normally only a very narrow band. Juveniles may also show a dark malar stripe, unlike adult females. The tips of the median coverts are broader and whiter in juveniles, and the dark centres show a long prominent tooth or are more pointed than in adults. After the post-juvenile moult, no reliable age differences in plumage are known between adult and first-year females, except more worn flight and tail feathers in first-year birds. Iris colour and skull ossification useful with experience.

MEASUREMENTS Wing: (max) male 72-82, female 68-78. Tail: male 53-59, female 51-56. Bill: (to skull) male 13.6-15.2, female 13.5-14.5. Tarsus: male 20.0-21.5, female 19.5-20.8. P6-P8 emarginated.

GEOGRAPHICAL VARIATION Two races described, showing differences in brightness of plumage, and in moult strategy.

> *E. a. aureola* (N Scandinavia to Kamchatka) Dscribed above. Populations on Kamchatka and around Sea of Okhotsk somewhat intermediate between nominate race and *ornata*.
> *E. a. ornata* (Japan, Sakhalin, Manchuria and southern parts of Russian Far East) Black forehead extends to above eyes. Darker above. Sides of breast blackish. Underparts on average brighter yellow. Differs from nominate in moult and migration strategies.

VOICE The song is delivered from an exposed perch in the top of a tree or bush. It resembles Ortolan Bunting in segmental structure, but is slower and higher-pitched, *djüü-djüü weee-weee ziii-zii*. There are many variations on the basic theme, but the song usually consists of 5-9 units, arranged in 3-4 short segments with 2-3 units each, rising in pitch between each segment, ending in a very variable phrase. In the many examples of different song types, some are simple variations of the basic theme, *drüü-düü dwee-dwee dwii-dwii zii-o*, others more varied and not always rising steadily in pitch, e.g. *dwee-di-dee wüüü cha-cha zreee*.

The call is a short metallic *tic*.

HABITS Breeding often does not begin until the second half of June, and there is usually only one brood. The nest is placed on the ground, on a tussock, in a depression, in roots, or slightly above ground in willow thickets, shrubs or other vegetation. It is built by female alone, of dry grass and stalks, lined with soft grass, rootlets and sometimes hair. Eggs 3-5, variable, glossy greyish-green or olive-grey to purplish-grey or purplish-clay colour, with dark markings varying from a few spots and short lines to the whole shell covered with dark spots and twisted and knotted lines, coarser and more numerous at the large end. Incubation 13-14 days, by both sexes. Young fledge after 11-14 days and are fed craneflies, grasshoppers, caterpillars, sawflies, beetles and other invertebrates. Diet of adults during the breeding season invertebrates such as beetles, caterpillars, dragonflies, flies, grasshoppers and spiders. Outside the breeding season, mainly cereal grain, rice and grass seeds. Gregarious in flocks, often of hundreds, even thousands, in winter.

STATUS AND HABITAT Common in low-lying wet meadows with tall herbage and scattered willow or birch scrub. Also found in other shrubby areas, particularly riverside thickets, areas with secondary scrub or sparse growth of young forest, birch forest edge, burnt areas and locally peat bogs. In winter frequents cultivations, ricefields, reedbeds, grasslands and scrubby arable land.

168

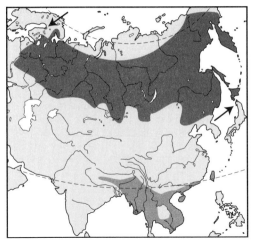

DISTRIBUTION AND MOVEMENTS Breeds in central Finland, from the Gulf of Bothnia to the south-eastern parts of the country. Range in European Russia generally between 53°N and 67°N, but occurs further north around the White Sea and on the southern Kola peninsula. In the Volga valley, found south to about 51°N in the region of Saratov. In the west, range extends to Novgorod in Russia, Smolensk in easternmost Belarus, and the Chernigov region in north-eastern Ukraine. Distribution extends eastwards to the Pacific Ocean, from the Anadyr area in the north, to Korea in the south including Kamchatka, Sakhalin, the Kuril Islands, and Hokkaido and northernmost Honshu in Japan. The northern limit of the range is mostly restricted to south of 65°N, but extends to north of Arctic Circle in the Indigirka and Kolyma basins. In western Siberia and northernmost Kazakhstan, normally found north of 53°N, but breeds further south in the Altai Mountains. Also northern Mongolia, Manchuria to Hebei, in China, and Korea.

Western populations vacate the breeding grounds between late July and early September, to migrate in an easterly direction. Northern and north-eastern populations follow the same timetable, but the race *ornata* leaves breeding grounds 6-9 weeks later than *aureola*. Japanese breeders migrate west to the continent directly, not via the main islands of Japan, although there are scattered records throughout the country to the southernmost Nansei Islands. In many parts of western Siberia, migration reaches a peak in late August, and in north-eastern China passage continues during a more prolonged period August-October. Stops over in large numbers to moult in the Yangtze Valley, from late August to October. Southward migration then recommences in October, with peak movement mid-October to mid-November. Arrives on the wintering grounds from October.

Winters commonly from central and eastern Nepal; Bangladesh; north-eastern India; Burma; and southern China, east to Guangdong; south to Indochina and Thailand, where it appears to be absent from the eastern parts of the country. Uncommon further south in peninsular Thailand and northern Malaysia. Uncommon in Taiwan in winter.

Northward migration begins in early April, with a few birds remaining until May. Peak migration through north-eastern China between end of April and end of May. In the south-eastern parts of the range, most birds reach the breeding grounds in early May, while in northernmost part of range and in the extreme west, the first birds normally do not arrive until early June.

Annual in Britain, Sweden and Norway. Vagrant to Iceland, Ireland, France, Belgium, the Netherlands, Germany, Spain, Denmark, Poland, Latvia, Estonia, Czech Republic, Italy, Malta, Greece, Cyprus, Turkey, Israel, Jordan, Egypt, Iran, United Arab Emirates, Oman, Pakistan, Nicobar Islands, Philippines, Borneo and Alaska.

REFERENCES Alström *et al.* (1991), Anon. (1993), Bezzel (1993), Cramp & Perrins (1994), Dementiev & Gladkov (1966), Dorzhiev & Jumov (1991), Harrop (1993), Johansen(1944), Stresemann (1969), Svensson (1992), Vaurie (1956), Wallschläger (1983).

28   CHESTNUT BUNTING
Emberiza rutila   Plate 11

Described as *Emberiza rutila* Pallas 1776. Monotypic.

The Chestnut Bunting is fairly common and its pleasant song is often heard from ridges in mixed Siberian forests.

IDENTIFICATION 14cm. The adult male is unmistakable. The head, breast and upperparts, including wing-coverts, are uniformly chestnut and the belly is yellow, sharply set off from the rufous breast. In fresh plumage in autumn and winter pale fringes obscure the rufous colour slightly, particularly on supercilium and throat. However, the male plumage is still obvious. What appear to be third calendar year males in spring are similar to adult males, but have paler throat, dark-centred wing-coverts and pale narrow wing-bars. First-year males in fresh plumage in autumn are very similar to females, differing only in that some rufous may be visible on ear-coverts or breast. After a pre-breeding moult in late spring they become more similar to adult males.

Females are relatively nondescript, but are characterised by combination of rufous rump, yellow belly and lack of white in the outer tail feathers. Female Yellowhammer is similar in some respects, but female Chestnut can be told by less heavily streaked breast and flanks, smaller size, different billshape, shorter tail and almost no white in tail. Unlike in Yellowhammer, the throat is never yellow. Female Yellow-breasted Bunting shares relatively small size and yellow underparts, but shows more distinct head pattern and white in the outer tail feathers. In Chestnut Bunting the head is greyish-buff and rather featureless, usually showing some contrast with the yellow underparts. The ear-coverts are rather uniform in colour, and the lateral and median crown-stripes are not very prominent. However, the malar stripe is usually quite prominent. In Yellow-breasted Bunting the crown-stripes and supercilium are prominent, and the ear-coverts pale with a narrow and distinct dark border, but the malar stripe is indistinct. The almost unstreaked rufous rump of Chestnut Bunting is strikingly different in colour from mantle. In female Yellow-breasted Bunting the rump is browner, only slightly more rufous than the mantle, and shows dark streaking. The wing-bars of Chestnut are buffish and rather indistinct, particularly on the median coverts, whiter and more prominent in Yellow-breasted Bunting. In Chestnut Bunting, the throat is buffish and never yellow, but the undertail-coverts always yellow. In Yellow-breasted Bunting, on the other hand, the throat and breast are often yellow, but the undertail-coverts whitish or buffish, only rarely yellow.

Juveniles are more heavily streaked than adults, and show less rufous on the rump. The supercilium is whiter and more prominent. This may make them appear more similar to Yellow-breasted Bunting, but they still differ by having more rufous on the rump and only very small amount of white in the outer tail feathers. The undertail-coverts are yellowish in Chestnut, whitish in Yellow-breasted. The heavier streaking of juveniles compared to adults also makes them more similar to Yellowhammer, but the streaking on the flanks is noticeably finer and more distinct.

DESCRIPTION

Adult male breeding Head, throat, entire upperparts, including lesser, median and greater coverts chestnut. Tertials similar, not showing typical *Emberiza* pattern, but with most of inner web brown. There may be a few dark markings on the mantle. Alula and primary coverts brown. Primaries and secondaries brown, the primaries with narrow pale edges and the secondaries with narrow chestnut edges. All tail feathers are uniformly brown and unusually pointed. There may occasionally be a very small white area on the tips of the outermost pair. Underparts lemon yellow, with dusky streaking on the flanks. Bill brownish- or bluish-horn. Tarsus pale brown. Iris dark chestnut-brown.

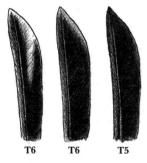

T6   T6   T5

Outermost (T6) and second outermost tail feathers (T5) of adult. Usually shows very little white in tail, feather on left indicating maximum extent of white pattern.

Adult male non-breeding Like adult male breeding, but chestnut part of plumage to some extent obscured by narrow pale fringes, most prominent on the throat and supercilium.

First-winter male Similar to females, but chestnut colour usually visible on crown, ear-coverts or breast. The throat is buffish or pale rufous-white centrally, without chestnut base to the feathers. The feathers on crown have dark centres. Mantle and scapulars olive grey-brown, streaked dark brown. The lesser coverts are often as in adult, but are sometimes tinged olive. Median coverts have dark centres and buffish tips. Greater coverts with dark centres and pale edges, becoming paler at the tip. Juvenile tertials are often retained. First set of adult tertials are not chestnut on the whole outer web.

First-summer male Similar to first-winter male, but worn, showing more chestnut on head and throat. The mantle and scapulars are still olive grey-brown, streaked dark brown. The wings are similar to female.

Second-winter male Birds very similar to adult male non-

breeding, but showing some features more similar to first-winter male are presumably second-winter males. They differ from adults by having broader fringes, obscuring the chestnut colours. The throat is buffish or pale rufous-white centrally, without chestnut base to the feathers. Median coverts have dark bases. Greater coverts have more extensive dark centres. Both median and, at least outer, greater coverts have pale tips wide enough to create faint wing-bars, a feature not present in adults.

Second-summer male Birds presumably this age similar to adult male breeding, but median coverts show dark bases, and greater coverts show dark centres. Both median and, at least outer, greater coverts have pale tips wide enough to create faint wing-bars.

Adult female breeding Crown greyish-brown with darker lateral crown-stripes, usually with some chestnut feathers intermixed. Lores grey. Supercilium buffish, relatively indistinct. Ear-coverts buffish-brown, slightly paler in the centre. Submoustachial stripe buffish-white. Throat whitish-buff. Malar stripe blackish. Nape greyish-brown, indistinctly streaked. Mantle greyish-brown, streaked dark, usually with some chestnut feathers intermixed. Back, rump and uppertail-coverts orange-rufous. Lesser coverts rufous-brown, tinged olive. Median and greater coverts dark brown with buffish edges and tips, forming wing-bars. Tertials dark brown with chestnut-buff edge forming *Emberiza* pattern on outer web, very narrow on inner. Rest of wing and tail like adult male. Breast, belly and undertail-coverts yellow. Breast and undertail-coverts often with some fine streaking. Flanks streaked dark.

Adult female non-breeding Very similar to adult female breeding, but plumage fresh and upperparts and breast browner.

First-winter female Very similar to adult female non-breeding, but the lesser coverts are grey-brown without any rufous tinge. There is no rufous on the crown, mantle or scapulars. The juvenile tertials are generally retained.

Juvenile Similar to adult female non-breeding. The crown is more distinctly streaked and the supercilium is more prominent. The streaking on the mantle is bolder and there is some blackish streaking on the back and rump. Lesser coverts greyish-brown or -rufous. Median coverts blackish-brown with buffish tips, the dark centre narrowing to a blunt tooth. Greater coverts with pointed blackish centre and pale buffish tip. Tertials blackish with rufous edge on the outer web, which shows *Emberiza* pattern. On the inner web the rufous edge is restricted to the tip. Primaries and secondaries like first-winter birds. Breast washed deep buff, prominently streaked blackish. Flanks, belly and undertail-coverts yellow, the flanks prominently streaked blackish.

Juvenile   **Adult**

Median coverts of juvenile and adult. Note long narrow 'tooth' at tip of dark centre in juvenile.

SEXING Unlike females, males always have chestnut bases to feathers of crown, ear-coverts and breast. In adults this is obvious, but in first-winter plumage inspection in the hand may be necessary. The lesser coverts are chestnut in all adult and many immature males, but are sometimes tinged olive, as in females, in first-year males. Females showing chestnut on crown are adults, and can be told from first-year males if correctly aged.

MOULT AND AGEING Juveniles undergo a partial post-juvenile moult July-September, involving head, body, lesser and median coverts, sometimes a few greater coverts and a few tertials. Immature males sometimes have a limited pre-breeding moult, involving at least crown and nape. The timing is insufficiently known, but moulting birds have been recorded in mid May. Adults moult completely August-September, sometimes during migration. Adult males probably attain breeding plumage by abrasion, without a pre-breeding moult.

Adult males are recognised by uniformly chestnut upperparts, throat and breast. Birds similar to adult male non-breeding, but differing most notably in that the median and greater coverts have dark centres and pale tips, are presumably second-winter males. First-winter males are most similar to females, but show some chestnut on crown, ear-coverts or breast. They differ from subsequent plumages by lacking chestnut base to the central feathers of the throat. The feathers on crown have dark centres, and the mantle and scapulars are olive grey-brown, streaked dark brown, without chestnut. The lesser coverts are often as in adult, but may be tinged olive. The rest of the wing is similar to female, often with juvenile tertials retained. Females are more difficult to age, but adults usually show some chestnut intermixed on the crown, and the lesser coverts are rufous-brown. In first-year females there is no chestnut on the crown, and the lesser coverts are grey-brown without any rufous tinge. Ageing according to the shape of the tail feathers is difficult, as the tail feathers are relatively pointed in adults, and there is some overlap in shape. However, the flight and tail feathers are relatively more worn in first-year birds than in adults. Iris colour and skull ossification are useful.

MEASUREMENTS Wing: (max) male 71-79, female 67-75. Tail: male 51-59, female 49-55. Bill: (to skull) male 12.3-14.5, female 12.0-14.3. Tarsus: male 18.4-19.9, female 18.4-19.4. P6-P8 emarginated.

GEOGRAPHICAL VARIATION None; a race *pamirensis* has been described from the Pamirs, but represents a straggler rather than an isolated population.

VOICE The song is usually delivered from a relatively inconspicuous perch on a branch in a tree. It is quite variable and somewhat similar to the song of Pallas's Leaf Warbler *Phylloscopus proregulus*, which is often heard from similar places. It is also reminiscent of part of Tree Pipit *Anthus trivialis* song: *wiie-wiie-wiie tzrree-tzrree-tzrree zizizitt*. The song of Black-faced Bunting is also similar, but usually lower pitched and more uniform, and rarely heard from the same habitat.

The call is a *zick*, quite similar to the call of Little Bunting.

HABITS Breeding usually begins first half of June, immediately after arrival on breeding grounds. The nest is placed on the ground among shrubs, and is built of grass blades, lined with thin black rootlets. Eggs c. 4, white, tinged blue-grey, with brown streaks, black curls and underlying pale violet-brown streaks. Feeds on caterpillars, other insects and seeds during breeding season, mainly seeds during rest of year. In flocks on migration and in winter. Feeds on ground, flying up into trees when disturbed. Relatively shy.

STATUS AND HABITAT At least locally fairly common or common in the southern taiga. Favours relatively open forest with shrubby ground cover. Occurs in both coniferous forest of pine or larch, deciduous of alder or birch, and mixed forest, often on ridges, hillocks or mountain slopes. In winter usually in open woodland, clearings or cultivated land with cover nearby, from foothills to 2500m. Reported from grain fields during migration.

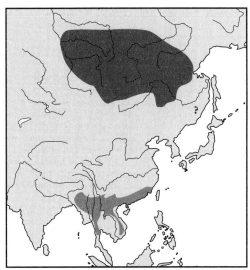

DISTRIBUTION AND MOVEMENTS Breeds in southern Siberia and Dauria. From the Krasnoyarsk area, perhaps as far north as the Podkamennaya Tunguska, eastwards, generally south of 60°N, to the eastern parts of the Stanovoy range. The southern limit of the range seems to include all of Lake Baikal and the Chita region, north of the steppe. Probably breeds in Kentei, Mongolia. Breeds in Greater Khingan Mountains in China, and possibly the Sikhote Alin in Ussuriland, Russia.

Leaves breeding grounds during August. The southward migration is rather slow, as the peak of the passage through NE China and Korea is September-October, in the lower Yangtse Valley October-November, and in Hong Kong October-December. The species is a rare but regular migrant in Japan in October, and has been recorded in winter.

Main winter quarters in central Burma, southern China, western Thailand, Vietnam and Laos. It is scarce but regular in winter in Manipur and northern Cachar, India, perhaps as far west as Sikkim, where recorded March-April.

Northward migration starts in March, with passage through Hong Kong March-April, eastern and north-eastern China and Korea April-May. Rare migrant in Japan in May. Returns to breeding grounds in late May and early June.

Vagrant Tajikistan, Nepal, Sikkim, Chitral, Ladakh, Netherlands, Norway, former Yugoslavia, Malta. Four records from Britain in June are of doubtful origin, but a September adult in 1994 may represent a genuine vagrant.

REFERENCES Alström *et al.* (1991), Anon. (1993), Cramp & Perrins (1994), Dementiev & Gladkov (1966), Dorzhiev & Jumov (1991), Osborn & Harvey (1994), Svensson (1992).

29   GOLDEN-BREASTED BUNTING
Emberiza flaviventris   **Plate 12**

Described as *Emberiza flaviventris* Stephens 1815.
Synonyms: *Emberiza flavigaster, Fringillaria flaviventris, Passerina flaviventris, Polymitra flaviventris.*

The most common and widespread of the African yellow-breasted buntings, occuring in a variety of lightly forested and bushy habitats.

IDENTIFICATION 16cm. A medium-sized bunting, with a bold black and white headpattern, orange-yellow breast, chestnut mantle, grey rump, and prominent white wing-bars. The crown is blackish, with a whitish median crown-stripe. The face pattern is characteristic, with prominent whitish supercilium and stripe on the ear-coverts, separated by blackish eye-stripe, extending onto the lores just in front of the eye. The lateral crown-stripes reach the bill, the eye-ring is black above the eye, and the moustachial stripe is broad, resulting in a different facial expression from other African buntings. The mantle is more or less uniformly chestnut when worn, streaked pale brownish-buff in fresh plumage, with scapulars similar in pattern and colour to the mantle. Females may show some dark streaking on the mantle. Individuals with prominent pale streaking may be confused with Somali Golden-breasted Bunting, which see for differences. The rump is uniformly grey, in obvious contrast with the mantle. At rest the rump is sometimes concealed by the folded wings, but the contrast with the mantle is obvious in flight. The wing-bars are broad and white, and prominent both on the median and the greater coverts. The throat is yellow, usually clearly demarcated from the orange-yellow breast, which fades to whitish on belly and undertail-coverts. The sides of the breast are greyish-pink. Besides Somali Golden-breasted, both Brown-rumped and Cabanis's Buntings, which see for differences, are superficially similar. Major field marks separating the African yellow-breasted buntings, described under respective species, are colour of lores and ear-coverts, colour and amount of streaking on mantle, colour of rump, and colour and extent of wing-bars.

   Juveniles are duller than adults, and differ from other species by combination of pale median crown-stripe, pale centres to the ear-coverts, unmarked breast, and prominent white wing-bar on the median coverts.

DESCRIPTION
Seasonal variation slight. Male and female difficult to separate on plumage. Juvenile slightly different from subsequent plumages. No age differences on plumage known for non-breeding birds.
Adult male breeding Crown black, with a prominent white median crown-stripe. Supercilium whitish. Lores mostly white, but black just in front of eye. Eye-ring pale buff below eye, blackish above. Ear-coverts black, except for whitish stripe from lores to below eye-stripe. Throat yellow. Sides of neck whitish-grey. Nape olive-grey. Mantle and scapulars chestnut, usually with narrow sandy-brown stripes. Back, rump and uppertail-coverts unstreaked grey. Lesser coverts grey, except for lower row which is white. Median coverts white with concealed blackish base. Greater coverts blackish with pale buffish edges and broad white tips. Tertials blackish with even chestnut edge on the outer web, but limited to the tip of the inner web. On the shortest tertial much of the outer web is chestnut. Alula

and primary coverts blackish. Primaries and secondaries blackish-brown, with narrow pale margin on the outer web. The tail feathers are dark brown, the outer three tipped white. Breast rusty-orange. Sides of breast greyish-pink. Flanks pale pinkish-buff. Belly yellow. Undertail-coverts whitish. Upper mandible dark brown, lower brownish-flesh. Tarsus pale brownish-flesh. Iris dark brown.

Tail pattern

Male non-breeding Plumage patterns as in breeding plumage, but crown-stripe and supercilium may be tinged pale rusty.
Adult female breeding Like adult male breeding, but dark pattern on head browner and crown-stripe tinged pale pinkish-buff. Mantle feathers have distinct dark shaft streaks. Back, rump and uppertail-coverts olive-grey, sometimes with broad streaking on the back. The lesser coverts are more brownish-grey than in male. The breast is darker than throat and belly, but not as dark as in male, less clearly set off from the throat.
Female non-breeding Plumage patterns as in breeding plumage, but rusty tinge on crown-stripe and supercilium more evident.
Juvenile Similar to adult female, but browner and duller. Dark parts of head browner and pale parts more strongly washed pale sandy-brown. The throat is sullied buffish-yellow. The mantle is sandy-brown, diffusely streaked dark brown. Back, rump and uppertail-coverts are brownish-grey. The lesser coverts are greyish, the lower row with narrow buffish fringes. Median coverts with relatively narrow white tips and blackish, rather square base, with a sharp tooth along the shaft. Greater coverts with blackish pointed centres and pale buffish-white tips. Tertials blackish with narrow chestnut edge, and dark centres more pointed than in adult. Alula and primary coverts brown, strongly rounded. Primaries and secondaries brown, with narrow pale margin on the outer web. Tail more or less like adult. Breast rusty-orange, with narrow collar of dark spots. Rest of underparts similar to adult female.

SEXING Males are brighter than females, with black and white head pattern. In adult males, the yellow throat is rather distinctly set off from the rusty-orange breast. The mantle is uniform in colour, except for pale fringes to the feathers.

   In females, the dark pattern on the head is browner, and the whitish parts show a buffier tinge than in males in corresponding plumage. Adult female has a duller and less distinct breast-band. The yellow colour of the underparts is less bright in females. Females usually show narrow dark shaft streaks on the feathers of the mantle.

MOULT AND AGEING Post-juvenile moult takes place after the breeding season, which occurs at different times in different parts of the continent (see Habits for summary). The extent of the moult is not entirely clear, but appears to be complete. However, at least some individu-

172

als apparently suspend the moult of the flight feathers. Adults moult completely after the breeding season, during same period as juveniles, but usually finish earlier. No limited pre-breeding moult recorded.

Juvenile differs from adults in several respects. The head pattern is brown and beige, instead of blackish and whitish. The lowest row of lesser coverts is mainly white in adults, but blackish with narrow, indistinct buffish fringes in juveniles. Rest with broad grey fringes and dark base. The white tip of median coverts is narrow and with pointed dark grey centre in juvenile. The dark centres of the tertials are more pointed, with narrower pale edges in juveniles. In adults, much of the outer web is chestnut. The underparts are paler than in adults, often with indistinct streaks. No age-related plumage differences found for certain once the post-juvenile moult is completed. Iris colour and skull ossification probably helpful.

MEASUREMENTS Wing (max): male 80.0-87.0, female 79.5-86.5, tail: male 67.5-75.5, female 68.5-74.5, bill: (to skull) male 13.8-14.4, female 13.8-14.8, tarsus: male 16.3-18.7, female 17.3-18.0. P5-P8 emarginated, sometimes faintly on P4.

GEOGRAPHICAL VARIATION The race north of the tropics is well-defined, but south of the equator the situation is less clear. Five races have been described, but differences relatively slight, and only three are recognised here. The colour of the mantle changes with wear and bleaching, and the difference between fresh and worn plumage in the same individual may be greater than the difference between birds in corresponding plumage from different regions.

E. f. flaviventris (From South Africa north to extreme S Sudan) Including *kalaharica* and *carychroa* (replacing *vulpecula*). Described above.

E. f. princeps (S Angola, Namibia) Very similar to the nominate race, but larger (male: wing 88-93, tail 74.0-80.5) and generally paler, with less prominent breast-band, and more extensively white on flanks. Not all birds from northern Namibia fit the description of *princeps*, and the status and validity of the race may require further study.

E. f. flavigaster (Distributed along the southern edge of the Sahara Desert, from Mali east to Eritrea) Mantle paler, more rufous than chestnut, with almost no black shaft streaks in female. The rump is paler grey, tinged sandy. The breast is paler rusty, similar between the sexes. Yellow colour of underparts paler, with whiter flanks. Nape pinkish-buff, not pale olivaceous grey. There is almost no black on the lores, just a tiny area in front of the eye.

VOICE The song, which is quite variable, is usually delivered from a perch in a bush or a tree. It is sometimes clear, sometimes rather dissonant, but usually a repetition of 4-5 similar phrases, although some song types can include more than one motif. Some examples of common variants could be transcribed as *trzee-trzee-trzee-...* or *sidiüü-sidiüü-sidiüü-...* or *ziziwüü-ziziwüü-zizi wüü-...* or *tr(z)ee-tr(z)ee-tr(z)ee-...* or *tsiew-tsiew-tsiew-...*or *siswüü-siswüü-siswüü-siswüü-si*. Several variants show a resemblance to song of *Parus*.

The flight call is a soft *tsüpp*. A contact call usually heard from perched birds is a buzzing dissonant *trzeeü* reminiscent of sections of song of Bullfinch *Pyrrhula pyrrhula*. Another variant, probably of similar function, is a short

buzzing warble, followed by a drawn-out rising *tüüüü*.

HABITS Breeds mainly during the wet season, but sometimes also before the onset of the rains. Nests may be found virtually year-round, depending on local climatic condition, and 2-3 broods are probably raised. The main breeding period of the nominate race in southern Africa is October-February, with November-December being the period of highest activity. In Zimbabwe the timing is similar, with breeding recorded October-April, with greatest activity October-January. In Zambia and Angola breeding begins in September or October. In much of Kenya, the breeding period starts in December and continues to July, with a marked peak in April. In Zaïre breeding takes place July-November. The race *flavigaster* breeds primarily June-September. The ragged, loose nest is cup-shaped and constructed with dry grass and light sticks or weedy plant stems, lined with fine grass and rootlets, often also with long hair from horse or cattle tails. It is placed in a fork in a sapling or bush 1-2m above the ground, often quite exposed. Eggs 2-3, glossy white, cream or pale greenish-blue, with a ring of black and sepia lines, interspersed with dots and dashes, at the large end. Incubation 12-13 days, fledging after 16-17 days. Diet of adults during the breeding season largely insects such as grasshoppers, ants, termites and beetles, and during remainder of year also seeds from grass, flowerbuds and weeds. Young are mainly fed insects, e.g. caterpillars, grasshoppers, termites and flies. Usually walks on ground, but sometimes hops. Unobtrusive and rather tame. Usually singly or in pairs, but flocks of up to 20may form outside breeding season.

STATUS AND HABITAT Although one of the most widespread of the African buntings, usually never really common. The race *flavigaster* is normally encountered in wooded acacia steppe and dry savanna, while the race *flaviventris* occurs in a variety of dry open woodland habitats, such as forest-savanna mosaic, wooded acacia steppe and mopane woodland, as well as in gardens.

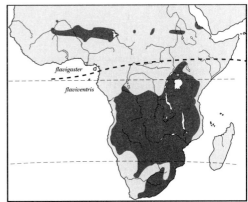

DISTRIBUTION AND MOVEMENTS Apparently resident or dispersive. Occurs in two disjunct populations over large parts of Africa south of Sahara. Avoids the equatorial forest region. The race *flavigaster* is found in a narrow belt, mainly between 12° and 15°N, just south of Sahara, in Mali and Burkina Faso; northern Ghana; southern Niger, east to Zinder; north-western Nigeria; around Lake Chad, and at Abéché in eastern Chad; in Jebel Marra and along 15°N in central Sudan; and northern Eritrea.

The nominate race is widespread south and east of the

equatorial forest, from southern and eastern Zaïre in the west and the extreme southern parts of Sudan and Ethiopia in the east, south to southern South Africa. In Kenya, mainly found above 1400m in the western and central highlands, and in Uganda mainly south and west of the Victoria Nile. Found throughout Tanzania, except coastal lowlands in north-east. Widespread in Zimbabwe, Zambia and Malawi. Distribution in Mozambique not well known, but recorded from most parts. Found throughout interior plateau of Angola, from Lunda, Malanje and adjacent Cuanza Norte, south to Bie and central Huila. Throughout northern Namibia, except coastal desert, south to the Windhoek area. In South Africa, widespread in northern, southern and eastern parts, apparently largely absent from the Karoo, the area between the Orange and Vaal Rivers and Lesotho. Casual in Cameroon.

REFERENCES Bannermann (1948 & 1953), Brown & Britton (1980), Chapin (1954), Ginn *et al.* (1989), Maclean (1985), Priest (1936), Skead (1960 & 1975), Traylor (1960b), Vincent (1949).

30 SOMALI GOLDEN-BREASTED BUNTING
Emberiza poliopleura   Plate 12

Described as *Fringillaria poliopleura* Salvadori 1888. Monotypic.

A bird of dry East African steppe and savanna, replacing Golden-breasted Bunting in much of Somalia and coastal East Africa.

IDENTIFICATION 15cm. A medium-sized bunting, most similar to Golden-breasted Bunting. Shares similar bold black and white head pattern, with broad black moustachial stripe, and prominent white wing-bars. Best difference is the more prominently striped mantle. Compared with Golden-breasted Bunting, the mantle is slightly darker chestnut, conspicuously streaked much paler greyish-buff. In males, the pale stripes are very pale greyish-buff, almost whitish, in females more buffish. There is often some darker streaking intermixed. Golden-breasted often shows some buffish streaking, but never as pale and contrasting as in Somali Golden-breasted. In Somali Golden-breasted, the scapulars are different from the mantle, dark-centred with narrow pale fringes, black with almost whitish edges in males, brownish-black with pale buffish edges in females. In Golden-breasted, the scapulars are similar in pattern and colour to the mantle. In Somali Golden-breasted the back and rump are contrastingly pale, the back with blackish dots. The supercilia almost meet over the bill, narrowly separating most of the lateral crown-stripes from the bill. In Golden-breasted, the lateral crown-stripes reach the bill. In Somali Golden-breasted the lores are white, unlike in Golden-breasted Bunting, where there is a small black area in front of the eye, and the eye-ring is white above the eye. In Golden-breasted, the upper half of the eye-ring is black. The upper wing-bars of Somali Golden-breasted are similar to Golden-breasted, but not quite as broad. The sides of the breast are grey and the flanks whitish and more contrasting than in Golden-breasted. In Golden-breasted Bunting the sides of the breast are greyish-pink, and the flanks not as pure white. In Somali Golden-breasted the yellow colour on

the underparts is paler on the breast and confined to a narrow stripe from the centre of the breast to the belly. The difference in colour between throat and breast is very slight, unlike in Golden-breasted, where there is often a clear division. The white in the outer tail feathers is less extensive than in Golden-breasted Bunting, restricted to the corners of the tail. The primary projection is shorter than in Golden-breasted Bunting, about one-third of the length of the tertials. In Golden-breasted Bunting, the primaries project about half the length of the tertials.

Golden-breasted Bunting, of the race *flavigaster*, shows a face pattern more similar to Somali Golden-breasted than does nominate Golden-breasted Bunting. The black area in front of the eye is tiny, and there is a narrow white area separating the lateral crown-stripes and the bill. However, in *flavigaster* the mantle is paler, more rufous than chestnut, and never appears striped like Somali Golden-breasted.

The juvenile resembles juvenile Golden-breasted, but is more contrastingly striped whitish on the mantle, and the underparts are whiter, with prominent dark spots or streaks on the breast.

DESCRIPTION
Seasonal variation slight. Male and female difficult to separate on plumage. Juvenile slightly different from subsequent plumages. No age differences on plumage known for non-breeding birds.

Adult male breeding Crown blackish-brown, with a prominent whitish median crown-stripe. Supercilium whitish. Lores white. Eye-ring pale buff. Ear-coverts white, with black moustachial stripe which is quite broad at rear. Throat pale yellow. Sides of neck whitish-grey. Nape olive-grey. Mantle chestnut with narrow, very pale greyish-buff stripes, and narrow dark shaft streaks. Scapulars chestnut with rounded dark centres and pale pinkish-buff edges. Back, rump and uppertail-coverts olive-grey, with some dark spots on the back. Lesser coverts grey, with dark base. Median coverts with blackish base. Greater coverts blackish with pale grey or buffish edges and broad white tips. Tertials blackish with even chestnut edge on the outer web, but limited to the tip of the inner web, and a narrow pale pinkish-buff fringe. On the shortest tertial much of the outer web is chestnut. Alula and primary coverts dark brown, the former with narrow whitish edge on outer web. Primaries and secondaries blackish-brown, with narrow pale edge on the outer web and distinctive whitish narrow tips on outer corner of the secondaries. Tail feathers are dark brown, the outer three comparatively narrowly tipped white. Breast yellow, washed rusty-orange, continuing as a narrow yellow stripe down the centre of the belly. Sides of breast greyish, sometimes with a few dark streaks. Flanks whitish. Undertail-coverts whitish. Upper mandible dark brown, lower fleshy-horn. Tarsus grey to yellowish-flesh. Iris brown.

Tail pattern

174

Male non-breeding Plumage patterns as in breeding plumage, but crown-stripe and supercilium may be tinged pale rusty.

Adult female breeding Like adult male breeding, but dark pattern on head browner and crown-stripe tinged rusty-buff. Mantle feathers have distinct dark shaft streaks. Scapulars browner than male. The breast is darker than male.

Female non-breeding Plumage patterns as in breeding plumage, but rusty tinge on crown-stripe and supercilium more evident.

Juvenile Head pattern similar to adult male, but black parts brown. Median crown-stripe, supercilium, lores and ear-coverts pale buff. Throat pale buffy-yellow. Nape olive-brown. Upperparts similar to adult, but paler and duller with sandy-brown stripes on mantle. Uppertail-coverts grey-brown, with indistinct shaft streaks. Lesser coverts brownish-grey, with dark base. Median and greater coverts with pointed dark centres and whitish tips. Tertials blackish with even rufous-brown edge, narrower and more symmetrical than in adult. Alula dark brown, with well-defined pale edge, extending to inner web. Primary coverts dark brown. Primaries and secondaries blackish-brown, with narrow pale margin on the outer web and distinctive white narrow tips on the secondaries. Tail pattern like adult, but less well-defined, particularly on third pair. The tail feathers are narrower and with more rounded tip than in adults. Breast pale yellow, with a brownish wash on the sides, sparsely spotted dark. Sides of breast greyish, sometimes with a few dark streaks. Flanks whitish. The narrow yellow stripe along the centre of the belly is paler yellow than adult. Undertail-coverts whitish.

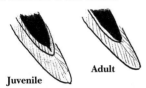

Juvenile   Adult

Pattern of lesser alula feather of juvenile and adult.

SEXING The differences are small, but males are brighter and cleaner in colour. In males, the lateral crown-stripes and border around the ear-coverts are black. However, particularly in fresh plumage the lateral crown-stripes have brown fringes also in males, making close inspection necessary. Males are on average larger than females.

Females are somewhat duller, and have browner lateral crown-stripes and border around the ear-coverts.

MOULT AND AGEING Both juveniles and adults appear to moult completely after the breeding period. The timing of the moult depends on local breeding season, with records of moulting birds from southern Ethiopia from June to August, from northern Somalia December to January, and from southern Kenya from March to April.

No age-related plumage characters are known after moult is completed. Skull ossification and iris colour should provide clues, but no information available.

MEASUREMENTS Wing (max): male 73.5-78.0, female 66.0-73.5, tail: male 65.5-69.5 , female 54.5-69.0, bill: (to skull) male 13.5-15.0, female 13.2-14.9, tarsus: male 16.6-18.0, female 16.1-17.5. P5-P8 emarginated, sometimes faintly on P4.

GEOGRAPHICAL VARIATION None.

VOICE The song is quite variable. It is very similar to the song of Golden-breasted Bunting, and no diagnostic differences are known. It is sometimes clear, sometimes rather dissonant, but usually a repetition of similar notes, although some song types can include more than one motif. Two examples of common variants could be transcribed as *chupi-chupi-chupi-chupi-chupi-chupi* and *treepwee-treepwee-treepwee-treepwee*.

The calls are not well known, but probably similar to calls of Golden-breasted Bunting.

HABITS The timing of breeding depends on local climatic conditions. Breeding records are few, but apparently breeds during and just after the wet season. In coastal and inland southern Kenya breeding activity seems to be at a peak between November and January, and in southern Ethiopia, Somalia, southern Sudan and north-western Kenya between April and June. In northern Somalia, probably breeds October to December. The nest is a cup of stiff grass stems lined with fine grass. It is placed in a fork of a bush. Eggs 2-3, glossy white, with a zone of blackish dots and scrawls and pale undermarkings. The food consists of insects and seeds. Often in small flocks or family parties. Tame.

STATUS AND HABITAT Fairly common in arid tropical sub-desert steppe, edges of wooded steppe, and coastal savanna. Often in thick dry thornbush and fairly open acacia scrub, or in dry scrub at the base of isolated kopjes, particularly in vicinity of water.

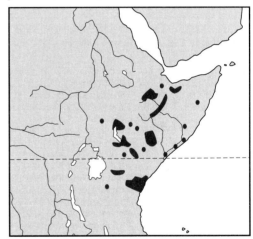

DISTRIBUTION AND MOVEMENTS Resident or dispersive. In Ethiopia, mainly found in the Rift Valley and in the south-eastern parts of the country. In Somalia, known to occur in the north-west and along at least the southern parts of the east coast. Occurrence in interior Somalia and in Ethiopian Ogaden province insufficiently known. Range just extends into extreme south-eastern Sudan. In Kenya most common in the dry north-west, north and east of the highlands, south to the Samburu area. Most common south-east of Lake Turkana. Also relatively common in the area north of Lake Magadi, and in the Tsavo area in the south-east, avoiding the central highlands. Range extends into extreme north-eastern Tanzania. Found in Uganda in the Moroto area.

REFERENCES Archer & Godman (1961), Brown & Britton (1980), Mackworth-Praed & Grant (1955).

31   BROWN-RUMPED BUNTING
Emberiza affinis   Plate 12

Described as *Emberiza affinis* Heuglin 1867.
Synonyms: *Fringillaria forbesi, Emberiza forbesi.*

The Brown-rumped Bunting breeds in dry open forest areas in a narrow belt across the African continent, south of the Sahel region.

IDENTIFICATION 14cm. The smallest of the African yellow-breasted buntings. The bold black and white crown pattern is superficially similar to Golden-breasted Bunting, but the face appears whiter, due to white lores without any black in front of or around eye, and obviously narrower dark lower border to the ear-coverts. In Golden-breasted there is a blackish area, which is connected to the eye-stripe, in front of the eye, and the moustachial stripe is broader. The race *flavigaster* of Golden-breasted, occurring to the north of the range of Brown-rumped, has no black on the lores, but otherwise differs from Brown-rumped in the same way as the nominate race. The bill of Brown-rumped is greyish, unlike Golden-breasted in which the bill is pinkish-brown. Both mantle and rump of Brown-rumped are reddish-brown, showing some faint diffuse streaking, usually appearing similar in colour. The uppertail-coverts are dark grey. When viewed directly from behind, the rump may appear paler and more greyish than the mantle, but never shows the strong contrast that Golden-breasted does. Western populations are paler above, showing more prominent streaking, particularly in fresh plumage. In Brown-rumped the wing-bars are faint or lacking in all plumages. All the other African yellow-breasted buntings show prominent white wing-bars. In hot weather, often holds the wings slightly lifted, with the carpal joint held away from the body in a way that exposes the lesser coverts. The whole wing then appears rather uniform in colour, showing some contrast with the more chestnut scapulars. With the exception of the whitish chin and undertail-coverts, the entire underparts are golden-yellow, with a reddish wash across the breast. In Golden-breasted Bunting the belly and the flanks are whitish or pale pinkish-buff, and the breast-band is more contrasting. The tips of the outer tail feathers are white, showing as white corners to the tail in flight.

The juvenile differs from other species by the same characters as adults, but note that slightly paler tips to median and greaters coverts may form inconspicuous wing-bars. Juvenile Golden-breasted shows little contrast between mantle and rump, but, among other things, differs from Brown-rumped by showing much broader white tips to the median coverts.

DESCRIPTION Seasonal variation marginal. Male and female difficult to separate on plumage. Juvenile slightly different from subsequent plumages. No age differences on plumage known for non-breeding birds.
Adult male breeding Crown black with distinct white median crown-stripe. Supercilium and lores white. Eye-ring white. Ear-coverts white with distinct narrow black border. Chin white. Throat yellow. Side of neck grey, tinged brownish. Mantle chestnut, pale fringes creating streaked appearance. Scapulars slightly darker than mantle. Back chestnut without streaking. Rump chestnut. Uppertail-coverts dark brownish-grey. Tail blackish, with white tips to three or four outer pairs. Lesser coverts grey-brown with

slightly paler edges and tips. Median and greater coverts grey-brown with slightly paler tips. Tertials blackish-brown with traces of pale edges. Primary coverts dark grey-brown. Primaries and secondaries blackish-brown with narrow pale edges. Breast bright yellow with a rusty tinge. Flanks and belly bright yellow. Undertail-coverts whitish. Upper mandible dark blackish-brown, lower light bluish-horn. Tarsus greenish-grey to fleshy-brown. Iris dark brown.

Tail pattern

Male non-breeding Very similar to adult male breeding. White parts of head, and particularly rear parts of median crown-stripe and supercilium, tinged rufous. Mantle more prominently striped due to broader pale fringes. Flight and tail feathers blacker. Tertials blackish-brown with broad chestnut edges on the outer- and tip of inner web.
Adult female breeding Very similar to adult male breeding. White parts of head tinged pale sandy-brown. Lateral crown-stripes and border around ear-coverts blackish-brown. Nape greyer. Mantle shows some dark streaking. The breast is faintly tinged buffish. The tips to the outer tail feathers are not as pure white as in males.
Female non-breeding Very similar to adult female breeding. Sandy-brown tinge to white parts of head slightly stronger. Lateral crown-stripes and border around ear-coverts perhaps a trifle browner.
Juvenile Lateral crown-stripes sandy chestnut, with some dark streaking. Median crown-stripe pale sandy-brown. Lores and supercilium pale sandy-brown tinged rufous. Ear-coverts pale sandy-brown with rusty-brown tinge. Border around ear-coverts dark brown. Chin and throat suffused pale rusty yellowish-buff. Nape rather pale buffish, streaked dark. Mantle more uniformly rufous-chestnut, more distinctly streaked dark than adults. Back, rump and uppertail-coverts unstreaked rufous-chestnut. Lesser coverts rufescent sandy-brown with slightly paler edges and tips. Centres of median and greater coverts pointed, grey-brown with diffuse sandy-brown edges. Greater coverts grey-brown with diffuse rufous edges of even width. Tertials blackish-brown with slightly narrower edges than adult. Primary coverts grey-brown. Primaries and secondaries blackish-brown with narrow pale edges. Underparts blotchy yellowish, tinged rusty particularly on breast. Undertail-coverts whitish.

SEXING The sexes are very similar. In males, the head pattern is black and white, but is tinged brownish or buffish in fresh plumage. Females have on average a stronger rusty- or sandy-brown tinge to whitish parts of head, particularly on the rear part of the median crown-stripe and supercilium, and the dark parts are browner. The dark streaks on the mantle are slightly broader. The demarcation between the white chin and the yellow throat is usually less well-defined in females. However, the differences are often marginal.

MOULT AND AGEING Details of the moult are few, but adults appear to undergo a complete moult after the breeding season, some time between September and January. First-year birds appear to moult during same period, but extent not known. As no specimen showing retained juvenile feathers has been found, the post-juvenile moult may be complete, as is apparently the case in the other African yellow-bellied buntings.

In juveniles the lateral crown-stripes are brown, and pale areas of head washed buffish. There is very little white in the outermost pair of tail feathers. After post-juvenile moult completed, no plumage characters helpful for ageing have been found. Ageing according to skull ossification and iris colour is probably useful, but has not been studied.

MEASUREMENTS Wing (max): male 69.5-76.5, female 68.5-75.5. Tail: male 59.0-66.5, female 54.0-69.0. Bill: (to skull) male 12.7-14.3, female 11.8-14.4. Tarsus: male 15.9-17.8, female 15.9-17.5. P4-P8 emarginated.

GEOGRAPHICAL VARIATION Variation mainly in colour of mantle, with relatively little difference between the races, except *nigeriae*, which is noticeably paler than the other three races.

    E. a. affinis (S Sudan, N Uganda and bordering areas of Zaïre). Decribed above.

    E. a. vulpecula (Adamawa Plateau in Cameroon and S Chad) More uniform, with a deeper shade of reddish-brown on the upperparts than nominate. Moults some time between September and March.

    E. a. omoensis (S Ethiopia) Upperparts darker and duller than nominate

    E. a. nigeriae (Gambia to E Nigeria and extreme N Cameroon) Includes *gambiae*. Paler above than other races, and with all-white submoustachial stripe.

VOICE The song is delivered from a perch in a tree or bush. Individual and geographical variation is unknown, and the following description is based on a few birds of the race *nigeriae*. It is a relatively short, slightly harsh warble *rijidi-durrrr-ridji-widjeri*, quite different from the monotonous song of Golden-breasted Bunting. A rapid, liquid and melodious *pidru-e-driliwi*, somewhat reminiscent of a miniature bulbul, is often heard from perched birds. It sounds almost like song, but is presumably a contact call. The flight call is a short *chip*.

HABITS Breeds during the early part of the wet season, roughly April to July, timing depending on local climatic conditions. The nest remains undescribed, but birds have been observed inspecting cavities in termite mounds, just at the beginning of the nesting season. Food insects, termites. Usually singly or in pairs, feeding on the ground. Hops.

STATUS AND HABITAT Widespread, but apparently nowhere common, in relatively moist open woodlands and forest. Often in areas with high termite mounds.

DISTRIBUTION AND MOVEMENTS Occurs in scattered localities from central Gambia eastwards to Ethiopia and Uganda. The distribution is imperfectly known, and most records in West Africa are from the wet season, May-September. The westernmost occurrences are in the Kiang West region in Gambia and in Guinea-Bissau. Other known localities are along the Niger in south-western Mali, scattered records in Burkina Faso, south-western Niger, north-eastern Ivory Coast and north-eastern Ghana. Widespread in eastern Nigeria, mainly during the wet season May to September; northern Cameroon; southern Chad;

north-western and south-western Central African Republic. In southern Sudan, northern Uganda and bordering areas of Zaïre the species is known from many places, in Uganda mainly in the north-west, but locally south-east to Mt. Elgon. Rather widespread in southern Ethiopia, in the area west of the Omo River and along the eastern edge of the Rift Valley; also recorded north of Ras Dashen in the north. There appears to be a short-distance migration, at least in West Africa. Birds appear to move north during summer, as indicated by local emigration from northern Ghana before the beginning of the wet season, April or May, roughly coinciding with arrival in Gambia at the beginning of the local wet season, starting around June.

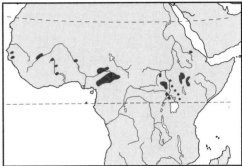

NOTE The name *Emberiza forbesi* is still in common use in the literature for this species. The original description under the name *Emberiza affinis* by Heuglin was of exceptionally poor quality. It was never meant to be a description, as he merely mentions that one individual, in a collection of what he considers to be Golden-breasted Buntings, lacks white wing-bars and is labelled *E. affinis*. The species was not officially acknowledged until it was described as *Fringillaria forbesi*, by Hartlaub in 1882.

REFERENCES Bannerman (1948 & 1953).

32   CABANIS'S BUNTING
Emberiza cabanisi   Plate 12

Described as *Polymitra (Fringillaria) cabanisi* Reichenow 1875.

Synonyms: *Emberiza cognominata, Emberiza orientalis, Fringillaria major, Fringillaria orientalis, Polymitra major.*

Cabanis's Bunting occurs in two disjunct populations, which are sometimes treated as different species. Usually found in woodlands and forest. In most places sparse, but locally fairly common.

IDENTIFICATION 17cm. Of the four species of African buntings with yellow underparts, Cabanis's is the largest, and the only one showing virtually uniformly black ear-coverts. In the nominate race from West Africa, the crown is dark, with no or inconspicuous median crown-stripe. The mantle is very dark blackish-brown with diffuse black streaking, and the rump is more or less concolorous with the mantle. In the race *orientalis*, from the southern parts of East Africa, the lateral crown-stripes are blackish, and the median crown-stripe whitish. The mantle is relatively pale greyish-brown with distinct dark streaking, always lacking reddish-brown colour-tone. The rump is greyish, but does not show any marked contrast with the mantle. Both Golden-breasted and Somali Golden-breasted Bunting show grey rump, obviously different in colour compared to the mantle. The underparts of Cabanis's are yellow with a faint greenish tinge, with no difference in colour between breast and belly. In Golden-breasted, the underparts are bright yellow, with breast washed orange. The wing-bars, especially on the median coverts, are not as broad as in Golden-breasted and Somali Golden-breasted. The juvenile resembles other yellow-bellied buntings, but show as dark ear-coverts.

Black-eared Serin *Serinus mennelli*, which has a similar face pattern and occurs in the same habitat as the race *orientalis*, completely lacks yellow on underparts, has a less striking crown and mantle pattern and narrower wing-bars.

Tail patterns of *E. c. cabanisi* (left) and *E. c. orientalis* (right).

DESCRIPTION Seasonal variation slight. Male and female difficult to separate on plumage. Juvenile slightly different from subsequent plumages. No plumage differences related to age known for non-breeding birds.
Adult male breeding Median crown-stripe very indistinct, dark smoky-grey. Lateral crown-stripes blackish-brown. Supercilium white, rather narrow, especially in front of eye. Lores and ear-coverts blackish-brown, the latter with a small white spot at the rear. Throat white. Sides of neck and nape greyish. Mantle and scapulars dark smoky-grey, diffusely streaked blackish-brown. Back and rump unstreaked dark smoky-grey. Uppertail-coverts dark brown. Lesser and median coverts blackish-brown, the latter narrowly tipped white. Greater coverts dark brown, edged smoky-grey, sometimes with traces of white tips. Alula, primary coverts, primaries, secondaries and tertials dark brown. Tail feathers dark brown, outer three or four pairs tipped white. Breast and belly yellow. Sides of breast greyish. Undertail-coverts white, with concealed dark grey base. Bill dark, with lower mandible fleshy horn. Tarsus fleshy horn. Iris brown.
Male non-breeding Very similar to adult male breeding, but dark parts blacker. May show a paler median crown-stripe. White wing-bar on median and greater coverts broader.
Adult female breeding Similar to adult male breeding. Crown, lores and ear-coverts dark brown, paler than male. Supercilium and throat tinged buffish. Central breast washed orange-brown, rest of underparts yellow.
Female non-breeding Very similar to adult female breeding, but white wing-bar on median and greater coverts broader.
Juvenile Crown uniform, rather dark brown. Supercilium pale rufous. Lores and ear-coverts dark brown. Throat whitish, tinged orange-brown. Sides of neck and nape brown. Mantle and scapulars dark brown, sometimes with

some diffuse streaking. Back, rump and uppertail-coverts unstreaked dark brown, tinged rufescent. Wings rather uniformly brown, with indistinct rufous double wing-bars. Tail similar to adult, but less contrasting. Dark on outer web paler and inner webs off-white. Breast orange-brown. Belly yellow. Sides of breast greyish. Undertail-coverts yellowish.

SEXING Males are characterised by dark grey and white head pattern, or black and white, depending on race. The central breast is concolorous with the belly.

In females the crown, lores and ear-coverts are paler brown and the supercilium and throat are tinged buffy. The central breast is washed orange-brown.

MOULT AND AGEING Both adults and juveniles appear to moult completely after the breeding period, August to December in nominate race, March to May in the south-eastern populations.

No ageing criteria found after moult completed. Skull ossification and iris colour probably helpful, but not studied.

MEASUREMENTS Wing: male 80.0-84.0, female 75.5-78.5. Tail: male 71.0-75.5, female 65.5-70.5. Bill: (to skull) male 14.6-15.8 , female 14.0-15.3. Tarsus: male 17.7-19.0, female 17.2-19.0. P5-P8 emarginated, sometimes faintly on P4.

GEOGRAPHICAL VARIATION Three subspecies have been described, one to the north and two to the south of the equatorial forest. The differences between the two regions are striking, and the two races occurring in the south are sometimes treated as a distinct species, Three-streaked Bunting *Emberiza orientalis*.
 E. c. cabanisi (Sierra Leone to NW Uganda, S Sudan and N Zaïre) Described above.
 E. c. orientalis (S Zaïre and Zambia, Tanzania and to N Mozambique) Has a paler buffy-grey mantle, with distinct blackish streaking, blacker lateral crown-stripes and ear-coverts, and a whitish-grey median crown-stripe. The wing-bars are broader, especially on the median coverts, where the visible part is all white, enhanced by white-tipped lower row of lesser coverts. The throat is yellow like the breast, with only the chin white. Juveniles are streaked on crown, mantle and breast, and have less white on the throat than the nominate race. The pale edges on the median coverts are slightly paler, making the pointed dark centres more prominent. Slightly larger than nominate (wing: male 83.0-88.0, female 78.0-83.5, tail: male 70.5-79.5, female 68.0-74.0). P4 emarginated.
 E. c. cognominata (Angola and along the lower Congo River) Like *orientalis*, but with more white on chin. Crown slightly duller and rump faintly streaked.

VOICE The song, which is usually given from an exposed perch, is a clear and penetrating repetition of the same note, similar to song of Golden-breasted Bunting and Somali Golden-breasted, but higher in pitch and usually starting with a thin, upwardly inflected note. The voice sometimes resembles Great Tit *Parus major*. Common variants could be transcribed as *sweey tswee-tswee-tswee -tswee-tswee*, or *suweeyo chuwee-chuwee-chuwee-chuwee-chuwee*, or *sweey tseweeo-tseweeo-tse weeo-tseweeo-tseweeo*. The song can also be given in a more rapid tempo: *sweey chewichewi-chewichewichewichewi* or *sweey twitwitwitwitwitwitwit*.

The call is a soft whistled *turee*. In flight also *tsipp*. The warning call is a drawn-out, high-pitched sibilant *seeeee*.

HABITS Breeding coincides with the wet season, roughly April to September in the north-western part of the range, and September to March, with a peak in November-December, in the south and east. The nest is placed in dense foliage in bushes, small trees or creepers, usually 1-2m above ground. It is a somewhat bulky cup made of strips of grass, rootlets, weed stems, dried leaves and twigs, lined with finer grasses or fibres. Eggs 2-3, white or pale green or cream, with scrawls and blotches of umber, sepia or grey, sometimes with lilac undermarkings. The food consists of insects, such as grasshoppers and beetles, and to a lesser extent seeds, millet and rice. Often in pairs or family parties on open patches on the ground in the forest.

STATUS AND HABITAT Rather sparse in scrub savanna woodland, forest and woodlands, with little or no undergrowth, often with ephemeral grasses, just north of the tropical rainforest. In the south usually confined to *Brachystegia* forest (miombo woodland), where it may be locally fairly common. Locally also on the edge of moist montane forest. At least in the south-east normally found above 800m.

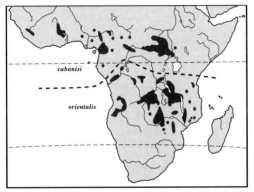

cabanisi

orientalis

DISTRIBUTION AND MOVEMENTS Mainly resident as far as known. Found in a fairly narrow discontinuous belt along and just north of the northern edge of the tropical rainforest, from Sierra Leone to Uganda. Seems to be localised in the west, with occurrence from Loma Mansa in Sierra Leone to Mt. Nimba, with a record from south-western Mali. Also in interior Ghana and Togo. Many scattered localities from southern Nigeria, where locally frequent, through Cameroon, Central African Republic, extreme northern Zaïre, extreme southern Sudan, to north-western Uganda south approximately to the Budongo Forest. In some areas apparently a wet-season migrant, occurring mainly May to September, but patterns of dispersion poorly known. More widespread south of the rainforest, in the west from Mt. Iboundji area in Gabon; along the lower Congo River; and throughout the central plateau in Angola; southern Zaïre; Zambia, except the Luangwa Valley and the south-west; northern and eastern Zimbabwe and Malawi, except central part, to northern Mozambique and western Tanzania, with additional populations across the central parts of the country, to the eastern Usambaras.

REFERENCES Bannerman (1948 & 1953), Chapin (1954), Ginn *et al.* (1989), Grote (1931), Maclean (1985), Priest (1936), Skead (1960), Vincent (1949).

33 BLACK-HEADED BUNTING
Emberiza melanocephala   Plate 13

Described as *Emberiza melanocephala* Scopoli 1769. Monotypic.
Synonyms: *Emberiza icteria, Euspiza melanocephala.*

The Black-headed Bunting is common in maquis, wooded steppe, fields and orchards in south-eastern Europe and Asia Minor. It shows many similarities to the Red-headed Bunting with which it hybridises in Iran.

IDENTIFICATION 16-18cm. The adult male is distinctive throughout the year. In breeding plumage the head is black, the upperparts rufous and the underparts bright yellow. Male Yellow-breasted Bunting shows similar distribution of colours, but is chestnut on crown instead of black, black on the throat instead of yellow, and shows chestnut breast-band and a prominent white flash in the wing. The bright breeding plumage of Black-headed becomes obscured by pale fringes after the partial post-breeding moult in summer, but is still easily recognisable. In the dullest individuals, much of the black colour on crown and eye-stripe may be obscured, but the lores, moustache and lower ear-coverts are always blackish, and the rufous colour of the mantle shows through.

A female in very worn plumage will show traces of male characters, such as greyish crown and ear-coverts, and a rufous tinge to mantle and rump, but is never nearly as bright as a male. The ear-coverts are sometimes greyish, but never blackish as in male.

Females in fresh plumage are easily distinguished from all other buntings, except slightly smaller Red-headed (which see for discussion), by combination of plain plumage, yellow undertail-coverts and lack of white in the tail. The face pattern is greyish-brown, without noticeable supercilium. The crown is faintly and uniformly streaked. The upperparts are pale brownish, streaked dark. The streaking is somewhat variable, usually indistinct, but may be quite prominent, particularly in fresh plumage. The colour of the underparts varies, and may be whitish, buffy or yellowish. The undertail-coverts are always yellow and often also the rump.

Cinereous Bunting of the race *semenowi* shows a varying amount of yellow on the underparts, and may appear quite similar, but always differs by showing white in the outer tail feathers. In Black-headed, the undertail-coverts are always at least as bright yellow as the brightest part of the belly and breast, whereas in Cinereous the throat and breast are deepest yellow, becoming paler towards the rear. The rump is always grey in Cinereous, often tinged yellow in Black-headed.

HYBRIDISATION Hybridises regularly with Red-headed Bunting in northern Iran.

DESCRIPTION
Adult male breeding Crown, supercilium, lores and ear-coverts black. Side of neck and throat bright yellow. Nape, mantle and scapulars rufous. Back and rump slightly paler rufous, tinged yellowish. Uppertail-coverts brown, often with a yellowish-olive tinge. Lesser coverts rufous. Median and greater coverts dark brown with pale buff edges, forming two wing-bars. Tertials dark brown with narrow even fringes. Alula, primary coverts, primaries and secondaries brown with narrow pale edges. Tail feathers brown, the outer one paler, but never white. Breast, belly and under-

tail-coverts bright yellow. The sides of breast are rufous, and there may be some faint rufous streaking on the flanks. The bill is steel-grey, lower mandible with paler cutting edge. Tarsus light brown. Iris dark brown.

Adult male non-breeding Like adult male summer, but especially upperparts obscured by greyish-brown fringes. The crown is rarely completely obscured by the sandy fringes. Instead it appears irregularly spotted. The lores and ear-coverts usually remain black, or at least obviously dark. On the mantle, there is frequently a mixture of female-type feathers, greyish-brown with dark streaks, and rufous feathers.

First-winter male Crown greyish-brown, streaked dark. Supercilium, lores, sides of neck and throat pale buff. Ear-coverts greyish-brown. Nape greyish-brown, faintly streaked. Mantle and scapulars greyish-brown, streaked dark brown. Back similar, but almost unstreaked. Rump like back, sometimes tinged yellow. Uppertail-coverts greyish-brown with dark shaft streaks. Lesser coverts greyish-brown. Median coverts brown with pale buffy fringes, the dark centre showing a tooth at the tip. Greater coverts with dark pointed centres and pale buffy fringes. Tertials brown with even, clear-cut, narrow, pale buffy fringes. Alula, primary coverts, primaries and secondaries with similar fringes. Breast tinged pinkish-buff, especially on the sides, slightly darker than belly, which is often washed pale yellow. Undertail-coverts pale yellow.

Adult female breeding Similar to first-winter male, but slightly paler and greyer. The edges of the feathers of the wings and tertials are more diffuse and less contrasting, without the clear-cut narrow pale buffy fringes characteristic of first-winter birds. Some show some characters of adult male, like rufous tinge to mantle, scapulars, back or sides of breast. The crown or ear-coverts may be relatively dark. Some females may have a rather prominent yellowish-green rump.

Adult female non-breeding The partial post-breeding moult is often very limited. Until the time of the complete moult on the winter quarters, similar to adult female summer, with mixture of varying amount of new feathers mainly on upperparts, and heavily worn wings, tail and unmoulted feathers. After the complete winter moult, there are two different, possibly age-related, plumage types. One is similar to first-winter male, but shows less contrasting edges to wing-coverts, tertials and flight feathers. The other is yellow on throat, breast, belly and undertail-coverts. Birds with whitish or pale buffy bellies are virtually identical to Red-headed in similar plumage, and there is virtually no difference in the colour of the wing-bars between the two species. In birds with yellow underparts, the throat tends to be of the same colour as the breast. The wing-bars are buffy, marginally paler than in Red-headed, sometimes whitish. The forehead and crown are streaked dark, on average more than in Red-headed, and never unstreaked. The rump usually shows less yellow than in Red-headed Bunting. In some individuals there is a rufous tinge to the mantle.

First-winter female Virtually identical to first-winter male.
Juvenile Crown pale golden-buff, with dark brown spots at the rear. Supercilium pale golden-buff. Ear-coverts slightly rufescent greyish-brown. Throat buff. Mantle golden-buff, heavily streaked, almost scalloped in appearance. Back and rump golden-buff with a few tiny spots. Uppertail-coverts slightly darker with dark brown centres. Lesser coverts golden-buff. Median and greater coverts, tertials,

primary coverts, primaries and secondaries brown with golden-buff edges. Breast golden-buff, with scattered spots. Belly and flanks pale buff. Undertail-coverts pale yellow.

SEXING Adult males easily identified throughout the year. Black head and bright yellow underparts of adult male in breeding plumage separate it from all females. After partial moult in summer, especially upperparts of male become obscured by greyish-brown fringes, but lores and ear-coverts remain black or obviously darker than in females. There is frequently a mixture of greyish-brown female-type feathers, and male-type rufous feathers on the mantle, but always males are easily recognised.

In very worn plumage some females often show traces of male characters, like rufous tinge to mantle, scapulars, back and sides of breast, and relatively dark crown and ear-coverts, but are never nearly as bright as males. Adult females in autumn are heavily worn until and during migration. In worn plumage some females to some extent ghost male plumage, but never to a degree that would make confusion with males likely.

First-winter birds are very similar and no sex-related plumage differences are known. Males are on average larger (wing: male 89-102, female 82-94).

MOULT AND AGEING The moult strategy of this species is different from that of all other buntings, except Red-headed. Juveniles attain first-winter plumage by partial moult within a few weeks after fledging. On the wintering grounds they again undergo a partial moult and attain a plumage similar to that of adult of respective sex. Adults moult partially between breeding season and southward migration. The extent of the moult is variable, often extensive in males, and may involve head and upperparts, throat, wing-coverts and tertials, but may be very restricted in females. On arrival on the wintering grounds, adults undergo a rapid complete moult, involving all feathers except those that were replaced after breeding.

In autumn, adult males are easily aged, as they show typical male plumage, albeit somewhat obscured, and worn primaries and tail feathers. Adult females are quite similar to first-year birds, and best age criteria are the heavily worn primaries and tail feathers. In first-year birds these are fresh. After complete moult on arrival on the wintering grounds, no age characters are known. However, it is probable that there is a difference in iris colour, although this has not been studied.

MEASUREMENTS Wing: (max) male 89-102, female 82-94. Tail: male 63-75, female 64-70. Bill: (to skull) male 16.4-18.4, female 16.2-18.5. Tarsus: male 21.3-24.0, female 21.2-23.0. P6-P8 emarginated.

GEOGRAPHICAL VARIATION None.

VOICE Usually sings from a tree, wire or other elevated point. Also has two kinds of song flights, the most common being similar to that of Corn Bunting, a level flight with shallow quivering wing beats and legs dangling. Occasionally also a pipit-like song flight. The song usually starts with a short series of dry *zrt* notes, accellerating into a melodious, quite harsh, more varied part *zrt zrt preepree chu-chiwu-chiwu ze-treeurr*.

On the breeding grounds a variety of call notes are heard, often given in random sequence. Many are similar to House Sparrow *Passer domesticus*, *chleep* or *chlip*, others may be slightly dissonant and similar to Bullfinch *Pyrrhula pyrrhula*, *dzüü*, or have a hard lark-like quality, *prriu*.

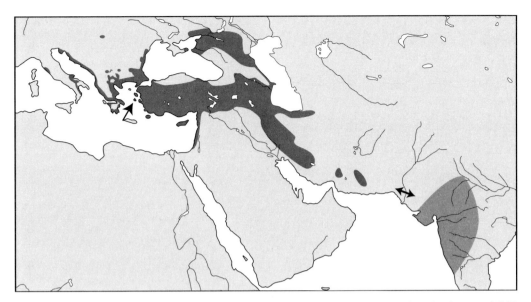

The flight call is a rather hard, deep *tchup,* reminiscent of Yellowhammer, a metallic *tzik,* or *plütt* like Ortolan or Goldfinch *Carduelis carduelis.* Both song and calls are very similar to those of Red-headed Bunting, which see for comparison.

HABITS Breeds from about mid May through June, somewhat earlier in southernmost part of range. The nest is usually placed below 1m in a thorny shrub or a vine, or against stem of thistles, occasionally on ground or higher. It is a loose construction of stalks of herbs, grass and leaves, often with brightly coloured flower-heads on the outside, lined with fine grass, stems, rootlets, hair and sheep's wool. Only one brood is raised. Eggs 3-5, sometimes up to 7, glossy, very pale greenish-blue, finely speckled and spotted with dull reddish-brown and underlying lavender-grey. Incubation 10-16 days. Young fledge after 14-16 days. Role of male in nest building, incubation and rearing of young unclear. Some observations suggest that males contribute very little in these respects, indicating possibility of polygyny; others report male participation. Young are fed invertebrates like crickets and beetles. Diet of adults consists of grass seeds and cereal grains during much of year. During breeding period also a variety of invertebrates such as beetles, wasps, crickets, earwigs, cicadas and larvae. Congregates in flocks at the end of the breeding season. During migration usually in flocks of 10-50, without mixing with Red-headed Bunting. In winter large flocks may form, now often associating with Red-headed Bunting. May roost in enormous concentrations, often together with Red-headed Bunting, Yellow Wagtail *Motacilla flava,* Rose-coloured Starling *Sturnus roseus,* House Sparrow or Yellow-throated Petronia *Petronia xanthocollis.*

STATUS AND HABITAT Common in open areas with scattered trees, scrubs and hedges, usually at lower elevations, but may ascend to 2000m locally. Also found in fairly dense maquis, wooded steppe and thickets. Often associated with cereal and sunflower fields, vineyards, orange groves and similar cultivated areas. Population densities of 30-50 pairs per km² not unusual in optimal habitat, and high concentration of 137 pairs per km² reported. Appears to be declining in areas where land use increases, particularly where hedges and scrubs are cleared or burnt and fields amalgamated for agricultural purposes. The use of pesticides also seem to affect the species adversly.

In winter in cultivated fields and scrubby areas.

DISTRIBUTION AND MOVEMENTS Breeds along eastern coast of the Adriatic Sea, from Slovenia in the north to Albania and Greece in the south. Locally common in southern Italy. Northern limit of range includes southern Serbia, Macedonia and southern Bulgaria and thence north along Black Sea coast to Danube Delta in Romania. Widespread on Aegean Islands, but does not breed on Crete. Widespread in Turkey, but absent from most of Black Sea coastlands. Breeds throughout Armenia and Azerbaijan, but in Georgia present only in the eastern parts. Absent from the Greater Caucasus range. In southern Russia north to eastern Crimea and lower Don, avoiding the arid areas along lower Volga. In the south found along eastern shores of the Mediterranean Sea, in western Syria, Lebanon, Israel and western Jordan, to about 100-150km inland. Further eastward, southern limit of range roughly coincides with southern border of Turkey, extending into mountanous regions of north-eastern Iraq. In Iran confined to the Elburz and Zagros mountains, and locally eastwards to Baluchistan. In the Elburz Mountains ranges east to about south-eastern corner of Caspian Sea.

Breeding grounds are vacated late July-August. Migration in south-easterly direction rather quick, with arrival in India already in August-September.

Winters in western and central India in Rajasthan, Gujarat, Madhya Pradesh (east to Saugor), Maharashtra (east to Nagpur and Nander) and Karnataka (south to Hiriyur). Scarce in Nepal, mainly eastern lowlands. Leaves wintering grounds March-April and, in most of range, arrives on breeding grounds in last third of April and early May.

Probably regular in low numbers during migration in Sinai and Saudi Arabia. Seems to have a propensity for overshooting, mainly in spring, with records from Iceland, Britain, Ireland, Netherlands, Belgium, France, Spain, Denmark, Norway, Sweden, Finland, Poland, Czech Republic, Switzerland, Austria, Malta, Morocco, Algeria, Tunisia, the Baikal area, Thailand and Japan, possibly also Borneo.

REFERENCES Ali & Ripley (1974), Bezzel (1993), Cramp & Perrins (1994), Dementiev & Gladkov (1966), Paludan (1940), Roberts (1992), Shirihai & Gantlett (1992), Stresemann & Stresemann (1969), Svensson (1992), Tucker & Heath (1994), Vaurie (1956).

---

34   RED-HEADED BUNTING
Emberiza bruniceps   Plate 13

Described as *Emberiza bruniceps* Brandt 1841. Monotypic.
Synonyms: *Emberiza icteria, Emberiza luteola, Euspiza luteola.*

The Red-headed Bunting breeds in thickets in open country in Central Asia. It is closely related to Black-headed Bunting and hybridises freely in some areas of overlap.

IDENTIFICATION 16cm. The adult male in summer is unmistakable, but perhaps superficially similar to a few species of weavers. The two most similar species, Rüppell's Weaver *Ploceus galbula* and Cape Weaver *P. capensis olivaceus*, differ in a number of details, most notably shorter tail, longer and more pointed black bill, and prominent yellow edges to the wing-coverts and flight feathers. In breeding plumage, male Red-headed Bunting shows chestnut head and breast and yellow underparts and rump. In some males the amount of chestnut on the head is more restricted, and the whole crown may be yellow. The mantle is yellowish-green, streaked blackish. Unlike adults of other Northern Hemisphere buntings, which undergo a complete post-breeding moult, adult Red-headed and Black-headed Buntings moult only partially before the southward migration. The extent is quite variable, often extensive in males, but may be very limited in females. After the partial summer moult, the bright colours of the male are often obscured to some extent, but still visible enough for a safe identification.

Females and first-year birds are more nondescript, characterised by plain plumage, yellow undertail-coverts and lack of white in the tail, almost identical to corresponding plumage of Black-headed, which see for general description and differences from other species.

Red-headed Bunting is slightly smaller than Black-headed, with a shorter, more conical bill. A bird with a wing shorter than 82mm and and bill shorter than 15.8mm is most probably this species (see Measurements), whereas a bird with wing more than 87mm and bill more than 16.8mm is most probably Black-headed Bunting. The primary projection is often slightly shorter in Red-headed, with four instead of five primaries showing, although there is some overlap. Individual variation and variation during the year make most plumage details difficult to use.

There are some subtle characters that may identify females and first-year birds in all plumages if seen well enough. In most birds there is a slight (or extremely slight) difference between the two species in contrast between the throat and ear-coverts. The ear-coverts of Black-headed are on average darker, often greyer, particularly below and in front of the eye. In Red-headed Bunting the ear-coverts tend to be browner, contrasting less with the throat. The edges of the median and greater coverts are on aver-

age buffier in Red-headed Bunting and whiter in Black-headed, but some individuals of both species show the colour typical of the opposite species. The colour of the wing-bars will in both species go from respective shades of buff when fresh to whitish when worn, and is consequently an unreliable character. The mantle is on average more distinctly streaked in Red-headed Bunting, but there is a great deal of overlap. The back, not to be confused with the mantle, often shows a rufous tinge in Black-headed. This is probably never the case in Red-headed, in which the back is sandy-brown.

After the complete winter moult, there are two different, possibly age-related, female plumage types in both Red-headed and Black-headed Bunting, one with most of underparts yellow, and the other with underparts mainly whitish or buffish, with yellow confined to the undertail-coverts. In birds with yellow bellies, Black-headed can often be told by the throat, breast and belly being of the same colour. In Red-headed, the throat is often whitish-buff or slightly paler yellow than the belly, and the breast is often washed a bit darker buffish. In winter and early spring, when the plumage is fresh, the difference in the colour of the wing-bars is not very pronounced. In both species the wing-bars are buffish, although slightly paler in Black-headed. In any case, they will not appear whitish in Red-headed at this time of year. The forehead and crown are on average less prominently streaked in Red-headed, in some individuals virtually unstreaked. In many Black-headed Buntings there is a perceptible difference in colour between a marginally greyer crown and the more rufous-tinged mantle. However, this difference is slight and, if present, only noticeable under the most favourable circumstances. The rump is usually brighter yellow in Red-headed Bunting.

In birds with whitish or pale buffish bellies, both species are extremely similar and most individuals will have to be left unidentified. In Red-headed, the mantle tends to be on average more prominently streaked, but the overlap is extensive. Besides this, the same differences as described above apply, but are even more subtle. However, there is virtually no difference in colour of the wing-bars, making this character useless in this plumage.

In late spring, with increasing wear, differences in head pattern become more pronounced, with the exception of the amount of streaking on the crown, which is very similar between the species during this period. In female Red-headed Bunting a brownish tinge on the forehead and a yellow tinge on the crown may already be visible. In birds with yellow bellies, the throat is usually noticeably buffier in Red-headed. Both white- and yellow-bellied Red-headed Buntings regularly show a diffuse brownish breast-band. In Black-headed Bunting the breast is usually pale, showing little contrast with throat and belly, but birds with buffish breasts occur. Birds with yellow bellies are also usually brighter yellow below than yellow-bellied Red-headed Buntings, including on the throat. This is the time of year when the colour of the median covert wing-bars is most useful. In most Black-headed Buntings the wing-bars are clearly whiter than in Red-headed.

As the plumage becomes increasingly worn, towards the end of the summer, these differences are further enhanced and traces of male characters become more apparent. A typical worn female Red-headed Bunting will show a rufous tinge on the forehead, a yellow tinge on the crown and mantle, greyish back and yellow rump. There is usually no difference in colour between crown and mantle, although the nape is paler. In contrast, Black-headed Bunting often shows darker and denser streaking on the crown, and the streaking tends to be more extensive towards the rear and shows stronger contrast with the nape than in Red-headed. The mantle is often tinged rufous. The back is tinged rufous and the rump is not as bright yellow as in Red-headed, in many individuals showing no yellow at all. As this is the time of the partial moult, relying on the colour of the median covert wing-bars requires knowledge of the state of wear and extent of moult in any particular individual. In both Red-headed and Black-headed Buntings adult females may moult the wing-coverts before southward migration or they may retain them until the complete moult on the wintering grounds. For example, an autumn adult Black-headed with fresh coverts will show wing-bars obviously buffier than a Red-headed with worn and bleached coverts, the opposite colour difference to what is normally the case.

Birds in first-winter plumage are extremely similar to first-winter Black-headed Buntings and differ from adults of respective species by showing some streaking on the breast, contrasting and sharply set-off whitish edges on the feathers of the wing, particularly visible on the tertials (which are blacker in base colour, compared to the bleached browner feathers of adults), and less yellow on the rump. The species are extremely similar, and most characters overlap to such an extent that they are only useful on series of specimens. There may be a tendency for Black-headed to show blacker and more distinct dark centres to the crown feathers. The contrast between ear-coverts and throat is perhaps less pronounced in Red-headed.

Cinereous Bunting, particularly of the race *semenowi* may appear quite similar, but always differs by showing white in the outer tail feathers. See Black-headed Bunting for further differences from Cinereous Bunting.

HYBRIDISATION Hybrids between Red-headed and Black-headed Buntings are known from the area south of the Caspian Sea. Virtually all certain hybrids are easily identified as such, being males showing a variety of intermediate characters. Many show a mixture of rufous and greenish on the mantle, while others show mantle colour similar to one of the parent species. In most hybrids, the mixture of characters is most prominently expressed in the head pattern. Those with mainly rufous mantle usually show a head pattern most similar to that of Black-headed Bunting, but with elements of yellow ranging from a few specks to a predominantly yellow crown. The ear-coverts are usually still extensively black. Hybrids most similar to Red-headed Bunting may show some rufous on the otherwise mainly greenish mantle, or elements of black in head pattern. As females are so difficult to identify as it is, female hybrids cannot be identified unless they clearly show characters diagnostic of both species.

DESCRIPTION

Adult male breeding Head and breast bright chestnut. In some individuals, only the lores, ear-coverts, throat and central breast are chestnut, with the crown bright yellow. Sides of neck golden-yellow. Nape yellowish-green, sometimes with faint streaking. Mantle and back yellowish-green. The scapulars are often brownish on the outer web. Rump bright yellow. Uppertail-coverts brown, often with a strong yellowish-olive tinge. Lesser coverts yellowish-green. Median and greater coverts dark brown with pale buff edges, forming two wing-bars. Tertials dark brown with narrow even fringes. Alula, primary coverts, primaries and secondaries brown with narrow pale edges. Tail feathers brown, the outer one slightly paler, but never white. Sides of neck and breast bright yellow. Belly and undertail-coverts bright yellow. Bill greyish, with slightly darker tip. Tarsus flesh-brown. Iris dark brown.

Adult male non-breeding Like adult male summer, but with a varying amount of new feathers with pale fringes obscuring the summer plumage. Individuals with a large number of new feathers show grey-brown crown and mantle, the latter streaked dark and often with a rufous tinge. Rufous colour of summer appearance is still visible on ear-coverts and breast.

First-winter male Crown sandy-brown, streaked dark. Supercilium, lores, sides of neck and throat pale buff. Ear-coverts sandy-brown. Nape sandy-brown, faintly streaked. Mantle and scapulars sandy-brown, streaked dark brown. Back similar, but almost unstreaked. Rump like back, often with a yellowish-green tinge. Uppertail-coverts sandy-brown with dark shaft streaks. Lesser coverts sandy-brown. Median coverts brown with pale buffy fringes, the dark centre showing a tooth at the tip. Greater coverts with dark pointed centres and pale buffy fringes. Tertials brown with even, clear-cut, narrow, pale buffy fringes. Alula, primary coverts, primaries and secondaries with similar fringes. Breast tinged pinkish-buff, slightly darker than belly, which is often washed pale yellow. Undertail-coverts pale yellow.

Adult female breeding Similar to first-winter male, but most show some characters of adult male, like rufous tinge to forehead, traces of yellowish-green on the crown, and rather prominent yellowish-green rump.

Adult female non-breeding The partial post-breeding moult is often very limited. Similar to adult female breeding until the time of the complete moult on the winter quarters, with mixture of varying amount of new feathers mainly on upperparts, and heavily worn wings, tail and unmoulted feathers.

After the complete winter moult, there are two different, possibly age-related, plumage types. One is similar to first-winter male, but shows less contrasting edges to wing-coverts, tertials and flight feathers. The other is yellow on throat, breast, belly and undertail-coverts. Birds with whitish or pale buffy bellies are virtually identical to Black-headed in similar plumage, and there is virtually no difference in the colour of the wing-bars between the two species. In birds with yellow underparts, the throat tends to be paler yellow or buffier than the breast. The wing-bars are buffy, slightly darker than in Black-headed, never whitish. The forehead and crown are sometimes virtually unstreaked, and on average less streaked than in Black-headed. The rump is usually brighter yellow than in Black-headed Bunting.

First-winter female Virtually identical to first-winter male.

Juvenile Crown pale golden-buff, with dark brown spots at the rear. Supercilium pale golden-buff. Ear-coverts slightly rufescent sandy-brown. Throat buff. Mantle golden-buff, heavily streaked, almost scalloped in appearance. Back and rump golden-buff with a few tiny spots. Uppertail-coverts slightly darker with dark brown centres. Lesser coverts golden-buff. Median and greater coverts, tertials, primary coverts, primaries and secondaries brown with golden-buff edges. Breast golden-buff, with scattered spots. Belly and flanks pale buff. Undertail-coverts pale yellow.

SEXING Adult males are characterised by bright chestnut head and breast. In autumn, after partial moult, adult males show a varying amount of new feathers, with pale fringes obscuring the typical male plumage. Adult males with a large number of new feathers show grey-brown crown and mantle, the latter streaked dark and often with a rufous tinge, but rufous colour of summer appearance is still visible on ear-coverts and breast.

Some adult females ghost male breeding plumage, by showing chestnut on the forecrown, face and centre of breast, but are never nearly as bright. Adult females in autumn are heavily worn until and during migration. In worn plumage male characteristics are more apparent, but still never to a degree that would make confusion with males likely.

First-winter birds are very similar and no sex-related plumage differences are known. Males are on average larger (wing: male 82-93, female 78-88).

MOULT AND AGEING The moult strategy of this species is different from most other northern passerines, except Black-headed Bunting, in that adults renew their flight feathers in the winter quarters. Juveniles attain first-winter plumage by partial moult within a few weeks after fledging. On the wintering grounds they again undergo a partial moult and attain a plumage similar to that of adult of respective sex. Adults moult partially between breeding season and southward migration. The extent of the moult is variable, and may involve head and upperparts, throat, wing-coverts and tertials, or be more limited, especially in females, with some individuals not moulting at all. On arrival on the wintering grounds, during the period September to December, adults undergo a rapid complete moult, involving all feathers except those that were replaced before the migration.

Birds in first-winter plumage are readily distinguished from adults by their plainer plumage, contrasting with clear-cut fringes on flight feathers and tertials. Unlike adults, they are usually streaked or spotted on the breast. The median and greater coverts have pale buffy fringes and pointed dark centres, showing a tooth at the tip on the median coverts. After the complete moult on the winter quarters no age-related plumage differences are known for certain. However, birds from this time of year appear to fall into two rather distinct groups, one with belly and breast mainly whitish, the other with these parts extensively yellow. It is possible that the paler birds are immatures and the yellow ones are adults, although this needs confirmation.

MEASUREMENT Wing: (max) male 82-93, female 78-88. Tail: male 59-72, female 62-65. Bill: (to skull) male 15.1-17.2, female 12.8-16.8. Tarsus: male 19.6-22.3, female 19.5-21.4. P6-P8 emarginated.

GEOGRAPHICAL VARIATION None.

VOICE Sings from elevated point, like top of bush or telephone wire, or in song flight reminiscent of that of Corn Bunting, but apparently without legs dangling. The song is a quite harsh, monotonous phrase. It is very similar to song of Black-headed Bunting, and diagnostic differences are difficult to point out. The phrase is often delivered in a more hurried tempo. As in Black-headed Bunting, the song often starts with some thin *zreet* notes, e.g. *zreet zreet zeeti-teezi-churri-churri-trrr*. The initial *zreet* notes are rather higher in pitch than the following song. In Black-headed Bunting, the song phrase does not appear to drop in pitch in the same way.

Call is slightly thinner than Black-headed, *twip* or *chip*. Several other call notes are known, e.g. a metallic *ziff*, a harsh *jüp*, similar to Yellowhammer, a *prrit*, and a sparrow-like *tleep*.

HABITS The breeding period is usually from around mid May to late July, males establishing territories about one week before females arrive. Two broods are regularly raised. The nest is probably built by the female alone, and is a cup of fresh weed stalks and grass, lined with dry grass blades and rootlets. It is placed in a bush, tall herbage or thick grass, usually 10-50cm above the ground, rarely higher than one metre, and never on the ground. Eggs 4-5, glossy, very pale bluish- or greenish-white, minutely speckled and spotted with umber and underlying lilac-grey. Dark lines or streaks are normally missing. Incubation 12-13 days, apparently by female alone. Young fledge after about 12-13 days. They are reared by the female alone, and are fed invertebrates such as grasshoppers, caterpillars and beetles. Diet of adults mainly cereal grains and grass seeds, but during the breeding season largely a variety of invertebrates, predominantly grasshoppers, caterpillars and beetles. Gregarious except during nesting period. Congregates in large flocks in winter, often mixing with Black-headed Bunting.

STATUS AND HABITAT In most areas within range common or even abundant in dry, relatively open country. Often found in cultivated areas, and in steppe and semi-desert, where it inhabits scrubby areas and thickets from lowlands to mountains, in extreme cases to 3000m. In winter mainly in cultivated areas, particularly grainfields.

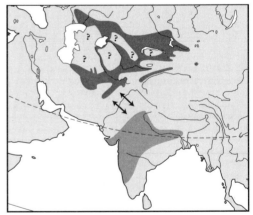

DISTRIBUTION AND MOVEMENTS Found in most of area enclosed between lower Ural River, southern Altai Mountains, western Xinjiang and north-eastern Iran. Boundary of northern distribution is approximately limited by a line along 50°N, from just north of the Caspian Sea, reaching the Volga River, but mainly within Kazakhstan boundary, eastwards to the southern Altai Mountains. In Altai Mountains extends into Russia. Distributed throughout Kazakhstan, Kyrgyzstan, Tajikistan, Uzbekistan and Turkmenistan, avoiding only the open deserts and high mountains. Further east extends into western Mongolia and north-western China, where recorded from most of Dzungaria and Tien Shan foothills in Xinjiang, south to Yarkant. In the south, breeds in north-eastern Iran and in north-western Afghanistan, but exact range in these parts not well known. Breeding has also been recorded near Quetta in Pakistan, but status as regular breeder requires confirmation.

On southward migration, first birds appear in Pakistan in late July and passage continues into September, along a slightly more northerly route than Black-headed Bunting. Most birds have deserted the breeding grounds by the end of August.

In winter distributed across much of India, east to Bangladesh, but only one record from Nepal. Apparently absent from southernmost parts of subcontinent and eastern coastal regions north to Bangladesh.

Northward migration begins in March, but main passage April and early May, arriving on territories during first half of May.

Appears to have a great capacity for extralimital occurence. Recorded as a straggler from all over Europe, including Iceland, but many of these are suspected to be escapes. In Asia, where ornithological activity is lower, recorded from south-eastern Tibet and Beijing, China, and from Japan. Records from Hong Kong (October) probably of this species, but Black-headed Bunting could not be ruled out.

NOTE The species was independently described under both the name *Emberiza bruniceps* and the name *Emberiza icteria* in 1841, but the latter description appeared a few months later. The name *icteria* has been in widespread use in the literature ever since.

REFERENCES Alström *et al.* (1991), Cramp & Perrins (1994), Dementiev & Gladkov (1966), Fairbank (1994), Haffer (1977), Mauersberger & Portenko (1971), Paludan (1940 & 1959), Roberts (1992), Shirihai & Gantlett (1993), Stresemann & Stresemann (1969), Svensson (1992), Vaurie (1956).

35   JAPANESE YELLOW BUNTING
Emberiza sulphurata   Plate 14

Described as *Emberiza sulphurata* Temminck & Schlegel 1848. Monotypic.

The Japanese Yellow Bunting is an inconspicuous inhabitant of Japanese submontane forests. It is uncommon and local.

IDENTIFICATION 14cm. A small, rather nondescript bunting, in summer largely uniformly yellowish-green in appearance, with mantle streaked dark and white double wing-bars. The head is uniformly plain greenish with a prominent white eye-ring. Male in breeding plumage may appear similar to the race *sordida* of Black-faced Bunting, especially when viewed from behind. However, the head of Japanese Yellow Bunting is paler and the throat and breast show no or insignificant contrast with the belly compared to males of *sordida*. The latter appears hooded, with obvious contrast between breast and belly. Blackish lores and small area on chin are similar in the two species, but more well-defined and restricted in Japanese Yellow Bunting.

In fresh plumage in autumn and winter, colour of plumage ranges from a more olive-green of adult males to browner with a rufescent tinge in first-winter females. Also in non-breeding plumage most similar to Black-faced Bunting, but head very plain with no or indistinct supercilium. Streaking on the underparts largely restricted to

flanks. Some birds may show a diffuse trace of streaking on the breast, but never as prominent as in Black-faced Bunting. The malar stripe of Japanese Yellow Bunting is short and indistinct, prominent in Black-faced Bunting. The bill is relatively uniformly blue-grey in appearance, whereas Black-faced Bunting shows a more obvious contrast between dark upper and pinkish lower mandible.

Females and immatures of extralimital Red-headed Bunting are bigger, but may show a superficial similarity. They lack *Emberiza* pattern on the tertials, have no white in the tail, no streaking on flanks and show yellow undertail-coverts.

Small size and greenish plumage may make confusion with Siskin *Carduelis spinus* conceivable. Among numerous differences, the longer bill and tail contribute to bunting-like jizz. The rump is never bright yellow, and the outer tail feathers show white pattern in typical bunting fashion.

DESCRIPTION
Adult male breeding Crown, superciliary area and ear-coverts uniformly greenish, with a grey tinge. Lores and chin blackish. Eye-ring whitish, broken both behind and in front of the eye. Throat dingy yellowish. No malar stripe. Nape green, tinged grey. Mantle and scapulars greyish-green, distinctly streaked black. Back, rump and uppertail-coverts greyish-green, with no or only very indistinct streaking. Lesser coverts greyish-green. Median coverts blackish with whitish tips. Greater coverts blackish with edges grey-green, tinged rufous and tips white, together with median coverts forming prominent double wing-bars. Alula and primary coverts dark brown. Tertials blackish-brown, with rather pale buffish outer edge, showing *Emberiza* pattern. Primaries and secondaries brown, with narrow pale edge on the outer web. Central tail feathers dark brown, tinged greyish-green. Remaining ones are blackish-brown, with large white wedge on second outermost pair, outer pair extensively white. Underparts dingy yellow, tinged greenish, except sides of breast which are smudged greyish-green. Rear flanks distinctly streaked blackish. Undertail-coverts pale yellow. Culmen dark grey, cutting edge of upper mandible and lower blue-grey, without great contrast. Tarsus pinkish-brown. Iris chestnut-brown.

T6   T5

Outermost and second outermost tail feathers (T6 and T5) of adult.

Adult male non-breeding Very similar to adult male breeding, but lores are greyish. The chin is concolorous with the throat. A tiny malar stripe is present. The crown, ear-coverts, sides of neck and nape are uniformly brownish, often tinged grey, and the mantle is faintly tinged brownish. The uppertail-coverts are tipped olive. The wing-bars are buffer and less prominent, particularly on the greater coverts.

First-winter male Very similar to adult male non-breeding, but brownish tinge stronger, particularly on breast. Breast tinged brownish. Flanks tinged greenish-grey. Flight feathers comparatively more worn. Lesser coverts tinged olive. Iris dull dark grey-brown.

Adult female breeding Similar to adult male breeding, but lores are paler, greyish, and there is no black on the chin. The upperparts are generally browner, less green, and the underparts are more buffish-yellow. The breast is tinged brownish, particularly on the sides.

Adult female non-breeding Similar to adult male non-breeding, but head and upperparts tinged browner still. Supercilium indistinct, but slightly more prominent than male, especially in front of eye. Central tail feathers dark brown, without greenish tinge. Underparts buffy-yellow, washed brownish on breast.

First-winter female Similar to adult female non-breeding, but head and upperparts tinged brownish-olive. Some are tinged rufescent. The breast is browner and may be faintly streaked. Lesser coverts tinged olive.

Juvenile Very similar to first-winter birds, except for differently patterned wing-coverts. The head may show some streaking on the forecrown, but is otherwise uniformly coloured, with virtually no contrast between ear-coverts and submoustachial stripe, unlike juvenile Black-faced Bunting. Lesser coverts dark grey with grey-green edges. Median coverts blackish with very pale grey-green tips. The dark centres of both median and greater coverts end in a blunt tooth, broader and more rounded than in adults. The wing-bars are narrower and less prominent compared to adults. The tertials are blackish-brown, with rather pale buff outer edge, showing "*Emberiza* pattern". Tail similar to first-winter birds. Underparts dingy yellowish-white, tinged greenish. Breast grey-green, duller than adult. Rear flanks distinctly streaked blackish. Undertail-coverts pale yellow.

SEXING Males are brighter green and yellow, with a more contrasting greyish back and rump. In worn plumage males have blackish lores and chin. The lores are usually darker in males throughout the year, but the difference is not always pronounced in autumn. The fringes obscuring underlying crown pattern in fresh plumage are olive-grey, relatively narrow and distinctly and squarely set off from the vivid greenish base. The contrast between fringes and feather bases may cause the crown to appear mottled, particularly when slightly worn. The edges of the central tail feathers are grey with a greenish tinge.

Females are generally browner than males. The fringes obscuring underlying crown pattern are broader than in males, and the transition between the brown fringes and the less vivid greenish bases is indefinite. Females are slightly browner on throat and breast, but first-year males may be similar to females in this respect. The breast is often faintly streaked, particularly in first-year females. The supercilium is indistinct in all plumages, but slightly more prominent in females, in which the anterior supercilium is yellowish and relatively well-marked above the lores. The edges of the central tail feathers are tinged brownish in females.

The wing length is useful for sexing. A bird with wing longer than 71mm is usually a male, while one with wing shorter than 69mm is most likely to be female.

MOULT AND AGEING Juveniles undergo a partial moult in July and August, involving body, lesser, median and greater coverts, tertials and often all tail feathers. Some individuals also moult some of the outer primaries. Adults have a complete moult during the same period. There is a limited pre-breeding moult, involving at least a small area in front of the eye.

There are age-related plumage differences, but overlap make these generally unreliable. First-year birds are usually a trifle browner than adults of respective sex, and first-year females usually show diffuse streaking on the breast. Juvenile tail feathers, if retained, are pointed and more abraded. The flight feathers are on average more worn in first-year birds. The iris colour is useful for ageing, but can only be determined in the hand. It is chestnut-brown in adults, clearly brighter than the dark grey-brown colour of first-year birds.

MEASUREMENTS Wing: (max) males 69.5-73.5, females 65.5-70.5. Tail: males 53.5-64.0, females 52.0-56.5. Bill: (to skull) males 11.7-13.4, females 11.9-13.5. Tarsus: males 17.3-19.1, females 17.0-18.6. PP 6-8 emarginated, sometimes with faint emargination on P5.

GEOGRAPHICAL VARIATION None.

VOICE The song is high-pitched and pleasant, usually delivered from an inconspicuous perch in the canopy. It is similar to the song of Black-faced Bunting but shorter, and also to some extent resembles the song of Common Reed Bunting. A singing bird usually alternates between a number of twittering phrases, e.g. *twee twee tsitsit prewprew zrii*, followed by *ziriritt zee-zee tew* and *psew zereret zeetew*. Phrases like this are sometimes followed by various twittering endings. The phrases often end with either a *zrii* or a more lowpitched *tew*. After the end of June, song activity declines markedly.

The call, a *tsip tsip*, is similar to that of Black-faced Bunting, but softer.

HABITS Breeding begins in second half of May, when leaves are fully grown. The nest is built of coarse grass and placed in the lower branches of a bush, usually below 2m, but never on ground. Eggs 3-4, pale brownish-white, more or less glossy, smeared and mottled lavender-grey and pale brown, with spots, streaks and short twisted lines. Diet is not well known. In winter and on migration often in small flocks. Rather unobtrusive.

STATUS AND HABITAT Formerly apparently more common, now rare in most places after decline during the last century. Listed as vulnerable by BirdLife International. Breeds in second growth and forest edge in deciduous and mixed forest in foothills and on the lower slopes of high mountains. Usually found between 500 and 1000m. Found in weedy and bushy areas in winter.

DISTRIBUTION AND MOVEMENTS Endemic breeder in Japan. Mainly found in the mountains of northern Honshu, particularly Mt. Fuji area and the Japanese Alps. Breeds locally in western Honshu. Breeding is also suspected locally in Kyushu. Leaves breeding grounds between late August and October. Most birds appear to leave Japan during winter, with scattered winter records from the southern half of Honshu south to the Ryukyu Islands. Southward migration may follow a more easterly route than northward migration, as autumn records from Korea and Hong Kong are few. Main wintering grounds unknown, but most winter records are from the northern Philippines, Taiwan or Guangdong, China. In Hong Kong mainly recorded during spring passage in first half of April, indicating regular wintering grounds further south. Several records on Shaweishan Island, Jiangsu, China, between late April and early June. Uncommon on passage in southern South Korea in April. First birds return to breeding grounds in late April, but main arrival in May.

REFERENCES Anon. (1993), Austin & Kuroda (1953), Brazil (1991), Collar *et al.*(1994), Jahn (1942).

---

36 BLACK-FACED BUNTING
Emberiza spodocephala   Plate 14

Described as *Emberiza spodocephala* Pallas 1776.
Synonyms: *Emberiza melanops.*

The Black-faced Bunting is widespread and common in a variety of more or less damp deciduous forest habitats in the southern Siberian taiga, China and Japan.

IDENTIFICATION 13.5-16cm. The breeding male is unmistakable. In birds from continental Asia, the head and breast are almost uniformly greyish or greenish, in obvious contrast with the pale yellow underparts. The loral area and chin are blackish, emphasising the rather large and partly pinkish bill. The upperparts are brown, streaked blackish, slightly greyer and unstreaked on the rump. Males from Japan, of the race *personata*, differ by being yellow on throat and breast and brighter yellow below. Adult females of all races in breeding plumage may be similar to non-breeding plumage, or resemble male of respective race, showing rather uniformly grey crown and ear-coverts. They differ mainly in that the lores and chin are never black and the submoustachial stripe and throat are pale. The supercilium may be rather faint, but is normally apparent. The breast may show a greyish wash, but the division from the belly is never as prominent as in male.

In non-breeding plumage females and first-winter males are similar, differing mainly in colour of the base of the crown feathers and in amount of streaking on breast. Adult males are similar to breeding plumage, but head pattern somewhat obscured by chestnut fringes. Female-type birds are rather featureless, lacking obvious distinguishing characters. The face pattern is non-descript, but typical of the genus. The bill is relatively large and pale. The supercil-

ium is marginally duller and less prominent than the submoustachial stripe. In the most similar species, the supercilium is at least as prominent as the submoustachial stripe. The upperparts are more or less similar in all plumages, throughout the year. The double wing-bars are relatively pale. The dark streaking on the underparts is more prominent on the flanks than on the breast.

Differs from non-breeding Common Reed Bunting by duller face pattern. The malar stripe is less prominent. The submoustachial stripe is marginally more conspicuous and paler than the supercilium, but both are less prominent than in Common Reed. The lesser coverts are grey-brown, not rufous as in Common Reed. The wing-bars appear whiter than in Common Reed, particularly noticeable on the median coverts. The streaking on the breast is relatively faint compared to the flanks, where it is blacker and often more prominent than in Common Reed Bunting, particularly compared to races of Common Reed occuring in range of Black-faced. The bill is larger and paler than in Common Reed, with straight culmen.

Dull Yellowhammers and Pine Buntings may appear similar to Black-faced, but show rufous, not unstreaked grey-brown rump. Female Cirl shows grey-brown rump, but differs from Black-faced by characteristic pattern of ear-coverts, uniformly streaked crown, brighter chestnut scapulars, finer streaking on the underparts and greyish bill.

The Song Sparrow shows a more striking head pattern, with particularly median crown-stripe, supercilium and malar stripe more prominent, is usually more heavily marked on the breast, and lacks white in the tail. The Black-chinned Sparrow of southern North America is superficially similar to adult male, but has all-pale bill, lacks contrast between breast and belly, lacks white in the tail, and does not show *Emberiza* pattern on the tertials.

The Dunnock *Prunella modularis* shows very little contrast in the head pattern, lacking median crown-stripe, supercilium and submoustachial stripe. Further differences are the dark and slender bill, the less prominent wing-bars, and lack of white in the tail.

DESCRIPTION
Adult male breeding Whole head grey, except lores and usually chin, which are blackish. The nape is tinged brownish. Mantle pale brown, streaked blackish. The central mantle and scapulars are slightly darker, tinged chestnut. Back brown, with a few indistinct dark streaks. Rump and uppertail-coverts grey-brown, unstreaked. Lesser coverts grey-brown. Median coverts blackish-brown tipped pale buff. Edges of greater coverts more grey-brown, tips almost as pale as medians. Tertials of similar colour as greater coverts, showing *Emberiza* pattern. Alula brown with ill-defined pale edge. Primary coverts dark brown with brownish edges. Primaries dark brown with narrow pale edges, the outer one with whitish edge. Secondaries dark brown, edges with a rufous cast. Tail feathers dark brown. Outermost pair extensively white, including inner parts of outer web. Second outermost pair with white wedge on inner web. Underwing-coverts white. Upper breast grey, continuous from the throat. The border between grey breast and pale yellowish belly is straight and well-defined. Flanks same colour as belly, streaked rufous, streaks becoming blacker towards the rear. Undertail-coverts yellowish-white with greyish base. Upper mandible blackish, with whitish-horn cutting edges, lower mandible pinkish, with small dark tip. Tarsus pinkish-brown. Iris dark

chestnut-brown.

Adult male non-breeding Similar to adult male breeding. The crown, and to a lesser extent the ear-coverts, are partly obscured by chestnut fringes, and streaked dark, but male appearance still apparent. Pattern of throat and breast slightly obscured by pale fringes. Faint supercilium and submoustachial stripe sometimes visible. Overall colour-tone slightly ruddier on upperparts. Belly with stronger yellowish tinge. Edges of wing-coverts more rufous, making wing-bars less contrasting.

First-winter male Wing and tail relatively more worn than in adults, but otherwise similar to adult male non-breeding, except pattern of head often more similar to that of female, due to broader brownish fringes, but separable by grey tinge to sides of neck. Grey breast concealed by pale fringes, throat and chin often without grey on bases of feathers. The streaking on the breast is less prominent than in females. Iris grey-brown.

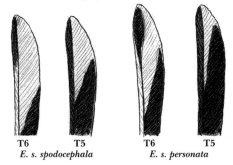

T6   T5   T6   T5
E. s. spodocephala   E. s. personata

Outermost and second outermost tail feathers (T6 and T5) of adult. Note more limited white pattern in *personata* than in nominate race, particularly on T5.

Adult female breeding Similar to adult male breeding, but with different head pattern. The amount of grey on the head varies, and in some females the crown is unstreaked grey, showing a pattern reflecting that of male, but usually the crown is streaked dark chestnut and the nape is browner. The supercilium, submoustachial stripe and throat are usually pale, but it is not unusual that there is some grey on the breast. The lores are never black.

Adult female non-breeding Crown grey-brown with darker brown lateral crown-stripes. Supercilium pale sandy-brown. Ear-coverts grey-brown, with darker brown borders. Submoustaschial stripe pale sandy-brown, paler than supercilium.Throat yellowish-buff, breast washed brownish. Malar stripe dark brown. Nape grey-brown, faintly mottled darker. Mantle pale brown, streaked blackish. The central mantle and scapulars are slightly darker, tinged chestnut. Back, rump and uppertail-coverts brown, with a few indistinct dark streaks. Rump and uppertail-coverts grey-brown, unstreaked. Lesser coverts grey-brown. Wing and tail similar to adult male non-breeding. Flanks washed brownish, streaked blackish-brown. Belly and undertail-coverts yellowish-buff.

First-winter female Similar to adult female non-breeding, but feathers of wing and tail more worn. Iris grey-brown.

Juvenile Similar to first-winter female, but crown almost uniformly grey-brown, indistinctly streaked dark brown. Supercilium and submoustachial stripe slightly darker and less prominent. Ear-coverts more uniform and darker brown. Malar stripe rather ill-defined. Throat finely spotted. Throat and belly with a browner tinge. Breast and

flanks relatively finely streaked dark brown. Mantle and scapulars duller due to more uniform streaking and browner base colour. Blackish centres of median and greater coverts pointed. Tail feathers tapered. Iris dark grey-brown.

Crown feathers of male (left) and female (right). Note well-defined squarely set off dark tip of male, and more extensive and diffuse dark tip of female.

SEXING In breeding plumage, males are characterised by uniformly grey or greenish head, including throat and upper breast. The lores and the feathering around the bill are blackish. In fresh plumage males are similar to females, the grey or greenish colour of head being concealed by brownish tips of feathers. The grey bases of the crown feathers often show through, creating a blotchy appearance. The grey colour is also often visible on the sides of the neck. In the hand, distinct and rather straight division between grey base and brownish tip of crown feather characteristic. The pattern of the crown feathers of first-year males is usually similar to adult male, but with broader tips to feathers. However, some come very close to pattern of female. These differ from first-year females by being less heavily streaked on the breast. They may be very similar to adult females, but will be possible to separate if correctly aged. Juvenile males of the race *personata* differ from juvenile females by their greener base colour on the crown. Males are on average larger than females (wing: male 69-77, female 66-72).

Adult females often show dark lateral crown-stripes and dark borders to the ear-coverts, but some show a plumage ghosting male, differing in lack of black lores and chin, and usually pale throat. In fresh plumage females may be identified in the hand by the base of the crown feathers not being as pure grey as in males, merging diffusely with the browner tips. The pattern of pale central crown-stripe and darker lateral stripes is always neat, without blotchy appearance. In juvenile females of the race *personata*, the base colour on the crown is brownish.

MOULT AND AGEING Juveniles undergo a partial moult late July to early October, involving head, lesser, median, and often all greater coverts, usually all tertials, usually at least central pair of tail feathers, often all. At least in Japanese birds, most juveniles moult some primaries. A majority moult 4-5 outer primaries, and a smaller percentage all or none. Usually some secondaries are moulted as well. Adults undergo a complete moult late July to early September. In males there is a limited pre-breeding moult in winter, involving feathering at base of bill, lores, supercilium, part of ear-coverts, chin and breast. In females this moult is more restricted or absent. The pre-breeding moult in first-winter birds is similar to that of adults, but less extensive.

In autumn, differences are relatively small between different age-groups. In adults, the primary coverts, primaries and tail feathers are less worn than in first-year birds, and the tail feathers are more pointed. Iris colour is useful in the hand and in good light, dark chestnut in adults, dark grey-brown in first-year birds. It should be noted that skull ossification proceeds slowly in this species, and adults frequently show incompletely ossified skull (stage D, Svensson 1992). First-year birds are usually in stage B as late as November. In spring, many first-year birds can be identified by showing primary coverts that are more worn, and with tips more pointed and frayed than in adults. Primaries and tail feathers are also relatively more worn than in adults. First-summer males usually show yellowish patches in the otherwise grey breast. First-summer females tend to be more boldly streaked than adults, and lack olive-grey on sides of neck and breast.

MEASUREMENTS Wing: (max) male 69-77, female 66-72. Tail: male 55-61, female 54-60. Bill: (to skull) male 13.0-15.0, female 12.4-15.1. Tarsus: male 18.9-20.1, female 18.3-20.9. P5-P8 emarginated, sometimes only faintly on 5th.

GEOGRAPHICAL VARIATION Varies mainly in base colour of head, colour of throat, saturation of yellow colour on underparts, amount of white in outer tail feathers, and to some degree size.

E. s. spodocephala (Siberia and N China) Head grey. In this race there is a clinal saturation from west (paler) to east (darker). Extreme western populations are very pale on belly, almost white, and sometimes separated as the race *oligoxantha*. Populations from extreme eastern Siberia are slightly smaller, with belly deeper yellow and demarcation between grey breast and belly more ill-defined, sometimes separated as the race *extremiorientis*. Some authors treat north-east Chinese and Ussuriland populations as part of the race *sordida*.

E. s. sordida (C China) Synonym: *melanops*. Similar to nominate race, but somewhat darker and brighter. The head is greenish-grey and the belly deeper yellow, and the streaking on the flanks blacker. Slightly larger than nominate race (wing: male 70-78, female 71-73).

E. s. personata (Japan, Sakhalin and the S Kuril Islands) Includes *sachalinensis*. Slightly smaller than nominate race (wing: male 65-76, female 62-73), but with heavier bill. Crown and sides of head tinged greenish. The head pattern differs from previous races in that both the submoustachial stripe, throat and breast are yellow instead of grey, with only a greyish smudge at the sides of the breast. The chin is black. The belly is lemon yellow, brighter than in other races. The white pattern on the outer tail feathers is less extensive than in other races. The female differs from other races by being bright yellow below, with more prominent blackish streaking than in nominate race.

VOICE The song is usually given from an inconspicuous perch inside a shrub or low tree. It is a lively and very variable succession of ringing chirps and trills, e.g. *chi-chi-chu chirri-chu chi-zeee-chu chi-chi*. The song of the Japanese race *personata* is similar, but is delivered at a slower tempo, is often broken up into shorter phrases, and is more monotonous. Both types may recall Common Reed Bunting, although the song of *personata* is perhaps most similar.

The ticking call note is similar to that of many other buntings, but with experience noticeably thinner and more sibilant, a sharp *tzii*.

HABITS Breeding usually begins between May and mid June, depending on location. There are regularly two clutches, fledglings occasionally appearing as late as early September. The nest is placed on the ground or low in a herb or bush, infrequently up to 1.5m above the ground (second clutches, when herbal cover denser, more often above ground). It is built of soft dry grass, lined with hair, mainly by the female. It is not clear whether male participates in building. Eggs 4-5, pale greenish- or bluish-white to pinkish-white, clouded and mottled umber or dull maroon, or with maroon and purplish-brown patches, covered with dark spots and lines. Both sexes incubate, but duration of incubation and fledging not studied, probably 20-25 days altogether. Diet of adults during breeding season mainly insects and larvae, such as bugs, small cicadas, flies, ants, caterpillars, beetles and spiders. Diet of nestlings presumably similar. During migration and in winter cereal grains and various other seeds seem to be most common food items. Outside breeding season usually in small flocks, usually staying in or near cover, sometimes mixing with other buntings, such as Yellow-browed or Grey, where these occur.

STATUS AND HABITAT Common in moist shrubby undergrowth, often mixed with a few spruce or firs, mostly along watercourses; from small streams to floodplains along the larger rivers. Also to a lesser degree in moist coniferous forest. Usually restricted to low altitudes, but ascends to 600m in the Altai Mountains. In Japan more regularly found in broadleaf mountain forest up to 1500m, sometimes in subalpine birch forest even higher.

In winter in foothills and lowlands. Usually found in hedges and shrubs near running water or bordering clearings and open habitats: like crops, stubble fields, edges of pools and riverbeds. Also in village gardens, forest undergrowth, tall grass, dwarf bamboo or sugar cane.

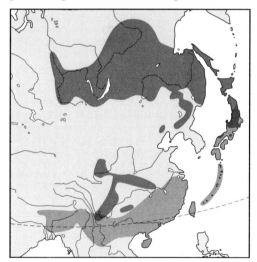

DISTRIBUTION AND MOVEMENTS Breeds in Siberia, from Novokuznetsk, Krasnoyarsk and the Sayan Mountains in the west to the southern Verkhoyansk range and Magadan in the north-east, and to Sakhalin and Ussuriland in the south-east. In the south, range roughly follows border with Mongolia, occurring south to Ulaanbaatar, extending to North Korea, and in north-eastern China in the Greater and Lesser Khingan Mountains and mountains of eastern Jilin and Liaoning. In Japan, a common breeder in northern half of Honshu and in Hokkaido.

Also breeds in the Kuril Islands, north to Urup. A separate population breeds in foothills and valleys in central China, from central Gansu, where found in the Nan Shan south to the Qingling Mountains, around the Red Basin, east to Hubei, and south along edge of Tibetan plateau to the Lijiang range in Yunnan. Generally found north of the Yangtze, but occurs further south in central Guizhou and western Hunan.

The breeding areas in Siberia are vacated by early September, and in Manchuria in October, but remains near breeding areas until October-November in Japan, where many winter in the southern parts of the country. Main autumn passage through Korea September-October, where Japanese race *personata* is scarce on passage and in winter.

Winters from eastern Nepal, where uncommon and local, north-eastern India, Bangladesh and north-eastern Burma, to southern China, where one of the most common buntings south of the Yangtze River in winter, northern parts of Vietnam and Laos, and Taiwan. Present on the wintering grounds from October to May. Vagrant west to Corbett National Park in India. Rare and local in northernmost Thailand.

Migrates through north-eastern China and Korea in April and May, arriving on breeding grounds in Manchuria in late April and in Siberia in mid-May. Returns to breeding grounds in Japan in early April

Half a dozen records from the western Palearctic probably represent vagrants, although captive origin possible. Recorded in Britain, the Netherlands, Germany and Finland, mainly in late autumn, but one record in March and one in May.

REFERENCES Alström *et al.* (1991), Anon. (1993), Bradshaw (1992), Cramp & Perrins (1994), Dementiev & Gladkov (1966), Dorchiev & Jumov (1991), Hough (1994), Ishimoto (1992), Jahn (1942), Satou (1989), Svensson (1992 & 1994), Suschkin (1925), Vaurie (1956), Wallschläger (1983).

---

37 GREY BUNTING
Emberiza variabilis   Plate 14

Described as *Emberiza variabilis* Temminck 1835.
Synonyms: *Tisa variabilis, Zonotrichia musicae.*

A secretive and uncommon bird of shady undergrowth in the temperate mountain forests of Pacific coast of Asia, from Japan to southern Kamchatka.

IDENTIFICATION 17cm. Adult male is unmistakable, almost uniformly dark slaty blue except on mantle, where streaked dark. Only other predominantly bluish Asiatic bunting is male Slaty Bunting, which is unstreaked on the mantle, white on the belly, and shows white in the outer tail feathers.

Female Grey Bunting shows the general bunting features, but differs from other *Emberizas* within its range, except Chestnut Bunting, which is very different in other respects, by lack of significant white pattern in outer tail feathers. Compared to most other buntings, the face pattern is rather dull. The supercilium is relatively inconspicuous, but the submoustachial stripe and malar stripe are fairly prominent. The crown is rather dark, with pale median crown-stripe. The mantle is streaked dark,

contrasting with unstreaked rufescent brown rump and central tail feathers. The underparts are whitish, with some relatively indistinct dark streaking and olive-brown wash on upper breast, sides of breast and flanks.

First-winter male Grey Bunting is basically similar to females on head and upperparts, but mottled blue-grey, particularly on underparts and rump. The breast and flanks are uniform in colour, or slightly mottled, but lack streaking. The head pattern is slightly duller than in females.

Female Tristram's may occur in similar habitat but shows a rufous rump, and a considerably more prominent face pattern, with whitish supercilium and submoustachial stripe, and well-defined dark-bordered ear-coverts. The sides of the breast are tinged rufous, instead of olive, and the contrast between the buffish-brown breast and white belly is more well-defined.

Black-faced Bunting is perhaps the most likely confusion species. The Japanese race (*personata*) of Black-faced Bunting, with which Grey Bunting most often associates, is strongly tinged yellow on the underparts. All races show a dull face pattern, similar to Grey, but differ in being more prominently streaked on breast and flanks. The uppertail-coverts are brown, instead of rufescent brown, and the central tail feathers are dark and do not appear similar in colour to the rump, as they do in Grey. The undertail-coverts are plain pale, not obviously dark-centred as in female Grey Bunting. Black-faced Bunting always shows white in the tail.

Female is similar to extralimital Song and Fox Sparrow, both of which lack white in the tail. Grey Bunting always shows *Emberiza* pattern in tertials, a feature which is absent in all American sparrows, including Song and Fox.

The Song Sparrow further differs by showing whiter and more prominently streaked underparts, and a medium brown instead of rufous-brown rump. The bill is dark.

The Fox Sparrow occurs in several forms, all very different from Grey Bunting, but possible to confuse if views unsatisfactory. In all races the breast is heavily streaked or flecked, and the upperparts vary from less prominently streaked than Grey to unstreaked. Western races also show more or less uniformly brown head, without crown-stripes or supercilium. First-winter female Grey Bunting shows a pale median crown-stripe, streaked mantle, and relatively indistinct streaking on the underparts. First-winter male Grey Bunting is entirely unstreaked below. In eastern races of Fox, showing a supercilium, the submoustachial stripe is always clearly whiter than the greyish supercilium. In Grey Bunting, the supercilium and submoustachial stripe are both olive-buffish, showing no obvious colour difference.

The Japanese Accentor *Prunella rubida*, which is also a bird of shady undergrowth in winter, has a uniform crown pattern, without a pale median crown-stripe. It lacks streaking on the underparts, ruling out female Grey Bunting, and lacks blue-grey colour on head and upperparts, ruling out male Grey Bunting.

DESCRIPTION

Adult male breeding Head, including throat and nape, uniformly slaty-grey, except for slightly darker lores. Mantle slaty-grey, streaked blackish-brown. Back, rump and uppertail-coverts slaty-grey. Lesser coverts slaty-grey, median and greater coverts with dark centres and slaty-grey edges. Tertials dark brown, the edges greyish on inner one, rufous-brown on outer, and intermediate on middle one.

Primary coverts dark brown. Primaries dark brown with grey-brown edges. Secondaries dark brown with brown edges. Tail dark brown, with blue-grey edges. Underparts slaty-grey, paler on the belly. Undertail-coverts slaty-grey, edged whitish. Upper mandible greyish-black, with pinkish-flesh cutting edge, lower pinkish-flesh with dusky tip. Tarsus pale brown. Iris dark chestnut-brown.

Adult male non-breeding Very similar to adult male breeding, but many fresh feathers edged brownish or buffish. Uniformly greyish head pattern to some extent obscured. Brown fringes may give impression of lateral crown-stripes, and sandy-buff fringes may create faint supercilium and median crown-stripe. Fringes on nape, mantle and rump not very prominent. Minute amounts of white in tail.

First-winter male Crown olive-grey, tinged rufous, with chestnut lateral crown-stripes continuing onto the nape, varying amounts of underlying blue-grey showing through. Supercilium, ear-coverts, sides of neck and throat slaty-grey, fringed olive-rufous. Mantle and scapulars olive grey-brown, chestnut in the centre, streaked dark brown. Back, rump and uppertail-coverts slaty-grey, broadly tipped rufous-chestnut, to a varying degree obscuring underlying colour. Lesser coverts dark greyish fringed olive-brown. Median coverts blackish with buffish tips. The dark centres extend like a short dark spike along the shaft. Greater coverts blackish with blue-grey edges and buffish tips, together with median coverts forming double wing-bars. Alula and primary coverts brown, with rufescent edges. Tertials blackish-brown, showing *Emberiza* pattern, with rufescent outer edge and tip on the inner web. Primaries and secondaries blackish-brown, with olive-buff edges, more rufescent on the secondaries. Central tail feathers rufescent brown. Remaining ones are blackish-brown, with narrow white tip on inner web of outermost pair. Sometimes minute white spot on inner web of second outermost pair. Breast, belly and flanks a mixture of pale buffish-white, slaty-grey and olive-buff, palest on the belly. Breast and belly unstreaked, but flanks sometimes indistinctly streaked dark. Undertail-coverts slaty-grey with whitish edges. Iris dark grey-brown.

First-summer male Similar to adult male breeding, with rather uniform greyish head, but generally with a brownish cast to plumage. Wings browner due to retained flight feathers, greater and primary coverts, and alula. Fringes of feathers of breast and mantle browner. Rump shows some rufous.

Adult female breeding Similar to first-winter male, but lacks slaty-grey mottling on head, rump and underparts. Median crown-stripe olive-buffish. Lateral crown-stripes chestnut-brown continuing onto the nape. Supercilium, lores and ear-coverts olive-buffish, the latter greyer below eye and bordered by narrow chestnut eye-stripe and moustachial stripe. Sides of neck olive-grey. Submoustachial stripe and throat greyish-white. Malar stripe greyish. Mantle and scapulars similar to first-winter male. Back, rump and uppertail-coverts uniformly rufous-chestnut. Wings and tail similar to first-winter male, but greater coverts with olive-grey edges and outer pair of tail feathers uniformly blackish-brown without white tips. Throat, breast, belly and flanks whitish, washed yellowish-olive, diffusely streaked dusky primarily on the breast and flanks. Belly whiter. Undertail-coverts brown with pale buff edges. Iris dark chestnut-brown.

Adult female non-breeding Similar to adult female breeding, but plumage fresh. Breast and flanks mottled greyish and olive-buff.

First-winter female Similar to adult female non-breeding. Upperparts generally more rufescent. Supercilium, submoustachial stripe and throat paler, rendering face pattern more contrasting. Outer pair of tail feathers show narrow white tip. Iris dark grey-brown.

Juvenile Central crown-stripe olive-buffish, relatively inconspicuous. Lateral crown-stripes grey-brown, darker than in subsequent plumages. Supercilium and lores olive-buffish. Ear-coverts uniformly olive-brown, diffusely bordered by chestnut eye-stripe and moustachial stripe. Sides of neck olive-brown. Submoustachial stripe and throat pale greyish-buff. Malar stripe dark greyish. Mantle more diffusely streaked than in subsequent plumages. Scapulars chestnut-brown, with diffuse dark centres. Back, rump and uppertail-coverts uniformly rufous-chestnut. Lesser coverts dark greyish fringed olive-brown. Median coverts blackish with buffish tips. The tip of the dark centre is blunt. Greater coverts with rounded blackish centres with olive-buff edges and buffish tips, together with median coverts forming double wing-bars. Alula and primary coverts brown, with rufescent edges. Tertials blackish-brown, showing *Emberiza* pattern, with rufescent outer edge and tip on the inner web. Primaries and secondaries blackish-brown, with olive-buff edges, rufescent brown on the secondaries. Central tail feathers rufescent brown. Remaining ones are blackish-brown, with narrow white tip on inner web of outer pair. Sometimes minute white spot on inner web of second outermost pair. The breast is olive-buffish, diffusely streaked blackish, more prominently than in subsequent plumages. The flanks are olive-buffish, diffusely streaked dark greyish. The belly is pale buffish, indistinctly streaked. Flanks indistinctly streaked dark. Undertail-coverts with diffuse brown centres and pale buff edges. The lower mandible may be rather dark initially, but gradually becomes pinkish-flesh at the base. Tarsus pinkish. Iris dark grey-brown.

SEXING Males of all ages show blue-grey on the underparts to some extent. Adult males are uniformly blue-grey on head and underparts. First-winter males are similar to first-winter females, but show a great deal of blue-grey colour in the plumage, unstreaked underparts and less distinct head pattern. The median crown-stripe, supercilium and submoustachial stripe are less prominent and the dark border around the ear-coverts and malar stripe are less contrasting. The feathers of the head, breast and upperparts have blue-grey bases which usually show through to some extent, and particularly the rump and uppertail-coverts appear mainly blue-grey with rufous-brown tips. The edges of the inner greater coverts are usually tinged blue-grey. The wings show a great deal of slaty-grey. Undertail-coverts slaty-grey with whitish edges.

Females lack the prominent blue-grey element in the plumage. Adult females may show a few blue-grey spots on the rump and uppertail-coverts, but in general the rump and uppertail-coverts are uniformly rufous-brown, without blue-grey bases. The edges of the inner greater coverts are usually tinged rufous-brown. The underparts are whiter than in males, with an olive wash particularly on the sides of the breast, and diffuse streaking on the breast and flanks.

MOULT AND AGEING Juveniles moult partially to first-winter plumage from July to September. This moult appears to include body feathers, lesser, median and greater coverts, and tertials. Some individuals retain parts of alula, or a few median or greater coverts. Occasionally the outer primaries may be renewed. Adults undergo a complete moult during approximately the same period.

Males are easily aged, as adults are predominantly blue-grey, and first-winter birds show broad rufous-brown or olive-brown tips, rendering them more female like. First-winter birds of both sexes show a whitish tip to the inner web of the outer pair of tail feathers. Adult females lack white tips to the tail feathers. Iris colour and skull ossification is useful. In adults, the iris is dark chestnut, dark grey in first-year birds, but this can only be ascertained in the hand with good light. Note that the skull ossification is very slow in this species (stage B in late autumn), and that adults only exceptionally are completely ossified.

MEASUREMENTS Wing: (max) males 82.0-90.5, females 75.5-84.5. Tail: males 66.0-71.5, females 61.0-70.0. Bill: (to skull) males 14.9-17.7, females 14.2-18.0. Tarsus: males 18.9-21.9, females 19.0-21.3. P6-P8 emarginated, usually also on P5.

GEOGRAPHICAL VARIATION None.

VOICE The song is a pleasant, rather simple phrase, usually given from an inconspicuous perch in bushes or undergrowth. It is variable to some extent, but usually starts with a soft drawn-out note, followed by a higher-pitched part in which a single note is repeated 2-3 times, *hsüüü twis-twis-twis*. Quicker versions, *hsüüü tsisisisisis*, or more variable phrases, *hui hui tie tie zizi*, are also given.

The call is a sharp *zhii*, similar to the call of Black-faced Bunting.

HABITS Breeds during June and July. The nest is placed in a low bush or on stems of dwarf bamboo, usually below 1m, and built of twigs, dead leaves of dwarf bamboo, and withered grass. Eggs 3-5, shiny greyish-white, with purple-greyish dashes at blunt end. Incubation by both parents 12 days. Young are fed by both sexes and leave the nest after 11 days. Diet insufficiently known. Solitary or in small flocks of up to half a dozen birds during migration and in winter. Sometimes in company of Black-faced Buntings. Usually forages on ground.

STATUS AND HABITAT Usually scarce, but locally fairly common, in mountains and hill country. Retiring habits and distribution in relatively rarely visited regions probably account for scarcity of breeding records. Usually confined to dense vegetation. In the north often in alder thickets, willows, and birch forest. In Japan prefers dense undergrowth of dwarf bamboo *Sasa paniculata* in dense subalpine coniferous or mixed forest. Locally fairly common in Japan during winter, when found in a variety of dense habitats. Usually found in evergreen forest undergrowth near streams in low-altitude hills, but sometimes in city parks and suburban gardens.

DISTRIBUTION AND MOVEMENTS Distribution is imperfectly known due to retiring habits. Breeds in southern half of Kamchatka, and the northern Kuril Islands, probably also, at least locally, in the southern Kuril Islands. Distribution in Sakhalin not known in detail, but apparently occurs throughout the island. In Japan principally in the Akan and Daisetsu Mountains in central Hokkaido, and Shiretoko Mountains in eastern Hokkaido, but also known from scattered localities in mountains of central and northern Honshu. Southward migration begins in late August in far north, but main passage through Kuril islands in September, with small numbers remaining into November. Winters in Japan mainly in southern half of

Honshu, Shikoku, Kyushu and Tsushima, regular perhaps as far south as northern Okinawa. Leaves winter quarters in March or April. Main northward migration through Kuril Islands during second half of May. Arrives on breeding grounds in Honshu in late April. Accidental throughout the Ryukyu Islands as far south as Iriomote and to Shaweishan Island on the east coast of China. Vagrant to Korea, Komandor Islands and the Vladivostok area, Russia, and Alaska. A record from the Ala Shan Mountains in central China 1908 is probably erroneous.

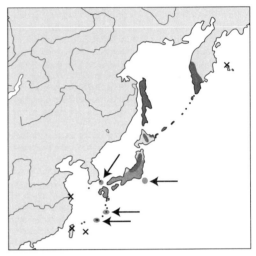

REFERENCES Anon. (1993), Anon. (1995), Austin & Kuroda (1953), Brazil (1991), Dementiev & Gladkov (1966), Fujimaki & Hikawa (1978), Haneda & Minochi (1969), Jahn (1942), Koblik (1993), Uramoto (1964).

38 PALLAS'S REED BUNTING
Emberiza pallasi   Plate 16

Described as *Cynchramus pallasi* Cabanis 1851 (originally *Emberiza schoeniclus* var. ß Pallas 1811).
Synonyms: *Emberiza alleonis, Emberiza canescens, Emberiza montana, Emberiza passerina, Emberiza polaris.*

Pallas's Reed Bunting is widespread in eastern Asia in such diverse habitats as Mongolian grasslands, arctic tundra and alpine meadows. Several races have been described, but the taxonomic treatment of the different populations is still subject to conflicting opinions.

IDENTIFICATION 14cm. Closely resembles Common Reed Bunting. The most important single character valid for all plumages is the colour of the lesser coverts, albeit often difficult to determine in the field. In Pallas's they vary from bluish-grey in adult males to greyish-brown in females. In very worn males they may even appear dark grey. In Common Reed Bunting they are some shade of rufous in all plumages. The distinct wing-bars, which are pale buff instead of pale rufous and relatively inconspicuous as in Common Reed, separate all plumages, but are unreliable in juveniles. The bill is two-toned, with upper mandible dark grey and lower pinkish, except during the breeding season, when it turns blackish. When the breeding season is approaching and the lower mandible starts

192

to turn dark the contrast between the upper and lower mandible may appear similar to that of Common Reed Bunting. Some Common Reed Buntings may also show a rather pale lower mandible, but it is then more bluish than pinkish.

Adult male in breeding plumage is similar to adult male Common Reed Bunting, and confusion with other species is unlikely, except possibly male Stonechat *Saxicola torquata*, if views poor. Further differences between breeding males are the much darker and colder colours of Pallas's Reed. When worn, the mantle becomes very dark, largely blackish with a few greyish stripes, contrasting strongly with the greyish-white rump. This strong contrast is never present in Common Reed. Some south-western races of Common Reed Bunting become very dark on the mantle when worn, but in these races the rump is also dark. Races that do have a pale rump, on the other hand, do not become as dark on the mantle as Pallas's Reed. The edges of median and greater coverts, tertials and flight feathers are a yellowish-buff in Pallas's instead of rufous, as in Common Reed.

In fresh plumage males and females are similar and difficult to separate in the field, except that the black bib may show through in males. Compared to western races of Common Reed in fresh plumage, Pallas's is much paler, with pale rump and very sparse streaking on the underparts, prominent pale double wing-bars, two-toned bill, with dark upper and pinkish lower mandible, and greyish-brown or blue-grey colour of lesser coverts. Some female Pallas's may show relatively distinct streaking on the breast and flanks, although still finer than in western races of Common Reed. The crown of female-type Pallas's is rather uniformly sandy-brown, with some faint streaking, while Common Reed shows fairly prominent dark lateral crown-stripes, except in very worn plumage when the whole crown may become dark. The ear-coverts in Pallas's are rather uniform in colour and relatively pale, with a dark spot at the lower rear corner and narrow dark moustachial stripe creating a distinct dark lower border. In western races of Common Reed, the ear-coverts are darker, more obviously bordered dark, particularly above. In Pallas's the supercilium appears indistinct, as it is not bordered either above or below by dark stripes, whereas Common Reed shows a more prominent supercilium. The bill is pointed with more or less straight culmen. However, there are races of Common Reed Bunting where the bill is small with a straight culmen. The races of northern Europe, and particularly central Siberia, often show a bill shape sufficiently similar to Pallas's to be possibe to misjudge.

Eastern races of Common Reed are much paler than western ones, and may be very similar to Pallas's, showing characters such as pale rump, almost unstreaked underparts and an ear-covert pattern almost identical to that of Pallas's. Again the two-toned bill, uniformly coloured crown, blue-grey or greyish-brown lesser coverts and paler and more prominent wing-bars of Pallas's will aid in separating the two species. In very fresh plumage the wing-bars in Pallas's may be darker buffish, approaching the colour of the wing-bars of Common Reed. However, the difference between the two species in this respect is usually pronounced.

The juvenile is streaked on the underparts, unlike most adults and first-winter birds. It is very similar to juvenile Common Reed. The pattern of the juvenile greater and lesser coverts is more similar than in subsequent plumage, and the wing-bars may appear whitish and equally prominent in both. In many other characters, the differences between juveniles of Pallas's and Common Reed resemble those of adults. The colour of the lesser coverts is similar to adults of both species, as is the shape and pattern of the bill. The pattern of the ear-coverts is similar between adult and juvenile Pallas's, but also similar to eastern races of Common Reed. The crown is rather uniformly dark in juvenile Pallas's, but usually shows a distinct pale median crown-stripe in juvenile Common Reed.

The juvenile is also very similar to juvenile Little Bunting, but the crown is uniform without pale median crown-stripe. In both species the ear-coverts are rufescent brown, with a pattern similar to that of adult of respective species. In juvenile Pallas's the lower border of the ear-coverts is dark with a dark spot in the lower rear corner, and the eye-stripe is concolorous with the central part of the ear-coverts. In Little the ear-coverts are bordered above by a dark eye-stripe, encircling the upper rear corner, while the lower border is concolorous with the central part.

DESCRIPTION

Adult male breeding Crown, superciliary area, lores, ear-coverts and throat black. Submoustachial stripe, sides of neck and nape white. The nape and sides of neck are initially yellowish-brown, wearing to whitish. Mantle blackish, with narrow pale buff and yellowish brown fringes, and two broader whitish stripes, becoming very dark as pale fringes wear off. Scapulars blackish with pale buffish edges. Back pale grey, tinged buffish, with some narrow black streaks. Rump pale whitish-buff, unstreaked. Uppertail-coverts pale whitish-buff with ill-defined greyish centres. Lesser coverts grey. Median coverts blackish with whitish-buff tips. Greater coverts blackish with pale whitish-buff edges and tips, together with median coverts forming double wing-bars. Alula and primary coverts brown, with slightly greyer edges. Tertials blackish-brown, showing typical *Emberiza* pattern, with pale whitish-buff outer edge. Edge on the inner web faint or absent. Primaries and secondaries blackish-brown, with narrow pale edge on the outer web, pale whitish-buff on the primaries, more rufous on the base of the secondaries. Central tail feathers are dark brown, with broad pale edges on the inner web. Rest of tail brown, outermost pair (T6) extensively white with relatively square border to dark base of inner web. Second outermost pair (T5) variable; usually shows approximately outer third of inner web white, squarely set off from dark base. Most birds are clearly different from Common Reed Bunting in tail pattern, but some are very similar. Breast, belly and flanks pale buffish-white, with a greyish wash on the sides of the breast and a few streaks on the flanks. Undertail-coverts whitish. Bill greyish-black. Tarsus flesh-brown. Iris dark chestnut.

Adult male non-breeding Crown sandy-brown, uniformly but faintly streaked, obscuring underlying black feather bases, which sometimes show through. Supercilium ill-defined, pale sandy-buff. Ear-coverts and lores sandy-brown, with a darker moustachial stripe, widening to a spot at the lower rear corner. Submoustachial stripe and sides of neck whitish-buff. Nape sandy-brown, underlying white bases not usually showing through. Chin buffish-white. Black colour of throat, imperfectly obscured by pale fringes, usually shows through. Mantle paler and browner than adult male breeding, with a stronger element of rufous. Back, rump and uppertail-coverts sandy-brown. Wings similar to adult male breeding, but fringes broader and buffier. Breast, flanks, belly and undertail-coverts with rather strong yellowish-buff tinge, unstreaked. Upper mandible dark grey, lower pinkish. Iris dark chestnut.

T6   T5   T5   T5

Outermost (T6) and three examples of second outermost tail feathers (T5) of adult. Usually shows less white in tail than Common Reed Bunting, but note range of variation in T5 in both species.

First-winter male Virtually identical to adult male non-breeding, but lesser coverts grey-brown instead of ash grey. Plumage slightly deeper buff and black head pattern more efficiently obscured. Tail feathers pointed. Both primaries and tail feathers are more worn than in adult. Iris dark grey-brown.

First-summer male Very similar to adult male breeding. Lower mandible paler. Often achieves breeding appearance somewhat later, so crown or ear-coverts may be more obscured than adults. Mantle slightly more rufous. Lesser coverts grey-brown. Tail feathers more pointed. Central tail feathers often browner and more abraded. Iris dark grey-brown.

Adult female breeding Very similar to first-winter male. Crown sandy-brown, with narrow uniform dark streaking. Supercilium whitish. Lores browner. Ear-coverts almost uniform sandy-brown, with darker moustachial stripe, widening to a spot at the lower rear corner. Submoustachial stripe and sides of neck whitish. Throat whitish. Dark brown malar stripe very prominent, almost encircling throat, but broken at the centre. Nape sandy-brown, indistinctly streaked. Colour of upperparts similar to adult male non-breeding, but rump with indistinct rufous-brown streaking. Wings and tail like adult male breeding, but lesser coverts grey-brown. Breast, belly, flanks and undertail-coverts dingy white. Sides of breast and rear flanks indistinctly streaked rufous-brown. Bill like adult male non-breeding, but appears to turn greyish-black during peak of breeding period. Iris dark chestnut.

Adult female non-breeding Very similar to adult male non-breeding. Lacks concealed black crown and throat pattern. Lesser coverts grey-brown. Crown indistinctly streaked rather then spotted, as in adult male. The malar stripe is prominent, resembling adult female breeding. The mantle is less prominently streaked than male.

First-winter female Virtually identical to adult female non-breeding. Tail feathers pointed. Both primaries and tail feathers are more worn than in adult. Iris dark grey-brown.

Juvenile Crown olive-brown with dark brown streaks. Supercilium sandy-buff, wearing to whitish. Ear-coverts rufescent brown, with a prominent dark spot in the lower rear corner, connected with the moustachial stripe that reaches the bill. Eye-stripe faint. Submoustachial stripe pale sandy-buff. Malar stripe usually prominent, blackish-

brown. Throat pale sandy-buff. Nape olive-brown, similar to crown, but less prominently streaked. Mantle pale sandy-buff with some rufous-brown intermixed, heavily streaked blackish. Scapulars blackish with pale sandy-buff edges. Rump pale sandy-brown, often quite prominently streaked dark brown. Uppertail-coverts olive-brown with dark brown streaks. Lesser coverts grey-brown. Median coverts blackish-brown with pale buffish tips. The shape of the black centres is more pointed than in adults and there is a characteristic rounded tooth. Greater coverts blackish-brown with similar pale buffish tips, together with median coverts forming narrow double wing-bars. Alula dark brown. Primary coverts dark brown, with pale rufous-brown edges. Tertials similar to adult female non-breeding, as are the primaries and secondaries. The tail feathers are similar to first-winter male. Breast yellowish sandy-brown, rather heavily streaked dark. Belly and undertail-coverts pale sandy-buff. Iris dark grey-brown.

SEXING Breeding males readily sexed by characteristic head pattern, which always differs from female by black crown, ear-coverts and throat. In non-breeding males the bases of feathers of crown and throat are extensively black, sharply and squarely set off from the buffish fringes. Adult males have blue-grey lesser coverts and first-year males have grey-brown lesser coverts.

In females the feathers of the central throat are whitish or pale buff and always lack black bases. The bases of the crown feathers may be blackish in females, but the dark centres are more pointed and the transition between the fringes and the bases more diffuse. This can often only be determined in the hand, but the black pattern of the throat is frequently visible in the field in males. All females have grey-brown lesser coverts.

MOULT AND AGEING Juveniles undergo a partial post-juvenile moult, involving head, body, lesser and median coverts, and usually a variable number of greater coverts, August-September. Adults moult completely late July to September. There is a limited pre-breeding moult on the wintering grounds, February-April, involving side of head and throat.

First-year birds retain primaries, secondaries, tail, primary coverts, alula and a variable number of greater coverts after the post-juvenile moult. These are more bleached than in adults, browner and less greyish-black. The tail feathers are also more pointed. The primary coverts differ from adults in colour and shape; see Common Reed Bunting. Iris colour useful. Sometimes migrates in juvenile plumage, recognised by heavily streaked breast.

MEASUREMENTS Wing: male 74-78, female 70-75. Tail: male 59-66, female 57-64. Bill: (to skull) male 11.9-12.8, female 11.9-12.5. Tarsus: male 18.1-18.9, female 18.6-18.7. P5-P8 emarginated.

GEOGRAPHICAL VARIATION There is some confusion concerning the races. Different sources give different ranges and allocate certain populations to different races. The populations east of the Kolyma River are sometimes included in *pallasi* and sometimes in *polaris*, or alternatively placed in their own subspecies, *latolineata*. In the south, the picture is just as complicated, with some populations breeding in alpine and others in steppe habitats. The morphological and vocal differences between races are incompletely known. The most widespread treatment is to acknowledge three subspecies, *pallasi*, *polaris* and *lydiae*. The latter is fairly easy to distinguish on the breeding grounds, but the plumage differences between the two former are less well understood. Both are variously claimed to be the darkest form in breeding plumage, and further studies may be needed to clarify the situation. Evidence that there are vocal differences between populations indicates that there may be reproductive barriers involved, but this needs further study. The most commonly acknowledged subspecies are listed below, without intention to resolve or indicate their status or validity, only to illustrate the complicated situation.

E. p. pallasi (The "southern" subspecies. Described from Transbaikalia, but Portenko also includes populations from the area between the Kolyma River east to the Chukotskiy Peninsula. Other authors separate these populations as *latolineata*, which in turn is often included in *polaris*). Populations from eastern Transbaikalia, eastern Mongolia, and the Amur area may belong here.

E. p. montana Synonym *suschkiniana*. (Tien Shan, Krasnoyarsk and Altai) Usually included in *pallasi*.

E. p. latolineata (Area between the Kolyma River and the Chukotskiy Peninsula) Usually included in *polaris*. Said to be darker and with more spotted rump than *polaris*.

E. p. polaris (The "northern" subspecies. NE European Russia and N Siberia, south to basins of Angara, Lena and Aldan Rivers. In the east to Chukotskiy Peninsula, or to approximately the Kolyma River depending on whether *latolineata* is included here or in *pallasi*) Probably more commonly found in lowlands than *pallasi*. Slightly smaller than the nominate race.

E. p. lydiae (The lacustrine depression of SW Mongolia, and possibly elsewhere) Differs by being more sand-coloured, including median and greater coverts. Wing-bars buffish. Mantle greyish-buff with brown streaks. Rump only slightly paler than mantle, faintly streaked.

E. p. minor (E Transbaikalia, E Mongolia, and possibly Manchuria) This race is sometimes recognised, but in fact probably refers to Common Reed Bunting, which see for discussion.

VOICE The song is delivered from the top of a shrub or from a lower position on a herb or tall grass. The song given by northern populations is a uniform repetition of a rather shrill note, *srrie srrie srrie srrie srrie srrie*, somewhat reminiscent of song of White Wagtail *Motacilla alba* in quality. A similar song, lacking the shrill quality, has been recorded from birds breeding near lakes in Inner Mongolian grasslands.

The common call note is a fine *chleep* or *tsilip*, recalling a Eurasian Tree Sparrow *Passer montanus*, but weaker. A call given in flight resembles flight call of Richard's Pipit *Anthus richardi*, but is weaker. A somewhat slurred *dziu*, reminiscent of both Common Reed Bunting and Yellow Wagtail *Motacilla flava*, has been recorded from birds breeding in steppe.

HABITS In northern parts of range, breeds in June and July, beginning when ground has dried out after thaw. In southern parts of range breeding also begins in June, but may last into August. The nest is built of grass and sedge, lined with fine grass and hair, sometimes dried larch needles. It is usually placed on the ground, hidden in a tussock or depression, or low in a bush. Eggs 3-5, similar to Common Reed Bunting, glossy creamy-pink to reddish-brown, with scattered dark spots and hairline streaks, and

greyish undermarkings and streaks. Incubation c. 11 days, mainly by female. Young fledge after c. 10 days and are fed by both sexes. Diet of young various invertebrates, like moths and craneflies. Diet of adults mainly invertebrates during breeding season, e.g. moths, craneflies, midges, larval sawflies and weevils. During remainder of year mainly various types of seeds, but at least some insects are taken. Near the breeding grounds crowberry, alder and grass, particularly feather-grass, make up substantial part of diet. Gregarious outside breeding season, when large flocks may form. Mixes freely with other buntings and Redpolls *Carduelis flammea*. May be rather inconspicuous.

STATUS AND HABITAT Widespread and locally common, even abundant, but scarce in many places. Occurs in a variety of habitats, primarily arctic and mountain tundra and steppe. Northern breeders favour areas of quite dense willow, alder or dwarf birch scrub, along rivers or near open wet sedge meadows, bogs or lakes. Also in wooded tundra. Southern populations are found in both mountains and steppe. In mountains generally found in tundra-like habitat above tree limit. Lowland populations inhabit different types of steppe, and have been recorded from (e.g.) rolling grassy hills with luxuriant vegetation, devoid of shrubs, areas of grass tussocks along lake shores in regions of dry short-grass steppe, and from areas with fairly tall scrubby vegetation.

In winter mainly found in reedbeds and shrubs near rivers and lakes and nearby grassy fields, rice fields and arable land.

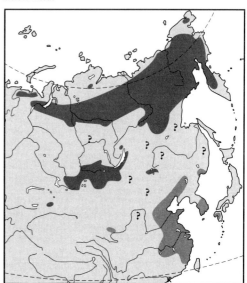

DISTRIBUTION AND MOVEMENTS Range divided into two principal regions, tundra area north of taiga belt, and mountains and steppe in southern Siberia and northern Mongolia, with distribution in intermediate areas insufficiently known. Northern populations breed from northeastern European Russia (Kara and Seyda rivers, Bolshezemelskaya tundra) eastwards through northern Siberia to the Chukotskiy peninsula, Koryakskiy mountains, Kamchatka and the northern shores of the Sea of Okhotsk. Reported south to basins of Angara, Lena and Aldan rivers, but doubtful whether distribution continuous south to range of southern populations. In the south, occurs from eastern Tien Shan, Altai Mountains and Khangai in northern Mongolia, north to Sayan mountains, Krasnoyarsk, and mountains north of Lake Baikal, eastwards through Transbaikalia to the Amur area, possibly south to the Greater Khingan Mountains in Manchuria and Sikhote Alin in Ussuriland. Although breeding has not been confirmed, an isolated population in Ordos, China, probably represents the southern limit of its breeding range.

Dispersion from breeding grounds may begin already in late July, but departure towards wintering grounds normally in August and September. Main passage through southern Siberia from mid-September throughout October. Main arrival and passage in north-eastern China in October. Winters in Xinjiang in western China, across northern China and probably in southern Mongolia, to eastern China, where it is found from central Manchuria south to Zhejiang, Jiansu and Fujian. Also in central and southern Korea, and in small numbers in southern Ussuriland, Russia and Kyushu, Japan. The wintering grounds are occupied between October and March, although odd birds may linger into May. Main northward passage through north-eastern China and southern Siberia during second half of April. Normally arrives on breeding grounds about mid June.

Vagrant Alaska, Britain and Hong Kong.

REFERENCES Alström *et al.* (1991), Alström & Olsson (1994), Anon. (1993), Cramp & Perrins (1994), Dementiev & Gladkov (1966), Dorzhiev & Jumov (1991), Grote (1931), Johansen (1944), Kozlova (1933), Ouwerkerk (1994), Portenko (1929), Shigeta & Mano (1979), Suschkin (1925), Svensson (1992), Vaurie (1964).

---

39   COMMON REED BUNTING
Emberiza schoeniclus   Plate 15

Described as *Fringilla schoeniclus* Linnaeus 1758.
Synonyms: *Cynchrami pallidi, Cynchramus alnorum, Cynchramus cannetti, Cynchramus cimicola, Cynchramus lacustris, Cynchramus lapponicus, Cynchramus microrhynchus, Cynchramus phragmitis, Cynchramus pseudo-pyrrhuloides, Cynchramus pyrrhuloides, Cynchramus riparius, Cynchramus schoeniclus, Cynchramus septentrionalis, Cynchramus stagnatilis, Emberiza arundinacea, Emberiza compilator, Emberiza durazzi, Emberiza intermedia, Emberiza palustris, Emberiza passerina, Emberiza pyrrhuloides, Emberiza scotata, Emberiza tschusii, Fringilla nortoniensis, Schoeniclus pyrrhulinus, Schoeniclus schoeniclus, Spizella pusio.*

The Common Reed Bunting is a widespread and common breeder over much of the Palearctic region in vegetation associated with wet ground. The complete range of variation is greater in this species than in any other species of bunting and many subspecies are recognised. The mantle varies from pale buffish in fresh plumage in the palest races to almost blackish-brown in the darkest ones when worn.

IDENTIFICATION 14-16cm. Males in breeding plumage are easily recognised by their characteristic head pattern. The head, including the throat, is black, except for a prominent white submoustachial stripe, and bordered behind by a conspicuous white nape. The mantle is grey-brown and rufous, streaked blackish, and the rump is greyish.

The wings are extensively rufous, with rather inconspicuous wing-bars. The underparts are whitish, with some dark streaking on the flanks. The outermost pair of tail feathers are extensively white.

In fresh plumage, in autumn and winter, the black colour of the head of male Common Reed Bunting is concealed, and males and females are virtually identical. The head pattern is then typically bunting-like. The crown is brown with a pale median crown-stripe. Supercilium, sides of neck, submoustachial stripe and throat are pale buffish. The ear-coverts and lores are relatively pale brownish, with eye-stripe, moustachial stripe and rear edge of ear-coverts darker brown. The malar stripe is dark brown, and quite prominent. The mantle is streaked dark, with base colour very variable between different subspecies. The colour of the rump also varies considerably. In the darkest western races, it is dark grey, whereas it is almost white in the pale eastern races. In common for all plumages and races is that the lesser coverts are rufous. This is a diagnostic difference from the two most similar species, Pallas's Reed Bunting and Little Bunting. The tips of the median and greater coverts are rufous-brown, somewhat paler on the latter, forming relatively inconspicuous double wing-bars. The streaking on the flanks and breast varies a great deal. Western races are prominently streaked, particularly on the sides of the breast and on the flanks, whereas some eastern races are virtually unstreaked below. The bill is blue-grey without prominent difference in colour between the upper and lower mandible. The culmen is usually convex, in some races very much so, but may be virtually straight.

In adult males in fresh plumage, the black bases of the feathers of the head often show through to some extent, particularly on the throat. The pale fringes wear off in the spring, and the black head pattern develops gradually. During this period parts of the feathering of the face (forehead, lores, anterior ear-coverts and chin), in which the bases of the feathers are not black, are moulted as well. Sometimes the wear proceeds faster than the moult, or vice versa, giving rise to strange and unexpected patterns (see illustration 39c on Plate 15). An intermediate plumage showing white supercilium and blackish ear-coverts, which is possible to mistake for Rustic Bunting, is frequently seen.

The degree of abrasion influences the general coloration. As the plumage becomes worn, the base colour of the upperparts turns darker and the underparts whiter. Dark streaking becomes more prominent. In females in very worn plumage, the crown pattern becomes darker, in some almost uniformly darkish.

In all plumages Pallas's Reed Bunting, which see for differences, is the most similar species, and often very difficult to identify with certainty. Japanese Reed Bunting of the far eastern Palearctic, which see, shows similarities in all plumages and could cause confusion. Little Bunting, which see, is very similar to Common Reed in fresh and female-type plumages.

DESCRIPTION
Adult male breeding Crown, superciliary area, lores, ear-coverts and throat black. Submoustachial stripe, sides of neck and nape white. Mantle a mixture of grey-brown and rufous, heavily streaked blackish. Scapulars blackish with rufous edges. Back grey, tinged brown with some dark streaking. Rump slightly paler gray, usually with dark streaking. Uppertail-coverts browner with ill-defined dark

shaft streaks. Lesser coverts deep rufous-brown. Median coverts blackish-brown with rufous-brown tips. Greater coverts blackish-brown with somewhat paler rufous-brown tips, together with median coverts forming double, not very prominent, wing-bars. Alula dark brown. Primary coverts dark brown, with rufous edges, greyer at the tip. Tertials blackish-brown, showing *Emberiza* pattern, with broad rufous-brown outer edge. Edge on the inner web rufous-brown at the tip. Primaries and secondaries blackish-brown, with narrow pale edge on the outer web, pale buff on the primaries, more rufous on the secondaries. The central tail feathers are greyish-brown, paler towards the edges and darker towards the centre. Remaining ones are blackish-brown, outermost pair (T6) with extensive white wedge on inner web. Second outermost pair (T5) with white wedge on inner web, usually differing in shape compared to Little and Pallas's Reed. Breast, belly and flanks dingy white, sides of breast with a greyish-brown smudge. The amount of streaking varies from a few streaks on the flanks to quite extensive streaking on sides of breast, central breast and flanks. Undertail-coverts whitish. Bill black. Tarsus usually dark brown, but sometimes paler, e.g. pinkish-brown. Iris dark chestnut-brown.

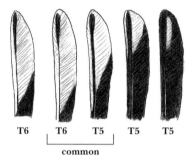

T6   T6   T5   T5   T5

common

Outermost (T6) and second outermost tail feathers (T5) of adult indicating range of variation. The most common pattern of each is indicated.

Adult male non-breeding Broad fringes of crown greyish-brown forming rufous-brown lateral crown-stripes, largely obscuring the underlying black feather bases, which sometimes show through. Supercilium rich buff. The ear-coverts and lores are relatively pale brownish, with eye-stripe, moustachial stripe and rear edge of ear-coverts darker brown. Submoustachial stripe and sides of neck whitish-buff. Nape grey-brown, with underlying white bases sometimes showing through. Chin buffish-white. Malar stripe blackish. Black feather bases of throat imperfectly obscured by pale fringes and often show through, particularly on the central breast. Mantle similar to adult male breeding, but slightly paler. Grey colour of back, rump and uppertail-coverts somewhat obscured by rufous fringes. Wings similar to adult male breeding, but fringes broader and less bleached. Breast and flanks tinged yellowish-buff, streaked brownish. Central belly and undertail-coverts whitish. Upper mandible dark grey. Cutting edge and lower mandible blue-grey.

First-winter male Virtually identical to adult male. Rump on average with stronger rufous tinge due to broader fringes. Minute differences in colour and structure of primary coverts detectable in the hand with experience (see ageing). Tail feathers pointed. Both primaries and tail feathers are more worn than in adult. Iris dark grey-brown.

Adult female breeding Crown dark brown, with varying amount of rufous-brown mottling, not always with obvious median crown-stripe. Supercilium whitish. Lores browner. Ear-coverts fairly uniformly brown. Submoustachial stripe and sides of neck whitish. Nape pale grey-brown, sometimes almost whitish. Throat whitish. Malar stripe blackish and prominent. Colour of upperparts similar to adult male breeding, but back and rump browner, with dark streaking. Uppertail-coverts browner. Wings and tail like adult male breeding. Breast, belly, flanks and undertail-coverts pale buffish-white. Breast and flanks distinctly streaked dark, with some rufous-brown blotches on the central breast. Bill blackish.

Adult female non-breeding Very similar to adult male non-breeding. Crown pattern appears streaked rather than spotted, as is often the case in adult male. The malar stripe is prominent and contrasts with the buffish throat. The breast and flanks are distinctly streaked. The nape is greyish-brown, without any white showing through.

First-winter female Virtually identical to adult female non-breeding. Age differences as in first-winter male.

Juvenile Crown chestnut, heavily streaked blackish. Supercilium buffish. Ear-coverts almost uniformly blackish-brown. Submoustachial stripe and sides of neck pale buff. Malar stripe broad, blackish. Throat yellowish-buff. Nape grey-brown, sometimes with a narrow, almost whitish collar. Mantle similar to adult female, but paler and with a few broad pale buffish stripes on the sides. Back, rump and uppertail-coverts yellowish-buff, streaked and spotted blackish. Lesser coverts buffish-brown. Median coverts blackish-brown with pale rufous-buff tips. The shape of the black centres is more pointed than in adults, showing a characteristic rounded tooth. Greater coverts blackish-brown with similar pale rufous-brown tips, together with median coverts forming narrow double wing-bars. Alula dark brown. Primary coverts dark brown, with narrow rufous edges. Tertials similar to adult female non-breeding, as are the primaries and secondaries. The tail feathers are similar to first-winter male. Belly and flanks buffish-white, darker buff on the breast, heavily streaked or almost spotted on breast and flanks. Undertail-coverts whitish. Bill flesh-grey with dark grey culmen and tip. Tarsus flesh-grey. Iris dark grey-brown.

♀   ♂

Crown feathers of female and male. Note rounded and sharply set off dark centre of male, and more pointed and diffuse dark centre of female.

SEXING Breeding males readily sexed by characteristic head pattern, which always differs from female by black crown, ear-coverts and throat. In non-breeding males the bases of feathers of crown and throat are extensively black, sharply and squarely set off from the rufous-brown fringes.

In females the feathers of the central throat are whitish or pale buff and always lack black bases. The bases of the crown feathers may be blackish in females, but the dark centres are more pointed and the transition between the fringes and the bases more diffuse. This can often only be determined in the hand, but the black pattern of the throat is frequently visible in the field in males.

MOULT AND AGEING Juveniles undergo a partial moult July to September, involving body, lesser and median coverts and usually all greater coverts. Some individuals moult all tertials, but in most cases at least some juvenile tertials are still present after the moult. A smaller percentage (about one out of ten) moult all tail feathers. Primary coverts, primaries and secondaries are not moulted. Adults moult completely July to September.

When juvenile greater coverts, tertials or tail feathers are retained, these will facilitate ageing. If all these are fresh, differences in structure and colour of primary coverts, abrasion, colour of iris and skull ossification should be examined. The unmoulted juvenile primary coverts of first-year birds are dark brown, with narrow rufous edges, loose in structure and with slightly frayed tips. In adults, the primary coverts are more firm in structure and have grey tips. These differences are still valid, but more difficult to judge due to wear, until the birds first complete moult the following summer. In first-year birds the primaries are slightly more worn than in adults. The change in colour of the iris has been studied in detail in Common Reed Bunting. First-autumn birds have a dark grey-brown iris that gradually changes to a dark chestnut colour. This change is so slow that it is sometimes possible to recognise birds in their second autumn. Naturally this can only be done with a great deal of experience. In spring the difference in iris colour between first-year birds and adults is still easily recognised by experienced examiners.

MEASUREMENTS Wing: (max) male 76-87, female 70-81. Tail: male 60-69, female 58-64. Bill: (to skull) male 10.9-13.5, female 10.4-13.2. Depth at base, male 4.7-5.8, female 4.6-5.6. Tarsus: male 18.7-22.0, female 18.0-21.7. P5-P8 emarginated.

GEOGRAPHICAL VARIATION With more than 30 subspecies described, this is the most variable bunting. However, the number of races is somewhat deceptive, as many are split on rather thin grounds. Most races are defined by slight average differences in bill size or wing length, or subtle colour differences. As a rule, northern forms are smaller and have finer bills, and southern forms are larger and more thick-billed. The difference in size between the large Central Asian forms and the small forms from northern Siberia is striking. In southern Europe thin-billed and thick-billed forms are largely separated by mountain ranges, and have been reported to breed side by side without mixing. The thick-billed forms are distributed from about north-eastern Spain, eastwards south of the Alps and Carpathians, but it appears as if the taiga belt largely separates thin-billed from thick-billed forms. These are also to some degree ecologically separated, by different diet and foraging technique (see Habits). In both thick-billed and thin-billed forms, there is a colour cline, going from dark in the west to very pale in eastern and central Asia. In view of apparently separate ranges, tentatively divided into three main groups, with an additional fourth group consisting of intermediate populations in south-eastern Europe and south-western Siberia.

'Northern group' - Relatively small size, relatively small bill:

    E. s. lusitanica (Portugal) The darkest of all races. Bill average size, finer than *witherbyi*.

    E. s. schoeniclus (N Europe) Including *goplanae*, *mac-*

kenziei, steinbacheri, septentrionalis and *turonensis*. Bill with almost straight or slightly arched culmen (see Measurements).

    E. s. passerina (NW Siberia between the Ural Mountains and Taimyr) A small race. Streaks on flanks finer than in nominate race, and rump and upperparts paler with narrower streaks on mantle. Wing: male 80-84, female 77-79. Bill slightly smaller than nominate race: male 10.4-12.5, female 10.4-12.5; depth at base, male 4.8-5.4, female 4.8-5.2.

    E. s. parvirostris (C Siberia) Including *pallidissima*. A small race. Pale, with little or no streaking on flanks, and reduced streaking on crown and mantle. Fine bill, with almost straight culmen: depth at base, male 5.0-5.3, female 4.5-5.0.

'Eastern group' - Medium size, proportionately large bill:

    E. s. pyrrhulina (NE Siberia, Kamchatka and Hokkaido) Includes *nortoniensis*. Paler than *parvirostris*, very similar to *pyrrhuloides* in general coloration, only slightly more rufous on mantle and wings, and with slightly greyer and less contrasting rump. The bill is relatively large, with convex culmen, similar to bill of *stresemanni*. Bill-length, sexes combined 11.2-12.5, depth at base 5.6-6.2. Wing: male 80.5-87, female 76-82.

    E. s. minor (Transbaikalia to Manchuria) It is not quite clear whether this is a valid subspecies or a synonym of *pyrrhulina*. There is also some confusion as to whether the name *minor* should be attributed to a race of Pallas's Reed Bunting or of Common Reed Bunting. However, the original, rather inadequate, description does mention rufous edges to upper wing-coverts, and thus obviously refers to *E. schoeniclus*.

'Intermediate group' - Medium size, intermediate bill:

    E. s. stresemanni (E Austria, Hungary and N Serbia) A relatively small race, similar to nominate race in both size and coloration, although slightly paler on the rump. Heavier bill than nominate, male 11.4-13.5, female 11.4-12.5. Depth at base, male 5.7-6.4, female 5.8-6.3. Wing: male 78-87, female 72.5-78.

    E. s. ukrainae (Ukraine and S Russia) Generally paler than nominate, with a heavier bill: male 11.5-13.5, depth at base, male 5.6-6.5.

    E. s. incognita (SE European Russia to N Kazakhstan) Including *palustris* Sarudny 1911. Bill, depth at base, male 5.5-7.5, female 5.0-7.0. Slightly greyer above than *pyrrhuloides*.

    E. s. pallidior (The basin of the Tobol and Irtysh Rivers in SW Siberia, south of the range of *passerina*) A medium-sized race, similar in colour to, and only slightly smaller than, *pyrrhuloides*. Bill significantly smaller: male 11.6-12.8, female 11.7-12.6, depth at base, male 5.1-5.7, female 5.4-5.8.

'Southern group' - Large size, large bill:

    E. s. witherbyi (Balearic Islands and Spain) Very dark, wing, male 79-82, bill large, similar to *intermedia*.

    E. s. intermedia (Italy, Corsica, along Adriatic coast of Croatia) Includes *canneti*, *palustris* Savi 1788, and *compilator*. A medium-sized race, with a relatively large bill. Wing, male 80-87, female 76-82. Bill, male 12.3-14.5, female 12.0-13.5, depth at base, male 7.0-7.8, female 6.9-7.7.

    E. s. tschusii (The Danube River in Bulgaria and Romania, and area north of Black Sea) Includes *othmari* and *volgae*. A medium-sized race. Paler than nominate,

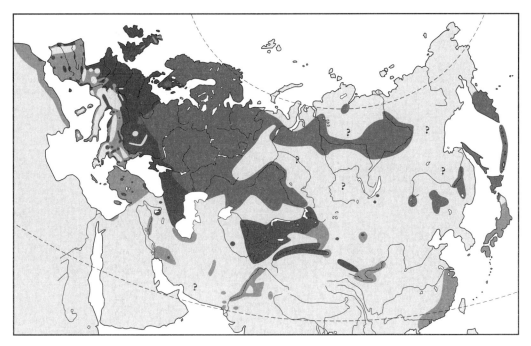

particularly on rump, with narrower dark streakings on upperparts. Bill, sexes combined 12.5-13.5, depth at base 6.4-7.4. Wing, male 81.5-87.5, female 78-84.

E. s. reiseri (SE Albania, NW Greece and S Macedonia and W Turkey) A large race. Very dark plumage. Massive bill, 13.4-14.7, depth at base 7.7-9.0, sexes combined. Wing, male 82-94, female 78-83.

E. s. caspia (E Turkey to W Iran and possibly Syria) A large race with a relatively large bill. Relatively pale, quite similar to *intermedia* in colour, but darker than *pyrrhuloides*. Bill, sexes combined 13.3-14.5, depth at base, 7.0-7.5. Wing, male 85-86, female 77-83.

E. s. korejewi (SE Iran) The status and validity of this race need further investigation. According to original description, similar in size to *pyrrhuloides*, but bill stronger and higher. Wing, sexes combined, 80-88. Bill, sexes combined 13.5-14, depth at base 7.2-8.7. Similar in colour to *pyrrhuloides*, but described as generally darker on mantle, wings and rump, and with narrower white submoustachial stripe.

E. s. pyrrhuloides (Northern parts of the Caspian Sea, from the Terek River, through C Asia, to Lake Balkash and S Kazakhstan) A large race. Bill, male 11.9-13.5, female 12.5-13.5, depth at base, male 7.2-9.3, female 7.6-9.0. Wing, male 86-94, female 79-84. Very pale. Slightly buffier above than *incognita*.

E. s. harterti (SW Mongolia, NW Xinjiang, China) A large race. Bill, male 12.5-13.5, depth at base 7.2-7.8. Wing, male 85-92. Very similar to *pyrrhuloides,* but perhaps marginally smaller.

E. s. centralasiae (Tarim basin east to Lop Nor, in Xinjiang, China) Bill, male 11.0-13.5, female 11.6-13.3, depth at base, male 6.8-7.6, female 6.6-7.4. Wing, male 80-90, female 75-83. Very similar to *pyrrhuloides*, but on average slightly smaller.

E. s. zaidamensis (Zaidam depression, Qinghai province, China) A large race. Bill depth at base 6.9. Wing, male 87-92, female 81-83. Similar in size to *pyrrhuloides*, but

buffier, less grey, in colour.

VOICE The song is delivered from a bush or a reed stem. It is a short series of relatively unmusical, tinkling units, e.g. *zritt zreet zreet zreet zritt zrüü* or *zreet zreet zreet zrühühü* often sounding uninspired and hesitant. Some song types are relatively simple and may resemble House Sparrow *Passer domesticus*, while some individuals give a more varied song. Each individual may have a repertoire of up to 30 different units that are combined into variable sequences. The introductory units are distinctive and invariable in each individual, and are probably used in individual recognition. Trills usually come at the end.

The common contact call, heard year-round, and which also serves as an alarm call, is a characteristic *seeoo*, falling smoothly in pitch. A hoarse *brzee* is mostly heard during migration, often from flying birds.

HABITS Breeding usually takes place May-June, but differs in different regions between late April to end of August. At least in some areas males are polygamous. The nest is built by female of twigs, moss, grass and sedges, lined with fine plant material, reed-flowers, moss, rootlets and sometimes hair or feathers. It is usually placed on the ground, in tussock or on pile of dead vegetation, sometimes also in bush up to 4m above the ground. Often 2-3 broods in a season. Eggs 4-5, glossy olive-grey to a relatively dark purplish-clay colour, relatively sparsely marked with dark spots and twisted and knotted lines, often with a blurred purplish edge, coarser and more numerous at the large end. Incubation 12-15 days, by both sexes. Young fledge after 9-12 days and are fed by both parents. Diet of nestlings a variety of invertebrates, such as spiders, flies, craneflies, mayflies, larval sawflies, caterpillars, beetles, grasshoppers, dragonflies and snails, but young switch to grass seeds as soon as they become independent. Diet of adults during breeding season a wide variety of invertebrates, such as caterpillars, midges, grasshoppers, beetles, spiders and dragonflies, but also to some extent seeds and shoots. Outside breeding season the diet of the small-billed forms switches largely to seeds, mainly of grasses and plants like goosefoot and knotgrass, whereas the large-billed forms continue to feed on invertebrates extracted from inside the stems of reeds. Small-billed forms take invertebrates opportunistically outside the breeding season, many of them larvae or pupae, but also adult springtails, spiders, bugs, beetles, midges and flies. Normal gait a hop. Often flicks tail when perched. After the last brood is finished, and throughout migration and winter, often congregates in loose groups, usually consisting of 8-100 birds.

STATUS AND HABITAT Common in marshy areas with scrubby or reedy growth or with tall herbage. Over vast geographical range with otherwise shifting conditions, the Common Reed Bunting is associated with consistent type of dense, prolific, fairly low vegetation, related to intense soil moisture rather than to any special need for water. In northern Siberia uncommon or absent from the taiga, being most common in willow thickets in floodplains in the forest-tundra. The *pyrrhuloides*-group is said to breed exclusively in reedbeds. Avoids closed forest and steep or broken ground. After breeding is finished, often feeds in fields and weedy areas adjacent to reedbeds. Outside the breeding season also found in open countryside and cultivated fields, weedy areas, along lake shores, woodland clearings and upland, often well away from water.

DISTRIBUTION AND MOVEMENTS Widespread throughout northern Europe, south to central France, Switzerland, Austria, Hungary and Romania. Occurrence south of this more fragmented. Possibly northern Morocco. In Portugal restricted to coastal areas north of Lisbon. In Spain, mainly in north-east, but also locally inland and in the south-west. In southern France, occurs in coastal areas, from Spanish border to the Camargue, more locally to the Italian border. In Italy, found throughout the Po Valley, and locally on Corsica. Local in Slovenia. Local in northern Croatia and along Adriatic coast. Breeds along the Danube and its tributaries in Serbia, Romania and Bulgaria, where also found locally in south-west and along Black Sea coast. North-western and south-eastern Albania. Distribution in Greece mainly Lake Prespa, and along north coast of Aegean Sea. Local in Turkey, primarily in central Anatolia, wetlands of Black Sea, and around Lake Van. From Europe, range continues eastwards through Russia, east to the middle Lena River in the north, and to Transbaikalia, the Amur River and Lake Khanka further south. Northern limit of distribution insufficiently known, but includes lower reaches of Ob, Yenisey, and Khatanga Rivers, and perhaps inland Taimyr peninsula. On Yenisey, found north of 60°N, being most common between 68-69°N, but occurs as far north as 70°N. Also found on Sakhalin, Kamchatka, the Kuril Islands, and in northern Japan, south to northern Honshu. In the south, occurs in Iran along the southern shores of the Caspian Sea, and possibly in the south-east. Range in Kazakhstan insufficiently known, but probably occurs in suitable habitat throughout. Breeds from northern coast of Caspian Sea, and the Ural and Emba rivers, eastwards to Lake Zaysan. Range also includes parts of the Aral Sea, and the Syr-Darya River, as well as scattered localities in much of the southern and eastern parts of the country. Range in Kirgizia and Tajikistan insufficiently known. Known from southern Uzbekistan, where it may also occur along the Amu-Darya River. Range in Turkmenistan insufficiently

known, but may occur along the Amu-Darya River, and on coast of Caspian Sea. Range in China disjunct. In west, found from Kashi to Hami, along northern edge of the Tarim basin. Isolated populations in Edsin Gol, north-western Inner Mongolia and in the Zaidam depression. In the north-east, breeds in northern Inner Mongolia and the southern parts of Heilongjiang province, possibly also locally in Jilin province.

Southern populations sedentary or dispersive. Populations breeding in Scandinavia, the Baltic states, eastern Poland, Belarus, Ukraine, Russia, northern Kazakhstan, and north-eastern China almost entirely migratory, but low numbers may winter locally in the southern parts of the breeding range during mild winters. Main southward migration between mid September and mid November. Winters in Great Britain, most of continental Europe, Morocco, coastal Algeria and Tunisia, the Mediterranean islands, western Turkey, Israel, southern Ukraine and European Russia, Transcaucasia, northern Iran, Iraq, Pakistan, and locally in north-western India, south-east to the Delhi area. In north-western China, winters in Xinjiang and in the Zaidam depression, and in scattered localities in Qinghai, northern Gansu, and western Inner Mongolia. In south-eastern China, winters in coastal regions from Guangdong to Jiangsu. Rare in winter in South Korea. Winters in Japan from northern Honshu to southern Kyushu, and occasionally in the Nansei Shoto, south to Miyako Island. Northward migration usually begins around mid-February or early March, and by April few, if any, are left on the wintering grounds. Migration through Siberia mainly in May and early June.

Vagrant to Iceland, Svalbard, Egypt, Kuwait, United Arab Emirates, Nepal, Hong Kong and Alaska.

REFERENCES Anon. (1993), Bezzel (1993), Cramp & Perrins (1994), Dementiev & Gladkov (1966), Dixon *et al.* (1994), Dorchiev & Jumov (1991), Eber (1956), Hartert (1910), Johansen (1944), Karlsson *et al.* (1985), Lessells (1994), Roberts (1992), Shigeta & Mano (1982), Steinbacher (1930), Svensson (1992), Vaurie (1956 & 1958).

40   JAPANESE REED BUNTING
Emberiza yessoensis   Plate 16

Described as *Emberiza minor* Blakiston 1873.
Synonyms: *Emberiza minor, Schoenicola yessoensis, Cynchramus yessoensis.*

A locally distributed inhabitant of such diverse habitats as mountain meadows and reedbeds in the Far East.

IDENTIFICATION 14.5cm. Adult male in breeding plumage is superficially similar to Common Reed Bunting and Pallas's Reed Bunting, but has head all black, lacking the white submoustachial stripe. However, in transitional plumage, white submoustachial stripe as well as a supercilium may be present. The nape is sandy chestnut-brown, instead of whitish as is typical of Common Reed and Pallas's Reed. The general coloration is also a warmer rufous-brown. Adult female in breeding plumage is similar to male, except for the face pattern, which is similar to female Common Reed, but with very dark brown crown, in some individuals almost a solidly dark cap, and almost uniformly dark ear-coverts. There is little streaking on the breast, but the malar stripes are prominent.

During the non-breeding season males and females are very similar in plumage, but the underlying black pattern of head in males may show through, particularly on the throat. In both sexes the ear-coverts and the crown are often strikingly dark and the malar stripe very prominent. The mantle is heavily streaked black in all plumages, contrasting with pale grey-brown rump. The central pair of tail feathers are strikingly pale compared to similar species, and when the tail is folded it appears rather uniform pale grey-brown, similar in colour to the pale unstreaked rump. The pale edges of the median and greater coverts are broad and only marginally paler at the tip. In combination with broad pale outer edges on the secondaries the whole folded wing appears more uniform in colour than in other buntings, with very inconspicuous wing-bars. The plain wing is usually in strong contrast with the heavily streaked mantle, but sometimes the dark centres of the inner greater coverts are visible, creating a streaked impression on the wing. In both sexes the underparts are pale, often with no or only faint streaking on the breast and flanks. Some birds in first-winter plumage may show quite prominent streaking on the breast and flanks.

In non-breeding and transitional plumage, confusion is possible with the pale eastern races of Common Reed Bunting and Pallas's Reed Bunting. Dark crown and ear-coverts, and heavy streaking on mantle, in combination with pinkish grey-brown rump, uniform wings with greyish lesser coverts and lack of white on nape, separate it from Common Reed. Pallas's Reed differs by same characters, except colour of lesser coverts which may be similar, but the wing-bars are even more prominent than in Common Reed.

Tristram's Bunting, which normally occurs in forest, may be superficially similar in certain plumages, but always shows more prominent wing-bars and streaking on breast and flanks. The breast is buffy-brown, contrasting with whitish belly. In Japanese Reed the underparts are uniform in colour. The mantle of Tristram's is always less heavily streaked than in Japanese Reed, and the rump is bright reddish-brown. In Japanese Reed the mantle is very heavily streaked blackish and the rump is always unstreaked pale pinkish grey-brown.

Yellow-throated Bunting, which may appear similar because of dark ear-coverts and inconspicuous streaking below, always lacks prominent malar stripe and shows greyish rump.

Siberian Accentor *Prunella montanella* may appear superficially similar to some plumages of Japanese Reed Bunting. Among other differences, thin bill and lack of prominent blackish streaking on mantle will prevent confusion.

DESCRIPTION
Adult male breeding Whole head black, including submoustaschial stripe. Nape greyish chestnut-brown, with a strong pinkish tinge. Mantle and scapulars a mixture of pale grey-brown and rufous, heavily streaked blackish. Back, rump and uppertail-coverts unstreaked grey-brown, with a strong pinkish tinge. Lesser coverts grey-brown. Median coverts blackish with rufous tips. Greater coverts blackish with very broad pale sandy-rufous edge on the outer web and tip. Tertials with blackish centres and pale buffy edge on the outer web, separated by a narrow zone of rusty-brown; pale edge on the inner web narrow. The characteristic *Emberiza* pattern is very well developed, and

the dark pattern on the outer web appears like dark spots, best visible on the longest tertial. Primaries and secondaries brown, with narrow pale rufous margin on the outer web. The central tail feathers are uniformly pale grey-brown. Outermost two pairs (T5-T6) with whitish tip and wedge on inner web, sometimes also on third outermost pair (T4), but usually third and fourth outermost pair show only slightly paler tip. Tail feathers very pointed. Underparts including undertail-coverts creamy, slightly darker on the breast. Sometimes very faint rufous streaking on the rear flanks. Bill blackish. Tarsus pinkish. Iris dark chestnut-brown.

T6   T5   T5

Outermost (T6) and two examples of variation in second outermost tail feathers (T5) of adult. Note that adults show pointed tail feathers.

Adult male non-breeding Like adult male breeding, but head pattern obscured by broad fringes. Crown blackish with pale grey-brown streaking. Supercilium pale grey-brown. Lores brownish. Ear-coverts and throat blackish, partly obscured by pale fringes, but always with prominent black malar stripe. Submoustachial stripe pale grey-brown. Upper mandible dark, with pinkish-brown cutting edge, often also paler at the base of the culmen. Lower mandible pinkish-brown, usually with dark tip.

First-winter male Similar to adult male non-breeding, but the black head pattern is more effectively obscured. Iris dull dark grey-brown.

Adult female breeding Similar to adult male non-breeding. The crown is very dark brown, streaked pale. In some individuals, the streaks are almost completely worn off, creating a solidly dark cap. The ear-coverts are uniformly dark brown and the blackish malar stripes are prominent. Throat pale buffish. The upperparts are darker and the mantle is very heavily streaked black, with a few pale stripes. There may be some rufous streaking or even some black spots on the sides of the breast. Bill dark brown.

Adult female non-breeding Similar to adult male non-breeding, but general coloration slightly darker. Dark pattern of crown browner, with more extensive pale streaking and a narrow pale median crown-stripe. The ear-coverts are also browner and there is no black on the throat. The malar stripe is prominent, but does not always reach the base of the bill. There is some rufous streaking on the sides of breast, extending to rear flanks.

First-winter female Similar to adult female non-breeding. Some individuals show indistinct dusky streaking on breast and flanks. Iris dull dark brown.

Juvenile Crown blackish with distinct pale grey-brown median crown-stripe. Supercilium pale grey-brown, more well-defined than in subsequent plumages. Lores brownish, slightly darker than ear-coverts, almost creating masked appearance. Ear-coverts brownish, blackish at rear.

Submoustachial stripe and throat pale grey-brown, sometimes almost whitish. Malar stripe faint. Nape yellowish-brown, faintly mottled. Mantle and scapulars yellowish-brown, the feathers with blackish centres, appearing heavily streaked or sometimes more spotted than in subsequent plumages. Back, rump and uppertail-coverts unstreaked yellowish-brown. Wings similar to subsequent plumages, except that dark centres of median coverts more triangular, and tips yellowish-brown. Greater coverts similar, with relatively narrow pale edges, and well-defined triangular tips of dark centres. Tail similar to first-winter male. Breast yellowish-buff, distinctly spotted blackish. Remainder of underparts unstreaked pale yellowish-white. Bill similar to first-winter birds, but initially somewhat paler. Tarsus pale pinkish. Iris dull dark brown.

Tertials of this species show a very prominent *Emberiza* pattern. The pale edge on the outer web is broad near the tip, but becomes very narrow about halfway along the feather.

SEXING In breeding males the whole head is black. In non-breeding plumage the base of feathers of crown and throat are black, sharply and squarely set off from the rufous-brown fringes.

In females the throat is whitish or pale buff and feathers of the central throat always lack black bases. The bases of the crown feathers may be blackish in females, but the dark centres are more pointed and the transition between the fringes and the bases more diffuse. This can often only be determined in the hand, but the black pattern of the throat is frequently visible in males.

MOULT AND AGEING Post juvenile moult best described as complete. Body and wing-coverts are moulted July to September, and flight feathers, tail feathers, and primary coverts are renewed in late autumn. Adults moult completely July to September.

Differences in structure and colour between adult and juvenile primary coverts, abrasion, colour of iris and skull ossification should be examined when ageing birds in autumn.

MEASUREMENTS Wing: male 64.5-69.5, female 60.5-67.5. Tail: male 59.0-66.5, female 54.5-62.5. Bill: (to skull) male 12.2-13.6, female 12.6-13.0. Tarsus: male 17.6-20.2, female 17.9-19.6. P5-P8 emarginated.

GEOGRAPHICAL VARIATION Two subspecies described, differing mainly in saturation of colour.
    E. y. yessoensis (Japan) Described above.
    E. y. continentalis (China and Russia) Slightly duller and paler in coloration, especially on neck, rump and edges of coverts. Shows more white in outer tail feathers.

VOICE The song is usually given from a tall herb or reed. It is a brief twittering phrase often containing a short trill. The extent of individual and geographical variation is insufficiently known. A common phrase could be transcribed *chuwi-chiwu sii-psere dsee*. Song of Japanese birds has been rendered *chui tsui chirin*. No diagnostic differences from mainland race are known.

The call is a short *tick*. In flight also a *bschet*, reminiscent of the flight call of Common Reed Bunting.

HABITS Breeds from May to July. The nest is a rather small cup built of dried grass stems and blades, lined with grass rootlets and hair, placed on or very close to the ground in grassy areas. Eggs 3-5, ochre-whitish, with brown patches and black lines, rather rounded. The fledging period is 11-12 days. A second clutch is usually started while still feeding the first brood. Both parents feed young. Food is insufficiently known, but seeds, beetles and caterpillars are known to be taken during summer. In winter grass seeds may constitute a major part of the diet.

STATUS AND HABITAT Everywhere uncommon and local. Seems to have been more common a century ago, but reason for apparent decline not known. Listed as near-threatened by BirdLife International. The species winters largely in coastal marshland areas, everywhere in Asia a heavily exploited habitat, so habitat destruction may be part of the explanation. Breeds in reedbeds and edges of marshes along rivers and lakes, but in highlands also in wet meadows and drier grasslands.

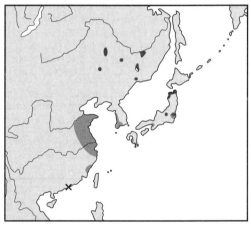

DISTRIBUTION AND MOVEMENTS Breeds locally in north-eastern China, in Ussuriland, Russia, and Japan. In China main occurrence in marshes and reeds in the Harbin and Qiqihar area. Also locally in western Jilin province. In both China and Russia along the Ussuri River, from approximately the confluence with the Amur River in the north, south to Lake Khanka. In Russia also further south, to the Posyet Bay area. Situation in North Korea unknown. Present day Japanese population restricted to northern half of Honshu, except for isolated occurrence on Mt. Aso, Kyushu. Breeding range in Honshu separated into three main areas. In the north, from Ogata and Hachirogata lakes in Akita to Jusan-ko and Rokasho lakes in Aomori. In the east in the Kasumigaura Marsh in Ibaraki. In central Honshu in highlands in Nagano and on Mt. Fuji. Breeding also recorded in Miyagi, Niigata and Chiba. Formerly said to breed in Hokkaido, but now vagrant there.

Winters along coast of south-eastern Honshu, from the

Kobe area to the Tokyo area, and in south-western Kyushu. In South Korea found in coastal areas in western and southern parts. In China, mainly found in lowland areas from the lower Yellow River in the north, south to the Hangchow area. Irregular further south to Fujian province. Vagrant to Hong Kong, with two November records in 1991 and 1992 respectively.

NOTE The species was originally described as *Emberiza minor* in 1873. The name *minor* is preoccupied, although it is not entirely clear whether it refers to a subspecies of *Emberiza schoeniclus* or of *Emberiza pallasi*. The name *Schoenicola yessoensis* was put forward by Swinhoe 1874 and is presently in use.

REFERENCES Anon.(1993), Austin & Kuroda (1953), Collar *et al.*(1994), Dementiev & Gladkov (1966), Jahn (1942), Nakamura *et al.* (1968 and 1970), Nakamura (1981a & 1981b), Nishide (1987).

MILIARIA

One species, of the western Palearctic. A rather large, nondescript species. It is often included in the genus *Emberiza*. Male and female are identical in plumage, but there is a marked sexual size dimorphism and juveniles undergo a complete post-juvenile moult, unlike the *Emberiza* buntings.

41   CORN BUNTING
Miliaria calandra   Plate 2

Described as *Emberiza calandra* Linnaeus 1758.
Synonyms: *Miliaria europea, Miliaria minor, Emberiza miliaria, Crithagra miliaria.*

The Corn Bunting is a bird of farmlands and grassy areas. In Europe primarily in the Mediterranean countries, where its characteristic song is one of the most typical sounds.

IDENTIFICATION 16-19cm. The largest and least distinctively plumaged bunting. Always appears bulky with a large head and proportionally short tail. The sexes are similar, generally grey-brown above and whitish below, streaked darker all over. The streaks often converge to form a dark spot in the centre of the breast. Differs from similar buntings by lack of white in outer tail feathers. Also lacks the typical *Emberiza* pattern on the tertials. The face pattern is plain and shows no notable features except a blackish malar stripe and a large pale bill. The ear-coverts are plain, sometimes a bit browner than the rest of the face, but particularly juveniles may show a pattern similar to that of female Cirl Bunting, but less prominent. The legs are quite pale, flesh-brown to straw yellow. Other similar buntings are slimmer-looking birds with finer proportions and proportionally longer tails. Possible confusion species include larks, sparrows and female rosefinches. Skylark *Alauda arvensis*, which occurs in the same habitat, is similar both in colour and to some extent in flight action, but has white outer tail feathers, shorter tail, smaller head and a thinner bill. Female Common Rosefinch *Carpodacus erythrinus* is much smaller, but superficially similar. The streaking both above and below is brown, not black, and noticeably less prominent, while the wing-bars are whiter and more prominent than in Corn Bunting. The characteristic call note of Corn Bunting, a dry *tuk,* is frequently heard and will aid in identification.

DESCRIPTION
First-winter birds are identical to adults. In fresh plumage the general colour is buffier; whiter and greyer in worn plumage. The sexes are similar in plumage, but differ in size.
Adult and first-winter, both sexes Crown grey-brown, faint-

ly tinged chestnut, uniformly streaked dark. Supercilium and lores pale buff. Diffuse eye-ring pale buffish. Ear-coverts pale grey-brown with a faint warm chestnut tinge, paler in the centre, finely streaked darker grey-brown. Submoustachial stripe and throat pale buff, the latter with sparse small dark spots. Malar stripe blackish and prominent. Sides of neck pale buff. Nape pale olive-brown, streaked dark. Mantle slightly darker and browner, more heavily streaked dark. Scapulars slightly browner still. Back and rump similar to mantle, but slightly paler and only diffusely streaked. Uppertail-coverts grey-brown, with whitish edges and a dark shaft streak. Lesser coverts grey-brown. Median coverts dark brown with buffy edges, broken at the tip, slightly tinged rufous on the outer web. Greater coverts dark brown with rusty-buff edges, slightly paler at the tips. Tertials dark brown with rusty-buff edges, not forming *Emberiza* pattern. Primary coverts dark brown with grey-brown edge on the outer web. Primaries and secondaries dark brown with narrow pale grey-brown edges. Tail dark brown, the outermost pair slightly paler at the tip. Underparts pale buff, with prominent streaking on flanks and breast, particularly at the centre where they may form a dark spot. Undertail-coverts pale buff with dark centres. Bill rather pale with darker culmen. The colour varies, usually yellowish-horn, but may be tinged pinkish, greyish or greenish. Tarsus straw yellow to flesh-brown. Iris dark chestnut-brown.

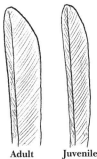

Adult   Juvenile

Outermost tail feather (T6) of adult and juvenile. Feather of juvenile is narrower than adult.

Juvenile Pale sections of plumage rusty- or yellowish-buff. Crown with prominent pale central stripe and dark lateral stripes. Supercilium broad, often rusty-buff. Lores pale. Ear-coverts uniform rusty-buff bordered by eye-stripe and moustachial stripe that do not connect at the rear. Malar stripe narrow and indistinct compared to adults. Sides of neck pale buff. Nape pale olive-brown, streaked dark. Feathers of mantle with rounded dark centres and even pale fringes giving spotted or scaly impression. Back with broader fringes looking even more spotted. Rump with more diffuse dark centres. Uppertail-coverts rusty-buff, with a dark oval subterminal spot. Lesser, median and greater coverts dark brown with pale rusty-buff edges. Median and greater coverts paler at the tip, forming double wing-bars. Tertials dark brown with distinct even rusty-buff edges. Primary coverts dark brown with even rusty-buff edge on the outer web. Primaries and secondaries dark brown with narrow pale rusty-buff edges. Tail dark brown, the outermost pair slightly paler. Breast with distinct elongated spots. Flanks less prominently streaked than in adults. Belly paler than breast and flanks. Undertail-coverts warmer buff than belly. The colour of the bill varies and it may be yellowish, pinkish, greyish or greenish, normally paler than adult, becoming yellowish towards the base. Iris grey-brown or chestnut brown. Tarsus similar in colour to adult, but slightly paler.

Adult   Juvenile

Median coverts of adult and juvenile. Tip of dark centre is blunt in adult, more like narrow spike in juvenile.

SEXING Males, at least in north-western populations, are significantly larger than females. In all but exceptional cases birds with wings longer than 98mm are males and those with wings shorter than 94mm are females. Weight is often helpful, but is less dependable than wing length. Males usually weigh more than 45gm, females less. Individuals with wing length in the overlap zone may be sexed as follows: birds with wing more than 95mm and weight over 46gm should be males, and those below should be females. Alternatively, those with wing length 95-97mm are males if weight is over 53g and females if weight is less than 45g. Note that these figures may not be useful in southern and eastern populations. Females on average seem to be slightly more heavily streaked on the rump and flanks, but differences are not big enough for sexing single birds.

MOULT AND AGEING Juveniles undergo a complete moult, starting at approximately five weeks, usually in July. Adult moults completely after breeding, mid July to early November. The duration of the moult is approximately 80 days. In some areas moult starts as early as mid June, in others end as late as December.

Juvenile plumage characteristic, more scalloped above and spotted rather than streaked on breast. After post-juvenile moult, first-winter birds are identical to adults and most cannot be aged on plumage. However, some first-year birds retain a few juvenile feathers on the rear part of the rump, with a dark pattern in shape of a spot rather than a streak. In early winter the bill may still be duller and greener than in adults. Skull ossification not studied, but may be useful. Differences in iris colour useful, but note that at least in some populations young juveniles have

more brightly coloured iris than usual in buntings.

MEASUREMENTS Wing: (max) male 91.5-107.0, female 85.0-101.0. Tail: male 62.0-77.0, female 54.0-70.5. Bill: (to skull) male 12.5-16.0, female 12.2-15.0. Tarsus: male 23.8-27.1, female 23.3-26.0. P6-P8 emarginated.

GEOGRAPHICAL VARIATION The variation is clinal and rather slight. It is usually impossible to assign single birds to a geographic area based on plumage characters, but there are average plumage differences between populations. The subspecies below are among those that are most often recognised, but the characters typical of each are not as different as they may sound and birds showing characters of a certain race are often found within the range of other races. The species is often regarded as monotypic, which seems to be a sensible position.

M. c. calandra (Most of Europe) Includes *graeca*. Described above.

M. c. clanceyi (W Ireland and Outer Hebrides) Slightly darker brown above and darker yellow and more heavily streaked below.

M. c. parroti (Corsica and adjacent parts of the W Mediterranean) Slightly smaller, slightly darker above and more heavily streaked below.

M. c. thanneri (Canary Islands) Smallest race. As dark as *parroti*, tawny yellow below and more heavily streaked over all.

M. c. buturlini (SE Turkey to E Kazakhstan) Paler and greyer above, with slightly blacker streaking on the mantle and less prominent streaking on the rump. The underparts are on average whiter with fewer dark streaks.

RELATIONSHIPS Often included in the genus *Emberiza*. The main reasons for a separate genus are the marked sexual dimorphism in size, but not in colour, the complete post-juvenile moult, differences in bill structure (curved cutting edge of mandibles) and behaviour. Whether this treatment reflects the true ancestry or not is unknown. Here placed after *Emberiza*, but placement before or after is arbitrary.

VOICE The Corn Bunting has an unusually long singing season from very early in spring through to the autumn. Sings from an elevated position, like a bush or a fence-post. Often sings in flight with dangling legs and uplifted wings. The song is distinctive and uttered persistently. It has been likened to the jangling noise made by a bunch of keys being shaken or a watch spring suddenly turned loose. Also likened to glass being ground. Several *zi* or *tuc* notes quicken into a harsh metallic scrabbling or rattling to produce a very characteristic sound, *zi zi zi zriss* or *trüc tüc tüc tictic tsrrzeesizizisirrsis*. Beware that Whinchat *Saxicola rubetra* often gives a similar phrase.

The call is a hard, dry *tuk* or *ptt*, often rapidly repeated. A rather Yellowhammer-like *trrp* may be given in alarm.

HABITS The breeding season varies a great deal according to local conditions and is often protracted. In north-western Europe often quite late, June-July, even into September, but may breed from mid May. In the Mediterranean area breeding may begin in already in mid February. The breeding strategy varies; some males are monogamous, while others are polygamous and may have half a dozen females. The nest is usually placed on the ground in grass or herbage, but sometimes in low bushes or trees. It is rather large and built of grass and roots,

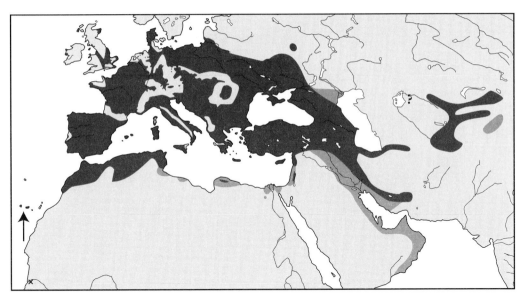

lined with finer grass, rootlets and hair. Up to three clutches have been recorded in a year. Eggs usually 3-6, glossy white, tinged blue, purple or buff, often diffusely speckled brownish, appearing dirty and quite dark, with a few bold dark blotches and scrawls. Incubation 12-14 days by female alone. Young are mostly attended by female and receive various invertebrates like flies, grasshoppers, moths and caterpillars, but also seeds such as unripe grain. Diet of adults a combination of seeds, buds and invertebrates such as grasshoppers, beetles and snails, depending on availability. Appears to take more animal food than one would expect, judging from shape of bill. Takes cereal grain especially during sowing and around harvest. Flight on breeding grounds often weak and fluttering, with legs dangling. Over longer distances the flight is undulating and strong but heavy. Hops on ground. Less agile in trees than other buntings. Gregarious outside the breeding season, when quite large flocks of 100 or more may form. Often in pure flocks, but may associate with other buntings, sparrows or finches.

STATUS AND HABITAT A common and sometimes abundant bird over much of its range, particularly in warmer regions. In cooler north-western areas it is a much more localised and declining species. In Ireland, Scotland, Wales and north-western mainland Europe there has been a marked decline since 1965 and the species has been lost as a breeding bird from much of its former range. In central Europe, the decline is less dramatic. It is likely that the reasons for this decline are both climatic and agricultural. Colder winters and wetter summers have been suggested as having a negative effect on Corn Buntings. A change in land use, from cereal crops to pasture, appears to be another reason for the decline in those areas. It is also reasonable to assume that the original cultivation of western Europe greatly benefited Corn Buntings, but that modernisation, including greater use of pesticides, has had serious detrimental effects on those same populations. Particularly the Swedish population has suffered severe decline from use of mercury-treated seed. Changes in agricultural practices, such as different time of sowing or harvesting, may have caused increased nest loss, or affect-

ed timing of food availability in a detrimental way. Loss of winter stubbles, as a result of a change from spring to autumn sowing, is yet another detrimental factor. The British and north-west European populations, being peripheral, will naturally be particularly susceptible to adverse change.

Usually found in steppe habitat or cultivated areas, especially cereal crops, downland and other grassland. Also grassy areas in semi-desert or coastal dunes, grassy scrubland and rough ground with some grass cover or low herbage. Trees, fences or wires will serve as song posts if available, but are not essential. In winter often in stubble fields.

DISTRIBUTION AND MOVEMENTS Breeds in suitable habitats across the western temperate and warm temperate zones of the western Palearctic, usually at low or moderate altitudes. Within range, apparently suitable areas sometimes rather arbitrarily avoided. From the British Isles, where absent from most western and northern areas, France, Spain, Portugal and the Canary Islands (except Lanzarote and Fuerteventura), east throughout the Mediterranean basin, from Morocco to Tunisia, and locally in Libya (Cyrenaica), through Europe, except in the Pyrenees, Alps, Carpathians and Tatra Mountains. In southern Germany and eastern Belgium largely absent from areas above 500m. Local in most of the Netherlands and north-western Germany. In the north to Denmark, extreme southern Sweden and Lithuania. Extinct in Norway and probably soon also in Sweden. Breeding range extends eastwards from southern Belarus, Ukraine and southern Russia east to the Caspian Sea and the Transcaucasian republics. In the south, occurs throughout Turkey east through northern Syria, Lebanon, northern Israel, northern Iraq, to the Elburz and Zagros mountains in Iran. Apparently disjunct population inhabits northernmost Afghanistan, south-eastern Uzbekistan, western Tajikistan, Kyrgyzstan, and southern Kazakhstan into extreme western China (Ili River basin, Xinjiang).

In north-west Europe Corn Buntings tend to abandon their breeding areas in winter but do not move far away. Mainly sedentary but migratory in the north-eastern parts of its European range. In the eastern parts of the Baltic states it is a summer visitor, and in Egypt, Jordan and southern Iraq it occurs only in winter. Vagrant Mauretania and Senegal and Pakistan.

REFERENCES Bezzel (1993), Cramp & Perrins (1994), Dementiev & Gladkov (1966), Donald *et al.* (1994), Harper (1995), Svensson (1992), Tucker & Heath (1994), Vaurie (1956).

CALCARIUS

Four species, similar to *Emberiza*, but plumper and more confined to open areas, where they forage exclusively on the ground. They show strong sexual dimorphism in plumage in the breeding season, and are all characterised by a long hind claw (hence the name longspur for the genus). All species occur in North America, but one species is also distributed across northern Eurasia.

42 MCCOWN'S LONGSPUR
Calcarius mccownii   Plate 18

Described as *Plectrophanes mccownii* Lawrence 1851.
Synonyms: *Rhynchophanes mccownii, Centrophanes mccowni.*

McCown's Longspur breeds on short-grass prairie in a rather limited area of north-central USA and adjacent Canada. It is still fairly common in some parts of its declining favoured habitat, but is generally rather scarce.

IDENTIFICATION 15cm. The breeding male is mostly grey, with black crown, moustachial stripe and breast patch, white throat and vent, and conspicuous chestnut median coverts, rendering it unmistakable. The female is a featureless grey-brown bird, with a rather large pinkish bill, broadly streaked on the upperparts, and unstreaked underneath. In worn plumage there is often a trace of a dark patch on the breast, ghosting male plumage, and the belly may become rather dark greyish. However, the underparts never show the more uniformly distributed small triangular spots and streaks, characteristic of breeding female Chestnut-collared. The moustachial stripe is dark and quite prominent, again ghosting male. The edges of the median coverts are often fairly extensively rusty, but may be inconspicuously pale buffish.

In non-breeding plumage the sexes are initially similar in the field, generally rather pale grey-brown, streaked dark on the upperparts, unstreaked underneath, but as plumage becomes worn males begin to show traces of black on crown and breast, and grey on rump. During fall and winter, McCown's is most similar to Chestnut-collared Longspur, but is generally paler, with large pale bill, less prominent wing-bars, contrastingly blackish alula and a faint brownish, almost crescent-shaped, patch on the breast contrasting with the whitish belly. The large pinkish bill of McCown's is a prominent feature compared to the small dark bill of Chestnut-collared. The face pattern is somewhat reminiscent of female House Sparrow *Passer domesticus*, because of rather prominent pale supercilium. The anterior supercilium, lores and area below eye form a pale area, bordered below by rather well-marked dark moustachial stripe. The border between the submoustachial stripe and the ear-coverts is thus quite well-defined. In Chestnut-collared, the facial expression is quite different, with indistinct supercilium, rather uniform ear-coverts and much less contrast between ear-coverts and submoustachial stripe. The median coverts are usually chestnut, which is never the case in Chestnut-collared, but this feature may

be difficult to see as the median coverts may be covered by scapulars and flank feathers. Furthermore, the chestnut element is not always prominent in females. In Chestnut-collared, the alula is similar in colour to the centres of the wing-coverts and flight feathers and does not stand out. The wing-bars are paler and more prominent in Chestnut-collared. The primary projection is usually more than half the length of the tertials in McCown's, but less than half the length of the tertials in Chestnut-collared. In McCown's, the underparts are unstreaked, but with a contrast between buffish breast and whitish belly. In Chestnut-collared, the breast is diffusely streaked and there is no noticeable contrast in base colour between breast and belly.

Told from Lapland and Smith's by large pinkish bill, nondescript face pattern, pale plumage, unstreaked breast, chestnut median but not greater coverts, inconspicuous wing-bars and striking tail pattern.

McCown's is often easier to see well on the ground in winter than both Smith's and Chestnut-collared, as it prefers more barren ground. Nevertheless tail pattern and flight calls are important for identification. The short tail shows much white, with an inverted blackish T in the centre. The flight feathers appear paler and more silvery in flight than other longspurs. Flight call is a soft rattled *chüpp chürüpp*, softer than Lapland, and quite different from the crystal-clear trill of Smith's or the squeaky twitterings of Chestnut-collared. In flight most easily separated from Horned Lark *Eremophila alpestris*, with which it often associates, by silvery flight feathers and tail pattern. Viewed from below, Horned Lark shows typical black tail, contrasting with white belly and underwing.

The juvenile is rather uniformly scalloped on the mantle and streaked on the breast, unlike adults. It differs from juvenile Chestnut-collared Longspur, other than in structure (bill size and primary projection, when wings fully grown) and tail pattern, also by having paler and more uniformly scalloped upperparts without whitish stripes on the central mantle often shown by Chestnut-collared. The breast is streaked in both species, but in McCown's the base colour of the breast is yellowish-brown, contrasting with whitish, unstreaked belly. In juvenile Chestnut-collared the underparts are uniformly buffy-brown, without contrast in base colour between the streaked breast and unstreaked belly. The median crown-stripe is whitish and more prominent in Chestnut-collared.

Female Dickcissel *Spiza americana* also shows chestnut median coverts, but is more heavily streaked on the upperparts and overall colour is a much more yellowish-brown. The malar stripe of non-breeding Dickcissel is always prominent. The jizz and behaviour are quite different from that of McCown's Longspur.

DESCRIPTION

Difference between male and female pronounced in worn plumage, slight in fresh. Juvenile clearly different from subsequent plumages.

Adult male breeding Crown black. Supercilium, lores and area below eye white. Ear-coverts pale grey, tinged brown. Moustachial stripe black. Throat white. Nape and sides of neck grey. Mantle and scapulars grey, diffusely streaked brownish-grey. Back and rump grey, mottled dark brownish-grey, not contrasting with mantle or uppertail-coverts. Uppertail-coverts dark brownish-grey. Lesser coverts grey, except lower row, which may be chestnut. Median coverts brownish-grey basally, visible part mainly chestnut with narrow buffish fringes. Greater coverts brown with paler brownish-grey edges and narrow whitish tips. Alula blackish. Tertials dark brown with paler edges. Primaries brown with narrow pale edges, slightly darker at the tip. Secondaries brown, slightly darker subterminally on outer web, tip whitish. Inner webs of both primaries and secondaries rather broadly edged white. All tail feathers, except central pair (T1), mostly white. The outermost pair (T6) are completely white, sometimes with small dark tip on outer web. The second outermost pair to second innermost (T5-T2) are white with similar amounts of blackish-brown at the tip. Breast brownish-black. Rest of underparts grey with some whitish mottling. Central belly and undertail-coverts white. Bill blackish. Tarsus pinkish-brown. Iris dark brown.

Crown feathers of male and female. Note sharply set off dark centre of male, and more pointed and diffuse dark centre of female.

Adult male non-breeding Crown pale buffish-brown, streaked dark brown, on forehead almost spotted. Dark centres of feathers often visible like irregular spots on crown. Feathers on rear crown whiter, sometimes producing a trace of a median crown-stripe. Supercilium, lores and submoustachial stripe whitish-buff. Ear-coverts greyish-brown, paler in the centre. Malar stripe very faint. Throat pale buffish-white. Mantle and scapulars pale buffish-brown broadly streaked brown, especially on upper mantle. Back, rump and uppertail-coverts also buffish-brown, but slightly less prominently streaked. However, rump turns greyer with increased wear. The uppertail-coverts have rather well-defined pale edges on the tips, creating a slight scalloping. Wings similar to adult male breeding, but fresh. The edges to the median coverts are broader and less well-defined. The greater coverts are brown with broad buffish-grey edges and tips. Tertials dark brown with diffuse pale edges, becoming gradually paler towards tips. The dark tip of the primaries are more prominent. Tail pattern like adult male in breeding plumage. Breast yellowish-buff, with underlying dark feather centres showing through. Sides of breast with some diffuse

streaking. Flanks with a dusky tinge. Belly pale buffish. Undertail-coverts pale cream. Bill dull pinkish to pinkish-red with diffuse dark tip.

First-winter and first-summer male Like adult male in corresponding plumage, but with less bright median coverts and browner rump. Dark breast patch less extensive. Less black on the crown feathers. Tail feathers tapered, more worn than in adults.

Adult female breeding Similar to adult male non-breeding, but plumage worn. The face pattern is more contrasting, with whiter supercilium and submoustachial stripe, and a more prominent moustachial stripe. The streaking on mantle and crown is blacker and more distinct. The colour of the median coverts varies from fairly extensively rufous to blackish with pale buffish fringes. The wing-bars are distinct but rather narrow. The bases of the feathers of the breast are dark grey. In worn birds a dark patch on the breast may ghost male plumage, but the patch is less well-defined.

Adult female non-breeding Like adult male non-breeding, but slightly paler on upperparts. Streaking on crown and mantle not quite as broad as in male, and also less distinct on back and rump. Lacks the male's spotted appearance on crown, created by the black feather centres. The malar stripe is slightly more prominent. Median coverts blackish with pale buffish fringes, only the outer ones with significant amount of chestnut.

First-winter female Very similar to adult female non-breeding, but tail feathers tapered and more worn than in adults.

Juvenile Crown dark brown, each feather with a neat thin pale fringe. The edging of the central ones slightly paler, creating a faint central crown-stripe. Supercilium, lores and submoustachial stripe whitish, the supercilium with thin blackish streaks. Ear-coverts faintly streaked blackish-brown, whitish in the centre. Malar stripe rather narrow, broken into spots on lower throat. Throat whitish. Mantle, scapulars, back and rump uniformly dark with pale narrow scalloping. The uppertail-coverts have dark brown centres and well-defined pale buffish-brown edges. Lesser coverts buffish-grey. Median coverts dark brown, with well-defined whitish edges. Greater coverts brown with broad well-defined sandy-grey edges and pale buffish tips. Tertials dark brown, paler than median coverts, with relatively narrow pale edges, more sharply set off than in adults. Flight feathers as in adults. Tail pattern like adult, but feathers obviously tapered. Breast yellowish-buff, distinctly streaked. Belly and undertail-coverts whitish. Bill paler pinkish-orange and with more obvious dark tip than in subsequent plumages.

Tail pattern. Tail appears very white, with black inverted 'T'.

SEXING Breeding male characterised by black crown and breast patch, and almost uniformly chestnut median coverts. In non-breeding plumage, dark patterns are obscured and the the sexes are rather similar. The median coverts are similar to breeding plumage, but with broader pale fringes. The concealed bases of the feathers of crown and breast are jet black, sharply set off from the paler fringes, sometimes showing through but sometimes only possible to determine in the hand.

Breeding females lack black crown and breast patch, and the median coverts are dark-centred with broader, less contrasting fringes, frequently with a chestnut cast of varying prominence. In non-breeding plumage, females are similar to males. The concealed bases of the feathers of crown and breast are blackish grey, more diffusely set off than in male. The difference between the bases of the feathers of the breast patch and surrounding feathers is small in females, but prominent in males. Wing length useful (male 89.5-97.5, female 86.5-92.0).

MOULT AND AGEING Juveniles acquire first-winter plumage by moulting body feathers, including wing-coverts, while still on the breeding grounds from July to September. Adults moult completely after the breeding season, from July to September. The breeding attire is acquired largely by wear, but there is also a limited moult of contour feathers in February to April, mostly restricted to the head.

The shape of the tail feathers and state of wear of wings and tail are useful for determining age. The tip of the tail in adults is truncate, while juveniles and first-year birds show a pointed tip. The flight feathers and tail of first-year birds are relatively more worn than adults throughout the first-year. Skull ossification completed between early November and end of January. Iris colour probably useful.

MEASUREMENTS Wing: (max) male 89.5-97.5, female 86.5-92.0, (chord) male 86-94, female 80-88. Tail: male 50.5-59.0, female 49.0-54.0. Bill: (to skull) male 14.6-16.1, female 13.6-14.8. Tarsus: male 17.2-18.5, female 17.2-18.6. Unlike the other longspurs, this species has only two emarginations (P7-P8). Primary projection approximately 25mm. P6 is 3-8mm shorter than P7.

GEOGRAPHICAL VARIATION None.

RELATIONSHIPS Because of its much larger bill and shorter hindclaw, many taxonomists have preferred to put this species in its own genus, different from the genus *Calcarius*, as demonstrated by the three synonyms above. These characters are, however, subject to strong selective pressure. All four longspurs share so many other similarities that it seems quite clear that they form a group of closest relatives.

VOICE The almost lark-like song is delivered from the ground or in flight. The song flight is unique within the range. The bird rises gradually with fluttering wings and hanging legs to 5 to 10m, then drops downward like miniature parachute with outspread unmoving wings and raised, spread tail, vigorously singing. The song strophes are often given with shorter intervals, making the song sound more continuous than other longspurs. It is a twittering jumble of notes, each strophe often starting with a descending *chup-iri-up*. Part of the song could be rendered *chup-iri-upchup chip-chu chip chup-iri-upchup chee...*

The flight call is a dry rattled *chüpp-chürrüpp*, very different from the call of Chestnut-collared, but reminiscent of call of Lapland. Sometimes a soft, almost metallic one-syllable *chüt* call is given from the ground or in flight. Sometimes a popping *poik*.

HABITS Breeds May to July. The nest is built on the ground, usually in natural prairie, often besides a small bush, but sometimes right out in the open, lacking any concealment. Locally also in wheat or fallow stubble fields. It is constructed of dried weed stems, woody fibre and blades, lined by finer grasses or wool, where available. Eggs 3-4, occasionally 5 or even 6. The colour varies a great deal and they may be whitish, pale green, clay and greyish-olive, with lines, spots and speckles of lilac, rusty-brown or blackish-brown. The female incubates for 12 days, and the young leave the nest about 10 days later, already flying short distances two days later. They are reared on insects, mainly moths, caterpillars and grasshoppers. Adults feed mainly on grasshoppers in the summer, but also other insects, weed seeds and grain, the latter two dominating in winter. Walks or runs. Rather tame. Outside the breeding season often in flocks, freely associating with Horned Larks and Lapland Buntings.

STATUS AND HABITAT Locally fairly common breeder on flat expanses of short-grass prairie, with prickly pear, sage and buffalo grass, often in areas with flat-topped buttes. The breeding habitat is subject to destruction and consequently the numbers are declining. If this development continues, McCown's Longspur will become increasingly threatened. During the present century, the breeding range has contracted significantly.

In winter on open ground, such as ploughed and stubble fields, short grass, dirt fields, dry lake beds and sandy prairie. Usually found on much more barren grounds than Chestnut-collared Longspur, with which it rarely associates.

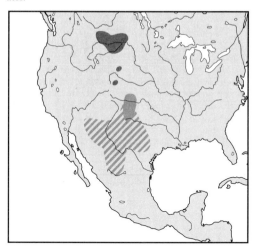

DISTRIBUTION AND MOVEMENTS Breeds in southern Canada and northern USA. Main breeding areas are in south-eastern Alberta and south-western Saskatchewan and Montana. Peripheral populations, subject to a great deal of fluctuation, have been reported from Manitoba, north-central North Dakota, north-eastern Colorado, where locally quite common on protected land, north-western Nebraska and south-eastern Wyoming. The species may well have disappeared from some of these areas today. Flocks form by early August, and by September most have deserted the breeding grounds.

Winters mainly from west-central Kansas and central Oklahoma south to western and south-central Texas. Smaller numbers winter in central Arizona and southern New Mexico south to north-eastern Sonora, Chihuahua, northern Durango, and north-western Coahuila. Leaves the southern portions of the wintering grounds around early March and about a month later further north. Most birds arrive on the breeding grounds in Montana in late April and in southern Canada in early May. During fall migration and in winter occurs in very small numbers in south-eastern and coastal California. On coast of southern California rare but regular in fall, casual in winter. Casual on coastal northern California and further north and west of its normal range to British Columbia, in the east to Illinois and Missouri. Accidental in Massachusetts, Minnesota, Michigan and Louisiana.

REFERENCES Bent (1968), Farrand (1983), Godfrey (1986), O'Brien (1995), Pyle *et al.*(1987).

43   LAPLAND LONGSPUR
Calcarius lapponicus   Plate 17

Described as *Fringilla lapponica* Linnaeus 1758.
Synonyms: *Plectrophanes lapponicus, Fringilla calcarata.*
Other name: Lapland Bunting.

The Lapland Longspur is one of the commonest passerines on the arctic tundra. In winter it inhabits seashores and open grassy areas.

IDENTIFICATION 16cm. The Lapland Longspur is rather bulky, with a large head and proportionately short tail, compared to *Emberiza* buntings, from which it also differs by long, nearly straight hind claw. The short bill is usually yellowish with a dark tip, but may be pale brownish in young birds. Often first brought to attention by characteristic rattling flight call *prrt ... chu*, resembling Snow Bunting but less melodious.

The breeding male is unmistakable, showing characteristic black face and breast, corn yellow bill, rufous nape and whitish zigzag pattern on the side of the head. The upperparts are relatively dark, blackish narrowly streaked pale buff. Breeding female is rather nondescript, but shows rufous nape and greater coverts. The head is very pale, with blackish lateral crown-stripes and prominent blackish border to ear-coverts. Pale lores, whitish supercilium and pale centres to ear-coverts create open-faced expression. Upperparts like adult male, underparts whitish, with blackish streaking on breast and flanks.

The almost lark-like habits and nondescript plumage of autumn and winter birds make these more difficult to identify. Non-breeding birds are similar to breeding female, but browner and paler on crown and mantle, and buffier on breast. Differ from buntings by combination of bulky appearance, usually yellowish bill, open-faced expression, chestnut greater coverts, and white wing-bars. The eye-stripe (behind the eye) and moustachial stripe, bordering the ear-coverts, are inconspicuous in front and broad, almost triangular at rear, bordered behind by whitish sides of the neck. The sides of the crown are dark, and the pale median crown-stripe conspicuous. The nape is pale rufous-buff, almost unstreaked (in males often with concealed rufous colour showing through), and contrasts with darker crown and heavily streaked mantle. The underparts are noticeably whitish, the breast washed buffish, with dark streaking. In non-breeding males, concealed black breast pattern often visible, causing breast to appear erratically spotted or even barred, rather than streaked.

Juveniles are duller and darker than adults. The mantle and crown are heavily streaked yellowish-brown and blackish, the nape similar in colour with no trace of chestnut. The breast is darker yellowish-olive and more prominently streaked than adults, clearly demarcated from the pale buffish belly. From other winter longspurs (which see for further differences) by tail pattern, element of chestnut colour in greater coverts, tertials and nape, and more prominent streaking on breast and flanks.

Non-breeding and juvenile Lapland may be confused with female-type Common Reed Bunting, but in all plumages the uniformly chestnut appearance of the greater coverts, contrasting with the rest of the wing and the mantle, and enhanced by two white wing-bars, are characteristic. The streaking on the breast is concentrated into a well-defined breast-band. The bill is yellowish or brownish. In Common Reed, the ear-coverts are darker and the malar stripe considerably more prominent. Common Reed Bunting shows rufous greater coverts, but these do not stand out as in Lapland, when compared to median coverts and edges of secondaries. The wing-bars of Common Reed are rufous and relatively indistinct. The underparts are not as white, and the streaking is diffuse and more extensive. The bill is greyish. The primary projection is longer in Lapland Longspur than in *Emberiza* buntings, and the hind claw is longer and straighter.

In North America confusion with Vesper Sparrow *Pooecetes gramineus* conceivable. Vesper is noticeably more uniformly grey-brown, with more heavily streaked breast, and lacks chestnut greater coverts. The lores and ear-coverts are darker, and the pale eye-ring prominent, creating a different facial expression. The lesser coverts are chestnut, but usually not visible, and the legs are flesh-coloured. In Lapland Longspur the lesser coverts are blackish or greyish (sometimes quite pale), and the legs dark brown.

Harris's Sparrow *Zonotrichia querula* is superficially similar, but occurs in different habitat and is sparrow-like in behaviour. It lacks white in the tail, and shows much less prominent dark borders around the ear-coverts, limited to the upper rear corner.

Easily told from all larks by very long primary projection, which is about equal to length of tertials. In flight chunky appearance and powerful flight separate it from more broad-winged and fluttering larks, as well as from e.g. Common Reed Bunting.

DESCRIPTION
Adult male breeding Crown black with some buffish-white at the centre rear. Supercilium pale buff, encircles rear of ear-coverts and reaches sides of breast, forming characteristic zigzag pattern. In front of eye, supercilium often very faint, never reaching the bill. Ear-coverts, lores, throat and upper breast black. Nape rufous. Mantle and scapulars blackish-brown, with some dark rufous admixed, prominently streaked pale sandy-brown. Back similar, but with less rufous. Rump rufous, streaked pale sandy-brown. Uppertail-coverts dark brown, with pale sandy-brown edges. Lesser coverts blackish with pale sandy-grey edges. Median coverts blackish with buffy-white edges, broadest on the outer web. Greater coverts blackish with chestnut edges and whitish tips. Primary coverts dark brown with rather broad whitish tips on the inner web. Primaries dark brown with narrow pale edges. Secondaries dark brown with rather broad rufous-buff edges, forming a wing panel, and whitish tips. Tertials dark brown with relatively broad chestnut edge on the outer web, forming typical

Emberiza pattern. Tail dark brown with white in the two outermost feathers. Sides of upper breast buffy-white. A narrow band of black from breast to flanks. Belly and undertail-coverts buffy-white. Bill corn yellow with dark tip. Tarsus dark brown. Iris chestnut-brown.

Crown feathers of male and female. Note sharply set off dark centre of male, and more pointed and diffuse dark centre of female.

Adult male non-breeding Crown streaked blackish-brown laterally, with a sandy-brown median crown-stripe. Supercilium and ear-coverts yellowish-buff. Lores similar, but paler. Eye-stripe and moustachial stripe blackish-brown, very broad, almost triangular, at rear edge of ear-coverts. Throat whitish or very pale buffish. Nape yellowish-buff with a varying degree of rufous. Upperparts similar to breeding plumage, but slightly less contrasting. Broader pale sandy-grey fringes on lesser coverts make these look more uniformly pale. Greater coverts with a stronger chestnut tinge. Remiges and tertials blacker. Upper breast barred or blotched blackish to a varying extent. Traces of a narrow band of black from breast to flanks. Bill yellowish with dark tip. Tarsus dark brown.
First-winter male Like adult male non-breeding, but rectrices pointed. Concealed rufous colour of nape and black on breast less apparent. Iris dark grey-brown.
First-summer male Very similar to adult male breeding, but rectrices pointed. Iris duller than adult.
Adult female breeding Very similar to adult male non-breeding, except that plumage is heavily worn. The lateral crown-stripes are blackish and median crown-stripe paler, more contrasting. The supercilium is pale buffish, whiter than the ear-coverts. Lores whitish. The eye-stripe and moustachial stripe are prominent. Breast whitish, usually with blackish gorget or irregular patch connected to the malar stripes. Nape tinged rufous with blackish spots. Upperparts pale sandy-brown, streaked blackish. Greater coverts pale sandy-brown, usually lacking chestnut tinge, but still warmer brown than surrounding areas. Remiges and tertials bleached and browner. Belly and flanks whitish, streaked blackish on the flanks. Bill tinged brighter yellowish.
Adult female non-breeding Similar to adult male non-breeding, but duller. Crown paler, supercilium and ear-coverts slightly paler. Eye-stripe and moustachial stripe brown and less prominent. Nape yellowish-buff with faint dark streaking, often with a faint rufous tinge. Lesser coverts more sandy-brown and less greyish. Breast and flanks pale sandy-brown, streaked dark brown. Belly and undertail-coverts buffy-white. Bill pale brownish with dark tip. Breast pale sandy-brown, usually unstreaked, but concealed dark bases to feathers sometimes visible.
First-winter female Very similar to adult female non-breeding, but rectrices pointed. The malar stripe tends to be more prominent and the breast often shows some fine dark streaking.

Juvenile Crown streaked blackish-brown and rufous. The edging of the central feathers slightly paler, creating a faint median crown-stripe. Supercilium pale yellowish-white, finely streaked blackish. Lores pale yellowish-brown. Ear-coverts rufescent brown, streaked blackish-brown. Malar stripe blackish-brown, broken into spots on lower throat. Submoustachial stripe and throat whitish. Mantle, scapulars, back and rump rufescent brown, streaked blackish. The uppertail-coverts have dark brown centres and well-defined pale rufescent brown edges. Lesser coverts dark grey, with pale buffish and rufescent tips. Median coverts with well-defined pale sandy or white edges, broken at the tip by pointed black centres. Greater coverts blackish-brown with broad well-defined chestnut edges and white tips. Tertials dark brown with paler rufous edges, more sharply set off than in adults. Flight feathers as in adults. Tail pattern like adult, but shape obviously tapered. Breast yellowish olive-brown, distinctly streaked. Belly and undertail-coverts pale buff. Bill pale brownish with dark tip. Tarsus flesh-pink or dull flesh-brown. Iris dark grey-brown.

Tail pattern. In flight tail appears dark with white sides, although white pattern is not very conspicuous.

SEXING Breeding males are characterised by black lores, throat, breast and ear-coverts, occasionally with traces of white fringes. The supercilium never reaches the bill. The nape is uniformly rufous. In fresh winter plumage, the black face and breast pattern are obscured by pale fringes. The best difference from females are black centres of the crown feathers, which are large and sharply set off from pale tips. Wing length is often useful.

Breeding females are usually much paler than males on ear-coverts and throat, and always have whitish and brown intermixed on throat, breast and ear-coverts. The supercilium usually reaches bill. The nape is considerably less rufous than in males, with dark centres to the feathers. In fresh plumage the amount of black on the base of the crown feathers is less extensive than in males, grading into the pale tips.

MOULT AND AGEING Juveniles undergo a partial moult July-September, starting about three weeks after fledging, involving body, lesser and median coverts and tertials, but not remiges or rectrices, before leaving breeding grounds. Adults moult completely, June-September, before leaving breeding grounds. The whole process takes about 50 days. There is a limited moult, involving ear-coverts, chin and lores, in March-May; rest of breeding plumage attained by wear.

Rather difficult to age after post-breeding moult completed. Shape of tail feathers is good indication of age. Central tail feathers often with more distinctive narrow grey edge in adults, but difference not always obvious. Iris colour useful. Skull ossification completed between mid November and end of January.

MEASUREMENTS Wing: (max) male 87-102, female 83-94. Tail: male 55-65, female 50-60. Bill: (to skull) male 12.1-15.0, female 11.0-13.6. Tarsus: male 19.5-22.2, female

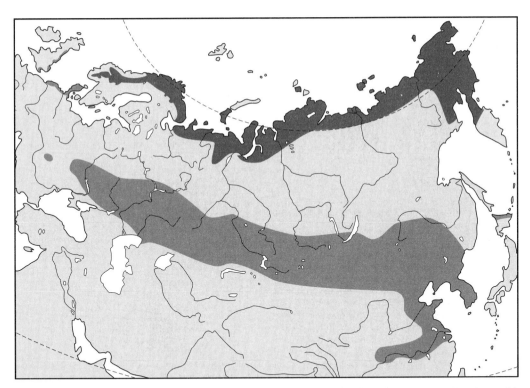

19.5-22.5. Primary projection approximately 25-30mm. P6 is 5-11mm shorter than P7. P7-P8 emarginated, often with faint emargination on P6.

GEOGRAPHICAL VARIATION The variation is slight and largely clinal. Main differences between races are size and intensity of colours of upperparts.

C. l. lapponicus (N Norway to E Siberia). Described above.

C. l. subcalcaratus (Greenland and N Canada, west to the Mackenzie River) Bill longer, heavier and deeper at base. Wing on average longer (male 98, female 92). Males tend to show less black on the sides of the breast, but females tend to show more black on the breast than the nominate race. The nape is slightly paler than the nominate race. The upperparts are slightly paler in breeding plumage and slightly darker than *alascensis*. However, the differences are so slight that it is difficult to define the geographical boundaries of these three races.

C. l. alascensis (Chukotskiy peninsula, islands of the Bering Sea, Alaska, east to the Mackenzie River) Upperparts paler than nominate race in both summer and winter plumage. Streaking of upperparts narrower, without rusty tinge. Bill heavier.

C. l. kamtschaticus (Sea of Okhotsk area and Kamchatka) Darker above than nominate, with richer rufous tinge.

C. l. coloratus (Komandor Islands; casual to Attu) Similar in colour to *kamtschaticus*. Largest race (male 93-100, female 88-94), with longest primary projection.

VOICE The song is delivered from an elevated point on the ground, a stone or a low shrub, or in flight. Has typical pipit-like song flight, where male ascends, usually silently, to about 10m, singing while gliding down, with wings and tail spread, to a perch on the ground. The song is a rapid succession of somewhat squeeky and jingling notes, and resembles to a varying degree Shore Lark *Eremophila alpestris*, Snow Bunting and Bobolink *Dolichonyx oryzivorus*. It is rather stereotyped in each individual, but varies geographically and between singers. Examples of common song types may be transcribed *djüü-tiiah-preeyu chirio-twi-trii tri-leeoh* or *towii-chü dowewichidow-e djüü-chürü-triiahli*.

The common flight call is a short, hard and tuneless rattled *prrt*, usually followed by a short clear whistled *chu*, sometimes deflected. Also a higher pitched *jeeb*, which is often heard from nocturnal migrants. A melodious *tee-uu* is often heard on the breeding grounds.

HABITS Mainly monogamous, but some males bigamous or even promiscuous. Nesting begins only a few days after the females have arrived on the breeding grounds. The nest is placed in a sheltered position on ground, often protected by a shrub. It is a well constructed cup of grass, moss, rootlets and lichens, usually lined with feathers, soft fibres and sometimes hair. Usually only one brood. Eggs usually 5-6 (numbers decrease later in the season), base colour pale greenish, greyish or buffish, but usually rather dark, heavily marked and usually largely obscured with olive-brown or rusty blotches, often with sparse black or purplish-black dots and scrawls. Incubation by female 11-13 days. Young are fed by both parents, mainly on adult and larval mosquitoes, craneflies, midges, and other insects and spiders according to abundance. Young reach 90% of adult weight after about 8.5 days, and leave the nest when 8 to 10 days old, 3-5 days before they are able to fly. During summer, adults' food consists mainly of insects and other invertebrates, especially adult and larval crane-

211

flies, mosquitoes, midges and beetles. Outside breeding season feeds mainly on seeds, from grasses, sedges and various herbs. Usual gait a quick run, but also walks and hops. Usually perches on ground or boulders, but also on low bushes, rarely in trees. Gregarious except when breeding. Often associates with Skylarks *Alauda arvensis*, Shorelarks, Snow Buntings or longspurs. Sometimes allows close approach but flocks may be wary.

STATUS AND HABITAT Common on moist open grassy and lowland tundra above treeline. Exceptional densities of 400 pairs per km² have been recorded. Often near lakes in damp valley bottoms or on plateaus with crowberries, dwarf birch and willows. In winter on a variety of open weedy areas, such as airfields, grass steppes, stubble fields, pasture near wetlands and coastal saltmarsh.

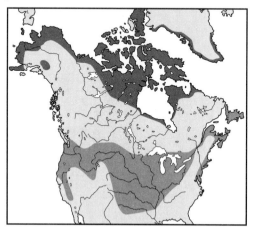

DISTRIBUTION AND MOVEMENTS Breeds in arctic region of northern Eurasia, Greenland and northern North America. Along the Arctic Ocean mainly found in areas north of the Arctic Circle, but occurs further south in Scandinavia, Greenland, and northern Newfoundland, breeding as far south as Churchill (Manitoba) and Cape Henrietta Maria (Ontario) in Canada. Occurs in Alaska south to the Aleutian chain. Absent from Iceland and Svalbard, where only accidental. Has bred in Scotland.

Autumn migration begins in August. First birds may arrive on wintering grounds already late August, but main migration period September and October. Often does not reach winter quarters until November.

Wintering grounds in Eurasia not well known. Most probably migrate in south-easterly direction. Lower numbers winter in coastal western Europe, from southern Scandinavia and Poland to Great Britain and France. In Central Europe rare, more common further east. Reoccurs in numbers in Ukraine. Winters eastwards through southern Kazakhstan, Mongolia and China south to the Yangtse, to Korea and Japan, where rare and sporadic during migration and in winter. In North America winters mainly on the Great Plains in southern Canada and northern and central USA. More sparsely east to the Atlantic seaboard, from North Carolina to Newfoundland, and west to the Pacific states, from California to British Columbia, largely avoiding the area between Sierra Nevada and the Rocky Mountains.

Withdrawal from southernmost parts of wintering area begins around mid February. Main departure in March. Last birds may remain until mid May, at which time first birds arrive on breeding grounds.

Accidental south of normal wintering area to Portugal, Spain, Malta, northern Caucasus, the Mexican Gulf coast and Florida in USA, and Mexico south to Veracruz and Yucatán.

REFERENCES Bent (1968), Bezzel (1993), Cramp & Perrins (1994), Dementiev & Gladkov (1966), Gabrielson & Lincoln (1959), Godfrey (1986), Harris *et al.* (1989), Kessel (1989), Svensson (1992), Vaurie (1956).

44　SMITH'S LONGSPUR
Calcarius pictus　　　　　　Plate 18

Described as *Emberiza (Plectrophanes) picta* Swainson 1832.

A Nearctic species, uncommon in sedge meadows in the transition area between the boreal forest and the tundra. In restricted winter range locally common in favoured areas of pastures.

IDENTIFICATION 15cm. Male in breeding plumage rather dark above and golden-buff below with unique black and white face pattern. The crown is black, the supercilium white and on the ear-coverts there is a bold black triangular pattern with white centre. White lesser coverts of male sometimes visible when perched, and obvious in flight. The bill is longer and more pointed than other longspurs. Plumage of female shows relatively limited variation between summer and winter and is very similar to male in winter as well.

Non-breeding birds are nondescript and almost always difficult to see well, due to preferred habitat of relatively tall grass. The face pattern is similar to that of other longspurs, but the dark border to the ear-coverts is narrow and well marked, and enhanced by a whitish submoustachial stripe that angles upwards behind the ear-coverts, being palest adjacent to the dark border. The crown and mantle, separated by a paler nape, are boldly streaked and give a very dark impression. The underparts are rather uniformly yellowish-buff, with limited but distinct narrow streaking on the breast and flanks.

In fall and winter most similar to Chestnut-collared Longspur. Unlike other longspurs, males of both species show white lesser coverts, although these are usually concealed. The underparts of Smith's Longspur are tinged yellowish, not as dingy brown as in Chestnut-collared, with streaking on breast and flanks narrow and well-defined, and restricted to a narrow band across the breast. In Chestnut-collared, the streaking is more extensive, but less distinct on the breast, and there is almost no streaking on the flanks. The contrast between the pale nape and the dark crown and mantle is pronounced in Smith's, but not very prominent in Chestnut-collared, in which the crown and mantle are paler. The primary projection in Smith's is approximately equal to the length of the tertials or more, much longer than on Chestnut-collared. The tail is proportionately longer in Smith's than in Chestnut-collared, with different pattern. The dark border around the ear-coverts is relatively narrow, making the face pattern more distinctive than in Chestnut-collared, in which the dark border to the ear-coverts is broader and more diffuse. The whitish submoustachial stripe makes the ear-coverts stand out more than in Chestnut-collared.

In fresh non-breeding plumage in fall, when upperparts

are less dark and there may be a rusty tinge to edges of coverts and tertials, Smith's Longspur may also be similar to the dullest Lapland Longspurs. In Smith's, the supercilium is whitest behind the eye, whereas in Lapland it is rather the other way around. The dark border around the ear-coverts is relatively narrow, of more even width and darker than Lapland. The submoustachial stripe in Smith's is whiter than in Lapland, making the ear-coverts stand out more. In Smith's, the inner part of the lower row of lesser coverts is white, whereas in Lapland the lesser covert area is more uniform greyish in colour, with no noticeable colour difference between inner and outer ones, sometimes appearing quite pale. The greater coverts and tertial edges are not as bright rufous in Smith's as in Lapland. The primary projection is similar in Smith's and Lapland, but the spacing of the visible primaries is uneven in Smith's. On the folded wing, the space between the tips of the second longest visible primary (P6) and the third longest primary (P5) is greater than the spaces between the other primary tips. In Lapland all primaries are about evenly spaced. The underparts are more uniformly buffish in Smith's, belly not as white as in Lapland.

Unfortunately Smith's Longspur is often next to impossible to see well on the ground, making the tail pattern and flight call crucial for identification. There is more white in the tail than in Lapland, but less than in Chestnut-collared and McCown's, restricted to the two outermost pairs, showing like white sides to the tail in flight. The lesser coverts of male Smith's are visible in flight as a white shoulder patch, similar to Old World Chaffinch *Fringilla coelebs*. The flight call is crystal-clear rattle, quite different from Chestnut-collared, sharper and more distinct than Lapland.

The juvenile is more contrasting than juvenile Lapland. The supercilium is whiter, the area below the eye darker and the central ear-coverts whiter. There is more white speckling on the nape and sides of neck. The contrast between the breast and belly is more prominent in Lapland.

DESCRIPTION

Seasonal variation mainly in male. Male and female difficult to separate on plumage except in late spring and summer. Juvenile slightly different from subsequent plumages.

Adult male breeding Crown black. Supercilium white. Lores white, except a small black spot in front of the eye. Triangular ear-covert patch black with white spot in the centre, bordered below and behind by thin white line. Throat golden-buff. Sides of neck and nape golden-buff, streaked black on the nape. Mantle, scapulars, back, rump and uppertail-coverts heavily streaked blackish and buffish-brown. Outer lesser coverts black with thin white edges, inner broadly tipped white, forming white shoulder patch. Median coverts blackish-brown with whitish tips. Greater coverts dark brown with olive-brown edges and whitish tips. Alula not contrastingly darker. Tertials dark brown with narrow paler edges. Primaries brown with narrow whitish edges on the outer web. Underwing-coverts white with a buff tinge. The two outermost pairs of tail feathers are largely white. The four central pairs uniformly dark brown. Breast and belly golden-buff, becoming slightly paler towards the rear. Undertail-coverts whitish, suffused with yellowish-brown. Bill dusky with pale brown, orange or yellowish base to lower mandible. Tarsus pale brown. Iris brown.

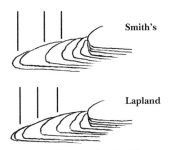

Primary spacing of Smith's and Lapland Longspur. Note uneven spacing of Smith's.

Adult male non-breeding Crown blackish-brown, streaked buffish-brown. Lores and supercilium pale buff. Eye-stripe dark and moustache brown, encircling pale buff ear-coverts. Submoustachial stripe yellowish, whiter next to ear-coverts. Malar stripe narrow, blackish-brown, does not reach bill. Throat pale orange-brown. Sides of neck and nape yellowish-brown, streaked dark, almost whitish immediately behind ear-coverts. Mantle blackish-brown with narrow pale buffish-brown stripes. Scapulars, back and rump slightly less heavily streaked. Wings like male in breeding plumage, but outer edge of greater coverts with chestnut tinge. Wing-bars created by white tips to median coverts and greater coverts more obvious. Tail pattern similar to adult male breeding, but base colour blacker. Breast and belly golden-buff, partly obscured by paler greyish-buff fringes. Narrow band of fine streaks across breast. Sides of breast and flanks streaked, most prominently on rear flanks. Undertail-coverts pale orange-brown. Upper mandible with a pink wash at base, lower mandible pink with tiny dark tip.

First-winter male Very similar to adult male winter. Tail feathers tapered and more worn than adults.

Adult female breeding Very similar to adult male winter. Crown darker and pattern on ear-coverts more prominent. The underparts are richer golden-buff. The upperparts are slightly darker. White area on lesser coverts restricted to inner ones of lower row. All wing-coverts, flight feathers and tail are heavily worn and browner. Pale fringes and wing-bars are narrow due to abrasion, compared to fresh plumage. Less prominently streaked on breast and flanks.

Tail pattern of Smith's Longspur. In flight, tail appears dark with white sides.

Adult female non-breeding Very similar to adult male winter. Slightly less contrasting on crown. Supercilium, lores, submoustachial stripe and throat whiter. Malar stripe very faint. Nape paler, without golden-buff tinge. Streaking on upperparts browner and less bold, particularly on back, rump and uppertail-coverts. Dark centres of scapulars not as sharply set off as in male, especially on the inner web. Lesser coverts brown, except for inner ones of lower row, which are white. Median covert wing-bar duller. Base colour of underparts paler and less bright. Band of streaks across breast broader. Streaks on breast and on flanks narrower, paler and less prominent.

First-winter female Very similar to adult female winter. Tail feathers tapered and more worn than adults.

Juvenile Crown blackish-brown, streaked chestnut-brown, with paler median crown-stripe. Face pattern may ghost that of adult male (perhaps only in juvenile males). Lores pale buff. Supercilium white. Area below eye and eye-stripe dark brown, encircling rear edge of ear-coverts, which are pale buff, whitish at rear. Submoustachial stripe whitish. Malar stripe inconspicuous. Throat pale buff. Sides of neck and nape yellowish-brown, streaked dark, with whitish streaking intermixed. Mantle blackish with whitish scalloping. Feathers of scapulars, back and rump with buff or chestnut edges. Median coverts blackish with white tips, the dark centres very pointed, reaching tip of feather. Greater coverts dark brown with rufous-brown edges and whitish tips. The dark centres are more clearly set off than in adults, and are more pointed. Breast and belly buffish. Breast more prominently and extensively streaked than adult.

SEXING Males are characterised by the white area on the lesser and median coverts being more extensive than in females. The outer lesser coverts are black with thin white edges, the inner ones broadly tipped white, forming uniformly white shoulder patch. The tips on the median coverts are whiter, broader and more sharply set off in males. In breeding plumage the head pattern of males is black and white.

In females, the lesser coverts are brownish, and the white area is restricted to the inner ones of the lower row. These feathers are not as broadly tipped white as in males. The tips of the median coverts are greyer and less distinct than in males. The head pattern of breeding females is dark brownish and pale buffish, rather than black and white, as in males. Wing length will aid sexing in many individuals (males 86.0-97.0, females 84.0-93.5).

MOULT AND AGEING Post-juvenile moult July to September, begins at 20 days of age and involves body feathers, including coverts. Tail and flight feathers are not replaced. In adults, non-breeding plumage is acquired by complete moult on the breeding grounds, starting around 10 July in males and about five days later in females. It is usually completed by September. Summer plumage is acquired by fairly extensive limited moult, involving head and underparts, just before the departure from the winter grounds or during migration.

Shape and wear of rectrices useful for ageing. Skull ossification completed between mid November and end of January. Iris colour probably useful, but not studied.

MEASUREMENTS Wing: (max) males 86.0-97.0, females 84.0-93.5, (chord) males 87-97, females 84-92; Tail: males 57.0-67.0, females 54.0-62.0; Bill: (to skull) males 13.3-14.5, females 13.1-14.6; Tarsus: males 18.8-22.0, females 18.0-23.5. Primary projection approximately 25-30mm. P6 is 0-4mm shorter than P7. P6-P8 emarginated.

GEOGRAPHICAL VARIATION None. Two races, *mersi* and *roweorum*, have been described. They were apparently based on individuals in different stages of wear, and are not recognised today.

VOICE The song, which is delivered from the top of a tree, shrub or other elevated location, varies from place to place. It starts out with some weak, high, whistled quavering notes, increases in loudness and ends with two characteristic harsh notes, the second of which drops abruptly in pitch at the end and is sometimes repeated: *sew seeyu wee tee tee dzee tzeeyu* or *seeyu wee tee tee dzee tzeeyu tzeeyu*. The song is rather similar to that of American Tree Sparrow *Spizella arborea*, but more forceful. Does not sing in flight, unlike other longspurs.

The flight call is a crystal-clear, slightly descending rattle of five or six rapidly repeated *tic* notes, recalling Serin *Serinus serinus* or Greenfinch *Carduelis chloris*. The last note drops abruptly in pitch. It resembles the rattle of Lapland Longspur to some degree, but is louder, sharper and with each note more distinct.

HABITS Breeds mid June to late July. This species has an unusual breeding strategy. Females mate with one to three different males and these males in turn mate with one to three different females, a behaviour called female-defence polygynandry. This results in a majority of broods being of mixed paternity. The females usually copulate with one male for the first days of the copulation period and then switch to a second. The first male is on average father to 2/3 of the offspring. The nest is placed on the ground, often next to a small bush or among tufts of sedge or grass. Eggs 2-5, usually 4, light clay-coloured or pale green with dark lines, dots and blotches of lavender or dark purplish. Female incubates 11-13 days. Young leave nest 7-9 days after hatching, but cannot fly until 12 days old. Young raised mainly on caterpillars, grasshoppers, mosquitoes and moths. Adults feed mainly on seeds of weeds and grasses for most of the year, but gradually switch to diet of invertebrates, which dominate during breeding season. In winter and on migration often in large flocks. Relatively unwary, but usually very hard to spot on ground, particularly in non-breeding season, when frequently first noticed when flushed. Walks or runs. Flight slightly undulating.

STATUS AND HABITAT Population density in Manitoba has been estimated to 0.20 birds/ha of suitable habitat. If this is true over the entire range, total population is unlikely to be more than 75 000 birds. In eastern part of range breeds in large wet sedge meadows, with scattered hummocks with conifers and scrubs, in the flat lowland areas where the forest peters out and the tundra begins. In the western part of range, mainly found in open grassy areas in valley bottoms and mountain passes, sometimes as high as 1000m above sea level. In winter and on migration favours pastures grazed by cattle. Also found in stubble fields, airports and grassy fields around lakes. Almost always found in longer grass than McCown's or Lapland, and rarely found in terrain open enough to allow an unimpeded view.

DISTRIBUTION AND MOVEMENTS Breeds from northeastern Alaska to southern Hudson Bay. An isolated population occurs in uplands of south-east Alaska and north-western British Columbia. From about Brooks Range in northern Alaska, east to Bathurst Inlet, mainly north of the Arctic Circle. From Bathurst Inlet, the narrow range extends to approximately Cape Eskimo, and thence along the southern coast of Hudson Bay to Cape Henrietta Maria in northern Ontario. In southern Alaska from Mt. McKinley NP to the Skagway area, and adjacent parts of Canada along the Alaska highway.

Autumn migration begins in August. Main arrival on

wintering grounds, from Kansas south to north-central Texas and north-western Louisiana, and east to western Tennessee, from late October to early December. Withdrawal from southernmost parts of wintering range begins first half of February. Main migration through Midwest states, east to Illinois and western Indiana, where casual in fall, from late March to late April. Arrives on breeding grounds late May to early June. Females arrive later than males. Casual to both west and east coasts of North America.

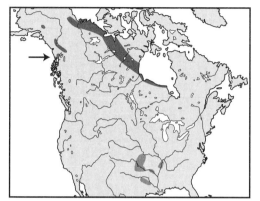

REFERENCES Bent (1968), Briskie (1993), Farrand (1983), Gabrielson & Lincoln (1959), Godfrey (1986), Pyle *et al.*(1987).

45   CHESTNUT-COLLARED LONGSPUR
Calcarius ornatus   Plate 18

Described as *Plectrophanes ornata* Townsend 1837. Monotypic.

The Chestnut-collared Longspur is common in the northern prairies of the United States and Canada. In winter congregates in sometimes large flocks that roam grasslands further south.

IDENTIFICATION 14cm. Breeding male unmistakable. Upperparts similar to Lapland Bunting, but underparts very different, with much of breast and belly black, and throat yellowish. The female is pale sandy-brown above, uniformly streaked dark brown, often with a trace of chestnut on the nape. The face pattern often ghosts that of male, with dark eye-stripe turning down around the rear edge of the ear-coverts, and moustachial stripe lacking. The breast, flanks and belly are covered with small triangular spots and streaks, making the underparts appear uniformly darkish at a distance, except for contrasting unmarked throat. The wing is rather uniformly brown, with two narrow wing-bars and some, usually concealed, white on the inner lesser coverts.

In non-breeding plumage a rather featureless dingy sandy-brown bird. It is superficially similar to the other three species of longspurs, but differs from all by short primary projection, only about half the length of tertials or less. The upperparts are rather heavily streaked dark brown and the underparts sandy-buff, with some diffuse streaking mainly confined to the breast. In males the concealed black breast and belly often shows through as irregular black blotches.

In fall and winter most similar to Smith's Longspur, which see for details. Both juveniles and non-breeding birds in fall and winter are similar to McCown's, which see for differences.

From Lapland Bunting by overall more uniformly sandy-brown plumage, lacking contrasting whitish belly and more white in tail. The outer lesser coverts are blackish, the inner ones white, although this is usually difficult to see. In Lapland, the lesser coverts are greyish with no noticeable colour difference between inner and outer ones, sometimes appearing quite pale. The greater coverts and tertials do not difffer significantly in colour from surrounding areas, and are never chestnut. The wing-bars are inconspicuous compared to Lapland. The primary projection is very short compared to Lapland.

As longspurs generally are difficult to see well on the ground, tail pattern and flight call are often crucial for identification. The tail appears mostly white with a relatively large inverted dark triangle distally in the centre. Flight calls of Chestnut-collared are soft, somewhat squeaky twitterings, often described as finch-like *kiddle kiddle*, quite different from the crystal-clear trill of Smith's or the more rattled call of McCown's, but may also give a soft rattle.

DESCRIPTION
Adult male breeding Crown brownish-black, with a greyish-white rectangular patch at the centre rear. Supercilium and lores white. Eye-stripe black, hooking down along rear ear-coverts. Ear-coverts, including moustachial area, yellowish-buff, with a white spot in the upper rear corner. Throat, submoustachial and malar area concolorous with ear-coverts. Nape chestnut. Mantle and scapulars pale greyish-brown, streaked blackish-brown. Back similar, but streaks browner and less prominent. Rump blackish-brown, mixed with greyish-white. Uppertail-coverts brown with paler edges. Lesser coverts blackish-brown, except inner ones in lower row, which are white. Median coverts dark brown with whitish outer edge, forming narrow wing-bar. Greater coverts greyish-brown with pale rather broad sandy-brown edges and whitish tips. Alula and primary coverts brown. Primaries brown with narrow greyish-white edges, inner four or five with greyish-white tips. Secondaries brown with pale sandy-brown edges (darker towards base on inner ones), and greyish-white tips. Tertials brown, edged pale sandy-brown. Tail extensively white, two outermost pairs (T5-T6) mostly white, third outermost pair (T4) with small dark tip, fourth (T3) and fifth (T2) outermost pairs with increasingly wide dark tip, and central pair (T1) largely dark. Breast blackish, often with some chestnut intermixed, sometimes also with traces of whitish fringes. Flanks and lower belly buffish-white, breaking up black breast pattern at the edges. Undertail-coverts buffish-white. Upper mandible blackish grey with yellowish cutting edge. Lower yellowish with blackish tip.
Adult male non-breeding Crown pale sandy-brown, streaked or spotted brownish-black. Concealed blackish bases of crown feathers sharply set off, often showing through to some extent. Supercilium sandy-buff, becoming whiter towards rear. Lores sandy-buff. Diffuse eye-stripe and area below eye greyish-brown, not very prominent. Ear-coverts sandy-buff, with some darker streaking and a trace of diffuse darker border along rear edge. Submoustachial stripe ill-defined sandy-buff. Malar stripe greyish-brown, rather narrow. Throat creamy-white or pale

buff. Nape sandy-brown, poorly marked. Concealed chestnut bases sharply set off, usually showing through. Mantle, scapulars, back and rump sandy-brown, streaked dark brown, less prominent towards rear. Uppertail-coverts brown with broad pale edges. Lesser coverts greyish-brown, except inner ones in lower row, which are whitish. Median coverts dark brown with broad pale rusty-brown tips. Greater coverts greyish-brown with broad pale sandy-brown edges and whitish tips. Alula and primary coverts brown with narrow pale edges. Primaries brown with narrow greyish-white edges, inner four or five with greyish-white tips. Secondaries brown with pale sandy-brown edges, and greyish-white tips. Tertials brown with rather broad, slightly paler tips. Breast pale dusky buff, with extensive blackish bases, usually showing through as dark blotches. Flanks and lower belly buffish-white, with some faint streaks on the rear flanks. Undertail-coverts buffish-white.

Tail pattern. Much white visible at base, but tail usually less spread in flight. Dark pattern then resembles a triangle as white on inner webs becomes concealed.

First-winter male Like adult male non-breeding. Differs in a number of minor respects. The crown is on average more streaked than spotted. The eye-stripe and dark border along rear edge of ear-coverts are less well marked. The partly concealed chestnut bases on the nape are on average less visible. The streaking on the upperparts is slightly less prominent. White patch on lesser coverts less extensive. Dark areas on second and third outermost pairs of tail feathers usually slightly more extensive. Tail as in juvenile, comparatively more worn than in adult.

Adult female breeding Crown greyish-brown, prominently streaked brownish-black, with pale spot at the rear. Supercilium and lores sandy-white. Eye-stripe brown, hooking down along rear ear-coverts. Ear-coverts pale brownish-buff, with a pale spot in the upper rear corner. Moustachial area almost concolorous with ear-coverts. Submoustachial stripe only slightly paler. Malar stripe ill-defined. Throat creamy-white. Nape tinged chestnut, streaked brown. Mantle, scapulars, back and rump sandy-brown, boldly streaked dark brown. Uppertail-coverts brown. Lesser coverts rather dark greyish-brown, with a small whitish patch on the inner ones in the lower row. Median coverts dark brown with pale sandy-brown tips. Greater coverts greyish-brown with narrow pale sandy-brown edges and whitish tips. Alula and primary coverts brown. Primaries brown with very narrow greyish-white edges, inner four or five with greyish-white tips. Secondaries brown with pale sandy-brown edges, especially about midway of feather, forming a pale patch, and greyish-white tips. Tertials rather uniformly brown. Tail pattern similar to adult male. Breast almost unstreaked, pale dusky buff, in the centre. Sides of breast, flanks and belly buffy-greyish, extensively covered with arrowhead-like brown streaks, which become more drawn out on the rear flanks and belly. Undertail-coverts buffy-white.

Adult female non-breeding Like adult male non-breeding, but mantle less contrasting and underparts slightly dark-

er, buffish-brown. The breast is diffusely streaked brownish, with no trace of underlying blackish bases. The primary projection is shorter than in males.

First-winter female Like adult female non-breeding, but dark pattern in tail more extensive and rectrices tapered. Second outermost pair of tail feathers has brown edge to tip of inner web.

Juvenile Crown pale rusty-brown, boldly streaked brownish-black, with a whitish median crown-stripe. Supercilium whitish. Lores pale sandy-buff. Eye-stripe blackish-brown. Ear-coverts whitish, with some narrow dark streaking and a darker moustache bordering lower rear edge, but not reaching bill. Submoustachial stripe whitish. Malar stripe an ill-defined row of dark brown spots. Throat whitish. Nape streaked dark brown, speckled white. Mantle and scapulars dark brown with pale sandy-brown fringes causing scalloped appearance. Fringes of central mantle whitish, sometimes creating white stripes. Back and rump dark brown, mottled sandy-brown. Uppertail-coverts brown with rather distinct pale sandy-brown edges. Lesser coverts pale rusty-brown, except inner ones in lower row, which have narrow whitish edges. Median coverts dark brown with whitish tips. Greater coverts greyish-brown with broad pale sandy-buff edges and white tips. Alula and primary coverts brown with narrow pale edges. Primaries brown with narrow buffish-white edges, inner four or five with slightly paler greyish-white tips. Secondaries brown with pale rufescent brown edges and greyish-white tips. Tertials brown with olive-brown outer web, becoming rufescent brown along the edge and with white tips. The tail pattern differs slightly from adults in that there is some brown along the shaft on the two outermost pairs. The edge on the inner web of the third innermost pair is brown. The feathers are also more tapered than in adults. Breast sandy-buff, prominently streaked blackish-brown. Flanks and belly buffish-grey, heavily streaked greyish-brown on the flanks. Undertail-coverts whitish.

SEXING In breeding plumage, males are characterised by more or less uniformly black breast and belly. Narrow pale buffish or chestnut fringes sometimes present. Males in non-breeding plumage show extensive black bases to feathers of lesser coverts, crown, breast and belly, sometimes with some chestnut admixed on the underparts. The breast may appear blotched. The lowest row of lesser coverts has broad white edges and remain white throughout the year, while rest wear to black. The feathers of the nape are uniformly chestnut, with pale fringes that wear off during spring. The primary projection is on average slightly longer in males.

During breeding season, when plumage worn, some females ghost male plumage, but dark areas are brown instead of black and the nape is less extensively rusty. The breast and belly are never as uniformly dark as in males. In non-breeding plumage, females never show as sharply set-off bases to either lesser coverts, crown, nape or breast feathers as males do. Wing length useful.

MOULT AND AGEING Juveniles undergo a partial post-juvenile moult, comprising at least body, lesser and median coverts, probably also greater coverts and tertials, July to September. Adults moult completely July to August. There is a limited pre-breeding moult February-April, more extensive in males, mainly restricted to forehead, lores, ear-coverts and throat.

Shape and wear of tail feathers useful for ageing. Skull ossification completed between mid November and end of January. Iris colour not studied, but probably useful.

MEASUREMENTS Wing: (max) male 81.5-89.0, female 79.5-82.0,(chord) male 81-91, female 76-85. Tail: male 55.0-61.5, female 49.0-55.5. Bill: (to skull) male 11.6-14.2, female 11.5-13.0. Tarsus: male 18.9-20.6, female 17.5-18.8. Primary projection approximately 10-15mm. P6 is 0-4mm shorter than P7. P6-P8 emarginated.

GEOGRAPHICAL VARIATION None.

VOICE The song is delivered from an elevated point on the ground or in flight. The song flight differs from that of McCown's Longspur in that the bird prolongs the flight by circling and undulating at the peak of ascent, and flutters as it descends. The song starts out with some fine clear whistled notes, followed by a short harsh warble consisting of a various number of elements, ending with a rattled trill: *si sely tiri dzre-ra trrrree*, or *si sely tiri dzre-i trrrree*, or *si sely tiri dzee-ra wee-ra trrrree*.

The common flight call differs from all other longspurs by being squeakier, and less dry and rattled. It is usually a double *cheedle cheedle*, or *chil-lip*. From small groups a variety of soft, somewhat squeaky twitterings, *twit-twe-twett tet*, can be heard. However, a soft rattle is sometimes given.

HABITS The nest is usually placed in a depression on the ground, often concealed under vegetation. It is constructed with grasses and weed stems and lined with finer grasses and hair. Eggs usually 4-6, glossy greyish-white, pale buffish- or greenish-white, spotted, speckled and lined with brown and lavender. Incubation by female 11-13 days. Young are fed by both parents, and leave the nest after about 10 days. The young are raised mainly on invertebrates such as caterpillars, worms and grasshoppers. Main food of adults is seeds of grasses and prairie plants, except in summer when diet is dominated by various invertebrates, e.g. beetles, grasshoppers, spiders and caterpillars. Walks or runs. This species and Smith's are the most secretive of longspurs, and tend to be found in denser cover than McCown's and Lapland. Often not detected until flushed. Quite gregarious in non-breeding season, when large flocks may form, but does not readily associate with flocks of Shore Larks *Eremophila alpestris*, unlike McCown's and Lapland.

STATUS AND HABITAT Has disappeared from large areas as these became cultivated. Still exists in good numbers

in rolling hills of short-grass plains, uncultivated grasslands, wasteland and prairie. Often in moister situations. In winter found in grassy areas, with denser cover than that preferred by McCown's.

DISTRIBUTION AND MOVEMENTS Breeds from southern Alberta and southern Manitoba south to north-eastern Colorado, northern Nebraska and south-western Minnesota. Southward migration usually begins in early September, the breeding areas being deserted by the end of the month. Arrives on southernmost wintering areas from mid October to December. Winters from northern Arizona, central New Mexico, and central Kansas, south to northern Zacatecas and San Luis Potosí, rarely south to Guerrero, in Mexico, and in southern Texas and northern Louisiana. Casual over large parts of North America, from British Columbia and southern California in the west and Nova Scotia, Newfoundland and Florida in the east, and south to Puebla and Veracruz in Mexico. In California regular in fall, and rare but annual in winter, sometimes in flocks of up to 50 birds. Departure from wintering grounds begins late February, with main departure in March. Usually arrives on breeding grounds during second half of April.

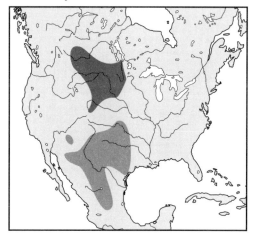

REFERENCES Bent (1968), Farrand (1983), Godfrey (1986), Pyle *et al.*(1987).

PLECTROPHENAX

Two arctic species, one of which has a complete circumpolar distribution, and the other one an extremely restricted insular breeding range. In both the males are largely white with a certain amount of black, showing a striking wing pattern. Females are similar but duller, with less white in the wing. In winter both species migrate, but some individuals endure the arctic winter close to the breeding areas.

46 SNOW BUNTING
Plectrophenax nivalis   Plate 19

Described as *Emberiza nivalis* Linnaeus 1758.
Synonyms: *Emberiza montana, Emberiza subnivalis, Plectrophenax borealis*.

In summer, a bird of high latitudes. Nests farther north than any other passerine. In winter in flocks along sea-

coasts and in open country further south.

IDENTIFICATION 15-18cm. Unmistakable throughout most of its range. In Alaska confusion possible with McKay's Bunting, which see. In summer both males and females are unmistakable, with heads and underparts predominantly white or whitish. The mantle is black in males, browner and less uniform in females. The wings are extensively white, with amount of black on the wingtips depending on age and sex. On the folded wing, white coverts and secondaries form a prominent wing panel.

In non-breeding plumage the dark parts of the plumage are largely obscured by pale fringes, strongly tinged rufous on crown, ear-coverts, breast and upperparts. Males are brighter and more contrasting than females, showing uniformly white primary coverts and lesser coverts. The scapulars often appear scalloped, due to extensively black bases and narrow pale fringes. The dark tip of the underwing is more sharply set off in males, a difference often visible in flight. In females, the amount of white in the wing is less extensive, usually restricted to whitish panel on secondaries and tips to greater coverts, and a whitish median covert wing-bar. In first-winter females, the amount of visible white in the wing may be restricted to double wing-bars, with wing panel very narrow. The scapulars of females are more similar to the mantle, and the dark tip of the underwing is diffusely set off.

The Snowfinch *Montifringilla nivalis* has a wing pattern similar to that of Snow Bunting, but the greater coverts are always white, eliminating possibility of confusion with female. The only plumage possible to confuse is juvenile male Snow Bunting. Juvenile Snowfinch is superficially similar to juvenile Snow Bunting, but the likelihood of confusion is nil on geographical grounds. Snow Buntings showing grey head (juveniles) are only seen on the breeding grounds, as they moult to first-winter plumage before they migrate. Most useful difference is the tail pattern, where Snow Bunting has all feathers, except dark central pair, largely white. Further differences are its longer pointed bill, all-black primaries, and often some black visible on the throat.

Female White-winged Lark *Melanocorypha leucoptera* can be surprisingly similar to first-winter female Snow Bunting in general coloration of upper parts. It is more heavily streaked on the crown and has an ill-defined malar stripe. There is usually a collar of fine spots on the breast and the flanks are streaked, particularly at the rear. The bill is longer and not conical. The lesser coverts are tinged orange-rufous and there are no prominent wing-bars on the folded wing. The alula and primary coverts are orange-rufous. The shape of the white bar on the trailing edge of the wing is different from Snow Bunting in that the inner primaries and secondaries are dark at the base, with the distal part white, lacking dark at the tip. In Snow Bunting the tips of the inner primaries and outer secondaries are dark, white pattern restricted to the bases.

Juveniles may appear superficially similar to Ortolan Bunting, due to the grey head and pale eye-ring. On close inspection similarities will vanish.

DESCRIPTION

Juvenile clearly different from subsequent plumages.

Adult male breeding Entire head white. Mantle, scapulars, back and uppertail-coverts black. Rump white. Lesser, median and greater coverts white. Alula black. Primary coverts white, sometimes with a small black spot at the tip. Tertials black. Primaries black with white base, amount of white increasing towards the inner ones. On the folded wing, the black colour on the outer webs almost reaches the tip of the primary coverts. Secondaries white. The three innermost pairs of tail feathers (T1-T3) black with whitish fringes. Three outermost pairs (T4-T6) mainly white, with some black near tip of outer web and along shaft. There may be some dark on the inner web of the third outermost pair (T4). Underparts white. Bill and tarsus black. Iris dark brown.

Tail pattern of adult (left) and juvenile (right). Note three central pairs (T1-T3) are predominantly dark. In the juvenile, the feathers are more pointed, and the outer pairs, particularly the third outermost tail feathers (T4), show more black at the tips than the adult.

Adult male non-breeding Crown and nape orange-brown, forehead quite dark, nape much paler, rather blotchy. The supercilium, sides of neck and throat are whitish, sullied very pale pinkish-brown. Mantle initially pale greyish-brown with dark streaking, but concealed jet black bases to feathers become more apparent as wear proceeds. Back a mixture of whitish and orange-brown, with some dark streaking. Rump and uppertail-coverts white, with varying amount of orange-brown blotching. Wings as in adult male breeding, but dark part of primaries jet black. The secondaries are mostly white, sometimes with small black marks near the tip of the outer web. Tail like adult male breeding, but whitish fringes broader. Underparts whitish, with a band of orange-brown across the breast. Bill yellowish-brown.

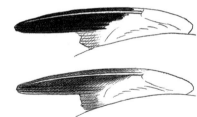

Pattern of underwing of male (top) and female (bottom). Dark pattern of male is blacker and more well-defined.

First-winter male Like adult male non-breeding. For differences in uppertail-coverts, tail and primary covert pattern, see Moult and Ageing. Tends to be darker above than adult, particularly on the nape and rump. The face and throat are not as pure white as in adults. In addition the greater coverts often show blackish bases.

Pattern of scapulars of female (left) and male (right). Dark centre of male's is blacker, more rounded and more sharply set off from the pale edge. In the female, shape of the dark centre may be very pointed.

Adult female breeding Crown dark grey, with narrow whitish edges. Supercilium whitish. Lores pale sandy-brown. Ear-coverts range from whitish to grey, tinged pale brown at the rear. Throat white. Nape white, contrasting with crown and mantle, streaked grey. Mantle, scapulars and back blackish, with varying amount of whitish fringes. Rump with varying amount of white, mostly on the sides. Uppertail-coverts blackish. The lesser coverts are blackish with white fringes. Median coverts mainly white. Greater coverts white with dark brown centres, visible as dark bar across wing. Alula and primary coverts mainly blackish with white edges. Outer primaries dark brown on outer web, the innermost ones (P1-P3) white basally. Secondaries white, with small dark subterminal markings on outer web of outer ones (S1-S4). Entire underparts whitish.

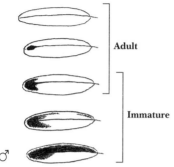

Primary coverts of adult and first year male. It is possible that males which show small black spots on the primary coverts, but are not first-year birds, may be second-year, or even third-year, birds.

Adult female non-breeding Similar to first-winter male. The whole head is more neatly patterned, without the blotching of males. The nape is sandy-brown, tinged rufescent, showing little contrast with the mantle. The mantle is very similar to first-winter male, but never shows any blotching caused by concealed black bases to feathers. The lesser coverts are black with greyish fringes. Median and greater coverts dark brown with white tips forming wingbars, the white tips of the greater coverts merging with white patch formed by secondaries.

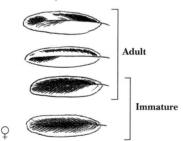

Primary coverts of adult and first-year female. 'Adult' females showing largely dark primary coverts may be second-year birds.

First-winter female Almost identical to adult female non-breeding. See Moult and Ageing for diagnosis in the hand.
Juvenile Whole head grey, often tinged olive, sometimes with paler throat. Relatively prominent pale eye-ring and submoustachial stripe. The mantle is somewhat brighter olive-grey, with indistinct dark grey streaks. The rump is of similar colour, without streaking. The lesser coverts are olive-grey in females, white in males. The median coverts are dark grey with white tips in females, white in males. Greater coverts blackish, with white tips in females, usual-

ly with at least outer web white in males. Tertials black, with dark chestnut fringes. Visible part of primary coverts brown in females, often with white base in males. Alula brown. Primaries dark brown, with some white basally on the inner ones. Secondaries white, with brown tips, extent varying individually, more extensively white in males. Breast varying from greyer in males to greyish-ochre, with some faint streaking in females. Flanks and belly whitish, washed greyish-ochre. Contrast with breast most pronounced in males.

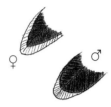

Pattern of longest uppertail-coverts of female and male. Dark centre of male is blacker, more rounded and more sharply set off from the pale edge. Dark centre of female is often very pointed and may appear more like a shaft streak.

SEXING This species shows a great deal of variation in the characters used for sexing. Intermediates occur, making it necessary to take all characters into consideration. Males are generally whiter and blacker than females of corresponding age. A bird with all white primary coverts is a male. The lesser coverts are uniformly white in males. In a few cases there are some small scattered spots. The secondaries are mainly white in males, sometimes with small black marks near the tip of the outer web. The dark tip of the primaries on the underwing is blackish and sharply set off in males. The dark centres of the scapulars are jet black, and the tips rounded or bluntly pointed in males, best visible on the middle ones. The dark centres to the uppertail-coverts are similar in this respect. They tend to end bluntly in adult males, and come to a point in first-year males, but intermediates occur. Males have less dark in the third outermost pair of tail feathers (T4) than females, very little in adults and usually restricted to the tip of the inner web of first-year males. Males are on average larger than females, and many can be sexed on measurements.

In females the primary coverts are mainly blackish, with white only on the edges. The lesser coverts are greyish-brown to blackish, with some off-white tips, never appearing as white as in males. The secondaries are white, with dark pattern on tips ranging from small dark subterminal markings on outer web in adults to about distal half of feathers. The dark tip of the primaries on the underwing is diffusely demarcated and browner. The tip of the dark centres of the middle scapulars is sharply pointed in females, and the base colour is browner or greyer than in males. The dark centres of the uppertail-coverts come to a point in females, often more so than in first-year males, but many are intermediates and the character is most useful in adults. In females, the dark pattern of the third outermost pair of tail feathers (T4) usually covers the entire inner web, the dark pattern normally dominating over white areas. Individuals showing intermediate characters occur. These are either first-winter males or adult females, so correct ageing should solve the most difficult cases.

MOULT AND AGEING Juveniles have a partial moult about three weeks after fledging, late July or August to September, involving head, body, lesser and median coverts, sometimes also inner greater coverts and tertials. Adults moult completely after breeding, between first half of July and mid September; duration 28-37 days. A limited pre-breeding moult involving head previously reported, but unconfirmed in recent studies.

Some birds are ambiguous, but most can be aged based on a combination of criteria. With progress of wear and bleaching ageing becomes more difficult. Ageing and sexing criteria to some extent interdependent. Beware of subspecies *insulae*, making up majority of British and Dutch wintering population. This race has on average more extensive dark patterning than other subspecies and therefore does not conform to the criteria below. Particularly first-year male may show characters typical of adult female of nominate race, such as all dark primary coverts, dark bases to greater coverts and dark tips to outer secondaries. Adult males frequently show dark tips to the primary coverts. **1. Tail feathers** Juvenile tail feathers, which are retained throughout the first-year, are more tapered than those of adults of both sexes. The tip of the dark centre of innermost pair of tail feathers (T1) is more pointed in first-winter birds. Between males of different ages there is usually a marked difference in the amount of dark on the third outermost pair of tail feathers (T4). In adults, the dark pattern is usually restricted to a relatively short dark patch along the shaft. There is often a limited amount of dark on the inner web, usually a narrow patch, isolated from the shaft patch. In first-year males, the dark pattern along the shaft is longer than in adults and the dark pattern on the inner web is more extensive and usually connected to the shaft streak. This difference is also useful in most females. A word of warning: black parts of feathers are more resistant to wear. Since the black centres are pointed, the rounded shape of adult tail feathers, which is mainly formed by white edges, can turn very pointed as these white edges are worn off, the resulting shape of the tail seemingly indicating first-year bird. **2. Primary coverts** Adult males often have the longest primary covert all white, sometimes with a small dark spot at the tip. Adult females often show a similar pattern, with a spot near the tip, but with a varying amount of dark on the outer web. Quite frequently the primary coverts of adult females are all dark, except for white base on the inner web. In first-year birds of both sexes, the outer web is often all dark. **3. Secondaries** In males and adult females, there is no black on the inner webs of the secondaries, except for a small dark spot near the tip of the outer one (S1) in some females, but first-year females usually show dark patches on the three outer ones (S1-S3). **4. Alula** In adult males, the alula is black, whereas it is dark grey in first-year males. **5. Uppertail-coverts** The dark centres of the longest uppertail-coverts tend to end more bluntly in adult males, and come to a point in first-year males. Intermediates occur. Not useful in females. **6. Primary colour** In adult males, the dark parts of the primaries are almost glossy black with sharply defined white fringes. Immature males have dark grey primaries, and the white fringes are often less well-defined.

Skull ossification is useful in autumn, but is completed in December. Iris colour should be useful with experience.

MEASUREMENTS Wing: (max) male 104-119, female 98-110. Tail: male 59-69, female 56-63. Bill: (to skull) male 12.4-15.8, female 11.9-14.9. Tarsus: male 20.0-22.7, female 19.1-22.3. Primary projection approximately 30-40mm. P7-P8 emarginated.

GEOGRAPHICAL VARIATION Variation largely clinal, comprising colour of fringes in fresh plumage and extent of black pattern in wings and on rump.

P. n. nivalis (From Alaska across arctic North America, Greenland, Svalbard, Faroes and Scandinavia to the Kola peninsula, grading into the following race further east). Described above.

P. n. vlasowae (From NE European Russia through arctic Siberia to Chukotskiy peninsula, south to Anadyr area, wintering west to Hungary and Romania) Generally paler than nominate race in fresh plumage. Particularly rump more extensively white than nominate race, including part of back and most of uppertail-coverts.

P. n. insulae (Iceland and Scotland) In all plumages somewhat darker than other races. The fringes of the upperparts are browner and darker in fresh plumage, and crown and breast deeper rusty. Shows more extensive black pattern in flight feathers and coverts. The rump is darker than in other races, usually without pale patch. Females in breeding plumage are very dark above, with less contrasting nape, and the fringes are olive-brown, sometimes chestnut on the rump and ear-coverts. The rump is all dark in breeding plumage. The lesser coverts are darker grey and the median and greater covert wing-bars are narrower. The primary coverts usually show no white in females, and there is on average more dark in the secondaries. The underparts are frequently marked with dark spots and streaks. Males often show a dark smudge on the hindneck in breeding plumage, and the ear-coverts are often tinged rusty.

P. n. townsendi (W Aleutian chain, Pribilofs and Komandor Islands, Kamchatka and along Siberian coast, north to about Anadyr area) Similar to *vlasowae* in general coloration, including pale rump, but slightly larger and with longer bill.

VOICE Sings from an elevated point, like a boulder, or in flight. In song flight, rises silently with rapid wing beats to about 10m and then begins to sing, while drifting back down to earth with wings spread and quivering. The song varies from place to place, but is usually similar to Lapland Longspur, but is more uniform and lacks the squeaky impression. It is rather monotonous, and often starts with one phrase, followed by a second, after which the first phrase is repeated, in turn followed by a third phrase. One example could be described as *terere dzüü weewa tererere dzüü tsee tsee.*

The common flight call is a soft ripple, *tiriririt*, often likened to voice of Crested Tit *Parus cristatus*, followed by a clear *pyu*. Both calls resemble call of Lapland Longspur, but are more melodious, less dry. Also a harsh *djeee.*

HABITS Breeds late May to July. Most males appear to be monogamous, but bigamy and promiscuity have been recorded. A fair proportion of the population may raise two broods. The nest is usually placed in a cavity, between rocks or under boulders; in areas where adapted to man also under roofs, in boxes, etc. It is a cup of grass, stalks, moss and lichen, and lined with fine grass, hair, wool and feathers. Eggs usually 4-6, slightly glossy, pale blue or greenish-blue, sometimes buffish, covered with reddish-

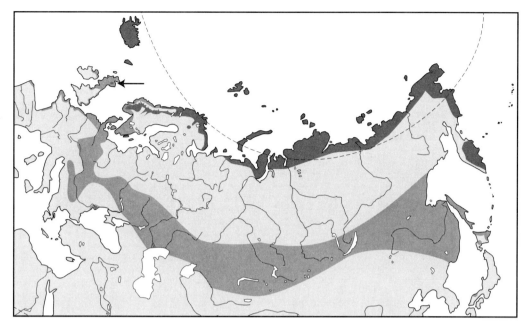

brown to purplish-black blotches, freckles and dots, usually with the markings concentrated at the large end. Incubation by female 12-13 days. The young reach 90% of adult weight after about 7.5 days, and leave the nest cavity after approximately 13 days. The young are raised on invertebrates such as mosquitoes, midges, crane-flies, moths and spiders. Adults will take invertebrates when available, in winter e.g. sandhoppers and sea slaters, gathered along the tideline. During much of the year a variety of seeds, berries and shoots dominate. Popular food items include knotgrass, crowberry, grasses, sedges and rushes. Gregarious except when breeding. Usual gait a quick run, but also hops. Usually perches on ground or boulders, but sometimes on wires or in trees. Sometimes seeks shelter in holes in the snow, during adverse weather. Usually does not associate with other species, but sometimes together with Shore Larks *Eremophila alpestris*, Twite *Carduelis flavirostris*, longspurs or occasionally other species. Often allows close approach but flocks may be wary.

STATUS AND HABITAT Common in most parts of range. In areas with plenty of suitable habitat, densities of 20-50 pairs per km² seem normal. Exceptional densities of up to 500 pairs per km² have been reported. Breeds further north than any other passerine. In isolated fringe areas south of main breeding range, such as Faroes and Scotland, populations often subject to marked fluctuations. Breeds in barren tundra, rocky terrain, scree and seacliffs. Has adapted to human settlements in some areas. A hardy bird which may winter far to the north. In winter on bare ground along sea coasts and in open country.

DISTRIBUTION AND MOVEMENTS Circumpolar distribution, mostly north of 68°N, but occurs further south, to about 51-60°N in Atlantic and Pacific coastal areas. From Aleutian chain, across arctic North America, Greenland, Iceland, Svalbard, Faroes, Scotland, northern Scandinavia (in Norway south to about 59°N), arctic Siberia, including islands of Arctic Ocean, to central Kamchatka and islands in the Bering Sea. Migration patterns seem to be fairly complex, with populations migrating in south-easterly direction often crossing the migration routes of other populations migrating in south-westerly direction, and vice versa. Leaves breeding grounds relatively late, some movement apparent at end of August, but main departure September to early October. In coastal regions, some birds may remain near breeding grounds all winter, if conditions permit, whereas others wander widely. Males apparently winter further north than females. Birds from western Greenland appear to winter in North America, whereas those from eastern Greenland migrate eastwards to Russia, to winter in the steppes, or to the British Isles. The Svalbard population also appears to migrate in a south-easterly direction, across the Kola peninsula. The race *insulae,* from Iceland, is partly resident, but also wanders, primarily to Britain and the Netherlands. The British and Dutch wintering populations are made up of about 70-85% and 63-64% respectively of *insulae* and the remainder by the nominate subspecies. In northern Germany about 20-25% of the wintering population appears to belong to *insulae*. Birds ringed in Alaska have been recovered in Yakutia, Siberia.

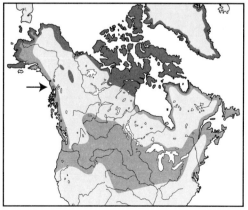

221

Main wintering grounds in steppes of central Asia and North American prairie. In Europe, winters in Iceland, the Faroes, northern Britain and Ireland, the Netherlands, southern Scandinavia, through eastern Europe to plains of southern Belarus, northern Ukraine, and eastwards through southern Russia and northern Kazakhstan, the range touching north-western China and northern Mongolia, to the Sea of Okhotsk and the Pacific coast south to Japan and north-eastern China, where uncommon and local. In southernmost parts of wintering range often only present in mid winter. Often returns as early as April to northern breeding grounds.

Accidental south to Canary Islands, Azores, Madeira, Morocco, Malta, Bulgaria, Turkey (where possibly regular in north), Bermuda, Florida, Texas and Hawaii.

REFERENCES Banks *et al.* (1990), Bent (1968), Bezzel (1993), Cramp & Perrins (1994), Dementiev & Gladkov (1966), Gabrielson & Lincoln (1959), Godfrey (1986), Kessel (1989), Pyle *et al.* (1987), Salomonsen (1931), Svensson (1992), Vaurie (1959).

47   MCKAY'S BUNTING
Plectrophenax hyperboreus   Plate 19

Described as *Plectrophenax hyperboreus* Ridgway 1884. Monotypic.

McKay's Bunting is common within its very restricted range on a few islands in the Bering Sea. It is found on tundra and along sea coasts.

IDENTIFICATION 18cm. McKay's Bunting is like a whiter version of Snow Bunting, differing in all plumages by having more white in the tail. The four outermost pairs are predominantly white, with significant amounts of dark restricted to the two central pairs. In Snow Bunting, the three outermost pairs are predominantly white, and the three central pairs dark. Unfortunately, this character is difficult to see in the field. McKay's Bunting also has more white in the wings than corresponding plumage of Snow Bunting.

During the breeding season the adult male is almost wholly white. In some individuals only the bill and the very tip of the wings are black, but normally there are at least traces of black on the central tail feathers and on the tertials. The amount of black in the plumage varies individually, and is to some extent related to age, but always differs from Snow Bunting by lacking significant amounts of black in the mantle. First-summer males are very similar to adult males, but show a varying amount of black on the alula, often restricted to the tip, and more extensive black pattern in wings and tail. Some individuals that show adult characters in wing but have scapulars, most of tertials and distal half of central tail feathers black may be second-summer males. It is also possible that hybridisation may account for atypical amounts of black in plumage, such as black scapulars.

The wing pattern of breeding female differs from adult male in that the alula is black and the primaries are more extensively black, but is very similar to that of first-summer male. However, breeding females can always be told from males by extensive dark pattern on mantle.

During the breeding season females are very similar to female Snow Bunting, particularly of the race *townsendi*, which occurs close to the range of McKay's, but are generally paler. Adult female McKay's are on average much whiter than Snow on nape and crown, and the contrast between head and mantle is more prominent. The crown and forehead are often all white, which is rarely the case in Snow Bunting. In the most typical adult female McKay's, the mantle is quite prominently striped black and white, with white dominating. The back (the area between the tertials) is usually obviously paler than the mantle, which is only rarely the case in Snow, and the rump is always white, creating a larger white rump patch than in Snow Bunting. In female Snow Bunting, the mantle is nearly uniformly blackish with some narrow white fringes, and rarely appears striped. The back is usually as dark as the mantle or very nearly so, with white patch limited to the rump, if present. Adult female McKay's differs from all female Snow Buntings in that the primary coverts are white, with at the most small dark spots at the tips. The white wing panel is formed by white inner primaries, secondaries and lesser, median and greater coverts, and is more extensive than in Snow. Often only three primaries are extensively black, but, unlike in Snow, the black pattern does not reach the tips of the primary coverts. The innermost primaries and all secondaries are white.

The darkest first-summer female McKay's are indistinguishable from the palest *townsendi* on colour of upperparts alone, as both head, mantle and back are on average darker than in adults, and the rump patch is consequently smaller. Individuals most similar in pattern of the upperparts can usually be separated by the pattern of the wings. First-summer Snow can be ruled out by much dark in greater coverts and secondaries, but first-summer female McKay's is very similar to adult female Snow. In both these the lesser coverts are greyish and the primary coverts appear dark, but the white wing panel is still larger in McKay's because of broader white tips to greater coverts, broad white edges to tertials, and mainly white inner primaries and secondaries. In first-summer female McKay's the bases to the outer greater coverts are often dark, but the tips are broad and the inner ones are usually white. In Snow there is usually a dark bar across the wing, formed by more extensively dark bases to all greater coverts. First-summer female McKay's show more black in the flight feathers than adult female, but less than in Snow Bunting. In both first-summer female McKay's and in Snow Bunting the dark pattern in the primaries reaches the primary coverts. McKay's differs from Snow in that much of the inner primaries are white, creating a narrower dark edge to the wing. Furthermore, in McKay's the entire outer web of the outermost primary is white or pale brown, whereas in Snow Bunting it is mainly dark, with a very narrow pale edge.

In autumn and winter, when the plumage is fresh, broad white or rusty fringes obscure underlying patterns. Nevertheless, all males of McKay's Bunting appear much whiter than Snow Bunting and never show any concealed black on the mantle, making sexing straightforward and confusion with Snow Bunting unlikely. In all Snow Buntings the underlying dark pattern is clearly visible. A few male McKay's, probably first-year birds, may show very narrow and sparse shaft streaks on the mantle, but never anything reminiscent of the pattern of Snow Bunting. The crown, ear-coverts and sides of breast usually show well-marked dark rusty patches. The extent of the rusty colour depends on age and wear (more extensive in young), and already in March adult males are mainly white again. First-year male McKay's Bunting differ from all Snow Buntings by showing a varying amount of white in the alula, and white bases to the central pairs of tail feathers. The dark part of the tail is usually restricted to approximately the outer half of the tail, or less.

Female McKay's in fresh plumage may be quite difficult to tell from female Snow Bunting. The black pattern on the mantle and back is partly concealed in both species, and the extent is difficult to discern, although McKay's is usually considerably whiter in appearance, and the streaking on the mantle more contrasting. The differences in wing and tail pattern are the same as described for breeding birds, although the wing of Snow may appear whiter when fresh, as the fringes are broader. Beware that adult female McKay's shows a wing pattern similar to that of first-year male Snow Bunting. The concealed black pattern of scapulars and mantle is more extensive in male Snow Bunting, and usually shows through, but may occasionally be difficult to determine in fresh plumage. The shape of the dark centres of the scapulars is blunt in male Snow, sharply pointed in female McKay's.

First-winter female McKay's shows a wing pattern similar to that of adult female Snow Bunting, but differs in the same way as described for first-summer female. Compared to first-winter Snow, the amount of white in the wing is significantly more extensive, and in all plumages McKay's shows almost uniformly white secondaries. At the most there may be small dark subterminal markings on the outer web of the outer secondaries. First-winter female Snow Bunting shows enough dark at the tip of the secondaries to be visible as a dark terminal bar in flight, and sometimes the outer secondaries are largely dark.

Juveniles are paler than most juvenile Snow Buntings, but almost identical in colour to the race *townsendi*, from which they differ by the same characters in the tail and wing pattern as do first-winter birds. Juvenile male McKay's is readily identified as it shows a varying amount of white in the alula, often all-white primary coverts, and white base to the dark central pairs of tail feathers.

Partly albino individuals of other species may appear similar, but should be possible to rule out on close inspection.

HYBRIDISATION Hybrids and probable hybrids between McKay's and Snow Bunting have been reported. These may show a variety of intermediate characters. Males with only the centre of the mantle white, and with the sides of the mantle and scapulars extensively black, are regularly seen, and are presumably hybrids.

DESCRIPTION
Seasonal variation mainly due to wear. Male and female possible to separate on plumage. Juvenile clearly different from subsequent plumages.

Adult male breeding Head, mantle, back, rump and uppertail-coverts white. The scapulars are sometimes black forming a V-pattern together with the tertial pattern. It is unclear whether this is an age-dependent character or just individual variation. Studies in other species have shown that males may change appearance with increasing age, and it seems likely that male McKay's Bunting becomes whiter with age. Lesser, median and greater coverts are white. Alula white. Primary coverts white, occasionally with minute dark spots near the tip. Primaries white with approximately distal third black in four or five outer primaries (P5 or P6 to P9). The black area is usually confined to the part of the primaries that extends beyond the

tip of the tertials on the folded wing. In some individuals there is very little black on the tips of the primaries. Secondaries white. There is a varying amount of black in the tertials, often restricted to the inner web of the two shorter ones, occasionally lacking altogether. Tail white, with black tips only on the two central pairs (T1-T2), sometimes reduced to subterminal spots or occasionally lacking. Underparts white. Bill and tarsus black. Iris dark.

Tail pattern of female. Note that only two central pairs are predominantly dark. Outer pairs are all white, with exception of fourth outermost tail feather (T3), which may be dark at the tip. In males, base of two central pairs white, or dark pattern further reduced and sometimes absent.

Adult male non-breeding Like breeding male, but broad white or rusty fringes to feathers obscure black scapulars, if present. Strongest rusty pattern confined to crown, ear-coverts and breast. Rusty or buffish feathers are also found on mantle, scapulars, tertials and rump. Bill yellowish with dusky tip.

First-winter male Like adult male non-breeding, but mantle, scapulars, tertials and rump often more strongly tinged rusty. In some individuals, there are faint shaft streaks on the mantle. There is more black in the wing than in adult male. The alula is white with black tip. The primary coverts are white, but often show some black at tip, similar to adult female. The distal part of the outer five to seven primaries (P3,P4 or P5 to P9) is black, the black reaching almost to the tip of primary coverts on the folded wing. There is more black in the central tail feathers than in adult male, usually covering distal half of the two central pairs of feathers.

First-summer male This plumage is insufficiently studied. It is similar to adult male breeding, but differs by showing the same differences in wing and tail pattern as described under first-winter male. There appears to be more black in the tertials, and the scapulars may be black.

Adult female breeding Head, back, rump, uppertail-coverts and underparts white. Mantle streaked black and white, usually, but not always, with white dominating. Lesser coverts white, sometimes with some dark at the bases. Median coverts white. Greater coverts usually white, but sometimes especially the outer ones may show some blackish at the bases. Alula black, primary coverts white with small black tips. White bases of primaries usually visible beyond primary coverts. Outer web of outermost primary white. Black tip on seven to eight of the outer primaries (P2 or P3 to P9). Secondaries white. Tertials blackish with whitish outer margin and tip. Middle pair of tail feathers (T1-T2) all dark except for pale edge, third innermost pair (T3) with small black subterminal patch and dark shaft. Outer pairs (T4-T5) with blackish edge of outer web, except outermost pair (T6) which is usually white on outer web, unlike first-year female.

Adult female non-breeding Similar to adult female breeding, but much paler, due to broad white or rusty fringes. Plumage suffused rusty, more strongly on crown, nape and ear-coverts. Throat white. Side of breast and neck with small rusty patches. Mantle feathers with sharply pointed blackish centres, edged pinkish-buff. Back almost unstreaked rusty-buff. Rump whiter. Uppertail-coverts white, except the longest pair, which are rusty. Inner tertials blackish with brown outer edge, outer ones with paler edge.

First-winter female Similar to adult female non-breeding, but darker above. The back often appears darker, making the pale rump patch smaller. Dark base of lesser coverts broader, giving overall greyish impression. Median coverts mainly white. Greater coverts, especially outer ones, with blackish or grey base. Inner tertials blackish with brown outer edge, outer with paler edge. Alula blackish. Primary coverts blackish with narrow pale edges. Dark areas in outer primaries reaches primary coverts. Outer web of outermost primary white, sometimes tinged pale brown. At least eight (P2-P9) of the outer primaries tipped black. Outer secondaries with brownish patches subterminally on the outer webs. Primaries relatively more worn than adult, brown or grey. Usually dark distal edge of outer web of outer tail feathers, unlike adult female.

First-summer female Similar to adult female breeding, but differs in having more extensively black in wing pattern as outlined under first-winter female. The crown is on average darker than in adult, and the dark streaking on the mantle usually dominates over white. The back is relatively dark, and the white rump less extensive than in adult.

Juvenile Head pale grey, tinged buffish-olive, throat paler. Eye-ring whitish. Submoustachial stripe pale buffish-grey. Mantle pale grey, tinged buffish-olive, with indistinct dark grey streaks. The rump is of similar colour, without streaking. Wing and tail like first-winter birds of respective sex. Breast buffish-grey, with some faint streaking. Flanks and belly whitish, with faint buffish-grey tinge. Males differ from *P. n. townsendi* by white base of central tail feathers and white alula.

SEXING Juveniles can be sexed by colour of primary coverts, white with dark tip in male and dark with narrow pale edges in female, and amount of dark on two central pairs of tail feathers (white base in males, all dark in females).

Males are characterised by extensively white plumage. Except in juvenile plumage when both sexes show similar pattern on the mantle, males can always be told by lack of concealed black on the mantle. Some individuals show dark shaft streaks which are occasionally distinct, but never similar to pattern of female. The lesser, median and greater coverts are white. The alula shows a varying amount of white depending on age. Primary coverts white, occasionally with minute dark spots near the tip; then similar to adult female. The black pattern on the primaries is more limited than in females, but varies individually and according to age. In the males showing the most extensive black pattern the distal part of the outer five to seven primaries may be black, the black reaching almost to the tip of primary coverts on the folded wing. Like that on the wings, the pattern of the tail varies with age. In first-year males showing most extensive black pattern on the two central pairs, there is white at least at the base, black on distal part usually covering half the tail or less.

Females differ from males by showing blackish streaking on the mantle. The longest uppertail-coverts have dark

centres. As in Snow Bunting, the dark parts of the primaries are greyer and less contrasting in females than in males, especially when viewed from below. Females always have blackish alula, and birds with visible dark bases to lesser and greater coverts are females. Females also show considerably more black in the primaries than males of the same age. However, the wing pattern of adult female is similar to that of first-year male. The central tail feathers are all dark in females.

MOULT AND AGEING Juveniles moult body feathers during July to September on the breeding grounds. Adults moult completely during same period, after breeding is finished. There is no certain evidence for a limited pre-breeding moult of body feathers.

Ageing and sexing criteria to some extent interdependent. Juveniles have more pointed tail feathers than adults. Adults can be told by their more rounded tail feathers. Note that the black centres of the tail feathers of adults are often very pointed. As black parts of feathers are more resistant to wear, the rounded shape, which is mainly formed by white edges, can turn very pointed as these white edges are worn off. The relative amount of wear is also useful. As a rule, first-year birds have primaries and tail feathers more worn than adults.

In adult males the alula is white, but shows a varying amount of black in first-year males. Furthermore, the dark parts of the primaries are restricted to a smaller area and to fewer feathers than in first-year males. It is possible that second-summer males can be told by traces of black in the alula, more black on the wing tips and more black in the tail than older males, but this requires further study.

Adult females show white base to the visible part of the primaries, unlike first-year females. A female showing mainly white primary coverts is adult. In first-year females, the primary coverts are blackish with narrow pale edges. Adult females show very little dark in lesser, median and greater coverts. First-year females have dark bases which are clearly visible on at least lesser and greater coverts. Dark bases of lesser and greater coverts in birds which, based on other criteria, appear to be adult may indicate second-year birds. Amount of white on mantle may also be age-related, increased amount indicating older bird.

Skull ossification is useful in autumn, but is completed around December. Iris colour should be useful with experience.

MEASUREMENTS Wing: (chord) male 108-122, female 101-113. Tail: male 65.5-75.0, female 64.0-68.5. Bill: (exposed culmen) male 11.2-12.7, female 10.7-11.7. Tarsus: male 21.1-23.6, female 20.8-23.1. P7-P8 emarginated.

GEOGRAPHICAL VARIATION None.

RELATIONSHIPS Sometimes treated as conspecific with Snow Bunting. However, although the restricted breeding range is completely surrounded by range of Snow Bunting, the lineages have remained separate long enough for the very distinctive appearance of McKay's to evolve, without Snow Bunting invading the core breeding area. In adjacent range of Snow Bunting, stray individuals of McKay's Bunting form mixed pairs with Snow, but there is no major hybridisation.

VOICE Both song and call are described as similar to those of Snow Bunting, but thorough studies appear to be lacking.

HABITS Breeds in June and July. The nest, which is made

of grass, is often placed in hollow driftwood along the shoreline, or in crevices in rocks. Eggs 4-6, light greenish, dotted with pale brown; incubation by the female 10-15 days. The young are said to leave the nest after a further 10-15 days. Food probably similar to that of Snow Bunting.

STATUS AND HABITAT Inhabits both shores and inland tundra on Hall and St. Matthew Islands, where reported to be common. No information on population trends found. In the Pribilofs usually found on tundra or scree.

DISTRIBUTION AND MOVEMENTS Main breeding area Hall and St. Matthew Islands in the Bering Sea (marked with arrows on map). Singing males in very small numbers are regularly recorded on St. Lawrence Island, and St. Paul and St. George in the Pribilof Islands. Migrates from breeding areas in easterly direction to the mainland, where it normally occurs from mid October to mid April, or exceptionally to the second half of May. Winters along Alaska coast from Kotzebue to tip of Alaska Peninsula. Accidental in British Columbia, Canada, and Washington and Oregon, USA. Not known from Siberian side although occurrence there seems possible.

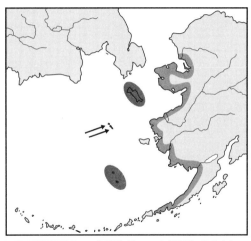

REFERENCES Bent (1968), Farrand (1983), Gabrielson & Lincoln (1959), Kessel (1989), Kessel & Gibson (1978), Lethaby (1994), Pyle *et al.* (1987).

CALAMOSPIZA

One species which is rather large and chunky and shows strong sexual dimorphism in plumage. The male is mostly black with a large white wing patch, the female is brown and streaky; despite this, the genus is thought to be most closely related to *Plectrophenax*. It is a bird of the American prairies, is gregarious at all seasons, and the male has a distinctive display flight.

48 LARK BUNTING
Calamospiza melanocorys   Plate 17

Described as *Fringilla bicolor* Townsend 1837. Monotypic.

A common and distinctive bird of the prairie region, generally seen in large flocks.

IDENTIFICATION 18cm. Male in breeding plumage is unmistakable, being jet black with highly contrasting white wing patches and white tips to tail feathers. Note also stocky build, fairly short tail and relatively large blue-grey bill. Non-breeding male resembles female but is darker and greyer above, whiter below and on the pale surrounds to the cheeks, has extensive black on the throat and retains the white wing patch. Female is similar in shape but is greyish-brown above with blackish streaks, and whitish below with distinct brown streaking and a buffy wash on the flanks. She also has dark grey-brown ear-coverts surrounded by pale buffy-white supercilium and patch on neck-sides, and a buffy-white wing patch in place of the male's white one. Juvenile resembles female but is buffier overall with a more scaly appearance to the back and more extensive streaking on underparts.

DESCRIPTION
Sexes differ; juvenile resembles female but is distinguishable.
Adult male breeding Body plumage jet black with broad white tips to undertail-coverts and narrow white fringes to the uppertail-coverts, mantle, scapulars and underparts in fresh plumage. Wings black with a large white patch formed by white outer greater and median coverts and

white outer webs to the inner ones. Tertials broadly edged white, remiges with narrow whitish edges. Tail black with outer web of outer feather white and white spots at the tips of all but the central rectrices, decreasing in size from outer rectrix to T2. Iris blackish. Bill bluish-grey, rather large and conical. Legs blackish-brown.
Adult male non-breeding Similar to female but has a large pale buff wing patch, throat mostly black, much heavier and blacker streaking on underparts and blackish (not brown) base colour to the wings.
Adult female Crown, nape and upperparts grey-brown, streaked blackish. Quite broad buffy-white supercilium extending to, or just beyond, rear edge of ear-coverts. Lores buffy-brown. Ear-coverts grey-brown, unstreaked. Submoustachial stripe buffy-white, extending round rear edge of ear-coverts. Malar stripe dark brown. Wings dark brown with broad pale buff edges to median and greater coverts forming prominent patch in wing (but smaller and less obvious than winter male's). Tertials have broad buff edges. Tail grey-brown with pale buff tips to the rectrices (pattern similar to male's). Underparts whitish with a buff wash on the breast and flanks, most noticeable on rear-flanks. Throat, breast and flanks moderately streaked dark brown.
First-year male In non-breeding plumage resembles adult female but averages whiter, especially on the wing patch, and has more white in the tail. Underparts are more heavily streaked with blackish (not brownish) and there is frequently some blackish mottling on the throat (though it is never mostly blackish as in adult male). Usually shows distinct contrast between fresh black outer primaries and worn brownish primary coverts and remainder of remig-

es, though occasionally they may all be retained juvenile brownish feathers; also frequently shows similar contrast between fresh and retained juvenile rectrices. Breeding black body plumage is frequently mottled grey (beware of adult male in early spring which is still assuming breeding plumage) and the retained juvenile remiges and rectrices are worn and brownish, contrasting with the moulted ones (as in non-breeding plumage).

First-year female Resembles adult female but wing patch averages buffier and less distinct, and there is often a contrast between moulted and retained juvenile remiges and rectrices as in first-year male (though the freshly moulted feathers are dark brown, not black, so the contrast is not so marked). Retained juvenile rectrices have indistinct whitish tips.

Juvenile Resembles adult female but is noticeably buffier overall, the upperparts appear scaled rather than streaked, due to whitish fringes to the feathers (most obvious on the scapulars) and the streaking on the underparts is slightly more extensive.

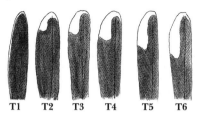

T1   T2   T3   T4   T5   T6

Tail feathers of adult; sexes similar, both rather variable. First-year female has indistinct whitish tips to retained juvenile rectrices.

MOULT AND AGEING The post-juvenile moult occurs in July-September, and is generally incomplete, including the outer four primaries and often a few rectrices as well as all the body feathers. The post-breeding moult occurs in July-October and is complete. These two, perhaps especially the post-breeding, appear to be suspended and completed on the wintering grounds. The pre-breeding moult occurs in January-April and is incomplete, including the tertials and usually all the greater coverts. Males can often be aged by plumage, but this is less useful for females; due to the incomplete post-juvenile moult, contrast between moulted and retained juvenile remiges and rectrices is also useful (see under Description). Retained juvenile rectrices average more pointed than moulted adult ones. Skull ossification complete in first-years from 15 November.

MEASUREMENTS Wing (chord): male (n30) 84-92; female (n30) 79-87. Tail: male (n16) 64.8-71.1; female (n6) 60.4-68.6. Bill: male (n16) 11.6-15; female (n6) 12.7-13.2. Tarsus: male (n16) 22.9-26; female (n6) 22.3-25.2.

GEOGRAPHICAL VARIATION None.

VOICE The song, often given in distinctive song flight (see under habits), is a rich, musical and varied series of whistles and trills. Calls include a distinctive, soft, two-note whistle, *hoo-ee*.

HABITS Nest is placed on the ground, usually hidden under a tuft of grass or small shrub; a loose cup of twigs, rootlets and grasses, lined with finer grasses and hair. Egg 4-6, pale blue and usually unmarked. The incubation period is 11-12 days and the young fledge after 8-9 days. Nests in large, loose colonies. Male sings either from the ground or, more often, during a peculiar display flight in which he flies several metres into the air and then glides slowly down with distinctive slow flaps of extended wings. Several males frequently display together in this way. Normally polygynous. Colonies are somewhat nomadic, moving around from year to year and frequently expanding the species's range during dry summers. Feeds on the ground, foraging for seeds and insects; feeds its young almost entirely on grasshoppers when these are in abundance. Generally found communally year-round and often in very large flocks in winter. These flocks generally move and feed together, with one bird acting as leader.

STATUS AND HABITAT Common to locally very common. Breeds in prairies, dry plains and sagebrush. Winters in weedy fields, agricultural land and semi-arid areas.

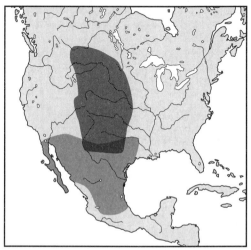

DISTRIBUTION AND MOVEMENTS Breeds in midwestern North America, from southern Alberta and (sporadically) Manitoba south to New Mexico and western Texas. Short- to medium-distance migrant, wintering from southern New Mexico and western Texas (where birds occur year-round) south to southern Baja California, and Jalisco and Hidalgo in central Mexico. Spring migration begins in early March and is quite leisurely, with birds arriving on breeding grounds from early April in south, late May in north. Autumn migration begins in July, with birds arriving on wintering grounds from late July, although it is also quite protracted and most arrive later. Casual in winter and on migration almost throughout US and southern Canada. Vagrant to Belize.

REFERENCES Armani (1985), Bent (1968), Dunn & Blom (1983), Ehrlich *et al.* (1988), Farrand (1983), Godfrey (1986), Oberholser (1974), Paynter & Storer (1970), Peterson & Chalif (1973), Pyle *et al.* (1987), Ridgway (1901), Terres (1980).

PASSERELLA

One species which shows considerable variation over its range (more than one species may actually be involved in the complex). All races are quite large, chunky and long-tailed, and have a bicoloured bill. Feeds mostly on the ground, scratching with its feet in leaf-litter. It was formerly included in the *Zonotrichia* genus.

49 FOX SPARROW
Passerella iliaca Plate 30

Described as *Fringilla iliaca* Merrem 1786.
Synonyms: *Zonotrichia iliaca, Emberiza unalaschcensis.*

This is a highly variable sparrow with 18 races recognised, covering much of northern and western North America. Although certain characters such as size and bill pattern seem fairly constant, plumage-wise the geographical variation is very marked and there may well be more than one species involved in the complex.

IDENTIFICATION 18cm. All races are large, stocky and fairly long-tailed with a bicoloured bill (dark above and pale yellowish-flesh to pale yellow below) and heavy, blotchy rufous- to dark brown streaks on breast and flanks, which merge to form a larger central spot on the breast. Eastern birds have 'foxy' reddish rump and tail, reddish covert and tertial edges, greyish head and upperparts with heavy rufous streaking, unstreaked grey supercilium and neck-sides, and whitish underparts with rufous streaks. Birds breeding in most of Alaska and north-western Canada are greyer on the head and upperparts, while those of the northern Rockies in British Columbia are duller and more uniform overall. Pacific coast races from the Aleutians to Washington are uniform dark brown above with reddish tones virtually or entirely lacking, and whitish, heavily streaked dark brown below. Birds breeding in the Rockies, from southern Canada south, show a noticeable contrast between grey, unstreaked head and mantle and reddish rump and tail. The dark races of coastal British Columbia are superficially similar to the dark rufous-brown races of Song Sparrow (50) which occur there but are distinguished by larger size, stockier build, larger bicoloured bill, darker brown upperparts and head, lacking any warm brown or rufous tones, and heavier, darker streaking on underparts. Juveniles of all races are slightly duller above than adults and have buffy underparts.

DESCRIPTION
Sexes alike; juvenile similar but distinguishable.
Adult/first-year Crown and nape grey with untidy rufous streaks. Broad supercilium and neck-sides grey, unstreaked, sometimes extending as a narrow band round base of nape. Lores mostly buffy-grey with small rufous patch just in front of eye. Eye-ring pale buff to whitish. Ear-coverts rufous-brown, variably but finely blotched and streaked whitish or pale grey beneath eye; more rufous and unstreaked on rear, sometimes extending back in upper rear corner to virtually separate supercilium and neck-sides. Broad submoustachial stripe white but often finely streaked rufous. Blotchy malar stripe rufous, contrasting with throat and submoustachial stripe and running into streaks on underparts. Mantle and scapulars grey, tinged olive and broadly streaked rufous. Lower back similar but virtually unstreaked. Rump and uppertail-coverts

bright rufous. Lesser coverts olive-grey, tinged rufous. Rest of wings blackish with rufous feather edges, broadest on greater coverts and tertials (tertials also tipped white on edges). Greater and median coverts narrowly tipped whitish forming two obscure wing-bars. Tail dark brown but with bright rufous feather edges (central feathers mostly rufous) so closed tail appears mostly rufous. Throat white, unstreaked. Rest of underparts also white with broad, rufous streaks on breast and flanks, those on lower breast generally slightly narrower and noticeably arrow-shaped. Iris dark reddish-brown. Bill mostly pale yellow with a dark greyish-horn culmen and tip. Legs dark flesh. Similar year-round but the rump and uppertail-covert feathers have narrow pale grey fringes in fresh autumn plumage, and the crown and mantle appear more rufous than in worn plumage due to more extensive rufous feather tipping.
Juvenile Similar to adult but upperparts noticeably duller, underparts buffy-white with streaking narrower and less blotched. Plumage texture is also looser, as in other juvenile sparrows.

MOULT AND AGEING The post-juvenile moult is partial and the post-breeding moult is complete; both occur in July-September on the breeding grounds, prior to migration. Some, but perhaps not all, birds have a limited pre-breeding moult, involving some head feathers, in March-April. Once the post-juvenile moult is completed first-years resemble adults in plumage, but have more pointed rectrices on average (although there is some overlap) and the rectrices also average more worn, especially by spring. Skull ossification complete in first-years from 1 December.

MEASUREMENTS Measurements for the three main groups detailed in Geographical Variation are given below. Northern and eastern group: Wing (chord): male (n10) 86.4-91.7; female (n7) 83.8-87.9. Tail: male (n10) 67-73.9; female (n7) 66.8-73.2. Bill: male (n10) 10.7-13; female (n7) 10.7-12.2. Tarsus: male (n10) 24.1-25.4; female (n7) 23.1-25.4. Maximum wing (*iliaca*): male (n14) 87-92; female (n7) 81-89.
Southern Rocky Mountain and Sierra group: Wing (chord): male (n27) 78.2-87.1; female (n14) 75.4-85.6. Tail: male (n27) 73.1-87.1; female (n9) 76.7-88.7. Bill: male (n27) 11.2-16.5; female (n14) 11.4-15. Tarsus: male (n27) 21.6-25.2; female (n14) 22.9-24.9 (*schistacea* is the smallest and *stephensi* the largest in bill size).
Northern Pacific coast group: Wing (chord): male (n42) 77.2-87.4; female (n26) 73.9-82. Tail: male (n42) 67-78.2; female (n26) 66-77.2. Bill: male (n42) 10.9-13.5; female (n26) 10.4-14. Tarsus: male (n42) 24.1-26.7; female (n26) 23.4-26.2 (*fuliginosa* averages the smallest-billed, *insularis* and *unalaschcensis* the largest-billed, although none in this group is as large-billed as the southern races of the Rocky Mountain and Sierra group).

GEOGRAPHICAL VARIATION Eighteen races described which vary widely in plumage but fall into three main groups. Differences within all three groups are clinal and the southern Rocky Mountain and Sierra group may be oversplit racially.

Northern and eastern group: greyish head and mantle, streaked rufous; bright rufous rump and tail; blotchy rufous streaks on underparts.

P. i. iliaca (Breeds in NE North America from N Ontario east to Newfoundland and locally in Nova Scotia, and winters in the SE USA, mainly from Mississippi and Illinois east) Described above.

P. i. zaboria (Breeds in N and NW North America from N Manitoba west to N and C Alaska, including N British Columbia. Winters in the S USA, mainly in Texas, Mississippi and Alabama) Similar to *iliaca* but averages darker and more greyish.

P. i. altivagans (Breeds on the eastern slope of the Rockies in C and SE British Columbia and SW Alberta, and winters in Oregon and California, occasionally also south to Baja California). It is similar to *zaboria* but duller, especially on the rump and tail, with less noticeable streaking above.

Southern Rocky Mountain and Sierra races: unstreaked grey or olive-grey head and mantle but otherwise similar to the previous group (although bill larger in southern races). Note that these two groups (races *altivagans* and *schistacea*) intergrade in the Rockies in SE British Columbia and SW Alberta. The races in this group are very similar in plumage (and are not generally distinguishable in the field except by breeding range) but the bill size increases from north to south and from east to west in the southern (Californian) races.

P. i. schistacea (Breeds from extreme SE British Columbia and SW Alberta south to Colorado, Utah and NE Nevada, and winters in the SW USA and N Baja California) The smallest-billed of the group.

P. i. olivacea (Breeds in SW British Columbia and Washington, and winters on the coasts of California and northern Baja California) Similar to *schistacea* but is more olive-grey on the head and mantle.

P. i. swarthi (Breeds in SE Idaho and NE Utah; winters to the south but range not known)

P. i. fulva (Breeds on the eastern slope of the Cascades from C Oregon south to NE California, and winters in SW California and N Baja California)

P. i. megarhyncha (Breeds from SW Oregon south to C California and in WC Nevada, and winters at lower elevations from C California south to N Baja California)

P. i. brevicauda (Breeds in the inner coastal mountain ranges of California, south of Trinity River, and winters in C and S coastal California)

P. i. monoensis (Breeds on the eastern slope of the Sierra Nevada in C California and adjacent Nevada, and winters in central interior and S California and N Baja California)

P. i. canescens (Breeds in CE California and C Nevada, south of *monoensis*, and winters in S California, Arizona and N Baja California)

P. i. stephensi (Breeds in the Sierra Nevada in S California and winters in S California at lower elevations) The largest-billed of this group and indeed of all the races.

Northern Pacific coast group: uniform dark brown above with very little or no rufous, and heavily streaked dark brown below. The races are very similar in plumage (and are not generally distinguishable in the field except by breeding range) but birds become paler and larger-billed from south-east to north-west.

P. i. fuliginosa (Breeds on the coast from SE Alaska south to NW Washington and winters from coastal S British Columbia south to California) The darkest of this group, uniform sooty brown above.

P. i. townsendi (Breeds in SE Alaska and on the Queen Charlotte Islands in British Columbia, wintering in the breeding range and south along the coast to central California) Similar to *fuliginosa* but slightly brighter and less sooty above.

P. i. annectens (Breeds in Alaska in the Yacugat Bay and Malaspina Glacier area, and winters on the coast from S British Columbia south to California)

P. i. sinuosa (Breeds on the Kenai Peninsula and in the Prince William Sound area, Alaska, and winters from coastal S British Columbia south to N Baja California)

P. i. ridgwayi (Breeds on Kodiak, Trinity and Afognak Islands in Alaska, and winters from coastal S British Columbia south to California)

P. i. unalaschcensis (Breeds on the Alaska Peninsula and in the Aleutian Islands, and winters from coastal S British Columbia south to California) The palest and largest-billed of this group.

VOICE The song, generally given from the top of a bush or a low branch in a tree, is rich, loud and melodious: 2 or 3 clear or slurred whistles, followed by a rapid series of short buzzy trills which usually descend in pitch. Varies somewhat according to race. Calls include a variety of 'chips' and a short, sharp whistle.

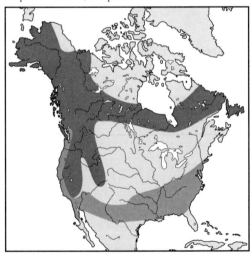

HABITS Nest is placed either on the ground under a bush or tree or low in a bush or tree; a cup of grass, twigs, moss and rootlets, lined with grass, hair, and often wool or feathers. Eggs 3-5, laid in May-July, bluish- or greenish-white and speckled or spotted with reddish-browns. The incubation period is 12-14 days and the young fledge after 9-11 days. Feeds on insects and sometimes berries, as well as seeds, generally foraging on the ground where it noisily scratches the leaf-litter with both feet together to expose food. May also sometimes forage low in bushes for berries. Outside the breeding season, single birds or small groups often join flocks of other sparrows; larger flocks may sometimes occur on migration.

STATUS AND HABITAT Fairly common to common throughout its range. Breeds in coniferous or mixed forest with a dense understorey, woodland thickets, riparian woodland and shrubbery, and chaparral and dense low scrub (especially in the west). Winters mainly in woodlots, forest and forest edges and other woodland habitats, generally those with a dense understorey, but also in undergrowth in parks and gardens.

DISTRIBUTION AND MOVEMENTS Breeds across northern Canada and Alaska and south through much of western North America. Short to medium or long distance migrant, wintering on the Pacific coast from southern British Columbia south to northern Baja California, and across the southern USA and adjacent extreme northern Mexico, north in the east to central Illinois and Connecti-

cut. See also under Geographical Variation. Spring migration starts in late February/early March in the east, March-April in the south-west, with birds arriving on breeding grounds from April. Autumn migration starts in late August/early September, with most birds reaching winter grounds by November. Casual in winter in southern Ontario. Vagrant to Japan (race *unalaschcensis* - 2 records) and to Europe (race *iliaca*) in Iceland (1), Ireland (1), Italy (1) and Germany (2).

REFERENCES Alström *et al.* (1991), Armani (1985), Bent (1968), Cramp & Perrins (1994), Dunn & Blom (1983), Ehrlich *et al.* (1988), Godfrey (1986), Paynter & Storer (1970), Peterson & Chalif (1973), Pyle *et al.* (1987), Ridgway (1901), Sibley and Monroe (1990), Terres (1980).

MELOSPIZA

Three species of medium-sized sparrows with relatively long, rounded tails which are often pumped in flight. They can be skulking, but generally respond well to 'pishing'. This genus was formerly included in *Zonotrichia*.

50   SONG SPARROW
Melospiza melodia   Plate 20

Described as *Fringilla melodia* Wilson 1810.
Synonyms: *Zonotrichia melodia, Melospiza fasciata, Zonotrichia fallax, Passerella melodia, Passerella rufina, Fringilla guttata, Ammodramus samuelis.*

This is one of the commonest and most familiar of the sparrows as well as being one of the most variable, with 39 races spread over most of North America (including Mexico).

IDENTIFICATION 15-18cm. A remarkably variable sparrow but all races share a long rounded tail, which is pumped in flight, greyish or whitish supercilium, pale median crown-stripe and broad dark malar stripe which separates the whitish submoustachial stripe and throat. Upperparts vary in tone but are always streaked, and the whitish underparts have variable dark streaking which, in adults of most races, merge to form a blotchy spot in centre of breast. Most also show greyish or grey-buff ear-coverts with darker edges, especially upper and lower edges (forming fairly distinct dark eye-stripe and moustachial stripe). Generally, geographical variation is as follows: eastern birds are grey-buff above, streaked darker, with warmer, more rufous-brown wings and tail, rufous-brown lateral crown, and moderately streaked underparts with a well-developed central spot. Western birds become progressively darker with most west coast races being dark rufous-brown above with heavier dark rufous to blackish streaking below. Birds get progressively larger, larger-billed and greyer above (streaked dark rufous) going north up the west coast, reaching an extreme in the Aleutians. Those of the south-western deserts are considerably paler rufous with quite light streaking underneath. Birds of the Mexican central plateau have more rufous in the wings and heavier, darker (blackish) streaking below than those fur-

ther north. Despite this variation Song Sparrow is quite easy to identify by its distinctive shape and certain constant plumage features (outlined above) and its equally distinctive song and call (see under Voice). Juveniles are similar but buffier overall with finer, fainter streaking underneath, lacking the characteristic central spot, and have a less distinct head pattern. Vesper Sparrow (77) has a noticeably shorter tail with white outer feathers, a bold white eye-ring, a more uniformly streaked crown, lacking a pale median stripe and chestnut lesser coverts (often difficult to see). Savannah Sparrow (61) also has a shorter tail, which is slightly notched rather than rounded, a less contrasting head pattern and lacks prominent rufous tones to the wings and tail; most specimens have a distinctive yellow or yellowish supraloral stripe on the front part of the supercilium and are more uniformy streaked underneath. Fox Sparrow (49) is considerably larger and bulkier than all but the distinctive Aleutian races of Song, is more heavily streaked below and has a distinctly bicoloured bill. Lincoln's Sparrow (51) is more similar to Song but adult has a shorter tail, a darker grey supercilium, much finer streaking on the breast, a distinct buffy wash to the breast and flanks, a distinct buffy (rather than whitish) submoustachial stripe and a narrower malar stripe. Juvenile Lincoln's is much more similar to juvenile Song but the crown is more heavily streaked with black and the throat is distinctly streaked. In the hand, note also the shorter tail and wing formula differences (make sure the wing is fully grown). Adult and first-winter Swamp Sparrows (52) are quite different from Song but juveniles of the two species can be exceptionally similar. Generally, juvenile Swamp has more obvious rufous tones to the wing and tail and a more heavily streaked crown (sometimes appearing almost blackish and usually lacking any pale median stripe). There is some overlap in both these features, however. With difficult individuals the best feature is the bill shape, which is slightly more slender, more pointed and less deep at the base in Swamp. In the hand, most juvenile Swamps can be told by the yellow or yellowish mouth lining and by differences in tail length (tail is usually longer in the races of Song Sparrow which overlap with Swamp) and wing formula (see under Measurements), but note that even here there is a small amount of overlap and differences in bill shape will still be useful.

HYBRIDISATION There is a record of hybridisation with White-crowned Sparrow (55).

DESCRIPTION

Sexes alike; juvenile similar to subsequent plumages but distinguishable.

Adult/first-year Crown dull rufous-brown, faintly streaked blackish and with a narrow greyish-white median stripe. Supercilium greyish-white, quite broad and reaching to rear of ear-coverts. Eye-ring pale buff. Lores and ear-coverts greyish-buff; ear-coverts bordered by a narrow dark rufous-brown eye-stripe (behind eye) on upper edge and a similar moustachial stripe on the lower edge; the rear edge is also often indistinctly darker. Broad submoustachial stripe whitish; malar stripe contrastingly dark brown, broadening on the neck-sides and not usually reaching base of bill. Nape and neck-sides greyish, faintly streaked dark brown. Mantle, back and scapulars grey-brown, heavily streaked blackish (the blackish streaks with rufous-brown edges). Rump more olive-brown and only faintly streaked darker, uppertail-coverts greyer and with a distinct dark brown central streak. Lesser coverts olive-grey, washed rufous. Rest of wings blackish-brown with warm brown (often slightly rufous) edges to all feathers, broadest on greater coverts and tertials. Greater and median coverts narrowly tipped pale buff forming two fairly obscure wing-bars. Tail warm brown, showing slight rufous tones, with narrow paler feather edges. Throat whitish, unstreaked and contrasting with the dark malar stripes. Rest of underparts also whitish, with dark rufous-brown streaks on breast and flanks which often merge to form a distinct spot in the centre of the breast. Iris dark reddish-brown. Bill dusky grey with most of lower mandible (except tip) horn. Legs pale flesh.

Juvenile Ground colour of upperparts buff rather than greyish. Head buffy with adult pattern only faintly outlined and narrow median crown-stripe lacking or virtually lacking. Crown buffy-brown, finely streaked darker. Underparts pale buff with relatively fine streaking on breast and flanks, not forming a central breast spot. Wings and tail as adult/first-year but wing-bars are buffier.

MOULT AND AGEING The post-juvenile moult occurs in July-November. In most southern sedentary populations it is complete, while in northern and migratory races it is generally incomplete, usually including the rectrices and the tertials, plus a variable number of remiges. The post-breeding moult is complete and occurs in July-October. There is no pre-breeding moult. In migratory populations, moults occur primarily on the breeding grounds and are usually completed by August; they are more protracted in the sedentary populations. Once the post-juvenile moult is completed, first-years resemble adults in plumage. Tail shape is not usually useful for ageing, as differences in shape are very slight and the juvenile rectrices are usually moulted anyway. Some birds may be aged in the hand by contrast between worn juvenile and fresher adult remiges. Skull ossification complete in first-years from 15 November in northern populations but from 15 October in some California races (and possibly earlier in more southern races). Note that some birds retain unossified 'windows' through to the first spring.

MEASUREMENTS This species is very variable in size and measurements for the separate groups outlined in Geographical Variation are given below.
Continental North America (but excluding the three groups below): Wing (chord): male (n196) 58.4-76.7; female (n138) 54.6-71.4. Tail: male (n196) 55.6-76.7; female (n138) 52.8-72.6. Bill: male (n196) 10.4-14; female (n138) 10.4-13.2. Tarsus: male (n196) 20.1-25.2; female (n138) 20.1-25.2. Maximum wing (*melodia*): male (n13) 64-70; female (n8) 62-67 (*cooperi* and *cleonensis* are the smallest races and *rufina* the largest). Bill depth (*melodia* n10) 6.8-8.1.
Aleutian/Alaskan group (races *caurina*, *kenaiensis*, *insignis* and *maxima* measured): Wing (chord): male (n36) 70.9-87.4; female (n21) 67.3-85.3. Tail: male (n36) 63.5-86.6; female (n21) 62.5-82. Bill: male (n36) 12.7-18; female (n21) 12.7-17. Tarsus: male (n36) 22.9-29.2; female (n21) 22.6-27.9 (*caurina* averages the smallest and *maxima* averages the largest in this group; there is no overlap between *caurina* and *maxima* in any of the measurements and *caurina* overlaps extensively in all measurements except bill with *rufina*).
San Fransisco Bay group (*samuelis* and *pusillula* measured): Wing (chord): male (n34) 54.6-63.8; female (n22) 53.6-61.5. Tail: male (n34) 50.3-61.7; female (n22) 52.1-59.7. Bill: male (n34) 10.2-12.7; female (n22) 10.2-12.5. Tarsus: male (n34) 19.8-22.4; female (n22) 19.8-21.8 (*pusillula* averages smaller than *samuelis* in all measurements but there is much overlap).
California/Baja California island group (*clementae* and *graminea* measured): Wing (chord): male (n16) 58.2-66; female (n11) 58.4-63.5. Tail: male (n16) 53.6-67.1; female (n11) 55.6-63.5. Bill: male (n16) 11.9-12.5; female (n11) 11.4-12.7. Tarsus: male (n16) 19.8-22.4; female (n11) 19.8-21.8 (*clementae* is longer than *graminea* in wing and tail with little or no overlap).
Wing formula: P9 < P5 by 6-12mm.

GEOGRAPHICAL VARIATION Thirty-nine races described. Many adjoining ones are very similar (and often not distinguishable in the field) but the overall variation is quite marked. Thirteen races can be grouped into three distinct groups; the rest have been united into a single continental group.
Continental North America group.
M. m. melodia (Breeds in E North America from E Ontario east to Newfoundland and south to Virginia. In winter it occurs throughout the SE USA. Found in the NE USA year-round but Canadian populations leave in the winter) Described above.
M. m. atlantica (Breeds on the Atlantic coast from Long Island south to N Carolina. In winter birds occur north to Maryland and south to Georgia) Very similar to *melodia* and some are indistinguishable, but others average slightly greyer above with darker and more distinct streaking; the song tends to have a more buzzy quality than *melodia*.
M. m. euphonia (Breeds in the Bruce Peninsula area of S Ontario and in the NC USA from Minnesota and Arkansas east to Ohio and Tennessee. The northernmost part of the range is vacated in winter, when birds also occur south to Texas and S Carolina) Very similar to *melodia* but the upperparts average slightly duller and greyer.
Z. m. juddi (Breeds in WC North America from EC

British Columbia and Wyoming east to W Ontario – James Bay area – and Michigan. Except for extreme southern populations it is migratory with birds wintering south to Texas and Virginia) Similar to *melodia* but the upperparts average slightly paler and greyer, the supercilium averages paler, and the underparts average whiter with fewer but more distinct dark streaks.

M. m. merrilli (Breeds in S interior British Columbia, extreme SW Alberta, E Washington, N Idaho and NW Montana. It is migratory, wintering mainly in California and Arizona) Noticeably darker and more uniform above than *juddi* with less noticeable streaking.

M. m. inexspectata (Breeds in NW North America in S Yukon, SE Alaska, interior NC British Columbia and W Alberta. It is migratory, wintering mainly from S British Columbia south to Oregon) Darker and sootier grey above than *juddi*. It is most similar to *rufina* but the upperparts are less rufous, more greyish-brown.

M. m. morphna (Breeds on the Pacific coast from SW British Columbia south to Oregon. It is mainly sedentary but occurs south to California in winter) Dark rufous above with heavy dark rufous streaking below.

M. m. rufina (Breeds on the Pacific coast from C British Columbia including the Queen Charlotte Islands north to SE Alaska. It is mainly sedentary but occurs south to Washington in winter) Darker and sootier than *morphna* and averages larger.

M. m. montana (Breeds in W USA in the mountains from Oregon and Idaho south to Nevada and New Mexico. In winter it also occurs south to Sonora and Chihuahua in N Mexico) Averages slightly darker and greyer than *melodia* with slightly longer tail and tarsus and a slightly smaller and more slender bill.

M. m. fisherella (Breeds east of the Cascades, from NE Oregon and extreme SW Idaho, south to EC California and W Nevada, and winters south to S California, rarely to S Arizona and adjacent N Sonora) Similar to *heermani* but is slightly larger, has somewhat paler and less rufous upperparts, and browner (less blackish) streaks on the underparts.

M. m. cleonensis (Resident from S Oregon south to N California) Similar to *samuelis* in proportions but more rufous; upperparts are olive-rufous, heavily streaked dark rufous-brown, and underparts have rufous-brown streaks which are blacker on the breast-sides. It is thus fairly similar to *morphna* but is more olive above and with blacker streaking on breast-sides.

M. m. gouldii (Resident on the C California coast) Similar to *cleonensis* but is less rufous above and has blacker streaking below.

M. m. mailliardi (Resident in the Central Valley of California) Similar to *heermani* but is slightly darker above and more heavily streaked above and below. It is thus also similar to *maxillaris* (the largest of the San Fransisco Bay group) but has a narrower (unswollen) bill.

M. m. heermani (Resident in Merced and Kern counties, California) Quite dark rufous above and quite heavily streaked with blackish above and below.

M. m. cooperi (Resident on the coasts of S California and N Baja California) Similar to *heermani* but slightly smaller, and paler and greyer above.

M. m. rivularis (C and S Baja California) Similar to *fallax* but averages larger, duller and less rufous above (rufous streaking fairly indistinct) and has a longer and more slender bill.

M. m. fallax (Arid areas from S Nevada and SW Utah south to N Sonora) Noticeably paler than *montana* with paler rufous streaking, but shares its slender bill; similar to *saltonis* but is slightly larger and darker looking.

M. m. saltonis (Extreme S Nevada, SE California and NW Baja California) Pale grey above, heavily streaked with pale rufous, has pale rufous wings and tail, pale rufous crown with a pale grey median stripe and is lightly streaked with pale rufous on the underparts.

M. m. goldmani (Resident in Durango, Mexico) Less heavily streaked above than the more southerly races; similar to *montana* but rather larger and darker, with less distinct streaking on the upperparts.

M. m. zacapu (Resident in Jalisco – Lake Chapala – and the Zacapu and Zamora regions of Michoacán, Mexico) Rufous above, similar to *adusta* and *yurira* but brighter.

M. m. villai (Resident in S Guanajuato and NE Michoacán in the area east of Lake Chapala, Mexico) The largest and darkest of all the southern races (noticeably sootier and less rufous above than *mexicana*).

M. m. yurira (Resident in the Acambaro region of SE Guanajuato, Mexico) Smaller, paler and more rufous above than *villai*, similar to *zacapu* and *adusta* but duller and less rufous above with greyer (less buffy) feather edges.

M. m. adusta (Resident in the vicinity of Lakes Patzcuaro and Cuitzeo, C Michoacán, Mexico) Similar to *zacapu* and *yurira* in being rufous above, and intermediate between these two in brightness.

M. m. niceae (Resident in the vicinity of Lakes Tecocomulco, Tulacingo and Zupitlan, Hidalgo, Mexico) Darker and less contrasting above than *azteca* or *mexicana*; most similar in colour to *villai* but slightly smaller and with paler, buffier flanks; the juvenile is slightly paler overall than juvenile *villai*.

M. m. azteca (Resident in the vicinity of Lake Zumpango, Distrito Federal, Mexico) Intermediate between *mexicana* and the dullest of the rufous southern races (*yurira*) in upperpart colour; the streaking on the upperparts also averages broader than in *yurira*.

M. m. mexicana (Resident in Mexico D.F., Tlaxcala and Pueblo, Mexico) Similar to *heermani* but darker, more olive-brown above, more heavily and blotchily streaked below, and has longer wings and tarsus and a more slender bill. It is also similar to *azteca* but is duller and greyer-brown above.

Aleutian/Alaskan group.

The following six races are found almost exclusively on coastal beaches; they are large and grey (with rufous streaks), and increase in size from south-east to north-west.

M. m. caurina (Breeds in SE Alaska in the region of the Glacier Malaspina and winters south to California) Similar to *rufina* but slightly larger and greyer; intermediate between *rufina* and *kenaiensis*.

M. m. kenaiensis (Resident on the south coast of Alaska in the region of Cadova and Boswell Bays) Intermediate between *caurina* and *insignis*, slightly larger and greyer than the former, and smaller and browner than the latter with darker streaking.

M. m. insignis (Resident on Kodiak Island, Alaska)

Paler and greyer than *kenaiensis*; compared with *sanaka* it is slightly smaller, and darker and more uniform brownish-grey above.

M. m. sanaka (Resident on Sanak, Unimak and Seguam Islands, Alaska) Larger and greyer than *insignis*; olive-grey above (almost ash grey when worn) with quite heavy brown streaking above.

M. m. amaka (Resident on Amak Island, Alaska) More heavily streaked than *sanaka* (similar to *maxima*) but has a smaller and stubbier bill than *maxima*, similar to *sanaka*.

M. m. maxima (Resident on the Aleutian Islands, from Atka west to Attu) The largest and largest-billed of all the races, but is otherwise similar to *amaka*.

San Francisco Bay group.
The following three races are all resident in saltmarshes in the San Fransisco Bay area; they are small and heavily streaked with blackish below.

M. m. samuelis (San Pueblo Bay and the north side of San Fransisco Bay, California) Very similar to *heermani* in plumage but is smaller and has a more slender bill.

M. m. maxillaris (Suisin Bay, California) Averages darker brown above and more heavily streaked below than *samuelis*, and is also larger with a stouter bill (which has a laterally swollen base).

M. m. pusillula (Southern side of San Fransisco Bay, California) Similar to *samuelis* but is even smaller, less rufous (more greyish-olive) above and on the lateral crown-stripes and even more heavily streaked below. The underparts are often tinged yellowish.

California/Baja California island group.
The following four races are restricted to and resident on various small islands off the coast of California/Baja California. They are all noticeably grey-looking.

M. m. micronyx (San Miguel Island, California) The greyest of these races, almost pure grey above and whitish below, with contrasting blackish streaks above and below.

M. m. clementae (San Clemente, Santa Cruz, Santa Rosa and Anacapa, California) Similar to *micronyx* but is browner-grey above and less heavily streaked.

M. m. graminea (Santa Barbara Island, California) Similar to *clementae* but is noticeably smaller.

M. m. coronatorum (Coronados Island, off the coast of N Baja California) Similar to *clementae* but has a smaller bill and tarsus. It is also similar to *cooperi* of the adjacent mainland but is paler above, is less heavily streaked and has a smaller bill.

VOICE The song, generally given from an exposed perch such as the top of a bush, fence post or overhead wire, is spritely and distinctive: 3 or 4 loud clear notes, followed by a buzzy *tow-wee*, then a trill which often ends with a short series of more distinct notes. It varies slightly according to race but is always distinctive and is familiar to most North Americans. Calls include a distinct nasal and slightly hollow-sounding *chimp* and a high-pitched *tsii* in alarm.

HABITS Nest is rather well hidden on the ground, in a grass clump, or situated low in a bush or tree; earlier nests are more likely to be on the ground. It is a cup of grasses, weeds, bark and leaves, lined with fine grass, roots and hair. Eggs 3-5, laid in February-August, pale bluish- to greyish-green, speckled or blotched with brown or reddish-

brown. Incubation period is 12-13 (rarely up to 15) days and the young fledge after 10 days, often leaving the nest before they can fly. Usually double- or triple-brooded. Feeds mainly on seeds, but also insects during the breeding season, and sometimes berries. Forages mainly on the ground, often in the open, flying into bushes when disturbed. Often visits feeders in suburban and rural areas. Long tail is pumped in flight, a habit shared with other *Melospiza* sparrows. Outside the breeding season usually occurs singly or in pairs or family parties, often with other species, but larger groups can occur on migration.

STATUS AND HABITAT Common to abundant in a very wide variety of non-forest habitats; open bushy and shrubby areas, hedgerows, overgrown fields, woodland edges, riparian growth (especially dense streamside or poolside thickets), shrubby mountain valleys, farms and large gardens and other open areas with shrubby cover. Also in semi-arid and arid areas with sufficient scrub in southwestern USA and the highlands of Mexico. Aleutian and coastal Alaskan birds are found almost exclusively on sandy and scrubby beaches, often foraging in driftwood and other wave-borne debris. The small, heavily streaked races in the San Fransisco Bay area are restricted to saltmarshes. Migrants favour much the same habitat year-round but may winter in more open areas.

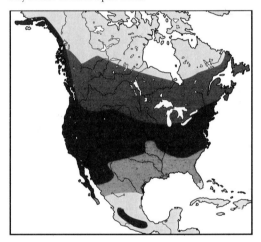

DISTRIBUTION AND MOVEMENTS Breeds across most of North America, including the Aleutian Islands, except for the northern tundra regions and the extreme southeastern and southern midwestern USA (although it does breed locally in Texas); also in central Mexico from Durango south to Michoacán and Puebla. Most of the west coast populations, and those of southern North America (north to about the Great Lakes region) are sedentary, but most of the interior Canadian and northern USA range is vacated in winter with birds moving south into the range of the sedentary populations and further south into the south-eastern USA and northern Mexico (the northern parts of Sonora, Chihuahua and Coahuila). See also under Geographical Variation. Spring migration begins in February with migrants arriving on breeding grounds from March. Autumn migration begins in June but is heaviest in September. Casual in winter north of mapped range. Vagrant to Britain (6 in April-June) and Norway (1 in May 1975).

REFERENCES Aldrich (1984), Alström *et al.* (1991), Armani (1985), Bent (1968), Cramp & Perrins (1994), Dhondt & Smith (1980), Dickerman (1963), Dunn & Blom (1983), Godfrey (1986), Paynter & Storer (1970), Pyle *et al.* (1987), Ridgway (1901), Terres (1980).

51   LINCOLN'S SPARROW
Melospiza lincolnii   Plate 20

Described as *Fringilla lincolnii* Audubon 1834.
Synonyms: *Zonotrichia lincolnii, Emberiza gracilis, Passerella lincolnii.*

A fairly common but rather unobtrusive sparrow, breeding across much of northern and western North America, but less often near human habitation than the other two in the genus.

IDENTIFICATION 15cm. Shorter-tailed than the other two *Melospiza* sparrows and often with a slight crested appearance, especially when agitated. Adults quite easily identified by combination of pale buff breast and flanks contrasting slightly but noticeably with whitish throat and belly; fine dark streaks on throat, breast and belly, noticeably finer than in similar sparrows. Broad grey supercilium, prominent and broad buff submoustachial stripe (contrasting with narrow blackish malar and moustachial stripes) and fairly prominent buff eye-ring are also distinctive, contributing to a characteristic facial 'jizz'. Crown is dark rufous-brown with a narrow greyish median stripe; both are finely streaked darker. Upperparts are dull brown, streaked blackish. Song Sparrow (50) has heavier, thicker streaks on underparts, a paler greyish-white supercilium, whitish submoustachial stripe, a noticeably longer tail and lacks contrasting buffy breast and flanks. No other sparrow shows broad grey supercilium and prominent buff submoustachial stripe. Juvenile is similar to adults but buffier overall, especially on the head, and lacks contrast on the underparts, the buff and white areas being less pure. Differs from juvenile Song in its distinctly streaked throat, smaller bill and shorter tail. Can closely resemble juvenile Swamp Sparrow (52) but is generally paler overall with less prominent rufous in wings, and has a distinctly streaked throat, buffy median crown-stripe and greyish inside of mouth. See also under Measurements.

DESCRIPTION
Sexes alike; juvenile similar to adult but distinguishable.
Adult/first-year Crown dark rufous-brown with a narrow grey median stripe; entire crown has fine, narrow dark streaks. Broad supercilium mid-grey, merging behind ear-coverts into greyish nape and neck-sides. Lores and ear-coverts grey, tinged buff, bordered above by a narrow dark brown eye-stripe (behind eye) and below by a narrow blackish moustachial stripe. Broad submoustachial stripe buff, often quite bright. Narrow malar stripe blackish. Eye-ring pale buff, quite prominent. Upperparts greyish olive-brown streaked blackish, most heavily on mantle. Lesser coverts grey-brown. Rest of wings blackish with buff-brown feather edges, broadest and brighter rufous-brown on greater coverts and tertials. Greater and median coverts narrowly tipped buff or buffy-white but only forming, at best, very indistinct wing-bars. Tail dark brown with buff- or dull rufous-brown feather edges, broadest on central rectrices. Throat whitish, breast and flanks pale buff contrasting both with the throat and with

whitish belly and undertail-coverts. Throat, breast and flanks have narrow but distinct black streaks; the under-tail-coverts are also usually indistinctly streaked with dark brown. Iris dark reddish-brown. Bill dark grey with a paler bluish-grey or dull horn lower mandible. Legs flesh.
Juvenile Resembles adult but is buffier overall. Median crown-stripe, supercilium, neck-sides and nape all buff or strongly washed buff so buff submoustachial is not as prominent. Bill paler horn on lower mandible. Inside of mouth grey or greyish-white.

MOULT AND AGEING The post-juvenile moult is partial and the post-breeding moult is complete; both occur in July-August on the breeding grounds, prior to migration. Some, perhaps most birds have a limited pre-breeding moult in February-April, involving some of the head feathers. First-years resemble adults in plumage once the post-juvenile moult is completed, and tail shape seems not to be very helpful for ageing as all birds have quite pointed rectrices. Skull ossification complete in first-years from 15 November.

MEASUREMENTS Wing (chord): male (n100) 57-69; female (n100) 53-65. Tail: male (n17) 57.4-66.6; female (n14) 54.6-62.2. Bill: male (n17) 10.4-11.9; female (n14) 9.6-11.7. Tarsus: male (n17) 19.8-21.8; female (n14) 18.8-20.6 (*alticola* averages the largest, and *gracilis* the smallest, in wing and tail, but there is much overlap).
Wing formula: P9 = P5 (to within 2mm either way).

GEOGRAPHICAL VARIATION Three races which are very similar and not distinguishable in the field.
   M. l. lincolnii (Breeds from Alaska across Canada, except in the Pacific coast districts, and south in the lowlands of the USA, west of the Rockies, to California and Nevada. Winters from the southern USA south to Guatemala, rarely to Panama) Described above.
   M. l. gracilis (Breeds on the south coast of Alaska and coastal British Columbia, including the Queen Charlottes and Vancouver Island. Winters from SW British Columbia south to C California and sometimes south to Arizona, Baja California and NW Mexico) Averages slightly smaller than *lincolnii* with heavier streaking, above and below, but the differences are slight.
   M. l. alticola (Breeds in the W USA in the Rockies and the Cascade and Sierra Nevada ranges. Winters throughout Mexico, except Yucatán, south to Guatemala and El Salvador) Very similar to *lincolnii* and may not be distinguishable from it, but averages slightly larger and is often slightly darker on the upperparts.

VOICE The song, given from an open perch, is a melodic, hurried and bubbling trill, somewhat reminiscent of the songs of both House Wren *Troglodytes aedon* and Purple Finch *Carpodacus purpureus*. Calls include a flat *tschup* or *chip*, repeated rapidly when agitated, and a buzzy *zeee*, sharper than the similar call of Swamp Sparrow.

HABITS Nest is hidden on the ground, generally in the middle of a dense clump of grass in the middle of a bog; a cup of coarse grass lined with finer grasses and rootlets. Eggs 4-5, laid in May-July; whitish or greenish-white, blotched and speckled with browns. Incubation period is 13 days and the young fledge after 9-12 days. Usually nests in loose colonies. Male sings from an open perch but otherwise birds are shy and sometimes elusive, foraging on the ground close to cover, or low in bushes, and flying into bushes when disturbed. Despite this they will often respond well to 'pishing' and when agitated, particularly near the nest, raise their crown feathers in a short crest and call continuously, with each call accompanied by a flick of the wings and tail. Feeds mainly on seeds but also insects, particularly in the breeding season, often scratching in leaf-litter with both feet together. Will visit the ground under feeders for seed. Pumps its tail in flight like other *Melospiza* sparrows, but as the tail is shorter this is not so obvious. Generally found singly or in pairs in winter, sometimes with other species, and sometimes in larger flocks on migration.

STATUS AND HABITAT Fairly common. Breeds in brushy bogs, moist mountain meadows with patches of alder and willow or stunted conifers and riparian thickets, up to 3500m. On migration and in winter favours brush piles, hedgerows, roadsides, woodland edges and various other brushy areas and open weedy areas that are close to scrub or brush.

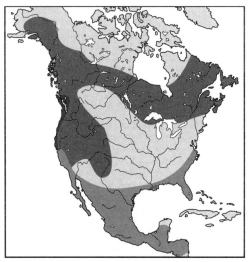

DISTRIBUTION AND MOVEMENTS Breeds in northern and western North America from Alaska east across Canada and through the northern Great Lakes region to Newfoundland and northern New England, and south in the west to southern California and northern New Mexico. Short- to long-distance migrant, wintering from the southern USA through Mexico (except Yucatán) south to to Honduras (casually to central Panama). See also under Geographical Variation. Arrives on breeding grounds from May and leaves for the winter grounds mainly during September. Casual in the Yucatán peninsula and in the West Indies (Bahamas and Greater Antilles) in winter and on migration.

REFERENCES Armani (1985), Bent (1968), Bond (1985), Dunn & Blom (1983), Ehrlich *et al.* (1988), Godfrey (1986), Peterson & Chalif (1973), Pyle *et al.* (1987), Ridgway (1901), Rimmer (1986), Stiles & Skutch (1989), Terres (1980).

52   SWAMP SPARROW
Melospiza georgiana   Plate 20

Described as *Fringilla georgiana* Latham 1790.
Synonym: *Zonotrichia georgiana*.

This common marshland sparrow is widely distributed across North America east of the Rockies, except for the largely cultivated USA prairie belt.

IDENTIFICATION 15cm. Smaller and slightly shorter-tailed than Song Sparrow (50) but otherwise fairly similar in shape, although adult plumage differs considerably. Noticeable rufous wing patch is distinctive in all plumages, although there is a small amount of overlap with eastern races of Song Sparrow in this feature. Breeding adults have a dark rufous crown, grey sides of head with narrow dark eye-stripe and moustachial stripe, and whitish throat and submoustachial stripe, separated by a narrow dark malar stripe. Upperparts are dull rufous-brown, heavily streaked black, with a rufous-brown tail and a large chestnut patch in the wing. Underparts are mostly greyish with buff flanks and whitish belly, and narrow indistinct streaks on breast and flanks. Females often average slightly duller with less contrasting rufous crowns. Non-breeding birds are generally duller and the crown is often brown, streaked black and with the rufous much reduced. First-winters generally have sides of head (especially ear-coverts) more brownish-buff and lack rufous in crown. American Tree Sparrow (71) is vaguely similar to adult Swamp in its head pattern but is paler above and has white wing-bars, a prominent black central breast spot and a more obviously bicoloured bill; note also the slimmer shape and notched tail of Tree Sparrow. Juveniles are similar to juvenile Song and Lincoln's (51) Sparrows. See Measurements and under Song Sparrow for differences from that species and note especially the bill shape on difficult individuals. Differs from juvenile Lincoln's by generally darker upperparts, crown with heavier black streaking, throat unstreaked, inside of mouth yellow or yellowish-white and edges to greater coverts, tertials and secondaries usually noticeably more rufous; see also under Measurements.

DESCRIPTION
Sexes slightly different but some individuals may not be sexable; juvenile clearly different from subsequent plumages. This species also shows seasonal variation.
Adult male breeding Forehead blackish with a pale grey median stripe which often extends back as a narrow indistinct pale median crown-stripe. Rest of crown quite bright rufous, often with some fine black streaking, and with narrow black edges on the lateral crown. Broad supercilium grey, lores and ear-coverts slightly buffier-grey. Eye-ring pale greyish-white. Eye-stripe (from behind eye) and narrow moustachial stripe (reaching to base of bill) blackish-brown, framing the ear-coverts. Submoustachial stripe whitish, narrow malar stripe blackish. Nape and neck-sides greyish, finely streaked darker. Mantle and scapulars dull rufous-brown, heavily streaked black and also finely streaked with pale straw/buff. Rump and uppertail-coverts more olive-brown, uppertail-coverts with broad, well-defined black central streaks. Lesser coverts chestnut. Greater and median coverts blackish with broad chestnut feather edges; greater coverts also have narrow buff tips. Alula and primary coverts blackish-brown, alula with narrow white edge. Flight feathers blackish with nar-

row grey edges to primaries, narrow rufous edges to outer secondaries and broader rufous edges to inner secondaries. Tertials blackish with rufous edges, becoming buffy-white round the tip. Tail rufous-brown with pale buff feather edges. Throat whitish. Breast grey with a few fine dark streaks, occasionally merging to form an obscure central spot. Belly pale greyish-white, flanks and undertail-coverts buff, flanks with obscure darker streaks. Iris dark reddish-brown. Bill dusky-grey with mid-flesh lower mandible. Legs flesh.

Adult female breeding Very similar to male and not always distinguishable, but tends to have less extensive rufous crown which is often more heavily streaked with blackish. Differences are most noticeable in mated pairs.

Adult non-breeding Similar to breeding but head rather duller. Crown noticeably less rufous and more heavily streaked black, often with a narrow pale grey median stripe. Ear-coverts also tend to be buffier. Sexes generally indistinguishable.

First-year In non-breeding similar to non-breeding adult but noticeably less grey and rufous on head. Crown has very little or no rufous and the narrow median stripe may be buffier. Supercilium and nape are brownish- or buffy-grey, not pure grey. In breeding usually identical to adults, although birds showing a distinctly streaked crown and an obvious greyish median crown-stripe are probably first-summer birds.

Juvenile Much buffier overall with black streaking on crown, nape, neck-sides, breast and flanks as well as mantle and scapulars. Streaking on crown usually quite heavy but can be be noticeably finer than that on upperparts. Bill flesh at first, rapidly becoming as adult's. Inside of mouth yellow to yellowish-white.

MOULT AND AGEING The post-juvenile moult is partial/incomplete and occurs from July-October; it may occasionally include the rectrices. The post-breeding moult is complete, also occurring in July-October. These moults usually occur on the breeding grounds, prior to migration in migratory populations. The pre-breeding moult is limited, involving the head feathers, and occurs in February-April. First-winters can usually be told by plumage and some first-summers may also be identified with caution by plumage (see under Description). First-years tend to have slightly more pointed tail feathers than adults but beware of first-years that have moulted the rectrices. Skull ossification complete in first-years from 15 November; some retain small unossified 'windows' through the winter.

MEASUREMENTS Wing (chord): male (n100) 56-65; female (n100) 52-63. Tail: male (n18) 53-65; female (n8) 52.3-61.2. Bill: male (n18) 10.2-11.9; female (n18) 9.8-11.9. Tarsus: male (n18) 21.3-22.3; female (n8) 20.3-22.1. Wing formula: P9 < P5 by 3-8mm. Bill depth: (n10) 5.8-6.5.

GEOGRAPHICAL VARIATION Two similar races.

M. g. georgiana (Breeds in the south-eastern part of the range, from the E Dakotas and Missouri east to Nova Scotia and Maryland, and also south in the Appalachians to western N Carolina. It winters in the southern part of the breeding range and south throughout the SE USA) Described above.

M. g. ericrypta (Breeds throughout the rest of the range: North-west Territories and extreme CE British Columbia east to NC Quebec and Newfoundland. It winters in the S USA from SE Arizona east to W Tex-

as, occasionally to Georgia and N Florida and in N Mexico, south to C Durango and Tamaulipas , occasionally to Jalisco and San Luis Potosí) Has brighter, paler upperparts than *georgiana* but the two are difficult to separate in the field.

VOICE The song, generally given from the top of a small bush or reed stem, is a slow musical trill on one pitch, similar to Chipping Sparrow (72) but more musical, slower and louder. Calls include a metallic *chip* or *chink*; also a long-drawn-out *zeee*, softer and less buzzy than the similar call of Lincoln's Sparrow.

HABITS Nests in loose colonies. Nest is placed low down in a tussock of marsh vegetation or a small bush; a cup of coarse grass and reeds, lined with finer grasses. 3-6 (usually 4-5) eggs are laid in May-July; they are pale bluish or greenish, speckled with browns. Incubation period is 12-15 days and the young fledge after 11-13 days. Double-brooded. Feeds on seeds, plus insects and other aquatic invertebrates, foraging on the ground, in reedbeds in low vegetation and in shallow water. Eats more insects than the other *Melospiza* sparrows and its more slender bill is probably an adaptation to this. Outside the breeding season, generally found in pairs or small groups, often with other sparrows. Shy and nervous, except when singing, generally flying to cover when disturbed. In flight, pumps its tail like other *Melospiza* sparrows.

STATUS AND HABITAT Fairly common over most of its range. Breeds in marshes and wetlands, including the margins of ponds, lakes and streams, with tall dense vegetation such as reeds, cattails and alder, willow or other low waterside scrub; will also breed in brackish coastal marshes. Favours marshes and wetlands on migration and in winter but also occurs in drier habitats such as weedy fields and woodland edges and clearings.

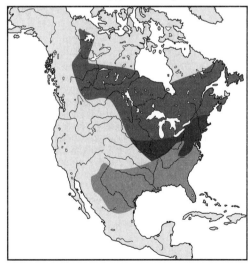

DISTRIBUTION AND MOVEMENTS Breeds across much of northern and central North America, from the Atlantic coast west in Canada to extreme eastern British Columbia and western North-west Territories, but in the USA only as far west as the eastern Dakotas, avoiding the cultivated prairie belt. Resident to long-distance migrant, wintering in the southern part of the breeding range and south through the southern USA (west to Arizona) and in northern Mexico. See also under Geographical Variation. Migrants arrive on breeding grounds from March or April and leave for the winter grounds mainly during September. Casual west of the Rockies, mainly in autumn. Vagrant to the West Indies - twice in November and once April.

REFERENCES Armani (1985), Bent (1968), Bond (1985), Dunn & Blom (1983), Ehrlich *et al.* (1988), Godfrey (1986), Peterson & Chalif (1973), Pyle *et al.* (1987), Ridgway (1901), Riggins & Riggins (1974), Rimmer (1986), Terres (1980).

ZONOTRICHIA

Five species of largish, relatively long-tailed sparrows with striking head patterns. Four species breed in northern North America and also winter almost exclusively in that continent, while the fifth (Rufous-collared) occurs widely throughout Central and South America, generally in mountain areas. They often form large flocks in winter.

53 RUFOUS-COLLARED SPARROW
Zonotrichia capensis Plate 22

Described as *Fringilla capensis* Müller 1776.
Synonyms: *Brachyspiza antillarum, Brachyspiza capensis, Fringilla matutina, Fringilla australis, Fringilla chilensis, Pyrgita peruviensis.*

The only tropical member of this primarily North American genus, it is a widespread species found from Mexico to Tierra del Fuego, but is largely restricted to mountains north of the Amazon Basin. It is also known as Andean Sparrow.

IDENTIFICATION 13.5-15cm. Similar in size and shape to the other *Zonotrichia* but differs in its distinctly crested appearance (recalling Rustic Bunting, but crest much more noticeable). Adult easily identified by broad rufous nuchal collar and black patches on sides of breast, forming a complete band in some races; over much of the range, the black and greyish-white striped head is also distinctive, but southern birds lack the black stripes and the head appears greyish. Birds of the Venezuelan tepuis are darker and dingier with darker heads. In all races upperparts are brown to rufous-brown, streaked darker, with two white wing-bars, and underparts are whitish. Juveniles are duller with a less distinct head pattern and streaked underparts.

DESCRIPTION
Sexes alike; juvenile clearly different from subsequent plumages.
Adult/first-year Crown black with narrow grey median stripe; feathers often raised in a short crest. Lores and supraloral blackish-grey. Eye-stripe black. Most of ear-coverts black with large grey patch in centre. Nape rufous, forming a prominent nuchal collar. Upperparts warm olive-brown, heavily streaked blackish on mantle, back and scapulars. Lesser coverts brownish, fringed grey. Rest of wings blackish-brown with broad rufous-brown edges to greater coverts and tertials, and narrower buff-brown edges to other feathers. Greater and median coverts tipped white forming two wing-bars. Bend of wing whitish. Tail blackish-brown with narrow buff-brown feather edges. Throat white, extending slightly round rear edge of ear-coverts and joining with rufous nuchal collar. Upper breast black, forming a prominent band which is narrower in centre but usually complete. Rufous patches on breast-sides, immediately below the black breast-band, join with rufous

collar. Rest of underparts whitish, washed buff on flanks. Iris dark reddish-brown. Bill blackish-grey. Legs flesh.
Juvenile Head and upperparts warm brown (upperparts buffier and less olive than adult's) with blackish-brown streaks; ear-coverts blackish with large buffy patch in centre, and rest of adult's head pattern may be faintly indicated. Crest is shorter. Nape is warm buff, streaked darker, but the rufous nuchal collar is lacking. Wing-bars buffy. Underparts buffy-white with blackish streaking on throat, breast and flanks.

MOULT AND AGEING Adults have a complete moult, probably following the breeding season, but the extent of the post-juvenile moult is not known. No ageing criteria are known once the post-juvenile moult is completed.

MEASUREMENTS Wing (chord): male (n19) 59.7-72.3; female (n11) 61-67.3. Tail: male (n19) 49.5-66; female (n11) 53.8-61. Bill: male (n19) 11.4-12.7; female (n11) 10.7-12.2. Tarsus: male (n19) 20.8-23.4; female (n11) 20.8-22.9.

GEOGRAPHICAL VARIATION Twenty-five races, which show quite marked variation, with the head becoming progressively greyer and less stripier in the southern Andes and southern S America, and darker and dingier on the Venezuelan tepuis.
> *Z. c. antillarum* (Occurs on the Cordillera Central of Dominican Republic) Similar to *septentrionalis* but the black breast-band is broader and more complete, the rufous collar is smaller and the bend of the wing is usually tinged with yellow.
> *Z. c. septentrionalis* (Occurs in highlands from Chiapas in S Mexico south-east to Honduras and El Salvador) Similar to *costaricensis* but the upperparts average less heavily streaked and the rufous collar is less sharply defined.
> *Z. c. costaricensis* (Occurs in highlands in Costa Rica and W Panama, the Santa Marta mountains of N Colombia, and the Andes from Lara in N Venezuela west and south to S Ecuador) Described above.
> *Z. c. orestera* (Occurs on Cerro Campana in W Panama and probably intergrades with *costaricensis* in Veraguas) Similar to *costaricensis* but averages darker and less buffy above with blacker streaking, darker grey on the head and paler on the underparts; the rufous collar is also slightly brighter.
> *Z. c. insularis* (Occurs on the islands of Curaçao and Aruba in the Netherlands Antilles) The palest race; closest to *venezuelae* but paler overall, including the

rufous collar, slightly greyer above and with less black on the breast-sides; it also has a less distinct head pattern than *costaricensis*, with the lateral crown-stripes less pure black.

Z. c. venezuelae (Occurs in the coastal mountains of N Venezuela from Yaracuy to Sucre; also at Quiribana de Caicara in NW Bolívar) Similar to *costaricensis* but has paler underparts; also similar to nominate *capensis* but has paler underparts and more black on breast-sides.

Z. c. inaccessibilis (Known only from the headwaters of Río Yatúa, Amazonas, Venezuela) Similar to *macconnelli* but has a darker and more extensive rufous collar, is darker and purer grey on the breast and flanks and has darker rufous wing feather edges. It differs from *roraimae* in the same way and also has slightly broader black head stripes.

Z. c. roraimae (Occurs on the tepuis and Gran Sabana of Venezuela, and adjacent Guyana and Brazil; also on the Sierra de la Macarena, Meta, Colombia) Similar to *macconnelli* but slightly smaller and paler overall, with slightly less black on the crown; darker and more heavily streaked above than *capensis* and *venezuelae*.

Z. c. macconnelli (Known only from the summit of Cerro Roraima, Bolívar, Venezuela) The darkest of the tepui races, with the crown appearing mostly black (the grey median stripe is very narrow and indistinct).

Z. c. capensis (Known only from the lower Oyapock River in French Guiana) Similar to *venezuelae* but has less black on the breast-sides and crown, and the underparts are slightly greyer. Very similar to *subtorquata* but the bend of the wing is white.

Z. c. tocantinsi (Occurs in Amazonia, Brazil, along the Rio Tocantins and probably along the lower Amazon west to Monte Alegre) Similar to *capensis* but has even less black on the breast-sides, browner (less grey) flanks and a slightly brighter rufous collar. Also similar to *roraimae* but slightly greyer above.

Z. c. matutina (Occurs in N Brazil from Mato Grosso east to Maranhão and Bahia; also in adjacent E Bolivia in W Santa Cruz) Similar to *capensis* but paler above and below, and with more grey and less black in the crown. This and the following three races have very little black on the breast-sides.

Z. c. subtorquata (Occurs in E and C Brazil from Espírito Santo and S Mato Grosso south, E Paraguay, extreme E Argentina in Misiones, and Uruguay) Similar to *capensis* but the bend of the wing is noticeably yellow, the underparts are whiter and the flanks are browner. Averages darker overall than *hypoleuca*, which also has white bend of wing.

Z. c. mellea (Known only from C Paraguay on the west side of the Río Paraguay, and in Formosa, NC Argentina) Very similar to *hypoleuca* and may not be distinguishable from it.

Z. c. hypoleuca (Occurs in E and S Bolivia from E Cochabamba and Tarija east to C Santa Cruz, and in the llanos of N Argentina south to Buenos Aires) Paler overall than *subtorquata* and has white, not yellow, bend of wing. Also similar to *matutina*, but slightly smaller and less rufous above, and to *pulacayensis*, but has a paler, more tawny-rufous collar.

Z. c. illescaensis (Occurs only on Cerro Illescas, Piura, N Peru) Recently described and similar to *huancabambae* and *peruviensis*.

Z. c. huancabambae (Occurs in the submontane zone

of the Andes in N Peru from Piura south to Junín) Similar to *peruviensis* but smaller (wing < 70mm) and darker above. Also similar to *costaricensis* but slightly paler on the underparts and with a slightly larger bill.

Z. c. peruviensis (Occurs in W Peru from the coast east to 4000m on the western slope of the Andes) Similar to *huancabambae* but larger (wing > 70mm) and more heavily streaked above, with whiter underparts. Also similar to *carabayae* but greyer and less rufous above.

Z. c. carabayae (Occurs on the eastern slope of the E Andes from Junín in C Peru south to La Paz and W Cochabamba in Bolivia) This and the following two races are quite bright rufous on the upperparts, with the rufous collar thus being less contrasting; *carabayae* is slightly duller rufous above than *pulacayensis* and more heavily streaked, with more black on the lateral crown; the underparts are also greyer, less buffy.

Z. c. antofagastae (Occurs in N Chile in Antofagasta and Tarapacá, from sea level to 2500m) Slightly smaller, brighter rufous and less heavily streaked blackish above than *pulacayensis*, and has a stronger buff wash to the flanks and undertail-coverts.

Z. c. pulacayensis (Occurs around Lago Poopó in Oruro, Bolivia) Intermediate between *peruviensis* and *antofagastae* in brightness.

Z. c. chilensis (Occurs at all elevations throughout most of Chile except the extreme north and in adjacent Argentina in W Mendoza aand W Neuquén; intergrades with *australis* in N Aysén in Chile) This race, *choraules* and *samborni* all have grey-looking heads, due to the very narrow black lateral crown-stripes. It averages darker and more rufous above than *choraules* with slightly more black on the lateral crown and breast-sides.

Z. c. sanborni (Occurs in the high Andes in Coquimbo and Aconcagua, NC Chile, and San Juan in adjacent Argentina) Similar to *chilensis* but slightly larger, with paler upperparts and a creamy wash to the underparts.

Z. c. choraules (Occurs in the lowlands and foothills of W Argentina in Mendosa, E Neuquén and Río Negro) Similar to *chilensis* but paler overall, especially on the head, and with narrower blackish lateral crown-stripes.

Z. c. australis (Breeds in S Chile and S Argentina and winters mainly in N Argentina and Bolivia) The head is fairly uniform grey, with the black on the lateral crown-stripes and ear-coverts more or less lacking.

VOICE The song is rather variable over its large range but quite distinctive; a series (usually 3-5) of clear whistles, followed by a cheerful trill or an accelerating stutter. In some areas, especially in Central America, the trill or stutter is lacking and the song consists of 3-6 drawn-out whistled notes. It is give from a prominent perch, often from the top of a building. Calls include a sharp *chip*, a whistled *ho-wheet* and, in alarm, a high-pitched *tsit*, regularly repeated.

HABITS Nest is placed in a niche in a wall or bank, hidden on the ground or low down (rarely to 5m) in a dense shrub or small tree; a compact or bulky cup of grasses and rootlets, lined with finer grasses and hair. 2-3 eggs are normally laid in the highlands, but the clutch size is generally 3-4 (occasionally 5) in southern and eastern lowlands; the eggs are pale greenish-blue and densely spotted and blotched with brown. It breeds throughout the year over much of its range but only during the austral summer in the extreme south. There are local peaks of breeding activity in mid-January and mid-June in the W Andes of Colombia and from February-April and June-August in parts of Costa Rica. In Colombia at least, this coincides with the onset of drier weather. Males sing, often year-round. Feeds mainly on grass and weed seeds, fallen grain and some insects. Forages on the ground, from which sometimes makes short flycatching sallies after low-flying insects. Breeding pairs remain on territories throughout the year; young birds and non-breeders wander locally in flocks.

STATUS AND HABITAT Generally common to abundant throughout its range, but less common and more local in the lowland savannas of the northern Amazon Basin. Found in gardens, parks, brushy areas, agricultural fields, forest edges and grassland; often occurs in villages, towns and cities in the highlands. Found in lowlands (down to sea level) in southern South America, the eastern Amazon Basin and locally in the Guianas but elsewhere largely restricted to mountains, mainly between 1500 and 3500m but locally somewhat lower.

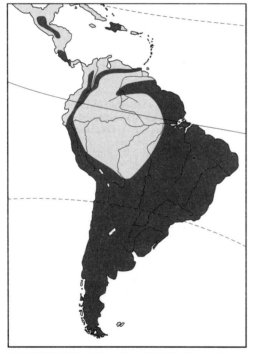

DISTRIBUTION AND MOVEMENTS Occurs in the mountains of Central America, from Chiapas (Mexico) south to Panama, in all the mountain ranges of South America except the northern ranges in Colombia and Venezuela and throughout eastern and southern South America; also in Hispaniola in the West Indies. Mainly sedentary but birds breeding in extreme southern South America migrate north for the austral winter. See also under Geographical Variation.

REFERENCES Armani (1985), Chapman (1940), Hilty & Brown (1986), Meyer de Schauensee & Phelps (1978), Paynter & Storer (1970), Ridgely & Tudor (1989), Ridgway (1901), Stiles & Skutch (1989).

54 HARRIS'S SPARROW
Zonotrichia querula Plate 22

Described as *Fringilla querala* Nuttall 1840.

This handsome and distinctively marked bird is less well known than the other North American *Zonotrichia* species, as it breeds only in the Canadian Arctic and migrates mainly through the central part of the continent to winter in the southern midwestern states. It is noted, however, for its habit of wandering in winter, with individuals turning up throughout eastern and western North America and often adding a bit of spice to backyard feeders.

IDENTIFICATION 19cm. A large sparrow, the largest of the genus. The pink bill and black on the crown, throat and upper breast are distinctive in all plumages. Breeding adult has black crown, front of face, throat and upper breast, contrasting with grey sides of head and neck (which have a noticeable black mark in the centre, on the rear edge of the ear-coverts). Upperparts are brown, heavily streaked black, and with two white wing-bars. Lower underparts are white with black mottling on flanks. Non-breeding adults have buffy, rather than grey, sides to the head, with the black central mark reduced or absent; some have nearly as much black as in breeding, but most have extensive white scalloping on the crown and many also have a variable white patch on the throat. First-winters have less black on the crown on average and normally a white chin and throat, with a black malar stripe and a broad, smudgy black breast-band. Juvenile has a brownish crown, streaked black, and fine dark streaks on the underparts with a blackish mark on the breast.

HYBRIDISATION Hybridisation has been reported with White-crowned Sparrow (55) (J. L. Dunn pers. comm.)

DESCRIPTION
Sexes alike; juveniles clearly different from subsequent plumages.
Adult breeding Crown, lores, throat and upper breast black, with ragged lower edge extending to a point in centre. Nape grey-brown to grey. Rest of head pale grey with black mark immediately behind rear edge of ear-coverts. Upperparts brown, heavily streaked black on the mantle and scapulars. Lesser coverts grey-brown. Median coverts black with broad white tips. Greater coverts blackish with pale grey-buff edges and white tips. The white tips to greater and median coverts form two prominent white wing-bars. Alula blackish with white outer edge. Primary coverts blackish with narrow grey feather edges. Flight feathers blackish with narrow greyish-white edges to primaries and narrow greyish-buff edges to secondaries. Tertials blackish with broad rufous-buff edges. Bend of wing white. Tail blackish grey-brown with paler feather edges and outer two rectrices broadly edged white on inner web. Lower underparts white with black blotchy streaks extending from breast along flanks; undertail-coverts washed buffy. Iris dark reddish-brown. Bill rosy pink. Legs brownish-flesh.
Adult non-breeding Duller on the head with sides of head greyish-buff. Amount of black variable: bright individuals have crown mostly black with narrow buff or whitish feather fringes giving a mottled effect, and retain solid black throat and upper breast; duller ones have broader fringes to crown feathers and a variable white patch on the lower throat, surrounded by black. Most winter adults have black

or blackish lores. Body plumage is much as breeding but underparts are washed buff, especially on the flanks, and the black mottling on the flanks is slightly less bold.

First-year In non-breeding (first-winter) crown is grey-buff, scalloped black; a few have an adult-type crown pattern. Lores are brownish. Throat is entirely white, bordered on the sides by a narrow black malar stripe and on the lower border by a wide but blotchy blackish band across the upper breast. Otherwise much as winter adult. In breeding (first-summer) generally indistinguishable from adults, although some average more brownish-black on the crown and face.

Juvenile Head and upperparts greyish-buff; upperparts (including rump) streaked with dusky blackish, crown more heavily streaked with black. Wing-bars buffier than adult's. Underparts whitish with buffy wash to breast-sides; breast and flanks streaked with dusky brown, throat un-streaked but bordered on either side by a narrow black malar streak (as in first-winter).

SEXING Sexes alike in plumage but many can be sexed in the hand by wing chord (see under Measurements).

MOULT AND AGEING The post-juvenile moult is partial and the post-breeding moult is complete; both occur in July-September on the breeding grounds, prior to migration. All birds have a partial/incomplete pre-breeding moult in March-May, which usually includes the two central rectrices. Most first-winters can be told by the all-white throat, brownish-buff lores and brownish-buff crown, streaked black, but a few may overlap with dull winter adults and are not safely aged by plumage. Note that birds showing a black throat with a white patch on the lower throat, fairly broad buff or whitish fringing to the crown feathers and blackish-brown lores are adults, but individuals intermediate between this and typical first-winter are best left unaged. Tail shape does not seem to be very helpful for ageing. Skull ossification complete in first-years from 15 November.

MEASUREMENTS Wing (chord): male (n55) 84-92; female (n50) 77-85. Tail: male (n30) 79.1-88; female (n13) 76.5-83. Bill: male (n30) 11.3-13.4; female (n13) 11-13. Tarsus: male (n30) 22.5-25; female (n13) 23-25.

GEOGRAPHICAL VARIATION Monotypic.

VOICE The song, given from an open perch, is a series of one or more clear, high wavering whistles, followed by another series on either a higher or a lower pitch. Calls include a strong, metallic *chink* or *weenk* and a musical twittering, often interspersed with harsh notes.

HABITS Nest is placed on the ground, well hidden underneath a thick bush or a small conifer, or in a mossy depression in a thick grass clump; a cup of twigs, grasses, mosses and lichens, lined with fine grasses. 3-5 eggs are laid in June-July; they are greenish or greyish variably marked with reddish-brown. Incubation period is 13.5 days; fledging period has not been recorded. Males often group together to sing at dusk. Feeds on the ground, scratching vigorously in the leaves and soil for seeds, flower buds, blossoms, insects and spiders, and small fruits and berries; regularly visits feeders. Usually found in flocks of up to several dozen in winter, but individuals regularly wander and turn up in flocks of other sparrows, often at feeders.

STATUS AND HABITAT Common, although widely scat-

tered in winter. Breeds in stunted coniferous forest and scrub, especially spruce woods, often by mossy bogs near the northern limit of tree growth in the forest-tundra ecotone. Migrates mainly through the prairies to winter in open woodlands, woodland edges and clearings, hedgerows, dense riparian thickets and brush piles. Regularly occurs at feeders in suburban and rural gardens in winter, frequently outside its normal wintering range.

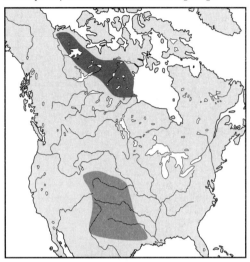

DISTRIBUTION AND MOVEMENTS Breeds in central northern Canada from western North-west Territories south-east to the western shores of Hudson Bay in south-eastern North-west Territories, north-eastern Manitoba and extreme north-western Ontario. Medium-distance migrant, wintering in the midwestern USA from eastern Wyoming and western Iowa south to northern Texas and Louisiana. Spring migration starts in late February, with birds arriving on breeding grounds in May, late May in the far north of the range. Autumn migration begins in September, with birds arriving on winter grounds from late October but mostly during November. Casual in winter more or less throughout the USA and southern Canada.

REFERENCES Armani (1985), Bent (1968), Dunn & Blom (1983), Farrand (1983), Godfrey (1986), Norment & Shackleton (1993), Oberholser (1974), Payne (1979), Pyle *et al.* (1987), Ridgway (1901), Rowher *et al.* (1981), Terres (1980), Woolfenden (1955).

55 WHITE-CROWNED SPARROW
Zonotrichia leucophrys   Plate 21

Described as *Emberiza leucophrys* Forster 1772.
Synonym: *Fringilla gambelii*.

Closely related to White-throated Sparrow (56), this species breeds across most of northern and western North America, wintering widely in the southern part of the continent. In Canada, its breeding range is more northerly than that of White-throated.

IDENTIFICATION 18cm. Slightly larger than White-throated Sparrow and also more slender-looking with a more erect posture, giving the impression of a longer neck. Black and white striped head and pink or pinkish-yellow bill make adults distinctive. Sides of head and underparts are a rather uniform pale grey, with throat, belly and undertail-coverts paler. Upperparts are grey, streaked with black and dark chestnut on the mantle and scapulars. First-winters are similar in bill colour and general pattern but the head is striped dark brown and greyish-buff/tan, the ear-coverts are brownish, and the ground colour of the upperparts is more buff with less grey and chestnut. The races *leucophrys* and *oriantha* have a black supraloral joining the two black head stripes; on the other races these are white or greyish, separating the two black head stripes and creating a subtly different facial pattern. Juvenile is quite greyish-looking and heavily streaked on the head and underparts as well as the upperparts; the adult's head pattern is vaguely indicated. It is similar to juvenile White-throated but is greyer, with the distinctive pale bill.

HYBRIDISATION There are single records of hybridisation with Song Sparrow (50) and Harris's Sparrow (54), and also at least two records of hybridisation with Golden-crowned Sparrow (57).

DESCRIPTION
Sexes alike; juvenile clearly different from subsequent plumages and first-winter birds also distinct.
Adult Forehead and broad lateral crown-stripe black, joined to narrower black eye-stripe by black supraloral. Median crown-stripe and supercilium (over and behind eye) white. All head stripes reach to rear of crown, not extending onto nape. Nape and sides of head pearly grey. Upper mantle grey, obscurely mottled dark brown. Lower mantle, back and scapulars boldly streaked dark chestnut and greyish-white, lower back and rump olive-grey, unstreaked; uppertail-coverts more olive-brown with paler feather fringes in fresh plumage. Lesser coverts grey-brown. Median coverts blackish narrowly edged rufous; greater coverts blackish, broadly edged rufous. Both are narrowly tipped white forming two thin but noticeable wing-bars. Tertials blackish, broadly edged rufous and with narrow white fringing. Rest of wing blackish with narrow buff feather edging. Tail dark brown with narrow buff feather edges. Underparts pearly grey but throat is usually paler greyish-white; belly is also slightly paler and flanks and undertail-coverts are washed buff. Iris dark brown. Bill pink, often with a small dusky tip. Legs dark flesh.

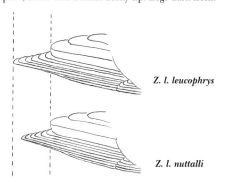

Z. l. leucophrys

Z. l. nuttalli

White-crowned Sparrow primary projection. *Gambelii* and *oriantha* are similar to *leucophrys*, and *pugetensis* is similar to *nuttalli*.

First-year In non-breeding (first-winter) head pattern as adult but black stripes replaced by dark brown and the white ones by greyish-buff. Ear-coverts are greyish-buff, contrasting slightly with greyer throat and neck-sides, and upperparts are duller: buff streaked dark brown on mantle and scapulars. In breeding (first-summer) as adult, although a few may retain the occasional buff or brown feather in the head.
Juvenile Appears darker and streakier than first-year; breast and flanks are heavily but diffusely streaked blackish, the crown also has fine dark streaks, there are narrow blackish moustachial and malar stripes, and the heavy streaks on the upperparts are black rather than brown.

MOULT AND AGEING The post-juvenile moult is partial and the post-breeding moult is complete; both occur in July-October on the breeding grounds prior to migration. All birds have a limited/incomplete pre-breeding moult, occurring in February-April; it is least extensive in *nuttalli* (usually restricted to the feathers on the front of the head) and most extensive in the races *gambelii* and *pugetensis* (usually including the tertials and central rectrices). The central rectrices are also often replaced in *leucophrys* and *oriantha*, and occasionally in *nuttalli*. First-winters of all races easily identified by plumage but only first-summer *nuttalli* can normally be told from adults by some retained first-winter head feathers. Tail shape does not seem to be useful for ageing but is unnecessary in autumn/winter. Skull ossification complete in first-years from 15 October in *nuttalli*, 15 November in other races.

MEASUREMENTS Wing (chord): male (n400) 67-84; female (n400) 63-80 (*nuttalli* and *pugetensis* average smaller than the other races - wing 63-75 - sexes combined). Tail: male (n37) 68-82; female (n29) 67-76.5. Bill: male (n37) 9.9-12.2; female (n29) 9.9-11.9. Tarsus: male (n37) 21.3-24.4; female (n29) 21.3-24.4. Maximum wing (*leucophrys*): male (n9) 77-86; female (n7) 72-80.

GEOGRAPHICAL VARIATION Five races, at least three of which can usually be distinguished in the field.
Z. l. leucophrys (Breeds in N Canada from NE Manitoba, where it intergrades with *gambelii*, east to Newfoundland, and winters in SE USA, also casually in the Greater Antilles) Described above. It builds the smallest nest of any of the races.
Z. l. oriantha (Breeds in W North America, mostly in the E Rockies, from S Alberta and extreme SW Saskatchewan south to S California and N Arizona and New Mexico; winters in the SW USA (rarely) and in Mexico south to Michoacán and San Luis Potosí, including Baja California) It is not always distinguishable from *leucophrys*, although females especially average marginally smaller, the upperparts average marginally paler and the bill may average slightly darker pink. It builds the largest nest of any of the races, averaging noticeably larger than that of *leucophrys*.
Z. l. gambelii (Breeds in NW North America from N Alaska south-east to CS British Columbia, where it intergrades with *oriantha*, and N Manitoba; winter range is similar to *oriantha* but apparently only as far south as Nayarit in W Mexico and it is more regular in the USA) Similar to *leucophrys* but has white (adult) or pale buff-brown (first-winter) lores and supraloral and a slightly thinner black (adult) or dark brown (first-winter) eye-stripe, giving a rather different facial jizz. It also has a paler, more orange-pink bill.
Z. l. pugetensis (Breeds in the coastal districts of W

North America from SW British Columbia south to N California; winters in the breeding range and south to SW California) Similar to *gambelii* in its head pattern but the bill is paler, duller and yellower, the breast is distinctly browner (especially in adults), the upperparts are browner and duller, lacking the grey and chestnut colouring of the preceding three races, and the bend of the wing is yellow (white, sometimes washed yellow in *gambelii*). The underwing-coverts are also washed yellowish (silvery-grey in *gambelii*) and the white head stripes are often tinged pale grey, giving a less 'clean' impression. This and the following race have a shorter primary projection than the preceding three races.

Z. l. nuttalli (Resident in coastal C California from Mendocino County south to Santa Barbara County) Very similar to *pugetensis* and the two are generally not distinguishable. First-winter birds often do not moult all the head feathers in late winter and first-summer *nuttalli* are often distinguishable by having a mixture of adult and first-year head feathers (mostly new adult ones on the front of the head and retained first-year ones on the rear). Care should be taken not to confuse this with first-years of other western races in early spring which may be in active head moult.

VOICE The song, given from a conspicuous perch at the top of a bush, is variable but typically a short series of thin whistled notes followed by a variable number of buzzy or twittering notes. Calls are similar to White-throated Sparrow, and include a *tsit*, and a sharp *pink* and a thin, high *seet*.

HABITS Nest is placed on or near the ground, generally hidden under a thick bush or shrub; a bulky cup of bark strips, grasses and twigs lined with fine grasses, rootlets and hair. 3-5 eggs are laid in April-August; they are greyish-white or greenish-blue marked with reddish-brown. Incubation period is 11-16 (usually 12-14) days and the young fledge after 7-12 (usually 10) days. Feeds on the ground, in undergrowth or in the open, searching for seeds and berries, often by scratching, towhee-style, in leaf litter; also takes insects, especially in summer. Active for longer periods in the north of its breeding range, where there is continuous daylight, than further south. Visits feeders in winter. Pairs and small groups occur in larger mixed flocks of White-throated or Golden-crowned Sparrows (57) and Dark-eyed Juncos (59) outside the breeding season, although large flocks often occur on migration, especially when grounded by adverse weather. Raises crown feathers when agitated, giving head a peaked appearance.

STATUS AND HABITAT Common, often abundant on migration. Breeds in subarctic and temperate areas in dense brush and scrub, especially near open grassy areas and often by lakesides or rivers, tundra where there is at least a thin bush cover, brushy areas on mountain slopes and in coastal areas, forest edges, wet meadows and chaparral; often around towns in the north. On migration and in winter found in open woodland and woodlots, grassland by woodland edges, parks and gardens, although it is generally not so much of a garden bird as White-throated Sparrow.

DISTRIBUTION AND MOVEMENTS Breeds across northern North America from the Pribilofs and western Alaska east across the tundra and northern boreal zones

(south to James Bay) to Newfoundland; and in western North America south to southern California and northern Arizona and New Mexico, and east to western and southern Alberta, Montana, Wyoming and Colorado. Winters mainly in the USA and in Mexico south to Michoacán and San Luis Potosí. In eastern North America in winter it occurs north to the southern Great Lakes area but is largely absent from Florida, the northern Appalachians and the southern Atlantic coastal plain. In the west there is a large overlap with the breeding range, with birds occurring west of the Rockies north to south-western British Columbia. See also under Geographical Variation. Spring migration begins in mid-April (slightly earlier in *pugetensis*) and is quite rapid, with birds reaching breeding grounds from mid-May in the north, slightly earlier on the west coast. Autumn migration begins in late August and is heaviest from late September to mid-October, with birds arriving on winter grounds from mid-September in the west, mid-October in the east. Casual in winter in Florida and the West Indies. Vagrant to Japan (4+ records in October-March, at least one of which involved the race *gambelii*) and to Iceland (1), Britain (2 - both in May 1977), France (1 - August 1965), The Netherlands (1 - December 1981 to February 1982) and Germany (1 - uncertain provenance), Greenland and Panama.

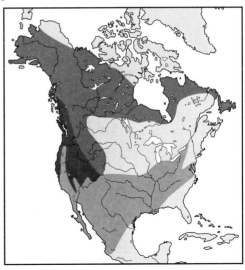

REFERENCES Alström *et al.* (1991), Armani (1985), Banks (1964), Bent (1968), Brazil (1991), Cramp & Perrins (1994), Dunn & Blom (1983), Dunn *et al.* (1995), Ehrlich *et al.* (1988), Fugle & Rothstein (1985), Godfrey (1986), Gray (1958), Kern (1984), King (1986), Mewaldt (1973 & 1977), Mewaldt & King (1978), Mewaldt *et al.* (1968), Morton & Welton (1973), Morton *et al.* (1969), Oberholser (1974), Paynter & Storer (1970), Peterson & Chalif (1973), Pyle *et al.* (1987), Ridgway (1901), Terres (1980).

56 WHITE-THROATED SPARROW
Zonotrichia albicollis   **Plate 21**

Described as *Fringilla albicollis* Gmelin 1789.

An abundant and familiar bird over eastern North America, where its distinctive whistling song is a characteristic sound of northern woodland and brush in the summer, and is also heard from migrants in early spring as they move north.

IDENTIFICATION 17cm. A chunky, relatively long-tailed sparrow; white throat (usually sharply defined) and yellow supraloral spot in a striped head are characteristic of all except juvenile plumage. Upperparts warm brown, streaked blackish, and with rufous edges to the coverts and tertials; underparts pale greyish, often obscurely streaked darker. Occurs in two distinct morphs, known as white-striped and tan-striped, with some birds intermediate between the two. White-striped birds have a boldly black and white patterned head with black lateral crown-stripe and eye-stripe and white median crown-stripe and supercilium, contrasting strongly with bright yellow supraloral. On tan-striped birds the dark stripes are browner and the pale ones are tan to pale greyish-buff; the yellow supraloral is also darker and duller. Juvenile lacks yellow lores, has a less distinct head pattern and is distinctly streaked on underparts; told from juvenile White-crowned Sparrow (55) by dark bill, more sharply defined whitish throat, brighter rufous edges to the coverts and tertials and warmer brown tone to upperparts generally. Juvenile Golden-crowned (57) lacks any noticeable head pattern and is duller brown above, lacking rufous tones. Juvenile Song (50) has a less contrasting head pattern, a much broader dark malar streak and is a different shape with, in particular, a noticeably rounded tail. Bright tan-phase birds with streaking on the underparts are rather similar to the Asian Yellow-browed Bunting (24) in winter plumage, especially regarding the pattern of the supercilium; the latter species is always distinguished by the dark framing to the ear-coverts (especially broad on the rear edge) and the characteristic white or whitish spot in the centre of the dark rear edge. It also has a different tertial pattern, with the rufous edge cutting in half-way down the feather, a broader and more distinct dark malar streak and a less obvious pale median crown-stripe.

HYBRIDISATION Occasionally hybridises with Dark-eyed Junco (59). Typically, hybrids resemble the junco in shape and general plumage pattern but have faintly streaked upperparts and a faint indication of the sparrow's head pattern. There is also one record of hybridisation with Golden-crowned Sparrow.

DESCRIPTION
Sexes very similar; juvenile clearly different from subsequent plumages.
Adult white-striped Median crown-stripe white and fairly narrow, lateral crown-stripe broader and black. Supraloral bright yellow, continuing behind eye as long and broad white supercilium. Eye-stripe black. All head stripes reach to back of nape. Sides of head and neck pale grey, setting off pure white throat and submoustachial area (sometimes separated by a very narrow dark malar stripe), which are generally bordered by thin black moustachial stripes and lower edge. Upperparts warm tan-brown, becoming grey-brown on rump, and heavily streaked with black on mantle

and scapulars. Lesser coverts grey-brown. Median and greater coverts blackish with tan-brown edges (more rufous on inner greater coverts); both are tipped white forming two narrow but noticeable wing-bars. Rest of wing blackish, most feathers narrowly edged pale buff but tertials broadly edged with rufous and with white at the tip. Bend of wing pale yellow. Tail blackish-brown with paler, grey-brown feather edges. Breast pale grey, concolorous with sides of head and neck and completely enclosing white throat. Rest of underparts also pale grey, becoming whiter on belly and undertail-coverts, often washed buff on flanks and sometimes with some obscure darker mottling/streaking on breast and flanks. May be slightly duller in non-breeding, mainly due to narrow grey-buff fringes to white head feathers and brownish fringes to black head feathers, but most are still distinct from tan-striped. Iris reddish-brown. Bill greyish-black with a horn base to the lower mandible. Legs flesh.
Adult tan-striped Body much as white-striped but underparts are more buffy-grey and some, probably females, have indistinct darker mottling/streaking on the breast and flanks. Head pattern is similar to white-striped but much duller; lateral crown- and eye-stripes are blackish-brown, median crown-stripe is pale buffy-grey and the supercilium is pale tan/grey-buff with a less distinct, darker and duller yellow supraloral. The ear-coverts and neck-sides are a more brownish-grey and there is usually a more obvious dark malar streak separating the (less pure) white throat and submoustachial stripe. Bare parts as white-striped.
First-year After the post-juvenile moult is completed, resembles adult but the iris is grey-brown, gradually becoming reddish-brown through the first spring. Many (especially tan-striped birds) have more extensive diffuse dark mottling/streaking on the breast and flanks and are slightly duller on the head with a smaller and duller yellow supraloral (sometimes quite indistinct) but, because of individual variation and polymorphic nature, these are not safe ageing characters. It is interesting to note that all birds in first-winter plumage are apparently tan-striped, with the black and white head feathers of white-striped birds appearing during the first pre-breeding moult.
Juvenile Resembles dull tan-striped adults but streakier overall. Head pattern is indistinct, ear-coverts have prominent dark edges, neck-sides are streaked blackish, and the underparts are distinctly buffy (whiter on belly and undertail-coverts) with prominent and well-defined blackish streaking on the breast and flanks (more distinct than the extensive but indistinct greyish-brown streaking of some first-years).

SEXING Females have slightly less yellow on the lores on average, more pronounced streaking/mottling on the breast, and the head pattern may average slightly duller, but there is much overlap and these are not safe sexing characters, especially considering the polymorphic nature of the species. Many birds can be sexed in the hand by wing chord: > 74 = male; < 67 = female.

MOULT AND AGEING The post-juvenile moult is partial and the post-breeding moult is complete; both occur in July-September on the breeding grounds, prior to migration. The pre-breeding moult is limited, involving mainly head and throat feathers, occurring in March-May. In autumn the iris of first-years is distinctly grey-brown, compared with the reddish-brown iris of adults. Young birds' irides gradually become reddish over the winter and first spring but many first-spring birds can still be told (at least in the hand) by a greyish outer circle to the iris (do not confuse this with the nictitating membrane). Tail feather shape is not very useful for ageing, but those of first-years average more pointed (there is much overlap however). There is a small amount of age/sex-related plumage variation but, because of the amount of individual and morphic variation, these should only be used as supporting characters to the above and the wing chord. Birds should not be sexed in the field except, perhaps, some mated pairs. Generally, exceptionally bright-looking white-striped birds with large, very bright, yellow supraloral will be adult males, and very dull-looking tan-striped birds with extensive streaking on the underparts and an indistinct buffy supraloral, not contrasting with the rest of the supercilium, are likely to be first-year females (compare with wing in both cases). Skull ossification complete in first-years from 15 December, but some may show small unossified 'windows' through their first spring.

MEASUREMENTS Wing (chord): male (n100) 68-79; female (n100) 63-73. Tail: male (n17) 68-77; female (n7) 68-73.7. Bill: male (n17) 10-12.2; female (n7) 11.2-11.7. Tarsus: male (n17) 23-24.1; female (n7) 22.3-23.9. Maximum wing: male (n10) 70-76; female (n10) 63-72.

GEOGRAPHICAL VARIATION Monotypic, but note that this species is polymorphic, with both morphs (and intermediates) occurring throughout the range.

VOICE Song, given from an open perch in a tree or bush, is a cheerful and very distinctive series of clear whistles; typically two short whistles followed by one or more longer triple whistles on a lower pitch, usually transcribed as 'pure sweet Canada, Canada'. Calls include a soft, lisping *tsssp* or *tseet* and a harder *chink*.

HABITS Nest is placed on or near the ground, often in a small depression and hidden in dense undergrowth, occasionally very low in a bush or conifer sapling; a cup of grasses, roots, twigs, bark strips, pine needles and moss, lined with finer grasses and hair. 4-6 (usually 3-5) eggs are laid in May-August; they are pale blue or greenish-white, heavily spotted with brown. Incubation period is 12-14 days and the young fledge after 7-12 days, often a few days before they can fly properly. Usually single-brooded. White-striped and tan-striped birds nest together on the breeding grounds with no segregation. Negative assortative mating usually occurs, i.e. most tan-striped males pair with white-striped females and vice versa. Males sing very late into the evening. Forages mainly on the ground, in or close to thick undergrowth, often scratching towhee-style for seeds. Frequently visits feeders in winter and on migration. Feeds on seeds, plus berries and insects, often ascending to bushes for the berries. Found in large flocks outside the breeding season, often with other sparrows, especially White-crowned and Dark-eyed Junco (59).

STATUS AND HABITAT Very common, often abundant on migration. Breeds in open coniferous and mixed woodland, birch and alder scrub and brushy clearings and edges. Winters in woodlots, scrub, and gardens and backyards, often in cities. Prefers wooded and brushy areas on migration.

DISTRIBUTION AND MOVEMENTS Breeds across southern and central Canada, and through the Great Lakes region, from south-eastern Yukon and north-central British Columbia east to Newfoundland and New England; also south in the Appalachians to W Virginia. Short- to medium-distance migrant wintering in the eastern and southern USA (also extreme southern Ontario) west to Arizona and south to northern Mexico. A small population winters in coastal California. Breeding and wintering ranges are generally separate but birds occur in New England year-round. Birds arrive on breeding grounds from April and leave for winter grounds mostly during September, moving south on a broad front. Vagrant to Iceland (5), British Isles (19), Netherlands (4), Finland (2), Denmark (1), Sweden (1) and Gibraltar (1). One of the most frequent sparrows to occur in Europe and, like the others, most records are in spring/early summer, although there are also several autumn/early winter records.

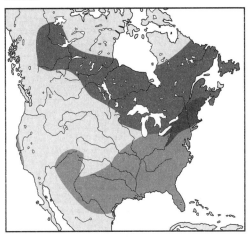

REFERENCES Alström *et al.* (1991), Armani (1985), Atkinson & Ralph (1980), Bent (1968), Cramp & Perrins (1994), Dunn & Blom (1983), Godfrey (1986), Knapton & Falls (1983), Kopachena & Falls (1993), Lowther (1961), Pyle *et al.* (1987), Ridgway (1901), Terres (1980), Vardy (1971), Watt (1986), Watts *et al.* (1984), Yunick (1977).

57 GOLDEN-CROWNED SPARROW
Zonotrichia atricapilla Plate 21

Described as *Emberiza atricapilla* Gmelin 1789.
Synonym: *Emberiza coronata*.

A western species which largely replaces White-throated Sparrow (56) on the coast and western mountains of North America. Unlike other North American *Zonotrichia* sparrows it is more of a mountain bird in summer, although it descends to southern coastal lowlands for the winter.

IDENTIFICATION 18cm. Breeding adults are easily identified by broad black lateral crown-stripes, reaching to nape, and enclosing a conspicuous yellow crown patch. Body plumage is similar to White-crowned Sparrow (55) but is slightly browner above and below. In winter the black on the head is replaced to a varying degree by dark brown, and the yellow crown patch is usually duller and more obscure, although some adults remain almost as bright as in breeding. First-winters typically have an obscure head pattern with brownish crown, streaked darker, and an obscure brownish-yellow crown patch, but many individuals are brighter and overlap with winter adults. Juveniles are very similar to juvenile White-crowned but are slightly buffier and less grey overall, and have a darker bill with a blackish upper mandible and dusky-straw lower one. Dull first-winters are easily told from first-winter White-crowned by the darker bill (often appearing slightly bicoloured and with a blackish upper mandible), trace of adult's head pattern, in particular lacking White-crowned's dark eye-stripe and noticeable pale supercilium, and browner underparts; but note that western White-crowned Sparrows are browner underneath than eastern ones. Hybrids occasionally occur between these two, however, and first-winters of these can be confused with very dull Golden-crowned Sparrows; one such bird resembled a dull Golden-crowned with only a trace of buffy-yellow on the forehead but had the pale bill of a White-crowned and 'messy' lateral crown-stripes giving a head pattern intermediate between the first-winter plumage of the two species.

HYBRIDISATION There are two or more records of hybridisation with White-crowned Sparrow and also one record of hybridisation with White-throated Sparrow.

DESCRIPTION
Sexes alike; juvenile clearly different from subsequent plumages.

Adult breeding Forehead and broad stripes on sides of head, reaching to nape, black. Crown patch pale yellow, nape grey. Ear-coverts and neck-sides uniform pale grey, sometimes with a faint brownish wash. Upperparts greyish-brown with a distinct olive tinge; mantle and scapulars heavily streaked with blackish-brown. Lesser coverts olive-brown. Median coverts dark brown, greater coverts dark brown edged rufous; both are tipped white forming two narrow but noticeable wing-bars. Tertials blackish, broadly edged with rufous and narrowly fringed whitish at the tips; rest of wing feathers blackish narrowly edged pale buff (alula edged white). Tail grey-brown with narrow buff feather edges. Throat and malar region pale grey, breast and flanks greyish-brown (warmer brown on flanks), belly and undertail-coverts whitish. Iris reddish-brown. Bill dusky-horn with a flesh lower mandible, usually appearing bicoloured. Legs greyish-flesh.

Adult non-breeding Variable but duller on the head, often considerably so. Bright individuals retain a breeding-type head pattern but are slightly duller with the black lateral crown-stripe faintly mottled with brown. Dullest individuals have an obscure yellowish crown patch and dark brown lateral crown-stripes which become paler and inconspicuous (pale brown streaked blackish) behind the eye, buffy-grey throat and sides of head, and paler, buffier underparts.

First-year In non-breeding (first-winter) bright individuals overlap with dull adults and are indistinguishable from them on plumage. Typical first-winters have brown crown, streaked darker (showing no obvious lateral crown-stripe but dark brown on supraloral) and a dull yellowish-brown crown patch, which may also be streaked darker. Note that birds showing a crown pattern intermediate between typical first-year and typical adult cannot be aged by plumage. Generally indistinguishable from adults in breeding (first-summer) but some may have some brownish mottling in the rear of the lateral crown-stripe.

Juvenile Similar to dullest first-winters but head pattern very obscure with crown pale buffy-yellow, streaked darker, lateral crown brown, streaked darker, ground colour of upperparts paler and buffier, and more uniform pale buff underparts with a narrow blackish malar stripe and fine but distinct blackish streaking on the breast and flanks.

MOULT AND AGEING The post-juvenile moult is partial, occurring on the breeding grounds in July-November; there is what appears to be a supplemental moult of some or most of the upperpart contour feathers on the winter grounds in October-November. The post-breeding moult is complete, also occurring in July-November; it is often suspended and completed on the winter grounds. The pre-breeding moult is limited/partial, occurring in March-May. First-years can often be aged by plumage in non-breeding plumage, but only very rarely in breeding (see under Description). Tail shape does not seem to be useful for ageing. Skull ossification complete in first-years from 15 November.

MEASUREMENTS Wing (chord): male (n30) 75-85; female (n30) 72-81. Tail: male (n17) 73.4-83.1; female (n7) 68.8-82.6. Bill: male (n17) 11.2-13.2; female (n7) 11.4-12.7. Tarsus: male (n17) 23.1-27.5; female (n7) 23.4-24.9.

GEOGRAPHICAL VARIATION Monotypic.

VOICE The song, given from an open perch in a tree or bush, is a short and melancholy series of 3-4 clear whistled notes, descending in pitch and usually in a minor key. Calls include a sharp, insistent *chink*, rather louder than other *Zonotrichia*, and a thin *seet*.

HABITS Nest is hidden on the ground or very low down in a young conifer or dense bush; a cup of twigs and moss lined with fine vegetable matter and hair. 3-5 eggs are laid in May-June; they are pale greenish-white marked with brown. Incubation and fledging periods have not been recorded. Feeds on seeds, plus some berries, fruits and insects in summer and autumn, hopping and scratching in dead leaves to search for seeds and only occasionally ascending to low bushes. Outside the breeding season usually occurs in flocks with other species, mainly White-crowned Sparrows; Golden-crowns tend to be more shy than White-crowns and flush to cover more easily.

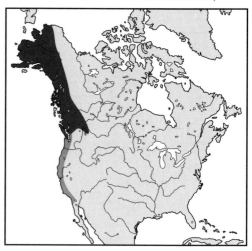

STATUS AND HABITAT Fairly common. Breeds in mountain and tundra areas, in alpine meadows with bushes and small trees, thickets and scrubby areas on hillsides, by streams, lakes and bogs; often above the treeline in the mountains and beyond it in the tundra, as long as there is sufficient scrub and small bushes. It also occurs on the edges of mountain coniferous forest. Winters in dry woodlands, brush and thickets, often in fairly arid areas.

DISTRIBUTION AND MOVEMENTS Breeds in north-western North America, from the Rockies west, from the southern half of Alaska south to southern British Columbia and extreme north-western Washington. Short- to medium-distance migrant, wintering in coastal districts, mostly west of the Cascade and Sierra Nevada mountain ranges, from extreme south-western British Columbia

(where there is a small overlap with the breeding range) south to northern Baja California. Spring migration starts in April, with birds arriving on breeding grounds in May. Autumn migration begins in late July/August, with birds arriving on winter grounds from September. Casual in winter in southern Baja, Sonora and northern Sinaloa. Vagrant to eastern North America, and to Japan (4, December-April).

REFERENCES Armani (1985), Bent (1968), Brazil (1991), Dunn & Blom (1983), Farrand (1983, Godfrey (1986), Gray (1958), Peterson & Chalif (1973)), Pyle *et al.* (1987), Ridgway (1901), Stewart (1972), Terres (1980).

JUNCO

Three species generally recognised at present, although Dark-eyed Junco occurs in several forms which were formerly considered separate species; one of these (Guadalupe Junco) is now generally thought to deserve specific status once again. Juncos are fairly small, slim sparrows with twittering flight calls; the northern species have conspicuous white outer tail feathers, which the southern Volcano Junco lacks.

58   VOLCANO JUNCO
Junco vulcani   Plate 24

Described as *Zonotrichia vulcani* Boucard 1878.

The southernmost of the three juncos, this species is restricted to the high volcanic mountains of southern Costa Rica and western Panama.

IDENTIFICATION 16cm. Pinkish bill and legs, yellow iris set off by black lores, pale grey underparts and dull brownish-olive top of head and upperparts, streaked darker, especially on mantle, render this a distinctive species. It lacks the characteristic white outer tail feathers of the other juncos and appears rather chunkier. It is the only junco in its range. Young birds have dark iris initially but are easily distinguished from young Slaty Finch *Haplospiza rustica*, the only other remotely similar species in these mountains, by pinkish, less slender bill, paler legs and conspicuously streaked upperparts.

DESCRIPTION
Sexes very similar; juvenile clearly different from subsequent plumages.
Adult Crown, nape and upper mantle dull grey with a faint olive tinge and faintly streaked darker. Rest of upperparts dull olive-brown with bold black streaks on mantle, scapulars and back. Lores and ocular area black. Sides of head and neck grey, unstreaked (ear-coverts with faint olive-brown tinge). Wings blackish-brown; remiges narrowly edged grey-brown, greater and median coverts and tertials coverts broadly edged tawny-brown. Tail blackish-brown with greyish-brown feather edges and pale grey tips to the outer feathers. Underparts pale grey, slightly paler on throat and tinged olive-buff, especially on rear-flanks and undertail-coverts. Iris bright yellow to orange-yellow. Bill pinkish-flesh, culmen sometimes tinged dusky. Legs flesh.
First-year Plumage as adult but iris is dark at first, becoming yellow through first-year. No details of the timing of this are known, but it is probably similar to Yellow-eyed Junco (60).

Juvenile Crown and upperparts brighter brown than adult's and with heavier black streaking on crown and nape. Covert and tertial edges are rufous, noticeably brighter than those of adult. Underparts pale grey-buff, paler on belly and streaked brown on throat, breast and flanks. Iris dark brown.

SEXING Females may average very slightly duller than males but this is only noticeable with mated pairs.

MOULT AND AGEING Few details known but adults have a complete post-breeding moult and juveniles have at least an incomplete (possibly a complete) post-juvenile moult, involving all the body feathers and tertials, probably the rectrices and perhaps the other remiges as well. First-years resemble adults in plumage after the post-juvenile moult but the iris changes to the adult colour gradually, so first-years can be told by darker iris probably for several months. No other ageing criteria are known.

MEASUREMENTS Measurements are provided of 3 specimens only (1male, 1 female, 1 unsexed); these are given together below. Wing (chord): 74.7-80.3. Tail: 69.1-73.2. Bill: 13.2-13.7. Tarsus: 25.9-27.7.

GEOGRAPHICAL VARIATION Monotypic.

VOICE The song is a series of short, choppy phrases of squeaky, burbling or buzzy notes. Calls are varied and include a thin, high *tsee*, a scolding, scratchy *whew* or *jeew*, a fast, rhythmical *cher-we, cher-we* and, when agitated, a repeated *tchup*.

HABITS Nest is placed on the ground, under a log, rock or bush, or in a niche in a mossy bank; a well made cup of grass stems, lined with hair and thistle floss, sometimes decorated on outside with moss. 2 (occasionally 3) eggs are laid in March-July; they are pale blue with a few brown or lilac dots near the large end. Usually found in pairs, occasionally alone or in family groups. Forages in the open on the ground, hopping and running; often by roadsides where they occur in its range. Feeds on various seeds and also fallen berries, insects and spiders. Flight is laboured and rather weak and fluttering; rarely flies far.

STATUS AND HABITAT Locally fairly common in high-altitude overgrown pastures, scrubby or bushy areas of páramo, bamboo thickets, roadsides and stunted second growth, generally at or above the treeline. Mostly above 3000m but down to 2600m on Cerro de la Muerte in south-central Costa Rica where forest clearing has provided habitat at lower elevation. There is also an isolated population at 2100m in Sabana Dúrika, an extensive upland bog in southern Costa Rica.

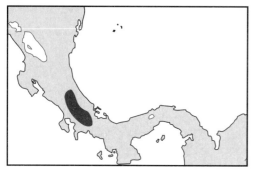

DISTRIBUTION AND MOVEMENTS Occurs in Costa Rica and western Panama. Sedentary, with little or no altitudinal movement.

REFERENCES Armani 1985, Stiles & Skutch (1989).

59   DARK-EYED JUNCO
Junco hyemalis   Plate 23

Described as *Fringilla hyemalis* Linnaeus 1758.
Synonyms: *Fringilla oregana, Struthus caniceps.*

A common and widespread species with many races, several of which were formerly considered separate species. One of these, Guadalupe Junco (59X), has recently been given specific status again by several authors, due to differences in morphology and vocalisations.

IDENTIFICATION 16cm. Very variable but all birds have conspicuous white outer tail feathers, fairly uniform grey, brown or blackish head and breast, and a distinctive twittering flight call. Most also have a pale pinkish bill and a white belly, sharply demarcated from the dark breast. Northern and eastern birds (Slate-coloured) have slate-grey (adult males) or brownish-grey (females) head, breast and upperparts contrasting with white belly. Most western birds (Oregon) have blackish hood contrasting with rufous mantle and flanks and white belly; those of the central Rockies (Oregon Pink-sided) have paler grey hoods with blackish lores, duller and paler greyish-rufous mantle not contrasting greatly with hood, and pale pinkish-cinnamon flanks. In the southern Rockies (Grey-headed), the head, rump, and underparts are all fairly uniform pale grey with a contrasting bright rufous mantle; in the extreme south, in Arizona and much of New Mexico, the bill is blackish with a pale blue-grey lower mandible, and the throat is greyish-white, slightly paler than the head. Finally, birds in the Black Hills area (White-winged) resemble Slate-coloured but are much paler grey and have two narrow but noticeable wing-bars. In all forms,

especially Slate-coloured and Oregon, females are noticeably duller than males and first-winter females are generally duller still. Generally unmistakable; Grey-headed forms (especially southern birds with a bicoloured bill) may be confused with Yellow-eyed Junco (60) but the iris is always dark. Juveniles are fairly uniformly brownish and streaked throughout; Grey-headed juvenile has a rufous mantle and is very similar to juvenile Yellow-eyed (see under Yellow-eyed Junco).

HYBRIDISATION There are a few records of hybridisation with White-throated Sparrow (56).

DESCRIPTION
Sexes differ slightly; juvenile clearly different from subsequent plumages.
Adult male (Slate-coloured) Head, upperparts, throat, breast and flanks uniform slate grey, occasionally with a very faint brown wash on mantle. Wings blackish with slate grey feather edges, broadest on greater coverts and tertials. Tail blackish with rectrices 5 and 6 entirely white, rectrix 4 variably white and rectrix 3 sometimes edged white. Belly and undertail-coverts white, contrasting with slate breast and flanks. Iris reddish-brown to dark ruby-red. Bill pale pink. Legs dark brownish or greyish-flesh. Similar year-round but bill may be tipped slightly darker in non-breeding plumage.
Adult female Pattern as male but hood and upperparts paler grey with a more distinct brown wash, especially on the mantle. Wing edges also browner, especially on the tertials, but no great contrast between the colour of the tertial and greater covert edges. Less white in tail on average. In the hand many can be told from males (especially first-years) by wing chord (see under Measurements).
First-year male Overall coloration as adult female but brownish-edged tertials often contrast with greyer edges to the newly moulted inner greater coverts, especially in fresh autumn plumage. Outer 1-5 greater coverts are often retained from juvenile plumage and show a distinct whitish tip (adult coverts can show an indistinct paler tip). Iris is grey-brown, becoming ruby-red (from the centre outwards) over the winter; many spring birds can be aged in the hand by a narrow grey outer ring to the iris. Rectrices average more pointed than in adults and the tail pattern is similar to adult female.
First-year female In autumn at least averages noticeably duller and browner than adult female, with distinct brown wash often extending over the hood as well as the upperparts. Less white in tail than adult female (rectrices 5 and 6 have broad dark edges). In spring more as adult female but averages duller. Tertial/greater covert contrast, eye colour, retained juvenile greater covert pattern and tail shape as in first-year male.
Juvenile Head and upperparts grey-brown, streaked dark brown (heaviest on mantle). Throat, breast and flanks pale buff, streaked dark brown. Belly and undertail-coverts whitish. Iris dark grey-brown.

MOULT AND AGEING The post-juvenile moult is partial and the post-breeding moult is complete; both occur in July-October, mainly on the breeding grounds prior to migration. The pre-breeding moult is limited to the head feathers and occurs in February-April. Iris colour is reliable as an ageing character at least through the winter but is very difficult, if not impossible to judge accurately in the field (see under Description). Plumage is useful for ageing but there is much overlap between adult fe-

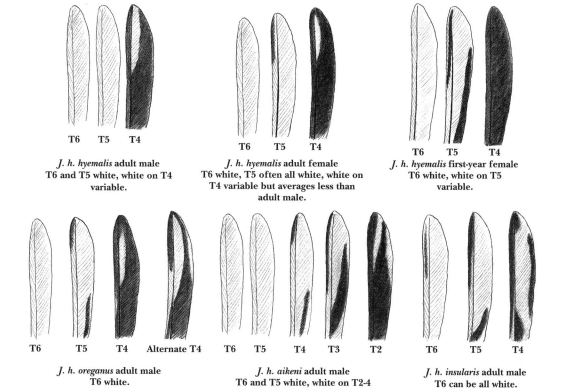

T6 T5 T4

J. h. hyemalis adult male
T6 and T5 white, white on T4
variable.

T6 T5 T4

J. h. hyemalis adult female
T6 white, T5 often all white, white on
T4 variable but averages less than
adult male.

T6 T5 T4

J. h. hyemalis first-year female
T6 white, white on T5
variable.

T6 T5 T4 Alternate T4

J. h. oreganus adult male
T6 white.

T6 T5 T4 T3 T2

J. h. aikeni adult male
T6 and T5 white, white on T2-4
variable (T4 often all white).

T6 T5 T4

J. h. insularis adult male
T6 can be all white.

Dark-eyed Junco tail patterns. Amount of white is variable; typical amounts are shown to illustrate racial variation and sexual differences in the nominate race.

male/ first-year male; for these check for contrast between tertials and greater coverts (see under Description). First-years have more pointed rectrices than adults on average but the difference can be subtle and there is considerable overlap. Skull ossification complete in first-years from 1 November throughout most of the range but from 1 October in some Californian (and probably other southern) populations.

MEASUREMENTS For ease of comparison between the sexes, measurements for all the forms listed above are given separately.

Slate-coloured Junco. Wing (chord): male (n32) 76.7-82.3; female (n23) 70.6-78.2. Tail: male (n32) 63.2-73.1; female (n23) 61.5-70.1. Bill: male (n32) 10.2-12.2; female (n23) 9.9-11.7. Tarsus male (n32) 20.3-22.6; female (n23) 20.3-22.9. Maximum wing (*hyemalis*): male (n11) 74-83; female (n10) 68-74 (*carolinensis* averages slightly larger than *hyemalis* in all measurements but there is much overlap).

Oregon Junco. Wing (chord): male (n41) 69.1-83.3; female (n31) 66.5-78.2. Tail: male (n41) 58.4-72.1; female (n31) 58.7-68.3. Bill: male (n41) 9.9-11.7; female (n31) 9.9-11.4. Tarsus: male (n41) 18.8-21.8; female (n31) 18.5-21.6.

Grey-headed. Junco Wing (chord): male (n36) 78-86.6; female (n31) 74.9-83.8. Tail: male (n16) 68.6-77; female (n11) 63-74.2. Bill: male (n16) 10.7-12.7; female (n11) 10.4-12.2. Tarsus: male (n16) 19.8-22.1; female (n11) 19.3-21.3.

White-winged Junco. Wing (chord): male (n28) 81.5-93;

female (n19) 79-86. Tail: male (n8) 75.2-78.7; female (n5) 71.1-76.2. Bill: male (n8) 11.7-13; female (n5) 11.4-12.5. Tarsus: male (n8) 20.8-21.8; female (n5) 19.8-21.1.

GEOGRAPHICAL VARIATION Fifteen races described. For convenience the races are listed under what were formerly the common names of the different species that were recognised within the complex. Within each group, the races are often very similar and hybridisation is also common between them, which can make racial identification difficult or impossible.

Slate-coloured Junco:

J. h. hyemalis (Breeds from C and N Alaska and WC British Columbia east across N and C Canada to Newfoundland and Nova Scotia and also through the Great Lakes region and New England. It winters from the southern edge of the breeding range in the east, south through E North America, mainly east of the Rockies, to N Mexico. Rare but regular west of the Rockies on migration and in winter) Described above.

J. h. carolinensis (Resident in the Appalachians from West Virginia and W Maryland south to N Georgia, but may move to lower elevations in winter; it intergrades with *hyemalis* in C Pennsylvania) Very similar to *hyemalis* but averages slightly larger and paler, bluer-grey; the bill is slightly darker (pale horn).

J. h. cismontanus (Breeds from SC Yukon south to C interior British Columbia and WC Alberta; winters through W North America) Similar to *hyemalis* and intergrades with it in NC British Columbia, but typical birds are blacker on the hood and slightly browner on the mantle, with females averaging more pinkish-brown on the flanks. In this they tend towards Oregon-type birds and they also intergrade with *oreganus* where their ranges overlap.

Oregon Junco:

J. h. oreganus (Breeds on the Pacific coast from SE Alaska south to C British Columbia; winters in the breeding range and south along the coast to C California and casually inland west of the Rockies) Very different to typical Slate-coloured; male has blackish hood, rufous-brown mantle and scapulars, grey rump, pinkish-cinnamon flanks; females are duller. Note that the hood does not extend onto the flanks as it does in the Slate-coloured races.

J. h. shufeldti (Breeds on the western slopes of the coastal mountain ranges from SW British Columbia south to C Oregon, intergrading with *oreganus* on Vancouver Island and with *thurberi* in C Oregon. It winters in the breeding range and sparsely further south and east) Very similar to *oreganus* but averages duller, with a greyer-brown mantle and paler, blackish-grey hood.

J. h. montanus (Breeds from central interior British Columbia and SW Alberta south to Idaho; winters throughout W North America south to N Chihuahua) Very similar to *shufeldti* but the wings and tail average shorter.

J. h. mearnsi (Oregon Pink-sided Junco) (Breeds from SE Alberta and SW Saskatchewan south to E Idaho and NW Wyoming; winters from just south of the breeding range south to NW Mexico) Similar to *shufeldti* but has a paler grey hood and paler, more pinkish sides.

J. h. thurberi (Breeds from S Oregon south to S California, intergrading with *pinosus* in the San Fransisco area and with *mutabilis* in SW California) Basically sedentary but moves to lower elevations in winter; some also move slightly south and south-east. Very similar to *mearnsi* but has a slightly darker hood on average (it is intermediate between Oregon and Oregon Pink-sided forms).

J. h. pinosus (Resident in the coastal ranges of C California) Very similar to *thurberi* but has a slightly paler grey hood on average, tending towards *mearnsi*.

J. h. pontilis (Resident in the Sierra Juárez of extreme N Baja California) Roughly intermediate between *thurberi* and *townsendi*, but tends to have pale pinkish sides like *townsendi* (paler than *thurberi*).

J. h. townsendi (Resident in the Sierra San Pedro Mártir of N Baja California but some move to lower elevations in winter) Similar to *mearnsi* but the pale pink sides are narrower on average.

J. h. mutabilis (Occurs in the mountains of S Nevada and SE California) Intermediate between the Oregon and Grey-headed groups, resembling *thurberi* (the adjacent race to the north) in having a dark (grey, not blackish) hood, and *caniceps* in its (duller) rufous mantle; it differs from both these races in its pinkish sides. Sexes are similar, but female averages slightly paler and duller.

Grey-headed Junco (this form resembles Yellow-eyed Junco in plumage pattern but the iris is dark):

J. h. caniceps (Breeds from S Idaho and Wyoming south to NE Arizona and N New Mexico, intergrading with *dorsalis* in the southern part of the range. It moves to lower elevations in winter; some also move slightly south and east) Head is mid-grey with blackish lores. Lacks hood, with underparts being only slightly paler than head; mantle is bright chestnut-brown and sharply defined.

J. h. dorsalis (Breeds in New Mexico, extreme W Texas and N Arizona, moving to lower elevations in winter and some also move slightly south) Similar to *caniceps* but the bill is noticeably larger and bicoloured, being blackish with a yellowish-flesh lower mandible. The underparts, including the throat, are also paler.

White-winged Junco:

J. h. aikeni (Breeds in the Black Hills area of W South Dakota and adjacent states; winters in the breeding area and also south to New Mexico) Resembles Slate-coloured but is paler and bluer-grey and normally has narrow but noticeable white wing-bars on the greater and median coverts. It is also noticeably larger than the other races (see under Measurements). Sexes are similar but the female averages slightly paler.

Guadalupe Junco *Junco (hyemelis) insularis* is described separately below.

VOICE The song, given from a prominent perch such as the top of a conifer, is a fast musical trill, occasionally interspersed with warbles, twitters and *chips*. Calls include a distinctive high-pitched twittering and a sharp *dit* or *chip*.

HABITS Nest is placed on or very near the ground and generally hidden beneath vegetation, under tree roots or a fallen tree; occasionally in the roots of an upturned tree, in a crevice in a stump or even on the verandah of a house. It is a cup of rootlets, grass and moss, lined with fine grasses, hair, rootlets, moss stems and, rarely, porcupine quills. 4-5 (occasionally 6) eggs are laid; they are whitish or pale bluish-white, speckled or blotched with reddish-browns and often purplish-greys. Incubation period is 11-12 days and the young fledge after 9-13 days. Northern populations at least are double-brooded. Feeds on the ground, gleaning seeds and insects. Often found in large to very large flocks in winter and especially on migration, frequently with other species. In certain areas in winter two or more forms may occur together in mixed flocks.

STATUS AND HABITAT Generally common to abundant throughout its range. Breeds in coniferous and mixed woodlands, especially clearings, edges and burnt-over areas. In winter and on migration found in a wide variety of habitats including woodland edges, weedy fields, gardens, roadsides and other open weedy areas, but seldom far from the cover of trees or bushes.

DISTRIBUTION AND MOVEMENTS Breeds across the whole of northern and western North America; in the east south to the Great Lakes area and New England and also south in the Appalachians to northern Georgia. Resident to long-distance migrant with northern birds occurring throughout southern Canada, the USA and northern Mexico in winter. Southern races are more or less sedentary but move to lower elevations in winter. There is considerable overlap in breeding and winter ranges with birds occurring in southern Canada and throughout the rest of the breeding range year-round. White-winged form is an altitudinal migrant, moving to lower altitudes in the Black Hills for the winter. See also under Geographical Variation. Generally, birds arrive on breeding grounds from early March in the south, late April in the north, and autumn migration begins in late September, with most birds on winter grounds by November. Vagrant in West Indies (Bahamas and Jamaica) in winter, and also to Iceland (1), British Isles (12), Holland (1), Norway (1), Poland (1) and Gibraltar (1), with most records being in spring; this is unusual for a North American landbird but the pattern is similar to White-throated Sparrow (56). As far as is known, all these vagrant records have involved the Slate-coloured form.

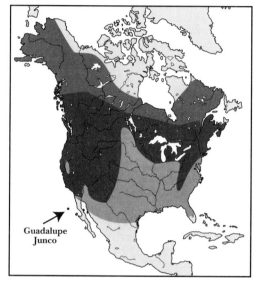

Guadalupe
Junco

REFERENCES Alström *et al.* (1991), Armani (1985), Balph (1975), Bent (1968), Blake (1964), Bond (1985), Brackhill (1977), Cramp & Perrins (1994), Dunn & Blom (1983), Godfrey (1986), Grant & Quay (1970), Paynter & Storer (1970), Ridgway (1901), Sibley and Monroe (1990), Terres (1980), Yunick (1972 & 1977).

59X GUADALUPE JUNCO
Junco (hyemalis) insularis   Plate 23

Described as *Junco insularis* Ridgway 1876.

Endemic to Isla Guadalupe off Baja California, this species has traditionally been considered as a race of the Dark-eyed Junco complex. However, its differences in morphology and vocalisations from that complex indicate that it is a species in its own right, forming a superspecies with Dark-eyed Junco.

IDENTIFICATION 16cm. Similar to Oregon form of Dark-eyed Junco but considerably duller and darker with longer bill and shorter wings and tail; head dark grey with black lores, mantle dull olive-brown, contrasting only slightly with head and with grey rump. Throat and upper breast paler grey than head but still forming a noticeable hood; rest of underparts buffy-white with pinkish-buff sides. Juvenile is streaked above and below, like other juncos, and is brighter brown on the mantle than adults, with warm brown flanks.

DESCRIPTION
Sexes alike; juvenile clearly different from subsequent plumages.
Adult Head dark grey, faintly tinged olive; lores black. Mantle and scapulars dull olive-brown, contrasting slightly with head and with grey rump and uppertail-coverts. Wings blackish with grey edges to coverts, broad pale buff tertial edges and narrow greyish-white edges to flight feathers. Tail blackish with rectrices 5 and 6 mostly white (narrowly edged dark) and rectrix 4 broadly tipped white on outer web. Throat and upper breast mid-grey, a shade paler than the head but still forming a noticeable hood. Rest of underparts buffy-white with pinkish-buff breast-sides and flanks. Iris dark reddish-brown. Bill yellowish-flesh with dusky culmen. Legs flesh.
First-year Probably differs from adults in iris colour, in the same way as Dark-eyed Junco; more study is needed on the usefulness and timing of this.
Juvenile Head and upperparts grey-brown, faintly streaked warmer brown; mantle is warmer brown with bolder streaks. Tertial edges brighter buff, greater coverts tipped whitish, forming an obscure wing-bar. Throat and breast grey-buff, streaked dark brown, breast-sides and flanks warmer buff (with a faint pinkish tinge), belly and undertail-coverts pale creamy-buff.

MOULT AND AGEING The extent of the post-juvenile moult is not known but, otherwise, moult and ageing are similar to Dark-eyed Junco.

MEASUREMENTS Wing (chord): male (n3) 67.8-69.9; female (n2) 63.5-64.5. Tail: male (n3) 58.2-59.2; female (n2) 53. Bill: male (n3) 12.7-13.2; female (n2) 12.7. Tarsus: male (n3) 20.8-21.1; female (n2) 20.6-20.8.

GEOGRAPHICAL VARIATION Monotypic.

VOICE The song is more varied and less trilling than in the other forms within this superspecies; it often includes buzzy notes and ends with a trill, and has been transcribed as *wheep-whit-whit-whit-wheep*. Calls resemble those of the other forms in the superspecies and include a sharp *chip*.

HABITS Nest is placed either on the ground, concealed under a bush, rock or fallen tree, or low down in a tree or bush; a cup of grass and mosses, lined with hair. 3 eggs are laid in March; they are pale greenish-white, speckled finely with reddish-brown. Incubation and fledging periods have nor been recorded. Feeds on seeds and insects, foraging on the ground and in the lower branches of trees, in a similar manner to the other forms.

STATUS AND HABITAT It occurs mainly in pine and cypress groves; the population size is not known but is presumably quite small.

DISTRIBUTION AND MOVEMENTS Endemic to Isla Guadalupe off Baja California, where it is sedentary.

REFERENCES Armani (1985), Bent (1968), Collar *et al.* (1992), Mirsky (1976), Ridgway (1901), Sibley & Monroe (1990).

Described as *Junco phaeonotus* Wagler 1831.
Synonym: *Junco cinereus*.

The southern counterpart of Dark-eyed Junco, replacing it as a breeding bird from extreme south-western USA through Mexico and western Guatemala. The southern Grey-headed form of Dark-eyed Junco approaches this species closely in plumage, but the two do not overlap in range.

IDENTIFICATION 16cm. Similar to Grey-headed form of Dark-eyed Junco but adults readily told by bright yellow eye. The inner covert and tertial edges, as well as the mantle, are rufous (grey in Grey-headed) and the bill is always bicoloured, but note that the race *dorsalis* of Grey-headed also has a bicoloured bill. Southern birds are duller than northern ones. Juvenile is very similar to juvenile Grey-headed (especially *dorsalis* race); the main difference is in the colour and pattern of the tertials and the greater covert colour. In Yellow-eyed the greater coverts are edged bright rufous and tipped white, and the tertials are uniformly edged bright rufous. In Grey-headed the greater coverts are edged pale buff and tipped whitish and the tertials are edged pale buff (with at best a pale rufous tinge), becoming whitish on the tip, resulting in a more contrasting effect.

DESCRIPTION
Sexes slightly different; juvenile clearly different from subsequent plumages.
Adult male Head and upper mantle mid-grey, contrasting with bright rufous mantle, back and scapulars. Lores black. Rump and uppertail-coverts olive-grey. Lesser coverts grey, median coverts rufous. Outer greater coverts greyish, inners rufous. Tertials blackish with broad rufous edges. Rest of wings blackish with narrow pale grey feather edges. Tail dark grey-brown with rectrices 5 and 6 mostly white. Throat, breast and flanks pale grey with a faint olive tinge and a stronger olive-buff tinge to the rear flanks. Lower breast, belly and undertail-coverts pale greyish-white. Plumage similar year-round but in fresh plumage crown and nape feathers have narrow darker grey fringes and the mantle feathers are narrowly fringed olive. Iris bright yellow to orange-yellow. Bill dusky with a pale yellowish lower mandible. Legs yellowish-flesh.

Adult female Sightly duller than adult male; rufous on upperparts duller, crown and nape washed olive, lores greyish-black (contrasting less with grey head) and flanks with a more extensive olive-buff tinge.
First-year male Iris is brown at first, becoming pale grey and then yellowish-grey (September-December) before becoming as adult after December (southern birds may differ in timing of iris colour change).
First-year female Iris as first-year male.
Juvenile Head brownish-grey, mantle and scapulars dull rufous, both streaked blackish. Underparts greyish-white, streaked dark brown on throat, breast and flanks. Iris dark brown. Wings much as adult but lesser coverts brownish.

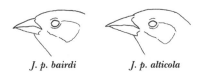

J. p. bairdi   *J. p. alticola*

Yellow-eyed Junco bills to show variation in size.

MOULT AND AGEING The post-juvenile moult is partial/incomplete, occurring in July-September: it usually includes the tertials and all the greater coverts, and sometimes the rectrices as well. The post-breeding moult is complete and also occurs in July-September. The pre-breeding moult is limited to some head feathers and occurs in February-April. The timing given for all the moults refers to the northern races only.

MEASUREMENTS Wing (chord): male (n63) 68.6-87; female (n56) 64.3-82. Tail: male (n33) 61-76.5; female (n24) 58.2-74.2. Bill: male (n33) 10.7-13.7; female (n26) 10.7-13.5. Tarsus: male (n33) 20.6-25.2; female (n26) 20.1-24.1 (*alticola* averages the largest and *bairdi* the smallest in all measurements; *fulvescens* and *alticola* are noticeably larger-billed than other races).

GEOGRAPHICAL VARIATION Five races, generally becoming duller, darker and larger-billed from north to south.

   J. p. palliatus (Occurs in the SW USA in S Arizona and SW New Mexico, and in NW Mexico from Sonora and Coahuila south to Jalisco and San Luis Potosí, intergrading with *phaeonotus* from Nayarit, Durango and Nuevo León south) Brighter than *phaeonotus* with a redder back, redder coverts and tertial edges, paler and purer grey head, whiter belly and more white in

T6   T5   T4

J. p. phaeonotus **adult male**
T6 is often all white

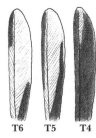

T6   T5   T4

J. p. palliatus **adult male**

T6   T5   T4

J. p. fulvescens **adult male**

Yellow-eyed Junco tail patterns. Amount of white is variable; typical examples are shown. Variation within each race may be age/sex-related.

the tail. Bill (12, sexes combined): 11.2-12.2.

J. p. phaeonotus (Occurs in C and S Mexico, from S Jalisco and Veracruz south to Oaxaca, intergrading with *palliatus* in the north) Bill (16, sexes combined): 10.7-12.5. Described above.

J. p. bairdi (Occurs in the Cape District in S Baja California) Paler overall than *phaeonotus*, with the cinnamon-brown mantle grading into the buffy rump, warmer brown flanks and less black on face (not extending behind eye); juvenile is less heavily streaked on underparts than juveniles of other races. Bill (7, sexes combined): 10.7-11.4.

J. p. fulvescens (Occurs in interior Chiapas, Mexico) Noticeably duller than the northern races with dull brown mantle, contrasting less with browner-grey head, olive-brown rump, brownish flanks, and less white in the tail. The song is also slightly different, being in two motifs and transcribed as *cher-cher-cher-chip-chip-chip*. Bill (10, sexes combined): 11.9-13.2.

J. p. alticola (Occurs in SE Chiapas and W Guatemala) Similar to *fulvescens* but slightly larger and darker (more olive) overall. Bill (14, sexes combined): 12.2-13.7.

VOICE The song, given from an open perch, is a series of clear whistles and trills, often in three distinct parts; much more musical and varied than the song of Dark-eyed Junco. Calls are similar to those of Dark-eyed Junco.

HABITS Nest is hidden on the ground under a low branch, log or fallen trunk; a cup of dried grass and rootlets, lined with fine grass and hair. 3-4 eggs are laid, which are bluish-white or whitish and either unmarked or with some reddish-brown blotches. Forages mainly on the ground but also in bushes and shrubs. Generally keeps close to cover but not shy and easily approached. Feeds mainly on seeds, but also insects and berries. Usually found in pairs or small flocks outside the breeding season, but seldom associates with other species, at least in south-western USA.

STATUS AND HABITAT Generally common in open coniferous and pine-oak forests, scrubby borders and pastures in mountains above 2000m, mainly from 2500-3500m. Sometimes also found in parks and gardens in villages and small towns.

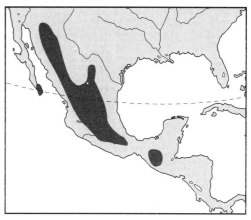

DISTRIBUTION AND MOVEMENTS Occurs in mountains from the south-western USA south through Mexico (including the southern tip of Baja California) to western Guatemala. See also under Geographical Variation. Sedentary, with very little, if any, altitudinal movement.

REFERENCES Armani (1985), Bent (1968), Davies (1972), Farrand (1983), Lamm & Leupke (1981), Peterson & Chalif (1973), Pyle *et al.* (1987), Ridgway (1901), Terres (1980).

PASSERCULUS

One species with four forms (or perhaps allospecies) within it; one of these has recently been split as a separate species (Large-billed Sparrow) by Sibley & Monroe (1993) and two other forms (Ipswich Sparrow and Belding's Sparrow) were also previously regarded as separate species from the widespread Savannah Sparrow, and may yet regain specific status. All the forms are fairly small and short-tailed sparrows, similar to *Ammodramus* (within which the genus was formerly included) but are slimmer, more round-headed and with a proportionally smaller head.

61 SAVANNAH SPARROW
Passerculus sandwichensis Plate 31

Described as *Emberiza sandwichensis* Gmelin 1789.
Synonyms: *Ammodramus sandwichensis, Fringilla savanna, Passerculus princeps, Passerculus rostratus, Ammodramus halophilus, Emberiza rostrata.*

A very widespread and highly variable species. The numerous races fall into four main groups, which were originally described as separate species. One of these groups (Large-billed Sparrow) has recently been given specific status again by Sibley & Monroe (1993), and it seems possible that the other two groups (Ipswich and Belding's) may also regain their specific status.

IDENTIFICATION 14-16cm. Has a short notched tail and is generally streaked above and below; streaking below may form an obscure central breast spot which is less prominent than on Song Sparrow (50). Most races have a yellow or yellowish supraloral which often extends over the eye onto the supercilium. Also tends to show a pale median crown-stripe, which can be quite obscure. Brown ear-coverts have darker edges, especially on the eye-stripe and moustachial stripe, and all races show a narrow dark malar stripe. Eye-ring is pale yellowish or whitish and quite noticeable, although less so than in Vesper Sparrow (77). Strength of yellow on supercilium and overall streaking and colour vary widely according to race. The widespread Savannah group is variable but is generally moderately streaked above and below and usually has a fairly bright yellow (sometimes whitish) supraloral. The race *princeps* (Ipswich Sparrow) of Sable Island and adjacent Nova Scotia is larger and noticeably paler with moderate streaking which is quite pale brown in colour. The races *beldingi* and *alaudinus* (Belding's Sparrow) of southern Californian and north-western Baja Californian saltmarshes are very heavily streaked, above and below, with blackish-brown. The *rostratus* group (Large-billed Sparrow), which is resident in coastal saltmarshes in Baja California and north-western Mexico, is pale and often almost unstreaked above with relatively light pale brown streaking below; it has a noticeably larger bill than other groups in the Savannah superspecies and a buffy-white supercilium. Song Sparrow (50) has a much longer rounded tail. Vesper Sparrow has white outer tail feathers, chestnut lesser coverts and a more prominent white eye-ring. Only other North American sparrows with yellowish or buffy supraloral are Seaside (62) and Grasshopper (67). Seaside Sparrow is very variable but always much more strikingly patterned than Savannah and has a long, deep-based and pointed bill. Adult Grasshopper Sparrow lacks streaking below. Juvenile Grasshopper is streaked below, and lacks the yellow bend of wing and greenish-yellow lesser coverts of the adult, but it is slightly smaller than Savannah and a different (chunkier) shape with a flatter forehead, (generally) a larger bill, and a pointed, rather than notched, tail. It also has a wider, more diffuse eye-ring, and paler lores.

HYBRIDISATION There is one record of hybridisation with Grasshopper Sparrow (67).

DESCRIPTION
Sexes alike; juvenile similar to adult but distinguishable.
Adult/first-year Crown and nape buff-brown, narrowly streaked blackish, and with an obscure pale buffy-white median crown-stripe. Supercilium yellow on supraloral, becoming pale yellowish-white behind eye. Lores buff. Ear-coverts with fine dark streaks and dark brown upper and lower borders (forming dark brown eye-stripe and moustachial stripe). Submoustachial stripe pale buff, narrow malar stripe dark brown. Neck-sides streaked dark brown and pale buff. Upperparts grey-buff, streaked blackish-brown; streaking is heaviest on the mantle and there are also some obscure and narrow pale rufous streaks on the upperparts. Lesser coverts greyish. Median coverts dark brown with pale rufous edges and whitish tips. Greater coverts dark brown with broad buff edges and whitish tips. Tips to greater and median coverts form two obscure wing-bars. Tertials dark brown with rufous-buff edges and whitish tips. Rest of wing dark brown with narrow pale buff or grey-buff feather edges. Tail blackish-brown with narrow pale buff feather edges. Underparts whitish with dark brown streaks on throat, breast and flanks. Iris dark reddish-brown. Bill blackish-grey with a flesh lower mandible. Legs flesh.
Juvenile Similar to adult but buffier overall and has broader pale tips to the greater and median coverts forming more prominent wing-bars.

MOULT AND AGEING The post-juvenile moult is partial and the post-breeding moult is complete; both occur in July-September, on the breeding grounds prior to migration. The pre-breeding moult is limited to some head feathers and occurs in February-April. First-years resemble adults once the post-juvenile moult is completed (even the juvenile is more similar to adults than in most sparrows). Some first-years can be told in the hand by relatively

pointed rectrices and outer primaries, and by the retained juvenile remiges and rectrices being relatively more worn, especially spring. Differences can be subtle, however, and there is some overlap in the feather shape. Skull ossification complete in first-years from 15 November.

MEASUREMENTS Measurements for the four main groups are given separately below.
Savannah Sparrow. Wing (chord): male (n30) 65-79.8; female (n22) 63.5-77.7. Tail: male (n30) 46-55.9; female (n22) 47-53.3. Bill: male (n30) 10.2-12.7; female (n22) 10.2-12.7. Tarsus: male (n30) 20.1-23.1; female (n22) 20.3-22.9. Maximum wing: male (n10) 70-74; female (n7) 67-70.
Ipswich Sparrow. Wing (chord): male (n7) 72.4-82.6; female (n7) 72.4- 82.6. Tail: male (n7) 52.8-64.8; female (n7) 53.3-56.9. Bill: male (n7) 10.4-10.9; female (n7) 10.7-11.1. Tarsus: male (n7) 21.6-24.1; female (n7) 21.8-24.1. Maximum wing: male (n23) 73.3-83.4; female (n15) 68.7-76.9.
Belding's Sparrow. Wing (chord): male (n56) 64-77.7; female (n39) 61-67.6. Tail: male (n56) 45.7-57.2; female (n39) 42.4-53.3. Bill: male (n56) 9.6-12.7; female (n39) 9.6-11.4. Tarsus: male (n56) 19-22.6; female (n39) 18.3-20.8 (*beldingi* averages smaller than *alaudinus*).
Large-billed Sparrow. Wing (chord): male (n28) 66-74.2; female (n27) 63.5-71.9. Tail: male (n28) 47-55.1; female (n27) 45.2-54.4. Bill: male (n28) 11.4-13.7; female (n27) 10.7-13.2. Tarsus: male (n28) 20.3-23.4; female (n27) 20.3-23.6 (bill averages largest in *rostratus*).

GEOGRAPHICAL VARIATION (This treatment follows Peters, although the Savannah group may be oversplit and more recent authors do not recognise the races *crassus*, *brooksi*, *rufofuscus* and *mediogriseus*): twenty-one races in four groups or allospecies within the superspecies. These four groups were originally described as separate species and one of them (the *rostratus* group) has recently been given specific status again by some authors, based on mitochondrial DNA studies. Within the different groups, the races are often extremely similar and individuals often cannot be identified in the field.

Savannah Sparrow group:
  P. s. sandwichensis (Breeds in most of Alaska, including the Alaska Peninsula and Fox Island, and winters in the western USA) Averages larger than other northern races, with relatively narrow brownish streaking on the underparts and a relatively long yellow supercilium.
  P. s. crassus (Breeds in SE Alaska, on the Alexander Archipelago and the adjacent mainland, and winters in the SW USA and rarely in W Mexico south to Guerrero) Very similar to nominate; the bill may average slightly stouter , but any differences are very slight.
  P. s. athinus (Breeds from N Alaska east through Yukon to W North-west Territories in the Mackenzie District, and south to SC interior British Columbia; winters from extreme SW British Columbia south through coastal W USA to N and W Mexico) Very similar to *brooksi*, but averages slightly darker and browner, and tends to have a more slender bill.
  P. s. brooksi (Breeds on the Pacific coast from British Columbia including Vancouver Island south to extreme NW California; Canadian populations are migratory, wintering in S California, Baja California and NW Mexico; populations on the USA coast are more sedentary) May average slightly smaller than other northern races and averages slightly paler and

greyer than *athinus*, intermediate between it and *nevadensis*.

P. s. nevadensis (Breeds from C British Columbia and E California east to W Manitoba and N Dakota, and winters from S Arizona and Texas south to C Mexico) The palest and greyest of the northern Savannah races and has a fairly slender bill.

P. s. oblitus (Breeds in NC North America, in E Northwest Territories in Keewatin District, E Manitoba, W Ontario, Minnesota, Michigan and Wisconsin; winters in NE Mexico) Darker than *nevadensis*, greyer than *mediogriseus* and darker and greyer than other northeastern races.

P. s. mediogriseus (Breeds from the southern parts of Ontario and Quebec south probably to Kentucky and W Virginia, and winters mainly in the SE USA) Fairly dark, like *oblitus*, but browner. This race is sometimes lumped with *savanna*.

P. s. labradorius (Breeds in NE Canada, Newfoundland, Labrador and Quebec south to St. James Bay and the north shore of the St. Lawrence, and winters in the SE USA) Similar to *mediogriseus* but averages slightly darker and browner.

P. s. savanna (Breeds in E Canada, in New Brunswick, Nova Scotia, Prince Edward Island and the Magdalen Islands, and in N New England, and winters mainly in the Yucatán area of Mexico and in the Greater Antilles and Bahamas) Described above. Paler than the other north-eastern races and also browner than *oblitus*.

The following three races are all relatively dark and rufous above:

P. s. rufofuscus (Breeds locally in CE Arizona, N New Mexico and Chihuahua; winter range incompletely known but there are records from Jalisco) Similar to *athinus* but averages smaller and darker. This race is sometimes lumped with *brunnescens*.

P. s. brunnescens (Resident in Mexico from Durango and S Coahuila south to Guerrero and Oaxaca) Very similar to *rufofuscus* but perhaps averages marginally duller and darker.

P. s. wetmorei (Resident in S Guatemala in SW Quetzaltenango) Very similar to *brunnescens* but averages even darker and browner above; the supercilium is entirely yellow, except at the extreme rear end.

Ipswich Sparrow:

P. s. princeps (Breeds only on Sable Island and winters on the Atlantic coast of North America from Nova Scotia south to Georgia) Noticeably larger and paler brownish-grey than any of the races in the Savannah group, the yellow on the supraloral is relatively pale, especially in autumn, and the streaking on the underparts is finer and paler brown than in other northern races.

Belding's or Saltmarsh Sparrow; small and very dark-looking, being very heavily streaked above and below with blackish:

P. s. alaudinus (Resident in coastal saltmarshes in N and C California) Similar to *beldingi* but slightly less heavily streaked above (thus often appearing less contrasting) and with a more slender bill.

P. s. beldingi (Resident in coastal saltmarshes from the Monterey area of California south to the El Rosario area of Baja California, including the Channel Islands and Todos Santos Islands) Averages darker (more heavily streaked) than *alaudinus* with a heavier-looking bill; a few are slightly paler and greyer and may resemble *nevadensis*, but are still smaller than that race.

Large-billed Sparrow; larger-billed than the other groups with a more convexly curved culmen, streaking on upperparts generally very faint or virtually absent, streaking on underparts generally pale brown and relatively faint, supercilium pale buffy-yellow to whitish; like the *beldingi* group, it is restricted to coastal saltmarshes):

P. s. anulus (Resident in WC Baja California from the El Rosario area south to the Sebastian Vizcaino Bay (including Isla Cedros) More heavily streaked than the other races in its group; it may appear similar to *beldingi* but is less heavily streaked, and has a shorter tail and a noticeably larger bill. This race appears to link the Belding's and Large-billed groups and has also been placed in the Belding's group.

P. s. sanctorum (Resident on Isla San Benito in the Sebastian Vizcaino Bay, Baja California) Has darker legs than the others in this group and a straighter culmen; otherwise similar to *rostratus* but the streaking on the underparts is slightly darker.

P. s. guttatus (Resident in W Baja California in the Laguna San Ignacio area, wintering south to S Baja California) Similar to *magdalenae* but slightly smaller-billed and has slightly darker olive-grey upperparts with less obvious darker streaking.

P. s. magdalenae (Resident on the west coast of Baja California in the Magdalena Bay area including Isla Magdalena, wintering south to S Baja California) Intermediate between *guttatus* and *rostratus* in size and bill size.

P. s. rostratus (Resident in the River Colorado delta area, from the Salton Sea in California, where it is now very rare, to the estuary in NE Baja California, and in extreme NW Sonora) Larger and larger-billed than *magdalenae*; also paler and greyer above with indistinct darker streaking and indistinct pale brown streaking on underparts.

P. s. atratus (Resident in NW Mexico from NW Sonora south to N Sinaloa) Averages larger than *rostratus*, darker and greyer above, and has darker brown streaking on underparts.

RELATIONSHIPS The monotypic *Passerculus* genus is closely related to *Ammodramus* and was formerly considered to be part of it.

VOICE The song, generally given from the ground (often from a prominent clod of earth or a rock) or a post or small bush, is a short series of *chip* notes followed by a long buzzy trill and ending with a shorter, more abrupt trill that is noticeably lower in pitch. Song of Ipswich Sparrow is said to be slightly lower-pitched and more musical with a longer trill at the end. A song of Large-billed Sparrow, heard in mid-winter, was described as being squeaky and unmusical, ending with a trill. Calls include a thin high *seep* and a harder *tsit.*

HABITS Nest is placed on the ground in a scratched-out hollow and usually sheltered by a grass clump, shrub or small tree; it is a cup (often with a roof covering the top) of grass, plant stems and sometimes moss, lined with finer grass. 3-6 (usually 4-5) eggs are laid in March-July; they are whitish and variously speckled, sometimes very heavily, with browns and often purples. Incubation period is 12 days and the young fledge after 7-10 (occasionally as long as 14) days. Birds tend to show strong site-fidelity. Feeds mainly on seeds, but also extensively on insects in the breeding season. Forages on the ground, hopping and walking (apparently *princeps* prefers to walk) in field edges, roadsides, saltmarshes and other open weedy or brushy areas. May also forage low in trees and hedgerows, especially in autumn. When disturbed it often hides in grass; if pursued it flies, low to the ground, before dropping into the grass and running further on. Flight is generally low, swift and slightly undulating. Outside the breeding season generally found in small groups, although very large flocks sometimes occur on migration when it may occur almost anywhere, even in city parks.

STATUS AND HABITAT Common to very common throughout much of its range but the race *princeps*, although common on its one tiny island breeding ground, is rare in numerical terms and may be threatened in the long term by the gradual erosion of Sable Island. Found in a wide variety of open habitats, with only extensive forest cover being shunned. The Savannah group occurs in grassland, tundra, boggy areas, semi-arid scrub, farmland and weedy or scrubby pastures, mountain pastures (to 4000m in the Rockies), sand-dunes and freshwater marshes, generally in highland areas in Mexico. Ipswich Sparrow breeds in coastal sand-dunes and winters on beaches and sand-dunes. Belding's and Large-billed Sparrows are restricted to coastal saltmarshes, in similar habitat to Seaside Sparrow (62) of the Atlantic coast.

DISTRIBUTION AND MOVEMENTS Breeds across virtually the whole of Alaska, Canada and the northern and central USA, along the Pacific coast south to Baja California, in north-western and central Mexico, south to Oaxaca, and in south-western Guatemala. Mexican and Pacific coast races are sedentary, other races are short- to long-distance migrants wintering in central California, the southern USA and Mexico and northern central America, and in the West Indies (Bahamas and Greater Antilles). See also under Geographical Variation. There is a slight overlap in breeding and wintering ranges in central-eastern USA. Birds arrive on breeding grounds from March

in the south, late April/early May in the north. Autumn migration begins in mid-August, with most leaving the breeding grounds during September. Vagrant to Japan (at least 10, all November-March), Costa Rica (1 record from Cocos Island) and to Britain (2, in April 1982 and September/October 1987). One of the British records (Portland Bill in April 1982) involved the rare race *princeps*; the bird was surely ship-assisted as this race is a relatively weak flyer.

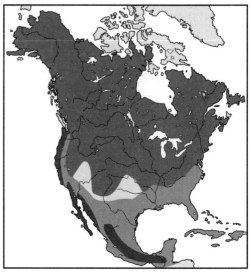

REFERENCES Alström *et al.* (1991), Armani (1985), Bédard & La Pointe (1984), Bent (1968), Bond (1985), Brazil (1991), Broyd (1985), Cramp & Perrins (1994), Davies (1972), Dickerman (1968), Ehrlich *et al.* (1988), Farrand (1983), Godfrey (1986), Paynter & Storer (1970), Peterson & Chalif (1973), Pyle *et al.* (1987), Ridgway (1901), Sibley & Monroe (1990 & 1993), Stiles & Skutch (1989), Terres (1980), Wheelwright & Rising (1993).

AMMODRAMUS

Eight species of small, rather chunky sparrows, generally with short 'spiky' tails and large-looking heads with flat crowns, and often a relatively large bill. Generally secretive and difficult to observe except when singing. Two of the species are exclusively South American.

62   SEASIDE SPARROW
Ammodramus maritimus   Plate 25

Described as *Fringilla maritima* Wilson 1811.
Synonyms: *Thyrospiza maritima, Passerherbulus maritimus*.

The only *Ammodramus* that is entirely restricted to coastal saltmarshes. It shows a surprising similarity to Red-winged Blackbird *Agelaius phoeniceus*, not only in its song but also in some of its habits and even its bill shape.

IDENTIFICATION 15cm. The largest *Ammodramus*, with a long, thick-based and spike-like bill. Plumage is variable but all adults have a distinct yellow supraloral, which of-

ten extends over the eye as a short supercilium, and a dark malar stripe which separates the whitish or buffy submoustachial stripe from the white throat. Gulf and Atlantic coast birds have olive-grey upperparts, rufous in the wing and obscure streaking on the underparts; Gulf coast birds are buffy on the breast whereas on Atlantic coast races the breast is pale greyish. The very local *mirabilis* race (Cape Sable Seaside Sparrow) of south-western Florida is much more olive above, more or less lacks rufous in the wings and has distinct streaks on the underparts. The recently extinct *nigrescens* race (Dusky Seaside Sparrow), formerly of Merritt Island, Florida, was blackish above and white below, heavily streaked black. Birds in western Florida are quite sooty above and quite heavily streaked below, but are not as blackish as *nigrescens*. Juveniles are distinctly buffy, with distinct dark streaking on the breast and flanks. They also lack the yellow lores and are buffy, rather than rufous, on the wing. They are told from juvenile Sharp-tailed Sparrow (63) by larger size and larger bill, lack of a distinct supercilium and lateral crown-stripe, and whiter throat bordered by dark malar stripe.

DESCRIPTION

Sexes alike; juvenile clearly different from subsequent plumages.

Adult/first-year Crown and nape mid-grey, lateral crown with faint brownish tinge. Sides of head also fairly uniform mid-grey except for bright yellow supraloral, which often extends over eye as short supercilium. Dark grey malar stripe separated from grey ear-coverts by whitish submoustachial stripe. Upperparts mid-grey with faint and obscure brownish streaking. Lesser coverts dark olive. Alula dark brown with white edge. Rest of wings mostly blackish-brown with rufous feather edges, broadest and brightest on greater coverts and tertials, and narrower and more olive-rufous on primaries and primary coverts. Bend of wing yellow. Tail blackish-brown with pale olive-rufous feather edges. Underparts pale greyish-white, with a faint buff wash on rear flanks, and wide but blurred greyish-brown streaks on breast and flanks. Iris dark reddish-brown. Bill blackish-grey, relatively thin and pointed. Legs dark flesh.

Juvenile Distinctly buffier than adult. Crown, nape and upperparts buff-brown, narrowly streaked black (streaks broader on upperparts). Sides of head buffier than adult on supercilium, neck-sides and submoustachial stripe. Supraloral spot pale buff. Underparts pale buffy-white, buffiest on breast and flanks and with sharply defined brown streaks on breast and flanks.

MOULT AND AGEING The post-juvenile and post-breeding moults are both complete, occurring in July-September (on the breeding grounds, prior to migration, in migratory populations). Some birds have a partial pre-breeding moult, involving some or all body feathers in March-April, but this does not occur in all birds. First-years resemble adults once the post-juvenile moult is completed and, as this moult is complete, tail feather shape is not useful for ageing. Skull ossification complete in first-years from 15 November in northern races, 15 October in southern ones.

MEASUREMENTS Wing (chord): male (n75) 56-65.3; female (n85) 53.6-64. Tail: male (n45) 48.5-59.1; female (n55) 47-58.4. Bill: male (n45) 12.7-15; female (n55) 12.4-15.2. Tarsus: male (n45) 20.8-24.1; female (n55) 20.8-23.4 (Atlantic coast races average longer-winged than Gulf coast and Florida ones).

GEOGRAPHICAL VARIATION Nine races, one of which is now extinct. Generally, Gulf coast races are buffier below than Atlantic coast ones, and the Florida peninsula races are darker and more heavily streaked than the others.

Atlantic coast races:

A. m. maritimus (Breeds on the Atlantic coast from Massachusetts south to N North Carolina and winters from Virginia south to NE Florida, occasionally north to Massachusetts) Described above.

A. m. macgillivraii (Resident on the Atlantic coast from N North Carolina south to S Georgia) Brighter than *maritimus* with a buffier breast, distinct brown lateral crown-stripes, greenish-yellow supercilium extending behind eye and a rufous-brown wash on mantle and neck-sides.

A. m. pelonota (Resident in NE Florida from the Georgia border south to New Smyrna) Very similar to *macgillivraii*, and may not always be distinguishable from it, but the central rectrices apparently lack the dark shaft streak that is present on *macgillivraii*.

Florida peninsula races:

A. m. nigrescens (Formerly occurred on Merritt Island and the adjacent mainland in CE Florida but is now extinct) Was the darkest race, almost blackish above and white below, heavily streaked black, with a sharply contrasting yellow supraloral.

A. m. mirabilis (Resident in the S Everglades and formerly occurred south-east to Cape Sable) Differs from other races in being distinctly olive on the head and upperparts, and heavily streaked with dark brown below.

Eastern Gulf coast races:

A. m. peninsulae (Resident in W Florida from Dixie County south to Old Tampa Bay) It is darker and sootier above than *maritimus* and has blurred sooty streaks on underparts.

A. m. junicola (Resident on the Gulf coast in NW Florida from Taylor County west to Escambie County) Slightly larger than *peninsulae* and also darker and browner above. The differences in these two races is clinal, however, with birds becoming progressively larger and darker from south-east to north-west, with birds from the central part generally not assignable to either race.

Western Gulf coast races:

A. m. fisheri (Breeds on the Gulf coast from Alabama west to San Antonio Bay, Texas, and winters southwest to Nueces County, Texas) Brighter than *maritimus* with a buffy breast and submoustachial streak (which extends round rear edge of ear-coverts, yellow supraloral extending behind eye as a greenish-yellow supercilium, warm brown lateral crown-stripes and grey crown-stripe (both narrowly streaked black), grey ear-coverts, warm brown wash to upperparts and brighter rufous edges to coverts and tertials.

A. m. sennetti (Breeds in S Texas from Aransas County south-west to Nueces Bay, and winters south-west to the mouth of the Rio Grande) Similar to *fisheri* but is slightly paler and greener above, duller rufous on head and wings, and has less of a buffy wash to the breast.

VOICE The song, generally given from a grass or reed stem but sometimes from the ground, consists of two short sharp notes followed by a longer buzzy *zhe-eeeeeeee*, quite similar to Sharp-tailed Sparrow and also reminiscent of Red-winged Blackbird. Calls include a *chack*, again rather similar to Red-winged Blackbird.

HABITS Nest is placed on or near the ground in a grass tussock above the high-tide line or low in a bush; a cup of grasses lined with finer grasses. 3-6 (usually 4-5) eggs are laid in April-July; they are white or bluish-white heavily marked with reddish-brown. Incubation period is 12-13 days and the young fledge after 8-10 days. Single-brooded, although many first nests are washed out by high spring tides, resulting in synchronised re-nesting immediately afterwards. Birds nest close together in favourable habitat, giving the impression of loose colonies. Secretive and difficult to flush, whereupon it flies a short distance before dropping back into the grass and frequently running further. It is inquisitive, however, and will often respond to 'pishing'. Feeds on young marine crabs, snails and other crustaceans as well as some seeds and insects, foraging on the ground along the edges of tidal creeks; generally keeps close to cover. Usually found in pairs or small groups outside the breeding season.

STATUS AND HABITAT Locally common throughout most of range but the race *mirabilis* is now very rare and considered endangered due to habitat loss. The race *nigrescens* recently became extinct for similar reasons. Found exclusively in coastal saltmarsh and tidal reedbeds, favouring the wetter tidal areas with *Spartina* grass or reedbeds. Race *mirabilis* occurs in marsh prairie.

DISTRIBUTION AND MOVEMENTS Breeds on the Gulf and Atlantic coasts of the USA, from Texas east and north to New England, but only patchily in Florida. Most populations are sedentary, but New England birds move further down the Atlantic coast in winter and some Gulf coast birds move south to south-eastern Texas in winter. See also under Geographical Variation. Vagrant north to Nova Scotia.

REFERENCES Armani (1985), Bent (1968), Dunn & Blom (1983), Ehrlich *et al.* (1988), Farrand (1983), Godfrey (1986), Marshall & Reinert (1990), Murray (1968), Paynter & Storer (1970), Pyle *et al.* (1987), Ridgway (1901), Terres (1980).

63 SHARP-TAILED SPARROW
Ammodramus caudacutus   Plate 25

Described as *Oriolus caudacutus* Gmelin 1788.
Synonym: *Ammospiza caudacuta.*

A small darkish sparrow with disjunct populations, which are genetically distinct (R. Knapton), in different habitats in the northern prairies, where it often occurs with Le Conte's Sparrow (64), on the shores of James Bay, and along the Atlantic coast, where it occurs with Seaside Sparrow (62). These three populations are in the process of speciating, as is indicated by the genetic, as well as morphological, differences between them.

IDENTIFICATION 13cm. A small, rather chunky sparrow

with a fairly flat head, slender pointed bill and a short spiky tail. Variable but all birds appear dark, noticeably darker than Le Conte's Sparrow, from which they further differ in having dark blackish-brown upperparts with whitish or pale streaks, unstreaked grey neck-sides, dark grey median crown-stripe and broad blackish or blackish-brown lateral crown-stripe. Most east coast birds have grey ear-coverts broadly surrounded by bright orange-buff and pale buff breast and flanks, distinctly streaked black, which contrast with whitish throat and belly. Coastal birds from the north of the range are noticeably duller with buff surrounds to the ear-coverts, pale streaks on back more or less lacking and indistinct streaking on underparts. Birds of the interior have distinct whitish streaks on mantle, a less distinct ear-covert patch and orange-buff on breast and flanks as well as surrounding ear-coverts; the streaking on the underparts is indistinct in these birds and is confined to the flanks. Juvenile is duller and buffier with orange and grey areas on the head lacking, buff edges to upperpart feathers (pale streaks lacking) and diffuse brownish streaking on breast and flanks. Seaside Sparrow is much larger, and has a noticeably larger and more pointed bill; it is also variable but adults have yellowish supraloral and all ages have a dark malar stripe and lack a broad dark lateral crown-stripe. Adults may get very worn in late summer, with the distinctive features of fresh plumage much less noticeable.

HYBRIDISATION There is a record of hybridisation with Le Conte's Sparrow.

DESCRIPTION
Sexes alike; juvenile clearly different from subsequent plumages.
Adult Forehead and broad lateral crown-stripe dark brown, streaked blackish. Median crown-stripe slate grey, finely streaked blackish. Lores and supercilium bright orange-buff. Ocular area and narrow eye-stripe dark brown. Broad submoustachial stripe bright orange-buff extending round rear edge of grey ear-coverts. Nape and neck-sides grey, tinged olive. Mantle and scapulars dark olive-grey, finely streaked with blackish and with three buffy-white lines (two on scapulars and one on the sides of the mantle). Rump and uppertail coverts warmer brown, finely streaked blackish. Lesser coverts olive-grey. Alula dark brown edged white. Rest of wings blackish with broad rufous-brown edges to greater and median coverts and tertials, and narrower buffy-white edges to other feathers. Greater coverts and tertials also narrowly fringed with white. Bend of wing pale yellow. Tail grey-brown with paler feather edges and faint darker cross-barring on central feathers. Throat and belly white. Breast and flanks pale buff with narrow but distinct blackish streaks; undertail-coverts pale buff. Iris dark reddish-brown. Bill dark grey. Legs dark flesh. Similar year-round but often considerably duller, through extreme wear, in late summer.
Juvenile Noticeably buffier overall than adult and with a less distinct head pattern. Median crown-stripe, ear-coverts and neck-sides dull grey-brown, washed buff. Surrounds to ear-coverts buff, concolorous with breast and flanks. Rest of underparts paler buff, whitest on belly. Upperparts olive-buff, heavily streaked black and with scapular and mantle lines lacking. Streaking on underparts more diffuse and browner than in adult.

MOULT AND AGEING The post-juvenile moult is incomplete and occurs in August-October; it includes the tail feathers and often some of the flight feathers. The post-breeding moult is complete, also occurring in August-October. Both these moults generally occur on the breeding grounds, before migration. All birds have a partial to incomplete pre-breeding moult in March-April, which includes the body feathers and often the tail feathers and outer 3-5 primaries as well. First-years resemble adults once the post-juvenile moult is completed, but some first-years may be told, especially in the hand, by contrast between new and retained juvenile remiges. Tail feather shape is not useful as the tail is moulted in the post-juvenile moult. Skull ossification complete in first-years from 15 November.

MEASUREMENTS Wing (chord): male (n30) 53-61; female (n30) 51-59. Tail: male (n33) 44.4-54.6; female (n23) 43.2-51.3. Bill: male (n23) 10.2-12.7; female (n23) 10.2-12.7. Tarsus: (n23) 18.3-23; female (n23) 20.1-21.8. Wing formula: P9 usually < P5 (cf. juvenile Grasshopper and Le Conte's).

GEOGRAPHICAL VARIATION Five races which differ mainly in overall brightness of plumage; proceeding from the north-west:

A. c. nelsoni (Breeds inland from SW North-west Territories and NE British Columbia south-east to NE South Dakota and NW Minnesota, and winters in coastal SE USA from S Carolina south to Florida and west to Texas, also casually in California) Brighter than *caudacuta* with more noticeable white lines on the upperparts, buffier-grey ear-coverts, breast and flanks orange-buff, concolorous with ear-covert surrounds, throat pale orange-buff, and streaking on underparts blurred, greyish and indistinct.

A. c. alterus (Breeds along the southern shore of Hudson Bay and along the shore of James Bay in N Ontario and W Quebec, and winters on the Atlantic USA coast from S Carolina south to N Florida, casually north to New York and west to Louisiana) Similar to *nelsoni* but is generally duller, intermediate between it and *subvirgatus*.

The following three races all intergrade where their ranges overlap, but form a group which is geographically and genetically distinct from the other two.

A. c. subvirgatus (Breeds on the Atlantic coast from the south side of the St. Lawrence river east to Nova Scotia and Prince Edward Island and south to Maine, intergrading with *caudacutus* in Sagadahoc County, and winters from S Carolina south to N Florida, casually to New York) The dullest and greyest of all the races; most similar in pattern to *caudacutus* but the ear-covert surrounds are duller buff, concolorous with the breast and flanks (not noticeably darker and brighter as in *caudacutus*), the pale lines on the upperparts are much less distinct and the streaking on breast and flanks is very indistinct.

A. c. caudacutus (Breeds on the Atlantic coast from S Maine south to New Jersey, where it intergrades with *diversus*, and winters from New Jersey south to Florida, casually north to Massachusetts) Described above.

A. c. diversus (Breeds on the Atlantic coast from S New Jersey south to N Carolina, and winters from S Carolina to N Florida, casually north to New York and west to Louisiana) Similar to *caudacutus* but pure birds have less whitish on the scapulars, more pronounced breast streaking and more of a buff wash to the breast.

VOICE The song, usually given from the centre of a bush but sometimes from an exposed perch or occasionally in flight, is a high-pitched, explosive and buzzy trill, transcribed as *pe-shhhhhhhhhh*, with the second part higher-pitched and fading at the end (R. Knapton).

HABITS Nest is placed on the ground and hidden in a dense tall grass, sedge or rush clump; a bulky, loose cup of grasses, rushes and (coastal breeders) seaweeds, lined with finer grasses. 3-7 (usually 3-5) eggs are laid in May-August; they are pale greenish or bluish-white, thickly speckled with browns. Incubation period is 11 days and the young fledge after 10 days. Often nests in loose colonies. May be somewhat nomadic, with colonies moving from year to year. Shy and secretive, foraging on the ground, in dense grass, and low in bushes. Often runs through the grass instead of flushing when disturbed. Flight is usually low and short, in typical *Ammodramus* fashion. Feeds on seeds, insects and aquatic invertebrates from margins of lakes and rivers. Outside the breeding season usually found singly, occasionally in pairs or small groups on migration.

STATUS AND HABITAT Fairly common. On the coast breeds in salt and brackish marshes and grassy meadows near salt water, often in areas with *Spartina* grass. In the interior breeds along grassy margins of lakes, marshes and pools, generally preferring wetter habitat than Le Conte's Sparrow. All races winter in coastal marsh and grassland.

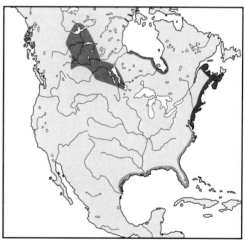

DISTRIBUTION AND MOVEMENTS Breeds in interior north-central North America, the southern shore of James Bay and along the north-eastern Atlantic coast. Short- to medium-distance migrant, wintering on the southern Atlantic and Gulf coasts of the south-eastern USA. See also under Geographical Variation. Arrives on breeding grounds in May-June and leaves for winter grounds in late September-October. Rare vagrant to western USA in autumn.

REFERENCES Armani (1985), Bent (1968), Dickerman (1962), Dunn & Blom (1983), Ehrlich *et al.* (1988), Farrand (1983), Godfrey (1986), Murray (1968), Paynter & Storer (1970), Pyle *et al.* (1987), Ridgway (1901), Terres (1980).

64   LE CONTE'S SPARROW
Ammodramus leconteii   **Plate 26**

Described as *Fringilla caudacuta* Latham 1790.
Synonym: *Emberiza leconteii*.

A small sparrow of wet areas in the northern prairies.
Unlike other *Ammodramus* sparrows with a similarly extensive range it is monotypic, showing no noticeable variation
over its wide range.

IDENTIFICATION 13cm. Shape similar to Sharp-tailed
Sparrow (63) but appears much paler. Head pattern is
distinctive with broad, bright buff supercilium reaching
to nape, blue-grey ear-coverts, black lateral crown-stripe
and whitish median crown-stripe. Nape and neck-sides are
pale grey, finely streaked with chestnut. Upperparts are
streaked blackish, pale buff and whitish. Underparts whitish with bright buff breast and malar area, and black
streaks on flanks. The *nelsoni* race of Sharp-tailed Sparrow is fairly similar but is much darker on the upperparts,
has a much broader black lateral crown-stripe, a grey
median crown-stripe and lacks chestnut streaks on neck.
Some fresh-plumaged Grasshopper Sparrows (67) are
quite buffy below, but never as bright as Le Conte's and
they lack its distinctive head pattern; they also have a larger bill and appear larger-headed and stockier. Juvenile is
duller overall with the breast as well as the flanks streaked
black; the buff areas are paler, the crown-stripe is buffy,
the lateral crown-stripe is streaked with whitish and the
nape and neck-sides are buffy with dark brown streaks.
Juveniles usually moult on the breeding grounds but sometimes migrate in largely juvenile plumage.

HYBRIDISATION There is a record of hybridisation with
Sharp-tailed Sparrow.

DESCRIPTION
Sexes alike; juvenile clearly different from subsequent
plumages.
Adult/first-year Median crown-stripe whitish. Fairly narrow lateral crown-stripe black, reaching to nape. Lores
and broad supercilium bright buff, also reaching to nape.
Postocular stripe black, narrow but broadening slightly
behind ear-coverts. Submoustachial area bright buff, extending round rear edge of ear-coverts. Nape and
neck-sides pale grey, finely streaked with dark chestnut.
Upperparts blackish with broad buff streaks and narrower rufous feather edges. Feather edges on scapulars
whitish, forming distinct 'tramlines'. Rump and uppertail-
coverts blackish with broad buff and rufous feather edges,
forming a rather variegated pattern. Lesser coverts brown.
Alula blackish-brown edged white. Rest of wings blackish-
brown with buff feather edges, broadest on greater and
median coverts and tertials. Bend of wing and underwing-
coverts white. Tail dark brown with buff feather edges;
individual feathers are very pointed. Throat pale buffy-
white, breast, flanks and undertail-coverts bright buff,
flanks with distinct but narrow black streaks. Belly white.
Iris dark reddish-brown. Bill bluish-grey, quite slender and
pointed. Legs flesh.
Juvenile Overall pattern similar to adult but duller. Crown-
stripe pale buff, lateral crown-stripe blackish, streaked/
mottled with whitish, buffy areas on the head paler with
the supercilium faintly streaked blackish. Nape and neck-
sides buff, faintly streaked dark brown. Upperparts less
intricately patterned than adult, appearing blackish heav-

ily streaked with buff. Underparts duller and more uniform than adult with streaking across breast as well as on
flanks. Bill flesh but bare parts otherwise as adult.

MOULT AND AGEING The post-juvenile moult is partial
and the post-breeding moult is complete; both occur in
August-October, either on the breeding or wintering
grounds and sometimes suspended over migration. All
birds have a partial to incomplete pre-breeding moult in
April-May, which usually includes the tertials, as well as
some or all of the tail feathers. This moult may be more
extensive in first-summer birds than adults and include
other flight feathers as well. First-years resemble adults
once the post-juvenile moult is completed, although many
first-year birds show retained juvenile feathers on their
autumn migration (some migrate in mainly juvenile plumage). Tail feather shape is not useful for ageing as all birds
have very pointed rectrices. Skull ossification complete in
first-years from 15 November.

MEASUREMENTS Wing (chord): male (n30) 50-56; female (n30) 48-54. Tail: male (n20) 44.8-52; female (n10)
46.5-55.9. Bill: male (n10) 8.4-10.1; female (n10) 8.4-9.9.
Tarsus: male (n20) 17-19; female (n10) 17.5-18.8. Wing
formula: P9 usually > P5 by less than 5mm (cf. juvenile
Grasshopper and Sharp-tailed Sparrows).

GEOGRAPHICAL VARIATION Monotypic.

VOICE The song, often given from the top of a grass stem
or small bush, is a high-pitched, insect-like buzz, about
one second in length, transcribed as *tse-bzzzz*. Calls include
a short *tseep*.

HABITS Nest is placed on, or just above, the ground in a
clump of dead grass and is usually concealed by a tangle
of vegetation; a cup of dry grass lined with finer grass and
hair. 3-5 eggs are laid in May-July; they are greenish-white
speckled with browns. Incubation period is 13 days; the
fledging period has not been recorded. Male often sings
from a conspicuous perch, but otherwise very secretive
and difficult to observe, preferring to run through the
grass rather than fly when disturbed. Feeds mainly on seeds
but also insects and their larvae, especially in the breeding season, foraging on the ground deep in grassy cover.
Outside the breeding season generally found singly, occasionally in pairs or small groups.

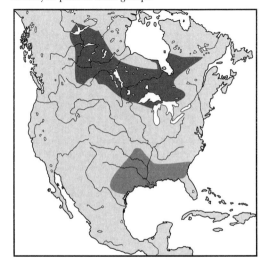

258

STATUS AND HABITAT Fairly common. Breeds in the prairies in moist sedge and grass meadows, marsh edges with shrub tangles and matted grass, and boggy areas with tall rank grass; also in open fens in boreal forest. Winters in similar habitat and also in dry grassland.

DISTRIBUTION AND MOVEMENTS Breeds in northern prairies from southern North-west Territories, extreme eastern British Columbia and extreme northern Montana east through James Bay and the northern Great Lakes to north-eastern Ontario and central Quebec. Medium-distance migrant, wintering in the south-eastern USA from eastern Texas and Kansas east to South Carolina and Georgia. Spring migration begins in March-April with birds arriving on breeding grounds in late April-May. Autumn migration begins in September with birds arriving on winter grounds from late September. Rare vagrant to western North America, especially California, in autumn.

REFERENCES Armani (1985), Bent (1968), Dunn & Blom (1983), Farrand (1983), Godfrey (1986), Murray (1968), Paynter & Storer (1970), Pyle *et al.* (1987), Ridgway (1901), Terres (1980), Tordoff & Mengel (1951).

---

65   HENSLOW'S SPARROW
Ammodramus henslowii   Plate 26

Described as *Emberiza henslowii* Audubon 1829.
Synonym: *Passerherbulus henslowii*.

An uncommon and local sparrow of damp grasslands in central-eastern North America. Colonies appear to be nomadic, breeding in different areas from season to season, although this may be a response to their specific habitat requirements.

IDENTIFICATION 13cm. A small *Ammodramus* but with a relatively large flat head and a short pointed tail. Adult has obvious dark streaking on the breast and flanks and olive back of head and nape, contrasting with distinctly rufous-toned upperparts. Head has distinct narrow black moustachial and malar stripes, separated by a broad buffy submoustachial stripe, a feature shared among the *Ammodramus* only with Baird's Sparrow (66), which is larger and has buff not olive on head and nape and much less chestnut on the upperparts (which appear paler and streakier overall). Broad lateral crown-stripes are blackish, crown-stripe and supercilium are yellowish-buff in front of eye, becoming olive and noticeably broader behind it and merging with olive nape. Upperparts are rufous, heavily streaked black and with whitish feather fringes which produce a complicated and variegated effect. Juvenile is generally duller, more or less unstreaked on underparts, and lacks the malar stripe. It is more similar to adult Grasshopper Sparrow (67), but should be easily distinguished by the distinct olive tone to the head and by the rufous tail and more pronounced rufous edges to coverts and tertials.

DESCRIPTION
Sexes alike; juvenile clearly different from subsequent plumages.

Adult/first-year Median crown-stripe yellowish-buff in front of eye, becoming olive and broader, streaked black, behind it. Broad lateral crown-stripes blackish, narrowly streaked olive-grey. Supercilium yellowish-buff in front

of eye, becoming olive behind it and broadening to merge with olive nape, neck-sides and upper mantle (nape and upper mantle finely streaked black). Lores and ear-coverts olive-buff streaked pale greyish-buff. Ear-coverts outlined in black, broadest in rear corners. Broad submoustachial stripe buff, separating black moustachial and malar stripes. Lower mantle and rest of upperparts streaked black and rufous with narrow whitish feather fringes creating a scaly effect. Rump and uppertail-coverts are paler rufous with narrower black streaks and lacking pale fringes. Lesser coverts pale rufous with olive fringes. Rest of wings blackish with rufous edges to greater and median coverts and tertials, and whitish fringes to tertials; flight feathers and primary coverts edged buff. Bend of wing pale yellow. Tail blackish with broad rufous feather edges central feathers are mostly rufous. Underparts whitish, strongly washed buff on breast, flanks and vent, and with distinct blackish streaks on breast and flanks. Iris dark brown. Bill dark horn with a flesh lower mandible. Legs flesh.

Juvenile Duller overall than adult, with underparts more uniform pale yellowish-buff and the streaking below either lacking or very indistinct. Upperpart feathers lack whitish fringes and are less rufous; the scapulars especially have paler and buffier edges. The black malar stripe is lacking and the bill is slightly paler than adults on upper mandible.

MOULT AND AGEING The post-juvenile moult and the post-breeding moult are both complete, occurring in July-September, mainly on the breeding grounds prior to migration. All birds have a limited pre-breeding moult in February-May, involving some head feathers. First-years resemble adults after the post-juvenile moult is completed. Tail shape is not useful for ageing, as the juvenile tail is moulted during the post-juvenile moult. Skull ossification complete in first-years from 15 November.

MEASUREMENTS Wing (chord): male (n64) 50-56.6; female (n47) 47-55.3. Tail: male (n34) 44.4-52.8; female (n17) 44.5-51.1. Bill: male (n44) 10.2-14; female (n17) 10.4-12.7. Tarsus: male (n44) 15-18.5; female (n17) 15.2-18.

GEOGRAPHICAL VARIATION Three similar races.
 A. h. henslowii (Breeds in the western part of the range from extreme SE North Dakota and E Kansas east to S Ontario, C New York and C West Virginia; winters on the SE USA coastal plain from Texas east to Florida and north to S Carolina) Described above.
 A. h. susurrans (Breeds in the eastern part of the range from C New York and New Hampshire south to E West Virginia and E North Carolina; winters on the USA Atlantic coastal plain from S Carolina to C Florida) Darker on the upperparts than *henslowii* and slightly buffier on the underparts.
 A. h. houstonensis (Only recorded from the type locality in SC Houston, Texas) The type locality was developed ten years ago; this race has not been recorded since and may be extinct (R. Knapton pers. comm.). It is darker above than *susurrans* and has a darker olive nape and upper mantle than *henslowii*; compared with *henslowii* it also has a darker rufous tail and a uniform supercilium, lacking a buffy-yellow supraloral.

VOICE The song, generally given from an exposed perch, is a loud, very short, almost explosive two-note song, with the accent on the second syllable; transcribed as *tsi-lick*.

HABITS Nest is usually placed on the ground but sometimes 15-50cm above it, and is generally hidden in a grass clump; a loosely woven cup of grasses, lined with finer grasses and often arched over with grass. 3-5 eggs are laid in May-August; they are whitish marked with reddish-brown. Incubation period is 10-11 days and the young fledge after 9-10 days. Usually nests in loose colonies; generally of 2-3 pairs but occasionally up to 40-50 (R. Knapton). May be double-brooded. Male sings most often at dusk, also regularly during the night and on cloudy mornings, but only infrequently during sunshine. Feeds on seeds and insects, foraging on the ground near dense cover. It is unobtrusive and often difficult to observe, preferring to run 'mouse-like' through the grass rather than fly when disturbed. When it is flushed the flight is rather weak and close to the ground; it generally drops quickly back into dense cover but may sometimes perch momentarily in the open before doing so. Outside the breeding season usually found singly, occasionally also in pairs or small groups.

STATUS AND HABITAT Uncommon, local and declining. Breeds in weedy fallow fields and meadows, and abandoned pasture with scattered scrub and good grass and sedge growth. Often found in damp or wet fields, although it is not restricted to such areas. It is very patchily distributed throughout its range with small scattered colonies and other apparently suitable areas remaining unoccupied. This, however, may be due in part to its specialised breeding habitat requirements: birds prefer to nest in areas where there is a lot of standing dead vegetation, as this inhibits grass growth and leads to an open but sheltered substrate which the sparrows prefer for feeding. Winters in similar habitat and also in pine woods.

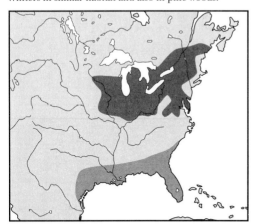

DISTRIBUTION AND MOVEMENTS Breeds in central-eastern North America and is a short- to medium-distance migrant wintering in the coastal plain of the south-eastern USA. See also under Geographical Variation. Spring migration begins in late March and early April with birds arriving on breeding grounds from late April. Autumn migration begins in early September.

REFERENCES Armani (1985), Arnold (1983), Bent (1968), Dunn & Blom (1983), Godfrey (1986), Paynter & Storer (1970), Pyle *et al.* (1987), Ridgway (1901), Terres (1980), Zimmerman (1988).

66   BAIRD'S SPARROW
Ammodramus bairdii   Plate 26

Described as *Emberiza bairdii* Audubon 1844.

An uncommon and local sparrow of short grass prairies that is becoming scarcer as its habitat disappears.

IDENTIFICATION 14cm. A largish *Ammodramus* but with the typical shape of the genus. Head pattern is quite distinct with rich buff median crown-stripe, supercilium and ear-coverts, and narrow dark brown eye-stripe, moustachial stripe and malar stripe. Upperparts are streaked black and grey-buff with some chestnut, especially on scapulars. Underparts are streaked across the breast and on the flanks. Outer tail feathers appear whitish in flight. Juvenile is very similar but head is paler buff, underparts are more strongly streaked and the back feathers have pale fringes, giving the upperparts a more scaly appearance. Henslow's Sparrow (65) is similar in head and underpart pattern but is much darker above and slightly smaller; the ground colour of the head is olive rather than buff and the upperparts (including wings) have chestnut rather than buff edgings. Juvenile Henslow's is virtually unstreaked below and juveniles of the other inland *Ammodramus* sparrows have much finer streaking below, are less scaly above and lack the dark malar stripe.

DESCRIPTION
Sexes very similar; juvenile similar to adults but distinguishable.
Adult/first-year Median crown-stripe rich buff. Lateral crown-stripes blackish, finely streaked with buff. Lores and broad supercilium rich buff. Eye-ring pale buff. Ear-coverts buff vaguely streaked greyish, and narrowly framed with blackish. Submoustachial stripe buff, extending round rear edge of ear-coverts. Narrow malar stripe blackish. Nape and neck-sides buff, streaked blackish. Upperparts pale grey-buff, strongly streaked blackish and with some chestnut, especially on scapulars and rump. Lesser coverts grey-brown with buff fringes. Alula dark brown edged white. Rest of wings blackish with pale buff feather edges, broadest on greater and median coverts and tertials. Bend of wing white. Tail dark brown with pale buff feather edges; the outer web of the outer feather is whitish. Throat buffy-white, breast and flanks pale buff streaked with blackish, belly and undertail-coverts whitish. Iris dark reddish-brown. Bill mostly flesh with a dusky horn culmen. Legs flesh.
Juvenile Resembles adult but the back feathers are broadly fringed whitish, giving upperparts a scaly rather than streaked appearance, the streaking on the underparts is more diffuse but more extensive, and the buff on the head is paler with the median crown-stripe narrowly streaked blackish.

SEXING Females may average slightly duller on the head than males but this is probably only noticeable with mated pairs and, even then, any differences are very slight.

MOULT AND AGEING The post-juvenile moult is partial and the post-breeding moult is complete; both occur in July-October, either on the breeding or the wintering grounds, and sometimes suspended over migration. All birds have a limited pre-breeding moult, involving some head feathers, in February-April. First-years resemble adults after the post-juvenile moult is completed, but note that many first-years migrate in full or partial juvenile plumage. Tail feather shape does not seem to be very useful for ageing, despite the fact that first-years retain the juvenile rectrices. Skull ossification complete in first-years from 15 November.

MEASUREMENTS Wing (chord): male (n30) 67-75; female (n30) 65-72. Tail: male (n18) 52.1-53.3; female (n5) 48.3-53.3. Bill: male (n18) 9.4-12.7; female (n5) 10.2-10.7. Tarsus: male (n18) 20-22; female (n5) 19.3-20.3.

GEOGRAPHICAL VARIATION Monotypic.

VOICE The song, generally given from a bush or weed stem, consists of 2 or 3 high, thin *zip* notes followed by a single warbled note and then a short musical trill at a lower pitch. Calls include a sharp, high *chip* and a low *tr-r-i-p*, used when young are threatened.

HABITS Nest is placed on the ground, generally hidden under a grass clump or low shrub but occasionally in the open; a cup of weed stems and grass, lined with finer grasses. 3-6 eggs are laid in June-August; they are white, spotted and scrawled with reddish-brown. Incubation period is 11-12 days and the young fledge after 8-10 days, often leaving the nest a few days before they can fly. Generally nests in small loose colonies. Male sings from the top of a weed stem or from either the top of or inside a low bush. Feeds on seeds and insects, foraging on the ground, usually in grass cover but sometimes in the open. Fairly shy and often difficult to approach, dropping into the grass or flying low through it when disturbed. May be difficult to find at all, especially on the winter grounds, although males are relatively easy to see on the breeding grounds when they are singing.

STATUS AND HABITAT Generally uncommon, local and declining, although it is still locally common (especially in southern Saskatchewan: R. Knapton) where there is undisturbed short-grass prairie. Breeds mainly in dry, upland short-grass prairie with scattered shrubs for song posts and matted vegetation. Also breeds in the bottoms of dried-out prairie sloughs, alkaline flats, abandoned weedy fields and occasionally in wheat fields in dry years. Winters mainly in dry weedy fields.

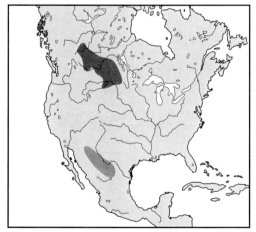

DISTRIBUTION AND MOVEMENTS Breeds in the prairie region from southern Alberta, Saskatchewan and Manitoba south to Montana and northern South Dakota. Medium-distance migrant wintering from extreme southeastern Arizona east to extreme south-western Texas and

in adjacent northern Mexico. Spring migration begins in late February, with birds arriving on breeding grounds from late April. Autumn migration begins in late August and early September, with birds arriving on winter grounds from October. Rare vagrant west and east of range.

REFERENCES Armani (1985), Bent (1968), Dunn & Blom (1983), Ehrlich *et al.* (1988), Farrand (1983), Godfrey (1986), Paynter & Storer (1970), Pyle & Henderson (1991), Pyle *et al.* (1987), Ridgway (1901), Terres (1980).

67 GRASSHOPPER SPARROW
Ammodramus savannarum   Plate 27

Described as *Fringilla savannarum* Gmelin 1789.
Synonyms: *Passerina pratensis, Coturniculus passerinus, Coturniculus savannarum.*

A variable and very widespread sparrow, occurring locally in South America as well as throughout much of North and Central America and the West Indies.

IDENTIFICATION 13cm. A small but chunky *Ammodramus* with the typical flat-headed and short pointed-tailed look of the genus, but appears stockier and larger-headed than Sharp-tailed (63) and Le Conte's (64), more like Henslow's (65). Very variable but all birds have streaked upperparts, unstreaked or vaguely streaked underparts (adults) with a variable buff wash to the breast and flanks, pale median crown-stripe and dark lateral crown-stripes, and a pale supercilium with a usually fairly obvious yellowish or buffy-orange supraloral spot. The greenish-yellow lesser coverts are distinctive but not normally visible in the field. Juveniles are streaked on the breast, and lack the supraloral spot and the greenish-yellow lesser coverts. Differs from juvenile Le Conte's in larger bill, less distinct supercilium and yellowish, not white, bend of wing. Note also different shape. Grassland (68) and Yellow-browed (69) Sparrows are smaller-headed and longer-tailed and lack the pale median crown-stripe. Savannah Sparrow (61) is more heavily streaked below than even juvenile Grasshopper and has a smaller bill and a prominent malar stripe, as well as a different shape and jizz.

HYBRIDISATION There is a record of hybridisation with Savannah Sparrow.

DESCRIPTION
Sexes alike; juvenile clearly different from subsequent plumages.
Adult/first-year Crown blackish-brown with grey-buff feather fringes and a narrow but prominent pale grey-buff median crown-stripe. Supraloral spot pale orange-buff, rest of supercilium pale grey-buff. Noticeable eye-ring whitish. Lores pale grey, ear-coverts grey-buff (buffier below eye). Narrow dark eye-stripe starts behind eye and extends round rear edge of ear-coverts. May show a trace of darker moustachial and malar stripes. Nape grey, streaked with rufous; neck-sides buffier grey, also streaked with rufous. Upperparts grey, streaked with blackish and rufous, and with two pale buff 'tramlines' down centre formed by broad feather edges. Lesser coverts (usually hidden) are mostly greenish-yellow (with small dark brown centres) and the bend of the wing is bright yellow. Alula dark brown edged white. Rest of wings dark brown with narrow whit-

ish fringes to primaries, and pale greyish edges to flight feathers and primary coverts. Greater and median coverts have greyish edges and buffy-white tips, forming two wing-bars. Tertials are blackish with broad rufous edges, the edges becoming whitish at the ends. Tail dark brown with pale grey feather edges. Underparts off-white with a pale greyish-buff wash on the breast and flanks, and sometimes some obscure streaking on the breast-sides. Iris dark reddish-brown. Bill bluish-grey with a flesh lower mandible. Legs flesh. Plumage similar year-round but more worn in spring/summer with many pale feather fringes worn off, so upperparts appear rather darker.

Juvenile Differs from adult/first-year most noticeably in distinct dark brown streaks on breast, but also lacks the buffy-orange supraloral spot and the greenish-yellow lesser coverts, has fine black streaks on the ear-coverts, blackish rather than rufous streaks on the nape, and more prominent pale fringes to the mantle and scapular feathers, which give the upperparts a more scaly look.

MOULT AND AGEING The post-juvenile moult is complete and occurs in July-October. The post-breeding moult is also complete and occurs in July-September. These moults usually occur on the breeding grounds, prior to migration, but the post-juvenile moult may be suspended and completed on the wintering grounds. All birds have a limited pre-breeding moult, involving some head feathers, in February-April. First-years resemble adults once the post-juvenile moult is completed, but note that some first-years retain some streaking on underparts and other juvenile features over the autumn migration. Tail shape is not useful for ageing as the juvenile tail is moulted during the post-juvenile moult. Skull ossification complete in first-years from 1 November in northern populations but from 1 October in southern USA populations.

MEASUREMENTS Wing (chord): male (n66) 53.3-67; female (n52) 56-64. Tail: male (n46) 37.3-51.3; female (n22) 39.4-50.8. Bill: male (n46) 10.2-12.4; female (n22) 10.2-11.9. Tarsus: male (n46) 17.8-21; female (n22) 18-20.8. Wing formula: P9 > P5 by more tham 5mm.

GEOGRAPHICAL VARIATION Eleven races described which differ in size and many plumage details but which all show the same basic plumage pattern. From the north:

A. s. perpallidus (Breeds in W North America from W Ontario and C Texas west patchily to S British Columbia and SW California. Winters from the SW USA south to Guatemala and El Salvador, and casually south to Costa Rica) Described above. Wing (20, sexes combined): 57.1-66.3. Bill (20, sexes combined): 10.2-11.7.

A. p. pratensis (Breeds in E North America from Wisconsin and NE Texas east to the Atlantic coast. Winters in the southernmost part of the breeding range and south to S Mexico and Guatemala, and in the Bahamas and Cuba) Darker above, larger-billed and brighter than *perpallidus* with rich orange-buff supraloral, buffier crown-stripe and buff throat, breast, flanks and vent contrasting with white belly; may have obscure rufous streaking on breast-sides. Wing (18, sexes combined): 58.4-62.7. Bill (18, sexes combined): 10.7-12.2.

A. s. floridanus (Resident in central peninsular Florida – *pratensis* also winters here) It is darker and greyer above than *pratensis*, has a broader and whiter crown-stripe and paler, less buffy underparts.

A. s. ammolegus (Breeds in S Arizona and N Sonora, Mexico. Winters in the breeding range and also south in Mexico and Guatemala) Resembles *pratensis* but is paler and more rufous on the upperparts and slightly buffier on the underparts, with more obvious rufous streaking on breast-sides and flanks.

A. s. bimaculatus (Resident in Central America from S Mexico south to W Panama) Resembles *pratensis* but the upperparts are slightly paler with less extensive rufous, supraloral spot is paler buff, and underparts are whiter, with relatively pale buff restricted to breast and rear of flanks.

A. s. cracens (Resident in NE Central America from N and E Guatemala south-east to NE Nicaragua) Noticeably darker above than other races with little, if any, rufous, and has an underpart pattern similar to *pratensis*.

A. s. caucae (Resident in the upper Cauca Valley of Colombia and, at least formerly, in N Ecuador) Similar to *bimaculatus* but the underparts average even paler, with the buff wash indistinct on the breast and more or less lacking on the flanks.

A. s. savannarum (Resident in Jamaica) Duller above than *perpallidus* (and noticeably duller than *pratensis*), with blackish streaks on nape and relatively dull brown streaks on upperparts. Wing (4, sexes combined): 56.1-57.7 Bill (4, sexes combined): 10.7-11.7.

A. s. intricatus (Resident on Hispaniola) Similar to *borinquensis* but has duller brown sides of head, upperparts, breast, flanks and undertail-coverts.

A. s. borinquensis (Resident on Puerto Rico) Similar to *savannarum* but averages smaller with richer buff median crown-stripe, edges to wing and upperpart feathers, sides of head, and breast, flanks and undertail-coverts.

A. s. caribaeus (Resident on Bonaire and Curaçao in the Netherlands Antilles) Averages slightly paler overall than the West Indian races.

VOICE The song, given from a low perch, is high, thin and insect-like; either 1 or 2 *chip* notes followed by a short buzz, or several wiry buzzy trills on different pitches, interspersed with staccato notes. Calls include high, thin, tinkling whistled notes and a piercing *tseee* or *tweeet* when alarmed.

HABITS Nest is placed on the ground and hidden in or under a clump of grass or low herbs; a cup of grasses, often arched over and lined with finer grasses, rootlets and hair. 3-6 (usually 4-5) eggs are laid in April-August, which are white speckled with reddish-brown at the round end (from North American data). In North America, the incubation period is 11-12 days and the young fledge after 9 days. North American birds are double-brooded. Probably breeds April-July in Costa Rica (from song and breeding condition specimens). Male sings from a grass stem, small shrub or a boulder, mostly in early morning and late evening. Feeds on seeds and insects, especially grasshoppers and small beetles, foraging on the ground usually in cover. Often rather shy, flushing a short distance with fluttering flight before dropping back into the grass or running 'mouse-like' through the grass when disturbed. Frequently cocks its tail and flicks its wings.

STATUS AND HABITAT Fairly common, but has decreased in recent years, especially in North America, due to loss of habitat. Breeds in hayfields and abandoned weedy fields, prairies with clumps of grass and weeds, palmetto scrub and dry, open savanna grasslands, often with scattered volcanic boulders; also wet brushy fields and pastures. Northern birds winter in similar open grassy habitat. In Florida (Kissimmee Mountains) it breeds up to 1300m; in Costa Rica it occurs at 100-800m; and in Colombia to 1000m (has occurred once at 3000m in its South American range).

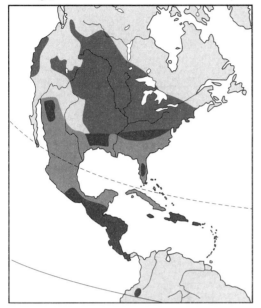

DISTRIBUTION AND MOVEMENTS Breeds in much of North America north to southern Canada, although more patchily in the west. Also occurs in Central America south to western Panama, the West Indies and locally in central Colombia and possibly northern Ecuador. Northern birds are migratory, wintering from just south of the breeding range and in the West Indies and Central America south to Costa Rica. See also under Geographical Variation. Arrives on breeding grounds from late March to early April in the south, early May in the north. Autumn migration begins in September but is quite leisurely, with some lingering to November.

REFERENCES Armani (1985), Bent (1968), Bond (1985), Dickerman (1968), Farrand (1983), Godfrey (1986), Hilty & Brown (1986), Oberholser (1974), Paynter & Storer (1970), Pyle *et al.* (1987), Ridgely & Tudor (1989), Ridgway (1901), Stiles & Skutch (1989), Terres (1980).

---

68 GRASSLAND SPARROW
Ammodramus humeralis   Plate 27

Described as *Tanagra humeralis* Bosc 1792.
Synonyms: *Myospiza manimbe, Myospiza humeralis.*

This and the following species are the only *Ammodramus* sparrows endemic to South America.

IDENTIFICATION 13cm. Crown grey, finely streaked blackish, upperparts grey to brownish-grey, streaked with blackish and chestnut. Supercilium grey with small but noticeable yellow supraloral spot. Eye-ring white. Rufous edges to tertials, inner secondaries and greater coverts form distinct patch in wing. Bend of wing yellow. Underparts pale greyish-white, washed pale buff, or sometimes pinkish, on breast and flanks. Yellow-browed Sparrow (69) with reduced yellow on face and heavy dark streaking above can be very similar and is best identified by song (see under Voice) but the following plumage points, taken together, should be reliable. In Grassland the crown has blacker streaking and the upperparts have more bold blackish streaking that is edged with chestnut (note that some races of Yellow-browed have quite dark streaking, but it is not edged with chestnut). The eye-ring is always white and relatively conspicuous. The edges to the tertials and inner secondaries are rufous, rather than warm brown. In addition, the ground colour of the upperparts tends to be greyer on Grassland and more grey-brown on Yellow-browed, but the latter can be quite grey above. Juveniles of these two are similar but Grassland has heavier and blacker crown streaking and distinct rufous edges to tertials and greater coverts. Grasshopper Sparrow is slightly smaller and has a 'spikier' tail, a heavier-looking head and a distinct buffy crown-stripe.

DESCRIPTION
Sexes alike; juvenile clearly different from subsequent plumages.
Adult/first-year Crown grey, washed brownish on sides and streaked blackish. Nape grey, with streaking finer and edged chestnut. Supraloral (in front of eye) yellow, supercilium grey. Lores and narrow eye-stripe dark rufous-brown, extending slightly round rear edge of buffy-grey ear-coverts. Eye-ring white. Neck-sides and submoustachial area buffy-grey. Mantle and scapulars grey with bold blackish streaking which is noticeably edged with chestnut. Back, rump and uppertail-coverts slightly more brownish-grey with streaking slightly less bold. Lesser coverts brown with broad olive-yellow fringes. Outer edge of alula white. Rest of wings mostly blackish-brown with paler feather edges; tertials and inner secondaries are broadly edged with rufous, forming a patch in closed wing. Tertials also fringed whitish at the end. Greater and median coverts edged and tipped whitish; greater coverts also with outer webs largely rufous-brown. Bend of wing yellow. Tail dark brown with pale greyish feather edges. Underparts pale greyish-white, tinged grey-buff on breast and flanks. Iris dark reddish-brown. Bill pale horn. Legs flesh. Similar year-round but in worn plumage the chestnut edges to the upperpart streaks wear off, resulting in the streaking appearing much heavier and blacker.
Juvenile Distinctly buffier overall than adult with distinct blackish streaks on breast and flanks. Yellow supraloral and bend of wing lacking.

MOULT AND AGEING Adults have a complete moult, probably after breeding, but the extent of the post-juvenile moult is unknown. There is probably no pre-breeding moult. No ageing criteria are known once the post-juvenile moult is completed.

MEASUREMENTS Wing (chord): male (n20) 52-64; female (n11) 54-60. Tail: male (n10) 42-49; female (n8) 38-42. Bill: male (n10) 10.5-12; female (n8) 11-12. Tarsus: male (n10) 17.5-21.5; female (n8) 18-21.

GEOGRAPHICAL VARIATION Four similar races.
A. h. humeralis (Occurs in the Cauca and Magdalena valleys, and the Santa Marta area, in northern Colom-

bia, east of the Maracaibo Basin in north-western Venezuela, and from the llanos of eastern Colombia east through much of Venezuela and south-east through the Guianas and eastern Brazil, south to Paraná) Described above.

A. h. pallidulus (Occurs on the Guajira Peninsula of Colombia and Venezuela) The palest race with the least heavily streaked upperparts.

A. h. xanthornus (Occurs from extreme SE Peru and SW Amazonian Brazil south, but excluding E Bolivia, through Paraguay, Uruguay and extreme S Brazil in Rio Grande do Sul to C Argentina in Rio Negro) The streaking on the upperparts is darker than in *humeralis* with narrower chestnut edges, and the yellow on the supraloral is more extensive, extending over the eye.

A. h. tarijensis (Occurs in E Bolivia in Santa Cruz, Tarija and presumably also Chuquisaca) Similar to *xanthornus* but the upperparts are slightly browner and the breast and flanks are buffier (less greyish); the wing is also longer (> 59mm).

VOICE The song, given from an exposed perch, is a high, thin, quite musical *eee, telee teeee*, rather variable but always high and thin, lacking the buzzing quality of Yellow-browed Sparrow.

HABITS Nest is placed on the ground and hidden in a grass clump; a deep cup of dried grasses (possibly occasionally roofed over), lined with finer plant material. Eggs: 3-4, whitish. Breeding season April-August in northern part of range (Colombia and Venezuela). Male sings from a grass clump, fence or low bush, mostly early in the morning and in the evening. Feeds on seeds and insects. May forage in the open early and late in the day but mainly shy and secretive, foraging in dense grass, through which it hops and runs 'mouse-like' when disturbed. When flushed, generally flies low for a short distance before dropping into the grass again.

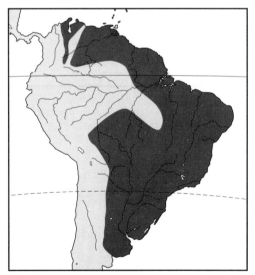

STATUS AND HABITAT Locally common where its tall grassland habitat is still intact. Occurs in tall grassy savannas, campos (open grassy plains, lacking trees, on the central plateau of Brazil), and cerrados (dense, tall grass savannas with scattered trees in central interior Brazil), but it will not tolerate heavy grazing or burning and dis-

appears if these habitats are thus modified. Generally occurs up to 1100m but found slightly higher in southern Venezuela.

DISTRIBUTION AND MOVEMENTS Found widely but patchily in South America east of the Andes, from Colombia and Venezuela south to central Argentina, but excluding most of western Amazonia. See also under Geographical Variation. Sedentary.

REFERENCES Armani (1985), Dunning (1987), Meyer de Schauensee & Phelps (1978), Ridgely & Tudor (1989).

69   YELLOW-BROWED SPARROW
Ammodramus aurifrons   Plate 27

Described as *Tanagra aurifrons* Spix 1825.
Synonyms: *Myospiza aurifrons, Myospiza cherriei.*

A South American *Ammodramus*, similar to Grassland Sparrow (68) and often difficult to separate from it except by song. It tends to occur in a wider range of grassland habitats and is generally less secretive and easier to see.

IDENTIFICATION 13.5cm. Very similar to Grassland Sparrow and slightly larger than Grasshopper Sparrow (67), with a less 'spiky' tail. Crown and upperparts grey-brown with dusky-brown streaking, underparts greyish-white. The South American race of Grasshopper Sparrow (*caucae*) has a buffy crown-stripe and is distinctly buffy on the throat and breast. Yellow-browed normally shows yellow on lores, supraloral, front part of supercilium (to above eye), eye-ring and the base of the submoustachial stripe. This yellow is much reduced on birds in Meta, Colombia, however, and also on birds in the Venezuelan llanos (which also have quite dark streaking above, similar to Grassland). Therefore sparrows of this type with yellow only on supraloral cannot automatically be assumed to be Grassland. Yellow-broweds with reduced yellow on the face are best separated from Grassland Sparrows by song (see under Voice) but the following plumage characters are also useful. The crown and upperparts appear less boldly streaked, with the streaks often being dusky brown rather than blackish and lacking chestnut edges. Birds in north-eastern Colombia, the llanos of Venezuela, south-eastern Colombia, south-western Venezuela and adjacent Brazil have blacker streaking above than western and southern birds (similar to Grassland Sparrow), but the streaks lack obvious chestnut edging. The tertials and inner secondaries are edged warm brown rather than chestnut. The eye-ring is normally yellowish (sometimes pale or indistinct) and is probably never noticeably white as in Grassland.

DESCRIPTION
Sexes alike; juvenile clearly different from subsequent plumages.
Adult/first-year Crown and nape grey-brown, finely streaked blackish. Supercilium, to behind eye, eye-ring, front part of ear-coverts and upper part of submoustachial stripe normally yellow (but the yellow is sometimes reduced to the supraloral and eye-ring). Remainder of ear-coverts and neck-sides grey-brown, unstreaked. On brightest birds, neck-sides are washed yellowish. Upperparts grey-brown with blackish-brown streaks, edged with dull brown, most prominent on mantle and scapulars. Lesser coverts dark brown with broad olive-yellow fringes.

Rest of wings blackish with dull to warm brown feather edges, broadest and warmest on greater coverts and tertials. Greater and median coverts tipped whitish, forming two obscure wing-bars. Bend of wing yellow. Tail dark brown with pale greyish feather edges. Underparts whitish, lightly washed greyish on breast and grey-buff on flanks. Iris dark reddish-brown. Bill horn with darker culmen. Legs flesh.

Juvenile Distinctly buffier overall than adult with fine brownish streaks on breast and flanks. Yellow on face and bend of wing lacking (on face replaced with pale grey-buff).

MOULT AND AGEING Adults have a complete moult, probably after breeding, but the extent of the post-juvenile moult is not known. There is probably no pre-breeding moult. No ageing criteria are known once the post-juvenile moult is completed.

MEASUREMENTS Wing (chord): male (n22) 53-61; female (n18) 52.5-60. Tail: male (n22) 39.5-47; female (n18) 38-44. Bill: male (n22) 10.5-12.5; female (n18) 10.5-12.5. Tarsus: male (n22) 20-23; female (n18) 20-21.5.

GEOGRAPHICAL VARIATION Four similar races, which vary mainly in the strength of streaking on the crown and upperparts and the amount of yellow on the face.

A. a. apurensis (Occurs in NE Colombia in Norte de Santander, Santander, Boyacá and Arauca, and east through the llanos of Venezuela to the Amacuro delta) Similar to *cherriei* but has blacker and heavier streaking on the upperparts.

A. a. cherriei (Occurs in the llanos of Meta, C Colombia) Has less yellow in the face than *aurifrons*.

A. a. tenebrosus (Occurs in SE Colombia in E Vaupés and Guainía, SW Venezuela in SW Amazonas and the adjacent area of Brazil) Darker than the other races, with streaking on crown and upperparts heavier and blacker than even *apurensis* and darker grey sides.

A. a. aurifrons (Occurs from SE Colombia south on the east of Andes to C Bolivia and east through N Amazonia to the Atlantic coast; also locally in the S Amazonian area of C Brazil) Described above.

VOICE The song, generally given from an exposed perch such as a fence post or small bush, is a high insect-like buzzing *tic tzzz-tzzzzz*, with the first note short and faint. It is repeated monotonously throughout the day.

HABITS Nest is usually placed in a grass clump, but occasionally in the lowest branches of a bush or shrub; a cup of dried grasses, lined with finer plant material. 2-3 whitish eggs are laid. Other breeding details, all from Colombia, include three breeding condition males in June, and a breeding condition male plus a juvenile in May, all in Caquetá, begging juveniles in February at Mitú and in September at Leticia, and a male wth food in August at Leticia. Feeds on insects and their larvae as well as seeds. Forages on the ground, often in grass but also in the open, and is not as shy as Grassland Sparrow.

STATUS AND HABITAT Generally common throughout its range. Occurs in a wide variety of open grassy habitats on roadsides, in towns and agricultural areas, riparian areas, llanos and sometimes in large grassy clearings in forested areas. Found mainly in lowlands but to 1000m on the eastern slope of the Andes; in Ecuador it is recorded regularly to 1500m and occasionally to 2000m (C. Rahbek).

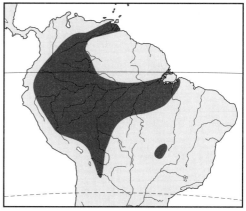

DISTRIBUTION AND MOVEMENTS Occurs in South America, from the eastern slope of the Andes (Colombia south to Bolivia) east across the Venezuelan llanos and northern Amazonia (very locally also in southern Amazonia). See also under Geographical Variation. Sedentary.

REFERENCES Armani (1985), Dunning (1987), Hilty & Brown (1986), Meyer de Schauensee & Phelps (1978), Ridgely & Tudor (1989).

XENOSPIZA

One species which is restricted to central Mexico, where it is rare, local and threatened through habitat loss. It is similar to the *Ammodramus* sparrows in shape, although the tail is rather longer and less pointed than in many of them.

70 SIERRA MADRE SPARROW
Xenospiza baileyi   Plate 31

Described as *Xenospiza baileyi* Bangs 1931.
Synonym: *Ammodramus baileyi*.

An uncommon and local sparrow of north-central Mexico. It was formerly included in the *Ammodramus* genus but has now been replaced in the monotypic genus under which it was originally described.

IDENTIFICATION 13cm. Extensive rufous in wings, combined with rufous-brown crown and blackish-streaked upperparts, plus whitish underparts with extensive blackish streaking, is distinctive, but this species is skulking and difficult to see well. Pale greyish-white supercilium, contrasting with dark ear-coverts, is also noticeable on perched birds. On flushed birds, the rufous wings and the heavily streaked rufous upperparts are good marks. Of the sparrows with streaked underparts that may occur in its range, Vesper (77) has conspicuous white outer tail feathers, Song

(50) has a noticeably longer tail and Savannah (61) normally has yellowish on the supraloral. Savannah and Vesper also lack the extensive rufous tones of this species. Some Mexican races of Song Sparrow are quite similar (showing some rufous in the wing and heavy black streaking on underparts) but are a different shape, with particularly a noticeably longer tail and longer wings (Sierra Madre Sparrow is very short-winged). Mexican Song Sparrows also have less intricately patterned upperparts, heavier and blotchier black streaking on the underparts and a broader and more prominent malar stripe.

DESCRIPTION

Sexes very similar; juvenile distinguishable from subsequent plumages.

Adult/first-year Crown and nape rufous-brown, streaked blackish and with an obscure greyish central crown-stripe. Supercilium greyish, quite broad. Eye-ring pale grey-buff. Lores greyish-buff. Ear-coverts brownish-grey, becoming rufous in the upper rear corner, and streaked with grey-buff. Neck-sides grey-buff, finely streaked blackish. Upperparts rufous-brown, heavily streaked blackish (more lightly streaked in female) and with pale grey-buff feather edges. Lesser coverts rufous. Alula blackish-brown edged white. Rest of wings blackish-brown; flight feathers and primary coverts with narrow buff edges, greater and median coverts with broad rufous edges and pale buff tips, and tertials with broad rufous edges and white fringes. Bend of wing pale yellow. Tail dark brown with paler greyish-rufous feather edges. Throat and submoustachial stripe whitish, separated by a narrow blackish malar stripe. Remainder of underparts whitish, washed pale buff on flanks and undertail-coverts, and with heavy black streaking on breast and flanks; lower throat often also finely streaked. Iris brown. Bill horn with slightly paler lower mandible. Legs flesh. Similar year-round but crown, ear-coverts and upperparts appear darker, with less rufous, in worn plumage.
Juvenile Similar to adults but the underparts have a more extensive buff wash and the streaking is browner.

SEXING Female is often noticeably less heavily streaked on the underparts but there may be some overlap; it is probably most discernible on mated pairs.

MOULT AND AGEING Adults have a complete moult, probably after breeding, but the extent of the post-juvenile moult is not known. There is probably no pre-breeding moult. No ageing criteria are known once the post-juvenile moult is completed.

MEASUREMENTS Wing (chord): male (n3) 58-64; female (n3) 60-63. Tail: male (n3) 51-52.1; female (n3) 48-51.2. Bill: male (n3) 10.5-11.5; female (n3) 10.5-11.5. Tarsus: male (n3) 20-21; female (n3) 19.5-20.5.

GEOGRAPHICAL VARIATION Monotypic.

VOICE The song, generally given from an exposed perch, is quite melodious; a series of short, chirpy and buzzing notes on different pitches. Calls include a buzzy note, repeated regularly.

HABITS Nest is placed close to the ground, hidden in or between zacatón clumps. 3 eggs are laid (from one clutch). Little is known of its breeding biology but singing has been heard from late March to late May (mainly in late May) and in August, and juveniles have been seen between June and September. Sings from an exposed perch, usually a tall grass blade but sometimes overhead wires. Spends most of its time on the ground; sometimes perches briefly on bushes or low branches before dropping back into the grass. Feeds on seeds and insects, foraging on the ground inside tall grass clumps where it is very difficult to observe. Seldom flies; even when flushed it soon drops back into the grass. Generally found in pairs or family parties rather than flocks.

STATUS AND HABITAT Status little known but appears to be rare and very local, and has suffered a recent decline through loss of habitat to cattle-grazing and crops. It is considered threatened by BirdLife International and the total population may number no more than a few hundred pairs. It appears to be restricted to areas of bunchgrass or zacatón and is found primarily in open areas containing bunchgrass and scattered pine trees in the mountains and high plateaux from 2285 to 3050m, mainly from 2800 to 3050m.

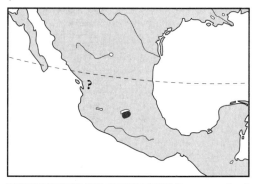

DISTRIBUTION AND MOVEMENTS Occurs very locally in the highlands of central Mexico. It formerly occurred in three disjunct populations in southern Durango, northern Jalisco and northern Morelos/Distrito Federal, but recent records have come only from the latter area; there is little or no suitable habitat left in the other two areas. It is sedentary, although there may be some very localised post-breeding dispersal.

REFERENCES Armani (1985), Collar *et al.* (1992 & 1994), Delaney (1992), Dickerman *et al.* (1967), Peterson & Chalif (1973), Sibley & Monroe (1990).

SPIZELLA

Six species are generally recognised, although two forms (Worthen's Sparrow and Timberline Sparrow, which are presently considered races of Field and Brewer's Sparrows, respectively) probably also deserve specific status. The *Spizella* sparrows are small and slim with fairly long, notched tails; they often form small flocks in winter.

71   AMERICAN TREE SPARROW
Spizella arborea   Plate 28

Described as *Fringilla arborea* Wilson 1810.
Synonym: *Spizella monticola*.

The most northerly of the *Spizella* sparrows, breeding only high in the tundra region and wintering entirely in North America north of Mexico.

IDENTIFICATION 16cm. Slightly larger than other *Spizella* but with the same overall shape; small and slim with a fairly long, notched tail. Most similar to Field Sparrow (75) but easily distinguished by bicoloured bill (black above and yellowish below), blackish legs, brighter overall plumage (in particular more sharply defined and brighter rufous crown) and variable but distinctive blackish spot in centre of breast. Sides of head pale grey with a rufous eye-stripe (behind the eye) and a narrow rufous malar stipe. Underparts also pale grey, with whiter throat and distinct rufous patches on the breast-sides, as well as the black breast spot. Upperparts tawny-rufous streaked with black, and with two white wing-bars. Juvenile has dark streaks on the head and underparts (somewhat obscuring the black central spot) and a duller head and bill pattern, but this plumage is moulted before the birds leave the tundra.

DESCRIPTION

Sexes very similar; juvenile clearly different from subsequent plumages.

Adult/ first-year breeding Crown rufous, sometimes with a narrow grey median crown-stripe, most obvious on the forehead. Nape pale grey, tinged rufous. Rest of head (including broad superciliary area) pale grey, with a narrow rufous postocular stripe which broadens at the rear and often extends slightly round the rear edge of the ear-coverts, and a very narrow and indistinct rufous malar stripe. Eye-ring whitish but fairly indistinct. Upperparts tawny-rufous (generally more rufous on the scapulars) with black streaks on mantle and scapulars. Rump and uppertail-coverts olive-grey, latter with dark brown streaks on feather shafts, and whitish feather fringes in fresh plumage. Lesser coverts greyish. Median coverts blackish edged dull brown, greater coverts blackish, broadly edged bright rufous; both broadly tipped white forming prominent wing-bars. Tertials blackish, broadly edged rufous and narrowly tipped white; other wing feathers blackish with narrow whitish or pale buff edges. Bend of wing white. Tail dusky blackish with narrow pale buff feather edges and outer web of outer rectrix mostly greyish-white. Throat pale greyish-white; rest of underparts pale grey, washed pale buff on flanks, and with a rufous patch on the breast-sides and a variable blackish or dusky spot in the centre of the breast. Iris dark reddish-brown. Bill blackish on upper mandible and tip of lower mandible, pale yellow on rest of lower mandible. Legs blackish.

Adult non-breeding Very similar but slightly duller; the crown feathers have narrow grey fringes and the greyish median crown-stripe is often wider and more noticeable, and the fresh uppertail-coverts have noticeable greyish-white fringes.

Juvenile Crown greyish-brown streaked darker. Sides of head slightly paler and buffier-grey than adult's, streaked dusky and with the ear-coverts narrowly outlined with dark brown. Underparts slightly buffier than adult's with dusky streaks on breast and flanks which obscure the dusky central breast spot. Upperparts much as adult but wing-bars are slightly buffier. Base of bill is duller yellow.

SEXING Sexes very similar; males may average marginally brighter than females, especially in non-breeding (winter), but this is complicated by geographical and seasonal variation.

MOULT AND AGEING The post-juvenile moult is partial, occurring in August-October. The post-breeding moult is complete, occurring in August-September. These moults occur mainly on the breeding grounds, prior to migration, although some first-years may retain a few streaked juvenile breast feathers through October, after starting their migration. All birds have a limited pre-breeding moult, involving some head feathers, in March-April. First-years resemble adults after the post-juvenile moult is completed but have more pointed rectrices, on average; these may also average more worn, especially in spring. Also a few first-years may be identified by some retained juvenile breast and flank streaking through October. Skull ossification complete in first-years from 15 November.

MEASUREMENTS Wing (chord): male (n96) 71-82; female (n90) 66-79. Tail: male (n76) 59-73.2; female (n55) 57-70. Bill: male (n76) 7.8-11.1; female (n55) 8.3-10.5. Tarsus: male (n76) 17.2-22; female (n55) 15.6-21.3 (*ochracae* averages longer than *arborea* in wing, but there is much overlap).

GEOGRAPHICAL VARIATION Two similar races.
   S. a. arborea (Breeds from C North-West Territories and N Saskatchewan east to E Quebec and Labrador, and winters mainly in the eastern part of the wintering range) Described above.
   S. a. ochracae (Breeds from W North-West Territories and NW British Columbia west through Yukon and Alaska, and winters mainly in the western part of the winter range) It is slightly larger and paler overall than *arborea* and has a richer buff wash to the flanks.

VOICE The song, given from a prominent perch such as the top of a small bush, a small hillock or the top of a grass clump, consists of several high, clear *seet* notes, followed by a variable warble. Calls include a high *tseet* and a musical *teedle-eet*, both quite distinct from calls of other North American sparrows and enabling this species to be picked out in mixed flocks.

HABITS Nest is usually placed on the ground under a

dense shrub or in a grass clump, occasionally low in a shrub or small tree and rarely up to 1.7m from the ground; a bulky cup of grass and weed stalks, moss, lichen and bark, thickly lined with feathers, hair and sometimes moss. 3-6 (usually 5) eggs are laid in May-July; they are pale bluish or greenish speckled with browns. Incubation period is 11-13 days and the young fledge after 8-10 days, often leaving the nest before they can fly properly. Feeds almost entirely on seeds, foraging on the ground and sometimes in small bushes and shrubs. Outside the breeding season generally found in flocks, usually with other species, which may roam over large areas. Quite shy, flying into bushes when disturbed, but regularly visits feeders in rural areas. It is a very hardy sparrow and can withstand temperatures of -28°C if food is available.

STATUS AND HABITAT Common throughout its range, the total population has been estimated as 10-20 million pairs. Breeds in open willow, alder and dwarf birch scrub along streams and in bogs on the edge of the tundra and above the treeline in open scrubby areas in western mountains; also sometimes in open areas with scrub conifers. Winters in weedy and scrubby fields, gardens in villages and around farms, marsh and woodland edges and other areas which provide an abundance of weed seeds.

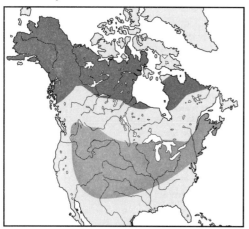

DISTRIBUTION AND MOVEMENTS Breeds in the far north of North America, from Alaska and north-western British Columbia east across the Hudson Bay area to eastern Quebec and Labrador. Medium-distance migrant wintering in southernmost Canada and the interior USA, generally north and east of the coastal mountains and plains, but range extends east to the Atlantic seaboard, from Nova Scotia south to Virginia, and sometimes west to coastal southern British Columbia. See also under Geographical Variation. Spring migration begins in March-April with birds arriving on breeding grounds in May. Autumn migration begins in September with birds arriving on winter grounds from October in the north, November further south. Casual on the west coast of North America in spring and autumn.

REFERENCES Armani (1985), Bent (1968), Dunn & Blom (1983), Ehrlich *et al.* (1988), Farrand (1983), Godfrey (1986), Heydwieller (1936), Naugler (1993), Pyle *et al.* (1987), Ridgway (1901), Terres (1980).

72 CHIPPING SPARROW
Spizella passerina   Plate 29

Described as *Fringilla passerina* Bechstein 1798.
Synonym: *Spizella socialis.*

This is a widespread and common bird over the whole of North America south of the tundra, although it is resident only in the southern USA and Central America; it is one of the more familiar sparrows in North America as it is often found round human habitation in suburban and rural areas.

IDENTIFICATION 14cm. Like other *Spizella* sparrows appears small and slim in the field with a fairly long notched tail. Breeding adults are easily identified by the distinctive head pattern of bright rufous crown, long and prominent white supercilium and black eye-stripe; bill is black, unlike many other small sparrows. Nape and sides of head are pale grey, forming a distinct collar. Underparts are a fairly uniform greyish-white, paler on throat; upperparts are buff-brown, heavily streaked black, with a contrasting unstreaked grey rump (quite obvious as the bird flies away). Coverts and tertials are edged pale rufous-brown and there are two fairly obscure wing-bars. Non-breeding (winter) adults are duller on the head; crown is less rufous and is streaked darker, eye-stripe and supercilium are less distinct and the bill becomes paler (dark flesh). First-winters resemble winter adults but lack rufous in crown and are washed brownish on the underparts, especially the breast and flanks. Juveniles have dark streaking on the crown, nape, breast and flanks as well as the upperparts, the rump is brownish and streaked and the covert and tertial edges have less obvious rufous tones. They also have flesh bills. First-summer birds resemble breeding adults. Non-breeding (winter) Clay-coloured Sparrow (73) is similar to first-winter Chipping but has rump uniform with mantle, a more noticeable grey patch on the neck-sides, buff-brown ear-coverts outlined with darker brown, a pale median crown-stripe, a prominent dark malar stripe contrasting with whitish throat and sub-moustachial stripe, and whiter underparts with a pale buff wash to the breast, flanks and vent. The lores are also pale, giving a 'softer' facial jizz. Juvenile Field Sparrow (75) is rather similar to juvenile Chipping but has noticeably less heavy streaking on crown, nape and underparts. After the post-juvenile moult birds resemble winter adults but the underparts have a pale brown wash, and the crown lacks any rufous. However, the post-juvenile moult is prolonged and first-year Chipping Sparrows may be encountered well into October (in eastern North America) or January (in the west) with brownish rumps, faint streaking on the flanks and no rufous in the crown. These are the ones most likely to be confused with juvenile/first-winter Clay-coloured Sparrow; the following are the best points of difference: Chipping has dark lores and a less prominent eye-ring giving a 'sterner' expression. The ear-coverts are grey-brown rather than buff-brown and lack a prominent dark moustachial stripe on the lower border. The pale sub-moustachial and dark malar stripes are not nearly so well marked as on Clay-coloured. The greyish collar is not as obvious or contrasting as on Clay-coloured. The underparts have a more uniform brownish wash (those of Clay-coloured are whiter with a pale buff suffusion restricted to the breast, flanks and vent).

HYBRIDISATION There is one record each of hybridisation with Clay-coloured Sparrow and with Brewer's Sparrow (74).

DESCRIPTION

Sexes very similar; juveniles clearly different from subsequent plumages. First-winters may also be distinguishable but overlap with winter adults so care is required.

Adult breeding Forehead black, extending slightly back towards eyes on the sides, with a narrow whitish stripe, extending back onto the forecrown, in the centre. Rest of crown bright rufous, sometimes with some fine black streaking (especially in females). Supercilium white, extending to rear edge of ear-coverts. Eye-stripe black, noticeably narrower than supercilium. Ear-coverts, neck-sides and nape pale grey. Mantle and scapulars quite bright tawny brown, heavily streaked with black; rump and up-pertail-coverts mid-grey, uppertail-coverts with obscure darker grey centres. Lesser coverts grey. Rest of wings blackish with pale feather edges; greater and median cov-ert and tertial edges are broad and bright tawny with a distinct rufous tinge, other wing feathers have narrow, pale buff edges. Greater and median coverts are tipped white or whitish forming two narrow but conspicuous wing-bars. Tail dark brown with narrow, pale buff feather edges. Underparts mostly pale grey, slightly but noticeably whiter on the throat and malar area. Iris dark reddish-brown. Bill black with a dark flesh base to the lower mandible, legs flesh.

Adult non-breeding Duller overall but especially on the head. Ear-coverts and supercilium are pale greyish-buff, eye-stripe is indistinct, the crown is tawny brown, streaked with black and generally with a trace of the breeding forehead pattern; there is often, but not always, some rufous in the crown. There is also a vague dark malar stripe separating the pale grey submoustachial stripe from the buff ear-coverts. The bill is more extensively flesh, but usually with a blackish upper mandible.

First-year Resembles adult but in non-breeding (winter) generally has a brownish wash to the underparts and lacks rufous in crown. Bill is all flesh, gradually darkening over the winter. Note also that the race *arizonae* of western North America has a post-juvenile moult which occurs mainly on the winter grounds, so birds will be in juvenile plumage through the autumn and will show traces of it through the early winter; first-years of other races (including the nominate) will also show traces of streaking underneath through much of the autumn. First-summer birds are similar to adults; they may average slightly duller, especially in the crown, but this is complicated by slight sexual variation in this character.

Juvenile Crown, nape, neck-sides and underparts fairly uniform pale greyish-buff; mantle and scapulars pale tawny-brown, rump and uppertail-coverts pale grey-brown. Crown, nape, neck-sides, breast and flanks with fine blackish-brown streaking (browner on underparts). Bill mid-flesh. Otherwise much as adult/ irst-winter but tertials and coverts generally with less of a rufous tinge.

SEXING Sexes very similar in plumage and size. Females average very slightly duller, especially on the crown (which may have some very fine black streaking); this is unreliable for single birds but may be noticeable on mated pairs. Note that there is a similar variation according to age and race.

MOULT AND AGEING The post-juvenile moult is partial/incomplete, often including the tertials, and occurs in June-November, possibly to January. The post-breeding moult is complete, occurring in June-November. Of the two migratory races, eastern *passerina* generally completes the post-juvenile and post-breeding moults on the breeding grounds, prior to migration. In western *arizonae* they are either suspended or occur on the wintering grounds, after migration. All birds have a limited pre-breeding moult in April-May. First-years resemble adults once the post-juvenile moult is completed, but the race *arizonae* in particular retains traces of juvenile plumage until well into the winter (see above). Tail feather shape is not very useful for ageing, despite retention of the juvenile tail, as the feathers are pointed in all ages. Skull ossification complete in first-years from 1 October.

MEASUREMENTS Wing (chord): male (n66) 66-76.2; female (n60) 63-75.7. Tail: male (n46) 53.3-65.3; female (n30) 51-63. Bill: male (n46) 8.9-10.4; female (n30) 8.6-10.4. Tarsus: male (n46) 15.7-18; female (n30) 15.5-17.8 (*passerina* averages shorter than the other races in all measurements, but there is considerable overlap).

GEOGRAPHICAL VARIATION Seven races generally recognised, with an eighth (*S. p. cicada*) also described from the pine forests of northernmost El Salvador. The races vary mainly in overall brightness, with southern breeding birds generally being brighter than northern ones.

S. p. passerina (Breeds in E North America, from CN Ontario and Nova Scotia south to E Texas and Georgia. Winters in the SE USA, including Florida, and in NE Mexico. Found throughout the year in SE USA, in N Florida and most of the Gulf coast) Described above.

S. p. arizonae (Breeds in W and C North America, from SE Alaska, SW North-west Territories and W Ontario south to N Baja California and the Mexican border, but apparently excluding a small area in N Texas, W Oklahoma and C Kansas. Winters in the southern parts of California, Arizona and New Mexico and SW Texas, and in W Mexico south to Oaxaca) It averages marginally larger than *passerina* and has a slightly paler rufous crown (although there is some overlap due to slight sexual variation in each race).

S. p. atremaeus (Resident in the highlands of N Mexico from Chihuahua south to Nayarit and east to Nuevo León) Similar to *arizonae* but averages darker and brighter above with heavier streaking, and darker grey on the breast (contrasting more with the white lower underparts). It has a greyer (less buffy) breast than *mexicana* in breeding plumage, but this difference is obscured in winter.

S. p. comparanda (Resident in NC Mexico, from Nayarit east to N Veracruz) Darker rufous above than *repetens*, but paler than *mexicana*.

S. p. repetens (Resident in Oaxaca and Guerrero in SC Mexico) Slightly paler above than *comparanda* but with slightly darker and browner (less greyish) sides of head.

S. p. mexicana (Resident in the highlands of S Mexico and adjacent NW Guatemala) Has a slightly but noticeably brighter and darker rufous crown than *passerina* and is also brighter above.

S. p. pinetorum (Resident in the highlands of Guatemala, Honduras and N Nicaragua, and also in the coastal lowlands from Belize to NE Nicaragua) Has a slightly darker rufous crown than *mexicana* and is also slightly brighter and 'cleaner-looking' overall.

VOICE The song, given from a prominent perch such as the top of a tree, is a monotonous trill of dry *chip* notes on one pitch. Although distinctive among the sparrows it is similar to the songs of Dark-eyed Junco (59) and Pine Warbler *Dendroica pinus*. The song of Worthen's Sparrow (75X) is also rather similar to Chipping's song. Calls include a short *tsip* or *chip*.

HABITS Nest is placed 1-3m (occasionally up to 8m) up in a thick bush, conifer sapling or vine tangle, or very occasionally on the ground; a thick cup of grasses, stems and rootlets, lined mainly with hair but also rootlets and fine grasses. 3-5 (usually 4) eggs are laid in March-August; they are pale blue, normally marked with brown or reddish-brown. Incubation period is 11-14 days and the young fledge after 8-12 days. Sometimes double-brooded. Feeds on seeds, and also on insects and their larvae in the breeding season. Forages mainly on the ground, in weedy fields and field edges, and on lawns; also in bushes. Sometimes visits feeders, especially in winter. Outside the breeding season generally found in flocks, often with other sparrows.

STATUS AND HABITAT Common throughout its range and found in a wide variety of habitats from subarctic and boreal through to tropical ecotones. In North America occurs mainly in open coniferous, oak and pine-oak woodland, forest edge, brushy field edges and brushy areas in towns and gardens; breeds up to 3700m in the southern Rockies. In Central America it is found in highland pine and pine-oak forests, edges and clearings, and also in lowland pine savanna from Belize to north-eastern Nicaragua.

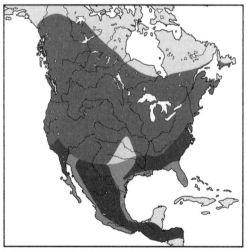

DISTRIBUTION AND MOVEMENTS Occurs from northern North America, south of the tundra, south through N and Central America to northern Nicaragua. Occurs only as a summer migrant in much of North America except the southern USA and the eastern seaboard north to Maryland. The two North American races are mainly migratory with birds moving south in the winter into the southern part of the breeding range and into northern and central Mexico; southern (including Central American) populations are sedentary. See also under Geographical Variation. Migrants arrive on breeding grounds from late March in

the south, early May in the north, and leave the breeding grounds from late September. Casual between October and April on Grand Bahama, Abaco, New Providence and Cuba in the West Indies. Vagrant to Costa Rica (1).

REFERENCES Armani (1985), Bent (1968), Bond (1985), Dickey and Van Rossem (1970), Dunn & Blom (1983), Ehrlich *et al.* (1988), Farrand (1983), Godfrey (1986), Kaufman (1990), Paynter & Storer (1970), Phillips (1966), Pyle & Henderson (1991), Pyle *et al.* (1987), Reynolds & Knapton (1984), Ridgway (1901), Terres (1980).

73   CLAY-COLOURED SPARROW
Spizella pallida   Plate 29

Described as *Emberiza pallida* Swainson 1832.

This close relative of Chipping (72) and Brewer's (74) Sparrows breeds mainly in the prairies and grasslands of north-central North America, wintering mainly in Mexico. It has been increasing its range eastwards recently and now breeds regularly in the Great Lakes region.

IDENTIFICATION 14cm. Slim and long-tailed, like Chipping Sparrow, but breeding adults with very different head pattern. Crown is brown, streaked black, and with an unstreaked pale buffy-grey median crown-stripe. Ear-coverts are buff-brown, bordered with darker brown, especially on the upper edge (eye-stripe) and lower edge (moustachial stripe). The broad supercilium is conspicuously whitish, the throat and submoustachial stripe are also whitish, separated by a narrow dark malar stripe, and there is a grey patch on the neck-sides. Rest of plumage is fairly like Chipping Sparrow but upperparts (including rump) are paler and buffer, underparts are tinged buff on the breast and flanks, and the wings lack rufous tones. Non-breeding adults are slightly buffer overall. First-winters resemble winter adults but average even buffer below, often with quite a contrast between buff breast, flanks and vent, and white belly and throat. Juveniles are streaked on breast and flanks; some or all the streaking is often retained through the autumn and very occasionally through the winter. Pale lores, pale median crown-stripe and lack of rufous tones in wings are good distinctions from most juvenile/first-winter Chipping Sparrows; see that species for other differences. Brewer's Sparrow is similar in all plumages but the crown lacks a conspicuous median stripe (it may occasionally have the appearance of a vague one) and is uniformly streaked blackish, the supercilium is more grey-brown and less well-defined and there is no prominent grey patch on the neck-sides (the grey neck-patch can be fairly obscure on breeding Clay-coloured but these always have a distinct crown-stripe, conspicuous whitish in summer, buffier and less conspicuous in winter). Brewer's is also slightly greyer overall, has a less contrasting face pattern, less buff (greyer) ear-coverts and a more prominent whitish eye-ring.

HYBRIDISATION There are records of hybridisation with Chipping and Brewer's Sparrows.

DESCRIPTION
Sexes very similar; juvenile clearly different from subsequent plumages.
Adult breeding Sides of crown buff-brown, heavily streaked black, contrasting with narrow but conspicuous, un-

streaked pale buffy-grey median crown-stripe. Supercilium broad, whitish, reaching to rear edge of ear-coverts. Lores and ear-coverts buff-brown, narrowly framed with dark brown; broadest on upper edge (forming a narrow eye-stripe from behind the eye) and the lower edge (forming a moustachial stripe). Throat and submoustachial stripe whitish, separated by a narrow dark malar stripe. Nape and neck-sides grey, narrowly streaked dark brown, often whitish adjoining rear edge of ear-coverts. Mantle and scapulars buff-brown, streaked with black; rump slightly greyer-buff and unstreaked, uppertail-coverts as rump but with fine blackish central streaks. Lesser coverts grey-brown. Rest of wings blackish-brown with pale buff feather edges, broadest on greater and median coverts, and tertials; greater and median coverts also tipped pale buff, forming two rather obscure wing-bars. Tail blackish-brown with pale buff feather edges. Underparts fairly uniform whitish, tinged pale buff on breast and flanks (forming a slight but noticeable contrast with the whiter throat and belly). Iris dark reddish-brown. Bill flesh with a dusky grey culmen and tip. Legs dark flesh.

Adult non-breeding Much as breeding but with a slightly stronger buff wash to the breast and flanks, slightly less conspicuous median crown-stripe, slightly buffier wash to the supercilium and a cleaner, more contrasting grey neck patch (unstreaked).

First-year Not always separable from adult by plumage but usually buffier on the breast and flanks in autumn, often with a clearer contrast between the buffy areas and the white throat and belly. Some may retain some juvenile flank streaking well into the autumn.

Juvenile Considerably duller and buffier on the head and breast (although has a dull version af the adult's head pattern) and has diffuse but noticeable dark streaking on the breast and flanks.

SEXING Sexes are similar; males average whiter on the supercilium and females buffier, but this is normally only noticeable in mated pairs and is of even less value in autumn when all birds may show a buff wash to the supercilium.

MOULT AND AGEING The post-juvenile moult is partial, occurring in July-October; it occurs mostly on the breeding grounds but some birds suspend their contour moult and complete it on the winter grounds. The post-breeding moult is complete and occurs in July-August on the breeding grounds. All birds have a partial/incomplete pre-breeding moult in March-May, which may include some remiges. Once the post-juvenile moult is completed all plumages are similar; many (but not all) first-winters can be identified by plumage, especially those which have retained some juvenile flank streaking (see under Description). Tail feather shape is not useful for ageing as all birds have quite pointed rectrices. Some first-summers may be told by relatively worn remiges and rectrices, but resemble adults in plumage. Skull ossification complete in first-years from 1 November.

MEASUREMENTS Wing (chord): male (n118) 58-66; female (n108) 56-63.8. Tail male (n18) 55.4-62; female (n8) 52.8-61. Bill: male (n18) 8.6-10; female (n8) 8.9-9.9. Tarsus: male (n18) 16.7-18.5; female (n8) 16.8-18.

GEOGRAPHICAL VARIATION Monotypic.

VOICE The song, given from an exposed perch, is a short series of 2-4 insect-like buzzes, on one pitch or varying only slightly. Calls include a weak *chip*.

HABITS Nest is placed low in a deciduous bush or low conifer, occasionally on the ground; a cup of grass and weed stems lined with fine grass and hair. 3-5 eggs are laid in May-July; they are greenish-blue spotted/speckled with brown and black. Incubation period is 10-14 (usually 10-12) days and the young fledge after 7-9 days, before they can fly. Sometimes double-brooded. Feeds mainly on seeds but feeds young on insects and their larvae. Forages on the ground in the open, and also searches for insects in bushes. Generally fairly confiding. Migrates in flocks of 25-100 birds and often found in small flocks outside the breeding season, which often form larger mixed flocks with Chipping, Brewer's and other sparrows. Out of range birds often associate with Chipping Sparrows.

STATUS AND HABITAT Locally common and extending its range east through the Great Lakes region. Breeds in scrubby grasslands, shrubby thickets of alder and willow, brushy overgrown fields, tall scrub along streams or at pond or swamp edges, in overgrown clearings in deciduous and coniferous forest and in prairies with tall bushes. Winters mainly in open semi-arid areas with scattered bushes or scrub.

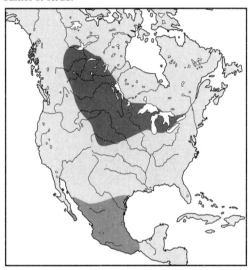

DISTRIBUTION AND MOVEMENTS Breeds in the prairie and southern boreal region of north-central North America from southern North-West Territories, eastern British Columbia and Wyoming east to the eastern Great Lakes region but excluding northern Ontario and the northern half of Manitoba. Winters in south-eastern Texas and through Mexico south to Oaxaca, occasionally western Chiapas. Most migration is through the centre of North America. Spring migration begins in late March with birds arriving on breeding grounds from early May. Autumn migration begins in late August. Casual in winter and on migration in the eastern and western coastal areas of North America; also in Guatemala and on Grand Bahama, New Providence and Cuba in the West Indies in late autumn and winter.

REFERENCES Armani (1985), Bent (1968), Bond (1985), Dunn & Blom (1983), Ehrlich *et al.* (1988), Farrand (1983), Godfrey (1986), Kaufman (1990), Knapton (1978 & 1980), Peterson & Chalif (1973), Pyle *et al.* (1987), Ridgway (1901), Terres (1980).

Described as *Spizella breweri* Cassin 1856.

Closely related to Chipping (72) and Clay-coloured (73) Sparrows but less well known, although it is common in sage brush and alpine meadows. The mountain race (*taverneri*) was originally described as a separate species and, although usually lumped with Brewer's Sparrow, it may deserve specific status; it is treated separately below as Timberline Sparrow (74X).

IDENTIFICATION 14cm. Shares the small, slim shape and longish notched tail with the previous two species but is greyer brown and more uniform on head and upperparts. Crown grey-brown, finely and uniformly streaked black with no pale median crown-stripe (although centre of crown may sometimes appear marginally paler); upperparts grey-brown, finely streaked darker except on rump and with two obscure buffy wing-bars; underparts whitish, washed pale grey-buff on breast and sides and whiter on throat and with a thin but noticeable dark malar stripe. Head pattern, apart from uniform crown, is similar to Clay-coloured but ear-coverts are paler and greyer-buff with a narrower dark outline (especially on the moustachial stripe), the whitish eye-ring is more conspicuous, the supercilium is greyer and rather less prominent and there is no conspicuous grey patch on the neck-sides. Further differs from Clay-coloured in its greyer-brown, rather than buffy, tone to the upperparts, breast and flanks. These grey-brown tones, with no rufous in the plumage, plus the pale lores and conspicuous whitish eye-ring, will easily distinguish it from non-breeding plumages of Chipping Sparrow. Juveniles are buffier overall and have dusky streaks on the breast and flanks. Timberline Sparrow is very difficult, perhaps impossible to distinguish from Brewer's in the field, although it averages slightly larger, and also slightly darker and greyer above. It has a distinct breeding habitat and there are apparently vocal differences, but the two are probably inseparable away from the breeding grounds.

HYBRIDISATION There is one record each of hybridisation with Clay-coloured Sparrow and with Chipping Sparrow.

DESCRIPTION
Sexes alike; juvenile clearly different from subsequent plumages. First-years may average slightly more buffy, especially below, than adults, but this should not be regarded as a reliable ageing criterion.
Adult/first-year Crown, nape and upperparts greyish buffy-brown; crown, nape, mantle, back and scapulars finely but noticeably streaked with blackish-brown. Rump is unstreaked but uppertail-coverts have obscure dusky central streaks. Supercilium pale grey-buff, reaching to rear edge of ear-coverts. Eye-ring whitish and quite conspicuous. Lores and ear-coverts greyish-buff with narrow dark upper and lower edges (forming obscure eye-stripe and moustachial stripe). Throat and submoustachial stripe whitish, separated by a narrow dark malar stripe. Neck-sides pale grey-buff with streaking obscure or absent but not forming a distinct patch. Lesser coverts grey-buff. Rest of wings blackish-brown with pale buff feather edges, broadest on greater and median coverts and tertials; greater and median coverts also tipped pale buff, forming two

rather obscure wing-bars. Tail blackish-brown with narrow buff-brown feather edges. Underparts whitish with a pale grey-buff wash to the breast and flanks, which contrasts slightly with the whiter throat. Iris dark reddish-brown. Bill dusky-horn with dark flesh lower mandible. Legs dark flesh. Similar year-round although pale grey-buff wash on underparts and supercilium is more noticeable in fresh autumn plumage, with first-years perhaps averaging more buffy than adults.
Juvenile Buffier on upperparts, supercilium, breast and flanks and with dusky streaks on breast and flanks. The wing-bars are also slightly broader and buffier. Some of these characters may be retained well into the autumn.

MOULT AND AGEING The post-juvenile moult is partial and the post-breeding moult is complete; both occur in July-August, mainly on the breeding grounds, although first-years sometimes retain a few juvenile feathers over the autumn migration. All birds have a variable pre-breeding moult, from just some head feathers to all the body feathers, the tertials and occasionally other flight feathers, in February-April. First-years resemble adults once the post-juvenile moult is completed, although some first-years retain traces of juvenile plumage well into the autumn (see above). Tail feather shape is not useful for ageing as all ages have pointed rectrices. Skull ossification complete in first-years from 15 October.

MEASUREMENTS Measurements for both Brewer's and Timberline Sparrow are included below, from Pyle *et al.* (wing) and Ridgway. Timberline averages longer than Brewer's in wing and tail, although there is considerable overlap. Separate measurements (from Oberholser) are also given.
Brewer's/Timberline Sparrow combined. Wing (chord): male (n39) 58-66; female (n40) 55.9-65.8. Tail: male (n19) 56.9-63.2; female (n10) 57.4-63.5. Bill: male (n19) 8.6-10; female (n10) 8.6-9.1. Tarsus: male (n19) 16.5-18; female (n10) 16.3-19.
Brewer's Sparrow. Wing (chord): male 60.5-64.5; female 57.4-59.9. Tail: male 58.4-67.1; female 57.4-59.9. Bill: male 8.1-8.6; female 8.1-8.6. Tarsus: male 16.8-18; female 16.3-17.5.

GEOGRAPHICAL VARIATION Brewer's Sparrow has traditionally been split into two races; however, recent research suggeasts that the two forms should be treated as separate species, based on differences in morphology, ecology and vocalisations. Brewer's Sparrow would thus become monotypic, with Timberline Sparrow also being a monotypic species.

VOICE The song, given from a prominent perch such as the top of a bush, a fence post or overhead wire, is a long and sustained series of buzzy notes and trills, changing frequently and abruptly in pitch and tempo. Calls include various nervous lisps and chip notes, the most frequent call being similar to Clay-coloured.

HABITS Nest is placed low in a sagebrush or other bush; a cup of grass and weed stems lined with fine grasses and hair. 3-4 eggs are laid in April-July; they are greenish-blue speckled with reddish-brown. Incubation period is 11-13 days and the young fledge after 8-9 days. Males may gather at dawn and dusk to sing in chorus. Feeds mainly on seeds but rears its young on insects. Forages on the ground, in tall grass and in bushes, especially sage bushes. Outside the breeding season usually found in small flocks, often with other sparrow species.

STATUS AND HABITAT Common throughout most of its range. Breeds on sagebrush flats and other open scrubby areas in the lowlands and plains of the Great Basin and the western prairies. In the Californian mountains, Brewer's nests up to 2000m and apparently birds nesting at high altitudes tend towards Timberline Sparrow in size and coloration. Winters in open, semi-arid areas and grassland.

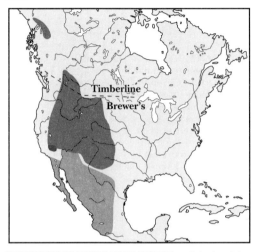

DISTRIBUTION AND MOVEMENTS Breeds in the plains and foothills of western North America, from extreme southern British Columbia and Saskatchewan south to south-central California and north-western Texas. Short- to long-distance migrant, wintering from just south of the breeding range in the south-western USA south to central Mexico. Casual on the west coast of North America on migration, more frequently in autumn.

REFERENCES Armani (1985), Bent (1968), Dunn & Blom (1983), Farrand (1983), Godfrey (1986), Kaufman (1990), Oberholser (1974), Peterson & Chalif (1973), Pyle & Henderson (1991), Pyle *et al.* (1987), Ridgway (1901), Sibley & Monroe (1990), Terres (1980).

74X TIMBERLINE SPARROW
Spizella (breweri) taverneri   Plate 29

Described as *Spizella taverneri* Swarth & Brooks 1925.

This form was originally described as a separate species from Brewer's Sparrow but has generally been regarded as a race of that species. However, its distinctly different breeding habitat indicates that Brewer's and Timberline might best be regarded as allospecies within a single superspecies. Recent research suggests that this form deserves specific status (J. C. Barlow pers. comm.).

IDENTIFICATION 14cm. This 'newly promoted' species can be readily identified by its distinct breeding habitat (very different to Brewer's) and there are also apparently differences in vocalisations. Note however that Brewer's and Timberline Sparrows are probably not separable in the field by plumage, at least not without extensive expe-

rience of both forms. Timberline Sparrow is slightly darker and greyer above than Brewer's with darker streaks on crown and upperparts but, while this may be apparent in a series of museum skins, it is probably not reliable for identifying birds in the field. Juvenile Timberline is apparently more heavily streaked on the underparts than juvenile Brewer's.

DESCRIPTION This species is very similar to Brewer's Sparrow and a full description is not repeated here.

MOULT AND AGEING As far as is known, moult strategy and ageing techniques are similar to Brewer's Sparrow.

MEASUREMENTS Wing (chord): male 61.5-66.3; female 59.6-62. Tail: male 62.5-68.1; female 59.6-62. Bill: male 7.1-8.6; female 8.1-8.6. Tarsus: male 17-18; female 17-18 (measurements from Oberholser). See also under Brewer's Sparrow; Timberline averages larger but there is overlap in all measurements.

GEOGRAPHICAL VARIATION Monotypic, but traditionally regarded as a race of Brewer's Sparrow.

VOICE Apparently differs from Brewer's but few details are known to the authors; the song of Timberline may be more interrupted than that of Brewer's with a regular sequence of trills and stops.

HABITS As Brewer's Sparrow except that the nest is built in a dwarf shrub or bush rather than in a sagebush, and it is said to be more wary, at least on the breeding grounds.

STATUS AND HABITAT Fairly common but local. Breeds in alpine meadows and scrubby valleys with birch and other scrub, high in the mountains at or above the treeline (above 1500m). Winters in open, semi-arid areas and grassland, probably with Brewer's Sparrow.

DISTRIBUTION AND MOVEMENTS Breeds in the mountains of south-western Yukon/interior north-western British Columbia and south-eastern British Columbia/south-western Alberta. Medium- to long-distance migrant wintering in the south-western USA and probably also in north-western Mexico. Nothing is known of its casual occurrences as it has generally been regarded as a race of Brewer's Sparrow with racial identification not being attempted.

REFERENCES Armani (1985), Bent (1968), Ehrlich *et al.* (1988), Oberholser (1974), Sibley & Monroe (1990), Swarth & Brooks (1925).

75   FIELD SPARROW
Spizella pusilla   Plate 28

Described as *Fringilla pusilla* Wilson 1810.

This bird is fairly common in south-eastern North America, north to the Great Lakes area, where its distinctive song is characteristic of brushy overgrown fields in summer. Worthen's Sparrow (75X) of north-eastern Mexico was originally described as a separate species and, although long regarded as a rare and little-known race of Field Sparrow, differences in vocalisations as well as plumage have strengthened the case for regarding it as a species in its own right, as Sibley & Monroe (1990) have done. It is described separately below.

IDENTIFICATION 15cm. Pink bill and narrow but conspicuous white eye-ring in a rather plain face are characteristic, giving the bird a 'gentle' facial jizz. Crown and nape rufous-brown, sides of head grey with ear-coverts faintly outlined in rufous. Upperparts brown streaked blackish and with two narrow white wing-bars. Underparts pale grey with a buff wash on breast and flanks. Juveniles are quite distinct with a paler, browner (not rufous) crown, buffier wing-bars and usually indistinct dusky streaks on the crown and breast; note however that juvenile Field is noticeably less streaky than other juvenile *Spizella* sparrows. American Tree Sparrow (71) is similar in overall pattern but is always easily distinguished by its bicoloured bill (black above, yellow below); it also has a variable blackish spot in the centre of the breast. Worthen's Sparrow is similar to the western race of Field Sparrow but is uniform grey on the sides of the head (lacking any rufous, even on the eye-stripe) and has a slightly bolder white eye-ring. It is also noticeably paler and greyer on the upperparts with a pronounced grey 'collar' on the nape and neck-sides and less of a buff tinge to the breast.

HYBRIDISATION There is apparently a record of hybridisation with Vesper Sparrow (77) but no details are known.

DESCRIPTION
Sexes very similar; juvenile clearly different from subsequent plumages.

Adult/first-year Crown and nape rufous-brown with a narrow and indistinct greyish median crown-stripe. Rest of head fairly uniform pale grey but with ear-coverts marginally browner-grey and outlined with rufous-brown, broadest in upper rear corner. Narrow but conspicuous white eye-ring. Mantle and scapulars pale buffy-rufous, streaked with blackish-brown. Back and rump pale grey-brown, unstreaked. Uppertail-coverts similar but with indistinct dusky centres. Lesser coverts grey. Rest of wings blackish with buff feather edges, broadest on greater and median coverts and tertials. Greater and median coverts also tipped white-forming two narrow but fairly conspicuous wing-bars. Bend of wing white. Tail blackish-brown with narrow grey feather edges. Underparts pale greyish-white, washed buff on breast and flanks. Iris dark reddish-brown. Bill pink. Legs pinkish-flesh.

Juvenile Averages buffier, especially on wing-bars, crown is pale brown, lacking rufous tones and usually with some indistinct dark streaking. Breast also generally has indistinct dusky streaks.

SEXING Female may average slightly duller and paler rufous on the head; this is unreliable for sexing single birds but it may be noticeable in some mated pairs in spring/summer.

MOULT AND AGEING The post-juvenile moult is partial/incomplete, occurs in July-October, and occasionally includes some of the rectrices. The post-breeding moult is complete, occurring in July-September. There is no pre-breeding moult. All moults occur mainly on the breeding grounds, but may sometimes be completed on migration in migratory populations. First-years resemble adults after the post-juvenile moult is completed, but have more pointed rectrices, on average; retained juvenile rectrices also average more worn by spring and some first-years may show a contrast between adult-type and juvenile-type rectrices through the first-year. Skull ossification complete in first-years from 1 November over most of range, 15 October in extreme southern populations.

MEASUREMENTS Wing (chord): male (n30) 62-72; fe-

male (n30) 58-67. Tail: male (n31) 58.4-71.9; female (n17) 54.3-62.2. Bill: male (n31) 8.6-9.9; female (n17) 8.6-9.9. Tarsus: male (n31) 17.3-19.8; female (n17) 17.3-18.3 (*arenacea* is larger than *pusilla* in all measurements, but there may be some overlap; a larger sample is required, especially of *arenacea*).

GEOGRAPHICAL VARIATION Two similar races.
S. p. pusilla (Breeds in E North America from New England and S Georgia west through the S Great Lakes region, including S Ontario and extreme S Quebec, and the Mississippi Valley. Winters in the breeding range south of the Great Lakes and in Florida, S Louisiana and Texas) Described above. Wing (18 males): 62.2-67.3 Tail (18 males): 58.4-65.3 Bill (18 males) 8.6-9.9 Tarsus (18 males): 17.3-18.3.
S. p. arenacea (Breeds from N Dakota and S Manitoba and W Minnesota south to N Texas. Winters in the central and southern parts of the breeding range and south through the rest of Texas and adjacent NE Mexico) It is slightly larger than *pusilla*, paler and greyer on the head, with less rufous outlining the ear-coverts and has a broader grey median crown-stripe. Wing (3 males): 68.3-71.1. Tail (3 males): 66-71.9. Bill (3 males): 9.4-9.9. Tarsus (3 males): 19-19.8.

Worthen's Sparrow *S. (p). wortheni* is described separately below.

VOICE The song, given from a prominent perch such as the top of a weed or bush, is a series of slow, clear whistles accelerating into a brief trill; the rhythm has been likened to a ping-pong ball being dropped on the ground. Calls include a rather weak *tsip.*

HABITS Nest is generally placed low down in a bush or small tree, sometimes also on the ground under a low branch or in a grass clump; a cup of grasses, weed stems and rootlets, lined with fine grasses, hair and sometimes thin bark strips. 3-6 eggs are laid in April-September; they are white or pale blue marked with reddish-brown. Incubation period is 10.5-17 (usually 11-12) days and the young fledge after 7-8 days, a few days before they can fly. Male sometimes sings at night, especially when the moon is full. Feeds mainly on seeds but rears its young on insects. Forages on the ground and sometimes low in bushes. Usually found in pairs or small flocks in winter, and often in larger flocks with other sparrows on migration.

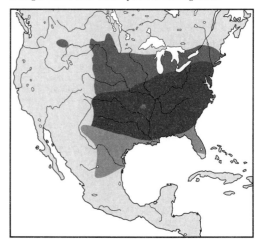

STATUS AND HABITAT Fairly common in neglected brushy fields, overgrown scrubby pastures, woodland edges, new plantations and other overgrown grassy areas with scattered bushes or trees.

DISTRIBUTION AND MOVEMENTS Occurs in eastern North America, north to the Great Lakes area. Northern populations (from the Dakotas and Nebraska east through the southern Great Lakes area and New England) are medium-distance migrants with birds moving into the southern part of the breeding range in winter, and also wintering south of the breeding range in southern Texas, coastal Louisiana, Florida and north-eastern Mexico (where they may overlap with the range of Worthen's Sparrow). See also under Geographical Variation. Migrants leave wintering grounds in March, arriving on breeding grounds from April, and leave the breeding grounds in September. Rare vagrant to California.

REFERENCES Armani (1985), Bent (1968), Dunn & Blom (1983), Godfrey (1986), Gray (1958), Peterson & Chalif (1973), Pyle *et al.* (1987), Pyle & Henderson (1991), Ridgway (1901), Schneider (1981), Sibley & Monroe (1990), Terres (1980).

75X WORTHEN'S SPARROW
Spizella (pusilla) wortheni   Plate 28

Described as *Spizella wortheni* Ridgway 1884.

This highly localised and relatively little-known sparrow of north-eastern Mexico has long been regarded as a race of Field Sparrow. However, differences in song and habitat, as well as in plumage, indicate that it is probably better treated as a separate species. It forms a superspecies with Field Sparrow.

IDENTIFICATION 15cm. Similar to Field Sparrow, especially the western race, but the sides of the head are entirely grey, with no rufous on the ear-coverts and no rufous eye-stripe. The white eye-ring is quite prominent, emphasised by the lack of eye-stripe. The crown is rufous, lacking a grey median crown-stripe, and the nape and neck-sides are grey, continuous with the ear-coverts, forming a noticeable collar which separates the rufous cap from the upperparts. The upperparts are paler and greyer than in Field Sparrow and the underparts have less of a buff wash.

DESCRIPTION
Sexes alike; juvenile apparently undescribed.
Adult/first-year Crown fairly pale rufous-brown. Forehead, lores, superciliary area, ear-coverts, neck-sides and nape grey, forming a noticeable collar on the nape. Eyering white. Mantle and scapulars rather pale greyish-buff with heavy blackish streaking (the streaks are narrowly edged with dull rufous). Back, rump and uppertail-coverts distinctly greyer with indistinct brownish streaking. Wings dark brown with pale grey-buff feather edges, broadest on greater coverts and tertials. Greater and median coverts also tipped greyish-white forming two obscure wing-bars. Tail dark brown with narrow pale grey feather edges. Underparts pale greyish-white with a very faint buff wash to the breast and flanks. Iris dark reddish-brown. Bill pink. Legs flesh. Plumage similar year-round but wing-bars may be even less distinct when plumage is worn (April-July).

MOULT AND AGEING The post-breeding moult is complete but the extent of the post-juvenile moult is not known. There is probably no pre-breeding moult. No ageing criteria are known once the post-juvenile moult is completed.

MEASUREMENTS Wing (chord): male (n7) 66.8-70.1; female (n2) 64.8-68.3. Tail: male (n7) 59.7-64.3; female (n2) 57.7-63.5. Bill: male (n7) 9.4-9.9; female (n2) 8.9-9.1. Tarsus: male (n7) 17.5-18.5; female (n2) 17-17.5.

GEOGRAPHICAL VARIATION Two races described, but there have been no records of the *browni* race since 1961, despite searches.
   S. w. wortheni (Occurs over most of the known range) Described above.
   S. w. browni (Has only been recorded from the vicinity of Sombrerete in NW Zacatecas) Slightly darker above than *wortheni*, with the base colour greyer and less buffy. The few specimens collected from San Luis Potosí are apparently intermediate between *browni* and *wortheni*.

VOICE The song, given from a small bush, is quite different from Field Sparrow, being a slow, monotonous trill on one pitch; it has been likened by several observers to a cross between the songs of Field Sparrow and Chipping Sparrow (72).

HABITS Nest is placed low in a bush or weed clump, usually 1-1.5m up but occasionally close to or even on the ground. 3-4 eggs are laid in May-July; they are apparently closer in appearance to those of Clay-coloured Sparrow (73) than to those of Field Sparrow. Little has been recorded of the food taken. Forages on the ground, generally in fairly high yucca grassland with clumps of juniper. Outside the breeding season found in flocks, generally of 8-12 birds (but occasionally up to 30-50). These flocks do not usually associate with other sparrow species but have occasionally been joined by single Clay-coloured and Vesper Sparrows. These winter flocks generally remain close to the breeding areas and break up in March, prior to breeding.

STATUS AND HABITAT Rare and local, it is considered threatened by BirdLife International. A detailed recent investigation has found that Worthen's Sparrow has probably declined significantly due to the destruction or modification of its shrubby grassland habitat. It is found in mesquite-juniper and yucca-juniper grassland, often where it borders open pine-oak forest, at 1200-2400m. It seems unable to tolerate agricultural improvement to, or overgrazing of, this rather specific habitat, and it seems unlikely that there are still large tracts of this habitat available within its historic range in north-eastern Mexico.

DISTRIBUTION AND MOVEMENTS More or less endemic to north-eastern Mexico, although there is one old record from New Mexico. It formerly occurred in Zacatecas, Coahuila, Nuevo León and Tamaulipas, with isolated records (possibly indicating now extirpated populations) from Chihuahua (1), San Luis Potosí (3), Veracruz (1) and Puebla (1) as well as the New Mexico type specimen. It is presently known only from south-eastern Coahuila and western Nuevo León. The two populations presently known are not migratory, with only local movements occurring in the non-breeding season. Thus the previous supposition that Worthen's Sparrow might be migratory (based on the isolated records from Veracruz and Puebla in the non-breeding season) may not be correct and those records may have represented the remnants of southern, more or less sedentary, populations.

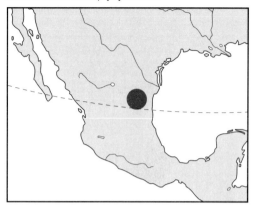

REFERENCES Armani (1985), Bent (1968), Burleigh & Lowery (1942), Collar *et al.* (1992 &1994), Delaney (1992), Ehrlich *et al.* (1988), Hardy & Wolf (1977), Peterson & Chalif (1973), Ridgway (1901), Sibley & Monroe (1990), Webster & Orr (1954), Wege *et al.* (1993).

76   BLACK-CHINNED SPARROW
Spizella atrogularis   Plate 24

Described as *Spinites atrogularis* Cabanis 1851.

Rather different in plumage from the other *Spizella* sparrows, this is a sparrow of arid brush and chapparal, found in the south-western USA and Mexico.

IDENTIFICATION 15cm. Shape similar to the other *Spizella* sparrows but plumage distinct, with grey head, rump and underparts contrasting with brown back, which is streaked blackish. Bill pink. Males have contrasting black lores and throat, especially in summer; females and winter males have these areas dark grey or greyish-black and not so contrasting. Juvenile is similar to adult but has the grey body areas more prominently washed brownish, lores and throat uniform with rest of head, faint darker streaking on underparts and buffier wing-bars. Readily told from Dark-eyed (59) and Yellow-eyed (60) Juncos by lack of white in tail.

DESCRIPTION
Sexes similar but separable by plumage, at least in breeding (summer); juvenile different from subsequent plumages.
Adult male breeding Whole of head pure grey with sharply contrasting black lores and throat, the black extending as a narrow band across the forehead. Upper mantle, rump, uppertail-coverts and breast also grey, underparts becoming paler greyish-white on belly and undertail-coverts. Lower mantle, back and scapulars bright brown, tinged pale rufous, and streaked blackish. Lesser coverts dark grey-brown with paler grey fringes. Rest of wings blackish-brown with pale buff feather edges, broadest on greater and median coverts and tertials. Greater coverts have more buffy-rufous edges and paler buff tips; these, combined with the buff edges to the median coverts, form two indistinct wing-bars. Tail blackish with narrow grey

feather edges. Iris dark reddish-brown. Bill pink. Legs dark flesh.
Adult male non-breeding Very similar but lores and throat are slightly duller greyish-black.
Adult female breeding Generally similar to male but lores and chin blackish-grey, merging into paler grey throat and forming a smaller, less contrasting dark patch. Grey head also often faintly washed brownish.
Adult female non-breeding Similar but lores and chin with more restricted blackish; often grey or buffy-grey, uniform with rest of head. Grey head may have a stronger buffy-brown wash. First-year female is generally indistinguishable from adult female in both breeding and non-breeding.
First-winter male As adult female and not generally distinguishable, although may average marginally darker on the throat and lores.
First-summer male As breeding adult male but may average marginally duller on the lores and throat.
Juvenile Similar to dull female in winter plumage in having lores and throat uniform with rest of head, but underparts are faintly streaked darker, head and rump are faintly mottled/washed brownish and wing-bars are broader and buffier.

MOULT AND AGEING The post-juvenile moult is partial and the post-breeding moult is complete; both occur in July-August. All birds have a limited pre-breeding moult, probably involving only some head and throat feathers, in February-April. Once the post-juvenile moult is completed, first-years are generally indistinguishable from adults by plumage; first-year males resemble first-year/ adult females in non-breeding (winter) plumage and become much as adult males in breeding (summer), although they may average marginally duller on the lores and throat. The shape of the rectrices does not seem to be very useful for ageing, with much overlap between adult and juvenile. Skull ossification complete in first-years from 1 November.

MEASUREMENTS Wing (chord): male (n45) 60-69.9; female (n43) 57-64.8. Tail: male (n15) 61.2-74.2; female (n13) 59.9-69.9. Bill: male (n15) 8.6-10.2; female (n13) 8.6-9.9. Tarsus: male (n15) 17.5-20.3; female (n13) 18-19.8.

GEOGRAPHICAL VARIATION Four races, which differ only slightly from each other and are not generally identifiable in the field.
S. a. evura (Occurs in SE California, S Nevada and extreme SW Utah, where it is a summer visitor; and in SE Arizona, S New Mexico, extreme W Texas, NE Sonora and Chihuahua, where it is resident). Winter range of migrant populations is incompletely known, but some winter in SE California, S Arizona and N Sonora) Similar to *atrogularis* but averages slightly smaller and male has less black on the lores.
S. a. cana (Breeds on the eastern slope of the coastal mountains, and on the western slope of the Sierra Nevada, from SC California in Monterey County south to N Baja California; winters mainly in S Baja California) Slightly darker, and less pure grey, than *evura*, especially in the south of its range; also averages slightly smaller but there is much overlap in measurements.
S. a. caurina (Breeds in the coastal ranges of C California, from Contra Costa County south to San Benito County; winter range not well known but recorded from Santa Cruz Island in winter) Very similar to *cana* but averages slightly greyer on the head, brighter on

the upperparts and less whitish on the belly.

S. a. atrogularis (Resident on the central plateau of Mexico, from Durango, S Coahuila and W Nuevo León south to N Oaxaca) Described above.

VOICE The song, given from an open perch, is a series of plaintive whistles which runs into a rapid trill. Calls include a faint *tsip* and a louder, sharp, high-pitched *tslip*.

HABITS Nest is placed low down in a thick bush; a cup of dried grasses, lined with finer grasses and sometimes hair. 2-5 (usually 2-4) eggs are laid in April-July; they are bluish-white, sometimes marked with reddish-brown. Incubation period is 13 days; fledging period is unrecorded. Nests in loose colonies. Feeds on seeds and insects, foraging on the ground and low in bushes and cacti. Shy and often difficult to observe; often sitting still for long periods hidden in the middle of a bush, especially if it has been recently disturbed. Flight is short and low. Generally found in pairs or small groups in winter, which may join mixed sparrow flocks.

STATUS AND HABITAT Uncommon to locally fairly common in arid scrub, brushy hillsides, chaparral, sagebrush and pedregal; mainly in highland areas at 1800-2300m.

DISTRIBUTION AND MOVEMENTS Occurs in the south-western USA, north to central California and extreme south-western Utah, and in Mexico south to Oaxaca.

Races *caurina* and *cana* and north-western populations of *evura* are short distance migrants, wintering in southern Arizona, extreme south-eastern California, southern Baja California and north-western Mexico. Other populations are sedentary. See also under Geographical Variation.

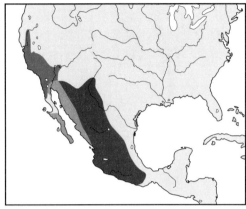

REFERENCES Armani (1985), Bent (1968), Peterson & Chalif (1973), Farrand (1983), Dunn & Blom (1983), Paynter & Storer (1970), Pyle *et al.* (1987), Ridgway (1901), Terres (1980), Oberholser (1974).

POOECETES

One species which is rather featureless apart from white outer tail feathers, conspicuous in flight. It also has a more conspicuous eye-ring than most North American sparrows and characteristic (but usually hidden) chestnut lesser coverts.

77   VESPER SPARROW
Pooecetes gramineus   Plate 31

Described as *Fringilla graminea* Gmelin 1789.

A fairly common bird across much of North America and characteristic of open farmland, prairie and sagebrush.

IDENTIFICATION 16cm. A fairly stocky, short-tailed sparrow with white outer tail feathers, conspicuous in flight. Chestnut lesser coverts are also distinctive, but are difficult to see (and are lacking in juveniles. More visible field marks are the dark ear-coverts, with pale surrounds and paler centre, and the conspicuous white eye-ring. Crown and upperparts are brown or grey-brown, streaked darker, and with obscure buffy wing-bars. Underparts whitish with dark streaking on breast and flanks. Bill quite conical with a straight culmen. No other North American brown streaked sparrow has obvious white outer tail feathers. Confusion is possible with female or first-winter Smith's Longspur (45), but these are much buffier, especially on the underparts, lack the bold eye-ring and chestnut lesser coverts, and have less prominent streaking on the underparts; the bill is also more slender.

HYBRIDISATION There is a record of hybridisation with Field Sparrow (75) but no details are known.

DESCRIPTION
Sexes alike; juveniles similar to adults but distinguishable. **Adult/first-year** Crown and nape greyish-brown, finely streaked darker brown. Supercilium pale greyish-buff, often with some very fine darker streaks. Lores and ear-coverts grey-brown with darker brown borders, noticeably broader in the upper and lower rear corners. Sides of neck pale buffy-white streaked dark brown. Submoustachial stripe whitish, joining with buffy-white neck-sides and pale grey-buff supercilium to form pale surrounds to ear-coverts. Upperparts grey-brown, streaked dark brown. Lesser coverts chestnut. Rest of wing dark brown with pale buff feather edges, broadest on tertials. Greater and median coverts also with pale buff tips forming two obscure wing-bars. Bend of wing white. Tail dark brown with narrow buff feather edges; T6 is mostly white and T5 is white on the distal half of the edge of the outer web. Narrow malar stripe dark brown, separating the whitish submoustachial stripe and the whitish throat. Underparts dull white with dark brown streaks on breast and flanks, and often some fine streaking on throat. Iris dark reddish-brown. Bill dusky horn with flesh lower mandible. Legs flesh. Similar year-round but upperparts appear paler and greyer in spring due to feather wear. Underparts may also have a faint buff tinge in fresh autumn plumage.
Juvenile Slightly buffier overall; wing-bars are broader and buffier and lesser coverts lack chestnut.

T6   T5   T5

Outermost (T6) and two examples of second outermost tail feathers (T5) of adult.

MOULT AND AGEING The post-juvenile moult is partial/incomplete (occasionally including the outermost primary), occurring in July-October. The post-breeding moult is complete, occurring in July-October. There is no pre-breeding moult. All moults occur on the breeding grounds, prior to migration. Once the post-juvenile moult is completed first-years resemble adults. Tail feather shape does not seem to be useful for ageing. Birds showing a contrastingly fresh outer primary in autumn are first-years (moulting adults moult the inner primaries first); this is probably less useful in spring due to wear of all feathers. Also some first-years may show duller chestnut lesser coverts, but this is not a reliable ageing criterion. Skull ossification complete in first-years from 15 November.

MEASUREMENTS Wing (chord): male (n62) 73.7-87; female (n60) 72-83.2. Tail: male (n42) 52.8-68.6; female (n30) 55.1-68.1. Bill: male (n42) 10.2-12.1; female (n30) 10.2-12.5. Tarsus: male (n42) 19.8-22.1; female (n30) 19.8-22.4 (*confinis* averages the longest and *affinis* the shortest in wing and tail).

GEOGRAPHICAL VARIATION Three very similar races, which are probably not separable in the field.
    P. g. gramineus (Breeds in E North America from E Ontario and Illinois east to Nova Scotia and N Carolina. Winters from the SE USA north to Virginia on the Atlantic coast and south through E Mexico, occasionally to Yucatán) Described above. Wing (27, sexes combined): 72.9-83.2. Tail (27, sexes combined): 55.1-66.
    P. g. confinis (Breeds from W Ontario and Missouri west to WC British Columbia and E California. Winters in the extreme SW USA and W Mexico, mainly in the highlands, south to Oaxaca) Similar to *gramineus* but averages slightly larger and paler and greyer on the upperparts, has a slightly more slender bill, and the streaking on the underparts is slightly paler brown. Wing (25, sexes combined): 76.2-86.6. Tail (25, sexes combined): 57.7-68.6.
    P. g. affinis (Breeds in the coastal districts of Washington and Oregon in the NW USA and winters from CW California to NW Baja California) Similar to *confinis* but averages smaller and slightly buffier (less grey) overall. Wing (10, sexes combined): 72.4-80. Tail (10, sexes combined): 52.8-60.5.

VOICE The song, generally given from a high perch in a tree or bush but sometimes in flight, is rich and melodious; it consists of two long slurred whistles followed by two higher notes and then a descending jumble of short trills and twitters. Calls include a fairly loud *hsip*.

HABITS Nest is placed on the ground, often hidden by a grass clump but sometimes in the open; a cup of grasses, rootlets and occasionally weed stems, lined with fine grass and hair. 3-6 (usually 3-5) eggs are laid in April-August; they are whitish, variously speckled and scrawled with browns and sometimes purplish-grey. Incubation period is 11-14 days and the young fledge after 7-14 days, often before they can fly. Double- or triple-brooded. Frequently sings late in the evening and even during the night. Males court on the ground and may fight vigorously for a female. Feeds on seeds and also insects and their larvae during the breeding season. Forages almost entirely on the ground in weedy fields and field edges, roadsides and other open areas, occasionally flying into trees or bushes when disturbed. Often found in small flocks on migration and in winter, sometimes with other species.

STATUS AND HABITAT Fairly common throughout its range. Breeds in open farmland, prairies and other grassland, weedy fields, sage brush, savanna, arid scrub and forest clearings; up to 4000m in the Rockies. Often found on roadsides in arable areas. In agricultural land, prefers field edges with hedgerows containing tall bushes and trees which it can use for song posts. Found in similar dry, open habitats on migration and in winter, including semi-arid scrub and weedy fields in the highlands of Mexico. Avoids dense forest and damp habitats.

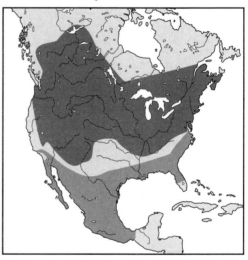

DISTRIBUTION AND MOVEMENTS Breeds across most of northern and central North America, south of the tundra, but only locally on the Pacific coast. Short- to medium-distance migrant wintering in the southern USA and through much of Mexico. See also under Geographical Variation. Arrives on breeding grounds from late March and leaves from early September. Casual in coastal south-western British Columbia in autumn, in eastern North America north to southern Ontario and Nova Scotia, and also in Yucatán, Mexico, in winter. Vagrant to Grand Bahama in the West Indies in autumn and winter.

REFERENCES Armani (1985), Bent (1968), Best & Rodenhouse (1984), Bond (1985), Dunn & Blom (1983), Ehrlich *et al.* (1988), Godfrey (1986), Gray (1958), Kaufman (1990), Oberholser (1974), Paynter & Storer (1970), Peterson & Chalif (1973), Pyle *et al.* (1987), Ridgway (1901), Terres (1980), Yunick (1984).

CHONDESTES

One species which is rather large and stocky, with a very boldly patterned head and tail.

78   LARK SPARROW
Chondestes grammacus   Plate 30

Described as *Fringilla grammaca* Say 1823.

A very distinctive sparrow which is common throughout much of the USA and northern Mexico, but scarce east of the Mississippi.

IDENTIFICATION 17cm. Fairly large and with a very distinctive head and tail pattern. The complicated pattern of chestnut, white and black on the head and the longish, rounded black tail with conspicuous white corners (especially noticeable in flight) make the adult unmistakable. Note also the black spot on the centre of the breast. Juvenile is streaked below and has a much duller head pattern but the tail pattern is still distinctive.

DESCRIPTION
Sexes alike; juvenile clearly different from subsequent plumages.
Adult/first-year Median crown-stripe white. Broad lateral crown-stripes chestnut, becoming black in front of eye and also narrowly bordered on lower edge with black. Long supercilium and broad crescent below eye white. Ear-coverts chestnut bordered above and below by black eye-stripe (including lores) and moustachial stripe. White submoustachial stripe, area behind ear-coverts and the supercilium form complete surrounds to the ear-coverts. Malar stripe black, broadening noticeably at lower end. Nape and neck-sides grey-brown, unstreaked. Upperparts greyish buffy-brown, heavily streaked with black on the mantle and scapulars. Lesser coverts grey-brown with paler grey-buff fringes. Rest of wings blackish with pale buff edges to all feathers, broadest on greater coverts and tertials. Greater and median coverts tipped pale buff or whitish, forming two fairly obscure wing-bars. The primaries are extensively pale buff to buffy-white at the base forming a prominent patch in the closed wing. Tail blackish with white spots at the distal end of all but the central rectrices; largest on rectrix 6 (distal half white) and decreasing in size to small white spots at the tips of rectrices 3 and 2. Throat white; rest of underparts whitish, tinged pale grey on the breast and pale greyish-buff on the flanks, and with conspicuous black spot in the centre of the breast. Iris dark reddish-brown. Bill dusky grey, slightly paler on lower mandible. Legs flesh. Similar year-round but tail may appear slightly more brownish in spring through wear and fading.

Tail pattern

Juvenile Sides of crown and ear-coverts dull rufous-brown, indistinct crown-stripe, supercilium and patch below eye pale buff. Black spot on breast lacking and breast and flanks, as well as crown and nape, are streaked black. The throat may also have a few indistinct streaks and the black malar stripe (along with the other black stripes on the head) are less distinct than in adult. Rest of plumage much as adult, but wing-bars are wider and buffier.

MOULT AND AGEING The post-juvenile moult is partial/complete, probably generally incomplete and occurs in June-October; it seems to be quite variable and occurs primarily on the breeding grounds, although a few may retain some juvenile streaking through to the following summer. The post-breeding moult is complete and occurs in June-September, primarily on the breeding grounds. All birds have a limited pre-breeding moult in February-April, which involves some head feathers. A few first-years may retain a little juvenile streaking through the first-year. Otherwise first-years resemble adults after completing the post-juvenile moult; they may average slightly duller but this is not reliable for ageing individuals. The rectrices average more pointed, and more worn in spring, on first-years than on adults. In addition, birds showing contrast between worn and fresh remiges are likely to be first-years, but in autumn beware of adults which may have started migrating before completing their moult. Skull ossification complete in first-years from 1 December over much of the range but from 1 November in Californian (and probably other southern) populations.

MEASUREMENTS Wing (chord): male (n86) 81.3-94; female (n64) 79-89.1. Tail: male (n66) 64-78.2; female (n34) 61-71.2. Bill: male (n66) 10.4-13.7; female (n34) 10.7-12.9. Tarsus: male (n66) 19.1-21.9; female (n34) 18.8-20.8.

GEOGRAPHICAL VARIATION Two races generally recognised; a third (*actitis* from Oregon) is now generally included in *strigatus*.
   C. g. grammacus (Breeds in the eastern USA, from Wisconsin and W New York, sporadically in S Ontario, south to NE Texas and W Carolinas, and winters from C Texas and the S Atlantic coast of the USA south to Guerrero and Oaxaca, casually to the Yucatán Peninsula and to Cuba and the Bahamas) Described above.
   C. g. strigatus (Breeds in the larger western part of the range and winters from the southern part of the breeding range south through Mexico, except Yucatán and the adjoining lowlands, occasionally reaching Guatemala and El Salvador) Similar to *grammacus* but the upperparts are paler and less heavily streaked, the chestnut on the head is paler, and there is slightly less black on the front of the face.

VOICE The song, generally given from a prominent perch such as the top of a small bush or fence post but sometimes in flight, is loud, melodious and variable, generally beginning with two loud, clear notes and followed by a series of melodious notes and trills, mixed with unmusical buzzes. Calls include a metallic *tink* and a sharp *tsit*, often repeated rapidly when agitated.

HABITS Nest is normally placed on the ground, generally in a small depression and hidden under a grass clump; occasionally it may be placed low in a bush. It is a cup of grasses and weed stems, lined with finer grasses, rootlets and hair. 3-6 (usually 4-5) eggs are laid in April-July; they are white, spotted and scrawled with blackish and often some purplish. Incubation period is 11-12 days and the young fledge after 9-10 days. Often breeds in loose colonies. Male is sometimes polygynous. In courtship display male sings from the ground with trailing wings and spread tail (showing off the white patches). Feeds largely on seeds but also on insects, especially grasshoppers, in the breeding season. Forages on the ground in the open. Generally tame and confiding, and will nest around villages and small towns if there is sufficient scrub. Generaly found in flocks in winter, sometimes with other sparrows.

STATUS AND HABITAT Fairly common throughout most of its range but scarce and local east of the Mississippi. It formerly bred east to New York and Maryland but the range has contracted in the east in recent decades. Breeds in prairies, savanna, farmlands, mesa, open woodland, forest edges and other open areas with scattered trees and patches of bare ground. Found in winter and on migration in similar open areas and also in brushy fields and semi-arid areas.

DISTRIBUTION AND MOVEMENTS Breeds throughout much of the USA east to the Mississippi and more locally east to Ohio, and western Carolinas and extreme northwestern Georgia (sporadically east to the sandhills area). Also breeds in southern Canada (southern British Columbia, Alberta, Saskatchewan, and sporadically in southern Manitoba and southern Ontario) and south to northern Mexico (Zacatecas). Populations in Mexico, most of Texas and California and the southern parts of Arizona and New Mexico are sedentary, but the others are short- to medium-distance migrants moving south in winter into the southern part of the breeding range and further south through Mexico, mainly south to Guerrero and Oaxaca but occasionally to the Yucatán Peninsula, Guatemala and El Salvador, plus the West Indies in Cuba and the Bahamas. See also under Geographical Variation. Migrants arrive on breeding grounds from late March and leave from late July. Vagrant to Britain but the two records, both in East Anglia (June-July 1981 and May 1991), probably involved ship-assisted birds.

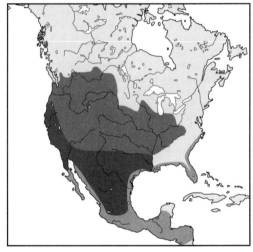

REFERENCES Alström *et al.* (1991), Armani (1985), Bent (1968), Brown (1991), Charlton (1991), Dunn & Blom (1983), Ehrlich *et al.* (1988), Godfrey (1986), Oberholser (1974), Paynter & Storer (1970), Peterson & Chalif (1973), Pyle *et al.* (1987), Ridgway (1901), Terres (1980).

AMPHISPIZA

Three species of medium-sized sparrows with distinctive head patterns; they are characteristic of arid and semi-desert areas in western and south-western North America. The genus *Amphispiza* was formerly included in the genus *Aimophila* but is currently thought to deserve independent recognition.

79 BLACK-THROATED SPARROW
Amphispiza bilineata   Plate 32

Described as *Emberiza bilineata* Cassin 1850.

The widest-ranging of the three *Amphispiza* sparrows and, like the others, found mainly in arid and desert country.

IDENTIFICATION 14cm. Black throat and breast, tapering to a point on the lower breast, and striking head pattern formed by black lores, dark grey cheeks and grey crown, contrasting with broad white supercilium and submoustachial stripe, make the adult unmistakable. Black tail with white tips to outer feathers is also distinctive. Juvenile has buffier brown upperparts and crown, warm buff wing-bars and tertial edges, and lacks the black throat and breast, but has fine brown streaking on breast and flanks. It is rather similar to juvenile Sage Sparrow (80) but has a broad, distinct and uninterrupted white supercilium, plain grey-brown crown (lacking dark streaks) and distinct white outer web of outer tail feathers and white spots in outer two feathers.

DESCRIPTION
Sexes alike; juvenile clearly different from subsequent plumages.
Adult/first-year Forehead blackish-grey, crown, nape and neck-sides brownish-grey. Supercilium white, narrow in front of eye but quite broad behind it, reaching just past rear end of ear-coverts. Narrow black line above supercilium. Eye-crescents white. Lores and ocular area blackish, rest of ear-coverts dark grey. Upperparts brownish-grey, with brown wash most evident on mantle and scapulars. Lesser coverts concolorous with upperparts. Rest of wings dark brown with grey-brown feather edges, broadest and brownest (buffy-brown) on greater and median coverts and tertials. Bend of wing white or whitish. Tail blackish with outer web of outer feathers white and the outer two

feathers also tipped white. Throat and breast black, separated from grey ear-coverts by white submoustachial stripe. Breast-sides whitish, black tapering to a point in centre of lower breast. Rest of underparts whitish, washed buff on flanks and undertail-coverts. Iris brown. Bill blackish. Legs dusky-flesh.

Juvenile Crown, nape and neck-sides grey-brown washed buff, upperparts more buffy-brown. Greater and median coverts edged warm buff and tipped pale buff, forming two obscure wing-bars. Tertials also broadly edged warm buff. Lores and ear-coverts grey-brown. Supercilium white, same shape as adults but lacking black border. Underparts whitish with fine brown streaks on breast and flanks, flanks and undertail-coverts with less of a buff wash than in adult. Bill slightly paler than adult's, especially on lower mandible.

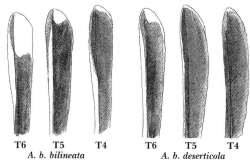

T6   T5   T4   T6   T5   T4
A. b. bilineata   *A. b. deserticola*

Tail feathers of adult to show racial variation.

MOULT AND AGEING The post-juvenile moult is quite protracted and often suspended over migration (in migratory populations), occurring in June-November; it is partial or incomplete, often including some flight feathers. Those which moult some flight feathers may be earlier-hatched individuals, but more study is needed on this. The post-breeding moult is complete and generally occurs on the breeding grounds, prior to migration (in migratory populations) in June-September. There is no pre-breeding moult. First-years can usually be told well into the autumn by remnants of the juvenile plumage. Once the post-juvenile moult is completed, first-years resemble adults but have slightly more pointed rectrices on average. The rectrices may also average more worn on first-years but there is much overlap with adults in this and it is difficult to judge on individuals. Skull ossification complete in first-years from 15 November.

MEASUREMENTS Wing (chord): male (n30) 61-70; female (n30) 55-67. Tail: male (n18) 57.7-68.3; female (n18) 55.4-64. Bill: male (n18) 9.6-10.7; female (n18) 9.1-10.4. Tarsus: male (n18) 17.8-19.8; female (n18) 17-19.6 (*deserticola* averages slightly longer than *bilineata* in wing and tail, and *grisea* averages slightly longer than *deserticola*, but there is much overlap).

GEOGRAPHICAL VARIATION Nine races, which differ only slightly from each other and are generally not identifiable in the field.

  A. b. bilineata (Resident from NC Texas south to E Coahuila, Nuevo León and NW Tamaulipas) Described above.

  A. b. opuntia (Occurs from SE Colorado and NW Oklahoma south through E New Mexico and W Texas to NW Coahuila. Northern populations from C New

Mexico north are migratory, wintering mainly in the southern part of the range.) Averages slightly larger and greyer above than *bilineata* and has slightly smaller white spots at the tips of the outer two rectrices.

  A. b. deserticola (Breeds from SE Oregon and SW Wyoming south through the Great Basin to the northern half of Baja California and NW Chihuahua, including Islas Cedros, Natividad and Angel de la Guarda, but not the north-western coastal region of Baja. Northern populations, from SC California and C Arizona north, are migratory, wintering in the southern part of the breeding range and south in Mexico to C Sonora) Slightly paler and browner above than *bilineata* and also has smaller white spots at the tips of the outer two rectrices (like *opuntia*).

  A. b. bangsi (Resident in the southern third of Baja California) Very similar to *deserticola* but averages slightly darker above and also slightly smaller, but with a relatively larger bill.

  A. b. tortugae (Resident on Isla Tortuga in the Gulf of California) The darkest race; dark slaty-grey above (with virtually no brown tinge) and greyish-white below, darker than the whitish of the other races.

  A. b. belvederei (Resident on Isla Cerralvo in the Gulf of California) Similar to *bangsi* but the upperparts are slightly darker and greyer and the upper mandible is usually slightly more curved.

  A. b. pacifica (Occurs in W Sonora and NW Sinaloa) Similar to *bilineata* but has smaller white tail spots; similar to *deserticola* in this respect, but is darker and slightly smaller than that race.

  A. b. cana (Resident on Isla San Esteban in the Gulf of California) The palest and greyest race, similar to *deserticola* but rather paler and greyer, especially on the upperparts; also slightly smaller and with a relatively shorter tail.

  A. b. grisea (Resident in N Mexico, from C Chihuahua, S Coahuila and SW Tamaulipas south to N Jalisco and Hidalgo) Darker and greyer above than *deserticola* and also slightly greyer above than *bilineata*.

VOICE The song, often given from the top of a bush but also from the ground, is rapid and high-pitched: two clear, metallic, bell-like notes followed by a trill. Calls include various high-pitched tinkling notes, often faint and rising slightly in pitch.

HABITS Nest is placed low in a thorn bush; a cup of dried grass, grass stems and bark shreds, lined with fine plant material, wool, hair and sometimes feathers. 3-4 pale blue or white eggs are laid in April-August. Incubation and fledging periods unrecorded. Feeds on seeds and insects, foraging mainly on the ground, but also in bushes. Calls constantly and often flicks its tail. Generally found alone or in pairs or small groups outside the breeding season.

STATUS AND HABITAT Fairly common in desert and semi-desert areas with thorn scrub, cacti, yuccas, mesquite and scattered juniper bushes; in flat areas and on hillsides.

DISTRIBUTION AND MOVEMENTS Occurs in the western USA (north to southern Oregon and south-western Wyoming) and northern and central Mexico (south to northern Jalisco and Hidalgo), but excuding the western USA coast and the high mountains. Northern populations of races *opuntia* and *deserticola* are migratory, wintering in the southern part of the species range. See also under Geographical Variation. Migrants arrive on breeding grounds from March and leave from late September. Vagrant to eastern North America, north to Ontario, in autumn and winter.

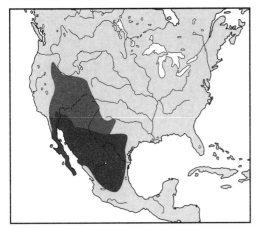

REFERENCES Armani (1985), Bent (1968), Dunn & Blom (1983)), Farrand (1983), Oberholser (1974), Paynter & Storer (1970), Peterson & Chalif (1973), Pyle *et al.* (1987), Ridgway (1901), Sibley & Monroe (1990), Terres (1980).

80   SAGE SPARROW
Amphispiza belli   **Plate 32**

Described as *Emberiza belli* Cassin 1850.
Synonym: *Poospiza belli*.

Like Black-throated Sparrow (79), this species has many races; it is characteristic of sagebrush country but is also found in chaparral and other arid and semi-arid areas.

IDENTIFICATION 16cm. Rather variable but all races have greyish head with white eye-ring, short white supercilium (sometimes restricted to supraloral), broad white submoustachial stripe and narrower black or blackish malar stripe, and whitish underparts with prominent black spot in centre of breast. Upperparts are grey-brown, browner than head. Flanks have variable dark streaking. Coastal range birds, west of the Rockies, are quite dark grey and unstreaked on the head and upperparts, and have a fairly broad black malar stripe. Interior birds are paler grey above and have dark streaks on the crown and upperparts; the malar stripe is also narrower and less conspicuous. Juveniles of all races are buffy-brown on the head and upperparts with pronounced dark streaking on crown, upperparts, breast and flanks. They are quite similar to juvenile Black-throated Sparrow but have a much less noticeable supercilium, streaks on crown and upperparts as well as underparts, and no noticeable white in the outer tail.

DESCRIPTION
Sexes alike; juvenile different from subsequent plumages.
Adult/first-year Crown, nape and neck-sides mid-grey. Eye-ring and supraloral white. Lores blackish. Ear-coverts mid-grey, bordered above by narrow and indistinct blackish eye-stripe and below by narrow blackish moustachial stripe. Broad submoustachial stripe white. Narrower (but still broad and noticeable) malar stripe black. Upperparts

grey-brown, appearing unstreaked in field although feathers have small indistinct dusky centres. Lesser coverts buffy-brown. Alula dark brown edged creamy-white. Rest of wings blackish-brown with buff feather edges, broadest on greater and median coverts and tertials; greater and median coverts also tipped buff, forming two obscure wingbars. Bend of wing pale yellowish-white. Tail blackish-brown with narrow paler feather edges, buff on most feathers but whitish on rectrix 6. Throat, breast and belly whitish, breast with prominent black spot in centre. Flanks and undertail-coverts buff, flanks and breast-sides with narrow dark brown streaks. Iris brown. Bill blackish, legs dusky-flesh to blackish.
Juvenile Crown and upperparts buffier than adult with darker streaks. Underparts buffy-white, whiter on throat, with brown streaks on breast and flanks; black breast spot lacking. Bill paler than adult's, dark horn.

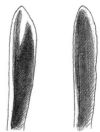

A. b. nevadensis   *A. b. belli*

Outermost tail feather (T6) to show racial variation.

MOULT AND AGEING The post-juvenile moult is partial and the post-breeding moult is complete; both occur in June-September, prior to migration (in migratory populations). There is no pre-breeding moult. First-years have slightly more pointed rectrices than adults, and these average more worn, especially by spring, but no other ageing characters are known. Skull ossification complete in first-years from 15 October.

MEASUREMENTS As the two groups are noticeably different in size (interior birds are considerably larger with very little overlap in wing and tail measurents), measurements for the two groups are given separately below.
Coastal group. Wing (chord): male (n30) 63-73; female (n30) 59-70. Tail: male (n19) 58.9-72.9; female (n14) 58.4-68.6. Bill: male (n19) 8.1-10.4; female (n14) 7.9-9.9. Tarsus: male (n19) 19.6-21.8; female (n14) 19.8-20.8 (*belli* averages slightly smaller than *cinerea* in wing and tail but there is considerable overlap).
Interior group. Wing (chord): male (n30) 74-82; female (n30) 70-78. Tail: male (n12) 70.6-78.5; female (n11) 67.3-75.7. Bill: male (n12) 9.4-10.4; female (n11) 9.4-10.4. Tarsus: male (n12) 20.8-22.6; female (n11) 18.8-22.4 (*canescens* averages smaller than *nevadensis*).

GEOGRAPHICAL VARIATION Five races, in two groups; the two groups are quite different and identifiable in the field, but variation within each group is much less marked.
Coastal group:
    A. b. belli (Resident in California on the western slopes of the C Sierra Nevada, in the coastal ranges, and also on the coast from Marin County south. It also occurs in NW Baja California where it intergrades with *cinerea*) Described above.
    A. b. clementeae (Resident on San Clemente Island,

off SW California) Very similar to *belli* but may average slightly paler above.

A. b. cinerea (Resident in C Baja California, from about 29°N south to about 26°N) It is paler above than *belli* with more of a buff wash and faint darker streaks on mantle; the malar stripe are also narrower and greyer and the black breast spot is smaller. In all these respects it is the most similar of this group to the interior group (it is similar in paleness to *canescens* but is more of a buffy-grey and the upperparts are less strongly streaked).

Interior group:

A. b. nevadensis (Breeds in the Great Basin from S Washington and extreme S Montana south to E California, NE Arizona and NW New Mexico; winters from CE California and S Nevada south to the northern parts of Baja California, Sonora and Chihuahua, and W Texas. Some southern breeders may be sedentary) Paler above than any of the coastal races, the malar stripe is narrow and dark greyish, and the upperparts have noticeable darker streaks.

A. b. canescens (Breeds in interior SC California and adjacent W Nevada; winters at lower elevations in the breeding area and also west to SW California and NW Baja California, and east to S Nevada and W Arizona) Similar to *nevadensis* but is slightly darker above with less prominent streaking, and has a more prominent black malar stripe; in these characters it tends towards the coastal group, especially *cinerea*.

RELATIONSHIPS The two interior races, *nevadensis* and *canescens*, have been found breeding in close proximity to each other with no sign of intergradation; this plus the differences in breeding habitat and genetics indicates that they may actually be distinct species, but more work needs to be done (and is in fact in progress). Similarly, the coastal populations may be specifically distinct from the interior ones, but there is, as yet, no direct evidence to support this.

VOICE The song, generally given from an the top of a low bush, is a jumbled series of rising and falling phrases which sound rather finch-like. Calls include a high-pitched twittering, reminiscent of a junco and also similar to Black-throated Sparrow.

HABITS Nest is placed low in a bush, normally a large sagebrush; a cup of dried grasses, lined with finer plant material and hair. 2-5 (usually 3-4) eggs are laid in March-July; they are pale bluish- or greenish-white, marked with reddish-brown. Incubation period is 13-16 days and the young fledge after 9-11 days. Twitches its tail while singing. Feeds on seeds and insects, foraging on the ground and also sometimes low in bushes. Unobtrusive, often sticking to sagebrush or other cover, but not as secretive as Five-striped Sparrow (81). When disturbed, may run through the scrub with tail cocked up, rather than flying. Will also briefly observe an intruder from the top of a bush before diving for cover. Occasionally visits feeders in winter in rural areas. Generally found in small groups or in flocks of 25-50 birds in winter.

STATUS AND HABITAT Generally fairly common, but the race *clementeae* is now very rare and considered endangered. Coastal birds are found mainly in chaparral on hillsides and mountain slopes. Interior birds breed mainly on alkaline flats with low sagebrush (*nevadensis*) or saltbush (*canescens*), and are also found in sandy and peb-

bly arid areas and deserts in winter. Breeds up to 3000m.

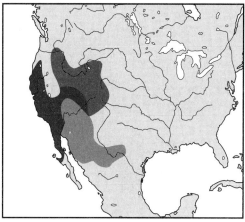

DISTRIBUTION AND MOVEMENTS Breeds in the Great Basin area of western North America, the Sierra Nevada slopes in California, and the coastal regions of California and northern and central Baja California. Coastal birds are mainly sedentary, while most interior birds are short-distance migrants wintering in the south-western USA and north-western Mexico. See also under Geographical Variation. Migrants arrive on breeding grounds from February/March and leave from September.

REFERENCES Armani (1985), Bent (1968), De Benedictis (1995), Dunn & Blom (1983), Ehrlich *et al.* (1988), Kaufman (1990), Oberholser (1974), Paynter & Storer (1970), Peterson & Best (1985), Pyle *et al.* (1987), Ridgway (1901), Terres (1980).

81   FIVE-STRIPED SPARROW
Amphispiza quinquestriata   Plate 32

Described as *Zonotrichia quinquestriata* Sclater & Salvin 1868.
Synonym: *Aimophila quinquestriata*.

This sparrow, until recently placed in the *Aimophila* genus, is the most southerly and localised of the three *Amphispiza* sparrows, basically endemic to western Mexico but also breeding just across the USA border in extreme southern Arizona.

IDENTIFICATION 15cm. A rather dark, dull sparrow with a distinctive head pattern. Crown, nape and upperparts darkish warm brown, underparts grey with white throat and belly, and small black spot in centre of breast. Sides of head grey with short, narrow white supercilium, white eye-ring, very broad black malar stripe (covering most of submoustachial area and contrasting with white throat) and narrow white submoustachial stripe, between grey ear-coverts and black malar. Head pattern is not dissimilar to Sage Sparrow (80) except that the black malar stripe is much broader than the white submoustachial stripe (other way round in Sage). Also shares black breast spot with Sage Sparrow but is easily distinguished by details of head pattern, brown crown (uniform with upperparts), mostly grey underparts and darker overall appearance. Head pattern is also fairly similar to Bridled Sparrow (82) but that species has a black throat bordered by broader white submoustachial stripes, is strongly streaked on the crown and upperparts, is distinctly rufous on rump and scapulars, has broad white wing-bars, lacks the black breast spot and is cinnamon-buff on flanks and undertail-coverts. Juvenile lacks the broad black malar stripe and has the belly pale yellowish; unlike most juvenile sparrows, it lacks streaking on underparts.

DESCRIPTION
Sexes alike; juvenile clearly different from subsequent plumages.

Adult/first-year Crown, nape, mantle, back and scapulars uniform warm brown. Short, narrow supercilium white, extending just past eye. Eye-ring white. Lores dark grey, ear-coverts and neck-sides slightly paler grey; ear-coverts faintly washed brown, especially on rear. Very narrow submoustachial stripe white, forming a narrow line immediately below ear-coverts, and bordered below by much broader black malar stripe (which also covers most of the submoustachial area). Rump and uppertail-coverts mid-grey, merging into brown back. Lesser coverts grey. Alula dark brown edged whitish. Rest of wings blackish-brown; flight feathers are narrowly edged with pale buffy-white, coverts and tertials have warm brown outer webs forming a brown area continuous with upperparts. Bend of wing white. Tail blackish-brown with narrow pale buff feather edges and very small white tips to the outer rectrices. Throat white, contrasting with broad black malar. Breast and flanks grey, belly white; there is a small black spot in centre of breast where the grey meets the white belly. Vent and undertail-coverts grey with paler greyish-white tips to feathers, creating a barred effect. Iris brown. Bill blackish-grey. Legs dark greyish-flesh.

Juvenile Similar to adult but the underparts are pale yellow, with a mottled brownish wash to the breast, the black malar stripe is lacking and the upperparts have faint darker streaks.

MOULT AND AGEING The post-juvenile moult is prolonged, occurring in August-December; it is partial to incomplete, sometimes including the tertials and rarely some of the primaries as well. The post-breeding moult is complete, occurring in August-November. There appears to be a limited/partial pre-breeding moult, at least in some birds, in April-June. No ageing criteria are known once the post-juvenile moult is completed, although tail shape may be useful with the juvenile rectrices averaging more pointed than adult ones; this requires more study. Skull ossification complete in first-years from 1 October.

MEASUREMENTS Wing (chord): male (n44) 63-73.3; female (n20) 60-71.1. Tail: male (n16) 66.5-72.4; female (n11) 61.7-72.9. Bill: male (n16) 11.4-12.7; female (n11) 11.4-12.5. Tarsus: male (n16) 19.6-20.8; female (n11) 19-21.1.

GEOGRAPHICAL VARIATION Two similar races.
A. q. septentrionalis (Occurs in NW Mexico, except the narrow coastal plain, from N Sonora south to C Sinaloa and W Durango, and also north to extreme CS Arizona. Principally sedentary, but extreme northern populations in Arizona and extreme N Sonora are migratory, with most birds moving south into the rest of the breeding range in winter) Described above.
A. q. quinquestriata (Occurs in W Mexico in N Jalisco) Similar to *septentrionalis* but is slightly darker overall and has a slightly larger breast spot.

RELATIONSHIPS The AOU transferred this species from *Aimophila* to *Amphispiza* in 1983, but its true relationships may not yet be fully resolved.

VOICE The song, generally given from an exposed perch, is quite variable but typically consists of two short buzzy notes, sometimes preceded by a softer higher note (difficult to hear), and followed by 2-4 rapidly delivered trilling notes; it is similar to song of Black-throated Sparrow. Calls include a soft, slightly metallic *tink*.

HABITS Nest is placed low in a thornbush or in the lowest branches of a shrub, usually very close to the ground; a cup of dried grass, lined with finer plant material. 3-5 white eggs are laid. Incubation period is 12-13 days and the young fledge after 9-10 days. Feeds on seeds and insects, foraging mainly on the ground but also in bushes. It is quite shy and difficult to observe, except when singing, feeding close to cover and disappearing into the brush when disturbed. Generally found in pairs or small groups outside the breeding season.

STATUS AND HABITAT Generally uncommon and local, and rare in Arizona (only 50-60 territorial males). Found in dense brushy and scrubby areas on grassy and rocky hillsides and canyon slopes, and in mesquite, generally in semi-desert and other arid areas.

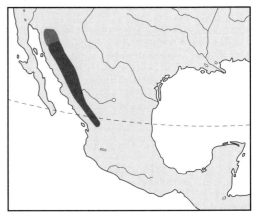

DISTRIBUTION AND MOVEMENTS Occurs in western Mexico, except the narrow coastal plain, from northern Sonora south to northern Jalisco; also in adjacent south-central Arizona. Most birds are sedentary, but extreme northern populations are migratory, moving south into the rest of the breeding range in winter. See also under Geograpical Variation.

REFERENCES American Ornithologists' Union (1983), Armani (1985), Dunn & Blom (1983), Ehrlich *et al.* (1988), Farrand (1983), Groschupf (1992), Hardy & Wolf (1977), Kaufman (1990), Paynter & Storer (1970), Peterson & Chalif (1973), Pyle *et al.* (1987), Ridgway (1901), Wolf (1977).

AIMOPHILA

Thirteen species of medium to large sparrows with long, rounded tails and generally rather flat crowns. They are mostly found in Mexico and Central America, but one species is endemic to the south-eastern USA and two are restricted to South America.

82   BRIDLED SPARROW
Aimophila mystacalis   Plate 32

Described as *Zonotrichia mystacalis* Cabanis 1852.

One of four *Aimophila* sparrows endemic to southern Mexico, this one occurs in arid thorn and cactus scrub at the southern edge of the Central Plateau.

IDENTIFICATION 15cm. A distinctive *Aimophila* with black lores, moustachial stripe and throat and contrasting white submoustachial stripe, supraloral and broken eye-ring. Rest of head dark grey with black streaks on crown. Upperparts grey-buff, broadly streaked with black; scapulars and rump rufous-chestnut. Wings with two bold white wing-bars. Underparts pale greyish on breast, becoming whiter on belly and cinnamon-rufous on flanks and undertail-coverts. Juvenile is duller overall, and has streaked breast and whitish throat. No other sparrow is really similar; Black-chested has white throat, broad black breast-band and rufous-chestnut on scapulars and mantle, not rump. Five-striped has fairly similar head pattern but has white central throat, unstreaked warm brown upperparts, lacking any rufous-chestnut, and greyish flanks and undertail-coverts.

DESCRIPTION
Sexes alike, juvenile clearly separable from subsequent plumages.
Adult/first-year Crown dark grey, blackish on forehead, with black streaks. Nape slightly paler and browner with finer streaking. Supraloral white, narrowly separated from broken white eye-ring. Lores, front of ear-coverts (below eye) and narrow moustachial stripe black. Prominent submoustachial stripe white. Rest of head grey with a suggestion of a darker postocular stripe. Mantle grey-buff with broad black streaks. Scapulars, rump and uppertail-coverts rufous-chestnut, unstreaked. Wings blackish with narrow greyish edges to lesser coverts, primary coverts and most remiges, broad buff edges to greater and median coverts and tertials, and broad white tips to greater and median coverts, forming two noticeable wing-bars. Bend of wing white. Tail blackish with narrow grey-buff feather edges. Throat black, contrasting with white submoustachial stripe. Breast pale grey, sharply demarcated from black throat, belly whitish, flanks and undertail-coverts cinnamon-buff. Iris dark brown. Bill blackish with flesh lower mandible. Legs flesh.
Juvenile Similar to adult but duller; upperparts grey-brown, washed rufous on scapulars, rump and uppertail-coverts, and streaked darker. Wing-bars buffier. Submoustachial stripe pale yellowish or buffy-white; underparts whitish with dark brown speckling on throat and dark brown streaks on breast and flanks.

MOULT AND AGEING Adults have a complete moult, probably after breeding, but the extent of the post-juvenile moult is unknown. There is no evidence of a pre-breed-ing moult, but more study is needed on this, and indeed on all aspects of moult, for this species and all other *Aimophila* sparrows, bearing in mind the complicated moulting strategy shown by Bachman's (88) and Cassin's (90) Sparrows, and the fact that at least two other *Aimophila* sparrows, Botteri's (89) and Rufous-winged (91), have a pre-breeding moult. No ageing criteria are known once the post-juvenile moult is completed.

MEASUREMENTS Wing (chord): male (n14) 63.5-72.4; female (n6) 64-68. Tail: male (n14) 74.2-82.6; female (n6) 73.7-80.8. Bill: male (n14) 10.9-13.5; female (n6) 11.4-13. Tarsus: male (n14) 21.3-22.9; female (n6) 21.6-22.4.

GEOGRAPHICAL VARIATION Monotypic.

VOICE The song, generally given from an exposed perch in a bush, is an excited series of jumbled high-pitched chirping notes, sometimes interspersed with softer notes. Pairs often duet.

HABITS Nest is placed on the ground, often under a cactus, or very low in a bush; a cup of dry grass and small twigs, lined with fine vegetable matter and hair. 3-4 pale bluish-white eggs are laid. Feeds on seeds and insects, foraging on the ground and in bushes. Will often feed in the open, but shy and disappears into cover when disturbed. Often found in small groups (family parties?) outside the breeding season.

STATUS AND HABITAT Locally fairly common in arid and semi-arid scrub, cactus scrub and thorn forest, often on rocky ground, generally from 1500 to 2000m.

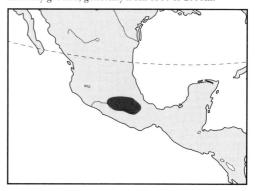

DISTRIBUTION AND MOVEMENTS Endemic to southern Mexico where it occurs in southern Puebla, west-central Veracruz, and northern and central Oaxaca. Sedentary.

REFERENCES Armani (1985), Hardy & Wolf (1977), Peterson & Chalif (1973), Ridgway (1901), Sibley & Monroe (1990), Wolf (1977).

83 BLACK-CHESTED SPARROW
Aimophila humeralis   Plate 35

Described as *Haemophila humeralis* Cabanis 1851.

One of Mexico's endemic *Aimophila* sparrows, occurring in western Mexico in arid scrub.

IDENTIFICATION 15cm. A very distinctive *Aimophila* with white throat and belly, separated by broad black breast-band, bright rufous mantle, back and scapulars (first two streaked blackish), dark grey head with black face and white loral spot, and prominent white submoustachial stripe and black malar stripe. Also note cinnamon-buff flanks and undertail-coverts, greyish rump and tail, and rufous wash on crown and nape (especially in fresh plumage).

DESCRIPTION
Sexes alike; juvenile clearly different from subsequent plumages.
Adult/first-year Forehead, lores and ear-coverts blackish with large white or whitish spot on lores. Crown, nape and neck-sides dark grey, crown and nape faintly streaked with dull rufous. Submoustachial stripe white. Broad malar stripe black, joining with black of breast. Mantle and back rufous, streaked blackish and with broad olive-grey feather edges. Scapulars rufous with narrow olive-grey feather fringes. Rump olive-grey with obscure, narrow, dull rufous streaks. Uppertail-coverts dark grey with pale greyish-white feather fringes. Lesser coverts dull rufous-brown. Alula blackish-brown, narrowly edged white. Rest of wings blackish-brown with olive-buff feather edges, broadest and brightest buff on greater and median covert, and tertials, and whitish on outer primary. The buff edges on the greater and median coverts are whitish at the tips (especially on the latter), forming a fairly noticeable wing-bar. Bend of wing whitish. Tail dark grey with narrow pale grey-buff feather edges. Throat white, completely enclosed by black malar stripes and broad black breast-band. The feathers of the breast-band have narrow pale grey fringes. Lower breast and belly white. Flanks, vent and undertail-coverts cinnamon-buff. Iris dark brown. Bill blackish-grey. Legs flesh. In worn plumage the feather edges and fringes largely wear off, resulting in a more contrasting appearance; the crown and nape appear darker, more blackish-grey, and contrast more with the brighter rufous mantle, and the breast-band is more solid black.
Juvenile Head and upperparts greyish-brown, washed rufous on mantle and scapulars. Underparts whitish, washed buff and streaked blackish-brown on breast and flanks.

MOULT AND AGEING Adults have a complete moult, probably after breeding, but the extent of the post-juvenile moult is unknown. There is no evidence of a pre-breeding moult; but see under Bridled Sparrow (82). No ageing criteria are known once the post-juvenile moult is completed.

MEASUREMENTS Wing (chord): male (n7) 65.3-70.1; female (n5) 58.4-66. Tail: male (n7) 69.8-81.8; female (n5) 66.5-76.2. Bill: male (n7) 12.4-13.5; female (n5) 12.4-13.2. Tarsus: male (n7) 19-22.1; female (n5) 20.1-20.6.

GEOGRAPHICAL VARIATION Monotypic.

VOICE The song, generally given from an open perch, is a rapid series of high-pitched, stacatto notes on one pitch,

sometimes preceded by a single note. Pairs often duet.

HABITS Nest is placed on the ground or very low in a bush; a cup of grasses and twigs, lined with finer plant material and sometimes with a thin domed roof of grass. 3-4 bluish-white eggs are laid. Feeds on insects and seeds, foraging on the ground, generally close to cover and often under bushes or cacti; also forages low in bushes. Generally shy and unobtrusive except when singing, disappearing into cover when disturbed. Often found in small groups (family parties?) outside the breeding season.

STATUS AND HABITAT Fairly common in arid scrub, semi-desert and rocky hillsides with dense cactus stands and scattered dense brush, to 1500m.

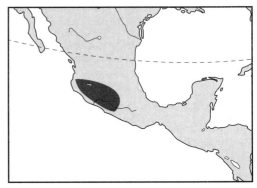

DISTRIBUTION AND MOVEMENTS Endemic to western Mexico, where it occurs from southern Jalisco south-east to southern Puebla and extreme western Oaxaca. Sedentary.

REFERENCES Armani (1985), Hardy & Wolf (1977), Paynter & Storer (1970), Peterson & Chalif (1973), Ridgway (1901), Sibley & Monroe (1990), Wolf (1977).

---

84 STRIPE-HEADED SPARROW
Aimophila ruficauda   Plate 35

Described as *Chondestes ruficauda* Bonaparte 1853.
Synonyms: *Haemophila acuminata, Haemophila lawrencii.*

This large sparrow is the most distinctive of the *Aimophila* sparrows; its boldly striped head is unique within the genus.

IDENTIFICATION 15.5-18cm. A large sparrow with a boldly black and white striped head, bicoloured bill (black above, straw/flesh below), warm brown upperparts, streaked darker, and longish, rounded rufous tail. Underparts whitish, white on throat, and with conspicuous cinnamon-buff flanks and undertail-coverts. Juvenile has black and white head pattern replaced by blackish and buff-brown and obscured by streaking, upperparts and tail paler rufous with less heavy streaking, less white throat and dark streaks on breast. Striped Sparrow (96) is similar but has a less contrasting head pattern (black cheeks are streaked greyish-white and the crown is brown, lacking an obvious crown-stripe); it also has an all-black bill, dull brown upperparts and tail, lacking rufous tones, and duller buff (not cinnamon-buff) flanks and undertail-coverts. White-crowned Sparrow (55) is superficially similar but lacks black cheeks, and has an all-pale bill and a dark brown, not rufous, tail; it is also noticeably different in shape.

DESCRIPTION

Sexes alike; juvenile clearly different from subsequent plumages.

Adult/first-year Crown black, faintly streaked rufous-brown and with broad white crown-stripe. Supercilium broad, white, often tinged buff on supraloral. Lores and ear-coverts black; ear-coverts with paler grey-buff centres. Nape and mantle grey-brown, streaked blackish, with the blackish streaks edged with rufous. Scapulars rufous. Back and rump pale rufous; uppertail-coverts pale rufous with pale buff feather fringes. Lesser coverts rufous. Rest of wings blackish-brown; primaries, primary coverts and alula have narrow pale buff feather edges, those of secondaries are more rufous. Greater and median coverts and tertials have broad rufous edges, becoming buffy-white towards the tip. Bend of wing white. Tail rufous. Throat whitish, breast and fore-flanks grey with narrow paler grey feather fringes. Belly whitish, rear-flanks and undertail-coverts cinnamon-buff. Iris dark brown. Bill black with conspicuous straw-flesh lower mandible. Legs flesh.

Juvenile Head stripes blackish and buffy, paler stripes with darker streaking, making head pattern more obscure than adult's. Upperparts paler, buffier and less streaked than adult's, tail paler rufous. Underparts whitish with buffy breast and pale cinnamon-rufous rear-flanks and under-tail-coverts; throat speckled dusky, breast streaked dark brown.

MOULT AND AGEING Adults have a complete moult, probably after breeding, but the extent of the post-juvenile moult is not known. There is no evidence of a pre-breeding moult; but see under Bridled Sparrow (82). No ageing criteria are known once the post-juvenile moult is completed.

MEASUREMENTS Wing (chord): male (n21) 63.5-79.5; female (n12) 63.7-72.4. Tail: male (n21) 74.9-94; female (n12) 72.9-88.9. Bill: male (n21) 12.7-16.3; female (n12) 13.2-16.5. Tarsus: male (n21) 21.6-24.9; female (n12) 22.9-24.1 (*lawrencii* averages the longest, and *acuminata* the shortest, in wing, tail and bill).

GEOGRAPHICAL VARATION Four races described which vary in size and overall brightness; generally, southern birds are larger and brighter than northern ones.

    A. r. acuminata (Occurs on the Pacific slope of Mexico from S Durango south to S Pueblo and SE Guerrero) Noticeably smaller than *ruficauda*, has blacker head stripes and ear-coverts, paler and less rufous upperparts and tail (than even *lawrencii*) and paler, more uniform underparts.

    A. r. lawrencii (Occurs in S Mexico on the southern side of the Isthmus of Tehuantepec) Larger than *ruficauda* with browner head stripes, greyer and less rufous upperparts and duller rufous tail.

    A. r. connectens (Occurs in E Guatemala, in the Río Motagua Valley) Intermediate between *lawrencii* and *ruficauda*; the upperparts are greyish (closest to *lawrencii*) but the tail is quite bright rufous (closest to *ruficauda*).

    A. r. ruficauda (Occurs on the Pacific slope from SE Guatemala south-east to NW Costa Rica) Described above.

VOICE The song, given from a conspicuous perch, is a long, jumbled series of dry, thin notes, often accelerating into a dry trill (*ruficauda*); or a series of double notes, transcribed as *pechew* (*acuminata*). Calls include varied hoarse, squeaky and nasal chipping notes, given continually from a group and rising to a crescendo when alarmed. Pairs greet each other with a chattering call and may also duet when singing.

HABITS Nest is placed 0.3-1.2m up in an isolated dense and often spiny shrub; a rather deep cup of coarse grasses and fine twigs, lined with fine grasses and hair. 2-4 pale blue eggs are laid in July-September (possibly to October). Nesting is often co-operative, with all members of the group attending a nest. Feeds mainly on grass seeds, but also takes insects and spiders. Forages mainly by hopping on open ground, flying into a low bush or hedge when disturbed. Flight is low and fluttering, with tail held low. Roosts in small compact flocks fairly high up in a tree. Generally found in social groups of 3-7 or more birds which feed, roost and nest together and are probably related to each other.

STATUS AND HABITAT Generally common in brushy savanna, weedy fields with hedgerows, open second growth and forest edges (but not in forest interior), often in semi-arid areas, on the Pacific slope; below 1800m in Mexico and below 800m in Costa Rica.

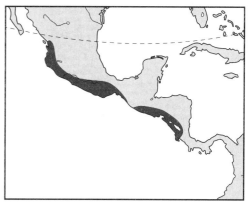

DISTRIBUTION AND MOVEMENTS Occurs in Central America, from southern Durango and Nayarit south to Peninsula de Nicoya in north-western Costa Rica. See also under Geographical Variation. Sedentary.

REFERENCES Armani (1985), Stiles & Skutch (1989), Paynter & Storer (1970), Peterson & Chalif (1973), Ridgway (1901), Wolf (1977).

85 CINNAMON-TAILED SPARROW
Aimophila sumichrasti   Plate 35

Described as *Haemophila sumichrasti* Lawrence 1871.

One of Mexico's endemic *Aimophila* sparrows; this one is restricted to arid areas in the southern part of the Isthmus of Tehuantepec.

IDENTIFICATION 17-17.5cm. Prominent black moustachial and malar stripes, together with the rufous tail, are distinctive. Crown dull rufous, streaked darker, and with grey median stripe. Upperparts grey-brown, heavily

streaked blackish. Ear-coverts pale greyish, further emphasising the black moustachial stripe on the lower border.
Underparts pale grey with whitish belly, flanks and undertail-coverts pale cinnamon-buff. Rufous lesser coverts are
also distinctive but are not normally visible. No other
Aimophila has combination of black moustachial and malar stripes and contrasting rufous tail. Rusty Sparrow (94)
has darker ear-coverts and is noticeably more rufous on
the upperparts and wings; it is also slightly larger. Oaxaca
Sparrow (93) is more similar in general appearance but
has a grey-brown tail and lacks the moustachial stripe; it
also has grey-brown, not rufous, lesser coverts.

DESCRIPTION
Sexes alike; juvenile clearly different from subsequent
plumages.
Adult/first-year Crown rufous-brown, streaked blackish,
and with grey crown-stripe. Supercilium grey. Lores blackish, post-ocular stripe dark rufous-brown. Broken eye-ring
white. Ear-coverts grey-buff. Moustachial and malar stripes
black, separated by pale greyish-white submoustachial
stripe. Nape and most of upperparts grey-buff, broadly
streaked blackish (the blackish streaks have narrow rufous
edges). Uppertail-coverts and tail rufous; uppertail-coverts with narrow buff feather fringes and tail with narrow
buff feather edges. Lesser coverts rufous. Rest of wings
blackish-brown; alula edged white, primaries and primary coverts narrowly edged pale buffy-white, edges to
secondaries more buffy-rufous. Greater and median coverts and tertials broadly edged buff and tipped white or
whitish, forming two obscure wing-bars. Bend of wing
white. Throat pale greyish-white. Neck-sides and breast
pale grey, faintly washed buff. Belly white, flanks and undertail-coverts pale cinnamon-buff. Iris dark brown. Bill
blackish with pale horn lower mandible. Legs flesh.
Juvenile Duller and buffier than adult; greyish-brown
above, streaked darker. Yellowish-buff below, streaked dark
brown on breast and flanks.

MOULT AND AGEING Adults have a complete moult,
probably after breeding, but the extent of the post-juvenile moult is not known. There is probably no
pre-breeding moult ; but see under Bridled Sparrow (82).
No ageing criteria are known once the post-juvenile moult
is completed.

MEASUREMENTS Wing (chord): male (n7) 66-68.8; female (n7) 63-66.8. Tail: male (n7) 66-71.9; female (n7)
63.5-69.9. Bill: male (n7) 14.2-15; female (n7) 13.5-15.2.
Tarsus: male (n7) 20.3-21.6; female (n7) 20.1-21.8.

GEOGRAPHICAL VARIATION Monotypic.

VOICE The song, generally given from an open perch, is
a rapid series of high-pitched, metallic notes. Pairs often
duet. Calls include a high-pitched double note.

HABITS Nesting habits are unknown. Feeds on insects
and seeds, foraging in bushes and the lower branches of
trees. Also forages by hopping on the ground, but always
close to cover. Shy and retiring except when singing; seldom flies far, preferring to disappear into cover when
flushed. Generally found in pairs or small flocks outside
the breeding season.

STATUS AND HABITAT Uncommon and local in arid
scrub and edges of cultivation, to 1000m.

DISTRIBUTION AND MOVEMENTS Endemic to southern Mexico where it occurs on the arid Pacific slope of

the Isthmus of Tehuantepec in south-eastern Oaxaca and
extreme south-western Chiapas. Sedentary.

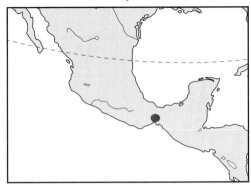

REFERENCES Armani (1985), Peterson & Chalif (1973),
Ridgway (1901), Sibley & Monroe (1990), Wolf (1977).

86   STRIPE-CAPPED SPARROW
Aimophila strigiceps   Plate 39

Described as *Zonotrichia strigiceps* Gould 1839.

The southernmost *Aimophila* sparrow and one of only two
that are endemic to South America.

IDENTIFICATION 16-17cm. A fairly large, slim and long-
tailed sparrow; the only *Aimophila* in its range. Grey head
with rufous lateral crown- and postocular stripes, and
short black malar stripe, are distinctive. Upperparts brown,
streaked blackish; underparts pale grey, whitish on throat
and submoustachial stripe, and washed buff on flanks and
undertail-coverts. Tumbes Sparrow (87) is fairly similar in
plumage but has pale yellow, not white, bend of wing and
is shorter-tailed, larger-billed and less slim-looking.

DESCRIPTION
Sexes alike; juvenile clearly separable from subsequent
plumages.
Adult/first-year Median crown-stripe grey, lateral crown-
stripes rufous, supercilium grey (whiter on supraloral),
postocular stripe rufous, forming stripy head pattern.
Lores dark grey, eye-ring white. Ear-coverts and neck-sides
grey. Nape grey-brown, finely streaked blackish (most of
the streaks narrowly edged rufous). Upperparts buff-
brown, heavily streaked blackish on mantle, back and
scapulars; uppertail-coverts have dusky central streaks.
Lesser coverts rufous. Alula dark brown edged white. Rest
of wings blackish-brown with pale buff feather edges,
broadest (and tinged rufous) on greater and median coverts and tertials. Greater and median coverts also tipped
buff, forming two obscure wing-bars. Bend of wing white.
Tail dark brown with pale buff feather edges. Throat and
submoustachial stripe white, separated by black malar
stripe. Breast pale grey, belly whitish, flanks and undertail-coverts pale buff. Iris dark brown. Bill blackish with
horn lower mandible. Legs flesh.
Juvenile Resembles adults but upperparts are duller brown
and underparts are yellowish-buff, streaked brown on
throat, breast and flanks.

MOULT AND AGEING Adults have a complete moult,
probably after breeding, but the extent of the post-ju-

venile moult is not known. There is no evidence of a pre-breeding moult ; but see under Bridled Sparrow (82). No ageing criteria are known once the post-juvenile moult is completed.

MEASUREMENTS Only two specimens measured, both male; nominate race *strigiceps* (first number), race *dabbenei* (second).Wing (chord): 68, 76. Tail: 66, 74. Bill: 12, 13. Tarsus: 20.5, 23.

GEOGRAPHICAL VARIATION Two races.
    A. s. strigiceps (Occurs east of the Andes in SC Paraguay and in Argentina from Formosa south to Córdoba and N Buenos Aires) Described above.
    S. a. dabbenei (Occurs along the eastern base of the Argentinian Andes in Jujuy, Salta and Tucumán) Larger than *strigiceps* and has blackish lores, warmer brown upperparts and distinctly rufous edges to the coverts and tertials.

RELATIONSHIPS Appears to be most closely related to Tumbes Sparrow.

VOICE The song, given from an open perch, is rather variable; typically a series of loud, ringing, metallic notes followed (at least in race *strigiceps*) by a trill. Calls include a sharp *chip* repeated regularly.

HABITS Nest is placed on the ground, in a grass clump, or low in a bush; a cup of dried grass lined with finer plant material. 3-4 pale blue eggs are laid. Often nests in loose colonies. Feeds on seeds and insects, foraging on the ground and also in bushes and trees. Generally flies into bushes or trees when disturbed. Usually found in pairs or small flocks outside the breeding season. Appears to be less shy and more easily seen than many other *Aimophila* sparrows.

STATUS AND HABITAT Locally fairly common in arid and semi-arid open woodland, scrubby hillsides and field edges with bushes, often near human habitation, to 1000m.

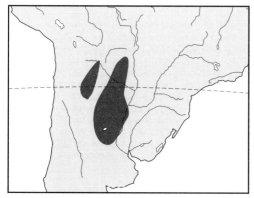

DISTRIBUTION AND MOVEMENTS Occurs in south-central Paraguay and northern Argentina. See also under Geographical Variation. Sedentary.

REFERENCES Armani (1985), Dunning (1987), Paynter & Storer (1970), Ridgely & Tudor (1989), Sibley & Monroe (1990).

87   TUMBES SPARROW
Aimophila stolzmanni   Plate 39

Described as *Haemophila stolzmanni* Taczanowski 1877. Synonym: *Rhynchospiza stolzmanni*.

A rather chunky and large-billed *Aimophila*, endemic to arid scrub and semi-desert in the Tumbesian region.

IDENTIFICATION 14.5cm. Resembles Stripe-capped Sparrow (86) in overall plumage pattern but is larger-billed, shorter-tailed and rather chunkier. Upperparts grey-brown, streaked blackish; lesser coverts rufous (as in Stripe-capped) but difficult to see. Bend of wing is pale yellow. Head pattern and underparts very similar to Stripe-capped Sparrow but supercilium and breast are slightly paler; note that these two are widely separated by range. The only other sparrow within the range of Tumbes is the very different Rufous-collared (53); Yellow-browed Sparrow (69) approaches it in range but is also quite different.

DESCRIPTION
Sexes alike; juvenile clearly different from subsequent plumages.
Adult/first-year Median crown-stripe grey, lateral crown-stripes rufous, faintly streaked blackish; both long, reaching to nape. Supercilium whitish, reaching to rear end of ear-coverts. Eye-stripe dark rufous (darker and duller on lores), also reaching to rear end of ear-coverts and often curving down slightly round it. Narrow eye-ring pale buffy-white. Ear-coverts grey, more or less unstreaked but area below eye is faintly streaked whitish. Upperparts grey-brown, washed with buff, heavily streaked with blackish-brown on mantle, back and scapulars. Lesser coverts rufous. Greater and median coverts blackish-brown with rufous-buff feather edges and pale buffy-white tips, forming obscure wing-bars. Tertials blackish-brown with broad rufous-buff edges and whitish fringes. Rest of wings blackish-brown with greyish-white feather edges. Bend of wing pale yellow. Tail blackish-brown with narrow pale greyish feather edges. Throat and submoustachial stripe whitish, separated by black malar stripe. Remainder of underparts also whitish, washed pale grey-buff on breast and flanks. Iris brown. Bill blackish with pale horn lower mandible, quite stout and conical. Legs flesh.
Juvenile Crown and upperparts buff-brown, streaked blackish on crown as well as mantle, back and scapulars. Underparts yellowish-buff, streaked dark brown on throat, breast and flanks.

MOULT AND AGEING Adults have a complete moult, probably after breeding, but the extent of the post-juvenile moult is unknown. There is no evidence of a pre-breeding moult ; but see under Bridled Sparrow (82). No ageing criteria are known once the post-juvenile moult is completed.

MEASUREMENTS Wing (chord): male (n4) 65-68. Tail: male (n4) 50-56. Bill: male (n4) 14-16.5. Tarsus: male (n4) 21-22.

GEOGRAPHICAL VARIATION Monotypic.

RELATIONSHIPS Appears to be most closely related to Stripe-capped Sparrow.

VOICE The song, generally given from an exposed perch, is a rapid series of metallic chipping notes, interspersed with trills and usually ending with a raspy or buzzing note. Calls include a sharp, high-pitched *tsip* repeated regularly.

HABITS Nest is placed on the ground, usually in a grass clump, or very close to it at the base of a bush; a cup of dry grasses and straws, lined with fine plant material and down. 4 white or pale bluish-white eggs are laid. Nests in loose colonies. Feeds on insects and seeds, foraging on the ground, generally close to cover, and also low in bushes and cacti. Although unobtrusive, it is not particularly shy or difficult to observe. Generally found in pairs throughout the year but may occur in groups outside the breeding season, which may join mixed flocks of other sparrows and finches.

STATUS AND HABITAT Fairly common in arid scrub, semi-desert with scattered bushes, cactus and trees, and dry, open woodland, mainly in interior valleys (C. Rahbek pers. comm.); not found in extensive grassland areas but often occurs by river margins and the borders of lakes and pools. Found from near sea level to about 1400m.

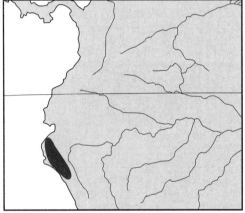

DISTRIBUTION AND MOVEMENTS Endemic to the Tumbesian region of north-western Peru (the Pacific slope from Tumbes south to northern La Libertad) and in adjoining south-western Ecuador (western Loja). Sedentary.

REFERENCES Armani (1985), Dunning (1987), Ridgely & Tudor (1989), Sibley & Monroe (1990).

88 BACHMAN'S SPARROW
Aimophila aestivalis   Plate 33

Described as *Fringilla aestivalis* Lichtenstein 1823.
Synonyms: *Fringilla bachmani, Peucaea illinoensis*.

This sparrow, closely related to Botteri's (89) and Cassin's (90), is the only sparrow endemic to the USA, although it has occurred as a vagrant in Canada. It was formerly called Pine-Woods Sparrow and occurs most commonly in open pine woods with a covering of scrub palmetto.

IDENTIFICATION 15cm. A typical *Aimophila* sparrow with a fairly large bill, flat forehead and longish rounded tail. Upperparts are greyish, strongly streaked with dark brown or rufous. Head often appears rather more strongly patterned than Botteri's and Cassin's, with the appearance of vague rufous or dark brown lateral crown-stripe and

narrow grey median crown-stripe. These are often fairly indistinct, but give the head a different appearance to Botteri's and Cassin's, which have grey crowns with more uniform fine darker streaking. Underparts with grey-buff or buff breast contrast quite sharply with whitish belly, unlike the following two species which show only a faint buff or grey-buff wash on the breast, which does not contrast with the belly. Tail appears fairly uniformly dark; the tips are paler brown with a small amount of whitish at the very end, but it is never obvious as it is on Cassin's. May have dark subterminal spots on the uppertail-coverts in fresh plumage, but they are not usually as large or well-defined as on Cassin's. Generally appears darker above and below than Botteri's and Cassin's but, apart from out-of-range vagrants, is unlikely to occur with them. Western birds are paler and more rufous above than eastern ones and have a distinct buffy breast, which contrasts noticeably with the whitish belly. A few Bachman's of the western races are very similar to the *arizonae* race of Botteri's and out-of-range birds may be difficult to identify; the sharp contrast between buff breast and whitish belly, more rufous and grey crown (usually lacking prominent blackish streaking) and blackish subterminal spots on the uppertail-coverts of Bachman's are the most useful pointers, but care is required (the uppertail-covert pattern in particular will be indistinct in worn plumage on all *Aimophila* sparrows). Juvenile Bachman's is usually noticeably darker above than juvenile Botteri's and Cassin's and has a more prominent whitish eye-ring.

DESCRIPTION
Sexes alike; juvenile clearly different from subsequent plumages.
Adult Crown grey, heavily streaked with dark chestnut and dark brown, especially at the sides. giving appearance of an indistinct greyish median stripe. Nape grey, streaked with chestnut. Supercilium greyish, becoming buffier on supraloral; lores also buffy-grey. Eye-ring pale buff. Ear-coverts buffy-grey, narrowly outlined with dark chestnut. Neck-sides and submoustachial stripe also buffy-grey, neck-sides narrowly streaked with dark chestnut. Malar stripe dark brown, narrow. Upperparts grey, strongly streaked blackish-brown and dark chestnut; streaking broadest and darkest on back and scapulars and more chestnut on mantle. Longest uppertail-coverts are chestnut with broad grey fringes and a blackish subterminal spot. Lesser coverts dark rufous with pale olive-grey fringes. Alula blackish edged whitish. Rest of wings blackish-brown, with rufous bases and broad grey edges to greater and median coverts. Flight feathers narrowly edged grey; tertials broadly edged rufous and with whitish fringes. Bend of wing pale yellow. Tail grey-brown with indistinct barring on central rectrices and pale buff-brown tips to the outer two rectrices (which may have small indistinct whitish spots at the very end). Throat pale grey-buff, breast darker grey-buff with some darker mottling at the sides; contrasts noticeably with whitish belly. Flanks, vent and undertail-coverts grey-buff. Iris dark brown. Bill dark horn with a paler lower mandible. Legs dark flesh.
First-year Bachman's (and Cassin's, and possibly some other *Aimophila* sparrows) have a complicated post-juvenile moult which occurs in two stages (see under Moult Ageing). First-years which have completed the first stage resemble adults but have a variable number of rounded 'spotted type' streaks on the breast. This 'spotting' is lost during the second stage of the post-juvenile moult (which

is really another, separate moult) in late autumn/early winter.

Juvenile Upperparts buffier than adult's, especially on nape. Crown and upperparts streaked blackish with little chestnut. Breast and flanks have distinct blackish streaks; throat also has fine dark streaks. Wing-coverts with buff, rather than grey, edges.

MOULT AND AGEING The post-juvenile moult is complete and occurs in two stages, in May-December. The first stage (May-August) involves the body feathers, the tertials and sometimes some rectrices, while the second stage (September-December) is, in effect, a complete moult, with those feathers moulted in the first stage being replaced again. The post-breeding moult is complete, occurring in June-October. All birds have a partial pre-breeding moult in March-August (extending into the breeding season), which often includes the central rectrices and sometimes some flight feathers. Once both stages of the post-juvenile moult is completed first-years resemble adults, but first-years often retain some 'spotting' on the breast until early winter (see under Description). Skull ossification complete in first-years from 1 October.

MEASUREMENTS Wing (chord): male (n30) 56-65; female (n27) 54-63. Tail: male (n39) 61-66.6; female (n9) 58.4-66. Bill: male (n39) 10.9-13.2; female (n9) 10.9-12.5. Tarsus: male (n39) 18.3-20.3; female (n9) 18.3-20.8.

GEOGRAPHICAL VARIATION Three races; *aestivalis* is generally distinguishable in the field from the other two.

A. a. illinoensis (Breeds from S Indiana and SE Illinois south through Arkansas and extreme SE Oklahoma to E Texas and Louisiana; winters in the southern part of the breeding range, mainly from S Arkansas south, and also along the Gulf coast to Mississippi) Paler and more rufous than *aestivalis* with rufous rather than dark brown and chestnut streaking on crown and upperparts, and a distinctly buffier breast; it also has more rufous in the wing-coverts and tertial edges.

A. a. bachmani (Breeds from extreme S Ohio and W Virginia south to Mississippi and W Florida; winters in the southern part of the breeding range, mainly from N Alabama and Georgia south, and also to C Florida) Very similar to *illinoensis* and the two are doubtfully distinguishable, although *illinoensis* averages paler and more rufous on the upperparts than *bachmani*.

A. a. aestivalis (Resident on the Atlantic coastal plain from N Carolina south to S Florida in Collier County) Described above.

VOICE The song, given from low in a pine tree or bush, on a grass stem, or in a short song flight, is a clear whistled note followed by a slow trill on a different pitch.

HABITS Nest is placed on the ground in a grass clump or at the base of a bush or palmetto; a dome-shaped structure of dried grasses, lined with finer plant material and hair. 3-5 white or pale bluish-white eggs are laid in April-July. Incubation period is 12-14 days and the young fledge after 10-11 days. Double- or triple-brooded. Male sings mostly in the morning and evening, and often continues singing well into the summer. Often breeds in loose colonies. Feeds on seeds and insects, especially grasshoppers and beetles, foraging mainly on the ground in cover, but also sometimes low in bushes. Generally shy and secretive

except when singing; it does not fly far when flushed, but soon drops back into cover and disappears. Generally found singly or in pairs throughout the year.

STATUS AND HABITAT Locally common but decreasing in northern part of range and has disappeared from many localities. Favours open pine woods with a ground covering of scrub palmetto in the south, but also found in open oak woodlands, brushy hillsides and weedy fields with developing scrub, especially in the north. It seems to require open mature forest with numerous clearings, a dense ground flora and a sparse understorey. Populations move on as clearings become forested and/or the ground flora or understorey becomes unsuitable, and therefore they need a steady supply of suitable habitat to sustain themselves. Such habitat is maintained naturally by sporadic fires, and controlled burning helps to maintain it.

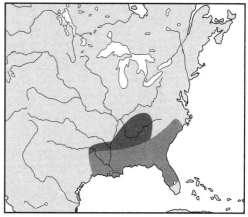

DISTRIBUTION AND MOVEMENTS Found in southeastern USA, from the southern parts of Indiana and Illinois, and N Carolina, south to the Gulf coast (eastern Texas to Florida), but excluding the higher Appalachian mountains. Resident in the southern part of the range, with northern birds moving into the southern part for the winter. See also under Geographical Variation. Vagrant north to Ontario.

REFERENCES Armani (1985), Bent (1968), Dunn & Blom (1983), Dunning (1993), Dunning & Watts (1990 & 1991), Ehrlich *et al.* (1988), Farrand (1983), Hardin & Probasco (1983), Kaufman (1990), Pyle *et al.* (1987), Ridgway (1901), Sibley & Monroe (1990), Terres (1980), Willoughby (1986), Wolf (1977).

89 BOTTERI'S SPARROW
Aimophila botterii   Plate 33

Described as *Zonotrichia botterii* Sclater 1858.
Synonyms: *Peucaea aestivalis, Coturniculus mexicanus, Ammodramus petenicus.*

A widespread and variable *Aimophila* with few relieving features, whose range just reaches the USA in the north.

IDENTIFICATION 14-15cm. A very plain sparrow with the largish bill, flat crown and longish rounded tail typical of the genus *Aimophila*. Head and upperparts greyish, streaked with rufous and blackish-brown, the different colours predominating in different races. Supercilium pale grey, relatively indistinct. Underparts whitish with pale buff or grey-buff wash on breast, flanks and undertail-coverts. In the northern part of the range may be confused with Cassin's Sparrow (90), but the tail is plain brown and lacks the white tips shown by that species (although Botteri's often shows paler brown tips to the tail feathers). Note also that the uppertail-coverts of Botteri's have a broad shaft streak (appear streaked) whereas those of Cassin's have a narrower shaft streak and a large dark subterminal spot (appear spotted). The upperparts of Botteri's are also streaked, whereas they are more variegated in Cassin's; these two features are of much less value in late summer, however, when the plumage is worn. Botteri's normally has a buffier wash on the breast than Cassin's, appears slightly bulkier and thicker-necked in the field, and lacks the faint dark streaks on the rear flanks which Cassin's usually shows. The songs of these two are quite different (see under Voice). It is also worth noting that Botteri's Sparrows never seem to get as excessively worn in late summer as Cassin's. Bachman's Sparrow (89) usually appears darker and more heavily streaked above than Botteri's. It also has a much more distinct grey or buffy-grey breast (which contrasts with the whitish belly), a more 'stripy' head and dark tips to the uppertail-coverts (like Cassin's Sparrow); some western Bachman's may, however, appear quite similar to Botteri's (particularly the *arizonae* race) especially in worn plumage. Bachman's also has a distinct song and the two do not overlap in range (but beware of extralimital birds). Other *Aimophila* sparrows have more distinct head patterns than Botteri's.

DESCRIPTION
Sexes alike; juvenile clearly different from subsequent plumages.
Adult/first-year Crown, nape and upperparts greyish, streaked dark brown (most streaks are narrowly edged with rufous). Supercilium grey, relatively indistinct. Grey-brown ear-coverts, faintly outlined darker; neck-sides paler and greyer with faint darker streaks. Lesser coverts olive-grey. Alula dark brown edged whitish. Rest of wings dark brown with pale rufous-buff feather edges, broadest on greater and median coverts, and tertials. Bend of wing pale yellow. Tail dark brown with narrow paler grey-buff feather edges. Throat and belly whitish, breast, flanks and undertail-coverts pale grey-buff. Iris dark brown. Bill dark brown with paler brownish-horn lower mandible. Legs dark flesh.
Juvenile Noticeably buffier than adult overall, breast and flanks with distinct dark streaks and throat also faintly streaked.

Tail and uppertail-covert pattern

MOULT AND AGEING The post-juvenile moult is complete and occurs in June-December; it may occur in two stages (as in Bachman's Sparrow). The post-breeding moult is complete and occurs in June-October. All birds (at least in northernmost populations) also have a partial/incomplete pre-breeding moult, involving all the body feathers and some tail feathers, in February-April. First-years resemble adults in plumage once the post-juvenile moult is completed and, as this is a complete moult, tail shape is not useful for ageing. Skull ossification complete in first-years from 1 October.

MEASUREMENTS Wing (chord): male (n127) 54.9-71; female (n44) 56.6-68. Tail: male (n13) 53.1-70.6; female (n6) 54.1-64.3. Bill: male (n21) 11.4-14; female (n14) 10.9-13. Tarsus: male (n21) 19.8-23.4; female (n14) 20.3-22.9 (*petenica* averages shortest in wing and tail, and longest in bill).

GEOGRAPHICAL VARIATION Nine races recognised in Peters; two others (*sartorii* and *tabascensis*) have also been described but are included under *petenica* in Peters. The four southernmost races (*petenica*, *spadiconigrescens*, *vantynei* and *vulcanica*) were formerly considered a separate species, Peten or Yellow-carpalled Sparrow.
  A. b. arizonae (Breeds in SE Arizona and in adjacent NW Mexico, south to S Sonora and N Durango; winters in the southern part of the breeding range, mainly south of C Sonora and has occurred south to Morelos) Distinctly more rufous on the crown and upperparts than *texana*, *botterii* and *mexicana*, and paler rufous above than *goldmani*.
  A. b. texana (Breeds in extreme SE Texas and adjacent E Tamaulipas; winter range is apparently unknown) Distinctly greyer above than *arizonae*, noticeably paler above than *mexicana*, and paler and greyer above than *botterii*.
  A. b. mexicana (Resident in the central highlands of Mexico, from SE Durango and San Luis Potosí south to Colima, Michoacán and Distrito Federal) A dark race, noticeably darker above (with broad blackish streaking) than other northern races.
  A. b. goldmani (Resident on the west coast of Mexico in S Sinaloa and Nayarit) A rufous race, like *arizonae*, but noticeably darker rufous above than that race.
  A. b. botterii (Occurs in the highlands of S and SE Mexico, from S San Luis Potosí south and south-east to W Chiapas) Described above. Wing (32, sexes combined): 58.4-69.9. Tail (32, sexes combined): 56.4-70.6 Bill. (32, sexes combined: 10.9-12.7.
  A. b. petenica (Resident in the lowlands of SE Mexico in E Veracruz, Tabasco, E Chiapas and the Yucatán Peninsula, N Guatemala and Belize) A small and very dark race, appearing mostly blackish above, and also very pale (whitish) on the underparts. Wing (10, sexes combined): 54.9-59.7. Tail (10, sexes combined): 53.1-57.9. Bill (10, sexes combined): 12.2-14.
  A. b. spadiconigrescens (Resident in pine savannas in the lowlands of N Honduras and NE Nicaragua) Similar to *petenica* in being very dark above, but the edges to the upperpart feathers are browner (less greyish) and it is not quite as pale on the underparts.
  A. b. vantynei (Resident in the highlands of C Guatemala) Quite dark brown above, but paler than the other southern races. The underparts are darker than *petenica* but paler than *vulcanica*.
  A. b. vulcanica (Resident in the highlands of Nicaragua and N Costa Rica) A dark race, similar to *petenica* but larger, slightly paler above and noticeably duskier below; it has the duskiest underparts of all the races, which contributes to a dark overall appearance.

VOICE The song, generally given from a low perch in a bush but sometimes in flight, is variously described as several pairs of short double notes followed by a trill and sometimes 1 or 2 final high-pitched whistled notes (Arizona); an unstructured medley of chirping and chipping notes and phrases (Costa Rica); a short, accelerating rattly trill, often preceded by two or more high sharp notes (southern USA). The main call is a sharp *tsit* or *swip*, either strong and rasping or weak and thin, but it is relatively silent outside the breeding season.

HABITS Nest is placed on the ground, low in a clump of grass or under the lower branches of a small bush; a deep, compact cup of dry leaves and grass stems, sometimes lined with finer grasses. 2-5 white eggs are laid in May-September. In Arizona at least, nesting appears to be timed to coincide with the onset of the rainy season. Very shy and secretive, difficult to observe in the open except when singing. Feeds on seeds and insects. Forages on the ground, generally hopping unobtrusively through grassy cover and running rapidly across open ground. Often cocks tail. Flight is low, fluttering and rather jerky. Found in pairs or small groups (family parties?), sometimes with other sparrows, especially Cassin's.

STATUS AND HABITAT Locally fairly common but rare in Costa Rica. Occurs in lowland semi-arid and arid grasslands, often boulder-strewn or with sparse cacti, live oak, mesquite or other scrub; also scrubby fields, grassland in highlands and coastal prairies. Found from sea level to 2700m but generally below 1100m.

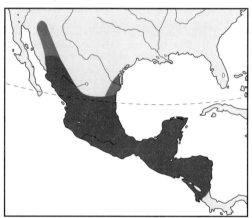

DISTRIBUTION AND MOVEMENTS Occurs from extreme south-eastern Arizona and extreme south-eastern Texas south through Central America to north-western Costa Rica. See also under Geographical Variation. Mainly sedentary, although northern populations are migratory, with most leaving USA and extreme northern Mexico in August and September, and returning in late April/May.

REFERENCES Armani (1985), Bent (1968), Dunn & Blom (1983), Farrand (1983), Kaufman (1990), Oberholser (1974), Peterson & Chalif (1973), Pyle *et al.* (1987), Ridgway (1901), Stiles & Skutch (1989), Terres (1980), Webster (1959), Wolf (1977).

90 CASSIN'S SPARROW
Aimophila cassinii   **Plate 33**

Described as *Zonotrichia cassinii* Woodhouse 1852.

A dull grey-brown *Aimophila* sparrow of the arid scrub and mesquite of the southern USA and northern Mexico.

IDENTIFICATION 15cm. A dull grey-brown *Aimophila* with rufous-brown streaking on the upperparts that is often quite obscure in worn plumage, and a longish rounded tail with whitish tips to the feathers that are usually conspicuous in flight. Greyish supercilium fairly distinct, grey-buff ear-coverts are narrowly bordered with dark brown. Underparts whitish, with whiter throat and a faint buff wash to the breast and belly. Botteri's Sparrow (89) is very similar but has obscure pale brown, rather than noticeable whitish, tips to the tail feathers. The *arizonae* race of Botteri's is noticeably more rufous than Cassin's, but the greyer *texana* race is similar to Cassin's in plumage as well as size and shape. In addition to the tail pattern, Cassin's upperpart feathers have dark subterminal spots or bars (giving a rather variegated look at a distance), rather than a dark central shaft streak; this is most noticeable on the uppertail-coverts but the pattern may completely disappear in worn plumage. Also in fresh plumage, the greater coverts have broader and paler tips than on Botteri's, forming a fairly noticeable wing-bar (this mark also disappears in worn plumage). The tail is generally more strongly barred than Botteri's (but less so in the eastern rufous populations) and the upperparts are more variegated. It is important to note that all these differences are more obscure and may not be applicable in worn plumage, when Cassin's usually appears more worn (often extremely worn in late summer) and less streaked above than Botteri's. In addition to these points, Cassin's tends to look somewhat slimmer and sleeker than Botteri's and has faint but distinct dark streaks on the rear flanks. Bachman's Sparrow (88) lacks whitish tips to the tail feathers (they have pale brown tips with white at the very end), are more heavily streaked above (always conspicuous, even in worn plumage) and have distinct buff or grey-buff breast and flanks. They also have a different head pattern, with the appearance of a rufous or dark brown lateral crown-stripe (streaked grey) and a grey median crown-stripe (streaked darker) rather than the greyish crown, fairly uniformly streaked with dark brown, of Cassin's. Juvenile Cassin's is very similar to juvenile Botteri's, especially the *arizonae* race, but is slightly paler and greyer (greyish-white rather than buffy-white) on the underparts, averages less heavily streaked on the breast, has a more variegated upperpart pattern (like adult), and has the adult's tail pattern.

DESCRIPTION
Sexes alike; juvenile clearly different from subsequent plumages.
Adult fresh Crown grey, finely streaked with rufous and some blackish-brown. Nape and neck-sides grey, streaked with rufous (little blackish-brown) except immediately behind ear-coverts. Supercilium grey, paler and buffer on supraloral. Lores pale grey, ear-coverts grey-buff, finely streaked whitish and narrowly framed with dark brown. Mantle and scapulars grey, the individual feathers with much rufous and a black shaft streak and anchor-shaped subterminal mark, giving a variegated, rather than

293

streaked, effect. Back and rump similar but less boldly patterned. Uppertail-coverts grey-brown with pale grey feather fringes, narrow indistinct darker shaft streaks and obvious dark anchor-shaped subterminal marks, similar to other upperpart feathers. Wings blackish-brown with pale grey feather edges, broadest on coverts, and whiter on tertials. Bend of wing pale yellow. Tail grey-brown; central rectrices with diffuse darker shaft streak and noticeable darker barring. Outer three rectrices have noticeable whitish tips, largest on the outer feather (rectrix 6) and smallest on rectrix 4. Underparts whitish, whitest on throat and belly and with a faint grey-buff wash on breast and undertail-coverts. Iris dark brown. Bill dark horn with a paler lower mandible. Legs dark flesh.

Adult worn Plumage becomes very worn in late summer and appears scruffy and much plainer, almost unstreaked, on the upperparts; the variegated pattern is lost and the wing feathers largely lose their greyish and whitish edges.

First-year Cassin's has a similar post-juvenile moult pattern to Bachman's Sparrow (which see) and first-years which have completed the first stage of the moult often (but not always) have some 'spotted type' streaking on the breast, which is lost during the second stage of the moult. This 'spotting' is very variable, often almost or completely absent and, if present, may very occasionally be retained into adult plumage. Therefore, only birds with noticeably heavy 'spotting' on the breast should be aged as first-year.

Juvenile Slightly buffier overall than adult; upperparts have less variegated pattern and underparts have indistinct darker streaking on breast and flanks.

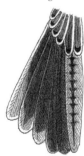

Tail and uppertail-covert pattern

MOULT AND AGEING The post-juvenile moult is complete, occurring in June-November in two stages, as in Bachman's Sparrow. The post-breeding moult is also complete, occurring in August-November. These moults occur on the breeding grounds or on post-breeding territories. All birds have an incomplete pre-breeding moult in February-June (often extending into the breeding season), which generally includes the tertials and central rectrices, and sometimes other flight feathers as well. Once both stages of the the post-juvenile moult is complete, first-years resemble adults, and some resemble adults after the first stage (see under Description). Tail feather shape is not useful for ageing, as the juvenile tail is moulted. Skull ossification complete in first-years from 15 September.

MEASUREMENTS Wing (chord): male (n30) 59-68; female (n30) 56-65. Tail: male (n20) 61-71.6; female (n5) 63.5-69.9. Bill: male (n20) 10.2-11.7; female (n5) 10.2-11.9. Tarsus: male (n20) 18.5-20.6; female (n5) 18.3-20.6.

GEOGRAPHICAL VARIATION No races described, but some birds (mainly in the east of the range) tend to be more rufous above, slightly buffier below, and have plainer tails with less obvious shaft streaks and barring on the central rectrices.

VOICE The song, generally given during a short, fluttering song-flight but sometimes from a perch on a low bush, is quite musical and very distinctive; it typically starts with a soft double whistle, followed by a trill, a low whistle and then a higher note. Calls include a trill of soft *pit* notes, a chittering used in territorial defence, a *tseep* note and a louder *chip*, but this species is relatively silent outside the breeding season.

HABITS Nest is placed on the ground, hidden under a bush, cactus or grass clump; a cup of dried grass, weed and grass stalks, lined with hair and fine plant material. 3-5 (usually 4) white or pale blue eggs are laid in April-July (mostly in May). Incubation and fledging periods unrecorded. Concentrations of territories occur in favourable habitat, which give the appearance of a loose colony. At least in Arizona, incidence of singing increases with the onset of the rainy season (D. Curson). Male sings mostly during a short fluttering song-flight, often through the night as well as the morning and evening (and through the day at a lower intensity). Feeds on seeds and insects, foraging on the ground, often inside cactus scrub or under bushes. Seldom drinks water and can seemingly go without doing so altogether. Generally shy and secretive, except when singing. Outside the breeding season generally found in pairs or small groups.

STATUS AND HABITAT Generally common. Occurs in arid grasslands and short-grass plains with scattered bushes, mesquite, cactus and yucca scrub; also sometimes in grassland with scrub bordering agricultural land. Found in lowlands and the lower grassy slopes of hills and mountains, up to 1800m.

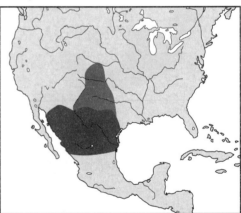

DISTRIBUTION AND MOVEMENTS Breeds in south-central USA, from extreme south-western Nebraska, eastern Colorado and western Kansas south to south-eastern Arizona and Texas, and in northern Mexico, from the USA border south to Sinaloa and Tamaulipas. Sedentary in southern part of range (from south-eastern Arizona, southern New Mexico and southern Texas, south to Mexico) with northern birds moving south to winter in the southern part of the range and possibly south to Guanajuato. Post-breeding dispersal occurs with vagrants recorded in western USA (especially California) and north to Ontario and Nova Scotia, in late summer and autumn.

Following post-breeding dispersal, migrant birds leave the breeding area in late October/early November and return from March, although they may not be noticeable until they start singing in late April or May.

REFERENCES Armani (1985), Bent (1968), Dunn & Blom (1983), Farrand (1983), Kaufman (1990), Oberholser (1974), Peterson & Chalif (1973), Pyle *et al.* (1987), Ridgway (1901), Terres (1980), Willoughby (1986), Wolf (1977).

91 RUFOUS-WINGED SPARROW
Aimophila carpalis   Plate 34

Described as *Peucaea carpalis* Coues 1873.

A small *Aimophila* sparrow, endemic to arid flat grassland areas with thorn scrub in north-western Mexico and southern Arizona.

IDENTIFICATION 14.5cm. A small, slim *Aimophila*, rather reminiscent of a *Spizella* sparrow but with the typical rounded *Aimophila* tail. Has fairly short but distinct moustachial and malar stripes which are prominent in pale greyish face. Crown rufous, broadly streaked with grey, narrow eye-stripe rufous. Upperparts greyish-buff with darker streaks. Two indistinct pale buff wing-bars and pale buff tertial edges. Underparts pale greyish-white. Distinctive rufous lesser coverts usually concealed. Juvenile is buffier overall and has dark, not rufous, streaks on crown and brownish streaks on breast and flanks. It shares the dark moustachial and malar stripes with the adult. Smaller than Rufous-crowned Sparrow with distinct moustachial (as well as malar) stripe, grey-streaked rufous crown, buffy wing-bars and tertial edges and buffier upperparts with more distinct and darker streaks. With its small size, buffy-grey upperparts and buffy wing-bars it is rather similar to the *Spizella* sparrows, but is readily distinguished from them by the rounded tail and relatively large bill.

DESCRIPTION
Sexes alike; juvenile clearly different from subsequent plumages.
Adult/first-year Crown and nape rufous broadly streaked with grey, especially along the median stripe. Long and broad supercilium pale grey, tinged buff, joining with grey neck-sides. Narrow eye-stripe rufous, curving round behind rear edge of ear-coverts. Narrow eye-ring whitish and fairly indistinct. Lores and ear-coverts pale buffy-grey, often separated from grey neck-sides by narrow rufous rear edge. Shortish narrow moustachial and malar stripes black, separated by pale buffy-grey submoustachial area. Upperparts greyish-buff, streaked dark brown on mantle and scapulars (the streaks are narrowly edged rufous). Lesser coverts rufous. Rest of wings dark brown with narrow grey-buff edges to remiges and primary coverts, and whitish edge to alula. Greater and median coverts broadly edged buff and tipped buffy-white, forming two relatively distinct wing-bars. Tertials broadly edged pale buffy-white. Bend of wing white. Tail grey-brown with pale greyish feather edges and sometimes a hint of darker cross-barring on the central rectrices. Underparts pale greyish-white, greyest on breast and faintly washed buff on flanks. Iris dark brown. Bill flesh-horn with paler yellowish-flesh lower mandible. Legs flesh.
Juvenile Buffier than adult, especially on face, upperparts,

wing-bars and tertial edges. Crown with dark brown, rather than rufous, streaking, and upperpart streaking lacks rufous edges. Eye-stripe dark brown rather than rufous. Breast and flank with dark brown streaks. Shares moustachial and malar stripes with adult but they may be dark brown rather than black. Bill less bicoloured than adult.

MOULT AND AGEING The post-juvenile moult is partial/incomplete, occurring in August-November, and often includes the tertials and sometimes other remiges. The post-breeding moult is complete, occurring in September-November. These moults occur after breeding and, as the timing of the breeding season varies from year to year, so does the timing of the moults. All birds have an incomplete pre-breeding moult in May-June which includes the central (and sometimes other) rectrices and often some or most of the remiges. First-years resemble adults once the post-juvenile moult is completed, but the juvenile plumage is often retained until late in the autumn, and a few birds may show some breast streaking through the winter; these can be aged as first-years. From November to April, birds showing symmetrical contrast between worn and fresh remiges can be aged as first-years; this is only useful in the hand and may be difficult to judge. Skull ossification normally complete in first-years from 15 November, but may be complete by 1 October in wet years when the birds breed earlier.

MEASUREMENTS Wing (chord): male (n36) 58-67; female (n36) 55-63.5. Tail: male (n6) 63.5-68; female (n6) 61.7-67.3. Bill: male (n6) 10.2-10.7; female (n6) 9.6-10.7. Tarsus: male (n6) 18.3-18.5; female (n6) 18.3-19.8.

GEOGRAPHICAL VARIATION Three similar races.
A. c. carpalis (Occurs in SC Arizona and NC Sonora) Described above.
A. c. bangsi (Occurs in S Sonora and N Sinaloa) More heavily streaked above than *carpalis*, has more rufous in the crown and slightly darker throat and flanks. In these characters it is intermediate between *carpalis* and *cohaerens*.
A. c. cohaerens (Occurs in C Sinaloa, intergrading with *bangsi* in the north of its range) More heavily streaked above than *bangsi*, darker on throat and flanks, and has more rufous in the crown, but intergrades occur.

VOICE The song, generally given from an exposed perch in a bush, is rather variable but typically a staccato series of *chip* notes, accelerating into a chipping trill. Calls include a sharp, high-pitched *seep*, repeated regularly.

HABITS Nest is generally placed low in a bush or tree; a cup of grasses and small twigs, lined with finer grasses. 2-5 (usually 4) pale blue eggs are laid in April-September. Incubation period unrecorded, but the fledging period is 8-9 days. Nesting season is timed to coincide with the onset of the rainy season and is thus quite variable, although the rainy season generally starts in late June/early July. Feeds on seeds and insects, foraging on the ground and in bushes and scrub. Rather shy and inconspicuous, and may be elusive when not singing. Usually found in pairs or small groups (family parties?) throughout the year; in the autumn, these often associate with Black-throated (79), Chipping (72) and Brewer's (74) Sparrows.

STATUS AND HABITAT Locally fairly common to common in semi-arid and arid areas of flat grassland mixed with thorn scrub, bunchgrass, mesquite or cholla, from sea level to 1200m.

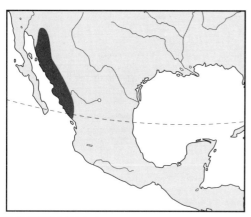

DISTRIBUTION AND MOVEMENTS Occurs in south-central Arizona and north-western Mexico, south to central Sinaloa. See also under Geographical Variation. Was apparently formerly more common and occurred in the south-western USA in New Mexico and south-eastern California as well as Arizona. Sedentary.

REFERENCES Armani (1985), Dunn & Blom (1983), Ehrlich *et al.* (1988), Farrand (1983), Paynter & Storer (1970), Phillips (1951), Pyle *et al.* (1987), Ridgway (1901), Sibley & Monroe (1990), Terres (1980), Wolf (1977).

---

92   RUFOUS-CROWNED SPARROW
Aimophila ruficeps   Plate 34

Described as *Ammodramus ruficeps* Cassin 1852.
Synonyms: *Peucaea ruficeps, Zonotrichia boucardi.*

One of the most widespread of the *Aimophila* sparrows, with twelve races generally recognised.

IDENTIFICATION 15cm. A smallish *Aimophila* with rufous crown and postocular stripe, sides of head mostly greyish, grey-brown upperparts with dull rufous streaks and pale grey-buff underparts with a noticeable black malar stripe. Rufous crown often has a vague greyish median stripe. Juvenile lacks rufous crown and is buffier overall with indistinct buffy wing-bars and dark streaks on breast and flanks. American Tree (71) and Chipping Sparrows (72) share the rufous crown but have a notched, not rounded, tail, white wing-bars, and lack a prominent black malar stripe; Chipping also has obvious white supercilium in breeding plumage and American Tree has a bicoloured bill, rufous breast-sides and a black spot in centre of breast. These two *Spizella* sparrows are noticeably different from Rufous-crowned in shape. Rufous-winged Sparrow (91) has rufous crown streaked with grey, black moustachial as well as malar stripe, buffier-grey upperparts with darker and more obvious streaking, rufous lesser coverts (usually concealed) and narrow whitish wing-bars and tertial edges. Oaxaca Sparrow (93) can be similar to Rufous-crowned; see under that species for details but note especially the all-black bill, blackish lores and ocular area, emphasising whitish supraloral and broken eye-ring, bright rufous tertial edges and the browner upperparts with darker, more prominent streaking, of Oaxaca. Rusty Sparrow (94) is noticeably larger than Rufous-crowned with a heavier bill; most individuals are considerably brighter than Rufous-

crowned with a stronger head pattern, rufous upperparts, a noticeably rufous tail, rufous edges to wing feathers and a distinct warm buff wash to flanks and undertail-coverts. North-western Rusty Sparrows (in Sonora, western Chihuahua, northern Sinaloa and north-western Durango) are duller and more similar to Rufous-crowned but are still noticeably larger with a darker, heavier bill, dull rufous-brown tail (tail on Rufous-crowned is normally grey-brown but may have dull rufous-brown feather edges), brown (not rufous) postocular stripe and broken eye-ring (at least in front of eye).

DESCRIPTION
Sexes alike; juvenile clearly different from subsequent plumages.
Adult/first-year Crown rufous, sometimes with a vague, narrow greyish median stripe from the forehead to above the eye. Long supercilium greyish, becoming whitish on supraloral. Lores dusky, eye-ring whitish and complete. Postocular stripe rufous, often indistinct. Ear-coverts dusky greyish, neck-sides greyish or buffy-grey, submoustachial stripe greyish-buff. Long and prominent malar stripe black. Nape and upperparts greyish, often with a faint olive tinge, and with broad but relatively indistinct rufous-brown streaks on nape, mantle and scapulars. Lesser coverts grey. Rest of wings dark brown with pale grey-brown feather edges. Bend of wing whitish. Tail dark brown with pale grey-buff to dull rufous-brown feather edges; central rectrices sometimes also have a hint of darker cross-barring. Throat greyish-white, breast slightly darker greyish, belly whitish, flanks and undertail-coverts greyish-buff. Similar year-round but rufous crown feathers may have grey fringes in fresh plumage. Iris dark brown. Bill dark grey with greyish-flesh lower mandible. Legs dark flesh.
Juvenile Buffier overall than adult and with dark streaks on breast and flanks. Rufous crown and postocular stripe lacking; crown is buff-brown, streaked darker, supercilium pale grey-buff, lores and ear-coverts buff-brown. Two indistinct buffy wing-bars; wing and tail feathers have more rufous edges than on adults. Shares dark malar stripe with adult.

MOULT AND AGEING The post-juvenile moult is incomplete, occurring in June-November and usually including the outer primaries, tertials and rectrices. The post-breeding moult is complete, also occurring in June-November. The exact timing of these moults depends on timing of breeding, which may vary from year to year. There is no evidence of a pre-breeding moult, but more study is required on this. First-years resemble adults in plumage once the post-juvenile moult is completed, but some may be told in the hand by slight contrast between old juvenile primaries and fresher adult ones, at least through to the first summer. Skull ossification complete in first-years from 1 October but many birds retain small unossified 'windows' through the first spring.

MEASUREMENTS Wing (chord): male (n93) 55.9-71; female (n59) 55.4-70.6. Tail: male (n63) 57.1-74.9; female (n29) 58.9-74.9. Bill: male (n63) 10.4-14; female (n29) 10.4-14. Tarsus: male (n63) 19-22.4; female (n29) 19-22.1 (*ruficeps* is noticeably smaller than most other races, especially in wing and tail).

GEOGRAPHICAL VARIATION Twelve races are generally recognised. The overall variation is quite marked, but adjoining races are generally very similar and often not identifiable in the field.

A. r. ruficeps (Occurs in C California on the coastal mountain ranges and on the western slope of the Sierra Nevada) Appears darker than *eremoeca* with darker and more distinct rufous-brown streaking on upperparts; it is also noticeably smaller. Wing (17, sexes combined): 55.4-61.

A. r. canescens (Occurs in SW California and extreme NW Baja California) Similar to *ruficeps* but averages slightly darker.

A. r. obscura (Occurs on Santa Cruz, Anacapa and Santa Catalina Islands, off SW California) Similar to *canescens* but averages slightly darker.

A. r. sanctorum (Occurs on the Todos Santos Islands off NW Baja California) The darkest of the coastal races, averaging darker (especially below) than *obscura*.

A. r. sororia (Occurs in the Cape District of S Baja California) The palest of the coastal races, averaging paler above and below than *ruficeps*.

A. r. eremoeca (Occurs from SE Colorado and NE Arkensas south through Oklahoma, E New Mexico and W Texas to N Chihuahua and C Coahuila. Most are sedentary but birds breeding in Oklahoma, W Arkansas, SW Kansas and SE Colorado move south for the winter, as far as Puebla and N Veracruz in E Mexico) Described above. Wing (13, sexes combined): 61.2-68.5.

A. r. scottii (Occurs from SE Nevada and extreme SW Utah south through New Mexico and W Arizona to N Sonora and NW Chihuahua) Very similar to *eremoeca* but averages slightly darker grey and with slightly narrower and darker rufous streaks on upperparts. Wing (22, sexes combined): 60.2-70.4.

A. r. rupicola (Occurs in the mountains of SW Arizona) Similar to *scottii* but slightly darker and greyer above (thus quite similar to the coastal California races).

A. r. simulans (Occurs in NW Mexico from SE Sonora and SW Chihuahua south to NE Jalisco and W Guanajuato) Averages rather more rufous above and paler below than *scottii* and other inland races (similar to *sororia* in plumage but with a smaller bill).

A. r. fusca (Occurs in W Mexico from S Nayarit south to Colima and Michoacán, intergrading with *simulans* in W Guanajuato and probably E Jalisco) Similar to *australis* but averages darker and more extensively rufous on the upperparts, and has a darker rufous crown which apparently never shows a grey median stripe. Wing (13, sexes combined): 58.4-66.

A. r. boucardi (Occurs in E Mexico from S Coahuila, where it intergrades with *eremoeca*, Nuevo León and S Tamaulipas south to N Puebla and CW Veracruz) Similar to *eremoeca* but averages darker, above and below, with the ground colour of the upperparts more brown than grey, and the streaking above is dull brown (not rufous). Wing (23, sexes combined): 60.4-70.6.

A. r. australis (Occurs in S Mexico in S Puebla, Guerrero and Oaxaca) Similar to *scottii* but averages smaller and may have a shorter and stouter bill. Wing (4, sexes combined): 59.7-64.

VOICE The song, generally given from the top of a bush or low in a tree, is a short, rapid, bubbling and jumbled series of *chip* notes. Calls include a distinctive nasal *dear* or *chur*, often repeated, and a thin *tsi*.

HABITS Nest is placed on or very close to the ground,

usually hidden in a grass clump but sometimes low in a bush; a cup of grasses and dried grass stems, lined with finer plant material. 4 white or pale blue eggs are laid in March-August. Incubation and fledging periods unrecorded. Often nests in loose colonies. Feeds on seeds, insects, berries and sometimes small lizards, foraging mainly on the ground, close to grass cover or rocky areas, but also low in bushes. Less shy and more easily seen than many *Aimophila* sparrows; often responds to 'pishing' and sometimes visits feeders in south-eastern Arizona. Seldom flies far when flushed. Usually found in pairs or small groups outside the breeding season.

STATUS AND HABITAT Locally common on rocky hillsides with short grass and scrub, chaparral, coastal sage scrub and short grass and rocky areas in open pine-oak and pinyon-juniper woodland; generally in semi-arid or arid areas, from near sea level (on California coast) to 3000m.

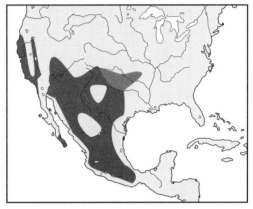

DISTRIBUTION AND MOVEMENTS Occurs in southwestern USA and Mexico, south to Oaxaca. Extreme north-eastern populations are short- to medium-distance migrants, moving south in winter as far as eastern Mexico. See also under Geographical Variation.

REFERENCES Armani (1985), Bent (1968), Dunn & Blom (1983), Farrand (1983), Paynter & Storer (1970), Peterson & Chalif (1973), Pyle *et al.* (1987), Ridgway (1901), Sibley & Monroe (1990), Terres (1980), Wolf (1977).

93   OAXACA SPARROW
Aimophila notostricta   Plate 34

Described as *Peucaea notostricta* Sclater & Salvin 1868.

A comparatively little-known *Aimophila* sparrow of arid interior Oaxaca.

IDENTIFICATION 15-16.5cm. A medium-sized *Aimophila*, similar to Rufous-crowned Sparrow but slightly larger. Crown and postocular stripe rufous; cheeks, supercilium and median crown-stripe grey. Bill and lores blackish, broken eye-ring whitish. Shares black malar stripe with Rufous-crowned and Rusty Sparrows. Upperparts warm brown with distinct blackish-brown streaks. Underparts whitish with greyish wash across breast and distinctly grey-buff flanks. Wings have rufous edges to tertials. Juvenile is more olive-brown above, lacks the rufous crown, is washed buff on the supercilium and submoustachial stripe, is streaked on the breast and flanks, and has a noticeably heavier cinnamon-buff wash to the breast-sides and flanks. Oaxaca is most similar to Rufous-crowned Sparrow; adults told from Rufous-crowned by all-black bill (lacking greyish-flesh on lower mandible), blackish lores and ocular area, emphasising narrow white or whitish supraloral and broken eye-ring, blackish streaking on upperparts (rufous-brown on Rufous-crowned), rufous edges to tertials (Rufous-crowned may have dull rufous-brown tertial edges, but they are more often grey-brown), warm buffy of buffy-grey flanks (grey or grey-brown on Rufous-crowned) and buff undertail-coverts (pale greyish-brown or greyish-white on Rufous-crowned). Juvenile Oaxaca has a heavier and more extensive buff wash to the flanks and undertail-coverts than juvenile Rufous-crowned (which has a pale greyish-buff wash) and is warmer olive-brown on the upperparts with brighter rufous tertial edges. Rusty Sparrow is also fairly similar to Oaxaca but is larger with a heavier-looking bicoloured bill (dark grey on lower mandible), a rufous tail (grey-brown on Oaxaca), more rufous-brown upperparts, rufous edges to primaries and greater coverts as well as tertials, and more contrasting underparts with whitish throat and belly, greyish-buff breast and quite rich buff flanks and undertail-coverts. Juvenile Rusty is noticeably more rufous on wings and upperparts than juvenile Oaxaca. Rusty Sparrow does not occur sympatrically with Oaxaca, but Rufous-crowned does.

DESCRIPTION
Sexes alike; juvenile clearly different from subsequent plumages.
Adult/first-year Crown rufous-brown, finely streaked blackish and with grey median stripe. Distinct grey supercilium, extending past rear edge of ear-coverts, becoming whitish on supraloral. Lores and ocular area blackish, emphasising broken whitish eye-ring. Postocular stripe rufous. Ear-coverts grey, neck-sides more grey-brown. Submoustachial stripe buffy-white, narrow malar strip black. Nape and upperparts warm brown; nape greyer in centre and finely streaked blackish, mantle and scapulars more heavily streaked with blackish (the blackish streaks narrowly edged with rufous). Lesser coverts dark brown fringed pale grey. Rest of wings dark brown, coverts and most other feathers edged grey-buff (buffier and broadest on greater coverts), but tertials and inner secondaries broadly edged rufous. When fresh, tertials have whitish spot at tip broken in centre. Tail grey-brown with paler feather edges. Throat pale buffy-white. Breast pale greybuff. Belly whitish. Flanks and undertail-coverts warm greyish-buff, undertail-coverts often pure buff. Iris dark brown. Bill black. Legs dark flesh.
Juvenile Upperparts more olive-brown than adult's, underparts more buffy throughout, with a heavier buff wash on flanks and undertail-coverts, and dark streaks on breast and flanks. Crown olive-brown, ear-coverts dark greybrown, supercilium greyish-buff (including supraloral) and relatively indistinct, submoustachial stripe buffier. Lores dusky-greyish. Bill dark horn.

MOULT AND AGEING Adults have a complete moult, probably after breeding, but the extent of the post-juvenile moult is not known. There is no evidence of a pre-breeding moult ; but see under Bridled Sparrow (82). No ageing criteria are known once the post-juvenile moult is completed.

MEASUREMENTS Wing (chord): male (n4) 68.6-71.1;

female (n1) 62.2. Tail: male (n4) 76.2-83.2; female (n1) 71.1. Bill: male (n4) 11.9-13.5; female (n1) 12.7. Tarsus: male (n4) 22.9-24.9; female (n1) 23.4.

GEOGRAPHICAL VARIATION Monotypic.

VOICE The song, generally given from an exposed perch, is a single note followed by a series of *chip* notes which sometimes runs into a short warble. Higher-pitched than song of Rusty Sparrow. Calls include a monotonous, rather insect-like chatter, a dry scolding, and a thin, high-pitched *tik*.

HABITS Nest and breeding undescribed. Feeds on seeds and insects, foraging on the ground or low in bushes and usually in dense grass or scrub cover. Shy and retiring, seldom flying far over open ground, although male generally fairly conspicuous when singing. May feed in the open but disappears into thick cover when disturbed. Generally found singly or in pairs, but in winter may occur in small groups, sometimes with other sparrows.

STATUS AND HABITAT Locally fairly common. Found in arid and semi-arid grassy hillsides with oak-thorn scrub, brushy ravines and other dry, scrubby areas, from 1600 to 1900m.

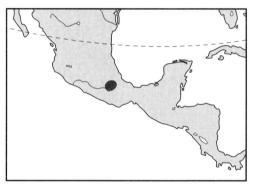

DISTRIBUTION AND MOVEMENTS Endemic to Mexico; it is only known from northern interior Oaxaca, but it may also occur in adjacent southern Puebla. As far as is known, it is entirely sedentary.

REFERENCES Armani (1985), Delaney (1992), Hardy & Wolf (1977), Peterson & Chalif (1973), Sibley & Monroe (1990), Wolf (1977).

94   RUSTY SPARROW
Aimophila rufescens   Plate 34

Described as *Pipilo rufescens* Swainson 1827.
Synonym: *Embernagra pyrgitoides*.

The largest *Aimophila* and also one of the most widespread, occurring from northern Mexico south to Costa Rica in a number of races.

IDENTIFICATION 16.5-20cm. A strikingly large *Aimophila* with a rufous cap (usually with a grey or grey-buff median crown-stripe), a distinct black malar stripe, and a relatively large bicoloured bill (black above, greyish below). Upperparts are rufous-brown to dull brown, often with darker streaks. Supercilium greyish with whiter supraloral. Face and breast pale grey, contrasting somewhat with buffy-white submoustachial stripe and whitish throat. Underparts whitish with a distinct ochre wash on flanks and undertail-coverts, Birds in north-western Mexico and Costa Rica are duller brown above than the others. Juvenile has cap duller and finely streaked with black, narrower and more distinct streaks on upperparts, and underparts washed with pale yellow and distinctly streaked dark brown on breast and flanks. In Costa Rica it is the only *Aimophila* sparrow with a rufous cap and prominent malar stripe. In Mexico could be confused with Rufous-crowned (92) or Oaxaca (93) Sparrow. Both are smaller, although Oaxaca can approach small Rusty in size. Rufous-crowned is distinctly smaller than Rusty, the upperparts are usually duller brown, the bill is proportionally smaller and paler, and the head pattern is less distinct (see also under Rufous-crowned). Oaxaca Sparrow is duller above than the allopatric race of Rusty Sparrow (lacking rufous tones), the upperparts are more heavily streaked with blackish and the bill is all black.

DESCRIPTION

Sexes alike; juvenile clearly different from subsequent plumages.

Adult/first-year Crown and nape rufous-chestnut with pale greyish median stripe. Supercilium grey, white on supraloral; often narrowly edged black on upper border. Broken eye-ring white. Lores black, eye-stripe dark chestnut. Ear-coverts grey, neck-sides grey-buff. Submoustachial stripe pale buffy-grey, prominent malar stripe black. Upperparts rufous, streaked/mottled with grey and with indistinct darker streaking. Lesser coverts olive-brown. Rest of wings dark brown; alula broadly edged pale grey, greater and median coverts and tertials edged rufous-chestnut (broadest on tertials) and fringed buff, remiges and primary coverts narrowly edged rufous. Bend of wing whitish. Tail rufous-brown with narrow paler feather edges. Throat and belly whitish, breast grey-buff, flanks and undertail-coverts warm ochre-brown. Similar year-round but median crown-stripe and streaking on upperparts often obscure in worn plumage. Iris dark brown. Bill black with grey lower mandible. Legs dull flesh.

Juvenile Crown rufous-brown, narrowly streaked blackish, and with indistinct buffy median stripe. Upperparts rufous-brown with narrower, darker streaks than adult. Face pattern less obvious than adults, supercilium and submoustachial stripe washed with pale yellowish. Underparts also washed pale yellowish and with narrow dark streaks on breast and flanks (flanks lack warm brown tone). Bill pale horn, legs slightly paler than adult's.

MOULT AND AGEING Adults have a complete moult, probably following the breeding season, but the extent of the post-juvenile moult is not known. There is no evidence of a pre-breeding moult; but see under Bridled Sparrow (82). No ageing criteria are known once the post-juvenile moult is completed.

MEASUREMENTS Wing (chord): male (n21) 71.1-78.7; female (n16) 66-73.7. Tail: male (n21) 71.1-78.7; female (n16) 69.8-77. Bill: male (n21) 14.7-17; female (n16) 14-15.8. Tarsus: male (n21) 22.3-25.4; female (n16) 22.6-24.4.

GEOGRAPHICAL VARIATION Seven races generally recognised which vary in size, overall brightness and prominence of streaking on upperparts.

   A. r. antonensis (Occurs on the Sierra de San Antonio in NC Sonora in NW Mexico) Similar to *mcleodii* but the breast, flanks, undertail-coverts and wing feather edges are paler and greyer.

A. r. mcleodii (Occurs in NW Mexico in E Sonora and W Chihuahua south to N Sinaloa and NW Durango) Slightly larger than *rufescens*, the upperparts are duller brown and less heavily streaked, the crown is duller chestnut, generally lacking the pale median stripe and the black stripe above supercilium (on edge of rufous crown), and the flanks have a duller, more olive wash.

A. r. rufescens (Occurs in W and SW Mexico from S Sinaloa and Guanajuato south-east to SW Chiapas) Described above.

A. r. pyrgitoides (Occurs on the Caribbean slope from E Mexico in S Tamaulipas south-east to W Belize, and south through the highlands of Honduras and N El Salvador possibly to N Nicaragua; intergrades with *pectoralis* in C Chiapas) Mottled buffy above and has distinct dark streaks on mantle and back; the underparts are distinctly buffier than on *rufescens*, especially on the breast and flanks.

A. r. pectoralis (Occurs on the Pacific cordillera from S Chiapas, Mexico east to W El Salvador, and also on Volcán San Miguel in E El Salvador) Similar to *rufescens* but the breast, flanks and undertail-coverts are greyer (less rusty) and the throat and belly are whiter, thus emphasising the breast-band.

A. r. discolor (Occurs in S Belize, NE Guatemala, N Honduras and NE Nicaragua) Smaller than *rufescens*, greyer on the head and neck, brighter and darker rufous on the upperparts with more distinct dark streaking, and has a richer and more extensive warm brown wash to the flanks.

A. r. hypaethrus (Occurs on the Pacific slope of the Cordillera de Guanacaste in NW Costa Rica) Similar to *rufescens* but has slightly darker upperparts with more conspicuous streaking and duskier lateral crown-stripes.

VOICE The song, generally given from a fairly conspicuous perch in a bush, is a variable but fairly short, throaty and emphatic series of rich clear notes, which has been transcribed as *chirup, chirup, chirup, see-bore.* Commonest call is a dry rapid chatter. Pairs sometimes greet each other with a mixture of squealing and churring notes.

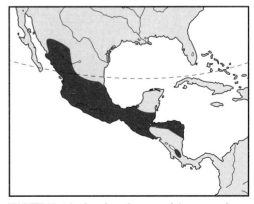

HABITS Nest is placed on the ground, in a grass clump, or up to 2.4m in a bush; an open cup of grasses. 2-3 (occasionally 4) bluish-white eggs are laid in May-July. Feeds on seeds, insects and other invertebrates; also takes small lizards. Forages mostly by hopping on the ground, often on tracks and roadsides, but also gleans insects low in bushes. Generally takes cover in bushes when disturbed. Flight is fluttering with pumping tail. Mostly seen singly or in pairs but also in family parties immediately after breeding.

STATUS AND HABITAT Fairly common to common over most of its range, but uncommon and local in Costa Rica. Found mainly on lower slopes of mountain ranges, forest edges, brushy second growth and scrubby clearings; also in more open grassland areas. Mainly associated with pine-oak forest but also occurs in more humid evergreen forest; from 600-900m in Costa Rica, 600-2700m further north.

DISTRIBUTION AND MOVEMENTS Occurs in highland areas from northern Mexico south to north-western Costa Rica. See also under Geographical Variation. Sedentary.

REFERENCES Armani (1985), Paynter & Storer (1970), Peterson & Chalif (1973), Ridgway (1901), Stiles & Skutch (1989), Wolf (1977).

TORREORNIS

One species which occurs in three disjunct races on Cuba; this is the only sparrow genus endemic to the West Indies. Morphologically it is similar to *Aimophila*, but in behaviour it more closely resembles *Pipilo* or *Zonotrichia*.

95 ZAPATA SPARROW
Torreornis inexpectata   Plate 35

Described as *Torreornis inexpectata* Barbour & Peters 1927.

The only sparrow endemic to the West Indies, Zapata Sparrow is found very locally on Cuba, where it is threatened by disturbance to its habitat. Although only known from the Zapata Swamp for many years, it has now been discovered from two other areas and the alternative name of Cuban Sparrow is thus probably more appropriate.

IDENTIFICATION 16.5cm. A distinctive, very short-winged sparrow with greyish-olive upperparts, pale yellow underparts and a striking head pattern of rufous crown, grey sides to the head, white supraloral, submoustachial stripe and throat, and prominent black malar stripe. Underparts are washed olive on sides. White throat sharply demarcated and separated from yellow underparts by a narrow indistinct greyish band across the upper breast. The upperparts have indistinct darker streaking. Eastern birds, from the coastal area of extreme eastern Cuba, have very little rufous in the crown and greyer upperparts than the other two races, more or less lacking streaking. Northern birds, from Cayo Coco, resemble western birds but have a more noticeable eye-stripe.

DESCRIPTION Sexes alike; juvenile clearly different from subsequent plumages.
Adult/first-year Crown rufous, finely streaked blackish and often admixed with grey, especially on the centre and rear. Supraloral white, lores blackish. Superciliary area, ear-coverts and neck-sides grey. Narrow, indistinct blackish moustachial stripe. Upperparts greyish-olive, indistinctly streaked blackish on mantle, back and scapulars. Lesser coverts olive-grey. Rest of wings blackish-brown with pale grey-buff feather edges, broadest on greater and median coverts and tertials. Bend of wing pale yellow. Tail blackish-brown with narrow pale grey-buff feather edges. Throat and submoustachial stripe white, separated by broad black malar stripe. Narrow band across upper breast grey, sharply demarcated from white throat. Rest of underparts pale yellow, heavily washed olive on flanks. Iris reddish-brown. Bill blackish. Legs flesh.
Juvenile Crown and upperparts uniform greyish-olive, secondaries and tertials with rufous edges. Underparts yellow with a stronger, more extensive olive wash than in adult.

MOULT AND AGEING Adults have a complete moult, probably after breeding, but the extent of the post-juvenile moult is not known. There is probably no pre-breeding moult. As juveniles have rufous-edged secondaries and tertials, birds in adult-type plumage but showing these rufous-edged flight feathers can be aged as first-year; it is not known whether these feathers are replaced in the post-juvenile moult or are retained throughout the first-year.

MEASUREMENTS Wing (chord): male (n1) 62; female (n1) 64. Tail: male (n1) 61; female (n1) 60. Bill: male (n1) 14.2; female (n1) 13.2. Tarsus male (n1) 22.5; female (n1) 20.5.

GEOGRAPHICAL VARIATION Three disjunct races, each represented by only very small populations.
T. i. inexpectata (Occurs locally in the Zapata Swamp area of S Matanzas) Described above.
T. i. sigmani (Occurs on the southern coast of Guantánamo, in extreme SE Cuba) Has less rufous in the crown than *inexpectata*, unstreaked upperparts which are purer grey, and slightly duller yellow underparts.
T. i. varonai (Occurs on Cayo Coco off the north coast of Cuba) Similar to *inexpectata* but tends to have a brighter and more noticeable rufous crown and a narrow dark rufous eye-stripe.

RELATIONSHIPS This monotypic genus appears to be most closely related to the *Aimophila* genus, although in its behaviour and shape it is more reminiscent of a *Zonotrichia* sparrow (G. Wallace pers. comm.).

VOICE A pulsating, rather insect-like, buzzing trill, interspersed with chattering notes; pairs often duet. Calls include a buzzing *zeee* and a thin *tsip* or *tsip-ip*, often repeated.

HABITS Nest (of *inexpectata*) is placed on or near the ground in a tussock of sawgrass *Cladium jamaicense* or other grass; a cup of dried grass leaves and stems lined with finer plant material. 2-4 bluish-white eggs are laid; breeding season is mainly March-June, at least for *inexpectata*. Feeds on invertebrates, seeds and berries. During the rainy season (May-October) *inexpectata* at least seems to specialise in eating the eggs and young of the snail *Pomacea palu-dosa*, and all races appear to take more insects and other invertebrates at this time. Race *sigmani* seems to be dependent on the seeds of coastal incense *Tournefortia gnaphalodes*, although it also eats molluscs during the rainy season. Forages on the ground and low in bushes (usually less than 2m off the ground), generally scratching in the leaf-litter with both feet together, in the manner of White-throated Sparrow (56) or Rufous-sided Towhee (99) (G. Wallace). Flight is rather laboured, with rapid bursts of wing beats, and the birds seldom fly far. Generally found in pairs, family parties or flocks of up to 10-12 individuals outside the breeding season.

STATUS AND HABITAT Locally common, but the populations of each race are very small. Race *inexpectata* is rare and endangered, although a recent increase has been reported where its habitat is protected in the Santa Tomás area; the population in 1982 was estimated at 250 individuals. Race *sigmani* has a total population of only 55-100 pairs (in 1982); although they occur mostly within a national park and there does not seem to have been a decline in numbers recently, this race is still threatened due to its tiny population and damage to its habitat through burning. Race *varonai* is common within its habitat on Cayo Coco and is the least threatened of the three races. The three races occupy rather different habitats. Race *inexpectata* occurs on the higher, drier parts of the Zapata Swamp where sawgrass is dominant and there are scattered bushes. Race *sigmani* occurs on the hot, dry, xerophytic coastal area of Guantánamo; it is apparently xrestricted to areas where coastal incense grows as the seeds of this plant form a major part of its food. Race *varonai* occurs in interior

semi-deciduous forest and forest edge, and in coastal xerophytic matorral (thorn-scrub) and mangroves (the latter two habitats possibly only during the winter). Fossil remains indicate that this species was formerly more widespread and probably occurred in arid scrub across much of eastern Cuba at least.

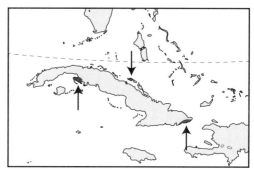

DISTRIBUTION AND MOVEMENTS Endemic to Cuba, where it occurs very locally in three disjunct and racially distinct populations. See also under Geographical Variation. Sedentary, although some individuals of the race *varonai* may move into adjacent mangroves and thorn scrub from the semi-deciduous forests during the winter.

REFERENCES Armani (1985), Bond (1985), Collar *et al.* (1992), Garrido (1985), González Alonso *et al.* (1982), Gonzáles Alonso *et al.* (1986), King (1978-79), Morton & González Alonso (1982), Paynter & Storer (1970), Pregill & Olson (1981), Regalado Ruíz (1981), Reynard (1988).

ORITURUS

One species which is similar to the *Aimophila* sparrows in shape and plumage; it is endemic to Mexico.

96   STRIPED SPARROW
Oriturus superciliosus   Plate 35

Described as *Aimophila superciliosa* Swainson 1838.
Synonym: *Plagiospiza superciliosa*.

This Mexican endemic resembles the *Aimophila* sparrows in many ways.

IDENTIFICATION 15-18cm. A largish sparrow, rather *Aimophila*-like but with a more pointed bill (which is all black). Blackish face and rufous-brown crown, separated by long broad white supercilium, give a distinctive head pattern. Narrow median crown-stripe greyish. Upperparts buffy-brown, heavily streaked with black; underparts pale greyish-white, whiter on throat and with a buff wash to the flanks and undertail-coverts. Tail quite long and rounded. Juveniles are buffier overall with dark streaking on the breast and flanks, and have dull brown crown. Superficially similar to Stripe-headed Sparrow (84) but easily distinguished by brown crown with less obvious (greyish) median stripe, all-black bill, plain buffy-brown upperparts (including tail) and duller, less contrasting buff flanks and undertail-coverts.

DESCRIPTION
Sexes alike; juvenile clearly different from subsequent plumages.
Adult/first-year Crown rufous-brown with a narrow grey median crown-stripe, both faintly streaked blackish. Supercilium white, long and broad, reaching to nape. Lores and ear-coverts black, ear-coverts streaked with white (giving a greyish look at a distance). Nape and neck-sides greyish-white, heavily streaked black. Upperparts buff-brown (washed rufous on mantle), heavily streaked with black (streaking heaviest on mantle) and with pale grey feather fringes, giving a rather variegated appearance. Lesser coverts warm brown with pale grey fringes. Alula blackish with broad white outer edge. Primary coverts blackish with quite broad pale buff edges. Greater and median coverts blackish with broad pale buff edges and whitish tips, forming two obscure wing-bars. Flight feathers blackish with narrow greyish-white edges to the primaries and narrow buff-brown edges to the secondaries. Tertials blackish with buff-brown edges (becoming whitish round the tips). Bend of wing white. Tail dark brown with buff-brown feather edges, broadest on central rectrices. Underparts pale greyish-white with a whiter throat and central belly, and a buff wash to the flanks and

undertail-coverts. Iris brown. Bill black. Legs flesh.
Juvenile Buffier above than adult's; underparts buffy-white, streaked dark brown on breast and flanks.

MOULT AND AGEING Adults have a complete moult, probably after breeding, but the extent of the post-juvenile moult is unknown. There is probably no pre-breeding moult. No ageing criteria are known after the post-juvenile moult is completed.

MEASUREMENTS Wing (chord): male (n10) 75.7-81.8; female (n10) 73.7-80.8. Tail: male (n10) 67.3-73.2; female (n10) 63.5-70.6. Bill: male (n10) 14.7-15.5; female (n10) 13.2-15.5. Tarsus: male (n10) 23.4-27.9; female (n10) 24.9-27.4.

GEOGRAPHICAL VARIATION Two very similar races.
   O. s. superciliosus (Occurs in NW Mexico, from E Sonora and Chihuahua south to Nayarit and W Zacatecas) Described above.
   O. s. palliatus (Occurs on the Central Plateau of Mexico, from Jalisco and WC Veracruz south-east to C Oaxaca) Very similar to *superciliosus* but averages slightly paler overall; paler and warmer brown above and paler and greyer (less buffy) on breast and flanks with whiter belly.

VOICE The song, given from a prominent perch, is a chattering trill, about one second in length.

HABITS Nest is placed very low down in a bush; a cup of twigs, grass and straw lined with finer plant material and hair. 3-4 eggs are laid, which are white, marked with greyish-brown and greyish-lilac. They are incubated by the female for 13-14 days. In courtship, the male displays in front of the female with wings and tail spread. Feeds largely on seeds through much of the year but switches to a largely insectivorous diet during the breeding season. Forages on

the ground, often in thick grass cover, and also low in bushes. Flight is usually short and low. Quite shy but sings from a prominent perch, and pairs or small groups will often perch on bush-tops or feed in the open unless disturbed. Generally found in pairs or small groups outside the breeding season.

STATUS AND HABITAT Fairly common in open grassland areas in the highlands, generally close to pine-oak forest and frequently in large grassy meadows in open pine-oak forest. Prefers areas where grass grows high and in thick clumps, and there are scattered shrubs. Found from 1800 to 4500m.

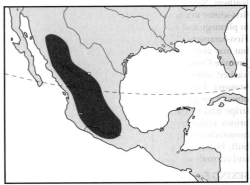

DISTRIBUTION AND MOVEMENTS Endemic to Mexico, where it occurs in the Sierra Madre Occidental and on the Central Plateau, from eastern Sonora and Chihuahua south to central Oaxaca. See also under Geographical Variation. Sedentary.

REFERENCES Armani (1985), Paynter & Storer (1970), Peterson & Chalif (1973), Ridgway (1901).

PIPILO

Seven species of large, distinctive sparrows known as towhees. They feed on the ground, scratching in the leaf-litter with both feet simultaneously to expose food items; this scratching may be audible for some distance.

97   GREEN-TAILED TOWHEE
Pipilo chlorurus   Plate 37

Described as *Fringilla chlorura* Audubon 1839.

A distinct and smallish towhee of dense brush and chaparral in western North America. It is the only towhee which is entirely migratory.

IDENTIFICATION 18cm. A distinctive towhee with olive upperparts, bright rufous cap, white throat, and grey face and underparts (whiter on belly). White submoustachial and black malar stripes are also conspicuous. Forehead grey, supraloral white. Females average slightly duller, especially the rufous cap, and all birds are slightly duller in winter. Juveniles are brownish, streaked darker, on the crown, nape and upperparts, and pale greyish-buff on the face and underparts, with dark streaks on the breast and flanks and a narrow dark malar stripe. Winter birds are

somewhat similar to the noticeably smaller Olive Sparrow (107) but have a distinct rufous cap (rather than dull rufous-brown lateral crown-stripes) and lack the prominent dark eye-stripe and pale supercilium of Olive Sparrow.

DESCRIPTION
Sexes similar but may be distinguishable; juvenile clearly different from subsequent plumages.
Adult/first-year Forehead grey, crown and nape bright rufous. Supraloral stripe white. Lores, superciliary area, ear-coverts and neck-sides grey, lores and area below eye faintly flecked white. Submoustachial stripe white, malar stripe blackish. Upperparts dull olive-green on nape, becoming dull olive-grey on rest of upperparts with faint grey-brown mottling. Lesser coverts bright yellowish-green. Alula blackish with narrow yellowish edge. Median coverts olive-green. Greater coverts grey-brown washed olive. Rest of wings blackish-brown with bright olive feather edges, broadest on tertials and narrowest on primary coverts. Bend of wing yellow. Tail blackish-brown with quite bright

but narrow olive-green feather edges. Throat white, bordered on either side by the blackish malar stripe. Breast grey, uniform with face. Rest of underparts paler grey (whitish on belly), washed buff on rearflanks and undertail-coverts. Similar year-round but slightly duller in winter with duller rufous cap (formed by narrow grey fringes to the feathers), upperparts more mottled with grey-brown and ear-coverts and lores sometimes very faintly washed with buff. Iris dark reddish-brown. Bill steely grey. Legs dull greyish-flesh.

First-winter Both sexes resemble winter adults but average duller, with broader grey fringes to the rufous crown feathers. Note that due to the slight sexual dimorphism, first-winter males are very similar to adult winter females in plumage and are not separable from them in the field. First-summers of both sexes are more similar to adults, but may average slightly duller on the crown.

Juvenile Crown, nape and upperparts grey-brown, faintly washed olive and streaked dark brown. Wing-coverts browner than adult's and tipped pale buff, forming two obscure wing-bars. Sides of head and neck, submoustachial stripe and throat pale greyish-buff, with a narrow dark brown malar stripe and a narrow, relatively indistinct moustachial stripe. Remainder of underparts also grey-buff, becoming buffier on flanks and undertail-coverts, and narrowly streaked blackish-brown on breast and flanks.

SEXING Females average very slightly duller than males, especially on the crown (first-years of each sex are duller than respective adults in this regard). This is not normally sufficient to sex individuals, but it may be noticeable on mated pairs.

MOULT AND AGEING The post-juvenile moult is partial and the post-breeding moult is complete; both occur in July-September, on the breeding grounds prior to migration. The pre-breeding moult is limited to the head feathers, occurring in February-May. First-years resemble adults after completion of the post-juvenile moult but have more pointed rectrices on average; these plus the retained juvenile flight feathers also average more worn and brownish-looking, especially by spring. Skull ossification complete in first-years from 15 November, but some birds may retain small unossified 'windows' through their first spring. First-years also tend to be slightly duller than adults, especially on the crown; this is complicated by the slight sexual variation but, for example, first-year females are generally noticeably duller than adult males, especially in direct comparison.

MEASUREMENTS Wing (chord): male (n30) 75-84; female (n30) 70-79. Tail: male (n11) 79.5-87.1; female (n8) 74.4-84.6. Bill: male (n11) 12.2-13; female (n8) 11.4-13. Tarsus: male (n11) 22.6-25.4; female (n8) 21.8-24.6.

GEOGRAPHICAL VARIATION Monotypic.

VOICE The song, generally given from an open perch, is a series of clear, whistled notes, preceded by a rather drawn-out *weet-chur* and ending with a raspy trill. Calls include a cat-like *mew*.

HABITS Nest is placed on or close to the ground, in or under a dense bush; a cup of grasses and twigs lined with finer plant material, rootlets and hair. 2-5 (usually 4) eggs are laid in May-July; they are bluish-white marked with brown and reddish-brown. Incubation and fledging periods are not known. Will run along ground with tail raised 'chipmunk-style' to distract predators from the nest. Feeds

on seeds, insects and some berries. Generally forages on the ground, often in dense undergrowth, where it searches leaf-litter by scratching with both feet simultaneously in typical towhee style. May also forage low in bushes. Frequently visits feeders in winter, particularly casual wanderers in eastern North America. Generally found in pairs or small groups outside the breeding season.

STATUS AND HABITAT Generally fairly common, but rare as a breeding bird in western Texas. Breeds in chaparral, dense brush and scrubby thickets on hillsides and mountain plateaux, and also in scrubby riparian woodland. Winters in similar scrubby and semi-arid habitats.

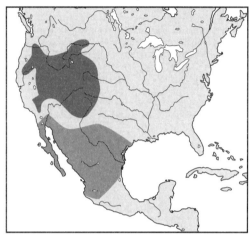

DISTRIBUTION AND MOVEMENTS Breeds in western North America from Oregon and central Montana south to southern California (but largely absent from the coastal mountains), and central Arizona and New Mexico; also locally in the Guadalupe Mountains of western Texas. Short- to medium-distance migrant, wintering in the southern parts of Arizona, New Mexico and Texas south through Baja California and Mexico to Jalisco and Hidalgo. Spring migration starts in February with birds arriving on breeding grounds from April. Autumn migration begins in September with birds arriving on winter grounds from October. Casual in eastern North America, north to southern Canada (Saskatchewan east to Nova Scotia but very rare), mainly in winter. Vagrant to Cuba in winter.

REFERENCES Armani (1985), Bent (1968), Dunn & Blom (1983), Godfrey (1986), Oberholser (1974), Pyle *et al.* (1987), Ridgway (1901), Terres (1980).

98   COLLARED TOWHEE
Pipilo ocai   Plate 36

Described as *Buarremon ocai* Lawrence 1867.
Synonyms: *Chamaeospiza alticola*, *Chamaeospiza nigrescens*, *Pipilo torquatus*.

One of two towhees endemic to Mexico, this one hybridises extensively with Rufous-sided Towhee (99) where their ranges overlap in central Mexico, to the extent that it is possible to see a hybrid cline, from Rufous-sided types in the east (Hidalgo and Veracruz) to Collared types in the west (Michoacán). Despite being morphologically distinct, the extent of this hybridisation has led some to question the validity of Collared Towhee as a distinct species.

IDENTIFICATION 21cm. Pure birds have a plumage pattern distinct among the towhees; black lores and cheeks, separated from black forehead and chestnut crown and nape by a narrow white supercilium, olive-green upperparts, and white underparts with a broad black breast-band and rufous undertail-coverts. The tail lacks white or pale spots. Collared x Rufous-sided hybrids are variable but often show the spotting on the upperparts of Rufous-sided, have a variable amount of rufous on the breast-sides and flanks, and have a blackish head with a variable chestnut patch on the nape and a variable number of white feathers in the throat (often forming a small white patch). As mentioned above, hybrids in Hidalgo and Veracruz are generally more similar to Rufous-sided, and those in Michoacán tend to be more similar to Collared. Juvenile is rufous-brown above (with contrasting olive wings and tail), with cinnamon wing-bars and whitish below with buff breast, flanks and undertail-coverts and blackish streaking on the breast. Chestnut-capped Brush-Finch *Atlapetes brunneinucha* is similar to Collared Towhee in general pattern, but has duller and darker green upperparts, lacks the rufous undertail-coverts and the white supercilium (but has a small white supraloral spot), has darker and duller (olive-grey) breast-sides and flanks, and has a narrower black breast-band. Some races of Collared Towhee (and hybrids) may show only a very indistinct white supercilium, but on these it is most obvious behind the eye and absent on the supraloral (cf. Chestnut-capped Brush-Finch).

DESCRIPTION
Sexes alike; juvenile clearly different from subsequent plumages.
Adult/first-year Forehead and forecrown black with a narrow white stripe through the centre. Rear-crown and nape chestnut, bordered on either side with black (which extends back from the forehead). Narrow supercilium white, reaching to rear edge of ear-coverts. Lores and ear-coverts black. Nape and neck-sides dull olive-green. Upperparts uniform dull olive-green. Lesser coverts olive-yellow. Rest of wings blackish-brown with dull olive-green feather edges, broadest on greater and median coverts and tertials, but brighter and more yellowish on remiges. Bend of wing yellow. Tail dusky olive. Throat and submoustachial area white. Upper breast black, forming a broad, solid band which separates the white throat from the rest of the underparts. Belly white; breast-sides greyish, becoming greyish-rufous on flanks and rufous on vent and undertail-coverts. Iris reddish-brown. Bill black. Legs flesh.
Juvenile Crown rufous-brown with black streaking (heaviest on forehead and lateral crown). Narrow supercilium pale buff (may be broken over eye). Ear-coverts blackish-brown. Upperparts rufous-brown, contrasting somewhat with olive wings and tail, and with indistinct blackish streaking. Greater and median coverts tipped cinnamon, forming two wing-bars. Underparts whitish with rich buff flanks and undertail-coverts and a buff wash across the breast; breast also streaked with black.

MOULT AND AGEING Adults have a complete moult, probably after breeding, but the extent of the post-juvenile moult is not known. There is probably no pre-breeding moult. No ageing criteria are known once the post-juvenile moult is completed, although iris colour may

be useful (as in Rufous-sided).

MEASUREMENTS Wing (chord): male (n11) 79.2-92; female (n9) 81.5-92. Tail: male (n11) 94.2-105.9; female (n9) 88.9-103.6. Bill: male (n11) 15.2-17.8; female (n9) 15-16.5. Tarsus: male (n11) 28.4-32.5; female (n9) 29.2-31.2.

GEOGRAPHICAL VARIATION Five races described which differ mainly in details of the head and breast pattern; impure Collared Towhees of one race may resemble other races.
   P. o. alticola (Occurs in W Jalisco and extreme NW Colima; hybridises extensively with the *griseipygius* race of Rufous-sided and pure birds apparently may no longer occur) Has a very narrow and indistinct white supercilium and usually lacks the narrow white line on the forehead of *ocai*; also has a broader black breast-band and more brownish-grey breast-sides than *ocai*.
   P. o. nigrescens (Occurs in NC Michoacán; hybridises extensively with the *macronyx* race of Rufous-sided and pure birds apparently no longer occur) Typical birds have some black in throat, lack the white supercilium and median stripe on the forehead, and have rufescent flanks; this 'race' is very variable, through hybridisation, and some birds lack the rufous crown patch, have an all-black throat and show signs of tail spots.
   P. o. guerrensis (Occurs in Guerrero) Has a rather narrower black collar than other races and the undertail-coverts are paler than in *ocai*; very similar to *brunnescens* but the flanks average browner.
   P. o. brunnescens (Occurs in C Oaxaca) Very similar to *guerrensis* but has slightly greyer flanks (it is intermediate between *guerrensis* and *ocai* in this respect). Apparently occurs sympatrically with the *oaxacae* race of Rufous-sided on Cerros San Felipe and Yucuyacua, and on Mt. Zempoaltepec, without hybridising with it (other races of these two species hybridise extensively where they occur sympatrically).
   P. o. ocai (Occurs in E Puebla and WC Veracruz; hybridises extensively with the *maculatus* race of Rufous-sided) Described above.

RELATIONSHIPS The extensive amount of hybridisation with certain races of Rufous-sided Towhee suggests a very close relationship between these two species, although two races of these species apparently occur sympatrically without interbreeding. '*Pipilo torquatus*' is one of these hybrid types.

VOICE The song, given from an exposed perch, consists of 2 notes followed by a long trill and terminating with a single longer note. Calls include a long, drawn-out and high-pitched *sweeee*, descending in pitch.

HABITS Nest is placed very close to the ground in a dense bush; a cup of twigs, dry grass and sometimes pine needles, lined with fine plant material, rootlets and hair. 4 pale bluish eggs are laid. Feeds on seeds, insects, berries and fruit, generally scratching in the leaf-litter in typical towhee style, but also foraging low in bushes. Often unobtrusive and generally found singly, in pairs or in small groups (family parties?).

STATUS AND HABITAT Fairly common to common in humid pine-oak and pine-fir forests with a dense understorey and on scrubby hillsides near forest edges, in the coniferous forest zone of the mountains. Where it is sympatric with Rufous-sided Towhee, it generally occurs at higher altitudes, although considerable overlap often occurs.

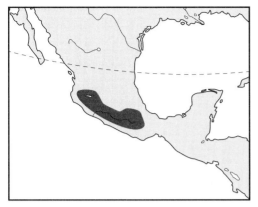

DISTRIBUTION AND MOVEMENTS Endemic to central Mexico, where it occurs from western Jalisco and north-eastern Colima east to west-central Veracruz, and northern and central Oaxaca. See also under Geographical Variation. Sedentary.

REFERENCES Armani (1985), Delaney (1992), Peterson & Chalif (1973), Ridgway (1901), Sibley (1950), Sibley & Monroe (1990).

99   RUFOUS-SIDED TOWHEE
Pipilo erythrophthalmus   Plate 36

Described as *Fringilla erythrophthalmus* Linnaeus 1758.
Synonyms: *Pyrigita arctica, Pipilo virescens.*

A highly variable species, with 25 races falling into four main groups, which were formerly considered separated species: Rufous-sided (eastern North America), Spotted (western North America and Mexico), Olive-backed (Mexico) and Socorro Towhee of Islas Revilla- gigedos off Mexico. There is much intergrading between all of the first three forms. Socorro Towhee is isolated and sometimes still given specific status. The voice of Rufous-sided Towhee is very variable and, despite the intergrading, there may well be more than one (or two) species involved in the complex.

IDENTIFICATION 22cm. Highly variable but distinctive and easily identifiable. Males of all the forms have a black hood, red eye, whitish underparts with extensive rufous on the sides, and a long, white-cornered black tail which is especially conspicuous in flight. Eastern North American Rufous-sided forms have a solid black back and a white patch at the base of the primaries, also conspicuous in flight. Western North American and Mexican Spotted forms have large white spots on the scapulars and sides of the mantle, and two broad white wing-bars. The central Mexican Olive-backed form has dark olive-green wings and upperparts, with pale yellowish spots on the upperparts and yellowish wing-bars. Females of the Rufous-sided and Spotted forms have a similar pattern to the males but the black is replaced with rufous-brown (Rufous-sided) or dark grey-brown (Spotted). Sexes of the other forms are more similar. Generally unmistakable, in Mexico told from

White-throated Towhee (103) by solid black or blackish hood, lacking any white or chestnut. Note that Rufous-sided Towhee hybridrises with Collared Towhee (98) with many intermediate types occurring in the zone of overlap between these two species (see under Collared Towhee for details).

HYBRIDISATION Some Mexican races of this species hybridise quite extensively with Collared Towhee where their ranges overlap; see also under Relationships and Geographical Variation.

DESCRIPTION
Sexes differ; juvenile clearly different from subsequent plumages.
Adult male Head, throat, upper breast and entire upperparts glossy black. Wings black with noticeable white patch at base of primaries and another smaller patch half-way down primaries. Tertials edged white. Bend of wing white. Tail black with white outer web of outer feather and large white tip to outer three rectrices, decreasing in size towards central rectrices. Centre of lower breast and belly white. Flanks rich orange-rufous, vent slightly paler orange-rufous, undertail-coverts buff. Iris dark red. Bill black. Legs flesh.
Adult female Plumage pattern as adult male but black replaced by warm to rufous-brown, white wing patches smaller and tertial edges pale buff to whitish.
First-year male Much as adult male but remiges and primary coverts brown or blackish-brown, contrasting with black greater coverts. Iris is grey-brown to dull red (but usually noticeably duller than adult's) to at least November, and some birds retain a trace of this colour through the spring. The tail has slightly less white on average, but there is much overlap with adult male (first-year males usually have the white tip on rectrix 4 less than 4mm long). Most have brownish rectrices which average more pointed than those of adults, but note that some may moult some rectrices during the post-juvenile moult.
First-year female Very similar to adult female and not always distinguishable. Most birds can be aged at least until November by iris colour (see under first-year male) but a few may be intermediate. Unmoulted rectrices average more pointed, remiges and primary coverts are more worn and paler brown than the greater coverts (but this can be difficult to judge, even in the hand), and the tail has less white on average (females with the white tip on rectrix 4 less than 3mm long are probably first-years).
Juvenile Head and upperparts brown with fine dark streaking, most prominent on mantle. Throat whitish, rest of underparts pale buff with warmer buff undertail-coverts; breast and flanks finely streaked dark brown. Males have blackish-brown remiges and rectrices, on females they are paler brown.

MOULT AND AGEING The post-juvenile moult is partial/incomplete (at least in North American races); occurs in July-September, and often includes some or all of the rectrices. The post-breeding moult is complete, occurring in June-August (North American races). There is no pre-breeding moult. First-years can usually be told by the contrast between worn, retained juvenile flight feathers and primary coverts, and fresh adult-type greater coverts; also sometimes by contrast between old and new tail feathers. First-years also have a duller eye (grey-brown to dull red) than adults, at least through the autumn. First-years have more pointed tail feathers, on average, than adults.

305

Skull ossification complete in first-years from 1 November in North American populations, possibly earlier in Mexican and Guatemalan ones.

MEASUREMENTS For ease of comparison, measurements for the four main groups are given separately below.
Rufous-sided Towhee. Wing (chord): male (n17) 83.6-94.5; female (n13) 76.2-83.8. Tail: male (n17) 88.4-99.3; female (n13) 80.5-89.4. Bill: male (n17) 13.5-14.7; female (n13) 12.9-14.7. Tarsus: male (n17) 27.4-29.7; female (n13) 26.2-28.2. Maximum wing (*erythrophthalmus*): male (n17) 85-95; female (n8) 82-87.
Spotted Towhee. Wing (chord): male (n147) 79.8-92.7; female (n85) 77-90.9. Tail: male (n147) 88.4-111.5; female (n85) 84.1-105.7. Bill: male (n147) 11.9-15.5; female (n85) 12.2-15.5. Tarsus: male (n147) 25.4-31.2; female (n85) 24.9-30.4.
Olive-backed Towhee. Wing (chord): male (n5) 88.9-94; female (n6) 86.6-90.6. Tail: male (n5) 104.1-111; female (n6) 95.2-104.7. Bill: male (n5) 15.2-16.5; female (n6) 13.8-15.5. Tarsus: male (n5) 30.7-32.3; female (n6) 30-31.8.
Socorro Towhee. Wing (chord): male (n5) 69.1-73.9; female (n3) 63.7-68.5. Tail: male (n5) 71.1-80.5; female (n3) 69.8-73.7. Bill: male (n5) 12.4-13.5; female (n3) 12.4-12.7. Tarsus: male (n5) 23.9-25.9; female (n3) 23.1-25.4.

GEOGRAPHICAL VARIATION Twenty-five races in four groups, which were formerly considered separate species. Within the different groups, races are often very similar and cannot be identified in the field except by breeding range.

Rufous-sided group: unmarked black upperparts, wings with white patch at base of primaries.
P. e. erythrophthalmus (Breeds in CE North America, from extreme SE Manitoba and Minnesota east through the Great Lakes region to New England and south to N Oklahoma and NW South Carolina. Winters from Illinois and S Pennsylvania, occasionally S Michigan and S Ontario, south to the Gulf coast, west to Texas and east to SC Florida) Described above.
P. e. rileyi (Occurs on the SE USA coastal plain, from SE Virginia south to SE Alabama and N Florida; basically sedentary but some may move out of the extreme north of the range in winter, and also occurs south to C Florida in winter) Similar to *erythrophthalmus* but averages slightly smaller and larger-billed, and the eyes are often paler and more orange, perhaps sometimes even paler.
P. e. alleni (Resident in C and S Florida) Has a whitish eye and is smaller than *rileyi*; has less white in the tail than *erythrophthalmus* and is slightly less pure black.
P. e. canaster (Breeds from E Louisiana north-east to CS North Carolina, but excluding the Atlantic coastal plain; winters throughout the breeding range and south-east to coastal South Carolina, SE Georgia and W Florida) Similar to *erythrophthalmus* in size but has a larger bill and less white in the tail; the eye colour varies from reddish to pale yellowish-white.

Spotted group: white spots on scapulars and sides of mantle, two white wing-bars; several of the Mexican races have dark olivaceous-grey (not black) upperparts, streaked black on mantle.
P. e. arcticus (Breeds from the southern parts of Alberta and Saskatchewan east of the Rockies south to NE Colorado and S Nebraska, and winters from Colorado south to S Texas and N Mexico in Chihuahua

and Nuevo León) The upperparts are a dull olivaceous-black and the spots on the mantle and scapulars are relatively large and extensive.
P. e. montanus (Breeds in the Rockies and the S Great Basin, from SE California, S Nevada and C Colorado south to NW Mexico in NE Sonora and NW Chihuahua; winters throughout the breeding range, except the extreme north, and south to the central parts of Sonora and Chihuahua) Resembles *arcticus* but the upperparts are purer black (more or less intermediate in colour between *arcticus* and *oreganus*).
P. e. curtatus (Breeds in the N Great Basin, from interior S British Columbia south to NE California and N Nevada; winters throughout the breeding range and south to SE California and S Arizona) Resembles *montanus* but the black averages still purer and less olivaceous.
P. e. oreganus (Breeds on the Pacific coast from SW British Columbia south to SW Oregon, wintering in the breeding range and south to S California) Resembles *curtatus* but is even blacker above; it is the blackest of the Spotted group and has relatively small white spots, not extending far onto the mantle.
P. e. falcinellus (Resident from interior SW Oregon south through the Sierra Nevada and the Sacramento Valley of California) Similar to *megalonyx* but the hind claw averages shorter, the white spots average larger and the rump is slightly paler and greyer.
P. e. falcifer (Resident in coastal N California) Similar to *falcinellus* in its short hind claw but the white markings above are smaller (it is only slightly more 'spotted' above than *oreganus*).
P. e. megalonyx (Resident in coastal S California, including Santa Cruz Island, and NW Baja California, south to about 32°N) Very black above (including the rump) and has small white spots above; very similar to the more northern *oreganus* but has slightly smaller white spots.
P. e. clementae (Resident on Santa Rosa, Santa Catalina and San Clemente islands, off SW California) Similar to *megalonyx* but the bill averages slightly larger and the upperparts (especially on the female) are slightly paler.
P. e. umbraticola (Resident in NW Baja California, from 32°N south to 30°N) Similar to *megalonyx* but the bill averages slightly smaller and the upperparts (especially on the female) are slightly darker.
P. e. consobrinus (Formerly resident on Isla Guadalupe off Baja California, but now extinct) Most similar to *oreganus* but had shorter wings and tail, a slightly longer hind claw, and was paler sooty black on the upperparts.
P. e. magnirostris (Resident in the mountains of S California) Similar to *megalonyx* but the sides are paler, more tawny-buff, and it has more white in the tail; it also has slightly shorter wing and tail, and slightly longer bill and hind claw, on average.
P. e. gaigei (Resident in the mountains of E New Mexico, W Texas, NE Chihuahua and N Coahuila) Similar to *griseipygius* but the rump averages greyer (less olive), with less black admixed; also similar to *montana* but has a noticeably less black rump and slightly smaller white spots on upperparts.
P. e. griseipygius (Resident in the Sierra Madre Occidental of Mexico, from SW Chihuahua south to Jalisco and N Michoacán; hybridises with Collared Towhee

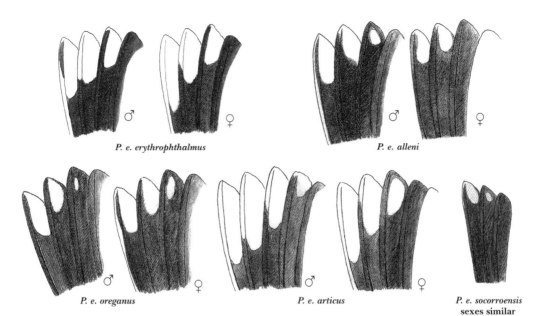

P. e. erythrophthalmus

P. e. alleni

P. e. oreganus

P. e. articus

P. e. socorroensis
sexes similar

Rufous-sided Towhee tail patterns. In most races the amount of white is quite variable; typical examples are shown to illustrate the variation within the species complex. There is some age/sex-related variation in the Rufous-sided and Spotted groups, with adult males averaging most white and first-year females the least, but there is much overlap in all age/sex categories.

P. ocai alticola in Jalisco and Michoacán) Similar to *gaigei* but the rump is slightly more olivaceous (less grey), the upperparts are more greyish-black and the flanks are slightly darker.

P. e. orientalis (Resident in the Sierra Madre Oriental of Mexico, from S Coahuila and C Nuevo León south to Querétaro and N Hidalgo) Similar to *gaigei* but the rump has more black admixed, the upperparts are more blackish, and the flanks are darker.

The following four races tend towards the Olive-backed group in upperpart colour and sometimes also in the colour of the spots.

P. e. maculatus (Resident in the Sierra Madre Oriental, from Hidalgo south to E Puebla and WC Veracruz.; hybridises with Collared Towhee *P. ocai ocai* on Mount Orizaba in Veracruz, where the two occur sympatrically) Has dark greyish olive-brown or brownish-olive upperparts which contrast slightly with the black (male) or dull sooty/brownish-black (female) hood, white spots on upperparts and tawny-rufous flanks with paler cinnamon-rufous vent and undertail-coverts.

P. e. oaxacae (Resident in the mountains of N and C Oaxaca; apparently occurs sympatrically with the *brunnescens* race of Collared Towhee without hybridisation) Similar to *maculatus* but the upperparts are paler and browner, the white spots are larger and the white on the tertial edges is more extensive.

P. e. chiapensis (Resident in the mountains of C Chiapas) Doubtfully distinguishable from *oaxacae* and possibly not a valid race; averages slightly darker above and the spots average buffier and less pure white.

P. e. repetens (Resident in SE Chiapas, on Volcán Tacaná and the Pacific Cordillera of Guatemala) Similar to *chiapensis* and *oaxacae* but the upperparts are less

buffy-brown (more blackish-olive) and the spots are whiter.

Olive-backed group: upperparts olive, contrasting with black hood, yellowish (not white) spots on upperparts.

P. e. macronyx (Resident in the mountains on the W and SW side of the Valley of Mexico, from E Michoacán east to Puebla; hybridises extensively with Collared Towhee *P. o. nigrescens* in E Michoacán) Has paler and more greenish-olive upperparts than *maculatus* and the spots on the upperparts (including tail) are distinctly yellow, not white; the bend of the wing is also yellow.

P. e. vulcanorum (Resident on the NW side of Mount Popocatépetl in Mexico) Similar to *macronyx* but duller olive, and noticeably streaked blackish, on the upperparts, and has larger, paler yellow spots.

Socorro Towhee:

P. e. socorroensis (Resident on Isla Socorro in the Islas Revillagigedo off W Mexico) Sometimes still regarded as a full species. Noticeably smaller than the other groups, both sexes are dark olivaceous-grey on head, throat, breast and upperparts, and the spots on the upperparts are relatively small.

RELATIONSHIPS It seems to be closely related to Collared Towhee (98) and the two frequently hybridise where their ranges overlap. There may be more than one species involved in the *P. erythrophthalmus* complex.

VOICE Male generally sings from an exposed perch, often at the top of a bush, and there are records of females singing. The distinctive song of the Rufous-sided group consists of 2 notes, the second lower, followed by a higher-pitched series of notes on one pitch; often transcribed as *drink-your-tea-ee-ee-ee*. The Spotted group has a more variable song, usually a buzzy trill preceded by softer notes which are only audible at close range. All groups usually sing from a prominent perch. The usual call of the Rufous-sided group is a rising, querying *to-whee* or *che-wink*. The Spotted group has more varied calls, including a whining *chee-ee* and a rasping mew.

HABITS Nest is placed on or close to the ground, or low in a bush; a rather loose cup of twigs, bark strips, weed stalks and grasses, lined with fine grasses and rootlets. 2-6 (usually 3-4) eggs are laid in April-August; they are whitish, speckled with reddish-browns and a little lavender. Incubation period is 12-13 days and the young fledge after 10-12 days. Double-brooded. Feeds mainly on seeds, and insects and their larvae, searching the leaf-litter by scratching with both feet simultaneously in typical towhee fashion. Sometimes also ascends to the lower branches of bushes and trees, where it eats some berries. Outside the breeding season often found in small groups, although sedentary populations probably remain on territory in pairs. Generally rather shy, keeping to the undergrowth, but easy to locate due to the rhythmic scratching noise it makes in the leaf-litter.

STATUS AND HABITAT Common throughout its range. Breeds in a variety of wooded and other habitats with dense undergrowth, including open forest and forest edge, second-growth woodland, riparian thickets, brush and chaparral. Southern birds in Chiapas and Guatemela occur mainly in undergrowth on the edges of coniferous forests, but also in more arid brush. Often found in parks and gardens which have a dense undergrowth. Migratory populations winter in similar habitat. Occurs in lowlands, foothills and in mountains up to 3500m.

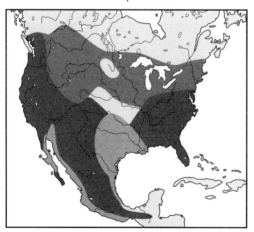

DISTRIBUTION AND MOVEMENTS Breeds in much of North America, except for much of Texas and parts of the Midwest, north to southern Canada, and south through the highlands of Mexico and Guatemala. Winters throughout much of the breeding range, except for the north-eastern part and the northern parts of the prairies and Rockies, and also in Texas and the lowlands of northern Mexico. Populations in New England, the Great Lakes region, and the Prairies and Rockies of northern USA and southern Canada are wholly or mainly migratory, moving south to the southern USA and northern Mexico in winter. Other populations are mainly sedentary although many northern breeders move south to the more southern parts of the breeding range in winter. The

Olive-backed and Socorro forms are entirely sedentary. See also under Geographical Variation. Migrants generally arrive on breeding grounds from March-April and leave in September. The Rufous-sided form has occurred as a vagrant to Britain (once, June 1966).

REFERENCES Armani (1985), Bent (1968), Cramp & Perrins (1994), Davies (1957), Dunn & Blom (1983), Godfrey (1986), Nichols (1953), Oberholser (1974), Paynter & Storer (1970), Pyle *et al.* (1987), Ridgway (1901), Sibley (1950), Sibley & Monroe (1990), Terres (1980).

100 CALIFORNIA TOWHEE
Pipilo crissalis   Plate 37

Described as *Fringilla crissalis* Vigors 1839.
Synonyms: *Pipilo fuscus* (in part), *Oriturus wrangeli, Pipilo albigula.*

Until recently this species was considered conspecific with Canyon Towhee (101) under the name Brown Towhee. Recent allozyme and morphometric evidence has shown, however, that they are better treated as allospecies.

IDENTIFICATION 21-22cm. Head and upperparts warm brown with a grey tinge. Throat rich buff, faintly streaked darker on the lower part and with a distinct gorget of dark streaks along the lower border. The rest of the underparts are pale grey-buff, whiter on the belly, and with contrasting rich cinnamon-buff vent and undertail-coverts. The tail is long and rounded, brown and unmarked. Juvenile lacks the gorget of streaks across the lower throat, and has rather obscure brown streaks on the underparts. Birds in southernmost Baja California have a distinct pale rufous crown, and are rather paler and greyer above and whiter below. Canyon Towhee has a paler buff throat than California Towhee, with a similar gorget of streaks surrounding it; it also has a dark spot in the centre of the breast, below this gorget, which California Towhee lacks. The colour of the crown is variable in both species; northern California Towhees have brown crowns, fairly uniform with the upperparts, but the crown is distinctly rufous in southern Baja birds. Canyon Towhees in the USA always have distinct rufous crowns, but in some Mexican races the crown is more or less uniform with the upperparts, the rufous tinge being very faint or lacking. The two also have quite different voices (see under Voice).

DESCRIPTION
Sexes alike; juvenile clearly different from subsequent plumages.
Adult/first-year Crown, nape and upperparts uniform warm brown, tinged grey. Lores, submoustachial area and ear-coverts similar, but ear-coverts faintly flecked with buff. Eye-ring rufous-buff. Lesser coverts greybrown. Rest of wings dark grey-brown with narrow grey-buff feather edges. Bend of wing white. Tail blackishbrown. Throat rich buff, faintly streaked dark brown on the lower part and bordered with a more distinct gorget of dark brown streaks. Breast and flanks pale grey-buff, becoming more buff on rear flanks. Belly greyish-white, rather paler than breast and flanks but not contrasting strongly; vent and undertail-coverts contrasting rich cinnamon-buff. Iris brown. Bill blackish with a paler and greyer lower mandible. Legs flesh.
Juvenile Resembles adults but is rather paler overall; the

underparts lack the gorget of streaks, are rather buffier and faintly but noticeably streaked with brown. Greater and median coverts have pale buff tips, forming two obscure wing-bars. Bill and legs are paler than adult's.

MOULT AND AGEING The post-juvenile moult is partial/incomplete, sometimes including some (rarely all) of the rectrices, and occurs in June-October. The post-breeding moult is complete, also occurring in June-October. There is no pre-breeding moult. First-years resemble adults after the post-juvenile moult is completed, but the flight feathers are paler brown and the rectrices average more pointed (there is often contrast between pointed juvenile rectrices and more rounded adult ones, but note that some first-years may moult all the rectrices during the post-juvenile moult). These differences are slight, are only useful in the hand, and are difficult to use in spring/summer when the plumage is worn and faded on all birds. Skull ossification complete in first-years from 1 September but some birds may retain unossified 'windows' through their first spring.

MEASUREMENTS Wing (chord): male (n27) 86.1-103.6; female (n16) 79-98.5. Tail: male (n27) 93.9-115.6; female (n16) 81.8-111.3. Bill: male (n27) 13.7-16.5; female (n16) 14.2-16.3. Tarsus: male (n27) 23.9-28.5; female (n16) 22.9-27.9.

GEOGRAPHICAL VARIATION Eight races, some of which are identifiable in the field.

P. c. bullatus (Occurs in SW Oregon and adjacent extreme N California) The largest race, greyer than *petulans* with the head and upperparts appearing noticeably greyish, especially in worn plumage.

P. c. petulans (Occurs in NC coastal California, from Humboldt County south to Santa Cruz County, and east to the western edge of the Sacramento and San Joaquin valleys) The most rufous of all the races and intermediate between *carolae* and *crissalis* in size.

P. c. carolae (Occurs in interior California, east of coastal mountains east to the foothills of the Cascades and Sierra Nevada Mountains, from Humboldt County south to Napa County, and also on the eastern side of the San Joaquin Valley south to Kern County) Similar to *crissalis* but averages darker and duller on head and upperparts and slightly paler on throat.

P. c. crissalis (Occurs in central coastal California, from Monterrey County south to Kern and Ventura Counties and east to the western edge of the San Joaquin Valley) Described above.

P. c. eremophilus (Occurs in east-central interior California in the Argus Mountains of SW Inyo County and NW San Bernadino County) Similar to *carolae* but slightly darker and greyer above, and also slightly smaller-billed and shorter in tarsus.

P. c. senicula (Occurs in coastal S California and NW Baja California, from approximately 34°N south to approximately 29°N) Slightly smaller, and noticeably darker and greyer overall, than *crissalis* (it is the darkest race).

P. c. aripolius (Occurs in C Baja California, from approximately 29°N south to approximately 26°N) Paler than *senicula*, and darker than *albigula* with a greyish crown.

P. c. albigula (Occurs in S Baja California, south of 26°N) The palest race, grey-brown above and whitish below with the cinnamon-rufous restricted to the undertail-coverts. Also has a noticeable pale rufous crown

which clearly contrasts with the upperparts (unlike other races of California), and the lower part of the throat (just above the necklace of streaks) is whitish.

RELATIONSHIPS Formerly considered part of the Brown Towhee complex with Canyon Towhee. Closely related to Canyon Towhee and forms a superspecies with it, although it now appears that Canyon Towhee is genetically closer to White-throated Towhee (103).

VOICE The song, given from an open perch, is an accelerating series of *chink* notes. Calls include a metallic *chink.*

HABITS Nest is placed low down in a thick hedge, bush or vine; a cup of dry grass and straw, lined with finer plant material and sometimes hair. 2-6 (usually 3-4) eggs are laid in March-September; they are bluish-white marked with black or reddish-brown. Incubation period is 11 days and the young fledge after 8 days. Very aggressive in the breeding season; pairs defend their territory year-round and probably mate for life. Feeds mainly on insects during the breeding season and seeds at other times; also takes vegetables and fruits from gardens and orchards. Forages mainly on the ground, scratching in leaf-litter in typical towhee-style, but not as vigorously or as persistently as Rufous-sided Towhee (99); also forages low in trees and bushes. Flight is generally over short distances and consists of quick wingbeats interspersed with glides. Generally found in pairs, also in family parties after the breeding season.

STATUS AND HABITAT Common in chaparral, brush, arid scrub, mesquite, riparian thickets and suburban gardens; frequently found around human habitation in towns and villages, where it will feed on vegetables and fruit grown in gardens.

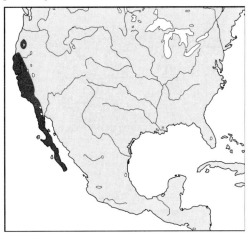

DISTRIBUTION AND MOVEMENTS Occurs in coastal western North America (east to the foothills of the Cascades and Sierra Nevada Mountains), from south-western Oregon south to the southern tip of Baja California. See also under Geographical Variation. Sedentary. Vagrant to the Chukotskiy Peninsula in extreme north-eastern Russia.

REFERENCES Armani (1985), Bent (1968), Davies (1951), Dunn & Blom (1983), Farrand (1983), Grinnell & Swarth (1926), Pyle *et al.* (1987), Ridgway (1901), Sibley & Monroe (1990), Terres (1980), Zink (1988).

Pipilo fuscus   **Plate 37**

Described as *Pipilo fusca* Swainson 1827.

This relatively 'new' species is formed by what used to be known as the interior populations of the Brown Towhee. Recent allozyme and morphometric evidence indicates that it is actually more closely related to the Mexican White-throated Towhee (103), with which it is partly sympatric, than to the California Towhee (100).

IDENTIFICATION 19-24cm. Similar to California Towhee, but all races have a paler buff throat and a dark spot in the centre of the breast, just below the gorget of dark streaks across the lower throat. It also has rather paler and greyer upperparts than most races of California Towhee (the race *albigula* is rather similar in this respect). USA birds have distinct rufous-brown crowns which contrast with the grey-brown upperparts (again, the *albigula* race of California is similar in this respect), but in many Mexican races the crown is more or less uniform with the upperparts, with the rufous cap lacking or very faint. The voices of the two are also different (see under Voice) and note that their ranges do not overlap. Juveniles have buffier underparts with obscure dark streaks and indistinct buffy wing-bars. White-throated Towhee is also fairly similar, and overlaps in range with Canyon Towhee, but it has a white (not buff) throat, lacks the dark spot on the breast and has a distinct rufous submoustachial area which often extends round the rear edge of the ear-coverts and sometimes also across the throat (there is often also a dark spot at the lower end of the malar area).

DESCRIPTION
Sexes alike; juvenile clearly different from subsequent plumages.
Adult/first-year Crown grey-brown, faintly tinged rufous. Lores buff, the buff also extending indistinctly round the ocular area. Ear-coverts grey-brown streaked buffy-white (especially under the eye). Submoustachial stripe pale buffy-brown. Nape, neck-sides and upperparts grey-brown, slightly paler than the crown and lacking any rufous tinge, but not contrasting greatly. Lesser coverts grey-brown. Rest of wings dark brown with narrow grey-buff feather edges. Bend of wing white. Tail blackish-brown. Throat pale buff, often with indistinct brown streaks on the lower part and bordered by a gorget of dark brown streaks. The throat is also bordered on the sides by a series of fine dark streaks which form a vague malar stripe. Breast and flanks pale grey-buff with a dark brown spot in the centre of the breast, just below the gorget of streaks. Belly whitish. Vent and rear flanks warm buff, undertail-coverts tawny-cinnamon to cinnamon-rufous. Iris brown. Bill blackish with a paler and greyer lower mandible. Legs flesh.
Juvenile Very similar to juvenile California Towhee but upperparts are slightly paler and greyer, as in adult.

MOULT AND AGEING As far as is known, the moult sequences and ageing details are the same as in California Towhee, although the timing of moults and earliest date of skull ossification may be different at the latitudinal extremes.

MEASUREMENTS Wing (chord): male (n43) 87.1-101.4; female (n23) 82-99.6. Tail: male (n43) 82.6-107.4; female (n23) 84.3-109.5. Bill: male (n43) 13.7-16.8; female (n23) 14.2-16.3. Tarsus: male (n43) 23.4-26.9; female

(n23) 22.9-26.9.

GEOGRAPHICAL VARIATION Ten races generally recognised; two other races have been described: *relictus* (which is now considered to be part of *mesoleucus*) and *tenebrosus* (which is now considered to be part of *fuscus*).

P. f. mesatus (Occurs in S USA in SE Colorado, NE New Mexico, extreme NW Oklahoma and extreme SW Kansas) Similar to *fuscus* but the crown is pale rufous.

P. f. mesoleucus (Occurs in SW USA and NW Mexico from Arizona and New Mexico, except north-east, south through extreme W Texas to N Sonora and NW Chihuahua) Similar to *mesatus* but the crown is slightly darker rufous and the upperparts are slightly greyer; the wing also averages slightly shorter.

P. f. texanus (Occurs in W and C Texas and in adjacent N Mexico in NE Coahuila) Similar to *mesoleucus* but the crown is slightly darker rufous and the tail also averages slightly shorter.

P. f. intermedius (Occurs in NW Mexico from NC Sonora south to extreme N Sinaloa) Similar to *fuscus* in its grey-brown crown, more or less uniform with upperparts, but the throat is paler buff; averages smaller than *mesoleucus* with darker upperparts.

P. f. jamesi (Occurs on Tiburón Island, Sonora, in the Gulf of California) Similar to *intermedius* but is smaller and paler tawny on the vent and undertail-coverts; the bill and feet are also relatively larger.

P. f. perpallidus (Occurs in N Mexico, from Chihuahua south through Durango to W Zacatecas; intergrades with *fuscus* in W Nayarit, northernmost Jalisco and SW Zacatecas) Similar to *fuscus* and *mesoleucus* but paler and greyer, and also averages slightly smaller than *mesoleucus*.

P. f. potosinus (Occurs in NE Mexico from N Coahuila, W Nuevo León and SW Tamaulipas south to NE Jalisco and Querétaro) Similar to *fuscus* but rather larger, paler and greyer above, paler buff on the throat, paler cinnamon on the undertail-coverts, and the crown has a stronger rufous tinge.

P. f. fuscus (Occurs in WC Mexico from Nayarit and N Guerrero east to Morelos and Distrito Federal) Intergrades with *perpallidus* (which see for details). Described above.

P. f. campoi (Occurs in C Mexico in Hidalgo, intergrading with *toroi* in NE Puebla and adjacent Veracruz) Similar to *toroi* in having the crown grey-brown, uniform with the upperparts, but is slightly darker overall with less extensive whitish on the belly.

P. f. toroi (Occurs in EC Mexico from Tlaxcala and WC Veracruz south to N Oaxaca) Intergrades with *campoi* but pure birds are paler and greyer (it is the palest and greyest of all the races).

RELATIONSHIPS Closely related to, and forming a superspecies with, California Towhee.

VOICE The song, given from an open perch, is a mellow chipping trill. Calls include a sharp *chiup* or *chud-up*.

HABITS Nesting and other habits similar to California Towhee.

STATUS AND HABITAT Common in brush, arid scrub, mesquite, riparian thickets and gardens in towns and villages; generally occurs at higher elevations than California and Abert's (102) Towhees.

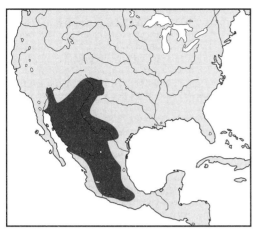

DISTRIBUTION AND MOVEMENTS Occurs in the southern and south-western USA and in northern and central Mexico. See also under Geographical Variation. Sedentary.

REFERENCES Armani (1985), Bent (1968), Davies (1957), Dunn & Blom (1983), Pyle *et al.* (1987), Ridgway (1901), Sibley & Monroe (1990), Zink (1988).

---

102 ABERT'S TOWHEE
Pipilo aberti   Plate 37

Described as *Pipilo aberti* Baird 1852.

A distinctive but very localised towhee, restricted to the south-western USA and adjacent north-western Mexico.

IDENTIFICATION 24cm. A large, buff-looking towhee with a distinctive black patch on the front of the face/throat. Upperparts are buffy grey-brown and underparts pale cinnamon-buff with rich cinnamon-rufous undertail-coverts. Tail long and rounded, brown and unmarked. Juvenile has paler underparts streaked with dark brown. It is larger and buffier than juvenile California (100) and Canyon (101) Towhees.

DESCRIPTION
Sexes alike; juvenile clearly different from subsequent plumages.
Adult/first-year Crown, nape and upperparts uniform buffy grey-brown, uppertail-coverts with pale fringes in fresh plumage. Forehead, lores, ocular area and chin black, forming a contrasting patch. Lesser, median and greater coverts buffy grey-brown. Rest of wings dark brown with narrow pale buff feather edges. Tail dark brown with narrow rufous-buff feather edges. Underparts cinnamon-buff, fairly uniform but slightly paler on belly; undertail-coverts brighter cinnamon-rufous. Throat is sometimes lightly streaked with dark brown immediately below the black chin. Iris reddish-brown. Bill pale flesh-horn. Legs dark flesh.
Juvenile Similar to adult on upperparts, but paler buff with dark brown streaks on underparts.

MOULT AND AGEING The post-juvenile moult is partial/incomplete, occurring in June-October; it may include some or all of the rectrices. The post-breeding moult is complete, also occurring in June-October. There is no pre-breeding moult. First-years resemble adults once the post-juvenile moult is completed but have more pointed rectrices on average. Some first-years may be told in the hand, with care, by more worn, paler brown flight feathers and contrast between juvenile and adult rectrices; this becomes very difficult to use in spring, however, when all birds have worn plumage. Skull ossification complete in first-years from 1 September, although some may retain small unossified 'windows' through their first spring.

MEASUREMENTS Wing (chord): male (n38) 88-97; female (n37) 82-92. Tail: male (n8) 105.9-119.9; female (n7) 100.8-109.5. Bill: male (n8) 15-16.3; female (n7) 15-15.8. Tarsus: male (n8) 27.9-29.2; female (n7) 26.4-29.

GEOGRAPHICAL VARIATION Two races recognised; a third race (*dumeticolus*) is now regarded as part of *aberti*. The two races are very similar and probably not identifiable in the field, except by range.
    P. a. aberti (Occurs from extreme SW Utah and S Nevada south to W Arizona, NW Sonora and NE Baja California) Described above.
    P. a. vorhiesi (Occurs in SE Arizona and extreme SW New Mexico) Similar to *aberti* but slightly more grey-brown (less buffy) on the upperparts and has slightly darker underparts.

VOICE The song, given from a bush or tree, is a chipping trill on various pitches. Calls include a sharp *peek*.

HABITS Nest is placed very close to the ground in a dense bush or a large grass clump; a cup of straw and dry grass, lined with rootlets and hair. 2-4 (usually 3) eggs are laid in February-September; they are bluish-white marked with blackish-brown. Nesting usually starts a week or two after the onset of the rainy season (usually March-April in Arizona), and birds will often nest again in the autumn if there are further rains at that season. Feeds on insects and seeds, and some berries. Forages on the ground, scratching with both feet and turning over leaves with its bill in typical towhee style, and also low in bushes. Shy and secretive, but may feed in the open, especially by the edge of streams in canyon bottoms. Generally found alone, or in pairs or family parties. Pairs normally stay together throughout the year and mate for life.

STATUS AND HABITAT Common in desert scrub, mesquite and woodland, especially near water, and in riparian thickets and in streamside vegetation in canyon bottoms; also occurs in citrus groves, suburban gardens and orchards. Generally found at lower elevations than Canyon Towhee. Sedentary.

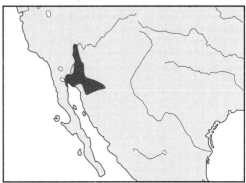

DISTRIBUTION AND MOVEMENTS Occurs in the south-western USA, from extreme south-western Utah and southern Nevada south to south-eastern California and extreme south-western New Mexico, and also in adjacent north-western Mexico in extreme north-eastern Baja California and northern Sonora. See also under Geographical Variation. Sedentary.

REFERENCES Armani (1985), Bent (1968), Dunn & Blom (1983), Finch (1984), Marshall (1963), Phillips *et al.* (1964), Pyle *et al.* (1987), Ridgway (1901), Terres (1980).

103 WHITE-THROATED TOWHEE
Pipilo albicollis   Plate 37

Described as *Pipilo albicollis* Sclater 1858.
Synonym: *Pipilo rutilus*.

This Mexican endemic is similar to the Brown Towhee complex and recent allozyme and morphometric studies have shown that it is very closely related to Canyon Towhee (101), with these two species more distantly related to California Towhee (100).

IDENTIFICATION 19cm. Fairly similar to Canyon and California Towhees but easily distinguished by the white throat and upper breast (with a vague necklace of dark marks separating the two) and the rufous-buff patch on the submoustachial area (which extends slightly onto the neck-sides and sometimes across the throat in a narrow band). There is often a small blackish spot at the lower end of the malar area, adjacent to the rufous-buff patch. The crown is greyish olive-brown, uniform with the upperparts, and never shows a warm brown or rufous cap (as many Canyon Towhees do). The underparts are whitish, with a vague necklace of dark spots across the breast, greyish lower breast and flanks, bright cinnamon-buff vent and undertail-coverts. Juvenile has buffy underparts with darker streaks.

DESCRIPTION
Sexes alike; juvenile clearly different from subsequent plumages.
Adult/first-year Head and upperparts fairly uniform greyish olive-brown. Submoustachial stripe whitish near base of bill, becoming rufous-buff lower down; the rufous-buff generally extends round the rear edge of the ear-coverts onto the neck-sides, and sometimes also across the throat as a narrow band. There is usually a small dark spot at the lower end of the malar area, adjacent to the rufous-buff. Lesser and median coverts greyish olive-brown. Rest of wings dark brown with narrow paler grey-buff feather edges; outer greater coverts are also obscurely tipped whitish. Bend of wing white. Tail blackish-brown. Throat and upper breast white, with a vague necklace of dark brown blotchy spots across the upper breast. Lower breast and flanks pale grey, separating white upper breast from white belly. Rear-flanks washed with buff; vent and undertail-coverts bright cinnamon-buff. Iris brown. Bill greyish with a yellowish-horn lower mandible. Legs dark flesh.
Juvenile Upperparts similar to adult but underparts buffy-white, streaked with dark brown.

MOULT AND AGEING Adults have a complete moult, probably after breeding, but the extent of the post-juvenile moult is not known. There is probably no pre-

breeding moult. No ageing criteria are known once the post-juvenile moult is completed.

MEASUREMENTS Wing (chord): male (n7) 82-92; female (n6) 79.8-84.1. Tail: male (n7) 82.3-100.8; female (n6) 87.6-94.2. Bill: male (n7) 15-17; female (n6) 15.2-16.7. Tarsus: male (n7) 26.9-29.5; female (n6) 26.7-27.9.

GEOGRAPHICAL VARIATION Two races described, which are very similar and not distinguishable in the field.
   P. a. albicollis (Occurs in S Puebla, E Guerrero and N Oaxaca, Mexico) Described above.
   P. a. parvirostris (Occurs in the vicinity of Mt. Zempoaltepec, Oaxaca, Mexico) Very similar to *albicollis* and may not be separable from it.

RELATIONSHIPS Within the *Pipilo* genus it is most closely related to Canyon Towhee.

VOICE The song, given from an exposed perch, often the top of a bush, is a series of high metallic notes.

HABITS Nest is placed close to the ground in a thick shrub: a cup of dry grasses and straw, lined with rootlets, hair and fine plant material. 4 eggs are laid, which are pale blue or bluish-white, marked with reddish-purple and blackish-brown. Feeds on seeds, insects and berries, generally foraging on the ground in the undergrowth and scratching in leaf-litter in typical towhee style. Will also forage low in bushes. Generally rather shy and unobtrusive, but more obvious in the breeding season, when noisy territorial disputes may occur. Generally found alone, or in pairs or small groups (family parties?) outside the breeding season.

STATUS AND HABITAT Fairly common in the highlands in semi-arid scrub and open pine-oak forest with a dense undergrowth. Sometimes also in parks and gardens in villages. Most common in semi-arid highland areas with dense scrub.

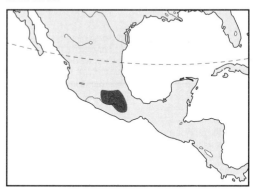

DISTRIBUTION AND MOVEMENTS Endemic to south-central Mexico, where it occurs in eastern Guerrero, southern Puebla and western Oaxaca. See also under Geographical Variation. Sedentary.

REFERENCES Armani (1985), Peterson & Chalif (1973), Ridgway (1901), Sibley & Monroe (1990), Zink (1988).

MELOZONE

Three species of fairly large ground-feeding sparrows which are dull olive above and paler below with striking head patterns. All are restricted to Mexico and Central America.

104 RUSTY-CROWNED GROUND-SPARROW
Melozone kieneri   Plate 38

Described as *Pyrgisoma kieneri* Bonaparte 1851.
Synonyms: *Melozone rubricatum, Atlapetes rubricatum.*

This species, endemic to western Mexico, forms a superspecies with Prevost's Ground-Sparrow (105) and is sometimes considered conspecific with it.

IDENTIFICATION 15-16cm. Bright rufous rear-crown, nape and neck-sides contrast with black forecrown and front of face. White supraloral and eye-ring conspicuous in black face. Rear part of ear-coverts grey, bordered above and behind by the rufous. Upperparts dark brownish-olive. Underparts white with a large black spot in the centre of the breast. Flanks and undertail-coverts cinnamon-buff. The Costa Rican race of Prevost's Ground-Sparrow is quite similar but has the rufous of the rear-crown and nape extending onto the rear of the ear-coverts, but not the neck-sides; it also has a larger black breast spot and a narrow black malar stripe. The more northern races of Prevost's have a mostly white face.

DESCRIPTION
Sexes alike; juvenile clearly different from subsequent plumages.
Adult/first-year Forecrown, lores, ocular area and front part of ear-coverts blackish, contrasting with rufous rear-crown, nape and neck-sides. Eye-ring white, supraloral buffy-white. Rear part of ear-coverts grey, washed olive. Upperparts olive-brown. Lesser coverts grey. Alula blackish-brown edged white. Rest of wings blackish-brown with narrow pale olive-grey feather edges, slightly buffier on coverts and tertials. Bend of wing white. Tail blackish-brown with narrow pale grey-buff feather edges. Underparts (including submoustachial area) white with a prominent black spot in the centre of the breast. Breast-sides grey, flanks olive-grey, undertail-coverts cinnamon-buff. Iris brown. Bill black. Legs flesh.
Juvenile Head and upperparts uniform dark buff-brown, lacking adult's head pattern. Coverts and tertials edged warm buff, noticeably brighter than on adult. Underparts as adult but with relatively indistinct dark brown streaks on throat and breast. Bill paler than adult's, horn-coloured.

MOULT AND AGEING Adults have a complete moult, probably after breeding, but the extent of the post-juvenile moult is not known. There is probably no pre-breeding moult. No ageing criteria are known once the post-juvenile moult is completed.

MEASUREMENTS Wing (chord): male (n10) 71.1-86.9; female (n12) 70.1-81.8. Tail: male (n10) 64-78.7; female (n12) 61.5-75.2. Bill: male (n10) 13.2-15.5; female (n12) 13.2-16. Tarsus: male (n10) 24.9-27.4; female (n12) 23.4-26.2.

GEOGRAPHICAL VARIATION Three races which differ only slightly from each other.

M. k. grisior (Occurs in NW Mexico, in extreme SE Sonora and N Sinaloa) Similar to *kieneri* but the forecrown and upperparts are slightly greyer and less olive-brown, the rufous rear-crown and nape are paler and the undertail-coverts are paler.
M. k. kieneri (Occurs in W Mexico, from C Sinaloa and W Durango south to W Jalisco and Colima) Described above.
M. k. rubricatum (Occurs in SC Mexico, from Guanajuato and Mexico south to Guerrero and W Oaxaca) Similar to *kieneri* but smaller and smaller-billed; also tends to have a slightly paler and brighter rufous rear-crown and nape.

VOICE The song is a series of clear, sweet notes, delivered slowly and often descending in pitch.

HABITS Nest is placed low in a bush or shrub, or in a grass clump; a cup of grass, twigs and rootlets, lined with finer plant material. 3-4 eggs are laid, which are bluish-white, sometimes marked with reddish. Feeds on seeds and insects. Often forages on the ground, scratching in the leaf-litter with both feet together (in a similar manner to the other ground-sparrows), but also sometimes very low in bushes. Shy and retiring, generally keeping to dense undergrowth. Flight is rather heavy; does not normally fly far. Generally found in pairs throughout the year, but also in small groups (family parties?) after the breeding season.

STATUS AND HABITAT Fairly common in arid scrub, dense brushy thickets, barrancas, dense brushy embankments and undergrowth in dry, open woodland, up to 2100m.

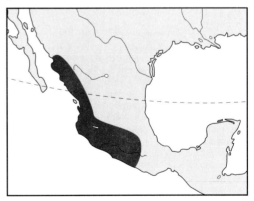

DISTRIBUTION AND MOVEMENTS Endemic to Mexico, where it occurs in the west and south-central parts of the country, from extreme south-eastern Sonora south to Guerrero and western Oaxaca. See also under Geographical Variation. Sedentary.

REFERENCES Armani (1985), Peterson & Chalif (1973), Paynter & Storer (1970), Ridgway (1901), Delaney (1992), Sibley & Monroe (1990).

105 PREVOST'S GROUND-SPARROW
Melozone biarcuatum   **Plate 38**

Described as *Pyrgita biarcuata* Prévost & Des Murs 1846. Synonym: *Pyrgisoma cabanisi*.

This species forms a superspecies with Rusty-crowned Ground-Sparrow (104) and the two are sometimes considered to be conspecific. As the southern race lacks the white face, the name Prevost's Ground-Sparrow seems more appropriate than the alternative name of White-faced; however, this southern race (or allospecies) has been considered as a species in its own right due to the differing head pattern and the fact that it is geographically widely separated from the more northern races.

IDENTIFICATION 15-16cm. All races have rufous nape, dark olive-brown upperparts, whitish underparts with buffy belly and undertail-coverts, and a distinctive facial pattern. Northern birds (southern Mexico, Guatemala, El Salvador and western Honduras) have sides of face white, large dull rufous-brown crescent on rear of ear-coverts, blackish forecrown and dull rufous rear-crown and nape; plain whitish throat and breast joins with white face. Southern birds (Costa Rica) have front of face black, with large white loral spot and obvious white eye-ring, and bright rufous rear-crown, nape and rear of ear-coverts. The breast has a large black patch in the centre and there is also a prominent black malar stripe. Rusty-crowned Ground-Sparrow is quite similar to the Costa Rican race of Prevost's but the rear part of the ear-coverts is grey not rufous, the rufous of the nape extends onto the neck-sides (behind the ear-coverts), the black breast spot is smaller, and the black malar stripe is absent.

DESCRIPTION
Sexes alike; juvenile clearly different from subsequent plumages.
Adult/first-year Forehead and forecrown black. Rear-crown and nape bright rufous. Sides of face (lores, superciliary and ocular areas and front part of ear-coverts) white. Rear of ear-coverts dark rufous-brown, continuous with rufous crown/nape. Upperparts olive-brown. Lesser coverts dark brown. Rest of wings blackish-brown with paler feather edges; narrow and white on alula, narrow and greyish on primaries, secondaries and primary coverts, and slightly broader and more olive-buff on greater and median coverts and tertials. Bend of wing white. Tail blackish-brown. Throat, breast and belly white, throat and upper breast faintly washed with buff. Breast-sides grey. Flanks grey-buff, vent and undertail-coverts cinnamon-buff. Iris dark reddish-brown. Bill black. Legs dark flesh.
Juvenile Head and upperparts quite bright buffy-brown, head lacking adult's pattern. Coverts and tertials edged rufous-buff. Underparts whitish with dark brown streaks on breast and fore-flanks; vent and undertail-coverts cinnamon-buff, similar to adult. Bill paler than adult's, horn-coloured.

MOULT AND AGEING Adults have a complete moult, probably after the breeding season, but the extent of the post-juvenile moult is not known. There is probably no pre-breeding moult. No ageing criteria are known once the post-juvenile moult is completed.

MEASUREMENTS Wing (chord): male (n8) 67.8-76; female (n4) 62-65.8. Tail: male (n8) 56.6-73.7; female (n4) 58.4-62. Bill: male (n8) 12.7-14.2; female (n4) 12.4-14.2. Tarsus: male (n8) 24.4-27.4; female (n4) 23.9-24.9.

GEOGRAPHICAL VARIATION Three races described; the southern one has a very different head pattern and a different song, and may represent a distinct species.

M. b. hartwegi (Occurs in the highlands of Chiapas, S Mexico) Similar to *biacuartum* but the upperparts are more greyish-olive.
M. b. biarcuatum (Occurs in the highlands and Pacific slope of Guatemala, El Salvador and W Honduras) Described above.
M. b. cabanisi (Occurs in the Valle Central in C Costa Rica) Differs markedly from the other races in head pattern. It has a brighter rufous rear-crown and nape (which extends onto the rear of the ear-coverts), the forecrown, front of the face and edges of the ear-coverts are blackish with a wide white eye-ring (extending a short way behind the eye) and a large white loral spot, and there is a noticeable black malar stripe, separated from the ear-coverts by a white submoustachial stripe. In addition, there is a large black central breast spot.

VOICE The song is usually given from a hidden perch in dense undergrowth. In Mexico it is a rapid series of chirping *chep* notes. In Costa Rica it is a high, thin, staccato sputter followed by a buzzy note and/or a slow trill, and finishes with 3-4 clear whistles. Calls include a weak, high-pitched *tsit*, regularly repeated, a sharp thin *pseer* in agitation or aggression, and a short series of sharp whistled noted duetted by pairs as a greeting.

HABITS Nest is placed 0.25-2m up in a large grass tussock or dense bush; a sturdy cup of grass, rootlets, stems and dead leaves, lined with finer grasses. 2-4 eggs are laid in May-September, which are white or whitish and heavily spotted with reddish-brown, dull red or lilac, especially at the larger end. Breeding is closely associated with the rainy season, at least in Costa Rica. Shy and retiring; males sing, often at dawn, from a hidden perch in dense undergrowth. Only sings in the wet season, at least in Costa Rica. Feeds mainly on seeds and small insects. Forages mainly on the ground, usually in thick cover, but will venture out in the open in the early morning. Hops and scratches with both feet simultaneously, towhee fashion, in leaf-litter, picking at seeds and insects.

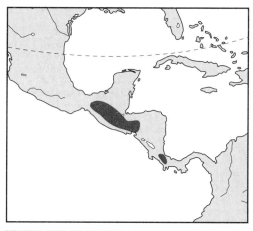

STATUS AND HABITAT Fairly common to common in

dense thickets and undergrowth in second growth, open woodland, forest borders, coffee plantations and hedgerows, on submontane and lower montane slopes from 600-2000m; the cover provided by a good undergrowth is the main requirement. Where it occurs with White-eared Ground-Sparrow (106), Prevost's tends to occur at lower elevations.

DISTRIBUTION AND MOVEMENTS Occurs from Chiapas, Mexico, to western Honduras, and in Costa Rica. See also under Geographical Variation. Sedentary.

REFERENCES Armani (1985), Paynter & Storer (1970), Peterson & Chalif (1973), Ridgway (1901), Sibley & Monroe (1990), Stiles & Skutch (1989), Winnett-Murray (1985).

106 WHITE-EARED GROUND-SPARROW
Melozone leucotis   Plate 38

Described as *Melozone leucotis* Cabanis 1860.
Synonym: *Pyrgisoma occipitale.*

This very distinctive ground-sparrow has a range fairly similar to Prevost's Ground-Sparrow (105). It is closely related to the other two ground-sparrows, but is not part of that superspecies.

IDENTIFICATION 17.5cm. The largest ground-sparrow, with an equally distinctive head pattern. Costa Rican birds have head mostly black with olive-green nape, broken white eye-ring, large white loral spot and another large white spot covering most of ear-coverts. Long, narrow patch behind ear-coverts bright yellow, extending along upper edge of ear-coverts as a narrow streak. Throat black, separated from black breast by a narrow rufous and white band. Rest of plumage similar to other ground-sparrows. Nicaraguan birds are similar but have more extensive black on breast, with white breast-band very inconspicuous. Northern birds, from El Salvador north-west to Chiapas, Mexico, have a broader yellow supercilium, from behind the eye to the nape, and breast mostly white, not black (but with a large black central spot).

DESCRIPTION
Sexes alike; juvenile clearly different from subsequent plumages.
Adult/first-year Crown dull blackish, becoming dark olive-green on nape. Large loral spot white. Eye-ring white but broken at front. Large white spot on rear of ear-coverts. Long narrow patch on neck-sides, immediately behind ear-coverts, bright yellow, extending a short way along top edge of ear-coverts as a narrow yellow streak. Rest of head, and throat, black. Upperparts greyish-olive on mantle, becoming browner on back and scapulars, and more olive-brown, washed buff, on rump and uppertail-coverts. Wings dark brown with olive feather edges, broader and buffier on the tertials than the other feathers. Bend of wing pale yellow. Tail dark brown with buffy-olive feather edges, broadest on central rectrices. Centre of upper breast black, separated from black throat by a narrow rufous band with an equally narrow greyish-white band immediately below it. Breast-sides grey, belly whitish, flanks, vent and undertail-coverts buffy-brown. Iris reddish-brown. Bill black. Legs horn.

Juvenile Head pattern similar to adult's but duller; black on face and breast duller and less extensive, white patches washed yellowish-buff, yellow patch dull buffy-yellow. Upperparts bright olive-brown with sooty feather fringes. Coverts and tertials edged cinnamon-buff. Lower underparts dull yellowish, lower breast and flanks streaked dark brown. Bill paler than adult's, horn-coloured.

MOULT AND AGEING Adults have a complete moult, probably following the breeding season, but the extent of the post-juvenile moult is not known. There is probably no pre-breeding moult. No ageing criteria are known once the post-juvenile moult is completed.

MEASUREMENTS Sexed specimens are race *leucotis*, unsexed ones race *occipitalis*. Wing (chord): male (n2) 74.2-79.3; female (n2) 74.2-78.7; unsexed (n3) 76.4-83.3. Tail: male (n2) 64.3-65.5; female (n2) 63.7-65; unsexed (n3) 72.4-81.8. Bill: male (n2) 14.2-14.7; female (n2) 14.7; unsexed (n3) 15-15.2. Tarsus: male (n2) 26.2-27.9; female (n2) 26.4-27.4; unsexed (n3) 26.2-28.5.

GEOGRAPHICAL VARIATION Three races described.
  M. l. leucotis (Occurs in N and C Costa Rica) Described above.
  M. l. nigrior (Occurs in N Nicaragua) Similar to *leucotis* but the black breast patch is broader, usually reaching the sides, and the white band between it and the black throat is very narrow and inconspicuous.
  M. l. occipitalis (Occurs on the Pacific slope in Chiapas, Mexico, Guatemala and El Salvador) Has a more prominent yellow supercilium (behind the eye) than *leucotis*, an olive-grey crown-stripe from the top of the crown to the nape, and a much smaller black breast spot, widely separated from the black throat (not separated only by a narrow whitish and rufous band).

VOICE The song is generally given from a hidden perch in the understorey. In Costa Rica it is a series of short, explosive staccato notes, interspersed with loud, hoarse or penetrating whistles, transcribed as *spit-chur, see-see-see, pseet-seecha seecha seecha*, etc. In Mexico it is described as a series of 5-15 fairly weak sibilant notes that fades towards the end (this may be the same as the greeting call described below). Calls include a high, piercing *tzip* and a characteristic series of buzzy sibilant notes, accelerating and descending, which is used as a greeting by mated pairs, at least in Costa Rica.

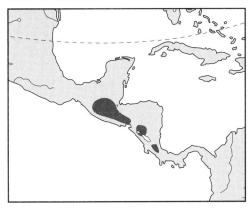

HABITS Nest is hidden on the ground or low in vegetation, especially banana plants and orchids; a massive bowl of dead leaves and stems, stout petioles and thin twigs, lined with finer stems and twigs. 2 (occasionally 3 or 4) eggs are laid in April-July; they are white, sometimes tinged bluish or greenish, and streaked and spotted with pale reddish-brown or cinnamon. Feeds on seeds, plus insects and other invertebrates. Forages mainly on ground or low in undergrowth, scratching in leaf-litter with both feet simultaneously, towhee style, and gleaning insects and seeds. Hops with a bouncing gait; tail is continually flicked up slightly and lowered slowly. Short flights are heavy and rather fluttering. Pairs remain on territory year-round; sometimes found in family parties for a while immediately after the breeding season.

STATUS AND HABITAT Uncommon and local to fairly common but shy and easily overlooked. Found in humid forest, dank ravines, forest edges and dense second growth with a dense understorey, from 500 to 2000m; generally above 1000m on the Caribbean slope in Costa Rica, and therefore at higher altitudes than Prevost's Ground-Sparrow.

DISTRIBUTION AND MOVEMENTS Occurs in Central America, patchily from Chiapas in southern Mexico south to central Costa Rica. See also under Geographical Variation. Sedentary.

REFERENCES Armani (1985), Paynter & Storer (1970), Peterson & Chalif (1973), Ridgway (1901), Stiles & Skutch (1989), Winnett-Murray (1985).

ARREMONOPS

Four species of plain olive-coloured sparrows with striped heads. This is principally a tropical genus but one species occurs north to extreme southern Texas.

107 OLIVE SPARROW
Arremonops rufivirgatus   Plate 39

Described as *Embernagra rufivirgata* Lawrence 1851.
Synonyms: *Arremon rufivirgatus, Arremonops superciliosa, Embernagra sumichrasti, Embernagra superciliosa.*

This smallish, secretive and rather drab sparrow is the northernmost representative of a group of a primarily Central and South American genus. The Pacific slope birds of western Mexico and north-western Costa Rica are sometimes treated as a separate species, Pacific Sparrow *A. superciliosus*; these two 'allospecies' form a superspecies which also includes Tocuyo Sparrow (108).

IDENTIFICATION 13.5-16cm. Basically olive-grey to olive-green above and pale buffy-grey below with paler, whitish, throat and belly. Head pattern quite variable. Caribbean slope birds (Olive Sparrow) have a greyish-olive median crown-stripe, uniform with upperparts, broad, dull rufous-brown lateral crown-stripe, broad buffy-grey supercilium and a narrow rufous-brown eye-stripe; they also have a relatively long tail. Birds in the Yucatán Peninsula and the Petén of Guatemala have darker and more distinct lateral crown-stripes which are streaked with blackish, brighter olive upperparts and whiter underparts. Pacific slope birds (Pacific Sparrow) are brighter olive above and have a more distinct head pattern, with more sharply defined, dark rufous lateral crown-stripe, grey or buffy-grey median crown-stripe and supercilium, and a relatively broad dark rufous eye-stripe. Juvenile is similar but duller; the head has a less distinct pattern and is faintly streaked brown, and there are two indistinct buffy wing-bars. Overlaps with the similar Green-backed Sparrow (109) in the Yucatán Peninsula and occurs in quite close proximity to Black-striped Sparrow (110) in Costa Rica; both differ in having black lateral crown and eye-stripes on a pure grey (not olive-grey or buffy-grey) head, and brighter green upperparts, which contrast noticeably with the grey head. Black-striped is also larger and has a blackish bill (dusky-horn in Olive Sparrow). Green-backed Sparrow occurs in more humid forests than the dry deciduous forests and scrub which Olive Sparrow prefers. Tocuyo Sparrow is very similar to Olive but has paler (buffy-white) median crown-stripe and supercilium; the two are greatly separated by range.

DESCRIPTION
Sexes alike; juvenile distinguishable from subsequent plumages.
Adult/first-year Median crown-stripe pale greyish-olive. Broad lateral crown-stripe dull rufous-brown and relatively indistinct. Both are long, reaching to nape. Supercilium pale buffy-grey, Neck-sides and ear-coverts buffy-grey. Narrow eye-stripe dull rufous-brown, darker on lores. Narrow eye-ring pale buff. Upperparts dull greyish-olive. Lesser coverts olive. Rest of wings dark brown with olive-green feather edges, broadest on greater and median coverts and tertials; edges of flight feathers are narrower but brighter yellowish-olive. Bend of wing yellow. Tail dark brown with narrow olive feather edges. Submoustachial stripe and throat whitish, separated by a narrow, faint dark malar stripe. Breast, flanks, vent and undertail-coverts grey-buff (buffier on undertail-coverts), belly whitish. Iris reddish-brown. Bill dusky with a pale horn base to the lower mandible. Legs flesh.
Juvenile Browner and duller above than adult with indistinct head stripes and faint brown streaking on crown, nape and neck-sides. Greater and median coverts are tipped buff, forming obscure wing-bars. Buffier on underparts. Juvenile of nominate race may be unstreaked, but juvenile of race *superciliosus* at least has dark brown streaks on breast and flanks and indistinct darker streaks on upperparts.

MOULT AND AGEING The following refers to the nominate race. The post-juvenile moult is partial, occurring in June-September. The post-breeding moult is complete, also occurring in June-September. There is no pre-breeding moult. In the other races, the timing of the moults may be different and the post-juvenile moult may be more extensive; more study is needed. Once the post-juvenile moult is completed, first-years resemble adults and no plumage criteria are known for ageing (tail shape does not seem to be very useful). Skull ossification complete in first-years (nominate race) from 15 September.

MEASUREMENTS Wing (chord): male (n39) 61.2-68.6; female (n30) 58-65. Tail: male (n18) 51.3-69.9; female (n11) 52.1-63.5. Bill: male (n18) 12.2-14; female (n11) 11.9-13.5. Tarsus: male (n18) 22.6-25.4; female (n11) 22.3-25.4. The Olive group has a longer tail (> 55mm) than the Pacific group (< 55mm).

GEOGRAPHICAL VARIATION Eight races described in two groups, which are sometimes considered separate species.

Caribbean group (Olive Sparrow): relatively ill-defined and pale rufous-brown lateral crown-stripe, greyish-olive upperparts and a relatively long tail.

A. r. rufivirgatus (Occurs in southernmost Texas and NE Mexico, from the USA border south to southern coastal Tamaulipas) Described above.

A. r. ridgwayi (Occurs in E Mexico in southern interior Tamaulipas, E San Luis Potosí, Hidalgo and N Veracruz) Intermediate between *rufivirgatus* and *crassirostris* and intergrades with both these races.

A. r. crassirostris (Occurs in E Mexico in C and S Veracruz, E Puebla and N Oaxaca) Brighter olive above than *rufivirgatus*, darker below, and has a bolder head pattern; in most of these characters it approaches *verticalis* but is darker below.

A. r. verticalis (Occurs in Mexico on the Yucatán Peninsula and perhaps also Tabasco, and in N Guatemala in Petén, and N Belize) Has a bolder head pattern than *crassirostris*, with darker rufous lateral crown-stripes which are streaked with black (the head pattern is not as distinct as in the Pacific group, however). It is also brighter olive above than *crassirostris*.

A. r. chiapensis (Occurs in the Central Valley of Chiapas, S Mexico) Intermediate in plumage between the Olive and Pacific groups and appears to link them (in range as well as plumage); plumage-wise it is closest to *verticalis* but the dark head stripes are not streaked with black and the underparts are buffier. It shares the relatively long tail with the other races in the Olive group.

Pacific group (Pacific Sparrow): well-defined dark rufous lateral crown-stripe, brighter olive upperparts and a relatively short tail.

A. r. sinaloae (Occurs on the Pacific coastal plain of Mexico from C Sinaloa south to Nayarit) The dullest of this group, similar to *sumichrasti* but greyer on the upperparts and also greyer (less buffy) on the median crown-stripe, supercilium and ear-coverts.

A. r. sumichrasti (Occurs on the Pacific coastal plain of Mexico from Jalisco south to the Isthmus of Tehuantepec in E Oaxaca; intergrades with *sinaloae*) Brighter olive than *sinaloae* with buffier-grey on the head, but noticeably duller above than *superciliosus*, with less buff on the head and underparts.

A. r. superciliosus (Occurs on the Pacific coastal plain of N Costa Rica, from the Nicaragua border south to the Peninsula de Nicoya and the Valle Central) The brightest of the Pacific group; quite bright olive above and noticeably buff-looking on the supercilium, ear-coverts, breast and flanks.

RELATIONSHIPS Forms a superspecies with Tocuyo Sparrow of northern South America.

VOICE The song, generally given from a concealed perch low in a tree or bush, is a series of dry *chip* notes, begin-

ning slowly and accelerating into a trill or rattle. In Costa Rica the pattern is the same but instead of dry *chip* notes, the series is of thin sibilant *tsew* notes that drop in pitch as well as accelerating; this is sometimes preceded by a few sharp clear whistles or staccato notes. Calls include a thin *tsip* often rapidly repeated.

HABITS Nest is hidden on the ground or under a fallen log in dense understorey; a globular structure with a side entrance built of rootlets and grasses. 2-5 white eggs are laid in April-July (Costa Rica) or March-September (Texas). Feeds on insects and other invertebrates and seeds, also some fruits. Forages mainly on the ground and low in dense tangles, hopping and gleaning seeds and insects, scratching noisily in leaf-litter. Often cocks tail. Generally found alone or in pairs, occasionally in family parties immediately after breeding.

STATUS AND HABITAT Genrally common throughout its range. Found in dense undergrowth in dry deciduous forests (especially live oak in Texas), brushlands, evergreen gallery forest and tall second growth; mostly in lowlands from sea level to 900m, but sometimes up to 2000m. Where it overlaps in range with Green-backed Sparrow, it prefers less humid and more open habitats with a dense undergrowth.

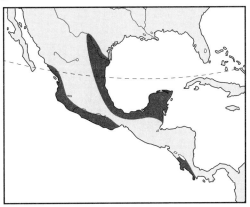

DISTRIBUTION AND MOVEMENTS Occurs on the Caribbean slope from southern Texas to northern Belize and in interior Chiapas (Olive Sparrow), and on the Pacific slope in western Mexico and north-western Costa Rica (Pacific Sparrow). See also under Geographical Variation.

REFERENCES Armani (1985), Dunn & Blom (1983), Monroe (1963), Oberholser (1974), Paynter & Storer (1970), Peterson & Chalif (1973), Pyle *et al.* (1987), Ridgway (1901), Sibley & Monroe (1990), Stiles & Skutch (1989), Terres (1980).

108 TOCUYO SPARROW
Arremonops tocuyensis   Plate 39

Described as *Arremonops tocuyensis* Todd 1912.

This little-known sparrow is the most restricted of the four *Arremonops* in range, being found only in north-western Venezuela and adjacent north-eastern Colombia. It is very similar to the more northern Olive Sparrow (107) and appears to form a superspecies with it.

IDENTIFICATION 13cm. Appears very similar to Olive Sparrow but is slightly smaller and the head pattern is more contrasting; the lateral crown- and eye-stripes are blackish and the supercilium and median crown-stripe are pale buffy-white (crown-stripe is slightly greyer than the supercilium). It overlaps in range with the nominate race of Black-striped Sparrow (110), which is larger, darker and brighter olive above, and has a mid-grey head with broader and blacker lateral crown- and eye-stripes.

DESCRIPTION
Sexes alike; juvenile distinguishable from subsequent plumages.
Adult/first-year Median crown-stripe pale buffy-grey, lateral crown-stripe blackish, admixed with brown at the rear. Supercilium pale buffy-white, slightly paler than median crown-stripe. Eye-stripe blackish, relatively narrow, and also admixed with brown at the rear. All head stripes are long, reaching to nape. Ear-coverts and neck-sides buffy-grey. Upperparts fairly uniform dull greyish- or brownish-olive. Wings dark brown with olive feather edges, broadest on coverts and tertials but brighter, more yellowish-olive on remiges. Bend of wing yellow. Tail dark brown with narrow olive feather edges. Underparts whitish on throat and belly with a grey wash to the breast and a buffy-grey wash to the flanks and undertail-coverts. Iris reddish-brown. Bill blackish with a horn lower mandible. Legs greyish-flesh.
Juvenile Duller and more brownish above than adult, and pale buff below. Head pattern indistinct and crown, nape and neck-sides finely streaked with brown.

MOULT AND AGEING Adults have a complete moult, probably after breeding, but the extent of the post-juvenile moult is not known. There is probably no pre-breeding moult. No ageing criteria are known once the post-juvenile moult is completed.

MEASUREMENTS (1 male) Wing: 72. Tail: 56. Bill: 15. Tarsus: 22.

GEOGRAPHICAL VARIATION Monotypic.

RELATIONSHIPS Closely related to Olive Sparrow and appears to form a superspecies with it.

VOICE The song, given from a concealed perch in the undergrowth or within the dense foliage low down in a tree or bush, is a series of thin, sweet notes terminating with a brief chatter reminiscent of House Wren *Troglodytes aedon*. The overall effect is similar to Black-striped Sparrow but thinner and sweeter.

HABITS Nest is usually placed on the ground under a bush, or very low down in a bush; a domed structure with a side entrance built of leaves, rootlets and twigs and lined with fine rootlets. 2-3 white eggs are laid. Feeds on seeds, insects and berries, generally foraging on the ground in dense cover, but sometimes also low in bushes. Shy and secretive. Generally found alone or in pairs.

STATUS AND HABITAT Generally uncommon but may be locally fairly common. Found in arid deciduous woodland with a dense understorey, and in dense scrub, in lowland areas (usually near the coast). In Venezuela it occurs to 1100m but in Colombia it is only found below 200m. It occurs in drier (less humid) woodlands, in more arid areas, than Black-striped Sparrow, although the two occur together in the Ríohacha area of Guajira, Colombia, at Mirimire, Falcón, in Venezuela and possibly elsewhere.

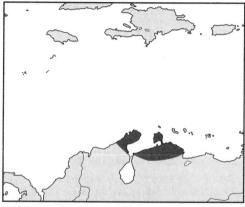

DISTRIBUTION AND MOVEMENTS Occurs in northwestern Venezuela in northern Zulia, Falcón and Lara, and in adjacent north-eastern Colombia in the Península de Guajira. Sedentary.

REFERENCES Armani (1985), Hilty & Brown (1986), Meyer de Schauensee & Phelps (1978), Ridgely & Tudor (1989), Todd (1912 & 1923).

109 GREEN-BACKED SPARROW
Arremonops chloronotus   Plate 39

Described as *Embernagra chloronota* Salvin 1861.
Synonym: *Arremonops chloronota*.

This *Arremonops* sparrow is restricted to Gulf lowlands in northern Central America. It is closely related to Black-striped Sparrow (110) and the two appear to form a superspecies.

IDENTIFICATION 14cm. Olive-green above and whitish below with greyish breast and flanks. Head is mid-grey with a broad black lateral crown-stripe and a slightly narrower supercilium. Juvenile is duller above, buffy below, and has an indistinct head pattern with fine brown streaking on the head. Green-backed is very similar to Black-striped Sparrow but is slightly smaller and has a different song and a less sharply bicoloured lower mandible; the dark stripes on the head are also marginally less pure black and may be streaked brownish, although they usually appear black in the field. The two are largely allopatric, although there may be a small amount of overlap in north-central Honduras. Also fairly similar to Olive Sparrow (107) but the head is much greyer, with prominent black (not rufous) stripes, and the upperparts are brighter olive-green; Olive Sparrow occurs in drier forest and scrub, rather than the more humid forest which Green-backed prefers.

DESCRIPTION
Sexes similar; juvenile distinguishable from subsequent plumages.
Adult/first-year Median crown-stripe mid-grey. Lateral crown-stripe dull black. Supercilium mid-grey, slightly paler and buffier on lores. Eye-stripe dull black, narrower than lateral crown-stripe. All head stripes are long, reaching nape. Narrow eye-ring pale buff. Ear-coverts, nape and neck-sides mid-grey, faintly washed with buff. Upperparts

uniform, quite bright olive-green, contrasting strongly with grey head. Lesser coverts green, brighter than the upperparts. Rest of wings dark brown with olive feather edges, broadest on greater and median coverts and tertials, but brighter and more yellowish-olive on remiges. Bend of wing yellow. Tail dark brown with olive feather edges. Throat whitish, sometimes faintly washed with buff. Breast and flanks grey, breast faintly washed with buff and rear flanks with olive. Belly white, undertail-coverts buffy-olive. Iris reddish-brown. Bill dusky horn to blackish, paler at the base of the lower mandible. Legs flesh.
Juvenile Duller than adult; more brownish-olive above and buffy below. Head pattern less distinct and crown, nape and neck-sides faintly streaked with brown.

MOULT AND AGEING Adults have a complete moult, probably after breeding, but the extent of the post-juvenile moult is not known. There is probably no pre-breeding moult. No ageing criteria are known once the post-juvenile moult is completed.

MEASUREMENTS Wing (chord): male (n4) 65.5-68.1; female (n4) 63.5-68.6. Tail: male (n4) 58.9-61; female (n4) 57.1-58.4. Bill: male (n4) 14.2-15.7; female (n4) 14-14.7. Tarsus: male (n4) 23.4-24.1; female (n4) 22.1-23.9.

GEOGRAPHICAL VARIATION Two similar races.
  A. c. chloronotus (Occurs in the Gulf lowlands in S Mexico in Tabasco and N Chiapas, the Yucatán Peninsula north to S Yucatán and C Quintana Roo, N Guatemala, Belize and NW Honduras) Described above.
  A. c. twomeyi (Occurs in the Gulf lowlands of NC Honduras in Yoro and Olancho) Similar to *chloronotus* but the head is paler grey, thus contrasting more with the black stripes, the upperparts average slightly brighter green, and the underparts are slightly paler with a buffy, rather than greyish, wash to the breast.

RELATIONSHIPS Closely related to Black-striped Sparrow and the two appear to form a superspecies.

VOICE The song, generally given from low in a bush, is a short series of short double notes which trail off as a trill at the end. Reminiscent of song of Tufted Titmouse *Parus bicolor* but less emphatic. Calls include a sharp *tchip*.

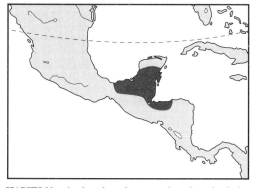

HABITS Nest is placed on the ground, under a bush, between the roots of a tree or in a bamboo clump; it is a domed structure with a side entrance, built of leaves, dried grass, rootlets and twigs, and lined with fine plant material. 3 (occasionally 4) white eggs are laid. Feeds on seeds, insects and berries, generally foraging on the ground in dense cover, but also low in the undergrowth. Shy and secretive. Generally found alone or in pairs, sometimes in small groups (family parties?).

STATUS AND HABITAT Fairly common in open humid forest and forest edges and second growth, and also in scrub and brushlands, although generally prefers more humid habitats than Olive Sparrow. Generally found below 700m.

DISTRIBUTION AND MOVEMENTS Occurs on the Gulf slope of northern Central America, from southern Mexico (Tabasco) south-east to north-central Honduras (Olancho). See also under Geographical Variation. Sedentary.

REFERENCES Armani (1985), Hardy & Wolf (1977), Monroe (1963), Paynter & Storer (1970), Peterson & Chalif (1973), Ridgway (1901), Sibley & Monroe (1990), Todd (1923).

110 BLACK-STRIPED SPARROW
Arremonops conirostris   Plate 39

Described as *Arremon conirostris* Bonaparte 1851.
Synonyms: *Embernagra chrysoma, Embernagra striaticeps*.

A primarily South American species which extends north in Central America to northern Honduras. It closely resembles Green-backed Sparrow (109) and the two appear to form a superspecies.

IDENTIFICATION 15-18cm. Head grey with broad black lateral crown-stripes and narrower black eye-stripes. Upperparts olive-green; face and most of underparts pale grey with throat and centre of belly whiter. Most birds have the appearance of a pale grey breast-band separating the white throat and belly, but this is lacking in birds from eastern Panama and the Pacific slope of north-western South America. Juvenile is duller on the upperparts, has a less distinct head pattern, has two pale buff wing-bars, and is yellowish-buff on the underparts with indistinct dark streaking on the breast. Tocuyo Sparrow (108) overlaps with Black-striped in north-eastern Colombia and north-western Venezuela; it is quite similar but is smaller, has paler and duller brownish-olive upperparts and has pale buffy-white (not grey) supercilium and median crown-stripe. Olive Sparrow (107) is also smaller and duller, has rufous-brown (not black) lateral crown- and eye-stripes, little or no contrast between head and upperparts, and does not overlap in range with Black-striped, although the two may occur quite close together in Costa Rica. Both Olive and Tocuyo Sparrows frequent arid open country and scrub, whereas Black-striped prefers humid forest and other humid habitats with trees or scrub. Very similar to Green-backed Sparrow (109) but is slightly larger, has a different song and, in Central America, has a sharply bicoloured lower mandible (distinctly pale at base), whereas on Green-backed the pale base of the lower mandible grades into the tip. Black-striped also differs from Green-backed (and others in the genus) in having a much more distinct juvenile plumage. Black-striped and Green-backed are largely allopatric but they may overlap in northern Honduras.

DESCRIPTION
Sexes alike; juvenile clearly different from subsequent plumages.

Adult/first-year Median crown-stripe and supercilium grey, joining at rear with grey nape and neck-sides. Supercilium slightly paler and buffier on lores. Broad lateral crown-stripe black, narrower eye-stripe also black; both long, reaching to nape. Sides of head grey, finely streaked with whitish and sometimes tinged buffy on ear-coverts. Upperparts uniform olive-green, washed with grey. Lesser coverts green. Rest of wings dark brown with olive-green feather edges, broadest on greater and median coverts and tertials, but brighter on flight feathers. Bend of wing yellow. Underparts pale grey with whitish throat and belly, and rear flanks washed with olive-buff. Iris reddish-brown. Bill blackish. Legs greyish-flesh.
Juvenile Head yellowish-olive with dusky lateral crown- and eye-stripes; pale areas narrowly streaked dusky. Upperparts brownish-olive streaked dusky. Underparts yellowish-olive washed brownish-olive on breast, flanks and undertail-coverts, and streaked dark brown on breast. Bill black with yellowish base. Legs pale flesh. Iris probably greyer-brown than in adult.

MOULT AND AGEING Adults have a complete moult, probably following the breeding season. Extent of the post-juvenile moult not known; in Costa Rica, juveniles acquire adult plumage after 4-5 months. There is probably no pre-breeding moult. No ageing criteria are known after completion of the post-juvenile moult.

MEASUREMENTS Wing (chord): male (20) 70.6-81.8; female (n11) 70.6-80.8. Tail: male (n20) 62,2-74.9; female (n11) 63-71.6. Bill: male (n20) 14.7-17.8; female (n11) 14.7-16. Tarsus: male (n20) 25.9-30.5; female (n11) 26.7-30.5.

GEOGRAPHICAL VARIATION Six races described, which vary slightly in size and the tone of the upperparts and head stripes. The race of the upper Magdalena Valley in Colombia (*inexpectatus*) is noticeably duller than most of the other races and has a different song; it has been suggested that it may be a distinct species.

  A. c. richmondi (Occurs in Central America from E Honduras south to W Panama) Slightly smaller than *conirostris*, brighter olive-green above and purer grey on the head.
  A. c. striaticeps (Occurs in C and E Panama and on the Pacific slope of SW Colombia and W Ecuador) Brighter olive-green above and purer grey on the head than *conirostris* (like *richmondi* but marginally duller) and the underparts are whiter than either of those races, lacking the grey breast-band.
  A. c. viridicatus (Occurs only on Isla Coiba off Veraguas, Panama) Similar to *striaticeps* but has more extensive and darker grey on the breast and flanks, has darker undertail-coverts, and is slightly darker grey on the head and slightly darker green on the upperparts.
  A. c. inexpectatus (Occurs in the upper Magdalena Valley in Colombia) The smallest and dullest of all the races, brownish-olive above, but with brighter wing feather edges.
  A. c. conirostris (Occurs in N Colombia, E Colombia east of the Magdalena Valley and south to Meta, most of Venezuela and extreme N Brazil in N Roraima) Described above.
  A. c. umbrinus (Occurs in the Maracaibo Basin of N Colombia/Venezuela) A small, dull race, similar to *inexpectatus* but slightly larger and brighter above.

RELATIONSHIPS Closely related to Green-backed Sparrow and appears to form a superspecies with it.

VOICE The song, generally given from a concealed perch in a bush but sometimes from the top of a bush, varies. In Costa Rica (*richmondi*) it starts off with a long, accelerating series of slow, often throaty, alternating high and low notes, suddenly going into an accelerating trill which ends on an abrupt note. In Venezuela (*conirostris*) it is a slower series of rich notes, interspersed with doubled-up notes. The song of *inexpectatus* (Magdalena Valley, Colombia) is rather different, being shorter and transcribed as *tsu'leép, tsuk-tsuk-tsuk-tsuk*. Calls include a whistled *ho-wheet*, a metallic or nasal *chook*, and a series of whining notes, inflected upwards or downwards and preceded by thin, clear whistles or slurred notes, which is given in unison by a mated pair as a greeting.

HABITS Nest is usually placed 15cm to 1m off the ground in dense vegetation, rarely on the ground or up to 2m off it; a bulky domed structure with a wide side entrance (occasionally a bulky open cup), built of dry leaves, bark shreds, twigs and ferns, and lined with finer plant material and rootlets. 2 (rarely 3) white eggs are laid in January-October (mainly April-July). Incubation period is 13-14 days and the young fledge after 11-13 days. Two broods are often raised. Parents will feign injury to distract predators from nest or recently fledged young. In Colombia, eggs have been found in April-May and breeding condition birds have been found between May and December. Feeds on seeds, insects, other invertebrates and occasionally small vertebrates and berries. Forages by hopping and gleaning on ground, and in bushes and low trees. Shy and retiring but males sing from high up in a dense bush and may venture to the top of it. Generally found alone or in pairs; sometimes in family parties. Where undisturbed, often feeds in dense cover at the sides of paths and tracks.

STATUS AND HABITAT Fairly common to common throughout its range. Found in humid deciduous woodland with a dense understorey, thick hedgerows, brushy thickets, weedy fields, young second growth and shady plantations with thick cover; from lowlands to 1500m, occasionally to 2000m.

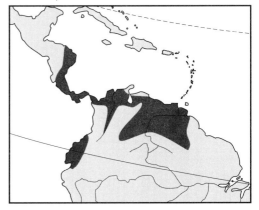

DISTRIBUTION AND MOVEMENTS Occurs from northeastern Honduras south to Panama and in South America south to south-western Ecuador and east to southern Venezuela and extreme northern Brazil. See also under Geographical Variation. Sedentary, although there may be some altitudinal movement with birds moving to the higher limits of the altitudinal range to breed.

REFERENCES Armani (1985), Hardy & Wolf (1977), Hilty & Brown (1986), Meyer de Schauensee & Phelps (1978), Monroe (1963), Ridgely & Tudor (1989), Skutch (1954), Stiles & Skutch (1989).

BIBLIOGRAPHY

Ali, S., & Ripley, S. D. 1974. *Handbook of the Birds of India and Pakistan.* Vol. 10. Oxford Univ. Press, Bombay.

Aldrich, J.W. 1984. Ecogeographic variation in size and proportions of Song Sparrows (*Melospiza melodia*). *Ornithological Monographs* 35: 1-134.

Alström, A., & Olsson, U. 1994. Identification of Pallas's Reed Bunting. *Birding World* 7: 15-20.

Alström, P., Colston, P. R., & Lewington, I. 1991. *A Field Guide to the Rare Birds of Britain and Europe.* Harper Collins, London.

American Ornithologists' Union. 1983. *Check-List of North American Birds,* 6th edition. AOU.

Anon. 1990. *ABA Checklist: Birds of the Continental United States and Canada.* Fourth Edition. ABA.

Anon. 1993. Bunting identification. *Birder* 7: 4-27.

Anon. 1995. Grey Bunting. *Birder* 9: 46-52.

Archer, G., & Godman, E. M. 1961. *The Birds of British Somaliland and the Gulf of Aden.* Oliver and Boyd, Edinburgh and London.

Armani, G.C. 1985. *Guide des passereaux granivores: Embérizinés.* Société nouvelle des editions Boubée, Paris.

Arnold, K.A. 1983. A New Subspecies of Henslow's Sparrow (*Ammodramus henslowii*). *Auk* 100(2): 504-505.

Åström, G., & Stolt, B. -O. 1993. Regional song dialects of the Ortolan Bunting *Emberiza hortulana* L. in Sweden. *Ornis Svecica* 3: 1-10.

Atkinson, C. T., & Ralph, C. J. 1980. Acquisition of plumage polymorphism in White-throated Sparrows. *Auk* 97(2): 245-252.

Austin, O. L., & Kuroda, N. 1953. The birds of Japan: their status and distribution. *Bull. Misc. Comp. Zool.* 109 (4): 279-613.

Baker, E. C. S. 1926. *The Fauna of British India.* Taylor and Francis, London.

Balph, M. H. 1975. Wing length, hood coloration and sex ratio in Dark-eyed Juncos wintering in northern Utah. *Bird-Banding* 46(2): 126-130.

Banks, R. C. 1964. The White-crowned Sparrow, *Zonotrichia leucophrys. Univ. Calif. Pubs. Zool.* 70: 1-123.

Banks, K. W., Clark H., Mackay, I. R. K., Mackay, S. G., & Sellers, R. M. 1990. Ageing, sexing and racing Snow Buntings in winter plumage. *Ringer´s Bull.* 7: 84-87.

Bannerman, D. A. 1948. *The Birds of Tropical West Africa.* Crown Agents, London.

— 1953. *The Birds of West and Equatorial Africa.* Vol. 2. Oliver and Boyd, Edinburgh and London.

Bates, R. S. P., & Lowther E. H. N. 1952. *Breeding Birds of Kashmir.* Oxford Univ. Press, London.

Beaman, M. 1994. *Palearctic Birds. A Checklist of the Birds of Europe, North Africa and Asia north of the foothills of the Himalayas.* Harrier, Stonyhurst, England.

Bédard, J., & La Pointe, G. 1984. Banding returns, arrival time and site fidelity in the Savannah Sparrow. *Wilson Bull.* 96(2): 196-205.

Benson, C. W. 1941. Nyasaland Birds. *Ibis* 83: 50-51.

— 1982. Afrotropical migrants. *Ostrich* 53: 44.

— , Brooke, R. K., Dowsett, R. J., & Irwin, M. P. S. 1971. *Birds of Zambia.* Collins, London.

Bent, A. C. 1968. Life Histories of North American Cardinals, Grosbeaks, Buntings, Towhees, Finches, Sparrows, and Allies. *U. S. Nat. Mus. Bulletin* No 237, parts 1-3, Washington D.C.

Best, L. B., & Rodenhouse, N. L. 1984. Territory Preference of Vesper Sparrows in Cropland. *Wilson Bull.* 96(1): 72-82.

Bezzel, E. 1993. *Kompendium der Vögel Mitteleuropas* AULA-Verlag, Wiesbaden.

Bianchi, V. 1907. *Material avifauna Mongoliya i vostotsnago Tibet* (in Russian).

Birckhead, H. 1937. The Birds of the Sage West China Expedition. *Amer. Mus. Novitates* No. 966.

Blake, C. H. 1964. Color and wing length in the Slate-coloured Junco. *Bird-Banding* 35(2): 125-126.

Bond, J. 1985. *Birds of the West Indies.* Fifth edition. Houghton Mifflin, Boston.

Bradshaw, C. 1990. Pine Bunting identification. *Birding World* 3: 316-317.

— 1991. Identification of Little and Rustic Buntings. *Birding World* 4: 309-313.

— 1992. Field identification of Black-faced Bunting. *British Birds* 85: 653-665.

— & Gray, M. 1993. Identification of female Pine Buntings. *British Birds* 86: 378-386.

Brackhill, H. 1977. Protracted prebasic head moult in the Dark-eyed Junco. *Bird-Banding* 48(4): 370.

Brazil, M. A. 1991. *The Birds of Japan.* Christopher Helm, London.

Bretagnolle, F. 1993. An annotated checklist of birds of northeastern Central African Republic. *Malimbus* 15: 6-16.

Briskie, J. V. 1993. Smith's Longspur, in *The Birds of North America,* Academy of Natural Sciences, Philadelphia.

Britton, P. L. 1980. *Birds of East Africa.* East Africa Natural History Society, Nairobi.

Brown, B. 1991. Lark Sparrow distribution changes. *Birding World* 4: 212-213.

Brown, L. H., & Britton, P. L. 1980. *The Breeding Seasons of East African Birds.* East Africa Natural History Society, Nairobi.

Broyd, S. J. 1985. Savannah Sparrow: new to the Western Palearctic. *British Birds* 78(12): 647-656.

Burleigh, T. D., & Lowery Jr., G. H. 1942. Notes on the birds of south-eastern Coahuila. *Occasional Papers of the Museum of Zoology, Louisiana State Univ.* 12: 583-586.

Buturlin, S. A. 1910. A forgotten bird. *Orn. Mitt. Moscow* I: 42-43.

Cadman, M. D., Eagles, P. F. J., & Helleiner, F. M. 1987. *Atlas of Breeding Birds of Ontario.* Univ. of Waterloo Press, Waterloo.

Cave, F. O., & MacDonald, J. D. 1955. *Birds of the Sudan.* Oliver and Boyd, Edinburgh.

Chapin, J. P. 1954. Birds of the Belgian Congo. *Bull. Amer. Mus. Nat. Hist.* 75B: 610-621.

Chapman, F. M. 1940. The post-glacial history of *Zonotrichia capensis. Bull. Amer. Mus. Nat. Hist.* 77: 381-438.

Charlton, T. 1991. The position of Lark Sparrow on the British list. *Birding World* 4: 156-159.

Cheng, Tso-hsin. 1987. *A Synopsis of the Avifauna of China.* Paul Parey, Hamburg & Berlin, and Science Press, Peking.

— & Stresemann, E. 1961. Ein übersehener Brutvogel der Palaearktis: "*Emberiza*" siemsseni (Martens). *J. Ornithol.* 102: 152-153.

Clancey, P. A. 1964. *The Birds of Natal and Zululand.* Oliver and Boyd, Edinburgh.

— 1971. *A Handlist of the Birds of Southern Moçambique.* Inst. Invest. Cientifica Moçambique, Lourenço Marques.

— 1989. Subspeciation in the Larklike Bunting of the southwestern Afrotropics. *Bull. Brit. Orn. Club* 109: 130-134.

— (ed.) 1980. *SAOS Checklist of South African Birds.* Southern African Ornithological Society.

Collar, N. J., Gonzaga, L. P., Krabbe, N., Madroño Nieto, A., Naranjo, L. G., Parker III, T. A., & Wege, D. C. 1992. *Threatened Birds of the Americas.* The ICBP/ IUCN Red Data Book, Cambridge, UK.

— , Crosby, M. J., & Stattersfield, A. J. 1994. *Birds to watch 2:*

The World List of Threatened Birds. BirdLife International, Cambridge, UK.

Collett, J. 1982. Birds of the Craddock District. *Southern Birds* 9: 58.

Conrads, K. 1976. Studien an Fremddialekt-Sängern und Dialekt-Mischsängern des Ortolans (*Emberiza hortulana*). *J. Ornithol.* 117: 438-450.

— & Conrads, W. 1971. Regionaldialekte des Ortolans (*Emberiza hortulana*) in Deutschland. *Vogelwelt* 92: 81-100.

Cramp, S., & Perrins, C. M. (eds) 1994. *The Birds of the Western Palearctic* Vol. 8. Oxford Univ. Press, Oxford.

Cumming, S. C., & Steyn, P. 1966. Observations on the breeding biology of the Rock Bunting *Emberiza tahapisi* Smith. *Ostrich* 37: 170-175.

Curry-Lindahl, K. 1981. *Bird Migration in Africa*. Academic Press, London.

Davies, J. 1957. Determination of age in the Spotted Towhee. *Condor* 59: 195-202.

Davis, L. I. 1972. *A Field Guide to the Birds of Mexico and Central America*. Univ. of Texas Press, Austin & London.

deBenedictis, P. A. 1995. Sage Sparrow mysteries. *Birding* 27: 134-136.

de Knijff, P. 1991. Little-known West Palearctic Birds: Cinereous Bunting. *Birding World* 4: 384-391.

Delaney, D. 1992. *Bird songs of Belize, Guatemala and Mexico*. Cornell Laboratory of Ornithology, Ithaca, New York.

Dementiev, G. P., & Gladkov, N. A. 1966. *Birds of the Soviet Union*. Israel Programme for Scientific Translation, Jerusalem.

Dhondt, A. A., & Smith, J. N. M. 1980. Postnuptial molt of the Song Sparrow on Mandarte Island in relation to breeding. *Canadian Journal of Zoology* 58: 513-520.

Dickerman, R. W. 1961. Hybrids among the fringillid genera *Junco, Zonotrichia* and *Melospiza*. *Auk* 78(4): 627-632.

— 1962. Identification of the juvenal plumage of the Sharp-tailed Sparrow *Ammospiza caudacuta nelsoni*. *Bird-Banding* 33(4): 202-204.

— 1963. The Song Sparrows of the Mexican Plateau. *Occasional Papers of the Minnesota Museum of Natural History,* No. 9. Univ. of Minnesota.

— 1968. A hybrid Grasshopper Sparrow x Savannah Sparrow. *Auk* 85(2): 312-315.

—, Phillips, A. R., & Warner, D. W. 1967. On the Sierra Madre Sparrow, *Xenospiza baileyi*, of Mexico. *Auk* 84: 49-60.

Dickey, D. R., & Van Rossem, A. J. 1938. The birds of El Salvador. *Zoological Series* 23: 1-609. Field Museum of Natural History, Chicago.

Dickinson, E. C., Kennedy, R. S., & Parkes, K. C. 1991. *The Birds of the Philippines*. BOU Checklist No 12. Tring, Herts.

Dinsmore, J. J., Koenig, D., Kent, T. H., & Petersen, P. C. 1984. *Iowa Birds*. Iowa State Univ. Press, Ames.

Dixon, A., Ross, D., O'Malley, S. L. C., & Burke, T. 1994. Paternal investment inversely related to degree of extra-pair paternity in the Reed Bunting. *Nature* 371: 698-699.

Donald, P. F., Wilson, J. D., & Shepherd, M. 1994. The decline of the Corn Bunting. *British Birds* 87: 106-132.

Dorzhiev, T. Z., & Jumov, B. O. 1991. *Ecology of Buntings* (in Russian). Buryatian Scientific Press, Ulan-Ude.

Dunn, J. L., & Blom, E.A.T. (chief consultants) 1983. *A Field Guide to North American Birds*. National Geographic Society, Washington.

—, Garrett, K. L., & Aldefer, J. K. 1995. White-crowned Sparrow subspecies: identification and distribution. *Birding* 27: 182-200.

Dunning, J. B. 1993. Bachman's Sparrow, in *The Birds of North America*. Academy of Natural Sciences, Philadelphia.

— 1991. Habitat Occupancy by Bachman's Sparrow in the Francis Marion National Forest before and after Hurricane Hugo. *Auk* 108(3): 723-725.

— & Watts, B. D. 1990. Regional differences in habitat occupancy by Bachman's Sparrow. *Auk* 107(3): 463-472.

Dunning, J. S. 1987. *South American Birds: a photographic aid to identification*. Harrowood Books, Pennsylvania.

Earlé, R. A., & Grobler, N. J. 1987. *First Atlas of Bird Distribution in the Orange Free State*. National Museum, Bloemfontein.

Eber, G. 1956. Vergleichende Untersuchung über die Ernährung einiger Finkenvögel. *Biologische Abhandlungen* Heft 13/14.

Ehrlich, P. R., Dobkin, D. S., & Wheye, D. 1988.*The Birder's Handbook*. Simon & Schuster, New York.

Elgood, J. H. 1982. *The Birds of Nigeria*. BOU Checklist No 4. Tring, Herts.

Etchécopar, R. D. & Hüe, F. 1967. *The Birds of North Africa*. Oliver and Boyd, Edinburgh and London.

— 1983. *Les Oiseaux du Chine, de Mongolie et de Corée: passereaux*. Société nouvelle des editions Boubée, Paris.

Fairbank, R. 1994. Black-headed Bunting identification. *Birding World* 7: 319.

Farnsworth, S. J. 1994. Corn Bunting *Emberiza calandra* in Mauritania and West Africa. *Malimbus* 16: 124-125.

Farrand, J., Jr. 1983. *The Audubon Society Master Guide to Birding*. Part 3. Alfred A. Knopf, New York.

Finch, D. M. 1984. Some factors affecting production in Abert's Towhee. *Wilson Bull.* 96(4): 701-705.

Forbes, H. O., & Ogilvie-Grant, W. R. 1903. *The Natural History of Sokotra and Abd-el-Kuri*. Free Public Museums, Liverpool.

Frandsen, J. 1962. *Birds of the South-western Cape*. Sable, Johannesburg.

Fugle G. N., & Rothstein, S. I. 1985. Age and sex related variation in crown plumage brightness in wintering White-crowned Sparrows. *Journal of Field Ornithology* 56(4): 356-368.

Fujimaki, Y. & Hikawa, M. 1978. The first breeding record of the Grey Bunting *Emberiza variabilis* in Hokkaido. *Misc. Rep. of the Yamashina Inst. for Ornithol.* 10: 172-177.

Gabrielson, I. N., & Lincoln, F.C. 1959. *Birds of Alaska*. Stackpole, Harrisburg.

Garrido, O.H. (1985) Cuban endangered birds. pp992-999 in *Neotropical Ornithology* (eds. Buckley, P.A., Foster, M.S., Morton, E.S., Ridgely, R.S. & Buckley, F.G.), Ornithological Monograph No 36, American Ornithologists' Union, Washington D.C.

Gartshore, M. E. 1975. Some aspects of the breeding biology of the Cinnamon-breasted Rock Bunting *Emberiza tahapisi*. *Bull. Nigerian Orn. Soc.* 11: 27-33.

Ginn, P. J., McIlleron, W. G., & Milstein, P. le S. 1989. *The Complete Book of South African Birds*. Struik Winchester, Cape Town.

Giraudoux, P., Degauquier, R., Jones, P. J., Weigel, J., & Isenmann, P. 1988. Avifaune du Niger: état des connaissances en 1986. *Malimbus* 10: 1-116.

Glaubrecht, M. 1989. Geographische Variabilität des Gesangs der Goldammer, *Emberiza citrinella*, im Norddeutschen Dialekt-Grenzgebiet. *J. Ornithol.* 130: 277-292.

Glaubrecht, M. 1991. Gesangsvariation der Goldammer (*Emberiza citrinella*) in Norddeutschland und auf den dänischen Inseln. *J. Ornithol.* 132: 441-445.

Godfrey, W. E. 1986. *The Birds of Canada*. Revised Edition. National Museums of Natural Science, Ottawa.

Goodman, S. M., & Meininger, P. L. 1989. *The Birds of Egypt*. Oxford Univ. Press, Oxford.

Gonzáles Alonso, H., de las Pozas, G., & Gonzales Bermúdez, F. 1982. Aspectos reproductivos y densidad poblacional de *Torreornis inexpectata inexpectata* (Aves: Fringillidae) en la Cienaga de Zapata, Cuba. *Ciencas Biologicas* 8: 123-129.

— Gonzáalez Bermúdez, F. & Quesada, M. (1986) Distribución y alimentación del Cabrerito de la Ciénaga *Torreornis inexpectata* (Aves Fringillidae) en la Ciénaga de Zapata, Cuba. *Poeyana* 310.

Gore, M. E. J. 1990. *The Birds of the Gambia*. BOU Checklist No 3. Tring, Herts.

Gore, M. E. J., & Won, P-o. 1971. *The Birds of Korea*. Royal Asiatic Soc., Seoul.

Grant, G. S., & Quay, T. L. 1970. Sex and age criteria in the Slate-coloured Junco. *Bird-Banding* 41(4): 274-278.

Grant, P., & Mullarney, K. 1989. *The New Approach to Identification*. Ashford.

Gray, A. P. 1958. Bird hybrids. *Technical Communication No 13*, Commonwealth Agricultural Bureau, London.

Grimes, L.G. 1987. *The Birds of Ghana*. BOU Checklist No 9. Tring, Herts.

Grinnell, J. & Swarth, H.S. 1926. Systematic review of the Pacific coast Brown Towhee. *Univ. of California Publications in Zoology* 21(18): 427-433.

Groschupf, K. 1992. Five-striped Sparrow, in *The Birds of North America*. Academy of Natural Sciences, Philadelphia.

Grote, H. 1931. *Emberiza pallasi suschkiniana* nom. nov. *Ornith. Monatsber.* 39: 150.

— 1931. *Emberiza cabanisi cognominata* nom. nov. *Ornith. Monatsber.* 39: 91-92.

Haffer, J. 1977. Secondary contact zones of birds in northern Iran. *Bonner Zool. Monogr.* 10.

— 1989. Parapatrische Vogelarten der Paläarktischen Region. *J. Ornithol.* 130: 475-512.

Haneda, K., & Minochi, E. 1969. The breeding ecology of *Emberiza variabilis*. *Bull. Int. Nat. Educ. Shiga Heights* 8: 59-68.

Hardin, K. I., & Probasco, G. E. 1983. The habitat characteristics and life requirements of Bachman's Sparrow. *Birding* 15: 189-197.

Hardy, J. W., & Wolf, L. L. 1977. *Voices of Mexican sparrows*. ARA Records, Gainesville, Florida.

Harper, D. 1995. Studies of West Palearctic birds. 194. Corn Bunting *Miliaria calandra*. *British Birds* 88: 401-420.

Harris, A., Tucker, L., & Vinicombe, K. 1989. *The Macmillan Field Guide to Bird Identification*. Macmillan, London.

Harrison, C. 1982. *An Atlas of the Birds of the Western Palearctic*. Collins, London.

Harrison, J. M. 1954. Remarks on the Taxonomy of the Yellow Bunting, *Emberiza citrinella* Linnaeus. *Bull. Brit. Orn. Club*. 74: 105-112, 75: 6-12, 75: 17-21.

Harrop, H. 1993. Identification of female and juvenile Yellow-breasted Bunting. *Birding World* 6: 317-319.

Hartert, E. 1910. *Die Vögel der Paläarktischen Fauna*. Gattung *Emberiza*. Berlin.

Hartert, E., & Steinbacher, F. 1932-1938. *Die Vögel der Paläarktischen Fauna*, Ergänzungsband. Berlin.

Haydock, E. L. 1949. A study of the Cinnamon-breasted Rock Bunting *Fringilloides tahapisi tahapisi*. *Ostrich* 20: 126-130.

Heydweiller, A. M. 1936. Sex, age and individual variation of winter Tree Sparrows. *Bird-Banding* 7(2): 61-68.

Hilty, S. H., & Brown, W. L. 1986. *A Guide to the Birds of Colombia*. Princeton Univ. Press, Princeton.

Hockey, P. A. R., Underhill, L. G., Neatherway, M., & Ryan, P. G. 1989. *Atlas of the Birds of the Southwestern Cape*. Cape Bird Club, Cape Town.

Hollom, P. A. D., Porter, R. F., Christensen, S., & Willis I. 1988. *Birds of the Middle East and North Africa*. Poyser, Calton.

Holloway, J. 1990. Identification of female Pine Buntings. *Birding World* 3: 250.

— 1994. Identification of Pine Bunting. *British Birds* 87: 627-628.

Horváth, L., & Keve, A. 1956. On the Systematic Position of the Yellow Bunting, *Emberiza citrinella* Linnaeus, in Hungary. *Bull. Brit. Orn. Club*. 76: 92-95.

Hough, J. 1994. Identification and status of Black-faced Bunting. *Birding World* 7: 98-101.

Howell, S. N. G., & Webb, S. 1995. *A Guide to the Birds of Mexico and Northern Central America*. Oxford Univ. Press, Oxford.

Hubbard, J. P. 1974. Geographical Variation in the Savannah Sparrow of the inland south-west, Mexico, and Guatemala. *Occasional Papers of the Delaware Museum of Natural History* No 12.

Humphrey, P. S., & Parkes, K. C. 1959. An approach to the study of molts and plumages. *Auk* 76 (1): 1-31.

Inskipp, C., & Inskipp, T. 1991. *A Guide to the Birds of Nepal*. Christopher Helm, London.

Irwin, M. P. S. 1981. *Birds of Zimbabwe*. Quest Publishing, Salisbury.

Ishimoto, A. 1992. Sexing of Juv. (1W) Black-faced Bunting. *J. Yamashina Inst. Ornithol.* 24: 1-12.

Jahn, H. 1942. Biologie der Vögel Japans - Fringillidae. *J. Ornithol.* 90: 94-105.

James, D. A., & Neal, J. C. 1986. *Arkansas Birds*. Academic and Univ. Pub. Group, London.

Jehl, J. R. Jr., & Hussell, D. T. 1966. Incubation periods of some subarctic birds. *Canadian Field-Naturalist* 80(3): 179-180.

Jennings, M. C. 1995. *An Interim Atlas of Breeding Birds of Arabia*. NCWCD, Riyadh.

Johansen, H. 1944. Vogelfauna Westsibiriens – Fringillidae. *J. Ornithol.* 92: 67-92.

Jukema, J., & Fokkema, J. 1992. Herkomst van in Nederland overwinterende Seeuwgorzen *Plectrophenax nivalis*. *Limosa* 65: 67-72.

Kaiser, W. 1987. Zu Strophenformen im Gesang der Goldammer und ihrer Entwicklung, Teil 1. *Der Falke* 34: 102-105. Teil 2. *Der Falke* 34: 144-148.

Karlsson, L., Persson, K., & Walinder, G. 1985. Photographic documentation of age and sex differences in birds – aims, methods and examples of results. *Vår Fågelvärld* 44: 465-478.

Kaufman, K. 1990. *A Field Guide to Advanced Birding*. Houghton Mifflin, Boston.

Kern, M. D. 1984. Racial differences in nests of White-crowned Sparrows. *Condor* 86(4): 455-466.

Kessel, B. 1989. *Birds of the Seward Peninsula*. Alaska Univ. Press, Fairbanks.

— & Gibson, D. D. 1978. *Status and Distribution of Alaska Birds*. Studies in Avian Biology No. 1, Cooper Ornithological Society, Los Angeles.

King, B., & Peng, J. T. 1991. Some bird observations in Ganzi prefecture of extreme north-west Sichuan province, China. *Forktail* 6: 15-32.

King, J. R. 1986. The daily activity period of nesting White-crowned Sparrows in continuous daylight at 65° N compared with activity period at lower altitudes. *Condor* 88(3): 382-384.

King, W. B. 1978-79. *Red Data Book, 2. Aves,* Second edition. IUCN, Morges, Switzerland.

Knapton, R. W. 1978. Sex and age determination in the Clay-colored Sparrow *Bird-Banding* 49(2): 152-156.

— 1978. Breeding ecology of the Clay-colored Sparrow. *Living Bird* 17: 137-158.

— 1980. Nestling foods and foraging patterns in the Clay-colored Sparrow. *Wilson Bull.* 92(4): 458-465.

— & Falls, J. B. 1983. Differences in parental contribution among pair types in the polymorphic White-throated Sparrow. *Canadian Journal of Zoology* 61: 1288-1292.

Koblik, E. A. 1993. Mystery bunting from the collection of Kozlov's expedition. *Russ. J. Ornithol.* 2: 409-414.

Komeda, S. 1987. *Bird Banding Manual: Identification Guide to Japanese Birds. Emberiza cioides*. Yamashina Institute for Ornithology.

Kopachena, J. G., & Falls, J. B. 1993. Re-evaluation of morph-specific variations in parental behavior of the White-throated Sparrow. *Wilson Bull.* 105(1): 48-59.

Kozlova, E. V. 1933. The Birds of southwest Transbaikalia, northern Mongolia, and central Gobi. *Ibis* 75: 59-87.

Kretchmar, E. A. 1993. The breeding biology of the Little Bunting *Emberiza pusilla* in the middle reaches of the Anadyr River. *Russ. J. Ornithol.* 2: 415-426.

Kreutzer, M., & Güttinger, H. R. 1991. *J. Ornithol.* 132: 165-177.

Lamm, D.W., & Luepke, J.C. (1981) Iris changes in hatching year Yellow-eyed Juncos. *North American Bird-Bander* 7(3): 93.

Latouche, J. D. D. 1925-30. *A Handbook of the Birds of Eastern China.* London.

Lekagul, B., & Round, P. D. 1991. *A Guide to the Birds of Thailand.* Saha Karn Bhaet, Bangkok.

Lessells, K. 1994. Baby bunting in paternity probe. *Nature* 371: 655-656.

Lethaby, N. 1994. *A Bird Finding Guide to Alaska.* Santa Clara, California.

Lewington, I. 1990. Identification of female Pine Bunting. *Birding World* 3: 89-90.

Lewis, A., & Pomeroy, D. 1989. *A Bird Atlas of Kenya.* A. A. Balkema, Rotterdam.

Lindsay, A. B. 1908. Through eastern Tibet and Kam. *Geogr. J.* 31: 402-415, 522-534, 649-661.

Litwinenko, N. M., & Schibajew, J. W. 1966. Zur Brutoekologie von *Emberiza jankowskii* Taczanowski. *J. Ornithol.* 107: 346-351.

Louette, M. 1981. *The Birds of Cameroon: an annotated checklist.* Paleis der Academiën, Brussels.

Lowther, J. K. 1961. Polymorphism in the White-throated Sparrow, *Zonotrichia albicollis* (Gmelin). *Canadian Journal of Zoology* 39: 281-292.

Ludlow, F., & Kinnear, N. B. 1933. The Ornithology of Chinese Turkestan. *Ibis* 75: 670-675.

Mackworth-Praed, C. W., & Grant, C. H. B. 1955. *Birds of Eastern and North Eastern Africa.*Vol.II. Longman, London and New York.

— & — 1963. *Birds of the Southern Third of Africa.* Vol. II. Longman, London and New York.

— & — 1973. *Birds of the West Central and Western Africa.* Vol. II. Longman, London and New York.

Maclean, G. L. 1985. *Roberts' Birds of Southern Africa.* J. Voelcker Bird Book Fund, Cape Town.

Madge, S. C. 1979. A grey Yellowhammer. *British Birds* 72: 80.

Marshall, J. T., Jr. 1963. Rainy nesting season in Arizona. *Proceedings of the XIII International Ornithological Congress* 2: 620-622, American Ornithologists' Union, New York.

Marshall, R. M., & Reinert, S. E. 1990. Breeding ecology of Seaside Sparrows in a Massachusetts saltmarsh. *Wilson Bull.* 102(3): 501-513.

Martens, G. H. 1906. Eine neue Ammerart aus Südost China. *Ornith. Monatsber.* 14: 192-194.

Mauersberger, G. 1971. Ist *Emberiza leucocephalos* ein Subspecies von *E. citrinella? J. Ornithol.* 112: 232-233.

— 1972. Über den taxonomischen Rang von *Emberiza godlewskii* Taczanowski. *J. Ornithol.* 113: 53-59.

— & Portenko, L. A. 1971. *Atlas der Verbreitung Palaearktischer Vögel* 3. Berlin.

Mewaldt, L. R. 1973. Wing length and age in White-crowned Sparrows. *Western Bird-Bander* 48(4): 54-56.

— 1977. White-crowned Sparrow: Banding Worksheet for Western birds. Supplement to *North American Bird-Bander* 2(4).

— Kibby, S. S., & Norton M. L. 1968. Comparative Biology of Pacific White-crowned Sparrows. *Condor* 70(1): 14-30.

— & King, J. R. 1978. Latitudinal variation in prenuptial moult in wintering Gambel's White-crowned Sparrows. *North American Bird-Bander* 3(4): 138-144.

Meyer de Schauensee, R., & Phelps, W. H., Jr. 1978. *A Guide to the Birds of Venezuela.* Princeton Univ. Press, Princeton.

Mirsky, E. N. 1976. Song divergence in hummingbird and junco populations on Guadeloupe Island. *Condor* 78: 230-235.

Monroe, B. L. Jr. 1963. Notes on the avian genus *Arremonops* with a description of a new subspecies from Honduras. *Occasional Papers of the Museum of Zoology, Louisiana State Univ.* No. 28.

Morton, E. S., & González Alonso, H. T. 1982. The biology of *Torreornis inexpectata*, 1. A comparison of vocalisations in *T. i. inexpectata* and *T. i. sigmani. Wilson Bull.* 94: 433-446.

Morton, M. L., King, J. R., & Farner, D. S. 1969. Postnuptial and postjuvenal moult in White-crowned Sparrows in central Alaska. *Condor* 71(4): 376-385.

— & Welton, D. E. 1973. Postnuptial moult and its relation to reproductive cycle and body weight in Mountain White-crowned Sparrows (*Zonotrichia leucophrys oriantha*). *Condor* 75(2): 184-189.

Munford, R.E., & Keller, C.E. 1984. *The Birds of Indiana.* Indiana Univ. Press, Bloomington.

Murray, B. G. Jr. 1968 The relationships of sparrows in the genera *Ammodramus, Passerculus* and *Ammospiza* with a description of a hybrid Le Conte's x Sharp-tailed Sparrow. *Auk* 85(4): 586-593.

Musilek, J. 1928. Beitrag zur Verbreitung von *Emberiza jankowskii* Tacz. *Ornith. Monatsber.* 36: 74-76.

Nakamura, T. 1981. The breeding behaviour and territorial dispersion of Japanese Reed Bunting *Emberiza yessoensis. Misc. Rep. of the Yamashina Inst. for Ornithol.* 13: 79-119.

— 1981. Annual change and disappearance of a local population of Japanese Reed Bunting *Emberiza yessoensis* in Kirigamine grasslands. *Tori* 30: 57-74.

— Iijima, K., & Kagawa, T. 1968. A comparative study on the habitat preference and home range of four species of the genus *Emberiza* on peat grasslands. *Misc. Rep. of the Yamashina Inst. for Ornithol.* 5: 313-336.

— Iijima, K. & Ushiyama, H. 1970. Territoriality of *Emberiza yessoensis* in a high population density. *Misc. Rep. of the Yamashina Inst. for Ornithol.* 6: 82-102.

Naugler, C. T. 1993. American Tree Sparrow, in *The Birds of North America.* Academy of Natural Sciences, Philadelphia.

Newby, J., Grettenberger, J., & Watkins, J. 1987. The Birds of the northern Aïr, Niger. *Malimbus* 9: 4-16.

Newman, K. 1989. *Newman's Birds of Botswana.* Southern Book Publishers, Johannesburg.

Nichols, J. T. 1953. Eye-color in the Red-eyed Towhee. *Bird-Banding* 24: 16-17.

Nikolaus, G. 1987. *Distribution Atlas of Sudan's birds with notes on habitat and status.* Bonner Zoologische Monographen, Nr. 25.

Nishide, T. 1987. *Emberiza* species on Hachirogata reclaimed land. (1) Invasion and changes in distribution. *Strix* 6: 86-95.

Norment, C. J., & Shackleton, S. A. 1993. Harris' Sparrow, in *The Birds of North America.* Academy of Natural Sciences, Philadelphia.

Oberholser, H. C. 1974. *The Bird Life of Texas.* Volume 2. Univ. of Texas Press, Austin.

Ogilvie-Grant, W. R. 1912. *Catalogue of the Collection of Birds Eggs in the British Museum (Natural History).* London.

— & Forbes, H. O. 1899. The expedition to Socotra. Description of the New Species of Birds. *Bull. Liverpool Museums.* Vol. 2.

Olsson, U. 1995. Little-known Oriental bird: Koslov's Bunting *Emberiza koslowi. Bull. Oriental Bird Club* 21: 39-43.

Osborn, K., & Harvey, P. 1994. The Chestnut Bunting in Shetland. *Birding World* 7: 371-373.

Ouwerkerk, A. 1994. Bill colour of female Pallas's Reed Bunting. *Dutch Birding* 16: 154.

O'Brien, M. 1995. Photo Quiz: McCown's Longspur. *Birding.* 27: 398-399.

Paludan, K. 1940. *Danish Scientific Investigations in Iran.* II. Ornithology. Copenhagen.

— 1959. *On the birds of Afghanistan.* Videnskabelige

Meddelelser fra Dansk Naturhistorisk Forening i København. Dind 122. Copenhagen.

Panov, E. N. 1973. *Birds of South Ussuriland.* Novosibirsk.

Payne, R. B. 1979. Two apparent hybrid *Zonotrichia* sparrows. *Auk* 96: 595-599.

Paynter, R. A., Jr., & Storer, R. W. 1970. in Peters, J.L. *Check List of Birds of the World: Volume XIII.* Museum of Comparative Zoology, Cambridge, Massachusetts.

Paz, U. 1987. *The Birds of Israel.* Christopher Helm. London.

Peters, J. L. 1970. See Paynter & Storer (1970).

Peterson, K. L. & Best, L. B. 1985. Nest-site selection by Sage Sparrows. *Condor* 87(2): 217-221.

Peterson, R. T., & Chalif, E. L. 1973. *A Field Guide to Mexican Birds.* Houghton Mifflin, Boston.

Phillips, A. R. 1951. The molts of the Rufous-winged Sparrow. *Wilson Bull.* 63(4): 323-326.

— , Marshall, J. & Monson, G. 1964. *The birds of Arizona.* University of Arizona Press, Tucson.

— *et al.* 1966. Further systematic notes on Mexican birds. *Bull. Brit. Orn. Club* 86: 148-159.

Pinter, J. M. 1991. Cirl Bunting song types. *British Birds* 84: 198.

Portenko, L. A. 1929. [Taxonomy of Pallas's Reed Bunting] *Ann. Mus. Zool. Acad. Sci. U. R. S. S.* (Leningrad) 29: 78.

— 1930. Subdivision of the species *Emberiza rustica* into geographical races. *Auk* 47: 205-207.

Pregill, G. K., & Olson, S. L. 1981. Zoogeography of West Indian vertebrates in relation to Pleistocene climatic cycles. *Ann. Rev. Ecol. Syst.* 12: 75-98.

Priest, C. D. 1936. *The Birds of Southern Rhodesia.* William Clowes, London and Beccles.

Pyle, P.. & Henderson, R. P. 1991. The birds of South-east Farallon Island: Occurrence and seasonal distribution of migratory species. *Western Birds* 22(2): 41-84.

Pyle, P., Howell, S. N. G., Yunick, R. P., & DeSante, D. F. 1987. *Identification Guide to North American Passerines.* Slate Creek Press, Bolinas, California.

Rand A. L., Friedmann H., & Traylor M. A. 1959. Birds of Gabon and Moyen Congo. *Fieldiana Zoology.* 41: 221-411.

Reichenow, A. 1911. Über *Emberiza cia L.* und ihre Formen. *Ornith. Monatsber.* 19: 77-81.

Reynard, G. B. 1988. *Bird Songs in Cuba.* Cornell Laboratory of Ornithology, Ithaca, New York.

Reynolds, J. D., & Knapton, R. W. 1984. Nest-site selection and breeding biology of the Chipping Sparrow. *Wilson Bull.* 96(3): 488-493.

Richardson, C. 1991. *Birds of the United Arab Emirates.* Hobby, Dubai and Warrington.

Ridgely, R. S., & Tudor, G. 1989. *The Birds of South America: Oscine Passerines.* Oxford Univ. Press, Oxford.

Ridgway, R. 1901. *The Birds of North and Middle America, Part 1: Family Fringillidae - The Finches.* Government Printing Office, Washington.

Riggins, J., & Riggins, H. 1974. Ageing Swamp Sparrows by plumage. *IBB News* 46(1): 5-9.

Rimmer, C. C. 1986. Identification of juvenile Lincoln's and Swamp Sparrows. *Journal of Field Ornithology* 57(2): 114-125.

Ringleben, H. 1993. Isländische Schneeammer *Plectrophenax nivalis insulae* für Deutschland nachgewiesen. *Limicola* 7: 140-144.

Roberts, T. J. 1992. *The Birds of Pakistan*, Vol. 2. Oxford Univ. Press, Karachi.

Robson, C. R. 1986. Recent observations of birds in Xizang and Qinghai provinces, China. *Forktail* 2: 67-82.

Rogacheva, H. 1992. *The Birds of Central Siberia.* Husum Druck und Verlagsgesellschaft, Husum.

Rowher, S. A., Ewald, P. W., & Rowher, F. C. 1981. Variation in size, appearance and dominance within and among the sex and age classes of Harris' Sparrows. *Journal of Field Ornithology* 52(4): 291-303.

Rudebeck, G. 1958. A New Race of the Bunting *Fringillaria capensis* (*L.*) from Angola. *Bull. Brit. Orn. Club.* 78:129-132

Salomonsen, F. 1931. On the Geographical variation of the Snow Bunting (*Plectrophenax nivalis*). *Ibis* 73: 57-70.

Sarudny, N. 1907. *Cynchramus pyrrhuloides korejewi* subsp. nov. *Ornith. Monatsber.* 15: 83-84.

Satou, F. 1985. *Bird Banding Manual: Identification Guide to Japanese Birds. Emberiza fucata.* Yamashina Institute for Ornithology.

— 1989. *Bird Banding Manual: Identification Guide to Japanese Birds. Emberiza spodocephala.* Yamashina Institute for Ornithology.

Schekkerman, H. 1989. Herfsttrek en biometrie van de Ijsgors *Calcarius lapponicus* te Castricum. *Limosa* 62: 29-34.

Schneider, K. J. 1981. Age determination by skull pneumatization in the Field Sparrow. *Journal of Field Ornithology* 52(1): 57-59.

Schouteden, H. 1960. De Vogels van Belgisch Congo en van Ruanda-Urundi. *Ann. Mus. Congo Belg., Sér. 8vo.*

Schäfer, E. 1938. Ornithologishe Ergebnisse zweier Forschungsreisen nach Tibet. *J. Ornithol.* 86. 1-349.

Shigeta, Y., & Mano, T. 1979. Records of the Pallas's Reed Bunting *Emberiza pallasi* from Japan. *Tori* 28: 117-124.

— & — 1982. *Bird Banding Manual: Identification Guide to Japanese Birds. Emberiza rustica, E. schoeniclus.* Yamashina Institute for Ornithology.

Shirihai, H., & Gantlett, S. 1993. Identification of female and immature Black-headed Buntings. *Birding World.* 6: 194-197.

Sibley, C. G. 1950. Species formation in the Red-eyed Towhees of Mexico. *Univ. of California Publications in Zoology* 50(2): 109-194.

— & Monroe, B. L., Jr. 1990. *Distribution and Taxonomy of Birds of the World.* Yale Univ. Press, New Haven and London.

— 1993. *A Supplement to Distribution and Taxonomy of Birds of the World.* Yale Univ. Press, New Haven and London.

Sibley, C. G., Ahlquist, J. E., & Monroe, B. L., Jr. 1988. A classification of the living birds of the world, based on DNA-DNA hybridisation studies. *Auk* 105: 409-423.

Singh, P. 1994. Recent bird records from Arunachal Pradesh. *Forktail* 10: 65-104.

Skead, C. J. 1960. *The Canaries, Seedeaters and Buntings of Southern Africa.* South African Bird Book Fund, Durban.

— 1975. Drinking habits. *Ostrich* 46: 140-141.

Skutch, A.F. 1954. *Life Histories of Central American Birds: Families Fringillidae, Thraupidae, Icteridae, Parulidae and Coerebidae.* Pacific Coast Avifauna No 31, Cooper Ornithological Society, Berkeley, California.

Small, B. 1992. Ageing and sexing of Ortolan and Cretzschmar's Buntings in the field. *Birding World* 5: 223-228.

Smythies, B. E. 1986. *The Birds of Burma.* 3rd edition. Nimrod Press, Liss.

Steinbacher, F. 1930. Bemerkungen zur Systematik der Rohrammern, *Emberiza schoeniclus* (L.). *J. Ornithol.* 78: 471-487.

Stewart, R.M. 1972. Age and crown types in the Golden-crowned Sparrow. *Western Bird-Bander* 47(2): 32-33.

Stiles, F. G., & Skutch, A. F. 1989. *A Field Guide to the Birds of Costa Rica.* Christopher Helm, London.

Stolt, B. -O. 1977. On the migration of the Ortolan Bunting *Emberiza hortulana* L. *Zoon* 5: 51-61.

— 1993. Notes on reproduction in a declining population of the Ortolan Bunting *Emberiza hortulana. J. Ornithol.* 134: 59-68.

Stresemann, E. 1930. Neue Formen aus Nord-Kansu V. *Emberiza leucocephala fronto* subsp. nova. *Ornith. Monatsber.* 38: 90.

— & Stresemann, V. 1969. Die Mauser einiger *Emberiza-Arten*

I. *J. Ornithol.* 110: 291-313.

— & Stresemann, V. 1969. Die Mauser einiger *Emberiza-Arten* II. *J. Ornithol.* 110: 475-481.

Sundberg, J., & Larsson, C. 1994. Male coloration as an indicator of parental quality in the Yellowhammer, *Emberiza citrinella. Anim. Behav.* 48: 885-892.

Suschkin, P. 1925. Notes on Palaearctic Birds. *Proc. Boston Soc. Nat. Hist.* 38: 20-30.

Svensson, L. 1992. *Identification Guide to European Passerines.* 4th ed. Stockholm.

— 1994. Sexing and ageing of Black-faced Bunting. *Birding World* 7: 202-204.

— 1975. Dvärgsparv *Emberiza pusilla* och sävsparvhona – problemet att skilja dem åt i fält. *Vår Fågelvärld* 34: 311-318.

Swarth, H. S., & Brooks, A. 1925. The Timberline Sparrow: a new species from north-western Canada. *Condor* 27(1): 67-69.

Taczanowski, L. 1874. Ornitologischer Untersuchungen des Dr. Dybowski in Ost-Sibirien. *J. Ornithol.* 22: 329-331.

Tarboton, W. R., Kemp, M. I., & Kemp, A. C. 1987. *Birds of the Transvaal.* Transvaal Museum, Pretoria.

Terres, J.K. 1980. *The Audubon Society Encyclopedia of North American Birds.* Alfred A. Knopf, New York.

Thiollay, J. -M. 1985. The birds of Ivory Coast: Status and distribution. *Malimbus* 7: 1-59.

Thomsen, P., & Jacobsen, P. 1979. *Birds of Tunisia.* Copenhagen.

Ticehurst, C. B. 1932. On the scientific name of Crested Bunting. *Bull. Brit. Orn. Club* 53: 15-16.

Todd, W. E. C. 1912. Descriptions of seventeen new neotropical birds. *Annals of the Carnegie Museum* 8: 198-199.

— 1923. A synopsis of the genus *Arremonops. Proc. Biol. Soc. Washington* 36: 35-44.

Tordoff, H. B. & Mengel, R. M. 1952. The occurrence and possible significance of a spring moult in Le Conte's Sparrow. *Auk* 68(4): 519-522.

Traylor, M. A. 1960. A new race of *Emberiza striolata. Natural History Miscellania* No 175. Chicago Academy of Sciences.

— 1963. *Check-list of Angolan Birds.* Comp. Diam. Angola, Museo do Dundo, Lisbon.

Tucker, G. M., & Heath, M. F. 1994. *Birds in Europe: Their conservation status.* BirdLife International, Cambridge, UK.

Uramoto, M. 1964. The breeding record and breeding range of *Emberiza variabilis. Yacho* 29: 271-272.

Vardy, L. E. 1971. Color variation in the crown of the White-throated Sparrow (*Zonotrichia albicollis*). *Condor* 73(4): 401-414.

Vaurie, C. 1956. Systematic Notes on Palearctic Birds, No 22. Fringillidae: *Emberiza schoeniclus. Amer. Mus. Novitates* 1795.

— 1956. Systematic Notes on Palearctic Birds, No 23. Fringillidae: the Genera *Emberiza, Calcarius,* and *Plectrophenax. Amer. Mus. Novitates* 1805.

— 1958. Systematic Notes on Palearctic Birds, No 33. Additional notes on *Emberiza schoeniclus. Amer. Mus. Novitates* 1898.

— 1959. *The Birds of the Palearctic Fauna.* Vol. 1. H. F. & G. Witherby, London.

— 1964a. A survey of the birds of Mongolia. *Bull. Amer. Mus. Nat. Hist.* 127: 103-144.

— 1964b 'Bunting' in Thomson, A. L. (ed) *A New Dictionary of Birds.* pp112-114.

— 1972. *Tibet and its Birds.* H. F. & G. Witherby, London.

Vincent, A. W. 1949. Breeding habits of African birds. *Ibis* 91: 680-688.

Vincent, J. 1936. The Birds of Northern Portuguese East Africa. *Ibis* 78: 120-123.

— 1950. New races of the Cape Bunting from Southern Rhodesia and Basutoland. *Bull. Brit. Orn. Club* 70: 14-17.

Wallschläger, D. 1983. Vergleich von Gesangsstrukturen Zentralasiatischer Ammern (*Emberiza*). *Mitt. Zool. Mus. Berlin* 59: 85-116.

Watt, D. J. 1986. Plumage brightness index for White-throated Sparrows. *Journal of Field Ornithology* 57(2): 105-113.

—, Ralph, C. J., & Atkinson, C. T. 1984. The role of plumage polymorphism in dominance relationships of the White-throated Sparrow. *Auk* 101(1): 110-120.

Webster, J. D. 1959. A revision of the Botteri's Sparrow. *Condor* 61(2): 136-146.

— & Orr R. T. 1954. Summering birds of Zacatecas, Mexico, with a description of a new race of Worthen's Sparrow. *Condor* 56: 155-160.

Wege, D. C., Howell, S. N. G., & Sada, A. M. (1993) The distribution and status of Worthen's Sparrow *Spizella wortheni*: a review. *Bird Conserv. Internatn.* 3: 211-220.

Wheelwright, N. T., & Rising, J. D. 1993. Savannah Sparrow in *The Birds of North America.* Academy of Natural Sciences, Philadelphia.

White, C. M. N. 1963. *A Revised Checklist of African Flycatchers, Buntings, etc* pp 95-102. Government Printer, Lusaka.

Willoughby, E. J. 1986. An Unusual Sequence of Molts and Plumages in Cassin's and Bachman's Sparrows. *Condor* 88(4): 461-472.

Winnett-Murray, K. 1985. First reported nest of the White-eared Ground Sparrow (*Melozone leucotis*). *Condor* 87(4): 554.

Witherby, H. F., Jourdain, F. C. R., Ticehurst, N. F., & Tucker, B. W. 1948. *The Handbook of British Birds.* H. F. & G. Witherby, London.

Wood, D. S., & Schnell, G. D. 1984. *Distribution of Oklahoma Birds.* Oklahoma Univ. Press, Norman.

Wolf, L. L. 1977. Species relationships in the avian genus *Aimophila. Ornithological Monographs* 23: 1-220.

Woolfenden, G. E. 1955. Spring molt of the Harris' Sparrow. *Wilson Bull.* 67(3): 212-213.

Yamashina, Y. 1957. Notes on *Emberiza jankowskii* Taczanowski with special reference to its speciation. *Journ. Fac. Sci. Hokkaido Univ.* 13: 164-171.

Yunick, R. P. 1972. Variations in the tail spotting of the Slate-coloured Junco. *Bird-Banding* 43(1): 38-46.

— 1977. Eye color changes in the Dark-eyed Junco and White-throated Sparrow. *North American Bird-Bander* 2(4): 155-156.

Zhao, Z. J., Nickel, H., & Groh, G. 1994. Vorkommen und Gesang der Jankowskiammer (*Emberiza jankowskii*) in der chinesischen Provinz Jilin. *J. Ornithol.* 135: 617-620.

Zimmerman, J. L. 1988. Breeding season habitat selection by the Henslow's Sparrow (*Ammodramus henslowii*) in Kansas. *Wilson Bull.* 100(1): 17-24.

— & Patti, S. T. 1988. *A Guide to Bird Finding in Kansas and Western Missouri.* Kansas Univ. Press, Lawrence.

Zusi, R. L. 1978. The interorbital septum in cardueline finches. *Bull. Brit. Orn. Club* 98: 5-10.

INDEX OF SCIENTIFIC AND ENGLISH NAMES

Species are listed by their English vernacular name (e.g. Cirl Bunting), together with alternative names where relevant, and by their scientific names. Specific scientific names are followed by the generic name as used in this book (e.g. *cirlus, Emberiza*) and subspecific names are followed by both the specific and generic names (e.g. *nigrostriata, Emberiza cirlus*). In addition, genera are listed separately.

Numbers in italic type refer to the first page of the main systematic entry and those in bold type refer to plate numbers.

330